Mother Teresa's General Letters to Her Sisters

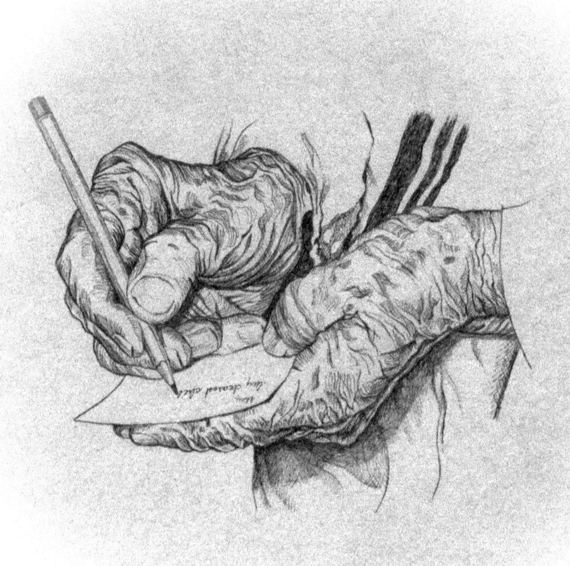

Mother Teresa's General Letters to Her Sisters

EDITED BY FR. BRIAN KOLODIEJCHUK, MC

MOTHER TERESA CENTER

San Diego, CA

The paper used in this publication meets the minimum requirements of American National Standards for Information Science—Permanence of Paper for Printed Library Materials, ANSI Z39.48-1984.

∞

Frontispiece: © Courtesy of Br. François Fontanié, CFR

LIBRARY OF CONGRESS CATALOGING-IN-PUBLICATION DATA
Names: Kolodiejchuk, Brian, editor.
Title: Mother Teresa's general letters to her sisters / edited by Fr. Brian Kolodiejchuk, MC.
Description: San Diego, CA : Mother Teresa Center, [2024] | Includes bibliographical references and index. | Summary: "Mother Teresa's General Letters to Her Sisters is a complete collection of Mother Teresa's circular letters to the members of her religious congregation, the Missionaries of Charity Sisters, from 1959 to 1997. The volume includes three appendices, footnotes, endnotes, a concordance, and an index. The editor's introduction explains the methodology of presentation and editing of the letters, some of which were originally handwritten"—Provided by publisher.
Identifiers: LCCN 2024026398 (print) | LCCN 2024026399 (ebook) | ISBN 9798989865710 (paperback) | ISBN 9798989865703 (hardcover) | ISBN 9798989865727 (ebook)
Subjects: LCSH: Teresa, Mother, Saint, 1910–1997—Correspondence. | Missionaries of Charity—Correspondence. | Nuns—India—Kolkata—Correspondence.
Classification: LCC BX4406.5.Z8 A5 2024 (print) | LCC BX4406.5.Z8 (ebook) | DDC 271/.97—dc23/eng/20240731
LC record available at https://lccn.loc.gov/2024026398
LC ebook record available at https://lccn.loc.gov/2024026399

CONTENTS

1963 / 31

1964 / 39

1965 / 55

1966 / 72

1967 / 81

1968 / 93

1973 *(continued)*

1974 / 183

1975 / 197

1976 / 212

1977 / 220

1983 / 302

1984 / 319

1985 / 325

1986 / 340

1987 / 355

1996 *(continued)*

1997 / 502

APPENDIX A / 521

APPENDIX B / 529

APPENDIX C / 533

PREFACE

Mother Teresa was born in Skopje, present-day North Macedonia, on 26th August 1910, to parents of Albanian descent, Nikola and Drana Bojaxhiu. Baptized the very next day, she was given the name Gonxha Agnes. For her father, a prosperous merchant, and her mother, a devout and diligent housewife, the wellbeing of their three living children was a priority. Years later Mother Teresa would reminisce: "we were a beautiful, united family."

The happiness of their home was cut short by Nikola's sudden death in 1919. Contrary to the customs of her social milieu, Drana started a small business of making and selling Albanian traditional clothes and thus supported her family. She provided for the education of her children but also inculcated into them Christan virtues, especially the care for the less fortunate.

Under the watchful eye of her mother and with the profound influence of the Jesuits who served in her parish, Gonxha grew into a deeply religious, very active and popular young girl. She distinguished herself in her studies. As a member of the Sodality of Our Lady, she organized, along with her companions, entertainment programs for various parish feasts and sang as a soloist on the parish stage. At the age of 18, she decided to join the Institute of the Blessed Virgin Mary (Loreto Sisters) with the intention of working as a missionary in India.

In September 1928, Gonxha left home to join the Loreto Sisters in Ireland and received the name Sister Mary Teresa, after St. Thérèse of Lisieux. After a several weeks there, she journeyed to India, arriving in Calcutta on 6th January 1929. After her first vows in 1931, she was sent to St. Mary's School in Calcutta. Through different responsibilities—teacher, headmistress, in-charge of the boarders—she showed extraordinary charity, courage, a great capacity for hard work, and a natural talent for organization. She lived out her consecration to Jesus with fidelity and notable joy, demonstrating deep faith and prayerfulness.

Mother Teresa's happy and for the most part predictable life took a new turn in 1946.

On September 10th, while on a train journey to Darjeeling for her annual retreat, she received "a call within a call," a divine inspiration to begin a new religious community whose aim was to "satiate the thirst of Jesus for love and for souls by labouring at the salvation and sanctification of the poorest of the poor." The radical lifestyle and total dedication to the poorest of the poor that she envisioned met with a time of testing. After an intense process of spiritual discernment involving her Loreto Superiors; her spiritual director, Fr. C. Van Exem, SJ; and the Archbishop of Calcutta, Rev. F. Périer, SJ, she obtained the necessary permission. Dressed for the first time in a white, blue-bordered sari, she left her beloved Loreto convent in August 1948 and plunged into the world of the poor.

After completing a short time of medical training, on 21st December 1948 she began her service in the slums of Calcutta. She visited families, cared for little street children, nursed the sick and dying on the streets, and sought food for those suffering hunger. Hands-on, she was immersed in the pain and misery of those on the fringes of society. Her mission of love flourished, benefactors began to assist the work and, one by one, her former students from St. Mary's joined her. Within a short time, Mother Teresa opened her first slum schools and medical dispensaries in several areas of the city. "The unwanted, the unloved, the uncared for" knew that from her and her dedicated followers they could expect help and solace.

The spread of her mission had something of "a wildfire effect," not just in Calcutta and India, but across the globe. The statistics show growth that confirmed divine involvement. A group of very young women, inexperienced and with limited education, albeit generous at times to the point of heroism, could have accomplished all they did only with God's help. The religious community was officially established in October 1950, counting 12 members. During that year, they attended 12,945 patients, in two mobile clinics; instructed 471 pupils in four slum schools; and cared for 369 dying in the Home for the Dying, besides other activities (e.g., Sunday schools, preparation for sacraments, sodality groups, etc.).

In 1997, the year of Mother Teresa's death, the community numbered 3,842 Sisters in 594 foundations in 120 countries. Their apostolic activities broadened to include greater numbers and a greater diversity of needs. In addition to over 1000 mobile clinics caring for over 3,000,000 people, over 250 Homes for the Dying with over 32,400 patients, 115 slums schools with over 10,700 pupils, 881 Sunday schools with over 68,600 pupils, the Sisters had over 120 malnutrition centres attending to over 47,200 children and babies, 25 homes for over 1,800 AIDS sufferers, 29 homes for over 1,400 patients with mental disabilities, while in over 600 soup kitchens over 617,300 needy persons were given food and care.

At that time, Mother Teresa's religious family included the Missionaries of Charity Brothers (founded in 1963), the Contemplative Sisters (founded in 1976), the Contemplative Brothers (founded in 1979), and the Missionaries of Charity Fathers (founded in 1984). Various groups of associates contributed to her apostolate: the Co-workers of Mother Teresa, Sick and Suffering Co-Workers, Lay Missionaries of Charity, the Corpus Christi Movement for Priests, volunteers, and others.

Mother Teresa, who wanted to remain unknown, came to be one of the most popular and admired women of her century. The extraordinary expansion and fruitfulness of her mission could not remain unnoticed. Numerous awards and honours, the esteemed Padmashri Award in 1962 in India, the Pope John XXIII Peace Prize in 1971, the prestigious Nobel Peace Prize in 1979, the Presidential Medal of Freedom in 1985, the Congressional Gold Medal in 1997, to mention just a few of the more significant ones, were bestowed on her, while she and her work increasingly garnered world-wide media interest. She received both prizes and attention "for the glory of God and in the name of the poor."

Yet, in the face of all the praise and attention, Mother Teresa remained remarkably humble, considering herself "just a pencil in God's hand," and all the accomplishments of her community "just a drop in the ocean." In her interactions with the poor, but even more so in her interaction with her Sisters, she could be aptly described simply as "Mother." This is how the members of her religious order referred to her, and that one word said it all. She could combine iron will and determination with the tenderness of a mother's heart. Each Sister was "her child," and she took keen interest in every detail of their life, in their growth, struggles, successes, failures, joys; she was there with them and for them through it all. Some of the dynamics of this deeply spiritual and surprisingly practical relationship between Mother Teresa and the members of her community come to the fore through her monthly circular letters. Her determined leadership, practical counsels, empathic concern, and above all, her profound love emerge through the words of these letters in all their richness.

The idea of presenting this compilation of the letters Mother Teresa wrote to the members of her religious congregation came about while the collection of *Mother's General Letters to the Sisters*—as the book is called by the Sisters—was being prepared. Though its publication was originally intended only for the MC Sisters, not for the public, nonetheless the realization that this material could prove to be a spiritual treasure for anyone interested in Mother Teresa and her legacy, or perhaps just desiring to delve into a book of sound and practical spirituality, prevailed over any concern for privacy. It is my hope that the reader will glean pearls of great value through the informal and unpolished style of these circular letters that Mother Teresa often hurriedly penned for the members of her community while travelling or sitting late at night at her desk.

ACKNOWLEDGMENTS

To complete this book took a lot of time and effort by many. It would not have been possible without their generous and competent help. First, I would like to thank the Sisters in various offices in Mother House who often and generously answered many of our questions and pulled out documents for fact-checking. A sincere thanks also to the Sisters in the Archives, both in Mother House and in Rome, who have kindly contributed with the scans and copies we needed. A heartfelt thanks also to the many Sisters in various mission houses across the globe whom we contacted many times and with many questions to get correct information for the footnotes and other study aids. Thank you, Sisters, for your generous collaboration; we can say that this project was a joint venture by all.

I would also like to express my gratitude to our literary agent, Claudia Cross, for guiding us through the process of finding the best options for bringing this book to publication, to Corey Field, our lawyer and friend for his professional expertise and friendly advice.

A very special thanks to Anne Needham, our editor, for her skilled and tedious work in navigating through the pages of Mother Teresa's particular style and structure. Thank you for helping us to clarify, without altering, the originality and authenticity of Mother's expression. Thanks also to Anne Kachergis and her team at Kachergis Book Design for their effort and dedication to excellence in designing this volume.

Last but not least, a hearty thank you to all of you (especially our MC Contemplatives Sisters) for supporting this project with your prayers and sacrifices.

Even with all effort made and the enormous amount of help we received, the possibility of errors remains. It is my hope they are minimal, but whatever they may be, full responsibility falls to me.

God bless you all!

Fr. Brian, MC
for the Mother Teresa Center of the Missionaries of Charity

CREDITS

When Mother Teresa wrote her General Letters to the Sisters, she wrote them exclusively for them and did not intend them for publication. Thus, she rarely acknowledged the authors of the works she quoted and paraphrased, as she was sharing the fruit of her own spiritual reading in a private way. Later, the Sisters who assisted her in preparing various materials for the spiritual enrichment or ongoing formation of the Sisters followed the same principle, again, intending the material only for internal use. In the process of publishing these letters for a broader audience, we have sought permissions where they seemed necessary.

We are especially grateful to the authors or the literary estates of the authors who have generously granted us the permission to quote their works in this volume.

John J. Carberry. *Mary, Queen and Mother: Marian Pastoral Reflection* (Boston: St. Paul Editions, 1979). © 1979, Daughters of St. Paul. Used with permission.

Louis Colin, CSsR, preface to *Lamps of Love: A Recall to the Principal Sources of Love*, trans. Sister David Mary, SNJM (Westminster, MD: The Newman Press, 1959).

Words of Abbe Gaston Courtois, © Fils de la Charité (Sons of Charity), 22 Rue Abbé Derry, 92130 Issy les Moulineaux, France. Used with permission.

Father Mateo Crawley-Boevey, SSCC, *Jesus King of Love*, 4th ed. (Washington, DC: National Center of the Enthronement, 1945).

Emile Guerry, *In the Whole Christ* (Staten Island, NY: Society of St. Paul, 1959).

Fr. Flann Lynch, OFM, Cap. *Come, Take Up Your Cross: The Practical Responsibilities of Christians Today* (Notre Dame, IN: Ave Maria Press, 1978).

Words of Abbot Columba Marmion, © Postulation of the Cause of Canonization of Abbot Columba Marmion, Abbaye de Maredsous, 11 rue de Maredsous, B-5537 Denée, Belgium.

INTRODUCTION

It is our joy to present this abridged volume of *Mother Teresa's General Letters to Her Sisters* from 1959 to 1997. Though there were excerpts of Mother Teresa's Letters in circulation in publications, they were incomplete and contained many errors. Preparing this volume has been an arduous task that has taken much time, and we would like to share with you some of the process so that you might better appreciate Mother Teresa's spiritual heritage, as well as her love for the Sisters of her community, the Missionaries of Charity (hereafter MCs[a]), as expressed in her general letters.

Though the volume of *Mother Teresa's General Letters to Her Sisters* is not new for the MCs, it is our hope that it will be very helpful for the members of her religious family and for many others interested in her spiritual legacy, for we have presented, along with the letters, some new discoveries and resource materials that will help us all to better understand, love, and appreciate Mother's spirituality and live her message more faithfully.

This abridged version contains all of Mother Teresa's General Letters to the Sisters. We have removed only some marginal, private matters specific to the Sisters' communities—mainly addresses, names of the Sisters and their assignments, operational details and schedules, matters of personal hygiene, clothing, and diet, and practices of private penances—that are not relevant outside of the Sisters' communities. These omissions do not affect the substance or the integrity of Mother Teresa's teachings. All the omissions have been marked with an ellipsis.

Some of the explanations and references are provided here for future generations who would not be aware of certain facts or circumstances the present generation is familiar with. Some of the notes were inserted in view of the external reader or for other members of the MC Family who are not familiar with the rules or customs of the MC Sisters.

a. MC is an abbreviation for Missionaries of Charity; it is also written after each member's name to designate that they are members of this religious congregation.

ORIGIN AND CIRCULATION OF MOTHER'S GENERAL LETTERS

As the houses outside Calcutta, and eventually outside of India, were opening, Mother[a] realized that her great desire to be with the Sisters was becoming an impossible challenge. On the other hand, the needs of the Sisters, who were exposed to the hardships of the expanding missions and facing the struggles of interacting with different cultural backgrounds and upbringing in the young Congregation, were becoming evident to her. She thus decided to be with the Sisters "through her general letters," which she proposed to write every First Friday of the month. Through her letters she had the opportunity to encourage, exhort, guide, and correct the Sisters. It was a vehicle to show her motherly love, but also a way to guide her growing congregation and to share joys and pains, as well as a means of communicating important news and decisions.

When Mother's letter arrived to a Community, it was read by the Superior in the refectory, with all the Sisters present. The Sisters would sit reverently and listen with great respect and attention to the message that came through the letter. The love they had for Mother was expressed in the way they treasured her letters.

We would like to explain the typical procedure of Mother's writing and sending out general letters. Mother would write a draft of the letter by hand, especially in the early years, and then hand the draft to the Sister typist (at times a Councillor and at times one of the Sisters working in the office). Especially in the early years, the letter was retyped with carbon paper in as many copies as were needed for the houses existing at the time. Then the letters (both the original handwritten drafts and the typed versions) were brought back to Mother for her signature. In the first years she would sign each copy of the letter and, normally, handwrite the name of the house at the top of the letter. At times she would also make a correction, or add a text or a *post scriptum* (PS) to the typed copy with a greeting or a message for a particular house. She herself disposed of the handwritten drafts, which means that most of the time she threw them in the dustbin or in the "chulha" (kitchen stove). As the number of

a. One of the customs and practices in the religious family of the Missionaries of Charity is to address or refer to Mother Teresa simply as "Mother." We have decided to respect this practice even in this abridged public version. This will contribute to the understanding of the spiritual dynamic underlying the letters. Mother Teresa was called "Mother," and she considered the members of her religious family as her spiritual children and often addressed them simply as "my dearest children."

houses increased, the letters were reproduced with a cyclostyle machine and later photocopied. Eventually Mother stopped signing the letters for each house.

It is interesting to note that she often wrote handwritten drafts on scraps of paper of all kinds and sizes, on used envelopes, at the bottom or on the back of the letters she received if there was space, literally on anything she found available. Many manuscripts show that she began a letter, was probably interrupted (and Mother would not refuse an immediate response to anyone who interrupted her) and then continued writing later. At times she added text between lines or in the margins. At times she jotted an asterisk or a number to indicate to the Sister typist to look on a separate sheet of paper for the continuation of the thought. Many of these letters reveal that she was "in haste" and trusted that the Sister typist would understand her speedy writing and her message. Some of the drafts were written on proper letter pads (which Mother evidently carried with her when travelling) and with neat handwriting. These were mostly the letters written while she was travelling, which she was sending back to Mother House to be retyped and mailed to the Sisters. It seems that she was more careful about her handwriting in these cases, as she was not there to clarify, if need be, a possible doubt.

Great credit goes to the Sister typists for their tedious work. Yet the unfortunate and regrettable result of this process was that most of Mother's handwritten drafts were ripped up and thrown away or burned after they were retyped, and most of the time by Mother herself. The few that were saved, thanks to the foresight and at times ingenuity of the Councillors and Sister typists, are of great value. Besides being a precious heritage of the Missionaries of Charity, these handwritten drafts were very useful in determining how faithfully Mother's letters were retyped. We were able to confirm that the contents of her handwritten drafts were faithfully transcribed when the letters were typed and sent out to the houses. In the early letters we frequently find that the Sister typists re-typed the text so faithfully that they retyped the dashes (instead of other punctuation marks), irregular or incorrect capitals, and even the grammatical errors that Mother had written. Her style is easily recognized in these letters. In this volume, we have reproduced that style as well; the only exception to this is the correction of a few obvious spelling or typing mistakes.

When Mother began to travel, she was at times sending her general letter from the house where she was; at other times she would send it to

Mother House. If the letter was sent to Mother House, the Councillors or Sister typists would then type the letter and send it out to all the houses. In those cases, they would retype her greeting and signature in capitals. In these instances, we have standardized the style of Mother's signature to the uniform italic used in the rest of this book.

As the MC mission expanded across the globe, Mother was becoming busier not only with the growing number of mission houses that were being opened but also with public engagements. Especially after receiving the Nobel Peace Prize in 1979, she became well known internationally; as a result, many awards were bestowed on her worldwide and more and more demands were made on her to speak at different public gatherings and functions. Therefore, she was often away from Mother House. At this time, the Councillors and the Sister secretaries in the Mother House office assisted Mother with the general letters, and more so in her last years when her health was failing.

Mother would then give only brief points, at times on a slip of rough paper, at other times just orally; the Sister responsible for the letters was supposed to "fill in the blanks." During this time the secretaries often copied from previous letters and added current updates on Society matters (e.g., new foundations, Mother's travelling schedule, professions, etc.). To the credit of those Sisters who helped with the letters during this time, they were able to keep faithful to her spirit and her mind. Mother would read these letters and frequently add a short message at the bottom before signing. In these letters, while copying parts of the old letters, the Sister typist usually corrected the punctuation, spelling, and grammar, and occasionally the sentences or the paragraphs were reordered.

It is important to mention that Mother had complete trust in the Sisters who helped her with typing and sending out the general letters. The following is the transcript of instructions given by Mother to Sr. M. Joseph Michael, MC, written in her own hand on the back of the last page of the handwritten draft of her letter dated 8th July 1976 (MGL 123), directing Sr. Joseph Michael to revise the draft of her general letter:

> *Sister M. J. Michael, please read this carefully—& correct & put things together—& also prepare as we did before the Meditation & the liturgy, reading, instruction, ex. of cons. [examination of conscience] on obedience. I think Sm. Bernard will be able to do it—if not you & Sm Caml. [Sr. M. Camillus] could get together & do it. The ex. of cons. in the new prayer book is well*

done—you could use it—& put in also that during these days we take growth [in] obedience as our particular Ex. [examen]. Let us more insist on that simple obedience—that helps to the awareness of God's presence. Let us be more busy with obedience than with disobedience.[c]

According to the directives we had received from the Congregation for the Causes of Saints at the beginning of Mother's cause of canonization, Mother's general letter is the letter that was signed by her and sent to the houses, not the draft of it that she had given to the secretaries to type from. We have followed this principle here, though from the historical and critical point of view it would have been interesting to have compared versions of the letters. Such study is not, however, within the scope of this volume. Scientific studies of the letters will be done at a later time; sufficient for now is to know, appreciate, and live Mother's legacy to us.

We have included a few sample pages of Mother's handwritten letters along with the typed version so that the Sisters can appreciate the spiritual riches of Mother's letters as well as the tedious work of the readers who assisted her with the preparation of the letters. Please see Appendix C, pp. 533–555 for these samples.

We owe heartfelt thanks to the Sisters who faithfully preserved Mother's Letters as well as to those who assisted her in any way in preparing them throughout the years.

DISCREPANCIES AND COPYING ERRORS

As we were preparing this volume, we noticed what appear to be discrepancies in the letters that you too may notice as you read them. Here is one example: The seventh paragraph of MGL 72 (19th April 1970, from Mother House) says: *"I will be away for quite a long time and will be moving about. Therefore please do not write to me, but remember me in your Holy Mass and Holy Communion. This will be enough for me."* In the very next letter, MGL 73 (7th May 1970, from Australia), the second paragraph says: *"Many thanks for all your welcome letters. I was so proud of you all who wrote. A number of houses did not write. You don't know what it means to get a letter from you in a new land."*

c. See Appendix C, p. 544–49, for the facsimile of this letter.

The simplest explanation might be the best in this case, namely, that both letters are correct. Perhaps the Sisters wrote anyway, even though Mother asked them not to, and she (possibly forgetting what she had written and pleased that the Sisters didn't listen) was happy to receive the letters. Mother meant not to write to her (personally), but perhaps the Sisters wrote to the Sisters of the newly opened house (which she always encouraged the Sisters to do); this gave her great joy and she praised it in her next letter. Possibly the Sister typist misunderstood what Mother wrote or, perhaps thinking of her busy schedule and of having to read and answer all these letters, might have taken the liberty to discourage writing. It is known that Sisters, especially the senior Sisters who were very close to Mother from the beginning, could be very (and, at times, overly) protective of her. Yet the instances of typists taking the liberty of writing something without previously consulting Mother seem to be rare and easily recognizable, as it could be in this example.

That said, the second letter is more consistent with Mother's mind: every time she wrote about the opening of a new house, she always encouraged the Sisters to write to the Sisters of the new foundation and provided the address of the new house; if she didn't know the new address, she asked them to address the letter in care of the Bishop's house.

In general, we may say, regarding such differences in the letters, that it is important to grasp that the completeness of the message has to be taken into account, not an isolated word or phrase, which, when taken out of context can lead to misunderstanding and confusion. This principle is important to keep in mind, especially when the Sisters who were assisting in typing the letters misunderstood what Mother asked them to write, or in an attempt to "improve" her English, conveyed something different from what she customarily taught. In those rare occasions, when the intent of the message could have been altered, its integrity is safeguarded through comparison with Mother's consistent teaching and lived example.

Some technical errors resulted during the copying of the letters before the letters were sent to the houses. This was especially the case when the general letters were retyped and not photocopied. Here are some examples:

There are two different typed versions of Mother's letter MGL 204 of 23rd July 1988. The one in our records seems to have been retyped from the original version, because the copy of the same letter that our office received from one of the houses has the last paragraph handwritten by Mother, while in the copy we had on file this paragraph was retyped. The signature is exactly the same in both copies—so it seems that in this case the signature has been cut and photocopied onto the letter. The text of the letter is identical in both versions.

There are also two different typed versions of MGL 207 of 9th December 1988. The one in our records has Mother's handwritten greetings for Christmas and the New Year and her signature written by someone else at the bottom of the letter (imitating Mother's handwriting and signature!). The copy of the letter we received from one of our houses is obviously a copy of the original letter that was sent to all the houses: it has Mother's greetings and signature in the middle of the letter and points from Constitution 156 on silence were added after she signed it. On the copy of this letter, as on a few other letters, someone went over Mother's greetings and signature with a thicker pen, as the stroke of the pen she wrote with did not copy clearly enough. But the content of both letters is identical except that one line was missed when the letter we have on record was retyped.

PREPARATION OF THIS EDITION OF *MOTHER TERESA'S GENERAL LETTERS TO HER SISTERS*

The letters in this volume are entered in chronological order, and each is coded (for easier reference) with its appropriate serial number (e.g., MGL 1, MGL 2, etc.).

Every original general letter written by Mother (handwritten copy and/or typed version that was originally sent to the houses) was compared to the copy found in the photocopied volumes of *Mother's General Letters* that all the Sisters' houses have in the refectories and that are read from at breakfast. We found that there are a good number of typing errors as well as words, sentences, entire paragraphs, or at times even entire letters that are missing. At times words have also been changed or added, probably in error or in an attempt to make clearer the meaning. When the meaning of some word or phrase was uncertain, we compared it to the handwritten original (if available). If this did not help to remove the doubt, we opted to leave it unclear (even though this may result in some awkwardness in the reading), instead of "guessing" what Mother might have meant.

In the bound books that are in the Sisters' refectories, the dashes, which are characteristic of Mother's writing style, were mostly changed to commas and periods. Irregular capitals, another characteristic of her style, were changed to lower case to reflect more standard English usage or, at times, the choice and preference of the typist. Some of the grammar also was corrected.

We have also included in this book of *Mother Teresa's General Letters* Mother's messages for *Ek Dil*,[d] that is, just the text written by her. These were added in their chronological order and marked with an appropriate serial number (e.g. ED 1, ED 2, etc.).

In the appendix, we added various documents as well as facsimiles of some of Mother Teresa's handwritten letters to help readers understand and appreciate her writing style. Finally, to help in study and research, we have added an index and a concordance of Bible citations used in Mother Teresa's letters.

EDITING PRINCIPLES FOLLOWED IN THIS VOLUME

The general principle followed in preparing this volume was to do as little editing as possible; only minimum changes were made to enable easier reading. It is important to note that this is not exactly a critical edition of *Mother Teresa's General Letters to Her Sisters*. However, we have attempted to make this edition as close as possible to the text Mother wrote, and it will eventually appear as part of a future critical edition, with very few changes (if any). The critical edition will contain much more information on versions (e.g., manuscripts, drafts, editions), sources, historical context, form, style, and other such matters that will help the reader to understand and appreciate the text, but the basic text of the letter as Mother wrote it will be the same as in the present edition.

Capitalization

As was done in previous publications (*Come be My Light*, *Where There Is Love There Is God*, *A Call to Mercy*) we have followed as faithfully as possible what could be termed "Mother's writing style." Her capitalization—or, better, irregular capitalization—is one of the key elements of that style.

Mother had the practice of capitalizing words that would not be capitalized in common English usage. She always capitalized "God" and the

d. Ek Dil (which in Hindi means "One Heart") is the MC Sisters' newsletter. See footnote to ED 1, p. 75, for more detail.

personal pronouns referring to Him, a practice that presently is not so common. At times she capitalized "She" when referring to Our Lady. She also capitalized the words that are related to the sacred and holy, as well as terms that were important to her, such as Sisters, "our Poor," (or "Your poor", when speaking of the poor that were under the care of the Sisters), "Smile," "Vow", "Poverty", "Chastity", "Obedience" "Wholehearted and Free Service", "Loving Trust", "Total Surrender", "Cheerfulness," and so on. This was her way of expressing respect for the sacred and emphasizing a certain reality that struck her. Sometimes she capitalized to stress a word or a point that she was trying to make. For example, "In all the houses and in the noviciate God is blessing the Generosity of the Sisters. Keep up this Generosity." At other times, she capitalized just because she got into the habit of writing that particular word in capitals; for example, she always wrote the personal pronoun "He" with a capital when it was referring to Jesus or any of the Persons of the Trinity, but at times she wrote "He" with a capital even when it was referring to any man.

However, Mother was quite inconsistent in the way she capitalized, and no rule can be applied to or derived from it. Even if we are not sure whether the capital letter meant something—had some spiritual reason behind it (respect for the sacredness of who or what it stood for)—or was just the result of her writing "in haste," we did not change it. We do believe that being faithful to her style and leaving most of the capitals wherever Mother had put them (even at the risk of being an annoyance to the reader), contributes to the authenticity of the text.

Mother was not in the habit of writing ALL CAPITALS (CAPS), and she very rarely underlined the text. However, when she wanted to emphasize a word or a phrase, at times she would write it on a separate line using bigger and clearer handwriting. The Sister typists at times reproduced this by typing it in ALL CAPS or by underlining the text. At times the typists also reproduced in ALL CAPS a word that she capitalized for emphasis. We have reproduced this, respecting the interpretation of the original typist, even if at times larger handwriting might have been just a result of writing in a hurry.

Dashes

The dash is a punctuation mark that characterizes Mother's writing style, not only in her personal notes and journals but also in her letters. It might be concluded that this excessive use of dashes as a predominant punctuation mark, in some way, reveals and portrays her dynamic personality. Many of the letters were written "on the go" (literally on the plane or train). Even when written on her desk, she frequently had a large stack of correspondence waiting to be answered, besides other matters that needed or claimed her attention. So, while writing, often late at night, she would hastily jot a dash to indicate a break in thought without being bothered which punctuation mark was required: a period, comma, colon or semicolon, an exclamation or question mark, or finally a dash itself. She was concerned about the essential—the message that she wanted to convey—so punctuation could be overlooked.

For the most part, we have kept the dashes as Mother wrote them. When it was necessary for the clarity of the text, we have replaced a dash or inserted additional punctuation.

Abbreviations

Using abbreviations was another characteristic of Mother's writing style, pointing to her "going-in-haste" mode: she tried to make the most of her time, navigating through the many demands of her busy daily schedule. She used many nonstandard abbreviations. The abbreviations were kept in the text as she wrote them, and a full word in square brackets, or an explanation in a footnote, has been added when required.

Mother always wrote numbers using digits, including at the beginning of a sentence when using a word would be grammatically correct. We have respected her style in this, even though it is contrary to conventional practice, except in those instances when the sentence begins with a number. In those cases, for easier reading, we have used the word rather than digits.

Mother also used the ampersand (&) very frequently. Some of the typists replaced it with its corresponding "and," while others left it as she had written it. However, there is no consistency in the way this was done, as at times in the same letter some ampersands were replaced, and others left as she wrote them. When the handwritten letter was sent out, we have left it as she wrote it; otherwise, we have respected the interpretation of the original typist.

Other Editorial Points

Mother used British spelling; we have respected it throughout this volume. If the Sister typist opted for an American spelling in the typed version of the letter, we have restored it to its original British spelling.

Only obvious typing errors, spelling mistakes, and incomplete or incorrect punctuation were corrected, using what is called "silent correction." For all other cases, we have added the customary [sic] after the misspelled word or explained the correction in the footnote. We have added missing words in square brackets to indicate that they are the editor's addition. Words mistakenly left out of the original typed version but found in Mother's handwritten drafts were added in italics and in square brackets. The paragraphs and formatting of the letters were left as much as possible as they appeared in the original writing.

Footnotes have been added to the letters to explain to whom or to what Mother was referring, especially regarding people, places, or events with which future generations of readers may not be acquainted (e.g., Fr. Van Exem, Eileen Eagan, East Pakistan, etc.). A brief description of world events, such as wars, riots, cyclones and the like, have also been included in the footnotes, as these put her words and work into historical perspective.

We believe that we are still at a point in time when all references to the names of Sisters who appear in any negative light should be removed, so we have replaced names with a long dash, for example, the names of the Sisters who left the Society.

In several letters, Mother refers to documents she is including with her letter (e.g., a talk given by a priest, "spiritual exercises", "juniorate programme," etc.). Most of these have been omitted as they might not be of interest to the general reader and in order to avoid an excessively large volume.

Some Standard Entries

For the sake of order and clarity, we have followed certain standard criteria for common entries. We provide here the explanation of the most common cases, while individual instances will be mentioned in the footnotes.

L.D.M.

Mother (and consequently MCs) started her correspondence with the initials LDM. However, there is a considerable inconsistency in her letters in the way LDM appears. It may be written as LDM or L.D.M.; +LDM or + L.D.M. or LDM or L.D.M. with the cross ("+") above the initials. In the handwritten letters she wrote LDM (without the cross and often without the periods in between). In the typed versions of the letters there are variations on how the initials appear, and in the bound volumes of *Mother's Letters* that are in the Sisters' refectories, the entry was standardized to "+ L.D.M.", probably to correspond to *MC Directory* no. 18.c ["We begin all our correspondence with a sign of the cross followed by the initials 'L. D. M.' (*Laudetur Deo Mariaeque*—Praise to God and to Mary)"]. The *Spiritual Directory* was revised and approved by the Extraordinary General Chapter in 1990, but it is evident that Mother continued her habit of writing LDM without the cross. In this volume, we have opted to respect the entry as it appears in the letter that was sent to the houses and to add a footnote when we have chosen a different format.

Dates

We have standardized the date of the letter to a day (dd)/month (spelled out)/year (yyyy) format, spelling out the last two letters of the day as spoken (e.g. 1st, 2nd, 3rd . . .). This was the way that Mother most frequently wrote the date in the early years, except that she usually used the short form for the month (e.g., in MGL 1, she wrote Sept. for September). Eventually, especially in later years, she wrote the dates with numbers divided with slashes (e.g., in MGL 11, she wrote 27/8/61) or with dashes (e.g., in MGL 92, she wrote 1-6-72), following the British format of writing the date. The spelled-out format was chosen to avoid any possible confusion between British usage (day first) and American usage (month first) in determining the date of the letter. The Sister typists frequently changed the date format, seemingly according to their personal preferences, as there is no consistency in the way they typed the date that Mother wrote.

Further, when the letter is dated as "First Friday in . . ." we have added in square brackets the actual date of the First Friday of that month, as, in some instances, this helps to place the events mentioned in the letter in their proper historical and chronological context. However, the fact that a letter is dated as "First Friday in . . ." does not mean that the letter was actually written on that day; from the content it is obvious that at times it was written before, and at times, after, the actual date of the First Friday of the month, but it was meant for the First Friday.

If the letter had only the month (and the year) and not the day, we have added in square brackets the date of that First Friday of that month as the reference date for that particular letter.

MC Letterhead

Some of Mother's letters were written on MC letterhead. We have opted for omitting it for the sake of saving space. In the instances that the letterhead of a particular MC house was used, only the name of the house from which the letter was actually sent is given, without the letterhead.

Mother House

Although the standard English word for the generalate of a religious order is "Motherhouse" (one word), Mother and the Sisters consistently wrote "Mother House" (two words, usually capitalizing "house" as well). This irregular usage has become conventional in Calcutta, so that even the venue (or site) is named "Mother House". Common people in Calcutta normally use the term to mean "Mother's house" (i.e., the house of Mother Teresa). Given this history, we have opted to adopt MC usage and have left this entry as two words, written with capitals, throughout this volume, even though it is at odds with standard English usage.

Mother's Signature

Mother's signature, and anything she added in her handwriting while signing a typed letter, whether it was meant for the whole Society or for a specific house, is italicized. If the note was meant for a particular house, a footnote with an appropriate explanation was added.

In her handwritten letters, Mother always wrote "SM. ____" or "Sr. M. ____," before the name of each and every Sister.[e] When her letters were typed, this was often changed to Sr. ____ or Srs. ____, ____ etc. We have changed these instances back to the original when the handwritten draft was available.

Any other changes that were made are explained in the footnotes, either on the first occurrence or as they arise.

e. The "M." stands for "Mary" in all cases and is the first part of the religious name of each sister; so for example Sr. M. Agnes is actually Sr. Mary Agnes, Sr. M. Gertrude, Sr. Mary Gertrude, etc., though it is only ever used in the abbreviated form, "M."

MOTHER'S QUOTING OTHER SPIRITUAL AUTHORS

During her years in Loreto,[f] Mother was formed in the practical and solid spirituality of the time. The Loreto nuns read from the works of Fr. Alphonsus (Alonso) Rodriguez, SJ, during breakfast;[g] and we can find echoes of this spiritual formation in her own spirituality, especially as expressed in her letters, but more so in her instructions to the Sisters.

In going through the books Mother read for her spiritual reading, we discovered that she made use of these spiritual sources in giving guidance to her Sisters by means of her general letters. She quoted and paraphrased from books by Louis Colin, CSsR, Abbé Gaston Courtois, Fr. Mateo Crawley-Boevey SSCC, Fr. Paul de Jaegher, SJ, Dom Eugene Boylan, OCSO, St. Therese of Lisieux, OCD, and Abbot Dom Marmion, OSB, among others. The writings of these spiritual authors rang true in Mother's heart, and as she put their spiritual counsels into practice in her own life, she considered it useful to pass them on to her followers. Endnotes have been added referring to the writings Mother quotes in her letters (primarily those of the 1960s).

Though the sources of these writings are acknowledged here, it is important to note that there is a great originality in the way Mother quoted or paraphrased these authors. In her visits to the communities she took a keen interest in the life of the Sisters and was very much aware of the needs of the Sisters or the challenges they were facing. Consequently, she usually first chose the theme or the issue that she needed to address, and then found that theme in the spiritual books she was reading. Generally, she made a résumé of a particular lesson presented by a spiritual writer and selected carefully what was appropriate for her and her Sisters, subtracting what she considered irrelevant to their way of life or changing a point to make it applicable.

In many instances, Mother was not quoting directly from other authors, but may have been inspired by their writings. She would assimilate the passages she read, giving them a personal flavour and often a new meaning. Thus, although some of the famous quotes attributed to her are

f. Loreto, here and hereafter, refers to the Institute of the Blessed Virgin Mary, commonly known as the Loreto Sisters. Mother was a member of this religious congregation for twenty years.

g. Fr. Alphonsus Rodriguez, SJ, (1526–1616), was a Spanish Jesuit priest and well-known spiritual writer. (He is to be distinguished from St. Alphonsus Rodriguez, SJ, the Spanish Jesuit lay brother.) He is the author of *The Practice of Christian and Religious Perfection*, a spiritual treatise in three volumes, in which he emphasizes the ascetical aspect of religious life.

actually quotes or paraphrases from other authors, she first "made them her own" by accepting them as true and practicing them in her own particular way of life. Consequently, when she shared them with her spiritual family, she shared them as reflecting her own lived experience, the fruit of her own interior depth and spiritual insight. By frequently adding a word or a phrase she would add a certain nuance to the original, thus giving it a somewhat changed meaning and proposing a different application. Her own way of acting validated the truth of her words; she spoke of what she lived. An anecdote that a Sister recounted shows how much those closest to her relied on the authenticity of her example: "Once when we were novices (in the 1980s), Fr. Bouché was giving a talk and he asked us novices, who said 'God loves a cheerful giver'.[h] We all said 'Mother'. Then he corrected us, 'St. Paul'. We saw in Mother [that she lived] everything that she said."

Another point needs to be mentioned regarding these quotes: Mother was becoming increasingly busier, with a growing number of responsibilities and numerous practical matters that needed her attention. As the Society kept growing, she also had to take care of the spiritual needs of an increasing number of Sisters. At the same time, she was going through her interior darkness. Under these circumstances, instead of providing original compositions with the counsels she wished to pass on to her Sisters, she opted for a more practical and time-saving alternative. As she did her spiritual reading, she either had a topic in mind or, while reading, chose a topic that she deemed would be helpful for the Sisters, and then incorporated and adapted that topic in her letters.

Therefore, especially in her early letters (of the 1960s), when instructing the Sisters on different themes (e.g., humility, joy, silence, or prayer), Mother would quote or paraphrase extensively from various authors on those themes, but would always adapt these spiritual lessons to the MC way of life and to the level of understanding of the Sisters (see, for example, MGL 23 of 27th December 1963; MGL 24 of 7th February 1964; MGL 25 of 6th March 1964; MGL 26 of 3rd April 1964). When quoting or paraphrasing other authors, be it late at night or in the occasional free moments of her busy day, it rarely crossed her mind to insert quote marks or to acknowledge and reference the author or the work she was quoting from.

h. Fr. Camille Bouché, SJ (1922–2002), was a Jesuit priest from Luxembourg, a member of the Calcutta province, who knew Mother from 1957 and who helped as a teacher and confessor in the formation of the novices in Calcutta.

She was not writing for an academic or public audience; thus the fact that it could be taken as plagiarizing did not cross her mind. She just did not think it important to add a reference in a letter addressed to her restricted audience, knowing that her Sisters (in her intention, the only readers of these letters) would not mind the origin of the quote, but would focus on its content, with which she—their spiritual mother and guide—wanted to enrich them. In this volume, however, we have referenced and acknowledged, to the best of our ability, the quotes and paraphrases that we found.

It is worth observing that with the passing of time (in fact, already in the early 1970s), Mother had almost entirely stopped quoting other authors. This was the time when she began travelling extensively and many of her general letters were penned on these journeys, either on the plane or on the train. This actually proved to be providential for the content of the letters, since on these long and frequent journeys she had much time to pray and reflect, without being disturbed. While travelling, Mother usually had a spiritual reading book with her, and undoubtedly these readings from spiritual authors or from writings of the saints influenced her own prayer and meditation. Yet, it seems that she preferred to write without the aid of these spiritual masters. These letters are very beautiful, profound and original in thought. They seem to be spontaneously springing from her heart in the moment they were written as the fruit of her own prayer and reflection, and these precious insights she shared with her Sisters as guidance and encouragement.

Mother used many quotes from the Scriptures, but not in a systematic, scholarly manner. Referring to the Bible, especially the Gospels, as a way of giving an example or making a point became natural to her. She was not in the habit of "looking up the references" but rather of quoting a verse or a passage from memory when it was applicable to the point she was making. References to Bible texts have been added in the margin at the place where Mother refers to it. However, these references do not imply that she is quoting precisely a Bible verse, but rather that she is referring to it and applying it. For practical reasons the customary and appropriate "see," in front of the reference, was omitted, although it is implied.

As a concluding thought to this introduction, we would like to quote the words of Louis Colin from his book, *Love One Another*, which Mother had read.

> A religious should always include his "saint-founder" amongst his favorite saints. He knows his virtue and his merits too well; he has received too many

favors from him; he has too close ties of spiritual parenthood with him not to have a marked predilection for him, and he should therefore practice a particular cult of veneration, and imitation, and have every confidence in him.... He should furthermore strive to follow in his founder's footsteps. He is an ideal to be studied and a model to be copied (p. 238).... The finest relic of him which we possess is not his shriveled body, but his spirit. Each of his sons should be a living monstrance for this relic (p. 242).... Let his sons, therefore, go to the works of the holy founder, drink therefrom and nourish themselves with his spirit. They should, however, cleave particularly to the teachings destined for his religious family. First, the rules and constitutions. This rule was the fruit of his prayers, sufferings, his experience and genius. We may say that, having borne it in his mind and heart, he subsequently made it, so to speak, incarnate in his person and his life.... The correspondence, circular letters and exhortations of the founder to his disciples should also be consulted. These documents are particularly instructive and revealing, because they are full of subtle feelings, intimate confidences and sometimes picturesque details, since the saint has put his whole self into them.[a]

Fr. Colin's words encourage each one of us to have a greater appreciation, love, and devotion to our "saint-foundress." It is our hope that this volume will elicit precisely this, and even more, namely, a greater imitation of our beloved Foundress and a more faithful living of the charism that she left us, her Missionaries of Charity family, and greater appreciation and renewed interest in her spirituality by many others, reviving in all the desire to live her maxim, "I will, I want, with God's blessing, [to] be holy."[i]

Saint Mother Teresa of Calcutta, pray for us!

Fr. Brian Kolodiejchuk, MC
for the Mother Teresa Center of
the Missionaries of Charity

a. Louis Colin, CSsR, *Love One Another* (Westminster, MD: The Newman Press, 1960), 243–44.

i. By the phrase "with God's blessing," Mother intended the Catholic understanding of grace: grace illumines the intellect and moves the will to fulfil God's commandments and counsels; without God's grace it is impossible to perform good works or to reach holiness.

Mother Teresa's General Letters to Her Sisters

1959

MGL 1. 20TH SEPTEMBER 1959

L.D.M.[a]

Delhi
20th September 1959[b]

My own dearest Sisters, Professed, Novices,
Postulants and Aspirants,

Seventh of October is a day of thanksgiving in our Society.[c] It is a day when the Good God erected our little Society into being.[d] As the Society is the sole Property of Our Lady, it was only right that on Her great day,[e] She would grant us the grace of living and growing. It is for us to grow into a straight—beautiful—fruitful tree. Let us all unite as one at the Feet of Our Mother[f] and thank Her and also promise Her—that, as She is the cause of our joy[g]—so we too will be the cause of Her joy.—For this we shall begin the novena of thanksgiving from the 27th Sept. in preparation for the 7th Oct. (Sing Magnificat[h]).

a. Mother began her general letters to the Sisters, as well as her other correspondence, with the initials L.D.M. (*Laudetur Deo Mariaeque*, Praise to God and Mary). Please see the introduction, p. xxxv, for more detail about this entry.

b. In order to avoid possible confusion in dating the letters, we have standardized the dates to the day (dd)/month (spelled out)/year (yyyy) format. For more information on dating the letter, please see the introduction, p. xxxii.

c. There are two extant copies of this letter. For more details, please see Appendix C, pp. 534–37. In one of the versions, Mother misspelled "seventh" (writing it as "seveth"); here and hereafter, we have corrected only such obvious spelling (or writing) mistakes without making a note of it, applying the rule of "silent correction".

d. Here, and hereafter, "the Society" (with capital) refers to the Society of the Missionaries of Charity, and the term is often used in the letters as an acronym for the Missionaries of Charity Sisters.

e. The seventh of October is the Feast of Our Lady of the Rosary.

f. In the second version of this letter Mother wrote, "at the Feet of Our Lady . . ."

g. "Cause of our Joy," one of the invocations in the Litany of Loreto, is a part of the title of Our Lady as the patroness of the Missionaries of Charity, "Immaculate Heart of Mary, Cause of our Joy and Queen of the World". All MC prayers end with the invocation: "Immaculate Heart of Mary, Cause of Our Joy, pray for us."

h. Our Lady's hymn of praise, Lk 1:46–55.

My dear children—there is so much in my heart to tell you—but these
Rom 16:3; 1 Cor 3:9 two things are uppermost—Charity and Obedience. Be a true Co-worker
of Christ.[a]—Radiate and live His life—be an angel of comfort to the
Jn 13:34, 15:12 sick—a friend to the Little ones and love each other as God loves each of
you with a special most intense love. Be kind to each other—I prefer you
make mistakes in kindness—than that you work Miracles in unkindness.
Be kind in words.—See what the kindness of Our Lady brought to her. See
Lk 1:28–37; Mt 1:20–23 how she spoke.—She could have easily told St. Joseph of the Angel's Message. —Yet, she never uttered a word—and then God Himself interfered.[b]
Lk 2:19, 51 She kept all these [things] in her heart—would that we could keep all our
words in Her heart. So much suffering—so much misunderstanding—for
what? Just for one word—one look—one quick action—and darkness fills
the heart of your Sister. Ask Our Lady during this novena to fill your heart
with sweetness.

Now that we have our 3 local Superiors—try to excel in Obedience—help them by your cheerful and prompt, blind and simple obedience.[c]—You may be more talented—more capable—better in many ways, even more holy—than your Superior.—All this is not required for you to obey.[d] There is only one thing for you—"She takes the place of God for you". Some Sisters think they can do the work better than what their Superior wishes or has told them to do.[e]—[Do] not be blind my children, the Good God has given you His Work to do it as He wants it to be done. He wants

a. "As each sister of this Society is to become a co-worker of Christ in the slums, she ought to understand what God and the Society expect from her. Let Christ radiate and live His life in her and through her in the slums. Let the poor seeing her be drawn to Christ and invite Him to enter their homes and their lives. Let the sick and the suffering find in her a real angel of comfort and consolation; let the little ones of the streets cling to her because she reminds them of Him, the Friend of the little ones" (*Constitutions of the Society of the Missionary Sisters of Charity of Calcutta*, 1954, Chapter XI, "Of the Practice of the Virtue," no. 92). This corresponds with no. 31 of the *Constitutions of Missionary of Charity*, 1988. Hereafter, all the references to the various versions of the MC *Constitutions* are referred to as "*Constitutions*" preceded by the year it was approved, e.g., "1988 *Constitutions*."

b. Although "interfered" is written in the original, it is much more likely that the correct reading is "intervened."

c ."Our obedience must be cheerful, prompt, and also blind and simple without question or excuse. All should remember that the Superior whom they obey takes the place of Jesus Christ Our Lord for Whose love they obey" (1954 *Constitutions*, Chapter VIII, "Of the Vow and Virtue of Obedience," no. 76). Corresponds with no. 60 of the 1988 *Constitutions*.

d. In the second version of this letter Mother wrote: "all these are not . . .".

e. In both versions Mother initially wrote ". . . their Superiors wishes or have told them . . ."; then she corrected it in both versions to the singular: ". . . their Superior wishes or has told them . . .". Also in both versions, Mother made an obvious mistake, "Be not be blind", which we have corrected to "Do not be blind", indicating the change with the parenthesis. She also misspelled "infallible" in both letters, and made a few more minor writing errors, which she herself corrected, probably when reading it a second time.

you to do His Work in His way and that is all.—Failure or success means nothing to Him—as long as you do His work according to His plan and His Will. Since the Constitutions are the written Will of God—what surer way can we follow—but the one pointed by our Superiors.—You are infallible when you obey.—The devil tries his best to spoil the Work of God and, as he can't do it direct[ly] to Him, he makes us do God's work in our way, and this is where he gains and we lose.

In all the houses and in the noviciate God is blessing the Generosity of the Sisters. Keep up this Generosity.—You have every reason to be happy. Keep Smiling at Jesus in Your Superiors, Sisters and Your poor.

Pray often, pray fervently for me.

God bless each one of you,
Mother[a]

a. One of the customs and practices in the religious family of the Missionaries of Charity is to address Mother Teresa or to refer to her simply as "Mother." We have decided to respect this practice even in this abridged public version. This will contribute to the understanding of the spiritual dynamic underlying the letters. Mother Teresa was called "Mother", and she considered the members of her religious family as her spiritual children and often addressed them simply as "My dearest children".

1960

MGL 2. [2ND] SEPTEMBER 1960

L.D.M.

First Friday[a]
[2nd] September 1960

My own dearest Sisters,

As the Society is growing it is but natural that a deep desire grows in my heart to be with you wherever you are—[to] love, help and guide you to become Saints. Since this is not possible, I shall try every First Friday to be with you through my letters.

My children, in the great world Jesus is loved so little—now as before
Lk 2:7 there is no room for Jesus. The world expects that we, at least, through our love, would repair this universal ingratitude. Alas, even among us professionals of sanctity and privileged ones of the Sacred Heart, how many of us are poverty-stricken in our love, our charity grown cold—lacking in response and generosity. Are we the intimate friends and true Spouses of Jesus? Are we His devoted ones, who, having given ourselves once and for all in a magnificent gesture of love, have never counted the price?[1]

"Thou shalt love the Lord thy God with thy whole heart, with thy
Mt 22:37 whole soul and with all thy mind". This is the command of the great God, and He cannot command the impossible. Love is a fruit in season at all times and within the reach of every hand. Anyone may gather it, and no limit is set.[2] Everyone can reach this love through meditation—spirit of prayer—and sacrifices, by an intense interior life.[3] Do I really live this life?

Am I convinced of Christ's love for me, and mine for Him? This conviction is like sunlight which makes the sap of life rise and the buds of sanctity bloom.[4] This conviction is the rock on which sanctity is built.[5]

a. The First Friday of each month is traditionally dedicated to the Sacred Heart of Jesus, and was very significant for Mother because of her great devotion to the Sacred Heart, her "first love."

What must we do to get this conviction? We must know Jesus, love Jesus, serve Jesus. We know Him through prayers, meditations—spiritual duties. We love Him through Holy Mass and Sacraments and through that intimate union of love.[6] We serve Him in His poor—by doing to them what we would like to do to Him.

Here, my children, is the sanctity hidden for us—in knowing Jesus—loving Jesus—serving Jesus. If we do this—the conviction will grow—and as the conviction will grow—we become a "Professional" in holiness.

Let me know if you want me to write to you on something else.

God bless you.

P.S. All letters to me must be closed. All letters to Sisters must be in English. You begin, "My dearest Mother" or "Sisters", and end "Your loving child" or "Sister" with your full name.

God bless you,
Mother

MGL 3. [7TH] OCTOBER 1960

L.D.M.

First Friday
[7th] October 1960

My dearest Sisters,

I was very happy to know from all the houses how all of you really desire to become "Professional in holiness".

The first step "to becoming" is to will it. St. Thomas says,[a] "Sanctity consists in nothing else than a firm resolve, the heroic act of a soul abandoning herself to God." "By an upright will we love God, we choose God, we run towards God, we reach Him, we possess Him." "O Good, good will, which transforms me into the image of God and makes me like to Him," so St. Augustine says.[b] My progress in holiness depends on God and myself—on God's grace and my will.[7]

a. St. Thomas Aquinas (1225–1274) was an Italian Dominican, Doctor of the Church, and one of the greatest theologians of the Catholic Church, best known for his masterpieces *Summa Theologiae* and *Summa contra Gentiles*, as well as his Eucharistic hymns, which are still in use in the liturgy (e.g., *Adoro Te Devote, Tantum Ergo*).

b. St. Augustine (354–430), born in Tagaste (present-day Algeria), became bishop of Hippo, philosopher and theologian, and Doctor of the Church; he is the author of numerous works, among which *Confessions* and *The City of God* are best known.

Often under the pretext of humility, of confidence, of abandonment, have we not forgotten the use of our strong will? We must have a real living resolution to reach holiness.[8] St. Teresa says that Satan is terribly afraid of resolute souls[a]—everything depends on these two words: I WILL or I WILL NOT.[b] Into this "I will", I must put all my energy.[9] "I will" said St. John Berchmans, St. Stanislaus, St. Margaret Mary,[c] and they did become Saints. What is a saint?—but a resolute soul—a soul that uses power plus action. Was not this what St. Paul meant when he said: "I can do all
Phil 4:13 things in Him who strengthens me."[10] With you, my sisters, I will not be satisfied by [your] being just good religious. I want to be able to offer God a perfect sacrifice. Only holiness perfects the gift.

To resolve to be a Saint, it costs much. Renunciation, temptations, struggles, persecutions and all kinds of sacrifices surround the resolute soul. One can love God only at one's own expense.[11]

"I will be a Saint" means—I will despoil myself of all that is not God; I will strip my heart and empty it of all created things; I will live in poverty and detachment. I will renounce my will, my inclinations, my whims and fancies and make myself a willing slave to the will of God.[12] Yes, my children, this is what I pray for daily—for each one—that we may become a slave to the will of God.

7th October is coming very close—our first ten years[d]—God has blessed.[e] Let us redouble our efforts to becoming more fervent, more close to God, and the coming ten years will be blessed with better and more lasting fruit.

I enclose the copy of the [Decree of] Erection of our Society.[f] It will help you to appreciate and love the Society more.

God bless you
Mother

a. St. Teresa of Avila (1515–1582), was a Spanish Carmelite nun, reformer of the Carmelite order, mystic, writer, and Doctor of the Church.

b. In this letter and in all the future instances, when the Sister typist chose to type various words and phrases in ALL CAPS, we have respected this original interpretation.

c. St. John Berchmans (1599–1621) was a Flemish Jesuit novice noted for his kindness and fidelity; he is the patron saint of altar servers. St. Stanislaus Kostka (1550–1568) was a Polish Jesuit novice, model of religious perfection; he is the patron saint of novices. St. Margaret Mary Alacoque (1647–1690) was a French religious of the Order of the Visitation in Paray-le-Monial (France) and the apostle of devotion to the Sacred Heart of Jesus.

d. Mother is referring to ten years since the Decree of Erection of the Society of the Missionaries of Charity, 7th October 1950.

e. Mother means "God has blessed our first ten years."

f. See Appendix A, p. 521.

MGL 4. [4TH] NOVEMBER 1960

L.D.M.

First Friday
[4th] November 1960[a]

My dearest Sisters,

On the 25th at 5:45 A.M.[b] I am leaving by P.A.A. [Pan Am Airways] and will be in America, God willing, on the 26th, 6:30 A.M. I go—but my heart and my mind and the whole of me is with you. It is the Will of God that I should go. Therefore let us all be happy, in spite of our feelings.[c]

During my absence Sr. M. Agnes[d]—the Asst. [Assistant] General—and
the Council General[e] will take all responsibility. God will take care of you Jn 17:11
all, my children, if you remain one; if you love each other as God has Jn 13:34; 15:12
loved you—with an intense love—as Mother[f] loves you with an undivided
love. Cling round the Society, because in the centre is Jesus. Be fervent and
loving with Jesus, and you are sure to reach great sanctity. Let Jesus' love
for you be the cause of your love for your Sisters and the poor.

a. This letter was actually written before 25th October, but sent to the houses as the letter for the First Friday in November.

b. The style for the time of day in Mother's letters varies. At times it is written with periods and at time with colons separating hours and minutes; furthermore, a.m. and p.m. are at times written in capitals and at times in lower case, seemingly depending on the choice and preference of the typist. Mother usually used 12 hours format and wrote am or pm without periods in lower case. We have standardized the style for the time of day for easier reading.

c. See Brian Kolodiejchuk, *Mother Teresa: Come Be My Light* (New York: Doubleday, 2007), 202 (hereafter *Come Be My Light*), for more details on the first trip abroad.

d. Sr. M. Agnes, MC (Shubashini Das), Mother Teresa's former pupil in Loreto, was the first to join the MC Society (on 19th March 1949). In this letter steeped in emotion as she is about to embark on her first trip abroad, Mother instructs the Sisters on Sr. Agnes's responsibilities, but she also gives them an exhortation on love for each other—a theme that seems to be uppermost in her heart. Sr. Agnes remained Mother's faithful disciple throughout her life and held various important offices in the Society, always remaining humble and somewhat hidden. She was faithful and loyal in her vocation as an MC, showing great love for Mother, for the Sisters, and especially for the poorest of the poor.

e. The Society was still very young, and the Sisters did not have the age required by the Constitutions (above thirty) for the convocation of a General Chapter, the election of a Superior General, a General Council, a Procuratrix and a General Secretary. Archbishop Périer recommended nominating Sisters for these offices, and he eventually nominated the Sisters according to the names suggested by Mother Teresa. The First General Chapter of the Missionaries of Charity was held in 1961, and the Assistant General and the Council General that Mother mentions here were actually "acting", that is, Sr. Agnes was acting Assistant General.

f. This is the first example in the general letters where Mother is referring to herself in the third person. She often referred to herself in the third person, especially in her instructions to the Sisters, but also in her general letters and in other correspondence. In the general letters (especially in later years), at times the typists added some information about Mother, usually after Mother's signature, obviously using the third person, but this does not seem to be the case here. Speaking in the third person is an adaptation of the custom prevalent among the Sisters in India, in which the speaker uses the third person even in direct speech, when addressing a person who is considered as worthy of high esteem, respect, and honour.

I am not afraid to leave you, for I know the great gift God has given me—in giving you to me. On my way back—that will be about the 15th Nov.—I shall go to Rome. Begin a Novena to the Sacred Heart, from our [MC prayer] book, from the 11th November. I am going to try and see our Holy Father and beg of him to take our little Society under his special care, and grant us a Pontifical recognition. As you know, we are not worthy of this great gift, but if it is God's Holy Will, we will get it. You pray and make many sacrifices. During this time it would make me very happy if the Seniors make sacrifices in Obedience; Juniors in Charity; Novices in Poverty; Postulants in Chastity.[a]

	SENIORS:	Obedience—	prompt, simple blind, cheerful—for Jesus
Phil 2:8			was obedient unto death.
	JUNIORS:	Charity—	words, deeds, thoughts, desires, feelings—
Acts 10:38			for Jesus went about doing good.
	NOVICES:	Poverty—	in desires and attachments, in likes and
			dislikes—for Jesus being rich made
2 Cor 8:9			Himself poor for me.

a. The stages of formation are as follows:

Aspirancy (aspirants, six months at the time of this letter, at present one year) gives the candidate the opportunity to see the life and work. The aspirants spend half day working along with the professed Sisters and half day studying. In the very beginning of the Society, in the early 1950s, there was no aspirancy as a separate period of formation. The candidates joined the postulancy, and after six months went to the noviciate. In the late 1950s they began aspirancy, which was less structured than other stages of formation and initially lasted three months. Until 1959, Mother was the only Finally Professed in the Congregation, and she was the Mistress of all the groups, though she had assistants; all the Sisters resided in Mother House.

Postulancy (postulants, six months at the time of this letter, at present one year) aims at mutual knowledge between the Society and the postulant. The postulants also spend half the day studying and half the day working with the poor.

Noviciate (novices, two years) aims at understanding the vocation and all that it implies. The novices spend the first year of their noviciate, the so-called canonical year, in prayer and study. During the second year, they work with the poor in the mornings and spend the afternoons in prayer and study.

Juniorate (junior sisters, five years) while deepening religious consecration, stresses the training for the apostolate and mission of the Church. Explicit formation during juniorate ("Junior courses") began only in 1988 with the six-month program in Calcutta. To avoid the difficulties of transferring so many Sisters every six months, it was subsequently decided to have the juniorate program in every region and to distribute it to a month per year over a five-year period, thus the Sisters are absent from their community for just over a month at a time, and the apostolate is less affected.

Tertianship (tertians, one year) is a special period of spiritual renewal and intense preparation preceding final profession. It is sometimes also called "third year".

Senior sisters, after final vows.

At the 1990 General Chapter the decision was made to introduce a period of *Pre-Aspirancy* (pre-aspirants, one year) that gives the candidate the opportunity to learn more about the faith, discern signs of vocation to the MC way of life and evaluate her aptitude to live it.

POSTULANTS: Chastity— in thoughts and affections, in desires and attachments, and in the streets in not looking at worldly pictures and magazines, in not listening to idle conversations, in faithfulness to the rule of touch—for Jesus is a jealous lover. Dt 4:24

Be faithful in little things, for in them our strength lies. To the good God nothing is little, because He is so great and we so small—that is why He stoops down and takes the trouble to make those little things for us—to give us a chance to prove our love for Him. Because He makes them, they are very great. He cannot make anything small; they are infinite. Yes my dear children, be faithful in little practices of love, of little sacrifices—of the little interior mortifications—of little fidelities to Rule, which will build in you the life of holiness—make you Christ-like. Mt 25:21, 23

To the feet of Christ's Vicar on earth,[a] I will carry each one of you—just as you are—and, I am sure, he, with his fatherly love, will bless each one of you and obtain for you the graces you need to become saints. Keep together round your Superiors—take care of them, love them, make your recreation resound with joy which no one can take from you—for a happy recreation is the best preparation for a fervent Holy Communion.[13] Jn 16:22

God bless you, my dear children,
Mother

a. Pope John XXIII.

1961

MGL 5. [6TH] JANUARY 1961

L.D.M.

First Friday
[6th] January 1961

My own dearest Children,[a]

We begin our New Year with one common resolution—to know, to love, to observe our Holy Rule. Fidelity to [the] rule is the most precious and delicate flower of love we religious can give to Almighty God.[14]

We must know the rule; we must know that the rule is the expression of the Will of God—to submit to it everywhere and always, down to the last breath. We must be convinced that the slightest unjustified violation wounds the Heart of Jesus and stains the conscience. When the rule becomes one of our greatest loves, then this love expands into a free and joyful service. Submission, for someone who is in love, is more than a duty—it is blessedness. This is the secret of the Saints.[15]

It was in the rule that the Saints found the quick and sure way to holiness—for it is love that sanctifies and is the greatest merit of regularity. We must observe the rule with a big and willing heart, faithful down to the last detail, and have a soul that has learned to see and love in even the least prescriptions the most Holy Will of God.[16] Fidelity in the least things not for their own sake, for this is the work of small minds, but for the sake of the great thing, which is the Will of God, and which I respect greatly in little things. St. Augustine says, "Little things are indeed little, but to be faithful to little things is a great thing." Is not Our Lord equally the same in a small

a. On the top of the copy of this letter Mother wrote "Asansol," (a town 140 miles northwest of Calcutta), indicating that this particular copy was meant for the Asansol community. When her general letters were retyped in order to make the bound books that are in the refectories, the letters were collected from different houses in order to make the collection more complete. These copies are now treated as manuscripts of Mother's letters.

Host as in a great one? The smallest rule contains the Will of God as much as the big things of life.[17] To be able to reach this knowledge, I must have faith in the rule—that it is of divine origin—that it is the echo of and a commentary on the Gospel. Faith in the rule is the foundation of the religious life. I must have trust that the rule is the means of my sanctification and the weapon of my apostolate, the source of Holiness, Peace, Joy, and a pledge of perseverance. I must cling to the rule as the child clings to its Mother.

I must love the rule with my will and reason, with my body and soul. It does not matter that the rule often seems unnatural, hard and austere. The sacrifice the rule imposes on us is a source of holiness for us and a sure means for our apostolate.[18]

It is perfect practice of the rule that makes the perfect religious. Remember, my dear children, if you believe in the holiness of the rule, you cannot help but respect it, trust it, love it; and if you believe in the divine origin of the rule, you must keep it faithfully and lovingly.[19]

It is this, my own dearest children, that Mother wants you to aim at during this year of grace.[a] God has been so very wonderful to us, and it is our duty to be very wonderful to God. Help each other to keep the rule.

You have been all such a great consolation to Jesus and to me during this last year. Let us try to be a greater consolation this year.

God bless you
Mother

MGL 6. [3RD] FEBRUARY 1961

L.D.M.

First Friday
[3rd] February 1961

My dearest Sisters,

We all want to do something beautiful for God during Lent[b]—because Jesus did so much during His Passion.—We look round and try to imagine all kinds of sacrifices and mortifications, but for us—dear Sisters—we need not go round seeking—just take your rules and try to live them with greater love for Jesus and with Jesus—and you will have all the sacrifices

a. *Year of grace* is a term used to refer to any calendar year in the Christian era, especially at the beginning of a new year.

b. Lent began on 15th February 1961.

your generous heart desires to offer to God. The sister who keeps the rule lovingly and strictly will make herself into a Saint. This is a direct way—no need to try to find other means.[20] St. Vincent compares the rules to "wings to fly to God".[a] A Sister, dying, asked, "What should I have done to be a Saint?" The Priest answered, "Aren't you familiar with this wonderful little book, your rule? If you had lived this rule, you would have been a Saint."[21] "Just think," says St. Alphonsus—"by the discharge of your ordinary duties you may become a Saint."[22] St. Vincent says—"Keep your rules and you will become Saints, for they are holy in themselves, they also can make you holy. They can make Saints of each and every one of you. The religious who keeps them well may rest assured that she will be happy in this life as well as in the next."[23] St. Francis de Sales writes[b]—"Walk on always in the punctual observance of your rules and you will be blessed by God—for He Himself will lead you with great care."

Nothing prevented Pope Benedict XIV[c] from canonizing a young novice because she had observed the rule perfectly.[24]

In the observance of the rule you will find strength for the purity of conscience, fervour to fill your soul and love which will inflame your heart.[25]

Buathier says[d]—"The rule is to our will what the arteries are to our blood." Holiness is only a very high degree of love. Obedience to the rule is the fullness of this love. The Sister who loves Christ will live according to His will—that is, according to the rule,[26] and he ends by saying: "Unhappy is the religious who rejects it. Outside the rule her life is wasted and miserable and day follows day in utter monotony."[27] Keep the rule and the rule will keep you.[28]

Yes, my dear children, let us all unite in helping each other to become

a. St. Vincent de Paul (1580–1660), known as the apostle of charity, was the French founder of the Congregation of the Missions (Vincentians) for the formation of the clergy and the relief of the poor, and co-founder, with St. Louise de Marillac, of the congregation of the Sisters of Charity.

b. St. Francis de Sales (1567–1622), bishop of Geneva, was a spiritual writer and Doctor of the Church known for his gentleness, kindness, and intelligence; his writings on the spiritual life, particularly the *Introduction to the Devout Life* and the *Treatise on the Love of God*, are considered spiritual classics.

c. Pope Benedict XIV (1675–1758) was pope from 1740 to 1758. Pope Benedict XIII (1649–1730) was pope from 1724 to 1730. He canonized St. Stanislaus Kostka (1550–1568), a Jesuit novice, on 31st December 1726. There are no novices canonized by Pope Benedict XIV, so probably "XIV" is an error in the original work, *The Practice of the Rule*, by Louis Colin, CSsR, from which Mother quotes. It should have been Pope Benedict XIII, and the canonized novice in question is St. Stanislaus Kostka. Please note that Mother (as it was her custom to paraphrase and adapt the text to the needs of the Sisters), in error, writes "she" instead of "he". The original work *The Practice of the Rule* does not specify whether the novice is "he" or "she"; however, neither Pope Benedict XIV nor Pope Benedict XIII canonized any female novice.

d. Father Jean-Marie Buathier (1850–1900) was a priest of the diocese of Belley, France, and author of the book *Le sacrifice dans le dogme catholique et dans la vie chrétienne*, quoted in *The Practice of the Rule* by Louis Colin, CSsR.

holy—for Jesus says—"Seek first the Kingdom of God and all the rest will be added onto you"—the Kingdom of God is holiness. Mt 6:33

In future you may write to the Sisters for their feast days—individually—but the general letters must be written as follows—one letter for all the houses—everybody must help in composing it, and the Superior or anybody she appoints writes—the copies can be made by the Sisters—or typed....[a]

You may also write and receive letters from your parents, brothers and sisters even during Lent and Advent. Those whose parents are here—may have visiting Sunday.[b]

For the [Lenten] fast do exactly what the Archbishop or Bishop has ordered for the Archdiocese....

If any Sister needs dispensation—the Superior may not give it—she must get permission from the Vicar General.

No recreation at tea time only during the Passion Week.

10 minutes adoration[c] must be added to the time-table of every house—6:50 to 7:00 P.M. is the best time.

When writing to me or our Sisters, please do not use "Rev." [Reverend]. Don't forget to add after my name, Sisters' name, or your own name—MC. Do not just put your number.[d]

All those who visit families, make sure that you get the family consecrated to the Sacred Heart. See that the family consecrated [has] a picture (however small) of the Sacred Heart in their home—however poor it may be. Do the visiting—thoroughly, and write particulars of each family in your book. Next time I visit the houses I want to see these books.

I have written much today.—Be holy—be good—be happy that you have been chosen to be holy.

God bless you all
Mother

a. The schedule for writing the general letters (i.e., the newsletters) has been omitted. There were, by this time, six MC houses—Mother House, Delhi, Ranchi, Creek Lane (which was later moved to Park Street), Agra, and Jhansi—in five cities in India

b. First Sunday of the month, when the Sisters could receive visits from their parents and family members.

c. This was actually a visit to the Blessed Sacrament (with benediction only on Sunday and day-in, when the confessor would come); one-hour community adoration began only in 1973. The day-in, usually Thursday, is a day when the Sisters stay at home and take more time for prayer, reflection, and study, as well as for house cleaning and other personal needs. The outside apostolate is avoided except in an emergency, and the care of the poor, especially of the residents in the homes, is delegated as much as possible to the workers or volunteers.

d. The number assigned to each Sister, used to distinguish her clothes, books, and other personal items.

MGL 7. 22ND APRIL 1961

L.D.M.

22nd April 1961

My dearest Sisters,

I would so much want you to read my first general letter I wrote.[a]—
How the devil is busy with you all.—My dear children, you are more busy
Lk 10:16 with your Superior as "she" than with Jesus—for whose sake you obey her.
It makes me very sad to think how many graces you are all losing because
of this want of obedience and submission. When you go to Heaven, Our
Lord is not going to ask you—was your Superior holy, clever, understand-
ing, cheerful, etc., but only one thing—"Did you obey Me?" What a wasted
life is ours if it is so full of self.—You spend yourself on her—instead of on
Him—your Spouse whose place she takes. Why don't you fix your eyes on
Jesus? If you can't see Jesus in your Superior how will you see Jesus in the
Mk 25:40 poor? How will you find Jesus in His distressing disguise? Tell me—how
1 Jn 4:20 will you love Jesus—you can't see, if you don't love your Superior you can
see? Where is your faith, my children? I am so afraid for you. The devil is
angry with the work of God—and not knowing how to spoil it—he will try
to spoil the instruments and so indirectly spoil the work of God. My children open your eyes wide—and don't allow yourselves to be deceived.—
Obey fully. Obey because you love Jesus—obey because you want to prove
your love for Jesus—obey—obey. Do not think that only because you love
and obey Mother—this is enough. It is easy to obey Mother. It is now that I
want to test your love for the Society and for me—by giving you the chance
to obey those I have put over you. Does not matter who they are or what
they are—as long as they are "HE" for whose sake you obey.

Lk 1:26–38 See how Our Lady obeyed the angel—"be it done to me according to
Thy Word".—Whose Word? Angel's—because he took the place of God—
Mt 2:13–15; 20–21 He was sent by God to her. She the Queen of Heaven obeys the Angel.—
See how she obeyed St. Joseph—with what love—and submission, without
an excuse.—To her—St. Joseph was—"HE" whose place he took.—Think
and pray over all [this] and you will see how much the devil has taken
from you. My children, obey lovingly—obey because you love Jesus.

Tomorrow we are going to Simla[b]—pray for this new foundation—that it be all for the greater glory of God.[c]

a. MGL 1 of 20th September 1959.

b. Capital of the State of Himachal Pradesh in Northern India. The house was opened on 23rd April 1961. Eventually this house was closed and the Sisters were moved to Ambala, where a new foundation was established on 22nd November 1961.

c. Motto of St. Ignatius of Loyola.

For the Month of Our Lady[a]—let us give Our Lady pure flowers of blind, simple, prompt and cheerful obedience. I would like these acts to be counted and sent to me—in the first week of June—so that I can offer them to the Sacred Heart, on His Feast.

God bless you
Mother

MGL 8. [2ND] JUNE 1961

L.D.M.

First Friday
[2nd] June 1961

My dearest Sisters,

As the month of June is the month of love[b]—I want you all to fill your hearts with great love.—Don't imagine that love, to be true and burning, must be extraordinary.—No—what we need in our love is continuity [in loving] the One we love.

See how the lamp burns—how the light burns—because of the continual consumption of the little drops of oil.—Let those drops be no more in
the lamp, there will be no light—and the Bridegroom has a right to say "I Mt 25:12
don't know you"—because there is no light. My children, what are those drops of oil in our lamp. They are the vocal and mental prayer—punctuality—those little words and acts of kindness—just a little thought for others—that fervour in saying the morning and night prayers—the way we genuflect—take Holy Water—make the Sign of the Cross—those little acts of silence, of look and thought, of word and deed. These are, my children, the very drops of Divine Love which make our religious life burn with so much light.

Don't search for Jesus in far Lands—He is not there—He is close to you—He is in you; just keep the lamp burning and you will always see

a. May is the month traditionally dedicated to Our Lady.

b. June is the month traditionally dedicated to the Sacred Heart of Jesus. On 24th June 1967 Mother would write to her spiritual director, Fr. Neuner, "Father, can you explain to me—when you have time—how to grow in the 'deep personal union of the human heart with the Heart of Christ.' From childhood the Heart of Jesus has been my first love.—Every Friday is the feast of the Sacred Heart for me. I love the Mass of the S H [Sacred Heart]—for in the words of the offertory re-echo the words of 10th Sept.—'will you do this for Me.' This M.C. is only His work." (See *Come Be My Light*, 257.) In the devotion of this month, her great love for the Sacred Heart found its desired expression, and she welcomed this yearly opportunity to draw closer to the Heart of Christ. She invited her Sisters to grow in this same love.

Him.—Keep on filling the lamp with all those little drops of love, and you will see how sweet is the Lord you love.

In this month of love, therefore, we will take for a special point—that fidelity to little things which will help us to know Jesus more clearly—to love Him more dearly—to serve Him more faithfully and ardently.[29]

All of you pray for our new foundation in Asansol. In your next general letters, give more news of the work in detail—so that our Sisters have a clear picture.

...

Keep close to Jesus with a smiling face.[a]

God bless you
Mother

MGL 9. [7TH] JULY 1961

L.D.M.

First Friday
[7th] July 1961

My dearest Sisters,

In all the houses there was a great increase in love and fervour during the month of June. I hope in the house in which you are, you tried to be a cause of joy to the Sacred Heart. I did feel very happy to be able to give the Sacred Heart a new Tabernacle in Asansol—from where, through our Sisters, He will radiate His love and life. It has also been a token of gratitude to Rev. Fr. C. Van Exem for all he has done for the Society.[b]

The Month of July is the month of the Precious Blood—the whole month is specially dedicated to the Holy Mass. Try during this month to increase your knowledge of this Mystery of Redemption.—This knowledge will lead you to love—and love will make you share through your
Mt 26–27, Mk 14–15, Lk 22–23, Jn 18–19 sacrifices in the Passion of Christ.

a. After the letter was retyped for the houses, Mother at times used to add, before her signature, a short exhortation for the Sisters of that house or the changes that concerned that particular house. Hereafter, these additions are reproduced in italics, and when necessary, a footnote was added to further explain the circumstance.

b. Father Céleste Van Exem, SJ, a Belgian Jesuit, was Mother's spiritual director from 1944 and guided her in the founding of the Missionaries of Charity (see *Come Be My Light,* 45ff). Born in 1908, he entered the Society of Jesus in 1927 and was ordained in 1940, in Kurseong, India. At the time of this letter, Fr. Van Exem was the superior of the Jesuit house and the parish priest in Asansol. From the beginning of the Society, he served as confessor of the Sisters in Calcutta. He died on 20th September 1993.

My dear children—without our suffering, our work would just be social work, very good and helpful, but it would not be the work of Jesus Christ, not part of the redemption—Jesus wanted to help us by sharing our life, our loneliness, our agony and death. All that, He has taken upon Himself, and has carried it in the darkest night. Only by being one with us He has redeemed us. We are allowed to do the same: All the desolation of the Poor people, not only their Material poverty, but their spiritual destitution, must be redeemed, and we must have our share in it.—Pray thus when you find it hard—"I wish to live in this world which is so far from God, which has turned so much from the light of Jesus, to help them—to take upon me something of their suffering."—Yes, my dear children—let us share the sufferings—of our Poor—for only by being one with them— [can] we redeem them, that is, [by] bringing God into their lives and bringing them to God.[30]

During this month let us take trouble to join in the Mass with great fervour and devotion—recite the Mass prayers with love and care. Let us take for spiritual reading—something about Holy Mass.—Often during the day say this prayer:

> "In union with all the Masses being offered throughout the world, I offer you this . . ."

Remember there are four Elevations every second.[a] Somewhere, at this very minute, Mass is being offered—so we are being prayed for the whole time. What a strength this conviction should be to us.

Remember me during your Holy Mass during the day.

God bless you
Mother

a. The elevation is the consecration at Holy Mass. Mother must have heard or read this statistic somewhere and shared it with the Sisters.

MGL 10. [4TH] AUGUST 1961

L.D.M.

First Friday
[4th] August 1961

My dearest Children,

The feast of our Society is very close, and I am sure we are all longing to be a cause of Joy to the Society, to do something great in her honour. The greatest offering we can make is a fervent heart.—If you really want
Rom 16:3; 1 Cor 3:9 to become a true Co-worker of Christ, keep the rule.

How beautifully our Vows [fulfil] the Spirit of our Society.[a] Total Surrender of all material and spiritual riches in Poverty—that Loving Trust in our Superiors in deep and perfect Obedience, and Cheerfulness because
Jn 15:16 we are consecrated to Him. Jesus Himself has chosen us for Himself, and what joy is ours that we can at all times be in close contact with Christ in His distressing disguise—in our work of Charity. Don't we fulfil the Gospel? "You did it to Me." Jesus says—"I was hungry, thirsty, naked,
Mt 25:34–40 homeless, sick, dying, unwanted and untouchable and you did it to Me." How great is our calling. How fortunate people would think themselves if they were given [the] chance to give personal service to the King of this world.[31] And here we are—we can touch, serve and love Christ all the days of our life. My Sisters, love your vocation above all, for in loving it you love God.

To prove our gratitude for our Great Vocation, this month we will take special care of our spiritual life. Take Rule 76 in all its details, meditate on it, take your P.E. [Particular Examen][b] on some special point [at] which you fail most. Read in the refectory about prayer, and how to pray better. Ask your superiors to help you with your spiritual life in a more concrete way. In one word, revive your spiritual life and make it a bright happy
Jn 12:32 reality. We can draw all to God only if we are lifted up.

Your work for the Poor will be done better if you know the way God wants you to do it, and you will know this only through Obedience. Cling to your superiors as [the] creeper clings. The creeper can live and grow

a. The Spirit of the Society is total surrender, loving trust, and cheerfulness.

b. The examination of conscience, considered by St. Ignatius of Loyola to be an indispensable spiritual exercise, consists of the general examen and the particular examen. The general examen is a review of one's thoughts, words, actions, and omissions over a period of time (typically the last six or twelve hours). The particular examen focuses on the practice of a particular virtue or the avoidance of a particular vice. The examination of conscience twice a day is part of the MC spiritual exercises, and Mother often referred to it in her letters as "examen" or with the abbreviation P.E.

only if it clings on[to] something. You also will grow and live in holiness only if you cling to Obedience.

I have noticed a number of Sisters are cutting their food.[a] I can say but one thing to them, "it is the beginning of your end", the beginning of a tepid life which ends in total selfishness. I have also noticed that as perfect obedience is declining, so is peace, joy and union with God growing weaker. Let us pull up during this month of our Society, and in the pulling remember to pray for your Mother.

God bless you and a very happy & holy feast to all.

Mother

MGL 11. 27TH AUGUST 1961

L.D.M.

Calcutta[b]
27th August 1961

My dearest Sisters,

On the 7th October 1961, we shall have our first elections for the Chapter General. That we may be able to know and do the things that are pleasing to God, we shall recite daily after Holy Communion:[c]

> "Come, O Blessed Spirit of Knowledge and Light, and grant that I may perceive the Will of the Father; show me the nothingness of earthly things, that I may realise their vanity and use them only for Thy glory and my own salvation, looking ever beyond them to Thee, and Thy eternal rewards. Amen."[32]

Also, we shall make three real sacrifices in honour of the Blessed Trinity. . . .

a. That is, reducing the amount of food they eat.

b. Some of Mother Teresa's letters were written on official MC letterhead. This is one of the first instances of a letter typed on MC letterhead. The letterhead is not reproduced here, or in the other instances when it was used, for the sake of saving space. This letter was typed on the letterhead of Doranda (Ranchi) house; however, along with the date, Mother writes Calcutta as the place from which the letter was written. There are various examples of letters written from one house on the letterhead of another house. It is possible that the Doranda house (or other houses) had extra printed papers and shared them with Mother House, as sharing among the houses was a common practice. In the beginning, Mother used to visit the Ranchi community (Doranda) every week, so she also might have taken the paper from there and written in the train on her way back. In all the instances that the MC letterhead was used, only the name of the house from which the letter was actually written is mentioned here, even when Mother used the letterhead of another house.

c. The following prayer is part of a Novena to the Holy Spirit; Mother chose the prayer for the fifth day, invoking the Spirit of knowledge.

Read Part II of our Constitutions, and you will find in 153 that every House has to elect a Deputy besides Sister Superior.[a] The Deputy must be of perpetual Vows. See also 157, and you will find how to do the election.[b] Sister Superior and the Deputy must be at the Mother House on the 27th September. They will begin the Retreat on the 28th, which Rev. Fr. C. Van Exem will preach.

My Children, this coming election is one more step towards the stability of our Society and so also nearer to the Pontifical recognition.

Try to pray often and fervently that we may all do all things for the greater glory of God.

God bless you—

God bless you
Mother

MGL 12. 23RD OCTOBER 1961

23rd October 1961[c]

My dearest Sisters,

As per [the] letter of His Grace,[d] the Good God has been pleased to bless our elections at our First General Chapter.

As we have all prayed and made many sacrifices to obtain God's blessing—now with the same fervour and love we shall offer our gratitude to God. Therefore, in all our Houses on the 29th, [the] Feast of Christ the King, we shall offer Holy Mass, and at the Benediction we shall recite

a. Constitution 153: "The deputies will be elected by all the professed sisters of the house, according to the rules laid down for the election of the Superior General in no. 157. To be validly elected deputy of a house the sisters must belong to that same house and be a professed of perpetual Vows." (1950–53 *Constitutions*; this corresponds with no. 161 of the 1954 *Constitutions*, which was in use until 1973.)

b. Constitution 157: "The Superior General is elected by secret ballot and by an absolute majority of votes. If after three scrutinies an absolute majority has not been obtained, a fourth ballot shall be taken in which only those two members will be eligible who had the greatest number of votes in the third ballot. In case more than two members had an equal number of votes in the third ballot, only the two older by first Profession and by age shall be eligible in the fourth ballot. In this fourth ballot these two member candidates cannot vote. Should this fourth ballot result in a tie, then the senior by first Profession is elected; and in case both have made their Profession on the same day, the senior in age is elected. The person who is elected cannot refuse the office unless the Chapter is willing to yield to her objections" (1950–53 *Constitutions*; this corresponds with no. 165 in the 1954 *Constitutions* and no. 176 in the 1988 *Constitutions*).

c. This is the first instance of a general letter where Mother did not write the initials L.D.M.

d. Mother Teresa is referring to Archbishop V. Dyer's letter regarding the result of the elections of the First General Chapter, at which Mother Teresa was elected as Superior General, and Sr. M. Agnes, MC, Sr. M. Gertrude, MC, Sr. M. Bernard, MC, and Sr. M. Dorothy, MC, as her Councillors.

the *Act of Consecration to the Immaculate Heart* (page 61[a]) and also sing the *Te Deum*.[b] (Superiors please get permission in time to have Benediction in case you don't have it.)

God is so good to us.—Let us live up to the trust [that] Our Mother, the Church, puts in us.

God bless you
Mother

a. This page number refers to the *MC Prayer Book* that was then in use; in the present *Prayer Book*, it is p. 73.

b. The *Te Deum* is a traditional liturgical hymn of praise sung in thanksgiving to God. The title derives from the first line of the original Latin text, "Te Deum laudamus," which is translated "We praise You, O God."

1962

MGL 13. 2ND JANUARY 1962

L.D.M.

Mother House
2nd January 1962

My dearest Children,

1962—Be all for Jesus and with Jesus—and you will be happy and holy throughout the year.

On the 31st December, as the siren sounded,[a] my thoughts were with each one of you. How my heart longed to offer to God a perfect sacrifice made of your hearts.—I offered to God each one of you and promised Him that I would work harder than ever to help you love Jesus with your whole heart and soul—especially through that complete obedience.—Yes, my Children, let us all try very specially not to criticise or grumble and cause endless disunion in our Family. Let us be the Apostles of Obedience spreading the Joy of Jesus in every house, wherever we may be.—One thing we must remember—we cannot help seeing the faults of our Superiors and Sisters—people and children, but we can help and we must not ever pass judgment on their intentions—the intention only Jesus knows. That is why Jesus is so very kind and full of Mercy, because He knows what we really mean each time.

My children—be kind to Jesus.—Don't hurt Jesus—for He loves you. He loves you through your Superiors—whom He has put in His place. If
Mt 10:42 He will reward a glass of water—how much more will He not reward your
submission[b]—your greatness of Heart—each time you obey—each time you submit your judgment to your Superiors in all things except sin....

God bless you
Mother

a. Mother is referring to the siren that sounded at midnight on New Year's Eve.
b. Meaning, "will He not reward much more your submission ..."

MGL 14. 9TH MARCH 1962

L.D.M.

Mother House
9th March 1962

My dearest Children,

As we begin Lent our thoughts naturally continually turn to the Passion of Our Lord—and we long to share with Him His pain. What is this Pain of Jesus? The pain of loving and not being loved.—He has loved us with an everlasting love—and what is our return?—Any little thing has the power to preoccupy our whole mind, and due to it—maybe [we] spend many hours without thinking of Jesus—and yet our heart and soul, body and mind belong only to Jesus. During this Lent let us improve our spirit of prayer and recollection.—Let us free our minds from all that is not Jesus.—If you find it difficult to pray—ask Him again and again—"Jesus come into my heart—pray in me and with me—that I may learn from Thee how to pray."—If you pray more you will pray better. Take the help of all your senses to pray. Pay special care—how you genuflect, how you join your hands, when passing by the chapel, going out or coming to the Convent, the taking of the holy water, using the holy pictures to lift your mind to God.—The Rosary in the street—should be a beautiful means to keep on praying. Take the trouble to say it fervently with your companion—and these are, my dearest Sisters, the little acts of special love we will offer to Jesus during this Holy Lent, and so share with Him His Pain.

Jer 31:3

During Lent and Advent you are allowed to write or see only your parents or the one who takes their place. In our home letters or when we see them let us try very specially to give Jesus to our loved ones.

Let your general letters vibrate with joy and fervour—let them be really the Community act of love to the Society.—Just as St. J. Berchmans said—a happy recreation helped him to make a fervent Holy Communion—so it should be with our letters—they should help us to love Jesus more in our Sisters.

I have seen Bhagalpur, Raigarh, Kanpur, and will soon go to Amravati—so pray very fervently—that Mother may know and do God's Holy Will in all things.

God bless you.
Mother

MGL 15. [2ND] JUNE 1962

L.D.M.

First Saturday
[2nd] June 1962

My dearest Children,

One day St. Margaret Mary asked Jesus, "Lord, what wilt Thou have me to do?" "Give Me a free Hand," Jesus answered.[33] He will perform the divine work of sanctity, not you, and He asks of you [only] docility.[a] Let Him empty and amend you, and afterwards fill the chalice of your hearts to the brim, that you, in your turn, may give of your abundance.[34] Seek Him fervently during this month of Love. Seek Him in the Tabernacle.—Fix your eyes on Him who is the Light—bring your hearts close to His Divine Heart—ask Him to grant you

the grace of Knowing Him,
the love of Loving Him,
the courage to Serve Him.

Knowledge will make you strong as death.[35] Love Him generously. Love Him trustfully, without looking back, without fear.[36]—Give yourself fully to Jesus—He will use you to accomplish great things, on the condition that you believe much more in His Love than in your weakness.—Believe in Him—trust in Him with blind and absolute confidence because He is Jesus. Believe that Jesus and Jesus alone is life—and sanctity is nothing but that same Jesus intimately living in you[37]—only then "His hand will be free with you". Give yourself unswervingly, conforming yourself in all things to His Holy Will,[38] which is made known to you through your Superior—Does not matter who they are or what they are—as long as they are " HE". Love Jesus with a big heart.—Serve Jesus with joy and gladness of spirit—casting aside and forgetting all that troubles and worries you.[39] To be able to do all these—Pray lovingly like children, with an earnest desire to love much and make loved the Love that is not loved.[40]

To thank Jesus for all His goodness to us, we shall make a special Novena to the Sacred Heart from the 12th June in preparation for the Enthronement of the Sacred Heart, which has to be made in each House on the 21st June, Corpus Christi.—We shall all do it, if possible, at the same time at about 5:00 or 5:30 P.M. Let me know if this is possible for you to

a. Mother wrote, "He asks only of you docility," but the grammatically correct phrase would be: He asks of you only docility.

arrange with the priest. I shall send you the prayers of Enthronement.—You must do it properly. After this start slowly to consecrate every family to the Sacred Heart, and see that the children start the 9 First Fridays.—You could arrange to bring them for Holy Mass.

Pray much for our new foundation at Amravati.—We are leaving Calcutta on the 14th June, God willing.

Pray much and often for me.

God bless you
Mother

MGL 16. 4TH AUGUST 1962

L.D.M.

Mother House
4th August 1962

My dearest Children,

From the 12th August we begin our Novena to the Immaculate Heart of Mary, Cause of Our Joy. This year we shall use as [our] prayer the *Act of Consecration*, page 61.[a]—Make the Novena after Dinner Prayer, with singing.[b] I hope great things from this Novena especially for the Grace to know how to thank God properly for all His Graces [that] He has given to each one of us through Our Society; and second, my dear children, let us beg from Our Lady to make our hearts—Meek and humble like her Son's was. It was from Her and in Her that the Heart of Jesus was formed. Let us all try during this month to pray for [this] again and again and [to] practice humility and meekness. We learn humility through accepting humiliations cheerfully. Do not let a chance pass you by. It is so very easy to be proud and harsh, moody and selfish—so easy—but we have been created for greater things.—Why stoop down to things that will spoil the beauty of our hearts? How much we can learn from Our Lady. She was so humble—because she was all for God. She was full of grace. She made use of the Almighty Power that was in Her—the Grace of God. Don't we, my dear children, get this Almighty Power daily at Holy Communion? Make use of it to become Meek and humble of heart. Let us often say during this month—"Jesus, meek and humble of Heart, make my heart

Mt 11:29

a. The page number refers to the *MC Prayer Book* that was then in use.
b. At this time the Dinner Prayer was prayed after the community's evening meal.

Jn 2:3 like unto Thine." Tell Our Lady to tell Jesus—"they have no wine"—the
wine of humility and meekness, of kindness and sweetness. She is sure to
Jn 2:5 tell us—"Do whatever He tells you, " accept cheerfully all the chances He
sends you—or makes especially for you.

Priests and religious are continually complaining that you do not greet them in the streets. It is true you must be busy with your Rosary, but if you take a little trouble to bow to Jesus in the Heart of the Priest or religious you meet—won't that help you to pray your Rosary with greater Love? A little act of Adoration will be like an extra coal put in the fire. Don't miss the chance. Be the first to greet, ALWAYS. It is also a small act of humility—so we will try our best, and tell me how many acts of Adoration you made in the streets, when I next see your smiling faces.

The Sisters, with the Superiors, begin their retreat on the 11th. Pray very fervently for them.

Pray also for Bhagalpur, which opens on the 23rd August, and Bombay on the 5th September.

God bless you
Mother

. . .

MGL 17. 28TH AUGUST 1962

L.D.M.

Hong Kong[a]
28th August 1962

My dearest Children, at the Mother House, 90 Park St., Ranchi, Delhi, Jhansi, Agra, Ambala, Asansol, Bhagalpur & Bombay.

Here I am far from you all—in body—but in my heart you are all there. In the plane all went well. I had plenty of time to make Meditation as my heart desired, as I was all alone in a place. Sometimes it is good to have "I" on your ticket,[b] because you get a special place and also you are left in peace.

In Hong Kong I arrived at 6 P.M. because of the change of time. Here are American Sisters with a very beautiful, big Convent, Chapel, and

a. Mother was on the way to Manila, Philippines, where she received the Ramon Magsaysay Award for International Understanding on 31st August 1962.

b. Mother was offered a business class ticket, which was at that time marked with the letter "I".

schools. Ours is really the little manger of Bethlehem. This is necessary for the glory of God[a]—just as much our little Society. God must be glorified in all His creatures. Lk 2:4, 7

Everybody had a good laugh at my suitcase[b]—it reminds me of home,[c] in all the riches that surround me. I have still to wash my clothes—I hope to do it before I go to bed, as I have to leave tomorrow by 10 A.M.

I hope everybody is keeping well—in Rangoon and Bangkok we stopped for one hour. From far everything is beautiful. Flying over the sea is the most beautiful part. You see only beautiful light blue up and down. Maybe on account of this Our Lady wears blue.

Keep close to Jesus with a happy heart.

God bless you
Mother

MGL 18. [2ND] NOVEMBER 1962

First Friday
[2nd] November 1962

My dearest Children,

I am sorry I have neglected you all—by not writing the First Friday letters, but I hope to do better in future.

As the work is growing, so also the spiritual life should grow. The practice and the living of our vows and rules should bring much fruit—the fruit of true holiness, which comes from a meek and humble heart.

Yes, my children, let us really take the trouble to learn the lesson of holiness from Jesus—Whose Heart was meek and humble. To learn the first lesson from this Heart is our Examination of Conscience. "Know thyself" says the Scripture[d]—and the rest—Love and service follow at once. Examen is not our work alone, but a Partnership between us and Jesus. We should not rest in a useless look at our own miseries—but should lift our

a. "This" refers to the "very beautiful, big Convent, Chapel, and schools" of the American Sisters which is necessary for the glory of God just as much as our little Society (with the poor and small convent that is comparable to the manger of Bethlehem) is necessary for the Glory of God.

b. Mother used a cardboard box to carry her personal belongings when travelling; she wittily called it "my suitcase."

c. Mother is referring to Mother House as "home."

d. "Know thyself" is not a Scripture quote but an Ancient Greek maxim (part of the collection of Delphic maxims), expanded upon by Socrates and other philosophers. "Know thyself" is at times quoted in spiritual literature as an incentive for self-knowledge as the basis of humility.

heart to God and in His light see ourselves. If we are sincere, we will let His light enlighten us and make Him free to have His way with us.

When you examine your Vows,[a] see—in your Poverty—is there not lessening of trust in Divine Providence—by gathering soap, clothes, pencils, etc. Is my attachment to Christ grown stronger because of [my] not clinging to small things? Is our joy great because we always try to get the worst things in the house—food, clothes, shoes, place in the church or dormitory. We must be poor like Jesus. His way of Poverty was simple; He trusted His Father completely.

In our Vow of Obedience—is there not lessening of our Faith—by seeing the human limitations of our Superior and forgetting the fact that
she takes God's place. Our Obedience, by being prompt, simple, blind and
2 Cor 9:7 cheerful, is the proof of our Faith. If God loves a cheerful giver how much
more would He not love an "Obedient giver"? We must obey like Christ
Phil 2:8 obeyed—unto death, even the death of the cross. He saw the will of His
Jn 14:31 Father—in everything and everybody—so He could say, "I do the things
Mt 26:57 that are pleasing to Him." He obeyed Caiaphas and Pilate because their
Jn 18:13, 14, 28; 19:11 authority was given from "above". He submitted to them with obedience
Mt 27:2–24; Mk 15:1–15; Lk 22:66–23:25; Jn 18:28–19:31 and dignity. He did not look at the human limitations of Caiaphas and
Pilate. He looked at His Father—for whose Love He submitted Himself to
them. Let us obey like Jesus, and our lives would become pleasing to God,
Mt 3:17; 17:5; Mk 1:11; Lk 3:22; 2 Pt 1:17 and He would say "This is my beloved child in whom I am well pleased."

During the time of war in India[b]—you must not speak about it with the outsiders—nor write in your letters. We must pray and try more and more to become very holy so that we can stop the war.

In my next letter for December, I will write about Chastity and Charity.

God bless you
Mother

a. Mother regularly misspelled the word "examine" as "examen"; we have corrected it here and throughout this volume.

b. The Sino–Indian Border War (or China–India Border War) between China and India was caused by a dispute over the Himalayan border in the Indian state of Arunachal Pradesh. It began on 20th October 1962 and ended with a cease-fire on 21st November 1962.

1963

MGL 19. 19TH MAY 1963

+[a]

L.D.M.

Mother House
19th May 1963

My dearest Children,

The greatness of Our Lady was in her humility.—No wonder Jesus, Who had lived so close to her, seemed to be so anxious that we learn from Him and her but one lesson—to be meek and humble of Heart. Mt 11:29

Humility is truth; therefore in all sincerity we must be able to look up and say, "I can do all things in Him Who strengthens me." Because of this Phil 4:13
assertion of St. Paul—you must have a certain confidence in doing your work—or rather God's work—well, efficiently, even perfectly—with Jesus and for Jesus. Be also convinced that you by yourself can do nothing, have nothing, but sin, weakness and misery; that all the gifts of nature and of grace which you have, you have them from God.[41]

If we have nothing, and if all that we have is from God—then why so much pride and self-love—that sensitiveness—which makes us so self-conscious—when corrected and found fault with—so bitter and hard—why allow unkind thoughts and bitter words, criticism, temptations against your vocation, discouragement and moodiness come in so quickly and lessen your love? And all that because of a correction given, a single look of disapproval or by something which is done by an individual or by the community even if not intended as offensive. Let us during the month of June practice:

a. This is the first instance when the cross (+) is typed above the initials L.D.M., most likely, the typist's preference.

24th May—1st Week: Not to utter any uncharitable remarks—but show meekness, patience, obedience, cheerfulness, when anyone blames us or speaks ill of us.

31st May—2nd Week: Not to allow feelings of dislike, revenge—to remain in our heart—but to speak well of everybody behind their back.

Mt 7:1 7th June—3rd Week: Not to judge rashly and uncharitably or interpret their intentions uncharitably but always find an excuse for their doing.

14th June—4th Week: If we commit a fault, let us be the first to say "sorry" and give a smile.

Let us during the month of June take special trouble to give our Sisters the living example of Charity. Let us all unite in getting rid of all uncharitable remarks, thoughts and actions, so that the Sacred Heart of Jesus will find in us the true consolation and reparation. Let us spread devotion to the Sacred Heart first at home, among our own Sisters, and then among our people.

The point I have given for each week—let us take it for P.E. [Particular Examen] for the whole Society, each house, each Sister individually. The Superior must write it out in big letters and put it up every Sunday, so that everyone could be reminded.

With God's blessing, Patna & Raigarh have started well.

Happy feast for the 24th.[a] *I hope you have a nice picnic that day.*

God bless you
Mother

MGL 20. 21st JULY 1963

+

L.D.M.

Mother House
21st July 1963

My dearest Children,

Tomorrow will be just one month before the feast of Our Society—as preparation I want each one of us to pay special attention to prayer.

It is not possible to engage in the direct apostolate without being a

a. May 24th, feast of Mary, Help of Christians, is the usual day on which the Sisters make their profession and renewal of vows, but it can vary according to circumstances. The corresponding day in December is the feast of the Immaculate Conception, the 8th.

soul of prayer, without a conscious awareness of and submission to the Divine Will. We must be aware of oneness with Christ, as He was aware of oneness with His Father. Our activity is truly apostolic only insofar as we permit Him to work in us and through us—with His power—with His desire—with His Love. We must become holy not because we want to feel holy, but because Christ must be able to live His life fully in us. We are to be all love, all faith, all purity for the sake of the Poor we serve. And once we have learnt first to seek God and His Will—our contacts with the Poor will become the means of great sanctity to ourselves and others.

Jn 10:30

Holiness is union with God—so in prayer and action alike, we come from God, in Christ and go to God through Christ.

Prayer, to be fruitful, must come from the heart and must be able to touch the Heart of God. See how Jesus taught His disciples to pray. Call God your Father, praise and glorify His name. Do His will as the Saints do it in Heaven—ask for daily bread, spiritual and temporal, ask for forgiveness of your own sins and that we may forgive others—and also [for] the grace not to give in to temptations, and the final grace to be delivered from the evil which is in us and round us.

Lk 11:1–11

Therefore let us take the trouble to pray well—with love and conviction—with faith and hope—with joy and humility.

The first week we shall take:

ADORATION: We shall pay great attention to acts of Adoration, genuflection, joining of hands in prayer, the attitude of the body during prayer, custody of the eyes in the streets.[a]

2nd Week: PETITION: Morning and Evening prayers, Office, Rosary, Visit,[b] Night Prayers.

3rd Week: UNION: Meditation—using the formula:[c] Night preparation—my last thoughts before sleeping—first thought on rising. Spiritual reading.

a. "Custody of the eyes" refers to the ascetical practice of controlling what one sees, refraining from seeing the things that could be disturbing or damaging and looking at things that are uplifting and edifying.

b. "Visit" refers to brief visits to the Blessed Sacrament, which Sisters would make during free moments throughout the day or before leaving the convent to go the poor and upon returning back.

c. Mother is referring to a "method" rather than a "formula" strictly speaking. More precisely she is referring to the Ignatian method of meditation, which includes a remote, proximate, and immediate preparation. The proximate preparation that she mentioned includes reading the gospel of the next day and preparing the points for the next day's meditation the night before and reviewing them upon rising.

4th Week: LOVE: to make as many spiritual Communions and visits to the Blessed Sacrament [as possible].

Pray for our Student Sisters....

God bless you,
Mother

MGL 21. 15TH OCTOBER 1963

+

L.D.M.

15th October 1963

My own dearest Children,

The first visitation having finished,[a] we must all unite and thank God for all the graces He has given to each one of us and through us to His Poor.

There are few points that are very common—I find the passing of remarks still very strong and, second, no punctuality.[b] In some houses there was not even a time-table which the Sisters knew.—Meals at any time—recreation for as long as they choose—sometimes more, sometimes less. Both these points are very important, and I think we should take this for our Particular Point. Each one of us owes the Community a great responsibility—to help keep the rules. School work not prepared due to want of regular time for study—books and registers kept very badly in some places. Many do not even know what the other Sisters in the Community are doing—or anything about the work of the Community. There should be more interest taken in each other's duties and in the Society in general. Each one should know how many sisters and houses we have—where the houses are.—You should remember the date of the opening of the house and offer Holy Mass and Communion for that house that day....

a. Mother is referring to the official visitation of the houses by herself as Superior General. As there were just a few houses at the time, she was able to visit the houses several times a year; with the increasing number of houses, she could visit the houses only once a year, and eventually later she had to send her delegate for visitation.

b. Mother is referring to uncharitable remarks and a lack of punctuality to the times for the apostolate, community prayers, meals, etc.

PRAYER: In most of the houses Community prayers are not in time—prayers recited very quickly and in a low tone. Spiritual reading not given full time—not made with enough zeal and desire for learning how to be holy.

POVERTY: In some houses—the place is kept very untidy and dusters and things very dirty. Things made for special feasts are made so much—that they can last for a long time. Sisters' clothes not properly mended in time. . . . Our Poverty is of choice—therefore we must be proud to be poor with Christ's Poor. A number of Sisters are so unfaithful to serving properly.[a] They allow the devil to cheat them, [depriving them] of the beautiful chance of eating like the poor do—the food of Christ's Poor—and also proving that they are happy to have all the health they need for God's work.

CHASTITY: There is too much talking—and very little recollection. Superiors and Sisters must be careful about the rule of touch and letter writing.[b] In the streets the saying of the Rosary has been very often neglected and yet the streets and not the slums are the dangerous places.

OBEDIENCE: Obedience has improved—but still I don't find that prompt, cheerful obedience. To obey with your whole heart and soul, like Jesus—He was obedient to them. Lk 2:51

CHARITY: There are still many places where the Sisters are allowed to pass remarks, to speak against this Sister or that Superior. There is still so much moodiness; there is so much careless service of the Poor. The Vow asks a "whole-hearted" service.

When speaking with the priests or brothers we must take great care to be very respectful—business-like and above all Mary-like. There should be no recreation after Confessions or any other day.

Let us pay great attention to recollection and union with God—during our work. We must learn how to pray always—by doing the work for Jesus and with Jesus. Lk 18:1; 1 Thes 5:17

The Professed begin their retreat on Monday the 21st. Pray for them.

God bless you,
Mother

. . .

a. "Serving properly" refers to taking the right amount of food needed to keep healthy.

b. According to the tradition in religious communities, as part of the practice of the vow of Chastity, the Sisters were not to touch each other either as an expression of emotion or in play. Mother is also alluding to the permission required to write letters (except to their family members).

MGL 22. 10TH NOVEMBER 1963

+

L.D.M.

10th November 1963

My dearest Children,

We will soon be beginning our preparation for the Coming of Christ. There will be soon in our chapel the empty crib.—This year we must prepare a better crib—a crib of poverty. It will be easy to fill the emptiness of the crib with Charity.

I find our spiritual life is not growing as fervently as it should—the reason for it—is not that we don't have enough spiritual exercises—but we do not make our examination of conscience, both General and Particular, with as much care and fruit as we should. Therefore this letter will be on how to make our spiritual life more fervent. We think we know ourselves enough—why should we spend twice a day so much time in self-analysis? We have so much to do and we believe we are doing it all for God—our very lives are all for God—therefore why spend so much time on ourselves? Yet, for all our reasoning, the examen is an essential feature in our spiritual life.—It is not that we do not make our examen—no, we do it, but we do it alone. We have to do it with Christ if we want to make it real.—Jesus is our co-worker—therefore it concerns Him just as much—my failures, my broken resolutions—my weakness to rise.—It is His concern too.

Our souls should be like a clear glass through which God can be seen. Often this glass becomes spotted with dust and dirt. [It is] to remove this dirt and dust that our examen is made—so that I become once more—
Mt 5:8 "clean of heart" and able "to see God". He can, and He will help us to remove this "dirt and dust" if we sincerely will allow Him to do it. The sincere will to let Him have His way—perhaps it has been the lack of this that has made our examens so fruitless.

There must be no excuse in our self-analysis—Our Vows, our duties, the virtues we should practice, our attitude to and our contacts with our neighbours—all provide us with food enough for reflection and after reflection action. If we think otherwise we are deceiving ourselves.—If we examine ourselves and find nothing to engage our attention—we need Jesus to help us detect our infidelities; then we shall be kept busy.

Our Examen is, after all, the mirror we hold up to nature, a poor weak human nature, no doubt, but one that all the more on that account needs the mirror to reflect faithfully all its deficiencies. If we undertake this work more sincerely, more generously, in partnership with Christ, perhaps we shall find what we thought to be stumbling-blocks transformed by Him into stepping stones. Our Examen will no longer have a lonely feeling, going alone, but with a Friend eager to help us. We may still discover in our daily examens plenty of "dirt and dust," but if faithfully we do our part—Jesus our Co-Worker and Friend will do the rest.

God bless you
Mother

MGL 23. 27TH DECEMBER 1963

+

L.D.M.

Mother House
27th December 1963

My dearest Children,

I hope you had a very holy and happy Christmas, and for the pilgrimage you will be able to go to a place where you can pray and enjoy yourselves.

In 1964 we will practice as Particular Point in January—"SILENCE".

God is the friend of silence. Before we continue to read this letter, let us adore Jesus in our hearts—Who spent 30 years out of 33 in silence; Who before He began His Public Life, spent 40 days in silence; Who often retired alone to spend the night on a mountain in silence. Let us adore Jesus (Mk 1:35; Lk 6:12) in the Eucharistic Silence. He Who spoke with authority, now spends His earthly life in silence.[42] We need to find God, and He cannot be found in noise nor in restlessness. See how the nature, the trees, the flowers, the grass grow, in perfect silence—see the stars, the moon and the sun how they move in silence.[43] Is not our Mission to give God to the Poor in the slums? Not a dead God, but a living, loving One. The Apostle said, "We will give ourselves continually to prayer and to the ministry of the word," (Acts 6:4) for the more we receive in silent prayer, the more we can give in our active life. Silence gives us a new outlook on everything. We need silence to be able to touch souls. The essential thing is not what we say, but what God says to us and through us.[44] Jesus is always waiting for us in silence. In that silence, He will listen to us, there He will speak to our soul, and there we will hear His voice. The interior silence is very difficult, but we must make the effort to pray.[45] In silence we will find new energy and true unity. The energy of God will be ours to do all things well. The unity of our thoughts with His thoughts, the unity of our prayers with His prayers; the unity of our actions with His actions; of our life with His life.[46] All our words will be useless unless they come from within—words which do not give the light of Christ—increase the darkness.[47] My children, let us begin first with that exterior "Silence"—not to speak out of time and when not necessary—when tempted to do so, I will say: "Silence of the Heart of Jesus, speak to me, strengthen me" or "Jesus silent in my heart, I adore Thee." Count all the times you have made the effort to turn to Jesus. Let us try our utmost for 2 weeks in this exterior silence of the tongue and eyes.

The other 2 weeks we will take the Silence of the mind and heart, and this interior silence—we will count—each time I make an effort to pray—to walk in God's presence—to see God in all those I come in contact with, to live my morning meditation throughout the day. In the streets especially I will radiate the recollection, the happiness of being able to belong to God, to live with God, to be His own. Therefore in the streets, in the slums, at work, I will always pray—pray with my whole heart—so I will
Mt 2:23 keep that silence, which Jesus kept for 30 years at Nazareth, and He keeps it even now in the tabernacle, always making intercession for us; praying
Lk 2:19, 51 like Mary did, for she kept all in her heart pondering, praying, and she still keeps on being our Mediatrix of all Grace. Yes, my children, let every month of the coming year—as it brings us closer to the end of our life on earth—it may also bring us closer to God—so close—that He may only
Mt 17:8; Mk 9:8 live in us—that our Poor when they look up see only Jesus.

More than ever I will do everything to help you, my children, to become holy—to become the real Apostles of the Love of God.—Silence will help us all to know God better—Love Him more tenderly—serve Him more perfectly.

Pray much for the new foundation in Jamshedpur. We will leave on the 3rd January. I hope you are all well. Pray for Sr. Mary Cecilia—who went Home to Jesus[a]—to hear Him [say], "I was hungry, and you gave me to eat;
Mt 25:35–36 I was thirsty, and you gave me to drink; I was a stranger, and you took me in; naked, and you covered me; sick and you visited me; I was in prison, and you came to me."

God's blessing on 1964.

God bless you
Mother

a. Sr. M. Cecilia, MC, died on 23rd December 1963, in Calcutta. Sr. Cecilia was the fourth Sister who died in the Society; however, she is the first one whose death is mentioned in a General Letter. Mother referred to Sr. Cecilia's passing away as "going home to Jesus."

1964

MGL 24. [7TH] FEBRUARY 1964

+

L.D.M.

[7th] February 1964

My dearest Children,

Our life, being so much in the public eye—has the more need of humility. We have been chosen by God from among thousands of others for a very great and beautiful vocation. The day we made our profession, we declared before God and the world that we will serve Him in Poverty, Chastity, Obedience and wholehearted Charity. We go about doing good to the Poor. People surround us with love and respect and trust.[48] This is why we need humility, to protect us in danger—to guard us from falls—to guarantee the fruitfulness of our works of Charity. Our ideal is no one but Jesus. We must think as He thinks, love as He loves, wish as He wishes. We must permit Him to use us to the full. It is beautiful to see the humility of Christ—"Who, being in the form of God, thought it not robbery to be equal with God; but emptied Himself, taking the form of a servant, being made in the likeness of man and in habit found as a man."[49]

Acts 10:38

Jn 13:34; 15:12

Phil 2:6–7

This humility of Jesus can be seen—in the crib, in the exile in Egypt, in the hidden life, in the inability to make people understand Him, in the desertion of His Apostles, in the hatred of the Jews—and all the terrible sufferings and death of His Passion—and now in His permanent state of humility in the tabernacle, where He has reduced Himself to such a small particle of bread that the priest can hold Him with his two fingers.[50] The more we empty ourselves, the more room we give God to fill.[51]

Lk 2:7; Mt 2:13–21
Lk 2:51
Mt 26:56; Mk 14:50
Mt 26–27; Mk 14–15; Lk 22–23; Jn 18–19

People do not want proud Sisters—for they are like a heavy instrument in the Hands of God—God will not use such a Sister for Himself.[52] An abrupt and rude Sister people do not want. The poor want to be treated like children of God—not like slaves.[53]

Our work brings many people round us—who wish to share in the work. If we are proud—we do not want, nor are we happy to have, people work with us. Maybe others do not know as well as we, maybe our Sisters are less talented than we, less capable, and yet it is given to you to accept with great joy whatever they can give and together with your offering—offer theirs also. It is a great virtue to practice humility without our knowing that we are humble.[54]

Let there be no pride nor vanity in the work.[55] The work is God's work. The Poor are God's Poor. Work for Jesus, and Jesus will work with you; Pray with Jesus, and Jesus will pray through you. The more you forget yourself, the more Jesus will think of you. The more you detach yourself from self—the more attached Jesus is to you. Put yourself completely under the influence of Jesus—so that He may think His thoughts in your mind—do His work through your hands—for you will be all powerful with Him who strengthens you.[56]

There are 3 signs of genuine humility—see if you possess these:

1) Deference, respect and obedience towards your Superiors.
2) The joyous acceptance of all humiliations.
3) Charity towards your Sisters, particularly towards those who are poor and humble.

A Sister is truly humble if she refuses to judge and criticise her Sisters, if she always fosters kindly thoughts towards them, if she rejoices in the good they accomplish for Jesus, if she finds an excuse for their failures, if she is happy and always cheerful with the poor, the sick and the dying.

If you have the qualities of deference for your Superiors, joy in the hour of humiliations and love for your sisters, you are truly humble after the Heart of Jesus.[57] Therefore for the first two weeks we will take for the Particular Examen:

1st Week: Deference and respect.

2nd Week: Prompt Obedience—without criticism.

3rd Week: Joyful acceptance of every chance of humiliation (When corrected I will accept it gratefully—I will speak my faults with love—I will not excuse myself when corrected for something I am not guilty of).

4th Week: Charity towards my Sisters—in patience—never to lose [my temper] or raise my voice in harshness—to give a smile always. To help my sisters by keeping the rule carefully—in the work and also by praying for them.

For each week I will count daily and mark my Particular Examen Book. Often to say during the day—"Jesus, meek and humble of heart— Mt 11:29
make this heart of mine like Thine—make it humble—make it kind—make it be all like Thine."

Mrs. Magsaysay will be coming to Agra to open Shishu Bhavan[a]—pray that all be only for the greater glory of God.

Your day for writing the General letter is 16th February.[b]

Please pray for the repose of the soul of Sr. Lourdes' mother, who passed away last month. Please also pray for our poor people who are homeless due to the trouble we had during the last few days.[c]

God bless you,
M. Teresa, MC

MGL 25. [6TH] MARCH 1964

+

L.D.M.

[6th] March 1964

My dearest Children,

Now that we have learned the need for Silence and Humility, we will be able to live a better life of Prayer.

We should be professionals in Prayer. The apostles understood this Acts 6:2, 4
very well—when they saw that they may be lost in a multitude of works—they decided to give themselves to continual prayer and to the ministry of the Word. We have to pray with those who pray and for those who do not pray.[58]

In reality, there is only one true prayer, only one substantial prayer: Christ Himself. There is only one voice which rises above the face of the

a. Mrs. Luz Banzon-Magsaysay (1915–2004) was the widow of Philippine President Ramon Magsaysay (1907–1957), who died in a plane crash three years after his election to the presidency. The Magsaysay Award was established in 1957 to "honour outstanding individuals and organizations working in Asia who manifest greatness of spirit in service to the peoples of Asia." Mother received this award on 31st August 1962. Shishu Bhavan is the MC home for abandoned children, literally "children's home". The first Shishu Bhavan was opened in Calcutta. Subsequently children's homes were opened in other places and each is also called Shishu Bhavan.

b. On the top of this letter the phrase "Letter for the month of February, Raigarh Community," is typed, which indicated that this particular copy was sent to Raigarh. At times on the typed copies of a letter there are minor additions meant only for that particular house. This is reflected here, where Mother reminds the Sisters from the Raigarh Community of the date when their newsletter is due.

c. Mother is referring to riots in Calcutta because of Hindu-Muslim conflict; some houses in Motijhil and other parts of the city were burned down.

earth—the voice of Christ. This voice re-unites and co-ordinates in Itself all the voices, even my own voice, raised in prayer.

There are many who do not know, many who do not dare, many who do not want to pray. In the Communion of Saints we act and pray in their name.

Often our prayers do not produce results—because we have not fixed our mind and heart on Christ—through Whom our prayers can ascend unto God. Often a deep fervent look at Christ may make the most fervent prayer. "I look at Him and He looks at me"—the most perfect prayer.

Perfect prayer does not consist in many words, but in the fervour of the desire which raises the heart to Jesus.[59] Jesus has chosen us to be "Souls of prayer". The value of our actions corresponds exactly to the value of prayer we make, and our actions are fruitful only if they are the true expression of earnest prayer. We must fix our gaze on Jesus, and if we work together with Jesus we would do much better. We get anxious and restless because we try to work alone without Jesus.[60] It is true we want so much to pray properly—and then we fail—we get discouraged and give up prayer. God allowed the failure, but He did not want the discouragement. He wants us to be more childlike, more humble, more grateful in prayer, and not to try to pray alone, as we all belong to the Mystical Body of Christ, which is praying always. There is always prayer—there is no such thing as I pray—but Jesus in me and Jesus with me prays—therefore the Body of Christ prays.[61]

For this month we will take for our Particular Examen PRAYER.

1st Week: Fervent fidelity and punctuality to the Community prayers. To say all vocal prayers intelligently, fervently—with devotion.

2nd Week: When I hear any bell ring—to say—"In union with all the Masses being offered throughout the world, I offer Thee Jesus for those in danger of dying without contrition."

3rd Week: To share everything I do, think and say with Jesus. Each time say—"Jesus let us do this, what do you think? Tell me what to say—or speak through me."

4th Week: Great efficiency and fidelity in the work I have to do—because this is my Mass—which I offer to God continually.—I will offer my work to God before I begin.

As this year will be the year of the Eucharistic Congress in Bombay, let us often say "O Sacrament most Holy, O Sacrament Divine, All praise and all thanksgiving be every moment Thine". Make a Spiritual Communion at the beginning of every work and try to make as many visits to the Blessed Sacrament as possible.[a]

Pray for the repose of the soul of Mr. Orzes, the father of Sr. Francis Xavier, who died last December. Pray also for the 2nd years and 3rd years who are preparing very fervently for their profession.

I am going to Goa for the meeting of the C.R.I. [Conference of Religious of India] and from there hope to go to South India.

Pray much for Mother.

God bless you
Mother

MGL 26. [3RD] APRIL 1964

+

L.D.M.

[3rd] April 1964

My dearest Children,

May the joy of [the] Risen Jesus Christ be with you. To bring joy into
our very soul—the Good God has given Himself to us. In Bethlehem, joy Lk 2:4,7
filled the cave: "I bring you good tidings of great joy" said the angel. In His Lk 2:10
life, He wanted to share His joy with His apostles, "That my joy may be in Jn 15:11
you." Joy was the pass-word of the first Christians. St. Paul—how often he
repeats himself, "Rejoice in the Lord always, again I say to you, rejoice." Phil 4:4
In return for the great grace of Baptism the priest tells the newly baptized, "May you serve the Church joyfully."[62]

Joy is not simply a matter of temperament. In the service of God and souls, it is always hard—all the more reason why we should try to acquire it and make it grow in our hearts.

Joy is prayer—joy is strength—joy is love.[63] Joy is a net of love by
which you can catch many souls.[64] God loves a cheerful giver. She gives 2 Cor 9:7

a. A Spiritual Communion is a prayer of desire for union with Jesus in the Eucharist, at the time when actual reception of Communion is not possible. It can be formulated with one's own words or with an established prayer such as:

"My Jesus, I believe that You are present in the Most Holy Sacrament of the altar. I love You above all things and I desire You in my soul. Since I cannot now receive You sacramentally, come at least spiritually into my heart. I embrace You as if You were already there and unite myself wholly to You; never permit to be separated from You. Amen."

most who gives with joy. If in the work you have difficulties and you accept them with joy, with a big smile—in this like in any other thing—they
Mt 5:16 will see your good work and glorify the Father. The best way to show
your gratitude to God and people: accept everything with joy.[65] A joyful
heart is the normal result of a heart burning with love.

Joy is a need and a power for us—even physically. A Sister who has cul-
Acts 10:38 tivated a spirit of joy feels less tired and is always ready to go about doing
good. Joy is one of the best safeguards against temptation. The devil is a
carrier of dust and dirt—he uses every chance to throw what he has at us.
A joyful heart knows how to protect herself from such dirt. Jesus can take
full possession of our soul only if it surrenders itself joyfully. "A saint who
is sad is a sad saint," St. Francis de Sales used to say. St Teresa was worried
about her Sisters only when she saw any of them lose their joy.[66] God is
1 Jn 4:8 joy—He is love.[67] A Sister filled with joy preaches without preaching. A
joyful Sister is like the sunshine of God's love, the hope of Eternal happiness, the flame of burning love.[68]

Sadness is like gangrene that eats up the very bone. Sad religious are
the greatest stumbling block to vocations, because young people, like
2 Cor 9:7 God, love a cheerful giver.[69]

In our Society, [a] Cheerful disposition is one of the main virtues required to be a Missionary of Charity.[70] The Spirit of our Society is Total Surrender, Loving Trust and Cheerfulness. That is why the Society expects us to accept humiliations readily and with joy;[71] to live the life of Poverty with cheerful Trust; to imitate the Chastity of Mary, the Cause of our joy; to offer Cheerful obedience from inward joy; to minister to Christ in His distressing disguise with Cheerful devotion. Therefore we will take for our Particular Examen:

1st Week: to accept humiliations readily and even with joy.

2nd Week: to accept in cheerful trust all the discomforts of Poverty.

3rd Week: to accept orders of Superiors and those in charge cheerfully and with promptness.

4th Week: to do the teaching, the leper work, the nursing at Nirmal Hriday or Shishu Bhavan with kindness,[a] [*cheerful devotion*][b] that comes from joy born of faith.

a. Nirmal Hriday, Bengali for "pure heart," in honor of Mary's Immaculate Heart, was the name of the first Home for the Dying in Calcutta. In other places, each home for the dying is also called Nirmal Hriday.

b. Mother added the words in italics in her handwriting to the already typed letter.

Please pray for the repose of Sr. Carmel's sister. In future, kindly send the news to the Mother House of the death of any relations of the sisters or benefactors of the House immediately, so that the whole Society may pray for them.

On the 4th—13 postulants, 12 novices and 8 professed will begin their retreat. The Final and First Profession will take place on the 14th at Christ the King Church and on the 13th the Reception at Baitakhana.[a]

Please pray for the new foundation at Goa, which will be housed in the Chapel of St. Francis Xavier.[b] The sisters will be leaving on 15th April.

God bless you
Mother

MGL 27. [1ST] MAY 1964

+

L.D.M.

[1st] May 1964

My dearest Children,

Mary's month is one of the most beautiful months—because it is all for the glory of Mary Our Mother. People all over the world offer her beautiful gifts, cover her altars with flowers—and as we have no material gifts to give Her, we shall offer Her in a special way flowers of kindness, of welcoming smiles and the purity of our tongue.

In the Gospel—we often see one word "COME, come to me ALL." Mt 11:28
"He that cometh to me I will not cast out." "Suffer little children to come Jn 6:37
to me." Always ready to receive, to forgive, to love and to make sure that Mk 10:14
we understand what He means[72]—[Jesus] says, "Amen, Amen, I say to Mt 25:40
you, as long as you did it to one of these my least brethren, you did it to Me." If sometimes we feel as if the Master is away, is it not because I may have kept myself far from some Sister? One thing that will always secure Heaven for us—acts of Charity and Kindness, with which we have filled

a. Church of Our Lady of Dolours, Calcutta.

b. When the Sisters arrived in Goa, at first, they stayed in a village called Corlim, in a house given by the diocese. They began a mobile clinic, visiting the poor and teaching Catechism. A year later they moved to another house in Carambolim, donated by the Bishop. Mother might be mentioning St. Francis Xavier's Chapel, as Carambolim is in the vicinity of the diocesan property surrounding the Basilica of St. Francis Xavier, where his body is venerated. St. Francis Xavier (1506–1552) was one of the first members of the Society of Jesus (Jesuits) and a great missionary in India and Japan.

our lives. We will never know how much good just a simple smile can do. We tell people how kind, forgiving and understanding God is—are we the living proof? Can they really see this kindness, this forgiveness, this understanding alive in us?[73]

Nothing gives our Sisters or the people so much scandal as our harshness, abrupt manner and lack of kindness. Often impatience, bad temper, lack of thoughtfulness has driven some Sister or a poor person to bitterness for life.[74] Often we hear people say: I will never go to Church, because this priest or that Sister was so unkind to me—treated me so badly.[75] When our poor come to beg or demand for something—how harshly we refuse them. It was said of Little Flower[a] that she had such a gracious way of refusing, that the refusal gave as much pleasure as the gift.[76]

Very often we hear ourselves say—I could not help it—I was so busy—or I was very tired—these poor people come again and again—and I lost my temper, I gave them a shout—I closed the door on them—I said things I should not have said. If I was the Poor—and the Poor was me, what would I feel if they did that to me?[77] They feel just what I would feel. We have no time to listen to the Poor—often they have to come again and again—walk long distances—sick—tired—in pain—to tell us of their want—of their suffering and we—because we are busy about many
Lk 10:40 things—we have no time to sit at their feet and listen.

To children and to the Poor, to all those who suffer and are lonely—give them always a happy smile—give them not only your ears but also your heart.[78]

Kindness has converted more people than zeal, science or eloquence.[79] We take a Vow to give wholehearted service to the Poor. Does this not mean—love, kindness, sweetness, humility unspoiled by selfishness. We are at the service of the Poor—the Poor are not at our service. If we want the Poor to see Christ in us we must first see Christ in the Poor.[80]

Be kind and merciful. Let no one ever come to you without coming away better, happier. Be the living expression of God's kindness. Everybody should see kindness in your face, in your eyes, in your smile, in your warm greeting.—In the slums we are the light of God's kindness to them.[81] You [are] a Missionary of Charity—a Carrier of God's love—a burning light. Are we really true to our vocation?[82] Has Jesus not had

a. Saint Thérèse of the Child Jesus and the Holy Face, more commonly known as St. Thérèse of Lisieux (1873–1897) or the "Little Flower" in the English-speaking world, was a French Carmelite nun, named Doctor of the Church in 1997. She was Mother's patron saint.

reason to be disappointed with me? Do I love my Sisters and the Poor with an intense love as God has loved me?[83] What is my love for the less-gifted; less-educated; less-attractive Sisters? Do I really sometimes show it by my behaviour, by my rudeness and impatience; by my partiality and cutting remarks that I disown her to be my Sister, the chosen Spouse of Christ?

To Our Lady I will give KINDNESS.

1st Week: EYES— will always smile joyfully.
2nd Week: EARS— will always hear patiently.
3rd Week: HANDS— will always work gently.
4th Week: MOUTH— will always speak kindly.

God bless you
Mother

MGL 28. 3RD JUNE 1964

+

L.D.M.

3rd June 1964

My dearest Children,

These days have been very trying for you all—as Mother has not been able to come to you—but all the more meritorious—as Faith—deep loving Faith is put more to the practice.

This month is the month of Love—Reparation and complete consecration to God. I want you to spend it with great fervour not in feelings—but in reality—the reality of your love for God in deeds. It is said that humility
is truth—and Jesus is the Truth—therefore the one way that will make Jn 14:6
us most Christ-like is humility. Let us not think that by hiding our gifts of God—by doing our work in an inefficient way—that this is the sign of humility. No—do and use whatever gift God has given you for the greater
glory of His name. Let them see your good works and glorify your Father Mt 5:16
who is in heaven. Do well—do with your whole heart—spend all yourself Col 3:23
in working for God—for we have but a short life—let us spend it all for
Him. In this month—we will take it for a particular point to be faithful in Mt 25:21, 23
little things—the faithfulness of the present moment—with Jesus, for Jesus.—If we do this—how much we will grow in love—how much we will be in love with God. My children, let us put all our energy into this month

Jn 14:14; 15:16; 16:23 of love to fall in love with God—say often this little prayer—"Eternal Father, in the Name of Jesus and for the Love of Jesus and because Jesus has said it— that if anything we ask you in His name it will be granted—grant me the grace of Loving you only—the grace of making my heart like the
Mt 11:29 Heart of Jesus—meek and humble."

You will be starting the school work again very soon.[a] Make your schools centres of radiating Christ. Teach your children, your sick, your lepers, the dying, to love God in their Poverty, and sickness—teach them to offer all to God.

I have been to Kerala—after opening our house in Goa—and what terrible suffering and poverty there is among the fishermen of Trivandrum. Six thousand of them are Catholics. I am most anxious to get our Sisters there. Pray that I be able to get at least 5 Sisters by the end of July to go and bring Jesus to them. We, SM. Regina and I, spent two days in their house,[b] where we met most of the parents of our Sisters. When I meet the Sisters I will give them all the news of their people.

The Noviciate building is not yet finished, so the new postulants have to practice poverty and hardship right from the beginning—which is the best way of learning to be a true MC. Due to the refugees,[c] my visit to Venezuela was postponed—but I hope to go by the end of this month—before that, I hope to see you.

During this month we will take for Particular Examen:

FAITHFULNESS IN LITTLE THINGS ESPECIALLY FAITHFULNESS TO THE PRESENT MOMENT.

Please pray for the repose of the soul of Sr. Rose's uncle, who died recently. [*SM. Theodore's father died on the 12th June '64.*][d]

God bless you
Mother

a. In India, the long school holidays are during the months of April and May, when the heat is at its peak. The school year normally begins in June, after holidays.

b. That is in the home of Sr. M. Regina and Sr. M. Stella. Actually, Mother stayed in their house for fifteen days.

c. Mother is referring to the so-called East Pakistan Riots of 1964. The violence that escalated drove thousands of Hindus out of East Pakistan (present day Bangladesh) to seek refuge in neighbouring West Bengal. The needs of the refugees became an acute problem in India, and Mother would not leave the country while help was so much needed.

d. This information was written in Mother's handwriting on the typed copy of this letter.

MGL 29. 15TH AUGUST 1964

+

L.D.M.

Mother House
15th August 1964

My dearest Sisters,

Today and on the 22nd will be one of the most beautiful feasts of Our Lady. She fulfils her role of Cause of our joy so beautifully—do we really do the same towards Her? And [do] you know why we love Our Lady so much? Because she was the spotless Mirror of God's love. Do we take the trouble to be free of deliberate sin—however small it may be—are we afraid of sin? Angels fell in the presence of God; Adam fell in Paradise—Judas fell near Jesus.[84] Am I afraid of falling? Afraid of hurting the Heart of Jesus, Who loved me and delivered Himself for me? How terrible sin must be—if it has the power to kill God's life in me—for mortal sin kills—it causes a mortal wound in the Heart of God, in me.[85] Let us rather die than ever wound God mortally.[86] Venial sin deliberately allowed to become a daily bread—a moral anemia—the soul becomes weak all 'round—the spiritual life begins to crumble and fall apart.[87] Henceforth no care is taken to avoid these little deceptions of the evil spirit; and what is this daily bread that causes moral anemia:

Wis 7:26

Rev 12:8–9; Gn 3

Mt 26:14–16; Jn 12:6

Gal 2:20

1) Stubbornly nourishing dislike for somebody and letting her know it through ugly, cutting remarks.
2) Carrying on a heedless opposition to those in authority—my Superior—criticising her, belittling her, often to the scandal of the other Sisters.
3) Not speaking to a Sister and refusing to pardon—keeping away from her—keeping in your heart little jealousies, hatred and bitterness—which show themselves often in uncharitable remarks. Keeping and hiding things of monetary value without permission. Giving little gifts without permission. Taking things [without permission] such as soap, not [eating] properly. Lazily doing one's work—carelessly. Lazily not answering the bell. Answering back when corrected. Harshness in manner, words and thoughts.[88]

Can I really be free of all these? Yes, with the grace of God and a strong determination to rather die than offend Jesus deliberately. St. Teresa says:

"God preserve us from deliberate sin, no matter how small it may be."[89] "Nothing is small when it means going against God—knowing that He is looking at us. Each time we sin, we say to God: 'Lord I know this hurts you, still I will do it. I know you are looking at me and you do not want me to do it—still I will do it.'"[90]

Let each Superior pray: "My God, let this Community be never stained by a venial sin, no matter how small it may be."[91]

St. [Claude] de la Colombiere writes:[a] "We see after one, two, or three years that the cowards are still cowardly, the irregular are still irregular; the angry ones have acquired no gentleness, the proud no humility; the lazy no fervour, the selfish no detachment from self, so that communities which ought to be fiery furnaces, where they would unceasingly burn for love of God and where the soul would become so Christ-like, so near to God, remain frightfully mediocre."[92] Accept and be happy when corrected—make reparation for them[b]—and you will never be caught unprepared.[93]

As the Society is growing, I find myself unable to see to the outward and inward growth. Therefore I have, with the Council, decided to keep the 2nd Councillor, SM. Gertrude, in the Mother House—to help with the exterior work of the Society. She will be my assistant for the works of the Society, while SM. Agnes remains my Assistant in all matters—spiritual and temporal. In future whenever you have any money matters or you need things for your houses, please write to SM. Gertrude. Mother will be the Acting Superior of Park Street.

PARTICULAR EXAMEN:

Avoidance of every deliberate venial sin, even deliberate fault.

God bless you
Mother

a. Claude de la Colombière (1641–1682) was a French Jesuit priest and the confessor of St. Margaret Mary Alacoque, known as the apostle of the Sacred Heart.

b. That is, for the faults for which you were corrected.

MGL 30. 1ST NOVEMBER 1964

+

L.D.M.

Mother House
1st November 1964

My dearest Children,

These three months have been very full—forgive me for not writing to you.

There are so many things I want to tell to you. Yet I come again and again on the same point—Silence and Charity. Silence will help you to pray better—because it will give you a chance to pray more—and charity will help you to become most Christ-like.

Silence of the tongue—will teach us so much—to speak to Christ—to be joyful at recreation and have many things to say. At recreation Christ speaks to us through the Sisters, and at meditation He speaks to us directly. Silence also makes us so much Christ-like—because He had a special love for this virtue.

Then we have the Silence of the eyes—which will always help us to see God. Our eyes are like two windows through which Christ or the world comes into our hearts—Often we need great courage to keep them closed—How often we say "I wish I had not seen that thing" and yet we take so little trouble to overcome the desire of seeing everything.

The Silence of the mind and of the heart—And Our Lady kept all these Lk 2:19, 51
things in her heart. This silence brought her close to God—she never had to regret anything. See what she does when St. Joseph was in trouble—one word from her would have cleared his mind.—She did not say that word,
and Our Lord Himself worked the miracle to clear her name. Would that Mt 1:18–21
we could be so convinced of this necessity of Silence. I think then the road to close union with God will become very clear.

Let us, for this month of Holy Souls, and also in union with their Silence, offer God many acts of Silence—in preparation for the coming of the Holy Father.[a]

In the month of December, we will offer many acts of Charity in thanksgiving for the Holy Father's visit.

I want you to make the children, the sick and the slum people make many sacrifices for the Holy Father.

a. Pope Paul VI visited Bombay from 2nd to 5th December 1964 for the 38th International Eucharistic Congress.

I am giving below the days for the General letter—and now as we open a house we will add it to the list. Don't write very long letters—but be very faithful to the writing about everything that will keep our Society a family.

. . .

God bless you
Mother

MGL 31. 13TH DECEMBER 1964

+

L.D.M.

13th December 1964

My dearest Sisters,

The Birthday of Jesus is coming very near. I want to be with each of you on this beautiful day—but as this is not possible I wish each one of you—A happy and holy Christmas.

Jn 8:12; 9:5 JESUS is the LIGHT
Jn 14:6 JESUS is the TRUTH
Jn 11:25; 14:6 JESUS is the LIFE

We too must be

The LIGHT of CHARITY
The TRUTH of HUMILITY
The LIFE of SANCTITY

Charity and humility are twins born of sanctity, or rather the fruit of charity and humility is sanctity. Neither of these can be ours if we are in darkness—if there is no charity. There has been so much uncharitableness in the past in each community—and in each one of us. We are the carriers of God's love.—Do we not often carry in our hearts—real darkness—caused by our tongue? In every house I go, I find charity so much hurt by words and remarks—said or repeated—faults and failings of the Sisters carried from one house to another—repeated—and very often made much greater than they really were. Even the Superiors discussing the faults of the Sisters—of other houses—or of their own. Sisters changed from one house to another make remarks about the Sisters of

the community from which they come—they make comparisons between one house and another, between one Superior and the other, between the Sisters of one community and another. A Sister may have made a mistake in one community—or a Superior may have treated a Sister unkindly in some house.—Is this not a matter for confession, rather than a topic of conversation at recreation? When I hear all the pain and suffering caused by these endless remarks and unkindness, I think of Our Lord, Who told the people near the sinful woman to throw the stone only if they were free Jn 8:2–11
from sin—and you know what happened, they all went away—because they knew that Jesus knew their sins. When we speak uncharitably—behind or in front;[a] when we make those hurtful remarks; when we bring the past failures of our Sisters or of our Superior—let us hear Jesus say to us—"throw the stone only if you are free from sin." Tell me who can do it? Jn 8:7

Let us, near the Crib—with hands joined, I beg you—promise to Baby Jesus and His loving Mother—that each one of us is going in a special way to control our tongue, so that no uncharitable word will pass our lips. Superiors, speak kindly and lovingly to your Sisters, love them because they are His—He loved them first. Sisters, obey cheerfully your Superi- 1 Jn 4:19
ors—never answer them back, and then all of us will have deep love and respect for each other. Superiors, look up and see Jesus in your Sisters. Sisters, look up and see Jesus in your Superior. And this is what we must look for in each other:

for JESUS in the LIGHT of CHARITY
for JESUS in the TRUTH OF HUMILITY
for JESUS in the LIFE of SANCTITY

Make your communities a true home of charity, humility and sanctity. Let us all take as particular Examen for January, February and March:

CHARITY—in words and deeds, especially words.
We will say this prayer during the day:

CHARITY OF THE HEART OF JESUS, FILL MY HEART.

. . .

a. That is, when we speak uncharitably to their faces or behind their backs.

This is how Christmas and New Year will be happy and holy: if we make

JESUS the LIGHT of CHARITY
JESUS the TRUTH OF HUMILITY
JESUS the LIFE of SANCTITY

Live His life in us.[a]

God bless you
Mother

a. These words were added in Mother's handwriting to the already typed letter. The intended meaning is: "Christmas and New Year will be happy and holy if we allow Jesus, who is the light of charity, the truth of humility, the life of sanctity, to live His life in us."

1965

MGL 32. 7TH JANUARY 1965

+

L.D.M.

7th January 1965

My dearest Children at the Mother House, Park Street and all over,

Thank you for all the good you have done in 1964—for all the times you have tried to be fervent and holy—for all the times you have been happy to be poor—for all the times you have kept your heart pure—for every act of obedience you have made—for all the works of charity you have done to Jesus in His poor.—But also let us say "sorry" to Jesus for all the times in 1964 when we preferred our own will—when we refused the little acts of sacrifice He asked of us. Let us this year very specially try to be a true MC.—A Carrier of God's love—in our own hearts, in the hearts of our Sisters and in the hearts of those we serve—God's Poor.

Let us all take one strong resolution: "I will not commit a single venial sin against Charity this year." I know this will be hard, but with Jesus we Phil 4:13
can do all things. Daily, as we get up in the morning, we will renew this resolution.

God has blessed our brothers in a special way, giving them Monsignor B. D'Cruz, Vicar General of Quilon, to be Brother Camillus. Let us all thank God for His great love for us.

I have started the visitation of houses. I went to Darjeeling, and I am now on my way to Goa, Trivandrum, Amravati, Bombay, Raigarh, Jamshedpur, then I must be home for the Novices' examinations.[a]

a. This refers to the canonical requirement of examining the Novices before admission to the profession of vows; a part of this examination was done by a priest appointed by the Archbishop, whose duty was to confirm the Novices' motives and their aptitude to live religious life in this particular community.

Our new Noviciate is just beautiful. I hope you will all have a chance to see it.—Really poor and simple and beautiful and big.

Keep very faithful to your penances and acts of sacrifice—for these strengthen our love for Jesus and souls.

God bless you
Mother

MGL 33. 15TH FEBRUARY 1965

L.D.M.

15th February 1965

My Dearest Sisters,

Dt 4:24 In the Gospel we read that God is a jealous lover.[a] We cannot serve
Mt 6:24 two Masters, for we will either serve one and hate the other. Well, this is what has happened; two of our Sisters, Sister M.—— and Sister M.——, have preferred something else to Christ. As in the natural way a person who has two wives is punished by God, so we who are wedded to Christ on the day we make our first Profession, we who become the Spouses of Christ, cannot allow any other love into our hearts without drawing down God's displeasure upon ourselves.

Mt 7:1 We must not pass judgment on what has happened. What we have to
do is to humble ourselves and say, "God preserve me. What has happened
Jn 15:16 to others can happen to me. What others have done I can do." God has chosen us; He has also the right to stop choosing us, but He will never do it of Himself but when we force Him to do it, when we prefer something else to Him. In our hearts we have given the one place to God, deliberately, knowingly, willingly; it belongs to Him. Temptations have to come, they will come; they purify us and give us the chance to prove our love for God. Do not judge, do not pass any judgment, but one thing I tell
Mt 25:21, 23 you, Be faithful to God in little things, do not play with your vocation, for when you will want to preserve it, you will not find the courage to do so.

Why do we have so many broken homes? Because of uncontrolled affections—wanting to have all the pleasures—two loves. By the vow of

a. Mother Teresa is actually referring not to the Gospel, but to the Old Testament (the book of Deuteronomy). At times Mother used the words "Bible" and "Gospel" synonymously without paying attention to Old or New Testament; thus she sometimes used the word "Gospel" to mean Bible in general.

Chastity we give up our hearts to Our Lord, to the Crucified Christ; the one place in our hearts belongs to Him. I do not want you to judge, and do not be busy with words. I deliberately brought the Sisters to the Mother House; I could have taken other steps. Why should I be afraid and have to hide these things from you? They should not affect your vocation. Is it because somebody has fallen that we are going to lessen our devotion to Christ? On the contrary, this is the time for us to show greater generosity, greater humility and [do] much penance. Pay attention to the little things, to the Rosary in the street, to the custody of the eyes; many of us pay little attention to the rules of punctuality, to the custody of the eyes, to the rule of touch, and so many other little things. It is by the loving acceptance of all this that we share in the Passion of Christ. We cannot be religious and have all comforts. Let us compare with family life. If in a home a member has gone astray, would not the other members cling more and more to each other? Let us be faithful to Christ. We cannot stand alone. Pray and be faithful.

Mt 26–27; Mk 14–15; Lk 22–23; Jn 18–19

"I would be happy today if a coffin had left this house," the family of the Sister told me. When we left home to enter the religious life, our parents made many great sacrifices to let us go, and when we are unfaithful to our vocation, it grieves them deeply.

Again I tell you, I do not want any curious talk; if you have any questions to ask, ask me. But there is really nothing to ask. The plain fact is that what has happened is the result of particular friendship. If Eve had not played with the snake, we would not have had original sin; if we do not play with our hearts, we shall not have to face such spiritual accidents. Let us all be afraid for ourselves; be faithful to Christ and pray, "Dear God, give me the grace of perseverance." Your vocation is God's gift to you. You either choose to be faithful and to die for it, or you give it up.

Gn 3

Another thing—be sincere with yourself. When you see that habitually you are disobedient, you are breaking the rule of touch, you have temptations against faith, against chastity, against poverty, speak in time; that is the golden rule for safeguarding your vocation.

What has happened is a big humiliation for the Society, but it is also a grace in disguise, for it should lead us to be more faithful in little things. Again I repeat, Sisters, I do not want you to judge; we do not know what goes on in the depth of souls, only God Almighty knows. But from the 24th of February, the mission houses will begin a novena of reparation.... We must say to ourselves, "Their weakness is our weakness, their fault is our fault." We must tell Jesus we want to make reparation to His Sacred Heart for so much infidelity on our part.

If the people outside ask anything just say: "Yes, they have gone home." If the people speak badly about them, do not allow them to do so. Never allow anyone to speak badly about priests and nuns. Let us ask Our Lord
Dt 4:31 to give them the grace to make up for what they have lost. God is the all merciful Father, He will forgive and forget and give the chance to make up in their lives. If we are feeling so sad, let us think what it must mean to the Heart of Jesus!

For our particular examination this month we shall try specially to
Mt 1:24–25, 2:13–23 imitate the faithfulness of St. Joseph in serving Jesus and Mary. Particular care we shall take of the rules on Chastity.

Pray much for Mother & the Society.

God bless you
Mother

MGL 34. 22ND MARCH 1965

+

L.D.M.

22nd March 1965

My dearest Children,

Glory and honour be to God Almighty for all He has done for us. The Holy Father has gladly granted us the Decree of Praise and so raised our Society to a Pontifical [Right].[a] To thank God for this great grace, we shall have the First Friday Novena, together with "My soul doth magnify the
Lk 1:46 Lord" (singing) after dinner from the 24th to the 2nd. On the 2nd May, we shall all offer Mass of Thanksgiving, and at the Mother House the Decree will be read publicly. Do not forget to pray for our beloved Archbishop Périer,[b] to whom after God we owe our existence, and also Rev. Fr. C. Van Exem. Let us remember our parents and benefactors, who have helped

a. The Decree of Praise was granted on 1st February 1965. For the text of the Decree of Praise, see Appendix A, pp. 522–23.

b. Archbishop Ferdinand Périer (1875–1968), a Belgian Jesuit, was ordained a priest in 1909 in India and bishop in 1921, appointed the coadjutor bishop of Calcutta in 1921 and archbishop in 1924, remaining in office until 1960. The book, *Come Be My Light,* shows the important role Archbishop Périer played in the founding of the Society.

us right from the beginning, the Government of India and especially the West Bengal Government, and our Sisters who have died in the Society.[a] [*and all our Sisters far and near who try to put the 'gift of God' the 'Decree of Praise' into love in action.*]

God love and bless you all
Mother

The yearly retreats will be as follows:

...

During the retreat, please be very careful about charity. As an act of Thanksgiving to God, we shall offer not to pass any remarks about Sisters or [the] Superior of our own houses and not to compare one Superior with the other or speak of their faults and failings to each other.

I shall be at every retreat house during the 8 days.

I hope all the Sisters to renew their Vows have received my letter—and the Superior, the authority to receive their vows.[b]

God bless you
Mother

MGL 35. 27TH JUNE 1965

+

L.D.M.

Mother House,
27th June 1965

My dearest Children,

Since April I have not written to you, but except for Trivandrum—I have seen all the Sisters during the retreat.

All these retreats have been such a great consolation to Jesus and to me. I am sure you are all keeping the resolutions faithfully and lovingly.

Remember that we are wedded to Christ, and so, as we belong to Him, we must therefore share His Passion also. The Vow of Chastity makes us cleave to Christ, and the fruit of our union with Christ is the Vow of

a. Continuing the sentence after the word "Society," Mother added these words in her handwriting to the already typed letter.

b. This means that the Superior should have received a letter authorizing them to receive the renewal of vows.

Charity, just as the child is the fruit of the Sacrament of Matrimony. We must love to be pure—we must use every means to keep ourselves pure—body and soul. Jesus must be able to use us fully. To enable the Vow of Charity to grow, we make the Vows of Poverty and Obedience.—Just as the lamp can't burn without oil—so the vow of Charity cannot live without the Vows of Poverty and Obedience, and all these three vows are because of Chastity—so live your Vow of Chastity. Ask Our Lady daily to teach you to know it better, love it better and live it better.

The General letters must be written—these keep the life of the family alive—so please begin again—this will be the list of writing. We all look [forward] to the news of our houses. So please begin writing.

. . .[a]

In future we will say the *Veni Creator* from the book *Sing and Pray*[b] no. 72, also the *Angelus* in English.[c]

Jn 19:28 We must make great use of the Precious Blood of Jesus to satiate His thirst for souls. Let us often sing "SWEET LORD."[d]

We are preparing to leave for Venezuela very soon—by the 5th. . . .

I will be going with them and will be away for about one month. During my absence SM. Agnes takes my place. I am sure you are all going

a. The schedule for writing general letters (i.e. newsletters), the travelling schedule and the transfers of the Sisters have been omitted. There were by now eighteen houses—Mother House, Ranchi, Delhi, Jhansi, Agra, Asansol, Park Street (in Calcutta), Ambala, Amravati, Bhagalpur, Bombay, Patna, Raigarh, Jamshedpur, Carambolim (referred to as Goa), Darjeeling, Trivandrum, and Cocorote (in Venezuela).

b. *Sing and Pray: A Daily Hymn Book, Voice-Parts* (London: Burns Oates & Washbourne, 1932) was a hymn book that the Sisters were using at the time; it contained English and Latin hymns and prayers.

c. After Vatican Council II (hereafter, Vatican II), as the liturgical reform began to take place, Mother asked the Sisters to pray this prayer in English instead of Latin.

d. "Sweet Lord, Thy Thirst for Souls . . ." (*MC Prayer Book*, 61) is a hymn composed by Sr. Trinita (the third Sister to join the Society but who left before first profession), according to the instructions that Mother gave to the Sisters. She took the tune of an existing hymn, "Sweet Lord, Grant by My Tears," and put in the lyrics that she wrote with Mother's help. The lyrics of the hymn "Sweet Lord, Grant by My Tears" are

Sweet Lord, grant by my tears, the sins of years
I may now wash out, O sweet Lord.
Thy mercies still, with healing power,
O Lord, on me pour.
  Never more will I from thee wander
  Never more holy graces squander, sweet Lord
  I've strayed from thee, pity on me, Jesus set me free.
Sweet Lord, bent at thy feet, spare, I entreat
Thy repentant child, O sweet Lord.
Alas for me, was pierced thy side, and thou crucified. *(cont.)*

to do your best. We are going to try to see the Holy Father on our way, and so you will all be in His blessing.

Pray much & often for Mother.

God bless you
Mother

MGL 36. 12TH JULY 1965

+

L.D.M.

Mother House
12th July 1965

My dearest Children,

On the 13th July—the day of Our Lady of Fatima—the Immaculate Heart of Mary, the Cause of our joy—we will take the plane at 11:30 A.M. to Delhi [and] at 2:30 to Rome. In Rome we will be 2 days, and from there SM. Joseph and I will go to England and the other four Sisters will stay in Paris for 4 days. We come back to Paris and then to Caracas. We will be in St. Felipe[a] on the. . . .[b] Write directly to St. Felipe as per address I gave you in the last General letter.

SM. Agnes will be fully in charge of the Society while I am away from India. All permissions and business must be arranged with her. I am sure you are all going to try your best during my absence and that more than ever you will love Jesus in His distressing disguise.—Love the Poor—Love

---

The lyrics of "Sweet Lord, Thy Thirst for Souls" are

Sweet Lord, Thy thirst for souls,
I satiate with my burning love,
all for Thee.
My chalice will be filled
with love, sacrifices made all for Thee.
Evermore, I will quench Thy thirst, Lord.
Evermore I will quench Thy thirst,
Lord, for souls.
In union with Mary, Our Queen,
I will quench Thy thirst.

a. The handwritten draft of this letter does not exist. On the typed version is written *St.* (in English) instead of *San* Felipe (the correct name of the city). In MGL 41 of 6th August 1965, p. 68, Mother wrote in her hand, "San Felipe", so it is possible that the Sister typist made a mistake when retyping this letter.

b. Mother did not write a date for this letter, probably waiting for the date to be confirmed, which she would add later. Mother and the Sisters arrived at San Felipe on 26th July.

the Society that gives you an opportunity to serve the poor. Forget yourself in all things and love to be Poor for His and their sake.

I know you will be all praying and making many sacrifices for us and for Venezuela—the one sacrifice I specially beg of each one of you—help each [other] to make your community burn with charity.—Let Christ's love be a living bond between you in each [house]—and between each house and the Society. By this the world will know that we are true Missionaries of Charity.

God bless you
Mother

MGL 37. 16TH JULY 1965

+

L.D.M.

Rome
16th July 1965

My dearest Sisters and Brothers,[a]

Yesterday on arrival we were told that it was arranged for us to see our Holy Father[b]—so we went to St. Peter's, where the Holy Father had the public audience. Thousands and thousands of people were there—of all kinds.—He spoke to the Priests and Religious on submission and obedience to the Church and Superiors—and also to the Superiors on being Servants to their Subjects. He spoke in Italian, French, Spanish and English. After the public audience we went, about 40 of us, for a private audience. As we were the last, we had his blessing. He showed great joy in seeing us—but no words would come to my mouth. He asked for prayers. He told me to write to him and also he would see me again—if not in Heaven. Not one of us could remember other things, as we were all only
Mt 19:29 looking at him. See the hundredfold—six little MCs, with nothing to their name, in the presence of the Vicar of Christ. How much we must love our Society, and show our gratitude by being what God and the Society expect
Rom 16:3; 1 Cor 3:9 of us—true co-workers of Christ. More than ever do your work for the

a. This is the first letter addressed to the MC Brothers as well. The Brothers were founded on 25th March 1963. Being far away from Calcutta, on the way to open the first foundation outside India, this letter is imbued with motherly care. She expresses more of her feelings and shares an abundance of recommendations and advice, being at the same time very supportive and reassuring.

b. Pope Paul VI.

Poor—with a humble devoted heart. Be kind and loving with each other, for you cannot love Christ in His distressing disguise if you can't love Jesus in the heart of your Sisters. Love, to be living, must be fed on sacrifice. Be generous with the penances and all the sacrifices that come from our Poverty—and you will be in all sincerity able to say MY GOD AND MY ALL. Mt 25:40

Postulants and Aspirants—learn well—because if you do not know the Society and her spirit you will not be able to love your vocation—which is one of Total Surrender, Loving Trust and Cheerfulness.

1st and 2nd Years & 3rd Years[a]—Pray well, because if you do not pray well and live the life of prayer—you will not be able to make that Total Surrender to God, that Loving Trust to your Superiors and Sisters and Brothers, and how would you work with cheerfulness and joy with God's Poor if prayer and sacrifice does not feed your soul?

Young Professed—Study well—not only those who are busy with secular study—but every professed sister—you must study the work you have to do—to be able to do it well—and see Christ in the distressing disguise. In the noviciate you have learned and prayed—now you have to put your heart and soul into putting into practice what you have learned and [what] you have prayed for.

Finally Professed Sisters—you must learn, pray, study and be the shining light of Christ to the young Sisters.[b] In you, let them see that total surrender to God—by accepting whatever He gives you—by giving whatever He takes from you. From your obedience—prompt, blind, simple and cheerful—let them learn what loving trust means. In your joy and smile, let them see how happy and grateful you are to God and the Society—to have chosen you to serve Him in His Poor. All of us, let us not forget the aim of our Society, that we are here to quench the Thirst of Christ for Souls. Jn 19:28

And all the Superiors of our Society—be what our Holy Father said in public—the Servant of the Servants of God. You are to serve and not to be served—the word "co-workers" fits each one of you more than any other Sister. Remember you are first for the Sisters. Help them to grow Christ-like.—Know each Sister better—you will love her more, and then only you will serve her with a devoted love—as Christ loved each one of us. Mk 10:45

a. The third years refers to the Tertians.

b. Mother is alluding to the call of Jesus, "Come be My Light," that she had received at the time of inspiration. See *Come Be My Light*, 98.

I am here—far, in land-distance—but my heart and very soul is with
Jn 13:34, 15:12 each one of you. Love one another—Help one another—be kind to one another. Speak gently and lovingly to one another—take care of one another,
Jn 13:35; Rom 16:3 and we will fulfil God's own desire. By this— "Love for one another"—
1 Cor 3:9 they will know you are the co-workers of Christ.

Tomorrow morning we are leaving for France—and then the same day SM. Joseph and I will leave for England. We shall return to Paris on the 22nd and on the 25th we all leave for Caracas. We shall be at St. Felipe on the 26th—St. Ann's feast.

Pray much—both Holy Father and Cardinal Agaganian blessed the new Foundation and each one of the Society.[a] We met also Rev. Fr. General of the Society of Jesus and now we have a strong friend in Fr. J. D'Souza.[b] All of you pray well and keep well.

God bless you
Mother

MGL 38. 19TH JULY 1965

L.D.M.

London
19th July 1965

My dearest Sisters & Brothers,

SM. J. [Joseph] & I are at last in England. As we arrived in Paris from Rome, Br. Marquiset & many other people met us.[c]—They told us that Fr. Gorrée was at Geneva with the Mission group & that we had to go[d]—so we took the first plane together with André & off we went to Geneva—without even realising that we had no visa for Switzerland.—At the

a. Cardinal Gregorio Pietro Agagianian (1895–1971) was the Prefect of the Congregation for the Propagation of the Faith (Propaganda Fide) from 1960 to 1970.

b. Spaniard Fr. Pedro Arrupe, SJ (1907–1991) was the Superior General of the Society of Jesus at the time. Indian Fr. Jerome D'Souza, SJ (1897–1977) was working at the Jesuit Curia as an assistant and adviser to the Superior General for Indian and Asian affairs from 1957 to 1968.

c. Armand Marquiset (1900–1981), French humanitarian, decided to consecrate his life to the service of the poor in 1931. He founded several charitable organizations, among others, Les petits frères des Pauvres (1946), dedicated to the care of elderly people, and Frères des Hommes (1965), inspired by Mother Teresa, who had first suggested the creation of Frères de l'Inde. One Christmas, wanting to give Mother and the Kalighat patients a surprise, he offered a red rose to each one of them.

d. Fr. Georges Gorrée (1908–1977) was a French missionary priest, a disciple of Saint Charles de Foucauld in the Sahara for five years, chaplain-captain during World War II, delegate of the pontifical missionary works. He directed the magazine *Amour sans frontières*, while assuming the position of vice-president of the International Association of the Friends of Mother Teresa.

airport—Fr. Gorrée & many girls & nuns were waiting.—They were all so very happy—& they made us feel so much [a part] of the same family. We left last evening—& again the whole troop came to see us off. Fr. Gorrée had tears in his eyes—when saying good bye.—I will have to tell you all so much about Geneva.

I have left Sister Joseph with her parents while I have come to London—for all the meetings etc. Mrs. Blaikie has been working very hard & preparing everything.[a]—

The other four Sisters are in Paris. André & Br. Marquiset are taking care of them. They will have time to see to their things & also learn Spanish. We will be back in Paris on Thursday about 3:00 P.M. & on Sunday we leave for Caracas.—

I have been out so often—I am just tired of meetings & talking, but, thinking of you all—and our Poor, it is worth doing it with Jesus and for Jesus.

In London I am staying with the Franciscan Missionaries of Mary.[b]—I think they have put me in a Bishop's room—with a huge [bed], I think 3 of ours put together.—

I hope you are all well and that you have received my general letter by now. I sent it from Rome.—In the whole world there is no place as our home—at 54A, or 90 P.S. [Park Street], Ranchi, Delhi, Agra, Ambala Jhansi, Jamshedpur Patna, Bhagalpur, Asansol Darjeeling, Raigarh Amravati, Bombay, Goa, Trivandrum & 78 L.C. [Lower Circular Road], the Brothers. So you see you are all very, very close to me. We are all longing to be [in] Venezuela—so pray very hard and make many sacrifices for us all.

God bless you
Mother

a. Mrs. Ann Blaikie (1916–1996) first met Mother in 1954 in Calcutta, where her family was living at the time. She began helping Mother through the Marian Society. In 1960 she, her husband John, and their three children moved back to London. Mother asked Mrs. Blaikie to be the head of the International Association of Co–workers of Mother Teresa. On 29th March 1969, Mother, Mrs. Blaikie, her husband John, and Josepha Gosselke went to Rome to present the *Constitutions of the Co-workers* to Pope Paul VI, who gave the Association his blessing. In 1988, Ann Blaikie retired as international link of the Co-workers.

b. The Franciscan Missionaries of Mary is an international congregation of women religious founded in India in 1877 by Mother Mary of the Passion. Mother was welcomed at their convent at 21 The Boltons, London. The room where Mother stayed was actually used to accommodate bishops visiting the nunciature.

MGL 39. 23RD JULY 1965

L.D.M.

Paris
23rd July 1965

My dearest children,

I hope you got my letters from Rome, London & this one from Paris.

All is well with us. This morning we are going for our Venez. [Venezuelan] visa. As we arrived from England we went to the Indian Embassy to get a certificate that we are not criminals etc.—They had a good laugh at the Embassy but they gave the certificate.

I can't tell you how everybody has been kind to us in England. There has been much writing in the papers.—I was really tired at the end after meeting & speaking to so many people—but this also is a part of the work, & somebody has to do it. On Monday we will write from Venez. [Venezuela]—

I hope you are all well. We depend very much on your prayers & sacrifices.

I hope SM. Michael and SM. Georgina are better. They can help us much by offering their sickness.

Keep smiling and love Jesus.

God bless you
Mother

MGL 40. 1ST AUGUST 1965

L.D.M.

Cocorote
1st August 1965

My dearest Sisters & Brothers,

Thank you for your letters of 19/7[a] which we received only on the 29th. All the letters from India took 10 days to come.—I hope you have received all ours we wrote from New Delhi, Rome, Paris, London & now from here.[b] Thank God you are all well and that everybody is doing & giving their best to Jesus.

I can't tell you how everybody is kind & helpful here. They are really

a. 19th July.

b. The letters mentioned here as coming from Rome, Paris, and London are above; however, the letter from New Delhi seems to be lost.

happy to have the Sisters.—The Sisters will, I am sure, give you all the news in detail. I will have many things to tell you when I return. To make sure that I return, they have given me a residential permit.[a]—The Sisters are simply delighted. Due to the not knowing the language, the Sisters have not yet been able to start the work. This morning they called the children for Holy Mass—they had over 100 children. Next Sunday I am sure they will be many more. How grateful we have to be to Jesus for our beautiful vocation.—Pray for each other, & each one for herself, & all of you for Mother, that we may all understand our vocation better, love it more & live it better & more fervently.

I am hoping to be home for the feast of the Society, but I am sure we will all make the sacrifice cheerfully if it be God's will otherwise.

I hope the Aspirants are growing in the knowledge and the love of the Poor—The Postulants in the love of the unwanted and suffering—The Novices in the knowledge & love of the Vows & Constitutions—The 3rd Years in the deep humility & love of Christ's meekness—The young Professed—in the efficiency of their Service to the Poor—The Finally Professed in that delicate love and attachment to Christ in His distressing disguise. Each one & every house, and all your Poor [whom] you love & serve, are everyday at the altar of God. There, there is no distance—no land—no sea—only Jesus.

We have a beautiful little chapel; now with Jesus with us—the Sisters feel strong & ready to do all that He will ask them[b]—for any sacrifice. Venezuela fully depends on your prayers & sacrifices.—You are just as much responsible for these Poor People as the five that are here.

I hope we get some news from home soon. Make sure somebody writes every week for the present.—The 2nd Years should begin their 2 months on the 19th August,[c] so their examinations should finish by that time—written 9th, 10th, 11th—13th oral—for the canonical, it will be done only after I come, as we have to have the Council meeting first.—Pray much & often for Venezuela.

God bless you
Mother

a. The Venezuelan government officials gave Mother Teresa a residential permit to ensure she would be able to return to Venezuela.

b. The meaning is: . . . now that Jesus is with us, the Sisters feel strong . . .

c. Mother is referring to the two months of intensive preparation before the first profession of religious vows. At that time the intensive preparation was two months, and the professions were normally in April and October.

MGL 41. 6TH AUGUST 1965

Sing for the Novena, "My soul does Magnify the Lord," and Prayer from the Novena in the Prayer Book.[a]

L.D.M.

San Felipe
6th August 1965

My dearest children, Sisters & Brothers,

[The] feast of the Immaculate Heart of Mary, Cause of Our Joy is drawing near.—Let our preparation for the great day be one of deep humble gratitude to God for all we have received during this year, specially the "Decree of Praise" which raised our Society to a Pontifical Right[b]—for all the vocations, and all the good done by the Good God through each one of us.

From Our Lady we will ask 2 special Graces—grace of perseverance in our beautiful vocation and a delicate love for God's Poor.—I know you all love the Poor—otherwise you would not join—but let each one of us—try to make this love—more kind, more charitable, more cheerful—let our
Mt 25:40 eyes see more clearly, in deep Faith—the Face of Christ in the Face of the
Poor. —

Here we have real spiritual slums; just as our people in India hunger & thirst for Food of the Body, our people here hunger & thirst for the Word
Lk 4:18 of God. Our Sisters will have really to preach the Gospel to the Poor.

I hope to be home for the feast of the Society—but in case I can't be I send you all—my blessing and prayers—for each one of you in the Mother House, Park St., Ranchi, Jamshedpur, Bhagalpur, Patna, Asansol, Darjeeling, Jhansi, Agra, Delhi, Ambala, Raigarh, Amravati, Bombay, Goa, Trivandrum, Brothers, Venezuela and the future houses of Ceylon, Madras, Bhopal.

Pray much for Mother. Happy & Holy Feast.

God bless you All always,
Mother

a. This line was added on the top of the letter, as it seems that Mother thought of it after finishing the letter and did not have space to add it at the end. We have reproduced it here as it was in the original, though it is a post script to the letter. Mother is referring to the novena to Our Lady for the Society Feast. We have selected this letter as a sample of the handwritten drafts; for the reproduction of this letter please see Appendix C, pp. 538–39.

b. On 1st February 1965, the Missionaries of Charity received pontifical recognition (Decree of Praise) whereby the congregation came directly under the authority of the pope instead of the diocesan bishop of Calcutta.

MGL 42. 9TH SEPTEMBER 1965

+

L.D.M.

Punjab Mail[a]
9th September 1965

My dearest Children,

Our Country and our people are in great need of prayers and sacrifices. Be generous with both. Do your penances with greater fervour—and pray—pray much.

I strictly forbid each and every one to discuss or pass any remarks about the war[b]—in general or private between yourselves or with the people outside. The heads of our country know their duty, and we have to pray for them, that they may fulfil their duty with justice and dignity. Let us pray for all those who are facing death, that they may die in peace. Let us pray for all those who are left behind to mourn their dead. Let us pray for all Sisters and Priests who may have to face hardships—for our Sisters, that they may be all brave and generous and face all sacrifices with a smile. Teach the poor people to do like this, and we will help our Country most.

Do not get excited, but be calm. Always remember that we are in the hands of God and that nothing can happen without His Will.

ALL the Sisters whose parents and relations are in Pakistan, please do not write to them. I will get news of them and let you know.

Pray much for me.

God bless you
Mother

a. "Punjab Mail" is the name of a train; obviously Mother was writing this letter while travelling.

b. This refers to the Indo-Pakistani War (also known as the Kashmir War) fought over the region of Kashmir, from 15th August to 22nd September 1965.

MGL 43. 30TH DECEMBER 1965

+

L.D.M.

30th December 1965

My dearest Children,

I hope you all got my letter for Christmas.[a] I am sure everywhere the children and you must have had a beautiful day. God has been so wonderful to each one of us, to have given us a chance to work for Him. So much has been done, yet there remains much more to be done.—Let us at the feet of Jesus offer this year—all that we have done and also all that we will do next year. There is so much to be done—do it well, with great love and intention, and you will have the joy of serving only Jesus.

This month we will take as a special point "Thoughtfulness for each
other and politeness towards each other". Thoughtfulness is the beginning of great sanctity. If you learn this art of being thoughtful, you will
Mt 11:29 become more and more Christ-like, for His heart was meek and He always thought of others.—Our vocation, to be beautiful, must be full of
Acts 10:38 thought for others. Jesus went about doing good. Our Lady did nothing
else in Cana—but thought of the needs of the others and made their need
Jn 2:1–11 known to Jesus. The thoughtfulness of Jesus and Mary and Joseph was so
Mt 2:23 great that it made Nazareth the abode of God most High. If we also have
that kind of thoughtfulness for each other, our communities would really
become the abode of God most High. How beautiful our Convents will
become—where there is this total thoughtfulness of each other's needs.
The quickest and the surest way is the "Tongue"—use it for the good of
others. If you think well of others, you will also speak well of others and
Lk 6:45 to the others. From the abundance of the heart the mouth speaketh. If
your heart is full of love, you will speak of love. There is sometimes so
much unhappiness in the house—only because of this want of thoughtfulness. Let us count all the acts of thoughtfulness in words, thoughts and
deeds. We shall all make this [a point for our] Particular Examen. It will
help us to become more Christ-like and also come closer to each other.

Sister Superiors—please help your Sisters to grow in this thoughtfulness by your example. Nothing will teach your Sisters so well as your example of thoughtfulness.

Madras was opened on the 3rd December. Bhopal will be opened on

a. The letter for Christmas that Mother mentions seems to have been lost.

the 2nd February. Pray for these two foundations—as both are important to the Church.

Due to bad health, SM.—— did not renew her vows on the 19th October; instead she went home.

Everybody at the Mother House is well, including Park Street and the Brothers. We had a most wonderful Christmas in Nirmal Hriday. Please send immediately your yearly report and accounts, as it has to be completed [for] the whole Society by the 15th January—the A/C [account for] 12 months and the work please send at once.[a]

This year has been a very sad year as 4 professed sisters left the Society. Let us pray for them.

A very happy and holy New Year. May God bless 1966—for you, your families and the Poor you serve.

God bless you
Mother

a. This refers to the statistics related to the apostolic work: e.g., the number of patients in MC homes; the number of persons helped spiritually, medically, or socially; the number of people helped with education, etc.

1966

MGL 44. 1ST JANUARY 1966

+

L.D.M.

Mother House
1st January 1966

My dearest Children,

A very holy and happy Christmas and God's blessing on 1966. [May] this year be for each one of you a year of prayer, of close union with God and a deep joyful Charity. Be a true Missionary of Charity in words, thoughts and deeds. Begin this with your Sisters, and it will overflow on the poor.

Jn 13:34, 15:12 Love one another—with a very real love—help each other to become holy.

God bless you
Mother

MGL 45. 6TH JUNE 1966

L.D.M.

Mother House
6th June 1966

My dearest Children,

All the time you are all so very close to me, and often I find myself praying:

"Soul of Christ, Sanctify them
Body of Christ, Save them
Passion of Christ, Strengthen them

Within Thy Wounds, Hide them
Never let them be separated from Thee"[a]

Yes, this is all I pray for each one of you.

During this month of the Sacred Heart try in a very special way to grow in charity. Often I have asked for this gift from you: "Never to pass an uncharitable remark". It is much better, but there is so much [uncharitableness] everywhere—and yet we have all come here to spend ourselves in serving God in His Poor out of pure charity.

Let us take this for our Particular Examen—"A delicate and thoughtful charity for my Sisters." Especially when you are hurt and you want to give back what you have received, say slowly: "Soul of Christ, sanctify her, etc.", and you will see what power of Love there will be in your heart.

Also our work—or rather God's work—we must try to do it more efficiently, more carefully and with greater [awareness of the] presence of God. The work is suffering much because there is not that intimate union:—For Jesus—with Jesus. There is not that thirst for souls—that living desire to satiate the thirst of Jesus for souls. Where is that burning Jn 19:28
zeal that gives without counting the cost? Where is that love for our slum children that takes the trouble to prepare the school work? to find the big children for First Holy Communion? Where is that eagerness with which to gather the children for Sunday Mass—the love to consecrate as many families to the Sacred Heart during the month of June—the joy to have the worst things in the house? Yes, my children, let us all once more during this month of love—especially during the Novena of the Sacred Heart—renew our offering with great determination to become true apostles of His Sacred Heart and learn from the Loving Heart of Jesus to be Mt 11:29
meek and humble of heart.

On the 31st May, we got 22 new aspirants. Together with the 11, we have now in Park Street 33 aspirants. At the Mother House we have 26 postulants; 63 novices and the 11 third years.

On the 27th June, I am leaving for Venezuela with SM. Pauline, SM. Paul and SM. Justin. During my absence, SM. Agnes, as Assistant General, takes full charge of the Society. I am sure you will all try your best to do all you can to help SM. Agnes. As I will be away, I have postponed the yearly retreats to September and October, so that I will be able to be with you.

a. This is an adaptation of "Anima Christi," a hymn from the fourteenth century by an unknown author, commonly attributed to St. Ignatius, that Mother Teresa and the Missionaries of Charity prayed daily after Mass.

For the month of July we will take for our Particular Examen "Joyful Obedience"—this is charity towards our Superior.

I hope you are all able to help the poor in a special way during these hard days.[a] Take the trouble to find out where are the most needy and get the permission in time to get the things they need. Fill your Shishu Bhavan and Nirmal Hriday with the sick and the hungry and take the trouble to pour your love on them.

Let us thank God continually for our holy vocation—and pray much for Mother.

God bless you
Mother

MGL 46. 5TH JULY 1966

L.D.M.

Cocorote
5th July 1966

My dearest Sisters,

Thank God we are home with our Sisters. Everybody in France was very kind to us. We were met by Rev. Fr. Gorrée, Br. Joch & (Little Brothers).—We stayed with the Sisters of Charity. Next day it was Fr. Gorrée's 35th anniversary of his first Mass—so we sang for him during his Mass. We got the Venezuelan visa and left for Caracas on Sunday the 3rd via Lisbon. The Sisters, SM. Joseph and SM. Dolores, were waiting for us.

Thank God for all the good the Sisters are doing in Venezuela. This morning they are having another 36 children for First Communion. Having so many centres—nearly every week they have First Communions. Something like Raigarh.—Pray very hard for Caracas—if it is God's Holy Will that we may have a house there.

I hope you are all well—and that everyone is giving your best to Je-
Mt 25:40 sus.—Young Aspirants—so full of love for Jesus—learn to see Jesus in the Poor you serve, for knowledge will teach you love, and the fruit of love is Service.—Happy Postulants—I can hear you in Cocorote—so earnestly wanting to love only Jesus.—Desire is a great sign of love, so keep

a. During this period the political situation in West Bengal was very difficult. The economy was in decline, it was hard to find things to buy and prices were rising; people were struggling and becoming poorer. So Mother is putting the Sisters on alert, encouraging them to be attentive and sensitive to the needs of the poor.

this desire burning in your hearts by letting others teach you the ways of love.—Smiling Novices—I can hear the music of your laughter of joy right here in Venezuela. Learn, my children, to be holy—for true holiness consists in doing God's Holy Will with a Smile.—Zealous young professed—the sound of your footsteps in search for souls must be like sweet music for
Jesus—keep the thirst for souls ever burning in your hearts—for only then Jn 19:28
we will be true MCs.—Humble Students—Humility is truth—and you are in search—keep this light of Christ, the Lamp, burning through your
books, ever full of oil—so that you may become a true light of Christ in Mt 5:14, 16
the slums.—Fervent 3rd Years—this is the fruitful time in your life—make sure that you let God's Grace work in your souls by accepting whatever He gives you and giving Him whatever He takes from you.—My faithful Finally Professed children—how pleased the Good God must be with each one of you—with your devoted, unselfish, intimate love for Jesus in His poor. Keep your light of fervour burning before our young Sisters—
who must be always able to look up and see only Jesus in us, through Mt 17:8; Mk 9:8
us. The Sisters are all very well here and do very much spiritual work. I found such a great difference in Cocorote among the people in this one year—thank God.—They were all very happy with all the things—especially the eatables.—The mango tree in our house is full—I wish it was at the Mother House where the tree would be clean in one minute.—I hope nobody is sick and that all are trying their best.

Pray much for me and the work in Venezuela.

God bless you
Mother

ED 1. JULY 1966[a]

a. *Ek Dil*, the Sisters' newsletter, had begun in 1966. From the time houses outside Calcutta began opening, Mother was encouraging the Sisters to share with each other about their works with the poor and so promote the family spirit among the different communities, as well as encourage each other with the edifying examples of good work each one was doing (e.g., MGL 8, MGL 14, MGL 24, MGL 30, MGL 35, MGL 55, etc.). At that time, the newsletters of the different communities were called "General letters," and Mother had assigned to each house the date for writing their contribution and sending it to the other communities. Eventually these letters were not sent to individual houses but rather to Mother House, where they were edited, compiled and then shared with other houses. Initially this compilation was called "Family News," then *Ek Dil Prem Pur* (Hindi for "one heart full of love"), while "Family news" was at times used as a subtitle; eventually it was called just *Ek Dil*. This particular newsletter does not have Mother's message (since she was abroad); however, it became customary that Mother would write a short message for every edition of *Ek Dil* whenever she was in Calcutta. Her messages have been reproduced in this

MGL 47. 30TH AUGUST 1966

\+

L.D.M.

Mother House
30th August 1966

My dearest Sisters,

I am sure you must have all had a happy and holy Feast of the Society. Each one of you was present at the altar. Let us thank God for all His Goodness to us.

For a long time I have been wanting to write this to you—but I have felt ashamed to write it. I begin by giving an extract from a Superior's letter: "I don't know what you have told the Sisters about the Superiors, but I know you always tell us to take great care of the Sisters and that, surely, I do. Even when I am very sick or very busy the Sisters won't touch my clothes. When one Sister wants to do it—the others remind her, 'Mother said not to wash Sister's clothes'. My clothes remain under my bed till noon when [I'm] sick and sometimes till night if I am out and busy. I have to wash sometimes after dinner. No one washes. If I am in bed at times, it happens that no chotta[a] was left for me—and I am so happy that I can tell Jesus, 'I am fully yours.'—But if this is done to every sick Superior, how will the love of mother and child grow? Not one Sister even asks, 'How are you Sister? Do you need anything?'" At least 10 Superiors have told me exactly the same thing, only in different ways and at different times. With one Superior it happened that when she was sick the Sisters never went near her, and so she nearly died of thirst. Another told me she washed her clothes at night because that day it happened that she had to go out twice and also there were some difficulties in Shishu Bhavan, and so she left straight after chotta and could not find time to do her washing—no one did it either—so she did it at night.

I don't know how anyone who has taken a Vow to give wholehearted free service could act like this—or how can a Sister love the Poor, the sick, the dying, the lepers if she does not love her Sister Superior or her Community? Charity must be in action not in feelings or words—it must begin at home. I feel shy to face the Superiors—who serve and love you

---

volume in the chronological order in which *Ek Dil* was sent to the houses. We have omitted the serial number of *Ek Dil* issues that did not include Mother's message.

a. *Chotta* is the Bengali word for "small, little"; in MC parlance (especially in the early years) it meant breakfast.

for the love of God. They often tell me—with you the Sisters are all sweetness, they act so differently—but with us they behave sometimes so badly. I do not know what to answer them or you. They often tell me—"if I correct a Sister, then she does not speak to me, nor sit near me, nor come for any permissions". Very often the only time a Superior sees a Sister privately is when she comes to renew her General permissions[a]—even for that at times the Superior has to send for the Sister. There is so much fault-finding. I know Superiors also are [at] fault, but this is not a reason for us to act towards our Superiors in this way.

My Sisters, remember whatever you do to your Superiors you do it to Mother. This letter I write with great sorrow—because it must hurt Jesus so much more if it hurts me, a human being—your Mother—so much. No, this is not that charity Christ expects from each one of you. This is not what Mother has taught you—what Jesus and the Society expect from each one of you.

Look up—wake up—be brave—and generous. Be what Jesus has accepted you to be—His Spouse. Love one another, love your "SISTERS". Jn 13:34, 15:12
In the midst of "SISTERS" is your Sister Superior. If this attitude does not change immediately, I will not allow any one of you to touch my things or do anything for me, but in future I will do all my work for myself—in reparation—and I hope my clothes also will remain unwashed and that the Sisters also will forget me; not take the trouble to take care of Mother; nor sit near Mother; nor address Mother—avoid Mother. Jesus said: "Whatever you did to one of these my least brethren, you did it to Me." Your Mt 25:40
Superior is not the least, she takes His place; therefore, what will He say to you? "Whatever you do to your Superior in unkindness, uncharitableness, harshness, rudeness, you did it to Me."

A priest asked a Sister, "Is it true that there is a general tone of dissatisfaction among the MC?"

God bless you
Mother

a. Renewal of General Permissions (sometimes referred to as GP), is a practice of asking the Superior's permission once a month (before the 7th) for all the things one needs. It is part of the practice of the vow of poverty, indicating that one with a vow of poverty owns nothing, thus needs to ask the permission to use everything she needs. During the same meeting with the Superior, the Sister "speaks her faults," that is, asks pardon for her faults and shortcomings. See also MGL 105 of 25th February 1974, pp. 183–85.

MGL 48. 31ST OCTOBER 1966

Waltair[a]
31st October 1966

My dearest Children,

On the 7th October, 1967, we shall have our 2nd Chapter General. During these months we must prepare ourselves in fervour and holiness, so that the General Chapter may bring much fruit.

15th Nov.–15th Dec. we shall take humility for a special point—in our thoughts, words and actions: In thoughts with God, in words with our Sisters and in action with our Poor. In every house during this month we will read about humility during breakfast, lunch and dinner.

The most wonderful part of redemption began in such a humble way. God did not send Gabriel to the palace of the great and rich but to the little girl Mary in the one-room cottage of Nazareth. She asked but one question—how could this be done? And when [it was] explained—she, full of
Lk 1:26–38 grace—offered herself as the Handmaid of the Lord.[94] Mary was chosen because, [she was] full of grace yet so full of humility. The coming of Jesus into her—generated in her zeal and charity. Zeal to give Jesus through works of charity. When her fullness of grace and the Word became one—the fruit of this union was service of love for the neighbour. She thought not of the grace, of the Son of God in her—of the joy and sorrow to be the Mother of God and men—she thought only how to serve, how to fulfil her vocation of the handmaid of the Lord. This life of Mary is so much like ours. When God first called us, He had prepared us through our parents and friends.—He sent His messengers, the Poor, to tell us of His choice of us.—Our first question also was—how could I become an MC? It was explained to us through the long years of postulancy and noviciate—and on our First Profession Day, we with Our Lady declared before heaven
Lk 1:38 and earth—"Behold the Handmaid of the Lord.—Behold I come to do the
Ps 40:7; Heb 10:9 Will of my God." Now that I am a professed Sister, now that His grace of vocation is in me, now that Jesus and I are one—has Jesus in me given me that zeal and charity as the fruit of our union? The Poor—in whose name I have made a vow to give them a wholehearted free service—do they re-
Lk 1:41, 44 joice—do their hearts leap with joy as St. John's did in his Mother's womb when Our Lady brought Jesus in his house? Do I really go to the Poor as

a. Waltair is the British colonial name for the city of Visakhapatnam (or Vizag), Andhra Pradesh. It is known for its Waltair railway station, after which the city took its name. Mother was obviously travelling to visit the houses in the south of India.

the Handmaid of the Lord, filled with Jesus, always ready to give only Jesus to the Poor I serve? Is my service of the Poor devoted, tender, intimate? Do I do to them what Mary did to Elizabeth?

How will I become humble? By accepting every humiliation that comes to me, accepting ourselves as we are and rejoicing at our infirmity. Naturally we don't like this, but confidence in God can do all things.[95] It is our emptiness and lowliness that God needs and not our plenitude.[96] A fervent Sister is conscious of her own weakness and tries to be happy when others see her weakness.[97]

These are the few ways how we can practice humility:

To speak as little as possible of one's self;
To mind one's business;
Not to want to manage other people's affairs;
To avoid curiosity;
To accept contradiction and correction cheerfully;
To pass over the mistakes of others;
To accept blame when innocent;
To yield to the will of others;
To accept insults and injuries;
To accept being slighted, forgotten and disliked;
Not to seek to be specially loved and admired;
To be kind and gentle even under provocation;
Never to stand on one's dignity;
To yield in discussion even though one is right;
To choose always the hardest.

All these are means and praiseworthy, but let us not forget that humility we owe God out of reverence to Him. Secondly, that it is not only an imitation of Christ, but a perfect way of giving oneself to Jesus, for to be able to accept with joy all these humiliations, love for Jesus becomes very intimate and very ardent.[98]

What is not humility:

Moodiness when humiliated, when corrected;
Trying always to excuse oneself;
Refusing to acknowledge one's faults; even [being] dishonest [with oneself];
Putting the blame on somebody;

Ambitious to acquire praise;
Yearning to be in charge of everything—to control all.

It is, however, in loving Our Lord and our neighbour that our Humility will flower, and it is in being humble that our love will become real, devoted and ardent.[99]

What is our Spiritual Life?—A love union with Jesus—the Divine and the human give themselves completely to one another. All that Jesus asks of me is to give myself to Him in all Poverty and nothingness.[100]

God bless you
Mother

1967

MGL 49. 18TH FEBRUARY 1967

+

L.D.M.

Mother House
18th February 1967

My dearest Children,

On the 25th February, I will be leaving India for Rome to attend the first International Union of Mothers General. I go as a delegate from India together with Mother Theodosia, AC.[a] Pray that all be for the greater glory of God and His Church.

I authorize SM. Agnes to take full charge of the Society during my absence. All permissions and business must be arranged with her. I am sure you will all try your best to help SM. Agnes in every possible way. On my way back I will be going to Malta and Tabora (E. Africa)—so I will need much of your prayers. I will not be able to go to Venezuela, as when I return I will have much to do to prepare for the Chapter General which will be on the 7th October, 1967.

During this Holy time of Lent, be extra careful of your penances. Make it a point to be faithful in small details. Penance, Jesus said, is nec- Mk 8:34; Lk 9:23
essary if we want to conquer the devil, the world and the flesh. Love to pray—feel often during the day the need for prayer and take the trouble to pray. If you want to pray better, you must pray more. Prayer enlarges the heart until it is capable of containing God's gift of Himself. Ask and Mt 7:7–8

a. Mother Theodosia, AC, was the Superior General of the Apostolic Carmelites. AC is the abbreviation for the Apostolic Carmel Sisters, a Congregation of Sisters affiliated to the Order of Discalced Carmelites (OCD). The Apostolic Carmel Sisters were founded in 1868 at Bayonne, France, by Mother Mary Veronica of the Passion. In 1870, Bishop Marie Ephrem, OCD, established the first community of Apostolic Carmelites in Mangalore, India. Apostolic Carmelites share God's love through education and other works of charity.

seek and your heart will grow big enough to receive Him and keep Him as your own.

Mt 7:1; Lk 6:37 Our Lord has so often said: "Do not judge," yet many of you, my children, pass judgment on everybody's actions. So much misunderstanding, disunion and real unhappiness is creeping in in many of our houses only because of these uncontrolled tongues. Words spoken in temper are carried from mouth to mouth. While [a Sister is] in temper, [the] words that are used are so below the dignity of a Religious. Common politeness and respect for each other are very often completely missing. Showing of hot tempers has been shameful in the past on both sides; the Superiors and the Sisters of the Community have used words which people in the world would feel shy to use. Often, also, Sisters' faults are made common topics of conversation. Every Sister has a right to her good name—therefore it is a sin of injustice to make such remarks. Sometimes a Sister comes from another house—though she is an MC still the difficulties of the Community are the family secret. She must not be told neither must she tell—even to the Superior of the house—the difficulties of the Community she left. I do not know how you can spend so much time and energy when there is work to be done. Use all we have for the Service of the Poor. I think this is why so much inefficient work is being done. There is so much less generosity in the joyful service of the Poor, because you get so preoccupied with what this one or that one has said or done, and so [you] have no time for Jesus and Him in His Poor.

I also find the joy of eating the food of the Poor is becoming less. Some Sisters have cut their food because they don't like it or because it is not chilly hot;[a] or avoid eating meat, pick and choose. We have come here to
2 Cor 8:9 be Poor with the Poverty of Christ—He, being rich, became Poor for us.
We all had our best at home—we have chosen this Poverty, because we want to do so. I, as your Mother, love each one of you with a deep personal love—it pains me to tell you, but unless you open your eyes and see—open your heart and believe that what Mother is saying is true and that I must change, you will lose that deep love you have for Jesus in His poor through your vocation as an MC. Therefore let us pray and do penance that Our Lord may have mercy on us.

When a Sister leaves a house—on arrival to the other house, she should send a letter of thank-you to the Community from where she has come. In future whenever a death occurs in any of our own families, please let me

a. That is, the food is not spicy.

know so that through my letters I can get the whole Society to pray for the departed soul.

Pray for me.

God bless you
Mother

MGL 50. 24TH MARCH 1967

+

L.D.M.

Mother House
24th March 1967

My dearest Children,

This brings you my love and prayers for a very happy and holy Easter.

Remember that the Passion of Christ ends always in the Joy of the Resurrection of Christ, so when you feel in your own heart the suffering of Christ, remember the Resurrection has to come—the Joy of Easter has to dawn. Never let anything so fill you with sorrow as to make you forget the Joy of Christ Risen.

Mt 26–27, Mk 14–15, Lk 22–23, Jn 18–19

Mt 28:8; Lk 24:41, 52; Jn 20:20

I am happy to be back home. It was very wonderful in Rome. Our Society being the youngest,[a] I felt like a little drop in a big ocean. Everybody has been very kind to me. I also went to Turin and Malta and so now let us pray that the 3 Maltese sisters add two zeros after their numbers and so make 300 aspirants from Malta. They are a real Catholic country. They live the life of Christ to the full. I saw SM. Joan's and SM. Frederick's people, but to my great sorrow I could not see SM. Victoria's, as they live far, and the day they were to have come, the weather was bad, and so they could not come by boat, but I spoke to them on the phone.

Pray for our Sisters who will make their final profession on the 14th April. The First Profession and Reception will be on the 24th May. SM. Anand has been given a special permission by the Holy Father to make Final Vows.[b]

a. Youngest among the religious congregations represented at the meeting of Superiors General that Mother was attending in Rome.

b. Sr. M. Anand, MC, was a doctor and member of the Community of Lay Missionaries in Fribourg, Switzerland. As a lay missionary, she came to India in December 1954, and worked as a mission doctor until she joined the Society on 7th October 1964. She joined the noviciate on 13th April 1965 and made her final profession on 24th May 1967 with special permission from Rome (after two years of noviciate, since she already had vows).

Our Brothers' Society will be canonically erected on the 26th—let us thank God.

SM. Gertrude, SM. Ignatius and SM. Philippa have been doing great good in Daltonganj. I hope we can continue the apostolate. In Jail Road, Ranchi, we have now a new community with SM. Helen as Superior, and SM. Genevieve is in Doranda.

The visa for Africa has just arrived, so pray that Mother does whatever He wants.

Be very careful in your talks with the people. Keep away from any conversation that involves the Government.[a] Whatever Government is in
Rom 13:1–7 power in our country, we will obey in all things except sin. Be careful of your letters—our work is to spread Love through works of love—we have no time for politics.

As we will have our Chapter General in October, I would like all the Sisters to make their retreat before October as preparation and also to pray very fervently for light and grace.

SM. Nirmala met Mother in Rome and went to Turin and Malta with Mother.[b] We are all happy to have her back in the Mother House, where she is preparing for her Final Vows.

In future, we shall say the following prayer before we leave the chapel in the morning after Holy Mass. This prayer is at the back of "What a Vocation Means" by Pope Paul VI.

> "Make us worthy, Lord, to serve our fellow men throughout the world who live and die in poverty and hunger. Give them, through our hands, this day their daily bread; and by our understanding love, give peace and joy."

The 3 H. Mary [*Hail Marys*] *& the other prayers will be said after Med.* [*meditation*] *instead of after H. Com.* [*Holy Communion*].

God bless you
Mother

a. Between 1967 and 1972 there was a period of political instability in West Bengal.

b. For Mother referring to herself in the third person, see MGL 4 of [4th] November 1960, p. 9, and corresponding footnote.

MGL 51. 13TH JUNE 1967

+

L.D.M.

Mother House
13th June 1967

My dearest Sisters,

Except for the Superiors, you have all made a very fervent retreat. You have had a chance to know your needs better through the seminars, so now with your hearts renewed and filled with the Spirit of God, go forward in closer and more intimate and personal following of Christ. You begin your regular life with the few changes that have been made; be happy and make it a special point to become God's sign of happiness in your Community. In all the houses I hope a real renewal of joy and fervour will take place. Do not let the past disturb you—just leave everything in the Sacred Heart, and begin again with joy.

We have all, of our free will, chosen to be more faithful to the poverty we profess. We have to be the "Sign of God" of that true Poverty of Christ—therefore we must radiate the joy of being Poor—but do not speak about it. Do not tell people of the hard life—just be happy to be poor with Christ.

In all my dealings with you during these retreats, I have found the root of all the trouble to be in every house the neglect of Prayer. The time-table must be carefully observed if you want to keep up your life of prayer—for at least 2 months or more we will take for our Particular Examen "I NEED PRAYER—I LOVE PRAYER—I PRAY". The first renewal in the Society must begin with Prayer. Second point is the improvement of punctuality.—Every house must make a time-table and it must be kept—with love and care. Do not expect the Superior to remind you of your duty to God and to your soul. Be careful of your weekly spiritual duties: Chapter and Instruction, Confession and Day of Recollection.[a]

Pray for Bellary and Poona, as on the 19th June the Sisters will leave for these two new foundations.

To be more like the Poor we have decided no longer to wear house

a. "Chapter" refers to the chapter of faults, which is a monthly meeting of the Sisters of the community, at which the Sisters publicly ask pardon of the community for public faults committed. General community matters are discussed, problems addressed, and decisions taken on how to improve. "Instruction" refers to the instruction the Superior gives to the Sisters once a month, to exhort them to greater fervour in living their consecration and greater fidelity to their particular mission of service to the poorest of the poor.

shoes—if any sister needs to wear on account of her health, she must get a special permission.

God bless you
Mother

. . .

MGL 52. [4TH] AUGUST 1967

[4th] August 1967

My dearest children, Superiors & Sisters, Novices & Postulants & Aspirants,

Lk 1:49 God has done marvels for us—Holy is His Name.

The Almighty works marvels for us—Holy is His Name. Yes, He has
Jn 14:12 done marvels and will do still greater things for each one of us—in each one and through each one—if we let Him do—in Total Surrender, Loving Trust & Cheerfulness. On the 7th November '67,[a] our second Chapter General will be held at the Mother House—for this great Grace we must prepare with a humble gratitude and love.—

Let each one learn this prayer by heart and say it as often as you wish—

> "We beseech Thee, O Lord, mercifully pour into our Society Thy Holy Spirit, by whose wisdom it was created, by whose providence it is governed and whose Love may kindle in the Society that same fire which Our Lord Jesus Christ sent down upon earth earnestly desiring that it should burn mightily. Amen."

During these 3 months of preparation—make at least 5 Sacrifices of real charity.—At each Holy Mass, [let] the first intention after the Church—be for the Society.—All our prayers & work we shall offer daily for the Society.—During these 3 months try very specially to make your Community Ekdil Prempur.[b]

. . .

a. Though the previous letters announced that the Chapter would be held in October, the date was moved to November because Mother had to attend the C.R.I. [Conference of Religious, India] meeting in Bangalore in October.

b. That is: One heart full of love. At times the Sister typist spelled it as two words (Ekdil Prempur) and at other times as four words, that is, Ek Dil Prem Pur; both mean the same thing.

[For the upcoming Chapter,] Each professed Sister in every house will be given a list with the names of the Sisters in her group; please mark the name of the Sister you think, with this mark ◯ round her name.—Only one Sister you must mark—put the list in the envelope given—close it—and give it to the Superior who will post all the envelopes together. When choosing the Sister—please ask the Holy Spirit to guide you—do not decide by your likes and dislikes—but who you think before God—will be of greater help to the Society and the Church.—

The Superiors and the deputies must be at the Mother House on the 26th Oct.; therefore, accordingly arrange things. There will be no passes[a]—so each house must pay for their tickets.

Both Poona & Bellary foundations have started well & [are] doing well.—Pray for them. I was sad to know that so few houses wrote to welcome our Sisters in their new homes.—You can always send the letter c/o Bishop's House—when you don't know the address....

I hope all of you, My Children, are well—and that joy and fervour fills your hearts and your Community.—Pray for Mother.

God bless you
Mother

a. "Passes" are free tickets that the Indian Railway gave to the MC Sisters twice a year. This concession was made by Indian Railways at Mother Teresa's request, as recognition for and contribution to the service that the Sisters offer to the underprivileged in India. The passes were issued yearly upon submitting a petition with the required documents. The passes were given in May/June and December/January (after the Sisters' transfers), so that with these tickets the Sisters could reach their destinations along routes that made stops at major cities (such as Ranchi, Guwahati, Mumbai, Delhi, Chennai, Ernakulam). As some Sisters would spend up to 3 days in the train, the Sisters in the Mission houses in the cities along the way would come to pick up the Sisters assigned to their community and drop off those who had been transferred. They also would bring meals for those continuing the journey. On the way back to Calcutta, the same procedure was followed. Apart from requiring skilful organization (at the time when all was done by an exchange of letters and several hundred Sisters would be on the move), these travels were a great opportunity for strengthening unity and boosting a family spirit among the Sisters. Indian Railways also provided a special free pass to travel by first class compartment to any part of India for Mother Teresa and her companion, as well as additional free passes for the Sisters travelling for urgent relief work in case of natural disasters. To date, the Indian Railway gives the passes to the Sisters twice a year.

MGL 53. 17TH SEPTEMBER 1967

LDM

Air India—across the Ocean[a]
17th September 1967

My dearest Children,

Once again I am crossing the ocean to prepare the way for you—in
Mt 25:40 search of God's Poor—In search of the hungry Christ—the Homeless Christ—the Sick Christ.—God's ways are very wonderful—as a very, very small child, I had longed to go to Africa & work for Jesus—but for some reason I did not join the Convent in Africa—& now today I go as an MC to fulfil the desire of God in my heart. I go with different hope, with different love—because of you—who will fulfil that hope & put that love into action for the Poor of Africa. It is also a beautiful preparation for our Chapter. God is so Good to us.

In reading Dom Marmion I find in him so much [of] what our Society expects of us: Holiness.[b]—He says: "Each religious order has its own beautiful spirit which delights the Sacred Heart.—If we have not the peculiar spirit & training of the order to which we belong, we are out of joint in the Community, and can never be good religious, nor truly delight the Heart of Jesus.— —[c] How to do this?—Through your noviciate—through your Superiors. All you have to do is to leave yourself absolutely in their hands—like wax—to cut away mercilessly all the unnecessary parts in me—that I may become a clean oblation on the altar of God's love—I would try to bear all for the love of Jesus Crucified."[101]—And when temptations to leave the order came to him—he prostrated himself before the tabernacle & cried out—"Let me be cut to pieces rather than leave the monastery."[102] "A religious profession faithfully observed leads infallibly to sanctity."[103] These are but a few sentences[d]—from his life of faithfulness to Christ—& we, my children, have made the same profession to the same Christ.—Are we as strong to be rather cut, than give up Christ? He achieved all [this] through his great love for his rules—to which he was so faithful in very

a. For the reproduction of the handwritten version of this letter, please see Appendix C, p. 540–41

b. Dom Columba Marmion, OSB (1858–1923), was an Irish Benedictine monk, abbot of Maredsous Abbey in Belgium, renowned spiritual director and author of numerous books (now considered spiritual classics), which made him one of the most popular and influential Catholic authors in the pre-Vatican II era. He was beatified by Pope John Paul II on 3rd September 2000.

c. Mother replaces the ellipses that are in the original with two dashes.

d. In this letter Mother mentions the author she is reading (probably *Abbot Columba Marmion, A Master of the Spiritual Life* or *The English Letters of Abbot Marmion*, or possibly another publication of Dom Columba Marmion that we did not find) and places the quotations in quote marks. In her letters that were meant for the Sisters, she did not often cite her sources.

small details.—He walked the way of the rules—and the observance of the rule brought him straight to God.—So many Sisters on account of a temptation or because the Superior has corrected them—or even because of some unknown feelings, so easily say—"I will go home." As in the world, so in the Convent; this is a great want of maturity.—We do not change our profession as we change our clothes.—Vows & Marriage are binding—we must use them only to fulfil God's Holy will in our regard.

Nowadays—everything is getting looser & looser—people are trying to loosen the most sacred bindings.—Are we to be guided by them—or
will we cling to the rock—Christ & the Church[?]—By being a true MC, 1 Cor 10:4
we are faithful to His Church.—

Improve your life of prayer & you will find your love for the rule increase, & by this increase your stability in His service will improve also. Be generous—love your vocation.—If you really love your vocation you
will appreciate & respect each other. You will love as He loves each one Jn 13:34
of you—with that deep sincere love. Everything will improve if you love your vocation.

God bless you
Mother

MGL 54. 30TH NOVEMBER 1967

+

L.D.M.

Mother House
30th November 1967

My dearest Children,

I am sorry for this delay in writing to you—as there has been so much trouble here—so pray for Calcutta.[a]

We have much to thank God for [for] all the graces He has bestowed on us[b]—during these days of grace. Our Chapter General ended by the elections which were made after much prayer:

a. Mother is alluding to political unrest.

b. Mother wrote, "We have much to thank God for all the graces . . ." This somewhat unusual sentence structure is quite frequent in Mother's writing. For the sake of avoiding stumbles during reading, we have added [for] in square brackets. However, it is possible that she meant "much" as a modifier for "thank," and the intended meaning is: "We have to thank God much for all the graces He . . . ," in which case an additional "for" would be redundant.

SM. Agnes	1st Councillor & Assistant General
SM. Frederick	2nd Councillor & Secretary General
SM. Joseph	3rd Councillor & Novice Mistress 2nd Years
SM. Nirmala	4th Councillor & Novice Mistress 1st Years

SM. Agnes is now the Superior of the Mother House.

At the Chapter, and before that in your retreats, we had all decided to improve our life of prayer and charity. Now that we have all realized the need for these two points in our life, let us all more than ever try to acquire them.

Jn 13:34 These words of Jesus: "Love one another, even as I have loved you"
should be not only a light to us, but they should also be a flame consuming
Jn 13:1 the selfishness which prevents the growth of holiness. "Jesus loved us to
the end" to the very limit of love, the Cross. This love must come from
within—from our union with Christ. It must be an outpouring of our love
Mt 6:9 for God—Superior and Sisters—a family—with the common Father Who
is in Heaven. Loving must be as normal to us as living and breathing, day after day until our death. The Little Flower said: "When I act and think with charity, I feel it is Jesus who works within me. The closer I am united with Him, the more I love all the other dwellers in Carmel." To understand this and practice it we need much prayer, which unites us with God and overflows continually upon others. Our works of charity are nothing but the overflow of our love of God from within. Therefore the one who is most united to Him loves her neighbour most. . . .[104]

As we are more and more involved working with priests, brothers and lay people, the Rule 137 has to be observed with greater care[a]—while working with them there must be no recreation. Be careful of letters. Don't discuss with people or write about Government matters. If questioned from where donations come, answer: Mostly from India, and [say] also that we are an Indian Congregation.

a. Rule 137: "As the sisters will be in frequent contact with the priest touring the mission, they must show great willingness to help and yet never depart from due reserve and discretion. They shall show him great respect and reverence, always anxious to oblige, business-like in their ways, without wasting time nor words" (1954 *Constitutions*, Revised).

PERSONAL QUALIFICATIONS[a]

(given on 5-point rating scale)

A = v. good; B = good; C = satisfactory; D = Improving; E = Unsatisfactory.

1. Adaptable____________________

2. Charitable____________________

3. Refined____________________

4. Courteous____________________

5. Sociable____________________

6. Neat about house & belongings____________________

7. Exercises good judgment____________________

8. Takes correction well____________________

9. Respect for authority____________________

10. Attends community exercises regularly____________________

11. Sense of responsibility____________________

12. Co-operation with authority & sisters____________________

13. Even temperament____________________

14. Shows initiative____________________

15. Recollected during the day____________________

16. Attitude in prayer____________________

a. This questionnaire was used as an evaluation sheet for the novices being admitted to profession and for the Junior Sisters before the renewal of their vows. Since this letter was actually a report of the Second General Chapter held in Mother House on 7th November 1967, this evaluation sheet was probably one of the outcomes of the Chapter.

17. Sincerity______________________________

18. Obedience to rule__________________________

19. Spirit of Poverty__________________________

20. Cheerfulness____________________________

21. Attempt to improve_________________________

22. Dealing with others (reserved?)____________________

Any remarks:_____________________________

Signature_______________________________

. . . .

We are leaving for Ceylon on the 8th December. All letters of welcome must be sent c/o Archbishop's House, . . .

God bless you
Mother

1968

MGL 55. 10TH JANUARY 1968

+

L.D.M.

Mother House
10th January 1968

My dearest Sisters and Co-workers,[a]

A Happy and Holy Year for 1968. I must ask you all to forgive me for not writing earlier and in time; I think this is the first time, and I hope it will not happen again.

We shall make this year a year of peace in a particular way.—To be able to do this, we shall try to talk more to God and with God and less with men and to men. Let us preach the peace of Christ like He did. He went about doing good: He did not stop His works of charity because the Pharisees and others hated Him or tried to spoil His Father's work. He just went about doing good. Cardinal Newman wrote: "Help me to spread thy fragrance everywhere I go—let me preach Thee without preaching, not by words but by my example—by the catching force, the sympathetic influence of what I do, the evident fullness of the love my heart bears to Thee."[105] Our works of love are nothing but works of peace. Let us do them with greater love and efficiency—each one in her own or his own work in daily life, in your home, in your neighbour. It is always the same Christ who says:

Acts 10:38

Mt 25:34–40

a. This is the first time that Mother writes a common letter to the Sisters and the Co-workers, although the International Association of Co-workers of Mother Teresa was officially established only a year later (their *Constitutions* were blessed by His Holiness, Pope Paul VI on 29th March 1969). She discontinued this practice except for a couple of instances in the 1990s. Instead, she wrote general letters addressed directly to the Co-workers.

I was hungry—not only for food but for peace that comes from a pure heart.

I was thirsty—not for water but for peace that satiates the passionate thirst of passion for war.

I was naked—not for clothes, but for that beautiful dignity of men and women for their bodies.

I was homeless—not for a shelter made of bricks but for a heart that understands, that covers, that loves.

This year let us be this to Christ in our neighbour, wherever the MC and their Co-workers be. Let us radiate the Peace of God [and] so light His Light and extinguish in the world and in the hearts of all men all hatred and love for power. Let the MCs and the Co-workers in every country, wherever they are, meet God with a smile everywhere they go and in everyone.

God bless you,
Mother

P.S. . . .

Also what to answer regarding funds: When asked, this answer [would] be better: "From all over the world, including INDIA."

The new foundation in Ceylon went off very beautifully. . . .

If possible, by the end of January please send each house a general letter on all that has been done or is being done in your house. Every house must try to send at least 2 or 3 Postulants; I do not think any of the houses are trying to get any girls; we must not force them, but we must be able to attract them by our example and love for Jesus in the poor.

Mother

MGL 56. 9TH APRIL 1968

+

L.D.M.

Mother House
9th April 1968

My dearest Children,

This will bring you the prayers and sacrifices offered for each one of you for a very Happy and Holy Easter. I have asked but one grace for you—that you may understand the words of Jesus, "Love one another as I have loved you." Can you tell me—how He loved you? Ask yourself and then see, do you really love your Sisters as He loves you? More and more I understand [that] unless and until this love is among us, we can kill ourselves with work, it will be only work, but not love. Work without love is slavery. We have so much to thank God for.—Let us, during these beautiful days of Easter, Rise with Christ to a life of greater love for each other. Jn 13:34; 15:12

"The Church wants 'renewal'—renewal does not mean—changing of habit and a few prayers. A renewal is faithfulness to the spirit of the Constitutions, a spirit which seeks holiness by means of a poor and humble life, the exercise of sincere and patient charity, spontaneous sacrifice and generosity of heart which finds its expression in purity and candour".[a]

Copy these words and meditate and see how each one of us understands this renewal which the Church expects from us. Let us begin "with sincere and patient Charity" first. We shall take each point and work it out.

These are a few changes that have been made:

1. Adoration in private (Professed Sisters)
2. No Stations of the Cross on Sundays and the week after Easter, Christmas and Pentecost.
3. Thursdays: 3:00 P.M. recreation, 3:30–4:30 P.M. FREE either to mend, play, read or sleep, etc.
4. Rosary in private for the novices & those who don't go out.
5. No rosary during washing, but there will be rosary while cutting the vegetables, etc., in the kitchen.

...

a. The original source of this quote is unknown, but a paraphrased version is found in the *Boletin Eclesiastico de Filipinas* (*The Philippine Ecclesiastical Review*) 43, no. 481 (April 1969): 276.

7. The Litany of the Infant Jesus only during the Christmas Week till the 6th January. Then again continue the Litany of the Name of Jesus. The Litany of the Passion only from Ash Wednesday till Holy Saturday.
8. Novena to St. Joseph—the big one from the 10th to the 18th March. The Wednesday prayer to St. Joseph on the other days of March and that after Visit Prayers.[a]
9. The 3 *Hail Marys* and the other prayers after meditation should be omitted. Begin the Office after meditation. Omit *Memorare* at Examen Prayer. No *Our Father* after office.

. . .

Pray much for Mother.

God bless you
Mother

MGL 57. 19TH MAY 1968

+

L.D.M.

Mother House
19th May 1968

My dearest Children,

I have just returned from Bombay, Goa, Poona, Bellary, Trivandrum, Madras and Ceylon. I hope soon to go to the other houses. My visits are always mixed with joy and sorrow. How much I long and pray that you would all appreciate and love sincerely your beautiful vocation, and [for] your loyalty to the spirit and life of the Society. How very often very small misunderstandings—repeated—becomes a cause of so much suffering. In the name of Jesus and for the love of Jesus, accept these little gifts from Him. Look up at that little hurt and see the gift of Jesus only. He had accepted so much suffering and humiliations because He loved you. Will you not accept the little correction or hurt because you love Him?

This year the Sisters will make their retreat in their own house together with their Superior. Have the retreat during the September–

a. Present-day *Midday Prayer* was then called *Visit Prayers*.

October holidays,[a] as these months are cooler. Let each Superior arrange for the priest and let me know the date of the retreat.

According to the changes, please write at once how many passes you need. Send the letter "Express", so that I can get everything in time.

Be careful of postage. Don't write useless letters. 2 or 3 Sisters can put their letters to me in one envelope if the corners are stuck,[b] or you can enclose it in your Superior's letter.

Same thing for travelling—everything has gone up by Rs. 4/- more.[c] Take more care of everything, especially the clothes and shoes.

Do not use the donations carelessly, because people are making many sacrifices to help us. Make sure you give out the food, clothes and medicine in time—don't allow it to get spoilt.

For your Sewing Classes please do not buy the most expensive material, because you won't be able to produce the best work, as our girls do not know enough.

The Sisters must not use the phone for themselves—each phone call is 30 np. [naya paisa[d]]—foresee things. Same thing for electric lights, soap, etc. We must feel the suffering of our people by taking care of all things.

> God loves those to whom He can give most,
> Those who expect most from Him,
> Who are most open to Him, need Him most,
> And rely on Him for everything.
> To be transfigured we have to be disfigured in our own sight.[106]

For seminars and meetings take it in turn to go. Never go alone anywhere. Do not accept any work which will take you away from the humble works of the Society. Help the people to start small home-industries, but do not start expensive and difficult things you are not able to do.

Same thing applies in your work with men—lay or Priests. Be very reserved. Never go to the Priest's house alone and without permission, nor enter his room. For your soul, use the confessional—for the work, use the parlour or office.

a. That is, during the public—or Puja—holidays.

b. This means that the letter should be folded and glued at the corners, so that the Sister would be assured that no one but Mother would read her letter. This was a simple means to safeguard the Sister's privacy and respect the confidentially of her correspondence with Mother, while at the same time keeping poverty.

c. That is, four Indian rupees.

d. One "naya paisa" (later just "paisa") equals one-hundredth of an Indian rupee. The *naya paisa* has since been demonetized.

New Sisters will be coming to your community. Make them feel they are welcome—you need them—you love them. Above all show your love by not repeating anything that was not nice, but help them to keep up their new fervour. Speak well of the Sisters that were in the Community. Do not speak evil of the Sisters who have left the Society, try to say something beautiful about them.

Be generous in the housework and finishing the left-over food.

Jn 10:17 Jesus said: "No one snatches my life from me. I lay it down myself, and because of that, My Father loves Me."

The capacity for faithfulness—makes saints.

Pray for Mother

God bless you
Mother

P.S. In some of the houses I notice that rabbit and chicken curry is cooked quite often for the Sisters and nothing for the children and the dying. As we share everything with Shishu Bhavan and Nirmal Hriday, i.e., condensed milk, etc., so also make sure you cook rabbit and chicken curry for them also on the day it is cooked for the Sisters or any other day.

MGL 58. 18TH JULY 1968

+

L.D.M.

Mother House
18th July 1968

My dearest Children,

These are days of grace for us. Let us keep very close to Jesus, for in Him alone is our strength.

Let us prepare in a very special way this year for the feast of Our Society, as a token of humble gratitude for all the Society has been to us, for keeping us, trusting us, loving us, for giving us the chance of

Feeding the Hungry Christ
Clothing the Naked Christ
Visiting the Sick Christ
Giving shelter to the Homeless Christ
Teaching the Ignorant Christ
Mt 25:35–40 "YOU DID IT TO ME"

We all long for Heaven, where God is, but we have it in our power to be in Heaven with Him right now—to be happy with Him at this very moment. But being happy with Him now means loving like He loves, Jn 13:34; 15:12
helping like He helps, giving as He gives, serving as He serves, rescuing as Mk 10:45; Jn 13:14
He rescues—being with Him 24 hours—touching Him in His distressing Mt 25:40
disguise.

My Sisters, what a great and wonderful vocation is ours, but you must know it to be able to love it and, if you love it, you will keep your word to God: "I want to be the Spouse of Jesus Crucified". Offer to God every word you say, every movement you make, every thought you think as an act of Love. To be able to become a true MC, we must more and more fall in love with God. Love Him with all the powers of body and soul. Let it Mt 22:37; Mk 12:30, 33
not be said that a woman in the world loves her husband better than we do Christ.[107] This love is our right and privilege—as women, we have been created to love.

Thank God, Jabalpur and Kanpur are well on their feet. The people have been extremely kind to us. By the 15th August, both [the sisters assigned to] Rome and Africa [will] have gone. Below are the addresses of the new houses. See what stamps you must put when you write.

We must be careful of the following things:

1. The Sisters must not travel from place to place without first getting the permission.

. . .

3. The printed letter paper should be used only for official letters. If any house can get the printing free, please do not put your address, so that we can use the same paper for the other houses.
4. Some Sisters have lost their parents but no one has informed the Mother House. I have already asked this to be done before. A post-card will do.
5. As everywhere there is so much unrest, please observe the rule of not going alone anywhere. Do not carry much money with you when travelling.
6. You may stop reading the Rules at chotta. Instead you may read from Fr. McNabb's books like "Listen Sister," etc.[a] There are about 12 books written by him. At dinner read the New Testament.

a. The book *Listen, Sister* and others in that series are written by John E. Moffat, SJ. Mother (or the Sister typist) made a mistake regarding the author.

7. In my last letter I asked you to curtail correspondence. I still find there is a lot of correspondence between houses. Please do not waste money on Express letters and trunk calls for little things.
8. The sisters should walk or cycle for short distances instead of using the ambulance.[a]
9. I have noticed in some of the houses that the Sisters have new shoes and umbrellas. What has happened to the old shoes? Umbrellas are left behind and the sisters ask for new umbrellas.
10. Read through Rules 66 and 137.[b] Be reserved with the priests and lay people. The people must not be involved in our family.
11. When Sisters are changed, no new things must be given to her except when it is necessary. This applies to the Superior also. Besides, the news must not be spread around that a Sister is being changed, because then the poor have to spend money to come and see you or give you a gift which you are not allowed to take. . . .[c]

God bless you
Mother

MGL 59. 5TH AUGUST 1968

Mother House
5th August 1968

My dearest Sisters,

A very holy and happy feast of the Society. Though I shall be away from the Mother House and India, you know you will be with us at the Altar in Rome. Pray for the Society and for each other, that we may know better the spirit of our Society,—love it better—and use it more fruitfully.

From the 17th August I will be away, and until I return SM. Agnes will

a. Mother Teresa warns the Sisters that they should not take advantage of their vehicles, which were used to transport the sick or dying (i.e., the ambulance), for their personal transportation but rather should walk whenever possible, especially short distances.

b. Rule 66: "All should avoid most carefully idle conversation or gossip when visiting and nursing the sick, thus guarding themselves against the danger of worldly views and ways" (1954 *Constitutions*, Revised).

Rule 137: See footnote to MGL 54 of 30th November 1967, p. 90, for the text of this Rule.

c. The addresses of the five new foundations (Jabalpur and Kanpur, India; Colombo, Ceylon; Rome, Italy; Tabora, Tanganyika) have been omitted.

take full responsibility. Address all letters to her so that there be no delay in answering.

THE QUESTION PAPER, I am sending for the sisters to renew their Vows; it would be good if you would all read it and see what answer you would give if you had to send me the reply.

Try to be a true MC in all things—and you will fulfil your vocation. Protect yourself from everything that may tarnish the beauty of your great vocation. You know the choice was His, when He chose you first. Jn 15:16

In my absence do not make it difficult for Sr. M. Agnes.

Pray for Rome on the 17th & for Tabora on the 24th.

God bless you
Mother

MGL 60. 21ST AUGUST 1968

LDM

Rome
21st August 1968

My dearest Sisters,

Everything went off very well—Bishop Hnilica was there to meet us.[a]—No one got sick [on] the journey.—From the airport, Bishop took us to St. Peter's to pray & thank.—Next morning he offered Holy Mass for us on the tomb of St. Peter.

We are still at Via Giusti with the Fr. Miss. of Mary [Franciscan Missionaries of Mary]. Yesterday we went round looking for a place—but
there was "no place in the inn." It was beautiful.—Today we hope to get a Lk 2:7
place. We are all praying & feeling like prisoners in this great & beautiful building. There is a possibility of getting an audience with the Holy Father tomorrow before he goes for Euch. [Eucharistic] Congress.[b] We must double our prayers for him. He really needs prayers.

The Sisters are learning Italian very fast. Everybody is trying to help them.—The trial of the house is a good preparation & a sign that Our Lord really wants us here. Sisters for Tabora are to leave on the 24th—with

a. Pavol Mária Hnilica (1921–2006), was a Slovak Jesuit priest, who was consecrated bishop clandestinely in then-communist Czechoslovakia (present day independent countries of the Czech Republic and Slovakia), where he exercised his ministry secretly before having to go into exile to Italy in 1952. In 1968 he helped Mother with the opening of the house in Rome (Tor Fiscale).

b. Pope Paul VI opened the 39th Eucharistic Congress in Bogota, Colombia, on 22nd August 1968.

the permit I got in Delhi—I do hope all will be well. I am sure you will [be] & are praying for these two houses. How we must love our Poverty and our Vow of Charity now more than ever—these two Vows are our strength and our protection & also [a protection] to the life of Obedience & Chastity. Let us all try to be very sincere in our Love for Jesus & our Vocation.—We must not allow ourselves anything which will take away from us the joy of loving Him only & being His only.

23rd Aug. 1968[a]

Yesterday Our Lady did the most wonderful act of love, as the Sisters will tell you. We have much to thank her for.—

We have our house right near the people. . . .[b]

It is a very small house. I think it is the poorest in the Society, but it is Good that it is so.—Franciscan Missionaries of Mary have been very, very kind to us. The Mother Vicar who was in Madras as Sup. [Superior]—she is now here & so she could not do enough for us.

We have blue beds with bulgur blue covers.[c] We shall soon make our
Lk 2:4, 7 mattresses with straw—so the Bethlehem home will soon be completed.—

I am leaving on the 4th midnight & will be in Dar-es-Salaam [on the] 5th [at] 9 A.M.

Everybody is well.—We saw Holy Father in public Audience & he went to S. Am.[South America]; he will [be] back on Sat. [Saturday] (tomorrow) & [we] will probably see him in Pr. Aud. [private audience] if God wants it.—Everybody prayed for the Society on the 22nd.

God bless you
Mother

a. Mother had not finished the letter and added a new date when she resumed writing.

b. The address of the new foundation in Rome has been omitted.

c. The bulgur grain donated by Catholic Relief Services (CRS) was usually sent to India in beige cotton sacks that were washed and used to make the Sisters' clothing (with washing, the cloth would become completely white, so that it could be used for making habits, etc.). At times the bulgur came in blue sacks. When making new foundations, the Sisters brought some essentials with them from India, including the bulgur sacks to make habits or bed covers. Mother is referring to the blue sacks here.

MGL 61. 11th OCTOBER 1968

+

L.D.M.

Mother House
11th October 1968

My dearest Sisters,

Every house and community has written for my feast. God love you and thank you.

By now most of you have finished your retreat, and I am sure Our Lord must have given many graces through which you know Him much better, will love Him more personally and serve Him with greater generosity.

One of the points, which I am sure you have all found during your retreat, that has to improve, is prayer and, from prayer, CHARITY for each other. It [is] difficult to pray if you don't know how to pray, but we must help ourselves to pray. The first means to use is SILENCE. Souls of prayer are souls of great silence.[108] We cannot put ourselves directly in the presence of God if we do not practice internal and external silence. Therefore we shall take as a special point: SILENCE of mind, eyes and tongue.

1) To restrain our wondering thoughts, especially those of uncharitable root.
2) To control our eyes from curiosity.
3) To hold back every single word of uncharitable remark or repeating.

This will need much sacrifice, but if we really mean and want to pray, we must be ready to do it now. These are only the first steps towards PRAYER, but if we never make the first step with a determination, we will not reach the last one—the Presence of God.

Prayer also will help us to love each other, because with Jesus with us, there will be no distraction. To love Him—to love one another with Him Jn 13:34, 15:12
among us, is one and the same thing, and it is easy. Since you are all doing hard work, the body is tired, and often sleep is the main obstacle to our prayer.[a] We in the Mother House bathe and wash and make our beds before Holy Mass, but we get up only [at] 4:40 A.M. You also try this in your

a. Mother means that sleeping or being sleepy during prayer is often an obstacle to concentrating on the prayers or on meditation. Yet the struggle itself to stay awake has its virtue and good effects as well, as we remember from the example of St. Thérèse.

community, but you must not get up earlier, and let me know if this has helped you. . . . As your meditation book, use the New Testament or a Life of Christ. Sister Superior will, I am sure, try to get one for each of you. The New Testament will help you to know Christ better, Love Him more tenderly and serve Him with great zeal.

Discontent, grumbling and criticism is prevailing throughout the world;[a] naturally it will find its place in our Society also. Let each one watch and pray, for it leads to infidelity and loss of fervour. You may represent by word of mouth or writing your desires but do not stoop down to criticising or grumbling, for it will do you great harm and also will lead you very far, as it has done to so many today in the Church.

In some of the houses the sisters keep increasing their works, the result is often the work is overpowering and done badly, and the sisters lose that wonderful contact with the poor. Joy and compassion are disappearing, and impatience and harshness are taking their place. We cannot do all the works of Charity—that is why we take the Vow of Charity according to Obedience. No new works must start until and unless the permission is received from me.

Some Sisters are being driven by the moving forces of development and are slowly by-passing the sick, the dying, the crippled, the lepers, the unwanted. They will soon not have time nor place for such as these. Our Consecration to God is to the Poorest of the Poor[b]—the unwanted.

To help you learn the language of the place, you may use the language of the place at the night recreation, but I am sure you will respect and be faithful to the rule of speaking English at all other times.

The Sisters in different houses must not order saris without asking Sr. M. Agnes. All saris will be provided from the Mother House.

Encourage the people to submission and joyful acceptance of Holy Father's Encyclical regarding Birth Control and do not engage yourselves in any contrary discussions or arguments.[c] We shall say the following prayer after Holy Mass in the morning, during Examen and after night prayers:

a. Mother may be referring not only to the world situation (1968 was a crucial year in the radical cultural changes that occurred in the decades that followed) but also to the criticisms, dissent and divisions that followed the publication of Paul VI's encyclical, *Humanae Vitae* (25th July 1968), notably among priests and bishops.

b. It is worth noting that Mother wrote "Poorest of the Poor" almost always with capital letters, at least in the letters for which we have handwritten drafts.

c. *Humanae Vitae*, the encyclical of Pope Paul VI on the regulation of birth, issued on 25th July 1968.

"May Our Lord preserve our Holy Father and give him life and make him blessed on earth and deliver him not to the will of his enemies who are refusing submission to his decision on family life and spreading it to others."

God bless you
Mother

1969

MGL 62. 28TH JANUARY 1969

+

L.D.M.

Mother House
28th January 1969

My dearest Superiors and Sisters,

As this concerns all of you, I am writing a joint letter.

All of you know how in every letter and instruction I have tried to teach you the same thing all these years. God has blessed the work and it has grown, but I have not been able to impart to you that love for each other which is the main strength of peace and unity.

In every house there is so much "Talk". There is no more that "SACRED SILENCE" which used to make people see and remember the
Jn 13:34–35; 1 Jn 4:7–12; 2 Jn 1:5 words of Jesus: "See how they love each other." Now in the Community the Superior often begins speaking of the faults of the sisters not present or comparing one Superior with another and sometimes even Mother.—The Sisters take that up and continue in the other houses wherever they may be sent. The regular topic of conversation is always "somebody absent",
Mt 10:4; 26:14–25, 47–49; Mk 3:19; 14:43–45; Lk 6:16; 22:3–4, 47–48; Jn 6:71; 13:2, 26–30; 18:2–5 and yet see the compassion of Christ towards Judas, the man who received so much love, yet he betrayed his own Master—the Master who kept the "Sacred Silence" and would not betray him to his companions. Jesus could have easily spoken in public as some of you do—and tell the hidden intentions and deeds of Judas to the others, but He did not do so.—He rather
Mt 26:50 showed mercy and charity and instead of condemning him, He called him
Lk 22:61 a "Friend", and if Judas would have only looked into the eyes of Jesus as Peter did, today Judas would have been the fruit of God's mercy. Jesus always had compassion. How many of our Sisters have to bear the cross of silent suffering because some Sister Superior or a Sister from the community has

discussed her faults in public? A Sister may have committed a fault in a house for which she may have already made reparation in that house—what right have the other houses to know of this sister's faults[?] Letters are exchanged telling of the Sisters' faults. I visited our houses last year and this year and in every house the younger sisters found it difficult because of the endless talking against somebody absent, including Mother. I wonder what pleasure you get in doing so—and why you should stoop so low.

There is so much harshness and pride in ordering and so much rudeness and criticism and grumbling in obeying. We have but one life and this we have dedicated to the Good God—why must we make it hard for each other? All of us have not got the same talents. It was Jesus, Mary and Joseph that made the Holy Family—not Jesus alone. For the family to be complete it was necessary to have Joseph the Carpenter besides the Mt 13:55
greatness of Jesus and the spotlessness of Mary—so in our community, our Superior or one or two Sisters may be very capable, but they alone do not make a community. We need the others to complete the team. Sometimes I hear: "this one is not good, that one is not capable", and I always like to ask the same question: "I wonder if you are born with all that you have now or was it not the Good God who gave you the ability to acquire and the Society the chance to grow!"

In some houses they have daily morning recreation, lunch lasts one hour and tea half an hour, and so often the Sisters miss their afternoon sleep or have to rush through their spiritual duties or omit them. You must all join together and try to help each other to keep the fervour, as each one of you wants to give ALL to God.

Let each Sister take this letter and read it personally and find out what part applies to her, and let her change that, for we are all here to do just that one thing—to become Saints; and this will be the renewal we will give to God in our Society. We don't have to make changes in clothes and work,[a] but we must all determine to change this deep uncharitableness which comes from wounded Pride.

Superiors and Sisters of each of our Communities, open your hearts to the Grace of God. Let us all give this to the Church this year:

"LOVE FOR EACH OTHER AS CHRIST HAS LOVED EACH ONE Jn 13:34; 15:12
OF US"

a. Mother seems to be subtly cautioning her community to be aware of the wave of exterior changes being made by numerous religious congregations after Vatican II, as she already had done in MGL 56 of 9th April 1968, p. 95: "The Church wants 'renewal'—renewal does not mean—changing of habit and a few prayers."

As the elections will be taking place soon,[a] let every Sister and Superior avoid speaking or getting involved. When you are asked anything regarding conversion or politics, just give a simple answer: "We are here to love and serve the Poor and nothing more." Please take this warning seriously.

I will be leaving India very soon, therefore, all business etc. must be addressed to SM. Agnes. Pray for our houses and the new ones to be made.

God bless you
Mother

MGL 63. 7TH MAY 1969

+

L.D.M.

Mother House
7th May 1969

My dearest Sisters,

It is after a very long time I write to you. Thank God much has been done, but still more remains to be done, and I am sure you are all trying to
Mt 5:16 do your best and give glory to God.

As our Society keeps growing, naturally there is a danger of that beautiful spirit of family diminishing, but it is for each one of us to protect it and make the life of love and unity, of humility and service, live and bring much fruit in each one of us and in the people we serve. The means to protect this family spirit of love and unity is spiritual life. We must be able to uplift each other and, through good example of a life of prayer and union with God, encourage and help [each other] to remain faithful to our vocation.

Our "Chapter" (weekly) must become more and more an exchange of grace which would help us to become more holy and Christ-like. Do not just keep telling your faults but aim at looking at the beautiful virtues in
Mt 11:29 Christ, in each other, and try to learn from Him to be more and more like Him. Bring Christ more into your own life and you will be surprised how much He will be able to use you and live His life in you, through you,
Gal 2:20 with you, and for you.

a. The elections for the West Bengal legislative assembly, held in 1969.

These are very difficult times in the Church,[a] but we must cling to the teaching and the guidance she gives us through our Holy Father.

Do not get mixed up in gossip conversations;—you hear of priests and nuns leaving, of many broken homes, but do not forget that there are thousands and thousands, priests and nuns, and happy families faithful unto death. This trial will purify the Church of her human infirmities, and she will come out of it beautiful and true. Now more than ever let us be faithful to our spiritual life through fidelity to our spiritual exercises and our vows. Let us remember that Christ, being rich, became poor that we 2 Cor 8:9
may be able to vow and keep poverty. Christ, being equal to His Father, went down and was subject to them,[b] that we may be able to surrender Lk 2:51
our will in obedience. Christ went about doing good that we may have Acts 10:38
the courage to continue giving wholehearted service to His poor. "I and my Father are one"—an undivided heart He kept [that] we may be able to Jn 10:30
keep complete consecration, through our vow of Chastity, unsullied and undivided.

The yearly changes will be soon coming, and I do hope and pray that each one of you will accept being changed or not changed as the will of God for you now; therefore pray and make sacrifices, that God may use Mother to express His will through her to you. We shall be soon making our new foundations in Bangalore, Lucknow, Melbourne, Bourke and Caracas. These are all very difficult and important places, therefore I want you all to pray very specially.

On the 13th May, 12 Sisters will be taking Final Vows, 31 novices will take First Vows, and 34 Postulants will become Novices, and about 80 aspirants become Postulants. Pray for all of them.

God bless you
Mother

a. Mother is alluding to the difficult period following the Vatican II, in which there were many adaptations and challenges, for example, changes in the Mass, changes in the norms and practices in religious communities, loss of vocations, etc.

b. That is, to Mary and Joseph.

MGL 64. 7TH AUGUST 1969

+

L.D.M.

Mother House
7th August 1969

My dearest Children,

Very soon we shall share the joy of our Society Feast. We have all tried in some way or another to be a real joy to Our Lady. So often during
Neh 8:10 the day, we call her "Cause of Our Joy"—and the joy of Her Son is our strength. Let us this year in wishing each other "Happy Feast" promise
Mt 2:23 that we will make our Community another Bethlehem—another Naza-
Jn 13:34, 15:12 reth. Let us love each other as we love Jesus. In Nazareth, there was Love, Unity, Prayer, Sacrifice and Hard Work, and there was especially a deep understanding and appreciation of each other and thoughtfulness for each other. We will all take this for a special point at every Chapter and Examination of Conscience—"U.A.T."

U—Understanding
A—Appreciation
T—Thoughtfulness

There will I am sure be real renewal within our souls and in our Society if we all help each other with U.A.T.

These are a few points for you to observe:

1. When the Bishops through their priests tell you to change something about Holy Mass in the chapel, you must do it, and you must all try your best to know and love and put into use the new Liturgy of the Mass.
2. Be careful about reading—see Rule 70[a]—and also regarding letters. No Sister is allowed to write without permission, except to the persons the rule puts clearly. The Sisters or the Superior must not correspond with the Sisters who have been in their

a. Rule 70: "No books, magazines and papers except those given for common use are to be read by ours. Should any other reading be found helpful or necessary, permission must be asked each time. Letters sent by, or addressed to, the sisters must be handed over to the Superior that they may be seen by her. All the sisters are at liberty to send letters exempt from every control to the Holy See and its Legate in the country, to the local Ordinary, to their own higher Superiors and to the Superior of the house if she be absent; and from all these they may receive letters likewise not to be seen by anybody." (1954 *Constitutions*; at present this rule corresponds to the *Spiritual Directory*, ch. 7, nos. 18a and 19.)

Community. Rule 70 does not apply to them.[a] There is too much correspondence going on after the Sisters have left the Community. You can write only one letter after leaving—to thank and no more—this also with permission.

3. When Sisters go from one community to another, they must not take anything without permission—see Rule 62.[b] So much suffering can be avoided if the Sisters observed this rule in spiritual matters also.
4. There is so much money going on travelling because the Sisters find it difficult to walk.[c]
5. Rule 99 says: "No Sister (including Superior) shall ever leave the house alone and without permission." Lately this rule has been neglected.—The Superior must tell the Assistant where she is going.
6. In some houses the Sisters are much more busy with money-making and deciding on big projects for which they ask money from different organizations. In future you must first consult me—and if I am not here, SM. Agnes—before you take any such steps.

I am enclosing the dates and the addresses of our houses. As our number are now 540,[d] it is not possible to keep the name-feast day except in the house where the sister is, but every house must write to the Community for the Anniversary of their foundation and for the sisters in that Community. Each sister will offer Holy Mass, Holy Communion, Rosary, Stations of the Cross and five sacrifices each for that Community. One common letter will be enough.

As we got many aspirants, we had to split them:

SM. Premila is in Madras with 39 aspirants
SM. Juliana is in Bombay with 25 aspirants
SM. Maria is in Delhi with 25 aspirants

a. Mother is reminding the Sisters that they must obtain permission before corresponding with the previous Superior or community members.

b. Rule 62: "The sisters shall never keep, give away or lend things without leave of the Superior. When a sister goes from one house to another, she is not to take anything with her without permission." (1954 *Constitutions* Revised; *Constitutions* 1988, no. 50, *Spiritual Directory* 22.d.)

c. Mother is objecting to the Sisters' spending so much money on transportation, when they could walk instead.

d. Mother is referring to the number of Sisters in the Society.

SM. Joseph has 40 postulants
and SM. Julia 40 postulants in the Mother House.

. . .

We must pray very specially for all our Sisters in India and out of India that we may all keep the beautiful lamp of our vocation always filled with [the] oil of Charity—that we may radiate Christ's love in action everywhere we go.

Mt 25:1–13

Pray much and often for me.

. . .

God bless you
Mother

MGL 65. 13TH SEPTEMBER 1969

L.D.M.

Melbourne
13th September 1969

My dearest Children everywhere,

Thank God all is well with us—one more tabernacle for Jesus—one more burning light among the people of Australia.—If we really live our total surrender to the full, what great things God will do for us and with us and in us. When I think what we are—and what He does through us—
Lk 1:38; 1:49 it makes my heart cry out with Our Lady, "Behold the handmaid of the Lord, for He has done great things for me."

Everybody has been so very kind and loving. The Superior General of the Sisters of Mercy met us at Sydney; Fr. Hart,[a] with a number of students, at Perth. He still loves Calcutta and remembers many of the Sisters to whom he gave the retreat. Bishop Warren[b] sent a telegram of welcome to Sydney Airport. So you see how God takes care of us.—Nobody got sick.

While I am away make sure you write to SM. Agnes for all you

a. Fr. John Harte, SJ (1931–2023), was an Australian Jesuit, who served at that time as a chaplain at the University of Western Australia (UWA) in Perth. As a chaplain, Fr. Harte took a group of students to Calcutta and stayed with the MC Brothers at Mansatala, since he had been in the Jesuit noviciate with Br. Andrew, MC. The students had the opportunity to volunteer at MC homes in Calcutta. After the opening of the houses in Australia, he helped the Sisters there.

b. Bishop Douglas J. Warren (1919–2013) was bishop of the Diocese of Wilcannia-Forbes, Australia, from 1967 until 1994. In 1969, at his invitation, Mother opened the house in Bourke to care for Aboriginal people.

need.—SM. Agnes and SM. Joseph I have appointed as my legal "attorneys", so any business, they will see to it.

I hope all the sick Sisters are better. . . .

I will write again soon.

God bless you
Mother

. . .

MGL 66. 4TH OCTOBER 1969

+

L.D.M.

Mother House
4th October 1969

My dearest Children,

One more tabernacle has been made for the Living God in Bourke among the people of Australia. I came back on the 1st, nobody expecting me, as I wanted to give you all a joyful surprise. Poor Sr. M. Gemma kept asking: "Who is there?" I said, "Mother"—"Our Mother?" "Yes, your Mother." In the morning everybody's head turned back to make sure if really it was "Our Mother" in the chapel.

As the Society keeps growing, I hope and pray you are all more and more conscious of your responsibility to the Church. You are the sign of God, the proof of His living love for men. Do not forget this and become preoccupied with your little difficulties which come in the community life. Be thoughtful of your Superior and each other. Today she takes God's place for you. She is me, your Mother, in your Community. I always look forward to seeing you, being with you, loving you. She too. Be kind to your Superior—do not let your mind and your heart be preoccupied with
her weakness. Do to her now what you would like the Sisters to do to Mt 7:12
you to-morrow, when you will be Superior. You will need love and trust then—give it to her now. When Christ was in the Community with His Apostles, He always was so loving; He trusted everyone, loved each one with a personal love. You would like the Sisters to give you this personal love—give it to your Sisters and to your Superior in the Community. Now, when the Superior has to correct, and maybe sometimes she forgets herself and her position, and may act so un-Christ-like, do not forget she is but

a human being. Be kind to her in her weakness, help her to overcome herself, help her to see only Jesus in you, in your kindness, in your compassion. In time of her weakness, your Superior comes and appears as Christ in His distressing disguise—she then needs your love, your humility, your
Heb 13:8 trust. Trust her with a loving trust, in spite of herself, for Jesus in her has not changed. He is the same, as there is only one Jesus. Her words may sometimes hurt you, her actions may surprise you, and you feel like giv-
Rom 12:19 ing her back what you have received. Never, never retaliate in that way.
Lk 23:34 Turn to Jesus in your heart, say with deep Faith: "Forgive her, she does not know what she says or does", "Soul of Christ, sanctify her". If in all these community difficulties you would turn to Jesus in Faith, Love and Trust, your Community will, I am sure, be a Living Tabernacle of God Most High, as Nazareth was.[109] When you are tempted to give back in bitterness and temper, touch your Cross—that is why you carry it on your left side, closest to your heart, and say: "Passion of Christ, strengthen me."
Mt 12:14; Mk 3:6 Never lower yourself to become a pharisee, who wanted to kill Christ.

Our Society is still young—20 years are but a very short time. Our Superiors are still without much experience. Have compassion on them, be kind to them. See the Hand of the Good God that is trying to write a wonderful message of Love to you personally using that bad pencil—maybe even a broken pencil, but it is the Hand and Mind of God you must try to understand, and not examine the pencil. Today He uses the pencil which is rough, and yet the loving message is there—always beautiful, always true, always thoughtful—only for you. Christ will use only that pencil in the place you are—for you. Therefore, kiss the Hand, but do not try to break the pencil.

Do not allow outsiders to get mixed in our family affairs. They don't understand—therefore may advise you the wrong way. Be careful, watch
Mt 26:41 and pray that you may not enter into temptation.

...

P.S. Be careful of people going to you with forged letters from C.R.S. [Catholic Relief Services] and Mother for supplies.[a]

God bless you
Mother

a. Catholic Relief Services (CRS) is the official international humanitarian agency of the Catholic Church in the United States, originally founded in 1943 by the American bishops to serve World War II refugees. Since then, CRS has expanded its relief work to reach more than 120 million people in more

MGL 67. 5TH NOVEMBER 1969

+

L.D.M.

Mother House
5th November 1969

My dearest Children,

To make the work of God grow and make it bring much fruit, the following points have been decided:

SM. Agnes, SM. Frederick and SM. Nirmala will act as "Regional Superiors" . . .[a]

1. They will receive all letters—renewal of General permissions and other internal spiritual uplift of the Community.[b] Also Sisters of the Communities may write freely to them. All these letters must be closed—also other permissions that may be necessary—for these too, the Superiors must ask of their acting Regional Superiors, and when they visit you, you must give them all respect.
2. All money and business letters must be written directly to SM. Camillus, our Procuratrix General.
3. All business regarding Shishu Bhavan and education must be addressed to SM. Audrey.
4. All letters regarding Medicine must be addressed to SM. Anand.

All letters for Renewal of Vows and any personal letters should be addressed to MOTHER. All houses outside India correspond direct[ly] with Mother.

As SM. Joseph, our 3rd Councillor, has to go to Venezuela as Superior, SM. Monica has been appointed as her substitute. She will also be the Novice Mistress of the 2nd Years.

---

than 100 countries on five continents. CRS began sending food supplies for the poor and needy under the care of the Missionaries of Charity in India from the early 1950s, when millions of refugees came to West Bengal, especially to Calcutta. Later, CRS assisted the poor in other parts of the world (e.g., Yemen, Ethiopia) and continue to do so. As this constituted a large network of food supplies all across the country, it was possible for other non-governmental organizations [NGOs] or individuals to go around with forged letters in order to get part of these goods for themselves.

a. By the end of 1969, there were thirty-four houses spread across India, Venezuela, Ceylon (now Sri Lanka), Italy, Tanzania, and Australia. Because of the number of communities, the houses in India were given Regional Superiors.

b. It appears that the Sister typist did not correctly understand Mother's original writing or may have omitted a line in error. Unfortunately, the manuscript of this letter is not preserved. A possible reading of this line could be: "... renewal of General permissions, and see to other internal and external matters; they will be responsible for the spiritual uplift of the Community."

As SM. Frederick becomes an acting Regional Superior, it will not be possible for her to remain in charge of the 3rd Years. SM. Joseph Michael takes her place.

We have made some small changes during the Seminar. I will send them to you with the Sisters when they return.

All your Superiors have made a very fervent Seminar, and I am sure the retreat also will be full of grace. Pray that we may all be able to answer to the grace of God with deep humility and love. From you, dear Sister, I ask but one thing—that you receive the work of the Holy Spirit in your Superiors with great joy and generosity. Help them to help you to become Saints, for we all want this grace only—to become Holy; you must forget and forgive all things of "Yesterday", and tomorrow has not yet come, but today you can love Jesus as He loved you, with a deep personal love. Do not be afraid—God will give you all the graces you need if you allow Him to make you Holy through prayer and sacrifice, through penance and hard
Lk 1:37 work. Nothing is impossible with God, as God is Love. He can give you
1 Jn 4:16 "Only Love", so let Him fill you with His Love, so that you can love Him in your Superior, your Sisters and your Poor. I know you all want to be a joy to the Holy Father and to the Church, so be generous and in Total Surrender, Loving Trust and Cheerfulness try to keep step with Christ climbing the Hill of Calvary once more.

God bless you
Mother

MGL 68. 25TH NOVEMBER 1969

L.D.M.

25th November 1969

My dearest Children,

By now all your Sister Superiors have returned to you with great love and humility to do great things for God with you. Be generous and help them to help you to become holy. Next week we begin with the Church—the Season of Advent. It is like Spring-time in Nature—when everything is renewed and so is fresh and healthy. Advent is also meant to do this to us—to refresh us and to make us healthy to be able to receive Christ in
Lk 2:6–7 whatever form He may come to us. At Christmas He comes like a little child, so small, so helpless—so much in need of His Mother and all that

[a] Mother's love can give. It was His Mother's humility that enabled her
to receive Jesus as a helpless Babe, Her humility that helped her to do the
work of a Handmaid to Christ—God of God, True God of True God, be- Lk 1:38
ing of one substance with the Father, by Whom all things were made. Let
us see and touch the greatness that fills the depths of their humility. We cannot do better than Jesus and Mary. If we really want God to fill us, we must empty ourselves through humility of all that is selfishness in us. To enable us to do this emptying, we shall also try to live the resolution made at the Seminar:[a]

1. To catch up with Christ your Son in Chastity, Poverty and Obedience.
2. To make my life a rivalry with Him in tender love for my Sisters and compassion for the poor, especially by understanding, appreciation and thoughtfulness.
3. To follow His footsteps in prayer and penance.
4. To overtake Him in total surrender, loving trust and cheerfulness.

Each one of us [is] going to make these our own aim during this Advent, Lent and throughout the year, so that with Mary we can say: "Behold the Handmaid of the Lord, be it done to me according to Thy word" Lk 1:38
and "The Word was made flesh and dwelt among us." This Total Surren- Jn 1:14
der to God will make His Word, Jesus, dwell in us and through us in our
Sisters and the Poor. The Loving Trust towards each other and our Poor
will make "The Word" breathe into us His Spirit of Love and unity. The
joy of the Lord will be our strength and light which will enable us to do Neh 8:10
great things with Him, for Him, for the greater glory of the Father, and
that all men may see our good works and glorify the Father. Mt 5:15–16

On the 8th December, 14 Novices are taking First Vows and 10 Final Vows.... Pray for them all.

SM. Agnes has gone to Kanpur to register the new house which is being bought for Shishu Bhavan and Convent. She will also go to Agra to be with the Sisters who are making the retreat and then go to Delhi to see off SM. Joseph, who will be the Acting Regional Superior and [who] is leaving on the 30th for Venezuela with SM. Josepha and SM. William.

SM. Frederick has left for Amravati and will see the Aspirants in Bombay and Madras, then she will go to Trichur, Kottayam and Palai to meet

a. The Seminar could have been on Our Lady, as the resolutions seem to be made to her.

the new Aspirants. Pray for her that she may do this important work with the help of the Holy Spirit.

The Novices are at the Mother House.

. . .

Pray for me.

God bless you
Mother

1970

MGL 69. 1ST FEBRUARY 1970

+

L.D.M.

Mother House
1st February 1970

My dearest Children,

During the year 1969—God has been so very wonderful to each one of you in using you to spread His fragrance of love everywhere. Many sacrifices have been made with great generosity, and most consoling of all is that there has been more understanding of each other, more thoughtfulness for each other, and more appreciation of each other, and so more unity and love in the community throughout the Society. 2 Cor 2:14

This year our Holy Father has proclaimed as a year of Hope, and we must, with him, look up and say: All will be well—because Christ cannot deceive us. All trials and sufferings are only means to greater love. No one will help us better and more than Our Lady—the Mother of the Church. She is our Life, our Sweetness and our Hope.[a] Let us listen to her, for she will tell us, as she said to the people at Cana—"Do what He tells you." He will always speak to us through His Vicar on earth—through our Superiors, who have their authority from above. Let us be brave and generous in our Total Surrender to God, in our Loving Trust with our Superiors, and that joy and cheerfulness with our Sisters and the People we serve. Let us for this reason improve our way of praying the Rosary and show greater fidelity in showing our love for Our Lady. Titus 1:2 Jn 2:5 Lk 10:16

a. Mother is referring to the prayer, *Hail Holy Queen*:

Hail holy Queen, Mother of mercy, our life, our sweetness and our hope. To thee do we cry, poor banished children of Eve; to thee do we send up our sighs, mourning and weeping in this valley of tears. Turn, then, most gracious Advocate, thine eyes of mercy toward us, and after this, our exile, show unto us the blessed fruit of thy womb, Jesus, O clement, O loving, O sweet Virgin Mary! Amen.

To be able to help our Sisters in the houses to do their teaching better, I have sent SM. Agnes, SM. Frederick, SM. Nirmala and SM. Dorothy to Bangalore to do a 2 month course in Catechetics. I am sure you will all pray for them—that they may do well. Please do not address any letters to them, as they will not have the time to answer them. I will be in Calcutta until their return.

...

SM. Barbara has been in hospital for a major operation.—Thank God, she is better now.

... Bangalore and Kanpur will soon have their own houses.

In Madurai the Sisters had a grand reception—everybody was happy. We have one of the houses built for the Poor by the Bishop,[a] so we are with our own people.[b]

We have started making [applications for] visas and passports for our Sisters, so pray very hard. I received a very urgent call for Sisters to go to the Holy Land to serve the refugees,[c] so please ask Our Lady to guide me to do the right thing—for this is such a great thing for our Society.

Do not get mixed up in useless discussions and arguments. Be careful of your reading. Renewal does not mean that you must eat everything anybody gives you—for us let it be enough, the Body of Christ and His Church.[d]—

There is a group of men who are posing as CRS [Catholic Relief Services] representatives, using CRS letterhead to get CRS supplies. Please do not give food to anyone under any circumstances, no matter what letter or telephone calls you may receive, even if they state that it is from CRS or any other Catholic Institution. Anyone who gives food will receive a bill from CRS for all food given to these imposters. If anyone approaches you, keep them and call the police.

Rev. Fr. Dominic George has been sent away from St. Dominic Mission Home & Orphanage, Mayannore, Ottapalam, Trichur Dt. He was a priest in the Jacobite Church and is actually a Muslim. He is not received in the Catholic Church. His real name is Dr. Maulana Mohamad Sulaiman, but

a. The meaning here is: We [are living in] one of the ...

b. The meaning here is: With the Poor.

c. From 1967 to 1970 a war involving Israel and Egypt, Jordan, the Palestine Liberation Organization (PLO), and their allies was going on. Mother received a call from Msgr. John G. Nolan, president of the Pontifical Mission for Palestine (from 1966 to 1987), asking to send the Sisters to take care of the Palestinian refugees.

d. Mother was warning the Sisters about the spread of post–Vatican II confusion about authentic renewal in religious life.

he moves about in the dress of a Catholic priest and is using the letterhead of the above Institution. Beware of him.

Please do not allow anyone to beg in the name of the Missionaries of Charity and also do not give in writing any permission to beg for us. If there is any begging to be done, you can do it personally and not through someone else.

Pray much for Mother.

God bless you
Mother

MGL 70. 19TH FEBRUARY 1970

+

L.D.M.

Mother House
19th February 1970

My dearest Children,

First week of Lent is nearly over and I hope each one is trying to enter
into the Passion of Christ with greater love. He still keeps looking out for Mt 26–27; Mk 14–15; Lk 22–23; Jn 18–19
"One" to console Him—to comfort Him. Do you try to be that "One"? To- Ps 69:20
day Christ in His Vicar and Church is being humiliated through pride in
acts of disobedience and disloyalty; scourged with evil tongues, crowned Mt 27:26; Mk 15:15; Jn 19:1
and despised, and Mt 27:29; Mk 15:17

Hungry for Love He looks at you
Thirsty for Kindness He begs from you
Naked for Loyalty He hopes of you
Sick and in Prison for Friendship He wants from you
Homeless for Shelter in your heart He asks of you Mt 25:35–40

Will you be that "One" to Him?

Christ obeyed because He loved His Father. He, being equal to the Lk 22:42; Phil 2:8
Father, did not feel it below His dignity to obey for He went down with Phil 2:6–8; Lk 2:51
them and was obedient to them. It was enough for Him that the Father Mt 26:62–66
had given His authority—be he the High Priest, Pilate or Judas. In Our La- Mt 27; Mk 15; Lk 23; Jn 18–19
dy's life we find the same—God the Father never spoke to her directly— Mt 26–27; Mk 14; Lk 22; Jn 13, 18
it was through the Angel or St. Joseph. Who more than they had claim Lk 1:26–38
not to be ordered about? Today much of the suffering in the Church and Mt 1:24; 2:13–21

outside is caused solely through misunderstood freedom and renewal. We cannot be free unless we are able to surrender our will freely to the Will of God. We cannot renew unless we have the humility and the courage to acknowledge what is to be renewed in us. Therefore be careful of people who come to you with wonderful speeches on freedom and renewal, but
Jn 15:11, 17:13 actually they deceive and take away from you the joy and peace of Christ,
Jn 14:27; 16:33; Eph 2:14 the Life, the Way and the Truth, for He alone is the Truth that cannot de-
Jn 14:6 ceive; He alone is the Way that will lead us to the Father; He alone is the
Jn 11:25 Life and Resurrection. To be able to keep on the Way to the Father, let us use our free will to choose and

> Follow Christ in Poverty
> Love Christ with undivided love in Chastity
> Obey, with full freedom in unity and submission with Christ,
> those who have authority from above
> Serve Christ in His distressing disguise through whole-hearted free service.

At the Mother House we are taking special care:

1. To bow our head at the name of Jesus, at the *Gloria Patri* and
   Jn 1:14 "the Word was made flesh."
2. Also tidiness and cleanliness and keeping things in the same place after use and not taking things without permission.
3. Weekly fidelity to the Chapter and Instruction.

Let us be faithful to Rule no. 137[a]—No young men or seminarian should be allowed to work in the dispensary alone with the Sisters.—Even Superiors should not [work alone with] such men. SM.—— has written to the Holy See for dispensation from her Vows, because she has been involved with a seminarian. Let us be careful—though this is the first case that has been knocked down by the devil, yet it is a sign that he is trying his best to catch any one of us—if we are careless in our observance of our vows and rules. Pray for her.

Pray also very much for our Holy Father and for me.

God bless you
Mother

a. Rule 137: See footnote to MGL 54 of 30th November 1967, p. 90, for the text of this rule.

MGL 71. 14TH MARCH 1970

+

L.D.M.

Mother House
14th March 1970

My dearest Children,

Calcutta is really sharing in the Passion of Christ. It is sad to see so much sorrow in our loved Calcutta. But just like Christ who, after the Passion, rose to live forever, so will Calcutta rise again and be the Mother of the Poor and the thousands of refugees that come flocking on all sides.[a] Pray for Calcutta and our people.

Mt 26–27; Mk 14–15; Lk 22-23; Jn 18–19

Mt 28:5–6; Mk 16:6; Lk 24:6–7; Rom 6:9

It has been a great joy for me to be with the Sisters at the Mother House. Everyone has really made the best use of this chance.

All the visas and passports are ready, and we hope our sisters will soon leave for Melbourne and Rome....

I am sure you will all with me thank God for the special loving grace He has given to SM.——, for before the dispensation had arrived she has deeply repented for her mistake and has begged to be allowed to return. I am sure Jesus would have done the same thing. I have written to her to return home to Mother House. I am sure this will be a great lesson for us all to learn never to play with our vocation. So many of us, for just a little inconvenience, speak so easily of giving up. Let us learn from her to appreciate and love our vocation—face death itself rather than give up. I am sure you will all pray for her and will never throw this fall to her face. This matter should be treated as a "Matter of conscience." Therefore, I am telling you everything, so that each one will know and there will be no need for further discussion between you or with others.

On the 19th March a new house will be started near Caracas.[b] I am not sure of the new address, but you can all write to the address in Marin,[c] and the sisters will re-address it....

I went to Raigarh to bring SM. Francesca to Calcutta, as she had fractured her leg and as she has to be in bed for 3 months. SM. Isabel will be the Superior of Raigarh. SM. Anna, due to continual fever in Darjeeling, was brought to Calcutta by SM. Josephine, who in the train had a beating

a. Because of the political tension between East and West Pakistan before the outbreak of war in 1971, refugees from East Pakistan were flocking to Calcutta.

b. The foundation in Catia La Mar, 34 km from Caracas, was opened on 19th March 1970.

c. Marin is a city in Venezuela, 80 km east of Caracas, where the house was opened on 17th July 1969.

on her face by a Communist girl.[a] SM. Josephine bled terribly and had to travel by 2nd class to avoid further beating.

Our Sisters in Ceylon and Africa are having much difficulties[b]—please pray for them. Shanti Nagar is really growing into a beautiful town of peace.[c]

In the Mother House during Lent we have taken only tea standing and in silence,[d] on Wednesdays and Fridays. Next year you can do it in the houses also....

I would be very happy if you would pay great attention to the new Mass and learn to offer it and join in it beautifully.[e] Utter every word with deep personal affection, devotion and meaning. Try to learn how to use your Bible with profit and love.

I will be soon going to our houses outside India, and I intend to stay a longer time in each house—therefore, the Regional Superiors will be able to act,[f] and as SM. Agnes is my Assistant she will be over all of them. I am sure you will all work harder and do your best to grow in the sanctity God and the Church expect of you.

During my absence especially it would console Our Lord and make Mother very happy if you would all try to understand and love obedience, for living under obedience is a great privilege, honour and a special grace. Obedience also begets in our soul unfailing peace, inward joy and close union with God. Help your Superior to help you to become holy.

Mt 28:8; Lk 24:41, 52; Jn 20:20 May the joy of the Risen Lord be your strength in the work, your way
Neh 8:10 to the Father, your light to guide you, and your Bread of life.
Jn 8:12, 9:5, 14:6
Jn 6:35, 48, 51

God bless you,
Mother

a. That is, Sr. Josephine received a beating on her face from the girl.

b. The Sisters were having difficulty in getting an extension of their visas.

c. Opened in 1969, Shanti Nagar ("City of Peace"), welcomes patients affected by Hansen's disease (leprosy) and their families. They are given medications and upon recovery are helped to live a regular life with their families and be self-supporting.

d. That is to say, the Sisters in Mother House decided to forego snacks and recreation at tea time, and to take their tea standing and in silence.

e. Mother is referring to the changes made to the Mass after the Vatican II, including the change from Latin to the vernacular.

f. The meaning is: the Regional Superiors will be able to exercise their authority without referring matters to Mother. If necessary, Sr Agnes, the Assistant General, is also available to the Regional Superiors.

P.S. Plastic paper given to the houses should be used to make pictures for the families and not to cover books. Once more I repeat: do not travel to the Mother House or from house to house for any reason either for accompanying patients or girls or even for necessary things.[a]

MGL 72. 19TH APRIL 1970

+

L.D.M.

Mother House
19th April 1970

My dearest Sisters,

On the 23rd April, we are leaving for Melbourne from Madras. I hope you will all pray that Our Lord will bless this, our new foundation. About the third week of June, I will take a group of 6 sisters to Palestine. We need lots of prayers for this work among the refugees.

The 5 sisters who have finished the course at Bangalore have been enriched with the riches of Christ and are most anxious to share with you all Eph 3:8
that they have received. Therefore when they come to your house, please make good use of this special grace and share with your people the gift of God.

...

Accept [your new Regional] Superiors with deep and humble faith and love. Do not let your minds dwell on their short-comings—rather be eager to learn from them how to love and serve Jesus with greater love. The Society will grow and bring much fruit only if we allow Jesus to use us Jn 15:5, 8
through them. Have for them that same love and confidence you have always had for Mother, and do not think you will give me less by giving them more.—No—because the love and confidence you gave me, you have given it to Jesus—in them also is the same Jesus. Do not compare nor pass remarks, but have this thought only in your mind—how well I can serve the Church through the Society? The Regional Superiors are given to you to enable you to serve the Church with greater love. Confide in them, write to them; your letters to them must be closed, and you will receive their letters closed. Pray daily for them that they may help you grow in sanctity through Total Surrender, Loving Trust and Cheerfulness.

a. Mother is warning the Sisters not to waste money and time travelling.

When Regional Superiors visit your house, they will give the blessing to the Community,[a] give the instruction and hold the Chapter, but in all matters of community life and permissions, these will be regulated by the Superior of the house. The Superiors of the houses will arrange all business and renew all general permissions with them. All Statistics must be sent to them. In the beginning maybe it will be difficult for you, but accept this as the will of God and everything will be alright for you.

If all the work is done by the Regional Superiors, what will Mother do? This must be a big question in your hearts. Mother will pray that you become Saints and so fulfil her promise.[b] Also I will be able to stay longer with our Sisters outside India and establish the Society. The MC must be-
Mt 28:19; Mk 16:15; Lk 24:48; Acts 1:8 come the witness of Christ in other parts of the world also. If you really love Mother, you will love your Superior and Regional Superior with the
Jn 13:34, 15:12 same love as He has loved you.

Do not get mixed up in politics nor discuss or write about this matter. Be careful of the excited crowd. Do your work with great love and effi-
Jn 14:27; 15:11; 16:33; 17:13; Eph 2:14 ciency and you will experience the peace and joy of Christ.

I will be away for quite a long time and will be moving about. Therefore please do not write to me, but remember me in your Holy Mass and Holy Communion. This will be enough for me.

As it is the wish of the Church that the Constitutions be re-written and the Spirit of the Vatican [II] be embodied in them, we shall have the Chapter General in January, 1971, as by February, 1972, we shall have to submit our Constitutions to the Holy See for the Final Approval, as per the decree of February, 1965. I shall be sending you some questions for your discussion as soon as they are ready. Do not speak of this to the people outside your community, but pray and make many sacrifices, that we may be able to know, love and do the will of God in all things.

...

God bless you

Mother

a. Mother is referring to the MC custom of the Superior (local, regional or general) "giving a blessing" to each Sister in the community in the morning and evening, by placing her right hand on the Sister's head and saying, "God bless you." She began this with the first group of Sisters, probably as an adaptation of the Bengali custom of taking a blessing from a respected person (a holy person, an elder, or a parent) by touching the person's feet with one's hands, and then placing one's hands on one's own head as a blessing. She was familiar with this custom from the time she came to India. "Giving a blessing" is one of the prerogatives of the Superior of the community.

b. Mother had made a promise to give saints to the Church, as she had written to Father Neuner: "When the work started— . . . Only one prayer I made—to give me grace to give saints to the Church." See *Come be My Light*, 212.

MGL 73. 7TH MAY 1970

Melbourne, Australia
7th May 1970

My dearest Children,

My sister is with me,[a] and we are on our way to Bourke.

Many thanks for all your welcome letters. I was so proud of you all who wrote. A number of houses did not write. You don't know what does it means to get a letter from you in a new land.

Our journey to Melbourne was like that of the Holy Family—just we—we stayed with the Loreto Nuns, as there was no place in the inn. His Lk 2:7
Grace[b] was not there either. A small house was shown which His Grace had shown me.—It was vacant of people, but full of dirt—leaking;—I have never seen anything like that. With the help of our co-workers and some young people it was ready enough to go in. We were all very happy in our Poverty. By Sunday morning we had Holy Mass in our Chapel and since then all is alright. Food and clothes have been pouring in. God has been so very wonderful to us. It is so beautiful to be Poor.

I hope all is well with you all and that you are helping Mother by your faithfulness to your life of prayer and sacrifice. Keep the love for the Poorest of the Poor always living. Do not let the present day talk take you away from the humble work of Nirmal Hriday and lepers. Our love for Jesus is poured out in action through these humble Mt 25:35–46
works. Do not think it is a waste of time to feed the hungry, to visit and take care of the sick and dying; to open [homes] and receive the unwanted and homeless. Oh no, this is our love of Christ in action. The humbler the work, the greater [must] be your love and efficiency. Be not afraid of the life of sacrifice that comes from the life of poverty.

Pray for me.

God bless you,
Mother

a. Mother is actually referring to her cousin, File (as is the custom in India, where one refers to one's cousin as one's "cousin-sister").

b. Mother is referring to James Robert Knox (1914–1983), an Australian cardinal who served as the Apostolic Internuncio in India from 1957 to 1967. He then became Archbishop of Melbourne (1967–1974), and from 1974 to 1983 he served in various offices in the Roman Curia, including the office of Prefect of the Congregation for Divine Worship and the Discipline of the Sacraments. He developed a close relationship with Mother while he was in India and helped with the opening of our houses in Australia. He is one of the few priests with whom she shared about her interior darkness.

MGL 74. 24TH MAY 1970

+

L.D.M.

Mauritius
24th May 1970

My dearest Children,

Today,[a] when in all our houses there is rejoicing, especially in the Mother House, where our Sisters take the first step of putting on the livery
Rom 13:14 of Christ[b]—the novices choose Christ as their Crucified Spouse and the Professed surrender themselves to God in Total Surrender, Loving Trust and Cheerfulness for life. I am sitting alone. Thank God there is perpetual adoration here, and so I am really not alone—in Jesus I have you all here very close.[c]

I hope to leave for Tabora on Tuesday[d]—then there will be no trouble at all. My hand is better, but I cannot use it for another week.[e] By that time I will be with my own and they will take care of me.

On the 20th His Grace came to Gore Street for Holy Mass,[f] and the Sisters renewed their Vows. It was his first time and so he was very happy. He spoke very beautifully and he encouraged the love the Society has for the Holy Father and the Church. I gave him the spiritual gift of all our works to send it to our Holy Father and I wrote in everybody's name including the lepers.

In Bourke the Sisters have done such good work[g]—there is joy in the faces of the people they have so lovingly cared for. The improvement is so visible. Thank God.

We hope to get some very good aspirants in Melbourne. The little

a. On 24th May, feast of Our Lady, Help of Christians (and on 8th December, feast of the Immaculate Conception), the Sisters profess and renew their vows, and those in formation move to the next stage.

b. Livery is a distinctive clothing or badge worn by a servant or official. Although the term has fallen out of use, in Mother's spiritual milieu, "livery of Christ" was often used to designate a religious habit.

c. Mother went to Mauritius to see about establishing a new foundation there and is writing from the convent of the Sisters of Marie Reparatrice, where she stayed from 22nd to 27th May 1970.

d. Tabora is a city in Tanzania, Africa. The house there was opened on 8th September 1968.

e. The Superior of the Sisters of Marie Reparatrice in Mauritius mentioned that Mother arrived with a broken arm, and the Sister who was taking care of the sick had the great privilege of helping her. In a letter to Eileen Egan dated 21st May 1970, Mother wrote: "I have fractured my left arm before I left India & so it is a little difficult for me to travel."

f. Mother is informing the Sisters that (His Grace) Cardinal Knox celebrated Mass at the MC house (at Gore Street) in Melbourne, Australia.

g. The house in Bourke, Australia, was opened on 16th September 1969; the Sisters were caring for Aboriginal peoples.

house in Gore Street will be soon too small, but I am glad they will be able to taste the joy of being poor. Bourke Sisters also have only 4 small rooms, and the other rooms are used for the work, as this was a St. Vincent de Paul Centre before. Both SM. Laetitia and SM. Christopher drive well. Most important is that there is joy, and great care is taken of their spiritual life by their confessors in both the places; as you know His Grace is very particular about this.

Here in Mauritius there are many poor, very much like our Venezuela people. The poor I visited are mostly from Indian or African origin. They still keep their own language, especially the old ones. There would be plenty of work for our Sisters.

The more I go round, the better I understand how very necessary it is for us to pray the work, to make the work our Love for God in action.—To be able to do that, how necessary it is to live that life of Total Surrender to God, Loving Trust in our Superior and each other, and that cheerfulness with the Poor. Let us be happy and show our humble gratitude to God for
this wonderful gift of being chosen by Him to be His MC. Don't allow Jn 15:16
the worldly spirit to enter your heart, your Community and your Society. 1 Cor 2:12; 1 Jn 2:15–17
Jesus in the Blessed Sacrament and in His Poor will always protect you if
you learn from Him to be meek and humble of heart. Mt 11:29

Pray much for Mother.

God bless you,
Mother

MGL 75. 6TH JULY 1970

+

L.D.M.

Rome
6th July 1970

My dearest Children,

Thank you for praying with such faith and love for Mother's Intention.

The intention was this: When our Sisters will no longer physically be able to go in search of souls, as the Rule 106 says[a]—we still have the better

a. Rule 106: "As the Society and all its members must be free to go in search of souls—to carry God's love amongst the poorest of the poor, it follows that no schools with regular curriculum, nor boarding-schools, nor hospitals or nursing homes can be accepted, except only those needed for the homeless destitute" (1954 *Constitutions*, revised; this was Rule 103 in the 1954 *Constitutions*).

part of our life to spend for Jesus—in silence and adoration—therefore we will spend it in perpetual adoration. These adoring Sisters, who will spend their days not in the slums in works of love, but in Silence adoring Christ in His Real Presence, will become the living food for the Sisters' apostolate. Also 1st years and 3rd years will share in this adoration.

Also in this group of adorers will be accepted young and old, crippled, etc., who because of their inability have never been able to consecrate their lives to God in Religious Life though they have been "chosen by Him". They will offer their sufferings through adoration and so share

Mt 26–27; Mk 14–15; Lk 22–23; Jn 18–19

in the Passion of Christ. They will be true members of the Society, as the Rule 7 says.[a]

In this group will also be accepted priests and nuns who, having spent their lives away from Jesus, want to return and make up to Christ by their lives of prayer and adoration.[b]

SM. Agnes will send you the few additions to our Constitutions which Cardinal Agagianian is most willing to approve after we have all accepted them and prayed over them.[c] I would like you—every house—to send me a common letter from your own Community—expressing in it your approval or disapproval—your joy or fear. Send the letter to Calcutta as I hope to be at the Mother House by the 1st August.

For the Society this will be a very great grace, as it will strengthen our union with God and with each other—and also our Faith in the Service of the Poor. We will have the support of the continual grace that will flow from Christ in the Blessed Sacrament—through the adorers to us, and so

Jn 17:11, 20–22

in all truth we will be—One.—

Do not speak of this to anyone outside your Community, as this is our

Mt 7:16

family matter. When we get all the permissions we need, then by our fruit they will all know.

a. Rule 7: "All the members of the Society form one family. All have the same obligations, the same privileges and work for the same purpose" (1954 *Constitutions*, revised).

b. Although this was Mother's intention, this group never came into existence. This intention is being realized in part in the active branch: the Sisters who are no longer able to go in search of souls have more time for prayer and are free to have extra time of Adoration, though there is no perpetual adoration. However, it is more fully realized through the contemplative branch, which Mother founded in 1976 with Sr. M. Nirmala, MC. The contemplative Sisters have more hours of adoration than the active Sisters and only two to three hours of apostolate, concentrating on the spiritual works of mercy. The possibility for priests who desired to return to the priesthood and make reparation was never made concrete; however, nuns who wished to return to religious life were welcomed by the contemplative branch.

c. Gregorio Agagianian (1895–1971) was an Armenian cardinal, head of the Armenian Catholic Church from 1937 to 1962 and Prefect of the Congregation for the Propagation of the Faith (Propaganda Fide) from 1958 to 1970.

The Sisters in Bourke, Tabora and Rome have done most wonderful work. The people of Tabora were very sad to lose SM. Damien. So are the people of Rome, where SM. Gertrude has done such good work. Due to her bad health and also as we have no one to teach our Sisters for the medical work, I am taking SM. Gertrude back to the Mother House. I am sure you will all be delighted, as she has taught most of you. We are leaving for Jordan on the 16th, and I hope to be home by the 1st August, God willing. I have been away so long.

Let us more and more be faithful to the Spirit of our Society—to that simplicity, humility and charity. Do not allow anyone or anything to become an obstacle to the living of your life—of a true MC. Often it must be very painful, but Jesus has said it: "If you want to be mine—take up the Cross and follow Me." Today's difficulties are the Cross—and the acceptance of the Cross with a smile is the sign of great sanctity. Do not pass judgment on others nor argue with them. Let every spirit bless the Lord. Be more than ever faithful to Poverty and Obedience—not because you have to but because you are in love with Christ and you want no obstacle which will prevent you from seeing Him in your neighbour. Everything that flies we cannot eat, so also everything that is printed we must not read.[a]

Mt 10:38; 16:24; Mk 8:34; Lk 9:23; 14:27

Mt 7:1

Ps 150:6

Be brave—and full of joy—because Jesus will never leave us alone. And now more than ever He wants to be our strength, joy and Faith—through His Real Presence. Holy Father has sent His affectionate blessing to each one of you and your families.

Jn 14:18

God bless you
Mother

a. The meaning here is that just as there are so many diverse flying creatures and not all of them should be eaten, so there are so many printed things, and not all of them should be read. Using this simile, she is warning the Sisters against a wide variety of reading material about religious life and the vows; they must be very prudent about what they read.

MGL 76. 6TH AUGUST 1970

6th August 1970

My dearest Children,

Thank God I am back home. Your prayers must have helped me most, for Jesus took great care of me.

From the 13th August we will begin our Novena in preparation for the Feast of our Society. This year we will prepare with greater love and unity and with humble gratitude.

Each day will be different. Therefore the reading, meditation, examination of conscience, instruction, etc., must be all based and prepared on the theme of the day and each day will be offered for a special group.

1st Day: Theme: CONTRITION—fruit of sorrow for sin—Chapter.

Ps 51:10 Prayer for the day: "Create a clean heart within me, O Lord."

Pray for our Aspirants and also for the Students of the world.

2nd Day: Theme: FAITH—declaration of faith. Give prominence to the Bible by installing the Written Word of God.[a]

Mk 9:24 Prayer for the day: "I believe Lord, increase my Faith."

Pray for our Postulants and also for the Seminarians in the world.

3rd Day: Theme: FAITH IN ACTION—Obedience. Fidelity to the Written Will of God—Our Constitutions.

1 Sam 3:9 Prayer for the day: "Speak Lord for Thy servant heareth."

Pray for our 1st year Novices and also for all Religious in the world.

4th Day: Theme: HOPE—the fruit of Prayer. Fidelity to the spiritual exercises of the day.

Ps 146:5–6 Prayer for the day: "Our hope is in the Lord, Who made heaven and earth."

Pray for our 2nd year Novices and also for the sick, the dying and lepers in the world.

5th Day: Theme: JOY—the fruit of Peace. Resist anything that leads to moodiness—to be in time for recreation.

Neh 8:10 Prayer for the day: "Let the joy of the Lord be my Strength."

Pray for our Tertians and also for all the Priests in the world.

a. By "installing" Mother means placing the Bible on a stand and keeping it in a prominent place near the altar, thereby giving due reverence to the book of the Word of God.

6th Day: TRUTHFULNESS—the fruit of humility—to act truthfully with God, with my neighbour and with myself.

Prayer for the day: "Christ is the Truth that cannot deceive." Jn 14:6

Pray for our Junior Professed Sisters and also our Government Officials.

7th Day: Theme: COURAGE—the fruit of Loving Trust. Not to be afraid to own up nor be afraid to stand by the truth.[a]

Prayer for the day: "I can do all things in Him who strengthens me." Phil 4:13

Pray for our Senior Professed Sisters and also for Lawyers and Doctors.

8th Day: Theme: HUMILITY—fruit of Purity of Heart. Great fidelity to the humble works of the Society.

Prayer for the day: "He, being equal to God, was not ashamed to become man." Phil 2:6–7

Pray for our Superiors and also Bishops.

9th Day: Theme: LOVE—fruit of Union with God through Faith.

A day of fasting—ending with a vigil in silent adoration from 9–10 P.M.

Prayer for the day: "Love of the Sacred Heart of Jesus, inflame my heart."

Pray for our Mother and the Councillors and also for the Holy Father and his Councillors.

Except for the times of recreation, be very careful of silence, so that you have time to reflect and pray for the different groups of people each day.

It will, I am sure, help us all to prepare for our Consecration to our Lady with greater love and purity. As much as I would love to come to you, still I am afraid it is not possible for me to do so before November,[b] as I have to go in October to Rome and USA as a delegate to the meetings.[c] On my way I will visit our Sisters in Venezuela also. Whenever I am away from India all Regional Superiors must inform [SM. Agnes of any important matters] and get permissions from [her].

a. To own up to something is to admit the truth.

b. Mother is referring to her visitation of the houses in India.

c. Mother went to Rome for the meeting of Superior Generals, as a delegate for India; in the USA she had numerous meetings with Co-workers.

Jn 15:11; 17:13 Jn 14:27; 16:33; Eph 2:14

Many thanks for all your loving letters. I hope you are all well. Let the Joy and Peace of Christ be always with you.

God bless you
Mother

P.S.: From the letter enclosed you will see that the Holy Father has sent us a candle as big as myself, as a token of love and appreciation, which will be used on the feast of the Society.

MGL 77. 25TH SEPTEMBER 1970

+

L.D.M.

Mother House
25th September 1970

My dearest Children,

On the 7th October [we] will complete 20 years of fruitful harvest. We have much to thank God for [for] all He has done for us, in us and through us. Make the 7th October a real thanksgiving day.

These days have been so difficult and so full of suffering for our people—the tension prevailing over the city and then the floods,[a] but our Poor are brave and generous. They accept the will of God with great trust. The situation is very much better now.

I would very much like you all to read *One with Jesus* by Paul [de] Jaegher, SJ. It will help you to [reach] that intimacy with Christ, which is the aim of every MC. Yes, only Jesus can satisfy the hunger and thirst for God and His Love. Be very careful of what you read—just pay attention to the rule, "No books, magazines and papers except those given for common use are to be read by us. Should any other reading be found helpful or necessary, Permission must be asked each time." The rule should be also carefully observed by the Superiors.

Another rule says: "In every house there shall be a part reserved for the exclusive use of the Sisters. No person of the other sex should be admitted into it. . . ." We have so little privacy, and if enclosure is not kept carefully, then that little also will be gone. In some houses people are allowed to

a. Mother is referring to the political tension between East and West Pakistan, which brought multitudes of refugees from East Pakistan to Calcutta, and to floods caused by heavy rains and the poor drainage system in the city. Floods caused millions of people to remain without food and drinking water, and to be subject to outbreaks of contagious diseases.

come inside the dormitory also. This must stop, as it may lead to difficulties we cannot overcome.

From Amman,[a] no news—only what we get from Newspapers, and this is really bad,[b] and yet Our Lord will, I am sure, take care of our Sisters. Pray much for them.

I will be leaving on the 5th October for USA, Rome, England, Venezuela, and hope to be back by the 20th November. I am sure you will be praying much for Mother. The CRS is paying for me. SM. Frederick will join me in England, as we have over 7000 co-workers and we want to arrange things as well as possible.

Some months back in one of my general letters, I mentioned not to allow individual young men to work with you alone in the dispensaries—it applies also for the Superior, not only when Sisters are in charge of dispensaries. I do not understand why there is such neglect in observing such a small wish of Mother's. In some houses these same people are allowed even to enter the interior of the house. Ordinary prudence and common sense require this of us. You will be surprised to hear how lay people pass remarks on such actions. People will naturally talk, but we must not give them reason to do so.

"Keep away from all party and political talk," as Mr. Talukdar says.[c] "You belong to God, therefore you belong to all parties.—Everybody must claim you as their own." It is a very beautiful sentence for a Hindu and lay man. There has been so much publicity given to "Kerala Girls"[d] etc. Many of our own Sisters are from that place—be careful not to hurt them, nor allow any group-forming in your community. I was told that the whole affair was pre-planned.

I hope each and every one of you [is] well and that you take the full amount of food and rest—in doing this you are really happy to be poor....

God bless you,
Mother

a. Amman is the capital of Jordan; Mother was concerned about the Sisters because of the ongoing war.

b. An armed conflict between the Palestine Liberation Organisation (PLO), under the leadership of Yasser Arafat, and the Jordanian Armed Forces, under the leadership of King Hussein, began in September 1970 and lasted until July 1971, resulting in the deaths of thousands of people.

c. Mr. J. C. Talukdar was the Home Minister of the West Bengal government, who generously helped Mother. His statement to Mother was in reference to the time of elections and voting for a certain party (as Mother could vote as an Indian citizen).

d. "Kerala Girls" refers to a scandal caused by articles published by many secular papers about a priest who was sending girls from Kerala to convents in Europe for large amounts of money. The articles claimed that the girls were joining to escape poverty and that the priest was making money on them. Many of the girls did enter convents, but some were employed as servants.

MGL 78. 11TH OCTOBER 1970

Plane to New York
11th October 1970

My dearest Children,

I am sure you are all anxious to know about our Sisters in Amman. They are all very well—and richer in fervour and trust—for instead of spending their days in fear & trembling, they prayed the Rosary continually. The result was on the 9th day—the troops stopped near our place—as the peace had been proclaimed. Again Our Lady has shown to be our Mother, the Cause of our Joy. In thanksgiving let us all pray our rosary with greater fervour & love.

I have left SM. Gertrude with them. She, being one of our oldest Sisters, will be able to encourage & help in case the trouble starts again—also, as a doctor, she will be a great help to the suffering people.

In the plane—where I happen to be alone in the 3 seats—I have had all the time to pray—& to read & to write.—My thoughts are naturally with each one of you—so brave so faithful—so full of love for God.—20 years of your devoted whole-hearted Service given to Christ in the Poor—has, I am sure, been a living proof to the Church that you are a living part in the Body of Christ and that Christ has been pleased with you and shared His love for His Father with you. Today, in the words of our Holy Father—every MC must be able "to cleanse what is dirty—to warm what is lukewarm—to strengthen what is weak—to enlighten what is dark."[a]—
Jn 13:34; 15:12 We must not be afraid to proclaim Christ's love and love as He loved. In the work we have to do—does not matter how small or humble it may be—make it Christ's love in action—do not be afraid to be poor—and so proclaim His Poverty.—Be not afraid—to keep a clean and undivided heart—and so radiate [the] joy of being the Spouse of Jesus Crucified.—Do

a. Mother is referring to the Address by Pope Paul VI to the College of Cardinals on the occasion of the fiftieth anniversary of his priestly ordination. Here is the excerpt: "The courage to proclaim the truth is also the first and essential charity that the shepherds of souls must practice. We must never accept, not even under the pretext of charity towards others, that a minister of the Gospel would announce a purely human word. The salvation of men is at stake. Therefore, in this still vivid remembrance of Pentecost, we want to appeal to all pastors who hold responsibility, that they may raise their voices, when it is necessary, with the power of the Holy Spirit (cf. Act. 1, 8), to clarify what is muddled, to straighten out what is distorted, to kindle what is lukewarm, to strengthen what is weak, to illuminate what is in darkness. This, more than ever, is the hour of clarity for the faith of the Church." The Holy Father is actually alluding to the seventh and eighth stanza of the Pentecost sequence. The translation that Mother read and quoted in her letter comes presumably from some local Catholic newspaper.

The Holy Father's address can be found online at http://w2.vatican.va/content/paul-vi/it/speeches/1970/documents/hf_p-vi_spe_19700518_sacro-collegio.html. Translation here is courtesy of the volume editor.

not be afraid to go down with Christ & be subject to those who have authority from above, and so declare Christ's obedience unto death—and rejoice—that once more Christ is walking through the world in you and through you, going about doing good. Lk 2:51; Heb 13:17 Phil 2:8 Acts 10:38

I know we all sometimes fail to see & touch Christ[a]—none of us has ever done it deliberately or with an "I don't care" attitude. Most of the time it has been tiredness or lack of understanding. Both [of] these, no one understands better than Jesus—for he had experience of them.

The Sisters in Rome have built a house—just like the people's. They have become first class builders—as the house is only a barrack it does not take much time. This living example of poverty has been a great grace for our barrack people & others.—With the help of the people now they are building a hall for the children. The work in Rome keeps growing & deepening spiritually.

Let us pray much for our Sisters in Ceylon—as their visas may not be renewed.—If so—they will have to leave by the 15th Oct. In Tanzania the family Consecra. [Consecration] to the Sacred Heart is spreading more & more.—In Venezuela—in both the houses—the apostolate of bringing the knowledge, the love and the service of Christ in the families is spreading to hundreds of families.—Our Sisters are doing all the works of the priest—except Confession & Consecration at Mass.

Our new work among the homeless old alcoholics keeps touching many hearts in Melbourne—and so also the Aborigines in Bourke have grown and radiate the joy of Christ. Let us thank God [for] the thousands you have brought in touch with Christ in India—through all the hard & demanding work you have all done with so much love & care. It is Good to remember all these—and Glorify the Father. Jn 15:11, 17:13 Mt 5:16

When you find life hard and you feel lonely and tired—this will fill you with courage—& new zeal for Souls. Look up—Jesus is always there—looking at you. Mt 17:8; Mk 9:8

I have not seen you all for so long.—I hope as soon as I return I will start visiting you—and be with you. Though this travelling to these meetings is one of the most difficult acts of Obedience I have to make—yet I must answer to [the] call of the Church and be the witness of Christ among the people He sends me to. I know you will pray for me—especially when in these meetings I have to speak—that I may give His message to them.

a. Mother is alluding to the Gospel passage of Matthew 25:31–46 and referring to seeing and touching Christ in the poorest of the poor.

On the 18th I will return to Rome for the meeting of the Mother Generals. Then on the 27th [I] will go to England with SM. Frederick to meet & organise fully the Co-workers—there are over 9000 Co-workers in England. From Eng. [England] I will go on the 8th Nov. to Venez. [Venezuela] to our Sisters whom I have not seen [for] nearly 2 years.

Pray much for Mother.—God love and bless each one of you.

Mother

1971

MGL 79. 17TH JANUARY 1971

17th January 1971[a]

My dearest Children,

At last Mother is back & will soon be coming to each one of you. It has been so long since I saw you—but now that the Society is growing these are the sacrifices of growth which you & I must make with a Smile.

The Award was most unexpected, & so I had no chance to let you know in time, as I knew only on the 23rd when I returned from Amman[b]—but I am sure each & every one of you were at the feet of the Holy Father—to receive his love & Gift.—It was all so very beautiful—when I come I will bring you for each house a copy of what was said.

For this year we are all going to try very hard to give glory to God
through Christ The Truth. Christ alone is the truth that Cannot deceive Jn 14:6
& the true way that leads to the Father—He alone is the true life—worth Jn 11:25
living—and He alone can love with a true and undivided love.

Jesus, the Truth—today & every day in 1971—wants to live His life—The Truth—in us and, through us, in our Community & in the Poor.—To be able to do so, we shall begin in a very simple way. Speak the truth—think the truth—act the truth—with God & His Church, with each other & with ourselves.—Let us be very sincere in our dealings with each other[c]

a. Mother did not write down the place from which she was writing, but obviously the letter was written from Mother House on a used envelope. She did not write "L.D.M." at the top of the page. We have one page (two sides) of this letter in Mother's handwriting. The rest of the original letter seems to have been lost, but we have it in the first typed version of *Mother's General Letters*, which we have added here. It begins after the footnote that notes the end of the transcript.

b. The first Pope John XXIII Peace Prize was awarded to Mother by Pope Paul VI on 6th January 1971 in Rome. When announcing the prize to the College of Cardinals on 22nd December, Pope Paul VI said: "We hold up to the admiration of all, this intrepid messenger of the love of Christ. This award is meant to be a public recognition of her apostolate of charity which is no longer restricted to the needy of India." *Progress Ukrainian Weekly*, vol. XII, no. 5, 31 January 1971.

c. End of transcript from copy of Mother's handwritten letter.

and have the courage to [accept] one another as we are. Do not be surprised or become preoccupied at each other's failings—rather see and find
Gn 1:27 in each other the good, for each one of us is created in the image of God.
Jn 15:1, 5 Also Jesus has said it so beautifully: "I am the vine, you are the branches and my Father is the vine-dresser." Let us try to see and accept that every Sister is a branch in Christ the vine. The same life-giving sap that flows from the vine (Jesus) through each of the branches (Sisters) is the same.

Due to some changes that have been caused by opening the Noviciate in London and in Calcutta, for the present the Regional Superiors will not be acting. Therefore, all matters regarding the houses, permissions must be written to me as before.

In a number of letters I have been warning you to be careful and prudent with young men and drivers of our ambulances. Two of our Sisters have been caught and left—Sr.—— and Sr.——. After much searching they have been found. Do not pass judgment on them. Pray for them and ask God to preserve and protect us in time of temptation. This is why we need truthfulness with ourselves and others, so that we have the courage [to see] the danger and speak of it in time.

God bless you
Mother

MGL 80. 7TH MARCH 1971

+

L.D.M.

7th March 1971

My dearest Children,

Mt 26–27; Mk 14–15; Lk 22–23; Jn 18–19 Lent is the time when we re-live the Passion of Christ. Let it not be just a time when our feelings are roused—but a change that comes through co-operation with God's grace in real sacrifice of self. Sacrifice, to be real—it must cost—it must hurt—it must empty us of self. Let us go through the Passion of Christ day by day. We often pray: "Let me share with You, Your Pain:[a] I want to be the Spouse of Jesus Crucified", and yet when a little spittle of uncharitable remark—or a stroke of pain—or a thorn of

a. This line is a paraphrase of a line from the "Stabat Mater," a thirteenth-century hymn that celebrates the sentiments of Our Lady at the foot of the Cross: "Let me share with thee His pain."

thoughtlessness is given to us—how we forget that this is the time to share with Him His shame and pain.

Of the 40 houses—I have visited 25 and I hope after the elections to
visit the rest.[a] God has done great things through each one of you—but Lk 1:49
I am sure if there [is] more meekness and humility towards each other—He will do still greater things. I am afraid much energy is used on petty things—on feelings let loose—on remarks passed from one to another—from community to community—through words said or written—and all this is due to the fact that we are preoccupied more with our feelings. If we could but remember that it is Jesus who gives us the chance through that Sister or circumstance to do something beautiful for His Father.

Superiors—try to look up and see Jesus in your Sisters. Your Sisters are Mt 17:8; Mk 9:8
His in a special way because He has chosen them and given them to you to Jn 15:16
take care of them and [to] lead them through holiness to His Heart. Have
COMPASSION ON THEM. Love them as you love Christ, for Jesus will Jn 13:34; 15:12
tell you: "You did it to Me." Guide them and lead them to the altar of God Mt 25:40
and offer them to His Father as a true sacrifice.

Sisters—look up and see Jesus in your Superiors, for they are His Fa- Mt 17:8; Mk 9:8
ther's choice for you. Through them He will make His will known to you.
"He who obeys you obeys Me," Jesus has said. Jesus has also said: "I am Lk 10:16
the Vine—you are the branch." In the Community, your Superior is the Jn 15:1, 5
Vine and you are the branch—and unless you and she are one and allow
His Father, the Gardener, to prune you, through suffering and trials— Gal 6:2
through bearing each other's burdens—neither of you will be able to bring any fruit. The Work for the Poorest of the Poor is the fruit. Only from this oneness with each other and with your Superior can you bring God into the hearts of suffering humanity.

During this Lent I want you to write for me and for yourself—all the Good you see in your Superior and each Sister of your Community. Only the Good, please. The houses I have visited, please send it to me in a closed inland [letter] marked "Personal"—and the houses I will be visiting—please keep till I come and give it to me then.

[For] a Chapter to be fruitful, you must come to it with a sincere and humble heart—coming face to face with each other—filled with one common desire to make your Community a real Nazareth—another living Mt 2:23; Lk 2:51–52

a. As the time of elections in India (either for the central government of the country or for the state government) could be a time of civil unrest, travelling could have been difficult, and Mother prudently would choose safer times to travel.

Jn 14:27; 16:33; Eph 2:14 Jn 15:11; 17:13 Jn 15:5, 8 tabernacle,[110] where LOVE, PEACE and the JOY OF CHRIST dwells. The faults of individual Sisters should not be pointed out during Chapter—only those points which prevent the Community as a whole to grow and bring much fruit.

On the 10th September it will be 25 years of the birth of our Society.[a] You could not give me a greater gift and show deeper gratitude than by thinking and speaking well of the goodness of each other—appreciating the good your sisters are doing—accepting each other as you are—and always meeting each other with a SMILE: for this is the GREATER LOVE.

I know your love for Mother has been always sincere and loyal. You have always given me of your best. Because of each one of you—[because] of your trust and loyalty—I have been able to go forward without fear [or] hesitation. My gratitude to you is my love for each one of you—a deep,
Jn 15:9 personal intimate love—as Christ has loved me—so I have loved you. Let
Gal 2:20 us all just be one heart full of love—and allow Jesus to live His life in each one of us to the full.

Pray for Mother.

God bless you
Mother

...

MGL 81. 29TH APRIL 1971

+

L.D.M.

Mother House
29th April 1971

My dearest Children,

The news of Bangladesh seems to become worse day by day—so many of our Sisters have their parents and their families there.[b] Up to now we have not received any news of them, but we pray that God may take care

a. Mother is referring to 10th September 1946 as the beginning of the Society, not 7th October 1950 (the official date of foundation); in fact, in the Entrance Book of the Society that records the personal data of the Sisters joining the congregation, under her own name Mother noted: "Entrance into the Society—10 September 1946."

b. Mother is referring to the "Bangladesh Liberation War," spurred by the attack on East Pakistan (now Bangladesh) by West Pakistan (now Pakistan). Hundreds of thousands of Bengalis were massacred by the Pakistan military from 25th March 1971 to 16th December 1971, and hundreds of thousands women were the victims in a systematic campaign of genocidal rape. An estimated ten million people fled to India for refuge.

of them. A group of our sisters have gone to do relief work on the Border of West Dinajpur.

Hatred and selfishness is destroying a whole nation. Let us be careful—lest we, being careless about the use of our tongue in uncharitable words and remarks, destroy the Society from its very roots.

Today, when our people are being tortured and suffer untold pain, let us reflect and control our tongue, which may cause deep wounds in the hearts of our Sisters—and so the Charity of Christ may no longer abide with us. The uncontrolled tongue may cause a wound in the weak vocation and so become the cause of leaving. In the Mother House we are determined to wipe away every uncharitable word from the house . . . , and for every charitable word we shall give 2 np [naya paisa][a] from our tea for the Poor.[b] I want you all to do the same. We must put all our real love and energy to uproot this evil from our Society. This uprooting of uncharitable words is a MUST for each one of us under obedience. Therefore, don't play with it nor neglect it. Jas 3:3–10

In future, Junior Sisters will be permitted to renew Vows only if Charity is alright—if not she will have to leave. Same will apply for Sisters preparing for Final Vows.

We shall make reparation for the past sins of our tongue, . . . beginning from the Friday you get this letter.

I am afraid God is punishing us because the worldly spirit of pride and neglect of poverty and also imprudence in our dealings with outsiders [have] slowly crept in.

Any sister who will not control her tongue in public must speak her fault in public the same night in the refectory.[c] The same applies to the Sister who repeats and carries tales from one to another—from one house to another. All of us must unite to free our Society from this terrible destruction.

God bless you
Mother

a. Two *naya paisa* was at the time equivalent to a few pennies.

b. Mother considers it a reward for an effort in charity in favor of the poor to give up the little delicacies (e.g., biscuits, etc.) the Sisters take with their tea.

c. Mother is referring to the custom of apologizing in front of the whole community and asking forgiveness for a public fault or faults committed during the day.

MGL 82. 19TH JULY 1971

+ L.D.M.

19th July 1971

My dearest Children,

More and more people are coming from Bangladesh, and there is so much suffering all around. We must pray for our people.

All of you have finished your retreat, and from what I have heard—you have made a fervent one. I am sure with the grace of God you will be able
Mt 22:37; Mk 12:30; Lk 10:27 to keep your resolutions. Have but one desire in your heart—to love Jesus with an undivided heart.

There are a few points I have to draw your attention to—which I am sure are not helping you to be a true MC:

1) In some houses—going to cinema and cinema conversation [have] become a regular thing. They make a big mistake to say that because somebody has paid for them, they are free to go. DEFINITELY NO. We do not accept Poverty because we are forced to be poor but because we choose to be Poor for love of
2 Cor 8:9 Jesus—because He, being rich, became poor for love of us. My Sisters, do not bluff yourselves.
2) The same thing with your hair. So many of you are letting your hair grow with the excuse of: I have no time to cut it, or I get headaches if I do not let my hair grow—and yet, all these years you had time to cut it—you had no trouble with your headaches. Now, because this is the fashion, you feel you also must do the same and try to follow it.
3) In some houses, the Sisters have started entertaining the priests—giving them special food, sending them food for feasts, washing and mending their clothes, having regular recreations on Thursdays instead of Instruction, etc. You all know that this is not done in the Society—for the simple reason that we have no right to use what belongs to the Poor; time, money, food, etc. belong to the Poor, and priests do not fall in the category of those who should receive our whole-hearted free service to the Poor;—or do the priests and rich come under this Vow? The next Superior will come—she will not do it—then WHO IS RIGHT? In these houses, there is very little time for the Poor—very little to give to the Poor—and what is more, unkindness and harshness [take] place instead.

4) Many Sisters have started eating and drinking in the houses of the rich and then pretend before the Poor: "We do not eat outside our convents." WHAT DECEPTION! We have chosen to eat the food of the poor. People think that you have not enough to eat, that is why you go to them. We take nothing in the houses of the rich to be able to tell the poor, when they offer us a drink: "We do not take anything outside." The TRUTHFULNESS OF OUR EXAMPLE will uplift them.

These were the beautiful sacrifices people loved in the MC. They loved
to see the Sisters in the company of Mary, rosary in hand, always in haste
to bring the good news—with Her going about doing good, for love of Lk 1:39
Her Son. Are we doing this today? Let every Sister in each community examine and resolve to renew her love for all that is beautiful in the Society and be faithful and loyal to the Society.

SM.—— has asked for freedom from her Vows for reasons of conscience. SM.—— did not renew her Vows in May. SM.—— was released [from] her Vows. Pray for all those who have been in the Society—that God may protect them and keep them in His love. Do not pass judgment—do not gossip—but show your love and kindness for them as you
would like others to do to you—if this had happened to you. Mt 7:12

I would very much like that all of you try very specially to get as many families consecrated to the Sacred Heart with the intention of obtaining fervent vocations for our Society.

God bless you
Mother

MGL 83. 10TH AUGUST 1971

+ L.D.M.

10th August 1971

My dearest Children,

May the happiness that gives peace and the holiness that gives joy be with each one of us for the 22nd, the Feast of our Patroness. May our Mother be a Mother to each one of us and so the Cause of our Joy—and may each one of us be Jesus to her and become the Cause of Her Joy.

No one has learned so well the lesson of humility as Mary did. She,
being the handmaid of the Lord, was completely empty of self, and God Lk 1:38

Lk 1:28 filled her with Grace—Full of Grace—Full of God. "HANDMAID" is to be at one's disposal—to be used according to someone's wish—with full trust and joy—to belong to someone without reserve—and this is one main reason of the Spirit of the Society:

Total Surrender:	to be at God's disposal
	to be used as it pleaseth Him
	to be His Handmaid
	to belong to Him.

Our Lady trusted the Angel, with deep loving trust, because he had
Lk 1:26–38 brought the good news. He was God's Messenger. This too is our Spirit:

Loving Trust in our Superiors and each other—for our Superiors give us the good news of God's will. She is the messenger of His will.

Cheerfulness and Joy was Our Lady's strength. This made her a willing handmaid of God, Her Son,—for as soon as He came to her—she went in haste. Only Joy could have given her the strength to go in haste
Lk 1:39–56 over the hills of Judea—to do the work of handmaid to her cousin. So with us too.

We too, like her, must be a true handmaid of the Lord and daily after Holy Communion go in haste, over the hills of difficulties we meet in giving whole-hearted service to the Poor. Give Jesus to the Poor as the Handmaid of the Lord.

Nearly all the houses have new and young Superiors. On both sides, we have a wonderful chance to be a true Handmaid of the Lord to each
Mt 2:23; Lk 2:51–52 other. Make your Communities another Nazareth.

Next month will be 25 years of the Beginning of the Missionaries of Charity.[a] You could not give me a greater joy nor love than by making your Communities a real Nazareth—a family of peace, joy and unity. I appeal to each one of you—to really put all your energy and overcome every obstacle to make your Community a true home of—MISSIONARIES OF CHARITY—.

All the Sisters whose parents and relations are in Bangladesh—each one of you have our full love—sharing your sorrow. No one has news, except SM. Francesca's sister and her family are dead. SM. Juliana's big brother is missing.

a. This letter was written on 10th August and "next month" is September. Mother counts twenty-five years because for her the beginning of the Society is 10th September 1946, not 7th October 1950 (the official date of foundation). See MGL 80 of 7th March 1971 and the corresponding footnote, p. 142.

Our Ceylon house has to close. Three [sisters] have been told to leave immediately; two [sisters] after a year, without replacement. As the two cannot do the work alone I am withdrawing all, and some congregation is taking over the work—so pray for our Poor in Ceylon.[a]

Be humble—love humility—empty yourself of self—and you will be able to love each other as He has loved you. Jn 13:34; 15:12

On the 19th August, we are leaving for Benares.

. . .

God bless you
Mother

MGL 84. 21ST AUGUST 1971

L.D.M.

Varanasi
21st August 1971

My dearest Children,

Thanks for all the nice things you had prepared—especially thanks to SM. J. [Joseph] Michael & the 2nd years for packing everything so well & with so much love. God bless you all.

The Bishop is in hospital in Bangalore.[b] He hopes to be back by the end of this month, & so two fathers & a Sister came to meet us. It was all very simple. SM. Mechilde & I went to see the place—& today we shall make the legal agreement & then take over the house.

The prayer "Radiating Christ" nowhere could be fully lived as here in Benares. I hope we will really be the Light of Christ—so many people just lying about, without a hand to serve them and a heart to love them—Our Sisters will have a beautiful work to do. Pray that they have the love and the courage to do it. Jn 8:12; 9:5

I am hoping we will be able to move in by tomorrow, & so the opening of Benares will be 22nd Aug.

I have never seen so [many] people anywhere nor so [many] disabled people on the roads. We will, I am sure, have an open Nirmal H. [Hriday] everywhere.—

a. Mother had to close the house in Colombo, Ceylon, because the government would not extend the Sisters' temporary residence visas. They had entered with academic research visas; these visas could not be renewed, since the Sisters were not doing academic research work. The Sisters handed over the Home of Compassion to the Active Carmelite Sisters on 25th August 1971.

b. Bishop Patrick Paul D'Souza (1928–2014) was ordained bishop on 8th August 1970 for the Diocese of Banaras; he served until 2007. The diocese was renamed as the Diocese of Varanasi in 1971.

I feel bad to have left you just before the feast—but I will make up to you when I return. I hope it will be very soon.—I did not realize how tired I was until we came here. I suppose when you have little to do—then you have plenty time for self.—Due to this maybe I will cancel my going to U.S. in Sept. & go there only in Oct. for the opening of the house.

Jn 13:34, 15:12 I am sure you are all trying in a special way to love each other as Jesus loves you—only with His love we can love one another. When we arrived here—it was raining—but by afternoon & today there is sunshine—and so we wash and dry. Don't worry about us all—everybody is well—& we are eating at the Bishop's table for as long as we are here.—I hope the things come by tomorrow.

Happy & Holy feast to all.

God bless you
Mother

MGL 85. 22ND SEPTEMBER 1971

+ L.D.M.

Mother House
22nd September 1971

My dearest Children,

Loving thanks for all your fervent prayers and wishes and cards for the 10th. It was really a family feast.

Thank God for all He and His Blessed Mother have done for us. As I am leaving on the 23rd with Sr. Andrea, Sr. Agnes will take full charge of the Society. My travelling will be:

23rd [September]—London	13th October–23rd—New York
2nd [October]–13th—Rome	23rd October–1st Nov.—Venezuela

The rest I will let you know. I have also divided the houses in 10 groups, and each Sister [in charge] will take [responsibility] of the house and its care as a part of her own [duty]. Though this will begin the 1st October so as to give you a chance to write to your Sister in charge and also she could write to you. Use this as a means to greater love and union among you in the group and among groups—in the Heart of Jesus. In the Society be open and sincere with each other. Avoid travelling, as it is becoming very expensive. Already I have been twice in most houses this year, except

Bhagalpore and Darjeeling—so it will not be necessary for the Sisters to visit the houses, unless something unforeseen happens. Do not use this for useless and uncharitable gossip and waste time and postage. I want you to feel that Mother wants you to learn to trust each other more—and make better use of each other.

Each sister in charge will send Sr. Camillus a full year's account of each house in her group and must always be ready to send any answers that are asked of her.

We all love the Society, so let us put our hearts into making her into a living and pleasing sacrifice to God. This is possible only through Charity Rom 12:1; Phil 4:18
and Unity.

1) All permissions, general and particular, the local Superior must get renewed with the Sister in charge of the group.
2) All money matters, etc. must be arranged with her—to her also must be sent the monthly accounts.
3) She must also have the names and the work of each Sister in each community.
4) She must also arrange for the yearly retreat of her group houses.
5) She must also foresee the need for changes and also propose to Mother the changes [that] need be made in her group.
6) At least once a month she must write to Mother and give a sincere opinion of the spiritual progress of the group, of what she has done to help her Sisters spiritually, and of the improvement of the work.
7) Every local Superior must, at least once in two weeks, write to her Sister in charge—tell her the good she has done, and also that which is not good, and what she is doing to improve.
8) Each Sister in charge will keep very close and intimate contact with Mother.

I feel this is going to help you much to unity and uniformity. Be faithful to your weekly instructions and chapters. Prepare for both with great love.

. . .

God bless you
Mother

MGL 86. 15TH OCTOBER 1971

+ L.D.M.

New York[a]
15th October 1971

My dearest children,

Here we are in Harlem. We have much to thank God for His love and goodness to us. The Negro Sisters have given us a separate part of their building and this will be our convent, with a lovely chapel. . . .[b]

I am sure you will be all very happy to hear that at the end of this month I am taking 4 sisters (if they all come from India) to Belfast, Northern Ireland. . . .

Make your communities more and more homes of love and peace. Do not let the devil cheat you by his evil ways and so be unkind and harsh
Jn 13:34; 15:12 to each other. Enjoy each other—"Love one another as Jesus has loved
Jn 15:9 you"—"As the Father has loved me, so I have loved you." "See how they
Jn 13:35 love each other," Jesus said.[c] Our Vocation is so beautiful—let us not spoil it. Holy Father spoke so beautifully. He said: "I am praying for you to persevere in your beautiful vocation. Pray for me much." Before his speech—while he was telling the people about the people who were there he said: "Our dear Mother Teresa is with us here." In this, like in everything else, he has so much love for each and every one of us. Let us be faithful to his teaching.

The news of [the] Calcutta cyclone is so hard to accept.[d] Our poor people are becoming poorer day by day. I beg you my sisters—be kind to them—be a comfort to the Poor and take every trouble to help them.

a. On the top of this letter the following was typed: "Franciscan Handmaids of Mary Convent, 15 West 124th Street, New York, N.Y. 10027 U.S.A. Please note that this is our address in New York." The Franciscan Handmaids of the Most Pure Heart of Mary is a religious community founded in Georgia in 1916 in response to the segregationist legislation which was seeking to prohibit white religious sisters (and other white teachers) from working in the education of black children or from providing any pastoral care to the black population. The members of the congregation are predominantly African-American. Their primary mission is the education of children of the African-American community. The Handmaids of Mary welcomed the MC Sisters in their convent in Harlem, and the Sisters stayed with them for about nine months.

b. "Negro Sisters" uses the term commonly accepted in the USA at the time; in the 1970s, "black" or "African-American" became the preferred terms.

c. Mother is alluding to the quote: "By this they will know that you are my disciples if you love one another" (Jn 13:35); while, in fact, she is quoting the phrase that is originally from Tertullian's *Apology*, ch. 31: "**See**, they say, **how they love one another**" (trans. S. Thelwall, in *Latin Christianity: Its Founder, Tertullian* [Grand Rapids, MI: Eerdmans, n.d.]). Often in exhorting her Sisters she would refer to the phrase, "See how they love each other," and the variations thereof.

d. This is a reference to the cyclone and tidal wave off the Bay of Bengal that hit Calcutta and the State of Orissa on 29th September 1971, causing mass destruction and taking the lives of thousands of people.

Open your eyes to the needs of the Poor. Put into a living reality your Vow—to give wholehearted free service to the poor—to Christ in His distressing disguise. It is Jesus in the poor that you feed, you clothe and you take into your homes. Do it all with a great undivided love. Do not spoil the work of God by your unkindness. How can you love Jesus in the poor unless you love Him in your Community? We must really make a real effort to make our community: Ekdil Prempur.[a] These two words are really the sign and the Light of Christ with us. Treat each other with great love and respect, and this will lead you to great love and union. If you really love Mother—make it a point to give me this joy—the assurance that each one of you [is] really going to give me this joy—of making your community Ekdil Prempur—only love—real personal love—the same love with which you love Jesus that you love your Sister in the community. Mt 25:35–40

We have a new Convent in Dum Dum.... Write to them care of Mother House, as the address is not yet known properly.

Pray for Mother.

God bless you,
Mother

...

MGL 87. 3RD DECEMBER 1971

+ L.D.M.

3rd December 1971

My dearest Children,

Thank God I am back.[b] All our Sisters are well and doing God's Work with great love.

In the world there is so much hatred and disunion. As we have just begun the New Year with the beginning of Advent[c]—let us in a special way make our houses real communities of love and union and so overcome this hatred. Love begins at home. Everything depends on how we love each other. Make your community live on this love, and spread the fragrance of His Love everywhere you go. Do not be afraid to love until it hurts, for this is how Jesus loved. 2 Cor 2:14

Love your Superiors—be one mind with them—be loyal to them. The

a. *Ekdil Prempur* means "One heart full of love." See ED 1, July 1966 and corresponding footnote.

b. The meaning is: back to Mother House.

c. Mother is referring to the new liturgical year.

Society will be what you, together with your Superior, make it: FERVENT
Jn 15:1–8 or TEPID—A FRUITFUL BRANCH OR A DRY BRANCH.

Jn 15: 1, 5 CHRIST—THE CHURCH is the Vine; the Society, the Branch; and we the fruit; His Father the Vine-dresser.

This thought is so beautiful. Let us meditate on it often. It will strengthen our Faith and our Love.

For this Christmas—my wishes and my prayer for each one of you is
Mt 22:37; Mk 12:30; Lk 10:27 that you may love Jesus with undivided love and that you may accept Him in your life—to live His life in whatever way He chooses.

I want also to thank each one of you:

for all the love and trust you have given me;
for all the generosity you have shown in serving the Poor with so much joy and love;
for your love and fidelity to the Spirit of the Society;
for the effort you have made to live the life of an MC through the observance of your Vows;
for trying your best to be a cause of joy to Our Lady and to
Jn 13:35 your Sisters in your community. By this Joy they will know that you are His disciples.

On the 7th there will be 40 Novices making their First Profession.
On the 8th, 15 Sisters will take Final Vows.
Pray for them all—that they may persevere unto death.

God bless you
Mother

1972

ED 2. JANUARY 1972

January 1972

My dearest Sisters,

Each one of you has been just wonderful in giving so much of yourself to God's Poor.

Let us never forget that in serving the poor we have a chance to do something beautiful for God, for, in spending ourselves in giving wholehearted free service to the poor, we really give it to CHRIST in the distressing disguise, for He has said "You did it to Me." Mt 25:40

God bless you
Mother

MGL 88. 26TH FEBRUARY 1972

+ L.D.M.

Mother House
26th February 1972

My dearest Children,

Forgive Mother for neglecting you so long. It has been nearly impossible to do anything else—besides what I have been doing.

We have been asked by [the] Bangladesh Govt. [government] to take care of the girls used by the Pakistan Army. What beautiful work we have to do for the Church. At the same time I want to draw your attention to the sentence Mujib Rahman said on behalf of these girls:[a] "They will be treated as heroines of the country because they suffered so much to

a. Sheikh Mujibur Rahman (1920–1975), often called the founding father of Bangladesh, served as prime minister (1972–1975) and then as president (1975) of Bangladesh.

protect their purity." These girls, Hindu and Muslim, purely from their natural love for purity—how they fought to protect themselves. Many committed suicide rather than lose the beautiful virtue of womanhood. We religious who have a chance to consecrate that beautiful gift to God in loving Him with undivided love—do we really take all the trouble to protect it and make it grow in beauty and strength? Many of us are still very careless in our dealings with men, who come with the intention of helping us in the work. In some houses—the would-be Co-workers are taking advantage and so are some of the sisters—neglecting their duties and spending much time in entertaining under the disguise of Co-workers. In no house must the Sisters engage themselves with the Co-workers (men) nor should you engage young drivers.[a] Remember the Bangladesh girls—how they fought to protect themselves! and how careless we are!

During this Lent we will take as a special point: TO FORGIVE. Unless
Mt 6:15 we forgive, we cannot be forgiven. If we do not forgive, then it is a sign that we have not been forgiven. Much of the hurt in our Communities comes from an uncontrolled use of words—said to anybody, anywhere—in front of any person. The result is a deep hurt and often unforgiven. Let us open our eyes, for we do much harm to ourselves, much more to others and above all to the Church and to our young Society. Be loyal to your
Mt 11:29 word [that] you have given to God, to Mother and the Poor. Learn to be meek and humble of heart.

Learn to trust each other—also to see the good that is in each one, the good that each Sister is doing, the virtue she practices, the sacrifices she has made and is making to follow her vocation. If we see all these, our Community life will be SOMETHING BEAUTIFUL FOR GOD.

Sr. M. Francis Xavier met with such a terrible accident, but thank God, as she says:—"Our Lady took care of her". She was saying the Rosary and had the rosary in hand when she gained consciousness. Sister is much better but is still in hospital with many head injuries. See, my Sisters, how Our Lady protected her. Let us love Her as our Mother.

I would be grateful if the books of Louis Evely are taken from the Library and not read for the present.[b]

a. The meaning here is: In no house must the Sisters **busy** themselves with the male Co-workers nor should you **employ** young drivers.

b. Louis Évely (1910–1985) was a Belgian Catholic priest and spiritual writer, and author of a number of books (e.g., *That Man is You; We Dare to Say Our Father; Suffering; The Gospels without Myth; In the Christian Spirit*). By this time, he had left the priesthood and married. Mother realized that his doctrinal teaching was questionable and thus asked that his books be removed from the community library, though she herself had quoted from his writings earlier.

I had no chance to tell you of our Dacca and Khulna foundations. Please write to them and welcome them in their new house …

God bless you
Mother

MGL 89. 19TH MARCH 1972

+

L.D.M.

Mother House
19th March 1972

My dearest Sisters,

On the 22nd March I am leaving for Australia, where on the 25th March we begin the Noviciate[a] & also Adoration for the old & the crippled. I am sure you will all pray much for Mother.

Holy Week will soon begin. Try to make it a real "Holy Week" in shar-
ing the Passion of Christ. We all have our cross to bear. "If you love me," Mt 26–27; Mk 14–15; Lk 22–23; Jn 18–19
Christ said, "Keep my Commandment":—LOVE GOD—LOVE YOUR Jn 14:15
NEIGHBOUR. These two—if we keep—we are then in love with Him— Mt 22:37–39
and He and His Father will come and abide with us. Jn 14:23

Today when everything is questioned & changed—let us go back to Nazareth. Jesus had come to REDEEM THE WORLD—to teach us the Love of His Father. How strange—that He should spend 30 years just doing nothing, wasting His time—not giving a chance to His personality or to His gifts. For we know [that] at the age of 12 He just silenced the learned priests of the Temple who knew so much and so well—who could discuss the law by heart, and for hours. Yet this little boy Jesus—silenced
them with His answer. But when His Parents found Him—He went down Lk 2:41–52
to Nazareth and was subject to them. For 30 years we hear no more of Lk 3:23
Him—[*only*] that the people were surprised when He came in public to
preach—He, a Carpenter's Son, doing just the humble work in a Carpen- Mt 13:55; Mk 6:3
ter's shop. [*The work of the MC is like that at Nazareth. Do I really love my vocation?*][b]

a. In the handwritten draft of this letter, Mother wrote Nov. (short for Noviciate); however, the Sister typist opted to insert the full word. She also added a few more minor corrections to the text. For example, she changed Mother's "only that the people" to "so that the people. . . ." We have restored the original here, marking it in parentheses. It is possible that the typist made the changes after obtaining Mother's approval.

b. The line in *italics* was the last line of the extant handwritten draft; the Sister typing probably

When I compare Christ's life in Nazareth—do I find its echo in my vocation as an MC? As long as I love doing the humble work of an MC—I am alright.

Same thing for prayer: I find the teaching of Christ so very simple—that even a little child can [grasp] it. "Teach us to pray," the strong men,
Mt 6:9–13; Lk 11:1–4 the Apostles said, and Jesus replied: "When you pray, say 'Our Father'. . . ."

You hear so much of "personality"—of "maturity"—of "maternalism,"[a]
Jn 13:33 etc.—and yet the Gospel is full of such words as "LITTLE CHILDREN", Jesus addressing His grown-up Apostles.

I am sending you the words of the Ceremony of Profession—they are so beautiful that I think we should all make a copy for our prayer book.

Jn 13:34; 15:12 Love Jesus with a deep Personal love and your Sisters with the same love as you love Jesus.

At the last meeting of Regional Superiors it was decided that the Renewal of Vows for one year or three years—will in future depend on the community. The Community will have to vote if the Sister should renew her Vows or not depending on how the Sister has been in the community and for the community especially regarding charity and love for her Vocation.

I hope to be back before the end of April. In the meantime, SM. Agnes takes all responsibility.

A HAPPY & HOLY EASTER TO YOU ALL.

God bless you,
Mother

ED 3. EASTER [2ND APRIL] 1972[b]

missed it by mistake. The rest of the handwritten draft of this letter did not survive. For the reproduction of the extant pages of this draft please see Appendix C, pp. 542–43.

a. Maternalism in this context has a derogatory meaning; the mother figure (in religious life, the superior) does not allow her child to mature and develop or take responsibility, but rather controls or commands the child according to her own ideas or goals. This was a common criticism of pre-Vatican II female religious life. Mother is concerned about how these ideas are fitting with Gospel simplicity.

b. *Ek Dil* 3 for Easter 1972 has an extract from MGL 14 of 9th March 1962 (beginning with "He has loved you with an everlasting love . . ." and ending with "special love we will offer to Jesus," p. 25) as Mother's message for this *Ek Dil* issue. As she was not in Calcutta, the Sister preparing *Ek Dil* might have consulted Mother or herself opted for this choice.

MGL 90. [AFTER 25TH] MARCH 1972

[Fitzroy, Melbourne]
Australia
[After 25th] March 1972

My dearest Sisters,

A very happy & holy Easter to you all. You must be praying very fervently for Mother—for everything went well. Our two novices and the 4 postulants had a big day on the 25th. Such a beautiful day to begin the life of Christ, or rather to say "Yes" to Jesus—like Mary did on this day. In the Lk 1:38
evening we started the adoration[a]—so many people came. Today again we shall have it at 5:00–6:00 [P.M.] & then 1:30–5:00 P.M. daily. I am trying to get as many Noviciates [as possible] to take one hour of adoration—so you must pray for this.—

I hope you are all well & that the heat is not too great. Here the cold is beginning, & so we have to wear extra things.

Pray much for Mother.

God bless you
Mother

MGL 91. 21ST APRIL 1972

+ L.D.M.

21st April 1972

My dearest children,

I came back on the 13th April—grateful to God for all His goodness to us all. All the Sisters—old and new—from Bourke and Melbourne send you their prayers and love. It was wonderful to see what God does with each one of you, when you let Him use you without reserve.

On the 25th March we started the Noviciate in Melbourne with 3 Novices and 6 Postulants;[b] also the Adoration—in Melbourne: 1:30–5:30 P.M.

a. Mother and the Sisters, with the help of the novices and postulants (several of whom had been members of other religious orders), started daily adoration at the convent at George Street, Fitzroy (Melbourne), which served as a noviciate as well. Mother had obtained prior permission of Archbishop Knox, who in turn asked her to have perpetual adoration in St. Patrick's Cathedral in preparation for the upcoming Eucharistic Congress (18th to 25th February 1973). The Sisters and lay people were taking turns to fill in the hours for round-the-clock adoration at the Cathedral.

b. In the previous general letter from Melbourne (MGL 90), Mother wrote "Our **two** novices and the **four** postulants had a big day on the 25th." At the time of this letter, one more Sister had been admitted to the noviciate and two more postulants had joined, but Mother adds them to the numbers, without mentioning that they arrived later.

daily and in Bourke from 6:00–7:00 P.M. So the Sisters keep on spreading
2 Cor 2:14 the fragrance of Christ's love.

On my return we had a Council Meeting: Of the 64 Novices, 55 in Calcutta and 2 in London will be Professed on the 13th May, and they begin their retreat on the 5th May. Rev. Fr. Henry will preach the retreat.[a] On the 24th May, 9 Sisters will make their Final Vows at the Parish Church of St. Mary's, Ripon St., Cal. [Calcutta], and Fr. Schepers, SJ, will give them their retreat. As you see we need your prayers and sacrifices for us all at the Mother House.

We have also decided a number of points:

1. [Regarding Noviciates:]
   a. For the sake of keeping unity in formation, and that the three Noviciates in Calcutta, London and Melbourne may keep very close to each other—according to Rule 214 (old 212),[b] they [the noviciates] will be directly under Mother, with:

      Sr. Agnes helping with the Postulants;
      Sr. Nirmala helping with all the Tertians and vocations
      Sr. Joseph Michael helping with the Noviciate.

   b. The sisters in the Houses outside India who are due for Tertianship will go to Rome or to the Noviciates in London or Melbourne as per Mother's decision.
   c. The Mistresses of Tertians, Novices and Postulants will write to Mother every month regarding the spirit in their own houses of Formation.
   d. Every three months [a] Formation Newsletter containing all their studies—portion covered, activities, anything special that has happened in their own house of formation that they would like to share with others, like lectures, seminars, etc., including the fun they have, will be sent [. . .] by:

a. Father Julien Henry, SJ (1901–1979), a Belgian Jesuit, ordained a priest in 1931, came to India in 1938 and began his apostolate at St. Teresa's Parish in 1940. He also served as spiritual father to the girls' Sodality in Entally, Calcutta. He supported Mother from the beginning of her work among the poorest of the poor (especially in the Motijeel slums) and was advisor and confessor of the MCs from 1949 to the end of his life. He was very zealous in spreading the devotion to Our Lady of Fatima.

b. Rule 212: "She [the Mistress of Novices] is under the authority of the Superior of the Society to whom she shall send every six months a written report about each novice and postulant. These reports should be composed only after fervent prayers, to avoid exaggeration and keep to strictest impartiality" (1954 *Constitutions*, Revised).

the postulants to the postulants

the First years to the First years

the Second years to the Second years

the Tertians to the Tertians.

A copy of each must be sent to Mother.

2. The decision was also taken to gradually bring a group of Finally Professed Sisters to the Mother House for at least 6 months of prayer and renewal, which will help them to know the teachings of the Church of the present day, so that they can share and enjoy the gift of faith and love offered today....

3. Every house must take means to get Vocations from their own place through prayer, sacrifice, and contact. If you need help regarding this, please contact Sr. Nirmala, who is in charge of Vocations.

   The Superior of each house may accept such aspirants, who must fill [out] the necessary forms and send them directly to Sr. Nirmala; and then, according to Constitution 25,[a] they must be kept in separate quarters (and not with the Community). After three months, if the girl decides to join the Postulancy, her formal application must be sent to Mother, on whose acceptance the girl will make her Postulancy at the place decided by Mother. In future, the increase of sisters in your community will depend on how many postulants you send from your place to the Mother House.

4. REGIONS: Houses outside India will be directly under Mother....[b]

Rome has released Sr. Joseph from her vows on grounds of ill-health, according to her application. Pray for her, as she has served the Society with great love for so many years.

God bless you
Mother

a. Rule 25: "For a period of three months before postulancy they [the candidates] will work as aspirants with the sisters in the slums and live at home or in the house of the professed in separate quarters" (1954 *Constitutions*, Revised).

b. Attached to this letter was a questionnaire that was to be answered by the Superior for each Sister due to renew her vows, and sent with the Sister's application:

1. Does Sr. play with her vocation by speaking of going home or running away at every difficulty?
2. Is she a cause of disunion and disturbance in the community through repetition, carrying of tales, finding fault, passing hurtful remarks, uncontrolled temper and criticism?
3. What is her contribution to the happiness of the community?

MGL 92. 1ST JUNE 1972

+ L.D.M.

1st June 1972

My dearest Children,

The Government of India has given our Society a new sign of love and appreciation by awarding me the Nehru Award for International Understanding.[a] We had a Mass of Thanksgiving in the Mother House. You also have it in all your houses if possible.

This month is the month of the Sacred Heart. Let us make a real effort to make this month one of True Love, Reparation and Forgiveness. Try to
Mk 6:31 make your Community a place where Our Lord can "come apart and rest awhile" with you. Make a real effort to get rid of all uncharitable words and thoughts. If anyone by mistake says something—do not answer or get excited or repeat. This is such a small thing I am asking you. I am sure you will give it to Mother.

Also try to get as many families as possible consecrated to the Sacred Heart.

Superiors, be kind and loving to your sisters. Sisters, be loving and trusting with your Superiors. You [must] accept each other as you are—for you need each other—you cannot do without each other.—Therefore it is
Jn 13:34, 15:12 most necessary that we love each other as Christ has loved each one of us.

We had a most beautiful ceremony of the Final Vows and so also the First Profession. I am going to Bangladesh, and on my return I will go to our houses in India. While I am away please contact SM. Agnes for all things—she is at the Mother House.

...

Also, Medicine that you have to buy—in future buy in your own place and only what you need at the time or for one month. The Regionals, if necessary, will give you the money, but they must not buy stocks of medicine for you. Foreign Medicine, we will share with you.

Many Superiors have expressed their wish to renew general permissions and to get spiritual help, both for themselves and their community, from Mother—but all business and money matters with their Regional.

a. The 1969 Jawaharlal Nehru Award for International Understanding was granted to Mother; however, her nomination for the award was announced to the public only in June 1972 and, because of her extensive travels, it was conferred on her by President V. V. Giri in a special ceremony in New Delhi on 15th November 1972. In his address at the ceremony, President Giri said, "In the troubled world of today, embittered by numerous conflicts and hatred, the life and work of people like Mother Teresa bring new hope for the future of mankind" (*The Herald*, 1st December 1972).

We could try this. All this is on experimental basis before the Chapter—when we hope to establish the regions in a more solid and permanent way.

There are a few changes in our Superiors....

God bless you
Mother

MGL 93. 18TH JUNE 1972

+ L.D.M.

Mother House,
18th June 1972

My dearest Children,

Jesus has promised to have the names of all those who spread the devotion to His Sacred Heart—written in His Heart.[a] In most of our houses it is so consoling to see the zeal of our sisters with which they spread this devotion to hundreds of families. Jesus cannot deceive us. Your names, my Children, are written in His Heart.

During this month let us ask from the Sacred Heart one very special grace—Love for Our Lady through all the work we do for Jesus, with Jesus, [to Jesus]. Ask Him to give and deepen our love and make it more personal and intimate for her:

– to love her as He loved her
– to be a cause of Joy to her as He was
– to keep close to her as He was
– to share with her everything—even the cross, as He did—when
she stood near the cross on Calvary. Each one of us has our cross to bear, Jn 19:25
for this is the sign of that we are His. Therefore we need her to share
with us.

Jesus wants us to be holy as His Father is. Mother has promised to give Mt 5:48; 1 Pt 1:16
saints to the Church. We can become very great saints if we only want to. Holiness is not a luxury of the few, but a simple duty for you and for me. HOLINESS: very great holiness becomes very simple if we belong fully
to Our Lady. Our sanctification is her main duty, She, as a first MC, went Lk 1:38–44
in haste to help Jesus sanctify John—and so it will be with you and me if

a. One of the promises of Our Lord to Saint Margaret Mary for souls devoted to His Sacred Heart.

we only love her unconditionally and trust her fully. The more we abandon ourselves to her totally and without reserve, the greater will be the number of great saints in our Society—for nothing is impossible for those whose Mother she is.[111] Often during the day, let us raise our heart to her and ask her how she would do this or that now if she was in our place[112]—and above all how to love God as she loved Him, that we too may love Him with her heart.

Love for Mary we can learn only on our knees and through our Rosary. All these years we have been together striving to become holy so that Mother can really offer to His Church: SAINTS—in its full meaning. I am sure each one of us have much to thank God for.

- For all the love we have received and given;
- for all the chances we have had to put that love in action for each other and our poor;
- for all the sacrifices we helped each other to make by our example of fidelity in little things;
- for the joy we have brought to our community life and in the service of the poor;
- for all the tiring journeys we have made by road, by train, by plane, by cycle in search of souls;
- for all the comfort we have given to the sick and the dying to the lonely and the unwanted;
- for all the delicate touch we have given in the service of the lepers;
- but above all, for all the joy we tried to spread throughout the world
Jn 13:34; 15:12 by loving as He has loved each one of us—as He has loved His Father and [His] Mother, us and His poor.

Let us, my children, give Our Lady full liberty to use us for the glory of her Son, for if we really belong to her, then our holiness is secure. Let us try to improve our praying [of] the Rosary when we are out of the house.

Failure and loss of vocation also come from neglect of prayer; and, as prayer is the food of spiritual life, neglect of prayer starves the spiritual life and so loss of vocation is unavoidable. Let us ask Our Lady in our own simple way to teach us how to pray—as she taught Jesus—in all the years
Mt 2:23; Lk 2:51–52 He was with her in Nazareth.

For the next day of recollection—let us take for our theme for the day: Our Lady, Mother of the Church and our Mother, Her Purity, Poverty, Obedience and Charity. Try to bring Our Lady fully in your own life, in the community and in the houses of the poor.

Once more I repeat that it would please Jesus and Mother very much if you would help girls to dedicate their lives to God through our Society. In some houses Obedience to Mother's wish has been very prompt.

Re. [Regarding] Accounts:—I am afraid this [is] not properly done. All money (does not matter how big or small)—even the money you get through selling all your rubbish,[a] or people give you like that, without intention—must be written in the book. So also every paisa you spend must be in the book. All money we receive belongs to the poor; therefore, we cannot use it in any other way but for the poor. Keep this clear in your minds and do not accept or allow people to buy for you things which you or the people should not use or do not need—for example, big expensive lights, toys, clothes, etc., nor accept any money in the dispensary work, however small it may be. Sh. [Shishu] Bhavan and Nirmal Hriday must be clean and simple but must not become showrooms. In our dispensary and leper work we must have the medicines we need for the poor—but not make of them shops where you store for years—and the most expensive medicines are allowed to get spoiled—and not given to the poor in time.

God bless you,
Mother

MGL 94. 15TH AUGUST 1972

+ L.D.M.

15th August 1972

My dearest children,

Many thanks for the letters you all wrote and Holy Masses you offered for my Mother.[b] Now more than before we have Someone our very own—together with the MCs, praying for the Society and each one of us. So let us thank God.

"And Our Lady pondered His words in Her Heart. . . ." Lk 2:19, 51

If we really want to be true MCs—we too, like Her, must learn that "Silence" which will enable us to ponder His Words in our hearts and so grow in love. We cannot love nor serve—unless we learn to ponder in our hearts—Knowledge of Christ and Him in His Poor will lead us to

a. This refers to recyclable items such as cardboard, plastic, glass bottles, etc.

b. Mother's mother, Drana Bojaxhiu, died on 12th July 1972 in Tirana, Albania. Mother never saw her mother again after she left home to join the Loreto Sisters at the age of 18.

Personal love. This love only can become our light and joy in cheerful
service of each other. Do not forget we need each other. Our lives would
Jn 6:33, 35, 48, 51 be empty without each other. How can we love God and His Poor—if we
do not love each other, with whom we live and break the Bread of Life
daily together.

This is my feastday greeting to each one of you:

—THAT YOU MAY KNOW EACH OTHER AT THE BREAKING OF BREAD
—LOVE EACH OTHER IN THE EATING OF THIS BREAD OF LIFE, and
—SERVE EACH OTHER AND HIM IN HIS POOR BY GIVING YOUR WHOLE HEARTED SERVICE, [*TO EACH OTHER & TO HIM IN HIS POOR.*]

When communicating with Christ in your heart after the partaking
of the Living Bread—remember what Our Lady must have felt when the
Holy Spirit overpowered Her, and she who was full of Grace—became full
with the Body of Christ. The Spirit in Her was so strong that immediately
Lk 1:28–39 She "rose in haste" to go and serve.

Each Holy Communion—each Breaking of Bread of Life—each shar-
Jn 1:14 ing should produce in us the same—for it is the same Jesus Who came to
Jn 1:4, 9 Mary and Was Made Flesh—Who comes to us and becomes our life. We
Lk 1:39–42 too, like her, should be in haste to give this life of Jesus to our Sisters and
Our Poor.

Lk 24:31 At the Breaking of the Bread they recognised Him: Do I recognise the
beauty of my Sisters, the Spouse of Christ, at the Breaking of Bread—in
the daily Mass we live together?

Our Lady was full of God because She lived for God alone—and yet
Lk 1:38 she thought of Herself only as the Handmaid of the Lord. Let us do the
same.

Let us pray much for [*our*][a] Sisters who will be soon leaving for our different houses.[b]

a. In the handwritten draft Mother wrote "our", which the Sister typist corrected to "the"; we have restored it here.

b. In the handwritten draft Mother wrote here: *"Same for Superiors and regionals—do not travel. Now I am going round the houses—it is not necessary for visits—people are passing remarks saying that we own the Railways since we are,"* but then crossed it out, without finishing the sentence. In several letters when Mother wrote something that seemed strong or possibly hurtful to the Sisters, she would cross it out, probably when re-reading the draft. Her aim was to help the Sisters improve. It was characteristic of Mother to write in a way that builds up and encourages, not in a way that hurts or puts someone on the spot. She was firm but always kind, like a mother.

Kindly cut down as much as possible the postage expenses. Also do not send express letters unnecessarily.

HAPPY AND HOLY FEAST OF OUR DEAR MOTHER MARY AND OUR SOCIETY.

. . .

God bless you,
Mother

ED 4.[a] AUGUST 1972

MGL 95. 5TH SEPTEMBER 1972

+ L.D.M.

5th September 1972

My dearest Children,

On the 6th September, SM. Tarcisia (Superior), SM. Probha, SM. Rikta and SM. Shubhra left for Mauritius. Write to them. . . .

Our Sisters in Varanasi have a new Home and a new address. . . . The opening and Blessing will be on the 7th Sept. [September] by the Maharaja of Varanasi. . . .

On the 24th September, Feast of Our Lady of Mercy—we are making a new foundation at Nellore in Andhra Pradesh. Write to them at. . . .

I will be leaving India on the 12th September. . . .

You will have to pray much for Mother. In my absence SM. Agnes takes full charge, therefore all letters and permissions must be sent to her.

Each Sister in your Community, after fervent prayer, will answer separately, in confidence, the questionnaire given below—about the sisters in your Community who are due to renew their vows in December, 1972. All answers should reach me in Calcutta by 21st October 1972.[b]

a. An extract from Mother's letter for that month (MGL 94 of 15th August 1972) was reproduced as Mother's message for *Ek Dil* 4. The reproduced paragraph is: "This is my feast day greeting to each one of you: THAT YOU MAY . . . like her should be in haste to give this life of Jesus to our Sisters and the Poor."

b. As Mother was out of Calcutta, the Councillors would in the meantime have prepared the reports to be ready upon her return. At this time (until the number of Sisters grew), Mother used to write to each Sister who was renewing her vows or making her profession a personal note on how

Questionnaire:

1. Does Sr.——play with her vocation by speaking of going home or running away at every difficulty?
2. Is she a cause of disunion and disturbance in the community through repetition, carrying of tales, finding fault, passing hurtful remarks, uncontrolled temper and criticism?
3. What is her contribution to the happiness of the community?

God bless you
Mother

MGL 96. 18TH SEPTEMBER 1972

+ L.D.M.

Jerusalem
18th September 1972

My dearest Children,

The MCs in the Holy Land! Each one of you [is] so very close to me. On my arrival I met Archbishop Laghi.[a] Tomorrow I will go to Gaza, where the Sisters are very, very necessary. Gaza is 1½ hours from here by air, so it will not be difficult. Please God, we shall be able to have the Tertians and Adoration in Jerusalem.[b] So pray very hard that we may be able to answer the call.

Yesterday after my arrival I went and made the Stations of the Cross ending at the Holy Sepulchre. It is all so different to what Calvary must have been; like all the hills round Jerusalem. Today we will go to Gethsemane and Bethlehem—to Gaza tomorrow early in the morning and then back to Amman.

The sisters in Amman are really doing God's work with great love—thank God. They are very happy to have SM. Helena, who already is trying to learn as much Arabic as possible.

---

to correct her weaknesses and grow in holiness; eventually, the letters were typed, and Mother used to sign them.

a. Pio Laghi (1922–2009) was an Italian cardinal who served as Apostolic Nuncio to several countries and later in the Roman Curia, as the Prefect of the Congregation for Catholic Education. From 1969 to 1973 he was the Apostolic Delegate to Jerusalem and Palestine.

b. Mother's intention was never realized.

By the time this letter comes, Nellore will be already on its feet.[a] All are praying here for Nellore.

I hope you are well and that you are all trying to pray the work by doing it with Jesus, for Jesus, to Jesus.

God Bless You,
Mother

MGL 97. 13TH DECEMBER 1972

+ L.D.M.

13th December 1972

My dearest Children,

MAY THE JOY AND PEACE OF JESUS AND HIS MOTHER BE WITH EACH ONE OF YOU DURING THIS CHRISTMAS FESTIVAL OF LOVE. Jn 14:27; 16:33; Eph 2:14

Thank you for all the letters you have written and the love you have given to each other and the Poor you have so lovingly served—during this year.

In the Coming Year we need much help from the Holy Spirit, as we shall have our Chapter General beginning on the 10th June. As the Holy Spirit is God of Love—He can fill and live only in hearts that are empty of all self-love: therefore, my dear children, let us with the Novena to the Baby Jesus—begin this great preparation and continue to the end of the Chapter General—asking for:

the Light to know the Will of God—
the Love to accept the Will of God—
the Way to do the Will of God.

The surest means to this—will be to deepen our love for each other—

knowing each other's lovableness—
feeling the need of each other—
speaking well of each other and to each other—
appreciate and know the gifts and the abilities of each other:

a. Nellore is a city located in the Indian state of Andhra Pradesh; Mother is referring to the new foundation there.

Jn 15:1, 5 In One Word—BE A REAL BRANCH ON THE VINE: JESUS.

From this Chapter General God expects great things, therefore we must be completely pure of heart—that is, free of all that is against love, so
Mt 5:8; 17:8 that we will be able to SEE HIM ONLY.

In my next letter I will send you more details as to what you have to pray and sacrifice for—so that with the help of the Holy Spirit we can together formulate the life and the work the Church has entrusted to the Society.

Let us all be very much aware of the responsibility we must share together in building up our Society as a living and fruitful Branch on the Body of Christ, His Church. It does not matter how small or how big your work is—as long as you are doing it with Him, for Him and to Him—and know that no one else will or can do that part of the work entrusted to you. Each one of us owes this sharing of responsibility, through the Society, to the Church.

We must also deepen our loyalty to Our Society and stand by our Constitutions—as they are for us the Written Will of God. For the people outside the Society—Our Constitutions mean nothing, therefore they may say anything; but for you and for me, they are the means of our Consecration to God—since we make our Vows according to these Constitutions.

During these months of preparation I would like you to read and pray your Constitutions—together with the Documents of Vatican Council, and it will help you much when you will realise how our Constitutions are so much part of the Vatican Council. Do not allow your minds to drift on useless thoughts—of what you have heard and what you have read. Some of us speak so carelessly and hold out attitudes which are [not] fit to the simplicity and humility of the life and work we have chosen—out of love for God. Much harm is done with this kind of talk, which is often the fruit of hidden pride or jealousy. That these things have to happen, Jesus has warned us already: "Woe to the world because of scandals. For it must needs be that scandals come; but nevertheless woe to the one by whom the scandal comes" (Mt 18:7).[a]

Woe to her through whom scandals are made: Wrong attitudes are leading some Sisters to worldliness, which is very much contrary to the

a. This is the first instance of Mother's letter including a citation of Scripture. It is possible that it was added by the Sister typist to Mother's text.

Poverty and Obedience of Christ we have chosen. It would be a shame for us to be richer than Christ, Who, being rich, became Poor and was "Sub- 2 Cor 8:9
ject to them" for love of us. Lk 2:51

Let us pray much for each other that we may help each other to greater love for God and our neighbour.

HAPPY AND HOLY CHRISTMAS AND GOD'S BLESSING ON 1973.

God bless you
Mother

This letter and preparation for Chapter is only for the Community. It should not be discussed with outsiders.

ED 5. DECEMBER 1972

December 1972

My dearest Children,

HAPPY AND HOLY CHRISTMAS!!

Nothing is Impossible with God, as God is love He can give "only Lk 1:37
love," so let Him fill you with His love so that you can love Him in your 1 Jn 4:8, 16
Superior, your Sisters and your poor.

We have to love each other with an "intense love" as "I have loved Jn 13:34, 15:12
you" Christ tells us. How will you show your love for your Sisters? By how
much you are ready to give yourself for and to them. Christ loved us to the Jn 13:1
extent of dying for us.

Allow your Sisters to use you, to become more holy because of you, to use the graces you have, the love you have, the everything you have. Always try to look at the good points of your Sisters. There is in each one something beautiful that has attracted the heart of God. For, each one,
He has called by her name. We are each one of us the branch on the same Is 43:1
Vine Jesus—the same loving hand of the Gardener—His Father takes
care of the Vine and each branch. That is why Jesus said—Love as I have Jn 15:1–8
loved you—as the Father has loved me—so I have loved you. Love one Jn 15:9
another. Jn 13:34; 15:12

Remember that each one of us is something beautiful for God, and the actions of each of us are the love for God put into action.

God bless you
Mother

2 Cor 2:14 *We shall spread the fragrance of Jesus' love, peace and joy during 1973.*

God bless you
Mother[a]

a. Mother wrote this additional line on the last page of this *Ek Dil* issue.

1973

MGL 98. 7TH FEBRUARY 1973

+ L.D.M.

Mother House
7th February 1973

My Dearest Sisters,

I hope and pray all went well with you during the Christmas and the New Year festival. I am leaving for Australia on the 9th. If all goes well we hope to start the house at Darwin for the Aboriginals. Also in Gaza, Holy Land, and we are preparing for Hodeidah, Yemen. All these 3 addresses I will send you in my next general letter.

From now on we begin the preparation for our General Chapter.

According to Constitution 164, the members of the Chapter General are:—

a) The Superior General
b) The Councillors
c) The Ex-Superior General
d) The Secretary and Procuratrix General
e) All the Superiors of the houses in which at least 12 Sisters with voice stay.[a]
f) All the Deputies chosen by the above houses.
g) The Deputies of houses which have not 12 Sisters with active voice.[b]

Constitution—165

The election of the Deputies (about whom see no. 164, letter 'f') is made by secret ballot, and the one who has obtained a relative majority of votes is con-

a. "Sisters with voice" refers to those Sisters who can vote and be voted for.

b. "Active voice" refers to Sisters who can vote and be voted for (i.e., the finally professed). "Passive voice" refers to Sisters who can vote but cannot be voted for (i.e., the junior professed).

sidered to have been elected. The Sisters of small houses (about which see no. 164 letter 'g') must be divided by the Superior General with the deliberative vote of her council in several electoral bodies comprehending at least 12 professed sisters, and each electoral body shall send from its midst to the Chapter two deputies, one of whom must be a local superior and the other not; the election, however, must be in each house by secret ballot papers which the local superior in the presence of the sisters with active voice immediately encloses in an envelope and sends to the Superior General. In the same way two substitutes of the Deputies may be elected.

We shall have the voting for the delegates to the Chapter on the 28th Feb. Everything regarding the voting must be kept perfectly confidential; even among ourselves there must be no discussion regarding it.

Herewith I enclose the names of the sisters for the houses to be voted for by you. There are two sides: you must choose one Superior and one deputy only from the Sisters whose names are on your paper. Near the name you choose, put this sign, ✓, carefully and clearly, then fold your paper in two and put into the envelope, which the local superior in the presence of the sisters with active voice immediately encloses and sends to the Superior General (one envelope for all papers, and not one envelope for each).

Every professed sister can vote, but only Finally Professed [Sisters] can be voted for.

Please do not put your name or the name of the house to which you belong on the paper—or any other mark.

Only one voting paper should be used by each sister; if you receive any extra papers, please destroy them.

All papers should be posted immediately the same day, in one envelope, and sent Registered by post and sent to me.

Pray, pray very fervently that you choose wisely.

a. From the 24th February to the 3rd March (both days inclusive) [do more] penances.
b. Our Adoration[a] and Rosary we shall offer for the same purpose—that we may choose the right person, whom before God we feel will be able to help at the Chapter General.

a. Initially the Adoration time was very short (actually, it was only a visit to the Blessed Sacrament (see MGL 6 of [3rd] February 1961, p. 15), in time it became fifteen minutes to half an hour, then one hour once or twice a week (on Sundays and Thursdays), and finally one hour daily in 1973. See MGL 100 of 26th March 1973 and corresponding footnote, p. 175.

Therefore, do not do the voting according to your likes and dislikes of the person but choose the person whom, before God, you think He wants you to choose, and for His glory.

Each day: Beginning from the day you receive this letter till the end of [the] Chapter, after Holy Communion and at Adoration we shall say the following prayer:

O Holy Spirit, Paraclete, perfect in us the work begun by Jesus: enable us to continue to pray fervently in the name of the whole world: hasten in every one of us the growth of a profound interior life; give vigour to our apostolate so that it may reach all men and all peoples, all redeemed by the Blood of Christ and all belonging to Him. Mortify in us our natural pride, and raise us to the realms of holy humility, of the real fear of God, of generous courage. Let no earthly bond prevent us from honouring our vocation, no cowardly considerations disturb the claims of justice, no meanness confine the immensity of charity within the narrow bounds of petty selfishness. Let everything in us be on a grand scale; the search for truth and the devotion to it; and readiness for self-sacrifice, even to the cross and death; and may everything finally be according to the last prayer of the Son to His heavenly Father. Amen.[a]

At the end of the Rosary each day say the following:

O Mary, Cause of our Joy, Help of MCs, whose tender love and care we have always experienced, bring everything by your aid to a joyful, favourable and successful conclusion.

Please arrange that all the Sisters, except delegates to Chapter General, finish their retreats by the end of May.

God bless you
Mother

a. Prayer taken from the Homily of Pope St. John XXIII, for Pentecost Sunday, 10th June 1962, in *Discorsi Messaggi Colloqui*, vol. 4 (Vatican City: Tipografia Poliglotta Vaticana, 1962), 350.

MGL 99. 16TH MARCH 1973

+ L.D.M.

Mother House
16th March 1973

My dearest Children,

I came back on the 12th. Thank you for all your prayers and sacrifices you made for Mother—all things for the greater glory of God. All the Sisters are very well and doing God's work with great love. We have now a third house in Australia....

We also have our Sisters in Holy Land...

They need many sacrifices and prayers.

In the second stage of preparation for the General Chapter I have appointed the Regionals to come to you with a questionnaire. After much prayer, try to answer it, so as to bring before the Chapter your hopes and desires for the renewal of the Society from within. I want you to be very humble—that is, very sincere and open and for the good of the Society, so that our renewal be a real work of the Spirit of God. Do not be afraid to write what you wish—only do it with great love and humility.

The questionnaire is as follows:

> For the greater glory of God and for the greater good of each of us in the Society and for our poor, do you suggest any changes in the Rules of:

1. Chastity
2. Poverty
3. Obedience
4. Community Life
5. Prayer
6. Penance
7. Works among the poor
8. Formation of our sisters
9. Profession and renewal of vows
10. Any other topic not mentioned above

Give reasons for each suggestion.

God bless you,
Mother

⁓ MGL 100. 26TH MARCH 1973 ⁓

+ L.D.M.

Mother House
26th March 1973

My dearest Sisters,

Since the papers of our houses outside India have not arrived—there will be some delay in giving you a list of all the delegates to the chapter—but enclosed please find in your envelope a small slip of paper giving you the name of the Superior and Deputy chosen [by] you.

Your two delegates will make their retreat at the Mother House starting 1st June—therefore they will not make it in their houses. The delegates should reach the Mother House by the 20th May. . . .

I am also sending to you your Regional Superior to visit your house in my name, to collect your written answers to the questionnaire I am sending you with them—which is a preparation for our General Chapter; to help you with your books and accounts and to get necessary information which we need very urgently.

I know you will receive your Regional Superior with great love and respect and do what Jesus and Mother want you to do with that same love and humility, realising your great responsibility towards the Church and the Society.

If you have no phone, please give the number that is closest or more convenient to you where you or we could phone in case of necessity.

Some of our Sisters lost their parents in the past few months, please pray for them and for their families. . . .

I would like every house to have one hour Adoration daily before the Blessed Sacrament Exposed,[a] at a time that is convenient to you. Your Regional Superior will help you to get the necessary permission from your Bishop to expose the Blessed Sacrament.

God bless you,
Mother

a. Mother was already encouraging the Sisters to have adoration from the time she visited the convent of the Sisters of Marie Reparatrice in Mauritius, in May 1970 (see MGL 74 of 24th May 1970, p. 128, and MGL 75 of 6th July 1970, pp. 129–30). In various communities the Sisters started having half an hour (or less, depending on their schedule) of prayer before dinner, however without exposition. In this letter Mother is asking the Sisters to have daily adoration, a practice later approved at the General Chapter of 1973; this rule was subsequently added to the *Constitutions* in the chapter on Prayer (1988 *Constitutions*, no. 132).

MGL 101. 3RD JULY 1973

+ L.D.M.

3rd July 1973

My dearest Children,

We have much to thank God—for all His Goodness and Kindness to us.

The retreat was really the preparation for the Coming of the Holy Spirit. The priest tried his utmost to make us realize the Goodness of God in giving us this wonderful vocation.

The Elections were made in deep recollection and full freedom and so everyone really felt the presence of the Holy Spirit. On the 10th June, in the presence of His Grace, we elected the Superior General. In the afternoon we voted for the six Councillors—but after considering the matter more fully, the Chapter decided to have only five:

SM. AGNES—1st Councillor, who becomes the Assistant General
SM. FREDERICK—2nd Councillor
SM. DOROTHY—3rd Councillor
SM. JOSEPH MICHAEL—4th Councillor
SM. CAMILLUS—5th Councillor

We have also divided the houses into regions....

We have tried to finish our Constitutions. They have now to go to Rome for approval. In the meantime I have sent each house a copy. Get together at least once a week and read them carefully. When the Regionals come to you they will help you do it with greater love and in more detail.

As the Regionals are Major Superiors—all letters written to them by the Sisters of her region must be received and given closed. If you read carefully on page 54 regarding Regional Superiors—you will find out what they and you have to do. As this is the beginning of regular regions, let us all try to help each other to do it with great love. Love your Regionals and help them to help you, together with your own Superiors to grow into a LOVE-CENTRED COMMUNITY WHERE JESUS WILL ALWAYS
Mk 6:31 COME APART AND REST AWHILE. You cannot show greater love for Mother than by accepting them with the same love and trust you have given me all these years. It is good that they be more and more involved with you and that Mother is less and less.

As Mother had been elected for the third time, permission had to be received from Rome. It was a joy for us all when His Grace, Dr. L. T. Picachy, SJ—on the 28th June, the day of the closing—at the thanksgiving Mass in the evening, read to us the telegram saying that Rome had approved of Mother's election.[a]

New Foundations:	12th July 1973	Vijayawada	
	16th August 1973	Coimbatore	
	10th September 1973	Yemen	
	24th September 1973	Lima (Peru)	. . .

God bless you
Mother

ED 6. JULY 1973

July 1973[b]

My dearest little Children,

We have so much to thank God for—especially for His fatherly Presence among us during the Chapter. I have never felt the Presence of God so vivid and so real as during the Chapter. Let us thank the good God Our Father for His kindness to us.

Another thing that struck me the other day was the smallness of Jesus in the Blessed Eucharist—for me to be able to hold with one hand. He, God of God, Light of Light, true God of true God, begotten not made, one in substance with the Father, by Whom all things were made—was in MY HAND. This is Christ's total Surrender to me and to you.

So my children, let us begin to put to life God's kindness towards each other and our smallness with the poor, so that even the smallest child [can] use us.

—Kindness and smallness
—Meekness and humility

Jesus gave to the world. Let us allow Him to continue this giving through us.

God bless you,
Mother

a. This paragraph seems to have been added (by a Councillor or a Sister typist), to share the joy of Mother's re-election and Rome's approval.

b. At this time *Ek Dil* was normally sent out to the houses three times a year (Christmas, Easter and Society Feast); however, this edition was sent out as a special "Chapter Edition." It contains mostly the news about the Chapter, the transcript of the telegram from Rome approving Mother's re-election, letters of the previous and new Councillors, feedback of the Chapter delegates, etc., except for a few pages with news about other houses.

MGL 102. 2ND AUGUST 1973

L.D.M.

Mother House
2nd August 1973

My dearest Children,

A very happy and holy feast of the Society to each one of you. As preparation for our Feast we shall have a Novena of meditation taking each day from our Constitutions one rule for our meditation with special care of the Practical Application.[a] The 3 days—19th, 20th, 21st, will be our triduum. Ask a priest or your confessor to give you [during the] three days a meditation on the spirit of the Society for which I am sending you the copy of our Constitution to give it to the priest who will give you the meditation.

[Four Sisters] are leaving for Rome on the 4th Aug. and will leave for Yemen, Hodeidah.... So pray for them....

I will be leaving India by the 7th Aug. and will be [back] only by the end of October. In the meantime SM. Agnes will take care with the help the Councillors and Regionals of the Society. I am sure you will all try your best and do good.

With great love, God bless you,
Mother

...

MGL 103. 24TH OCTOBER 1973

L.D.M.

Rome
24th October 1973

My dearest Children,

Thank you—for all the letters you have written for my feast and also all the prayers you have offered for my Sister.[b] We now have One more person praying for us at the throne of God, interceding for us.—We need their help & their care. So many of our Sisters' parents, brothers & sisters

a. In the 1973 *Constitutions*, some chapters had a section called "Practical Application" with several practical points listed after the Rules. In the subsequent edition of the *Constitutions*, these practical points were incorporated into the Rules or became part of the *Spiritual Directory*.

b. In 1973 Mother's sister Age passed away in Tirana, Albania, where she had lived with her mother.

have gone home to God during these years. I am sure they are making a new group of Co-workers in Heaven—and so the MCs are helped—by the glorious Co-workers of our families in heaven, by the suffering & the working Co-workers on earth.

From most of the houses I have received such beautiful letters thanking for the new Constitutions, which are so full of Jesus. They have been already approved and they bind us to observe them as now we make our vows according to this Constitution. At the Propaganda Fide I saw the priest who had read our Const.[Constitutions]. He said he liked them very much.—Some parts are too long & some repetition.—He found no mistakes about the vows & the teaching & said they are approved by the Church for us to live them and grow in holiness through them.

As you know I have taken the Sisters from Belfast.[a]— . . . It is necessary to have two houses close [to each other] in each country to keep the family spirit. In Ostia we are about 25 miles away from Rome—the place of St. Augustine & St. Monica.[b] . . . There is terrible poverty, not hunger for food but for God—people are starving for the knowledge of God. [In] Lima . . . [the Sisters] have the Norbertine Fathers to take care of them, especially Fr. Mulroy,[c] who is like a real Father to them. They will soon have a Nirmal Hriday—as there are plenty of people on the streets of Lima.

Yemen—Hodeidah, our Chapel the first Cathedral in that land—[the Sisters] have their hands full in spite of not yet knowing the language. One of the Gov. [government] officials wrote—"A new era of light & love has started in Yemen."—For all these new places we must make many

a. Mother made an unannounced three days' visit to Belfast and, after a meeting with the bishop, closed the house and took the Sisters with her the very next day, 17th September 1973. Mother and the Sisters spent the night packing up all their things to be ready for the departure. The Sisters' sudden departure upset the people, who blamed the local church. To salvage the situation and avoid further hostility, Mother decided to take the responsibility of closing the house. Mother left a statement, which was read at the Sunday Masses in St. John's Church and Corpus Christi Church, saying: "This is to state that I have decided to take the Sisters from Ballymurphy for two reasons. I need the Sisters for places where their presence is very necessary. Also, already the Sisters of Charity, who are well known and loved by the children, will be able to give them the same love and service. As I have stated above I am taking the Sisters from here—no one has forced me. We have nothing to do with the rumours that we have been forced to go."

b. St. Augustine was the son of St. Monica (c. 332–387), who is honored as a model of a Christian wife and mother. St. Monica prayed for the conversion of her son Augustine and followed him to Rome and Milan. After his conversion, they both were returning to their home in Africa, but Monica died on the way, at Ostia.

c. Fr. Richard Mulroy (1915–2001), a Norbertine priest, travelled to Lima, Peru, in the 1960s in response to the papal call to serve and evangelize in South America. He worked for nineteen years in service to Lima's indigent population, especially the imprisoned. Fr. Mulroy began assisting the Sisters and our poor in Lima and continued serving them generously until his return to the United States in 1986.

sacrifices. The brave group in New York, though only 4, the joy they radiate, through their works of love, is Wonderful.

The Sisters in Mauritius have established themselves as if they have been there for many years. The people love the Sisters. The Tabora Com. [Community] has done most wonderful work with the Burundi refugees.[a] Many non–Cat. [Catholics] & Cat. [Catholics] came to thank me for the Sisters—as through the work of the Sisters they have seen Christian love living through their actions. Thank God for our Sisters—

The World, my Sisters, expects from each one of us deep love for Jesus, fidelity to His Gift of love, our vocation—the life of prayer & action lived with Jesus in the appearance of Bread and in the distressing disguise of the Poor. It is very important for us to learn to pray the work by doing it with Jesus, for Jesus and to Jesus.

In future we shall say the MC prayer & also the Prayer for the Holy Father, etc. after our Med. [Meditation] prayer. The Sup. [Superior] will give the blessing morning & night as before.

We shall say the prayer "Soul of Christ" after Holy Com. [Communion].

I am trying to go to our Sisters in Gaza & Amman. I hope I will be able to make it. The news is very sad, as many lives have been lost.[b] I would be very happy if each one of you & every Com. [Community] make Chapter 15 of St. John your own, & we really live it. The full meaning of our MC vocation is there.

The Noviciate in Rome is a great blessing.—The Novices are very happy to be here.—SM. Valerie & SM. Felicia will be professed on the 1st Nov., both will go to Yemen to complete the two Communities.—

Jn 13:34, 15:12 I hope you are really trying to love each other as Jesus loves each one of you, with a deep, personal, tender love.

God bless you
Mother

a. Burundi gained independence in 1961, but tensions between Tutsis and Hutus persisted. In April 1972, mass killings of Hutus by the Tutsi-dominated Burundian army resulted in many people fleeing from Burundi to Tanzania, Zaire, and Rwanda. Mother is praising the Sisters in Tabora for their work with the Burundi refugees in Tanzania.

b. Mother is alluding to the Fourth Arab-Israeli War, or Yom Kippur War (6th to 25th October 1973), between Israel and Egypt, Syria, and their allies. The United Nations Security Council imposed a ceasefire on 25th October 1973.

MGL 104. 14TH DECEMBER 1973

+ L.D.M

14th December 1973

My dearest Children,

Thank God I am back home with you all. It has been wonderful to be with our Sisters outside of India. How much they all love each one of you. I do not think one recreation passes without their talking of you and the Mother House. It would make me so happy if you would write to these our new houses and let them feel how close you are to them. . . .

Any Sister who needs help for her own people in any way should write to Sr. Audrey and not directly contact any of our Co-workers or benefactors in India or abroad—to avoid any misunderstanding.

The coming of Jesus in Bethlehem brought joy to the world and every Lk 2:10
human heart. The Same Jesus comes again and again in our hearts during Holy Communion. He wants to give the same joy and peace. May His Coming this Christmas bring each one of us that peace and joy that He desires to give. Let us pray much for this grace of peace and joy in our own heart, in our Communities, in our Society and in the Church.

Our Holy Father has proclaimed the Holy Year as a Year of Reconciliation.[a] The word sounds long but it really means: FORGIVE AND LOVE.

Reconciliation begins not first with others but with ourselves: by allowing Jesus to clean us—to forgive us, to love us. It starts by having a
clean heart within. A clean heart always forgives and is able to see God Mt 5:8
in others and so love them. The Tongue, the part of our body that comes Jas 3:1–12
in such close contact with the Body of Christ, can become an instrument of Peace and Joy or of Sorrow and Pain. What do we want to use it for?

Forgive and ask to be forgiven: Excuse rather than accuse. Do not go
to bed when you remember "that your Sister has something against you," Mt 5:23–24
as Jesus said. Even if we are not guilty, still let us take the first step of reconciliation.

We have much to thank God for. You will be very happy to know that

a. On 9th May 1973, Pope Paul VI announced a Holy Year for 1975—"Today there is something we would like to tell you, something which we believe is important for the spiritual life of the Church. It is this: after having prayed and meditated, we have decided to celebrate in 1975 a Holy Year. . . . Now the Holy Year is oriented precisely to this personal and interior renewal . . . . This is the general theme of the next Holy Year, which is also centred upon another special theme that is oriented to practical living: reconciliation."

our Constitutions have been approved by Rome. I am giving you a few parts of Cardinal Rossi's letter:[a]

> The present Constitutions for the most part are quite good and very sound, with regard to both the doctrinal-spiritual element and the juridical element asked for by the "Ecclesiae Sanctae". The sections on "Consecration", the "Vows", "Prayer" and the "Cross" are very well done. In fact, the Constitutions breathe an air for spirituality that is much needed today. And they express a fidelity to and love for the Church and the Person of the Sovereign Pontiff that is very much in keeping with the public religious life in the Church.
>
> The text you have presented here binds all the Members of your Congregation—except where it may contravene Common Law—right from the moment of its promulgation.
>
> May I take this occasion ... to renew my sentiments of deep personal esteem and gratitude to you and your Institute for the very remarkable gospel spirit which you are bringing to the Church today. May God's Providence continue to bless your undertakings and make them ever more fruitful for the Kingdom of the Lord.

A VERY HAPPY CHRISTMAS AND GOD'S BLESSING ON 1974.

God bless you,
Mother

ED 7. DECEMBER 1973

December 1973

My dearest Children,

One wish, one prayer Mother has for each one of you—that you may
Jn 15:1–8 grow into a fruitful branch living on the 'Vine,' Jesus, and give to each other in your Community and to the world the fruit of Love, Compassion, Unity and Peace. Let us offer this our Gift to the Baby Jesus through the hands of Mary His Mother.

a. Cardinal Agnelo Rossi (1913–1995) was a Brazilian cardinal who served as the Prefect of Propaganda Fide from 1970 to 1984.

1974

MGL 105. 25TH FEBRUARY 1974

25th February 1974[a]

My dearest Children,

I hope you are all well and doing God's work with great love and so growing in holiness. By praying the work, we do the work with Jesus, for Jesus and to Jesus, and so we are in His Presence 24 hours. How beautiful is our Vocation if we really believe that He, Jesus, is in the appearance of bread and He, Jesus, [is] in the hungry, naked, sick, lonely, unloved, the homeless, the helpless, the hopeless. Our lives must be more and more woven with this deep Faith in Jesus, the Bread of Life, to be eaten with and for the Poor.

Mt 26:26; Mk 14:22; Lk 22:19; Jn 6:35, 48–58; 1 Cor 11:24

Jn 6:25; 48

It has been very consoling for Mother to visit our Sisters in all our houses *abroad*,[b] in the South and the few in the North [of India]. They all send you their "pouring love."

Yemen, Ostia, Addis Ababa, Lima, Gaza, Coimbatore, Vijayawada. Shivpur, Tiljala, Takdah—all these houses of 1973 send their greetings and love and beg each one of you to pray for them.

On the 28th SM. Stanislaus and 4 Sisters will be leaving for Shillong. . . .

On the advice received from Rome that Councillors should not hold the office of Regionals, SM. Lourdes replaces SM. Joseph Michael and takes over Uttar Pradesh, Union Territory (Delhi), Punjab and Madhya Pradesh without Raigarh. SM. Audrey replaces SM. Camillus and takes over Raigarh, Bihar, Maharastra and Union Territory (Goa). The rest is as usual until we get replacements.

This year being the year of Reconciliation, we will in every possible way take every opportunity to make up to each other before we go to

a. The draft of this letter was written on a used envelope.

b. Mother wrote by hand the word "abroad" in the typed version of the letter.

bed—if we have hurt or been hurt—does not matter how small or big the hurt was. For this to succeed, we need silence. Let us take this point as a special penance for Lent.

In our Communities, there are so many things that many people are going without because of the present difficulties. Is anything missing in our Community? Light, food, clothing? Should we not examine this as a Community? Many of us have very little knowledge of [the] value of things and money. Once a week we should examine our expenditures and at the end of the month, know the total amount. We must know the value of every article we wear and we use. It will help us. Same thing for the things we use for our work.

Once a month we must all help clean the go-down where food and relief goods are kept.[a] All the Sisters in the house must know what we have to be able to give to the Poor, but one Sister must be responsible and not everyone take at random. Also it will be good for us all, including the Superior—at least once a week to clean drains and toilets etc. and give a helping hand to clean the kitchen and—wherever there is a plot of land, make sure you work in the garden and put as [many] fruit trees as possible so that you can give the [fruit] to the Poor. This will help us to go back to that spirit of hard labour and sacrifice which has always been in the Society. On all the Fridays throughout the year we shall have only vegetable curry—and [with] the money so saved we shall buy fruit or fish for the sick in Nirmal Hriday or in the Slums, each week. Each house write to me, how did you do this and to how many people. You must use the money only of what you have saved.

For some months now at the Mother House we have only tea at tea-time except on Sundays and Thursdays. Maybe you could all try the same. My children, the suffering of the poor is very great all over the world. We also are the Poorest of the Poor. Are we really Poor? With Poverty which is freedom, charity will grow, and with Charity, our Love for Jesus will be more intimate and personal. As we come to know each other better, knowledge will lead us to love, love to service: one of kindness, joy and Peace.

1. It has been brought to my notice that more and more Sisters are asking to go home to see their relations, for all kinds of reasons. The Superior should not give the permission without

a. "Go-down" or "Godown" is the common word in India for a storage room.

first informing the Regional. We ourselves must have the spirit of sacrifice and not ask to go to visit our home. If we are really poor, then we must be truly so. Sisters will go home for two weeks only before they begin their Tertianship.

2. Also all general permissions and speaking of faults should be done in time, and we must not expect the Superior to send for us.[a]
3. Sisters must not keep money with them.

The Sisters in Australia have been very happy to have SM. Agnes for two months. Soon we hope to have a house in Papua, so pray hard.

God bless you
Mother

MGL 106. EASTER [14TH APRIL] 1974

+ L.D.M.

Mother House
Easter [14th April] 1974

My dearest Children,

A happy and holy Easter to you. May the joy and Love of the Risen Jesus be always with you, in you and among you—so that we all become the true witnesses of His Father's love for the world: "for God loved the world so much that He gave His Son." Let us also love God so much that we give ourselves to Him in each other and in His poor. Mt 28:8; Lk 24:41, 52; Jn 20:20 Jn 3:16

We can do this only by our fidelity to Christ, belonging to Him alone—and by our tender and thoughtful love for each other. How beautiful it is to see the love for each other a living reality. Young sisters, have deep love and respect for your older sisters. Older Sisters, treat younger Sisters with respect and love, for they, like you, belong to Jesus. He has chosen each one of you for Himself, to be His love and light in the world. The simplest way of becoming His light is by being kind and loving, thoughtful and sincere with each other: "by this they will know that you are His disciples." Ps 133:1 Jn 15:16 Mt 5:14–16 Jn 13:35

The small sacrifices we had offered to Jesus during Lent, we will no

a. As it is the responsibility of the Sister to ask for the renewal of her general permissions, Mother is reminding the Sisters not to expect their Superiors to call for them.

longer make them now. I was so happy to see and hear with what joy the Sisters in all the houses accepted Mother's desire of offering some little comfort to our poor by depriving ourselves. This spirit of sacrifice will always be the salt of our Society.

I have visited all our South and East houses—I have only the West and the North [to visit]. All the Sisters from all our houses are well and doing God's work with great love. The difficulties of food keep growing. Pray much for our people who, besides their Poverty, are victims of hunger and disease.

Our four Sisters did very well in Sudeep.[a] Sr. Leonie passed her Nursing. Our Brothers are preparing to go to Cambodia in place of our Sisters.

We are all happy to have SM. Agnes back with us. There are many Sisters preparing for First and Final Profession—many Postulants to join the Noviciate and as many Aspirants to become Postulants. So the month [of] May—Our Lady's month, will be filled with much love and offering.

God bless you
Mother

ED 8. APRIL 1974

April 1974

My dearest Children,

Mt 28:8; Lk 24:41, 52; Jn 20:20

Happy and Holy Easter. Let the joy of Risen Jesus be your strength and the bond of unity and love among you [and] all those you come in contact with.

God bless you
Mother

a. Sudeep Training Institute in Bangalore was a Catholic institution that offered short courses in theology and liturgy to Sisters from various religious congregations. Mother sent a number of Sisters for studies there. It is located in the vicinity of the National Biblical Catechetical Liturgical Centre (NBCLC), popularly known as the "Vatican area of Bangalore," and was renamed Bhakthi Bhavan in 1990 when its premises were occupied by the minor seminary.

MGL 107. 2ND JUNE 1974

Pentecost
2nd June 1974

My dearest Children,

We are in the month of June, and this year will be 300 years that the Sacred Heart opened itself once again to the world to be known and loved by you and me.[a] We have much to thank Jesus for [for] all He has been, is and will be to each one of us. Next year being the Holy Year,[b] and for us the 25 years of our existence—let us thank God for all things. We have nothing to offer as a token of thanks but our love—let each one of us offer during Holy Mass: our Tongue—that we will use it only for the "Word of God," for—

He is the Word to be spoken; Jn 1:1, 14
He is the Light to be lit; Jn 8:12; 9:5
He is the Way to be walked; Jn 14:6
He is the Life to be lived; Jn 14:6; 11:25
He is the Love to be loved. 1 Jn 4:8, 16

Therefore, my dearest children, let our life always give and receive Jesus. This same love applies to our Poor. How do we serve them? We exist because of them.

a. As Mother is writing this letter in June 1974, she is most likely referring to the second of the three major apparitions of the Sacred Heart to St. Margaret Mary, the apparition of the first Friday of 1674. In this apparition:

> Jesus appears to Sr. Margaret Mary while she is adoring the Blessed Sacrament. He shows her His wounds shining like suns and His chest like a fiery furnace. He complains of the little "return of love" that men show Him, after all He has endured to save them. He asks for two acts of reparation: communion on the first Friday of each month; Holy Hour on Thursday night, in union with His agony in Gethsemane. The first apparition took place on 27th December 1673, the feast of St. John the Apostle. Jesus has Sr. Margaret Mary rest for a very long time on His divine Heart. He reveals to her the wonders of His love. He chooses her to proclaim the intensity of this "ardent charity" to save souls. Jesus immerses the heart of Margaret Mary into His Heart, then gives it back to her all inflamed. From this experience, she will feel a pain in her side throughout her life.
>
> The third, the so called "Great Apparition" took place in June 1675. Jesus said to Sr. Margaret Mary: "Behold the Heart which loved men so much that He spared nothing, even to exhausting and consuming Itself, to show them His love. And in gratitude, I receive from most of them only ingratitude, by their irreverence and sacrileges, and by the coldness and contempt they have for Me in this Sacrament of Love. But what I feel most keenly is that it is hearts that are consecrated to me that treat Me thus."

(Fr. Gérard Dufour, Chaplain at Paray-le-Monial 1984–1993, *Sainte Marguerite-Marie, messagère du Cœur de Jésus,* http://www.sacrecoeur-paray.org/experimenter/le-message-de-paray-le-monial/de-jesus-a-sainte-marguerite-marie/.)

b. Pope Paul VI had announced a Holy Year for 1975; see MGL 104 of 14th December 1973 and the corresponding footnote.

Mt 25:34–40 They are hungry for bread and love;
They are thirsty for water and kindness;
They are sick with pain and loneliness;
They are homeless for lack of house and unwanted;
They are in prison between two walls and covered with ignorance.

Where are we Sisters—if we too are the poorest of the Poor? Do we know what it means to be

hungry and lonely?
thirsty and unloved?
sick and unwanted?
homeless and misunderstood?

We meet these people, our poor, every day. Do we know them? [Are we] really one of them? My sisters, it must hurt Jesus as it hurts Mother if we have become so rich as to have no time for the Poor. Do the Poor know us, do they love us? Are they happy in our Presence? Let us renew our love for our Poor. We will be able to do so only if we are faithful to the Poverty we have vowed, we have chosen. Nowadays, I see the sisters travelling with a big bedding plus one or two boxes. How rich we are! We must be ashamed to be richer than the Poor Jesus.

Our newly Professed and Finally Professed Sisters have left for their new houses—and I am sure it has been a great joy to you to receive them, because now you will be able to carry Jesus to many more of our poor people.

We have opened new houses in [Vellore, Guntakal, Kottayam, and Ernakulam]. . . .

Do not forget to pray for our Sisters in these new houses and write to them. Very soon we hope to open up houses in Cuttack and Nagpur, and also in Taiz, Palermo, and Papua.[a]

I will be leaving India on the 4th June to visit our Sisters and Co-workers and hope to be back by the end of September.

While I am away all matters should be seen by SM. Agnes.

God bless you
Mother

a. Cuttack here refers not to the city of Cuttack but to the Diocese of Cuttack in the state of Orissa (currently Odisha) which was established as the Archdiocese of Cuttack–Bhubaneswar just a few months earlier (24th January 1974). The new foundations Mother is referring to were to be Cuttack (Bhubaneswar) and Nagpur in India, Taiz in Yemen, Palermo in Italy, and Tokarara in Papua New Guinea.

MGL 108. 17TH JULY 1974

17th July 1974

My dearest Sisters,

It was wonderful to be with our Sisters in New York, Venez. [Venezuela] and Peru.

God love them, they are all well and are doing God's work with great love.

I am now in Rome; we have here 13 Novices, SM. Julia & SM. Martin, SM. Dominica and SM. Stella.

We are expecting the 3rd years, then we will have a big community. I will be going to our Sisters in Yemen, Amman, Gaza, and Addis Ababa. I do hope you keep praying for Mother. I hope you know that SM. Agnes takes full responsibility with the council when I am out of India—changes etc. she can do—therefore be one heart full of love with her and the council.

Let us all more and more insist on being loving and kind to each other. Show that we want and need each other, smile at each other and so show the love and compassion of Jesus for my Sister. Maybe in my own Community there is a Sister who is so lonely, unwanted, unloved. Do I know it? What am I doing about it? Am I happy when others insist [on] this?[a] Smile at each other, especially when I don't want to smile. The cold I had is nearly gone completely, so you need not worry for me. The Sisters here are all well and doing very well. The Cardinal of Naples is again and again asking for the Sisters, so I am going there tomorrow morning and be back by midday. I hope everybody is well and help each other to grow in love.

God bless you
Mother

a. Mother has written above: "Let us all more and more insist on being loving and kind to each other." So this sentence probably means: Am I happy when others (or Mother) insist on being loving and kind to each other?

MGL 109. 9TH AUGUST 1974

+ L.D.M.

Yemen
9th August 1974

My dearest Children,

A very Happy and Holy Feast of Our Lady. May the Immaculate Heart, Our Queen and Mother, be more and more our way to Jesus, the Light of Jesus, the love of Jesus and Our Life of Jesus in each one of us. In return for this great gift, let us more and more be a cause of Joy to each other, the way of peace to one another and the living Love of Jesus for each other. My children, how great, how kind, how gentle has been His love for each one of us and for the whole Society.

Let the poor and all those we come in contact with feel His touch in us and through us. As there are so many acts against Faith, Hope and Charity being made daily, we shall pray the whole morning prayer without the Our Father and Creed.[a] It does not take even 5 minutes to pray those acts. We will also, all of us, learn and relearn the prayers before dressing.[b] Renew your love for the penance and Stations of the Cross: though they are optional—which now means, I choose to do them—[in the same way], let us put greater love in praying the Rosary on the streets.

Since we do not have the Constitutions ready for each one, it will help us if one Sister reads 3 Constitution numbers for the community before the Spiritual reading, and do not neglect the meditation on Thursdays on the Constitutions.

No Superior nor sister must ask the Co-workers in any part of the world for money or things to purchase for them.

It is necessary that all our houses outside India send their Account paper to Sr. M. Stella every 3 months or, if it is more convenient, every month. Also acknowledge to her whenever you get money from Rome.

As Sr. Frederick will soon return to India and we will not be able to appoint anyone in her place as Regional—in future all letters must be written to [Mother House] and you will receive [news] from Mother House.

...

a. From the context it would seem that only some of the morning prayers from the MC Prayer Book were prayed. In the early days, the *Our Father, Hail Mary* and the *Creed* were prayed during morning prayer after the phrase, "Blessed be the holy and undivided Trinity, now and forevermore. Amen." From this time on, the *Our Father, Hail Mary,* and the *Creed* were not prayed within the morning prayer, but instead the *Act of Faith, Act of Hope,* and *Act of Charity* were prayed.

b. This refers to the prayers that the Sisters pray while vesting the habit, sari, etc.

Sisters, please take it as a real duty to write at least once a month to the Mother House. You may write [more] often if you need, but once a month is a Must. The Superiors and the Novice, Postulant and Aspirant Mistresses renew also their general permissions with the Councillors appointed for their houses.

If more or less you keep to the same date, you will be able to find out if the post is alright.

I am hoping to be home very soon. Pray much for me.

God bless you,
Mother

ED 9. AUGUST 1974

August 1974[a]

MGL 110. 29TH SEPTEMBER 1974

Paris
29th September 1974

My dearest Children,

I am at the last stop of Co-workers.—I hope to leave Rome on Wed., go via Amman & Gaza and then Cal. [Calcutta]. I hope to be with you the latest by the 15th Oct.

God has been very loving & shown Great love right through these 4 months. We have much to thank God for; I am counting the days to be with you all.

I hope you are all well and full of joy.

I am not bringing SM. Frederick with me—as she is very necessary for the work of the houses & also for the Co-workers to whom we owe greater care—than we have given them all these years.—She will be the best person to make these connections—at least for the present.—

All is well with me.—

God bless you
Mother

a. *Ek Dil* 8, Society Feast edition, has an extract from MGL 10 of [4th] August 1961 (the first two paragraphs, p. 20) as Mother's message.

MGL 111. 11TH NOVEMBER 1974

+ L.D.M.

Mother House
11th November 1974

My Dearest Children,

Thank God I am back. As Advent is approaching, let us prepare our hearts with greater love for His coming, through humility and meekness.

Therefore, every week we will take one line at a time of the prayer of peace—Lord, make me a channel of your peace—and use it during the whole day for that whole week. Pray the sentence again and again, as often as possible, and put it in action.

The line "that where there is error—I may bring truth" has been left out by mistake when printing the new prayer books. Please add this line after the line: "where there is discord I may bring harmony".

Start this preparation as soon as you receive this letter—and continue it during these weeks, even after Christmas if necessary, until you come to the end of all the lines in that prayer according to the pattern I give below.

FIRST WEEK: Where there is hatred—I may bring love.

1. Mark it on the board (or any other way you like) at the beginning of the week for all to know and remember.
2. Prepare the Mass at least once during that week (Thursday or the day you are all in) according to the sentence. Ask Father, if possible, to give a short homily on it.
3. Let the community prepare a meditation on it and have shared prayer.
4. Do the refectory reading on it.
5. Help each other to [make] up a short examination of Conscience on it for particular examen time.
6. Let each Sister write her own prayer about hatred and love. If it helps the community, maybe you could pray [it] at your adoration. When I come I will be happy to pray your prayer with you. If you wish, you could send it to me so that I can share your prayer with your other Sisters all over the world.
7. We will also do our penance with greater love and fidelity in reparation for all the hatred shown and felt; also in thanksgiving for all the love we have given.

8. At the end of the week, on Saturday—have chapter, during which each Sister will share 3 ways in which she has put that prayer in action.

I know you will be very sad, as I am—to hear that SM.—— and SM.—— left their houses without permission. Let us pray and offer our penance for our sisters that Jesus may help them to see. Do not judge but pray for them.

Neglect of the Rosary and worldliness can deceive many of us. So many of you are scarcely praying the Rosary in the streets; so many of you are spending so much time with your hair; so many of you are neglecting to do penance; yet the Constitutions are very clear: "We pray the Rosary on the Streets and we cut our hair completely at our profession." Just as for Samson in the Old Testament—all his energy was in his long hair, so Judg 16:16–17
maybe for us: our weakness and the beginning of refusal lies also in the keeping of our hair.

...These penances we will offer to obtain the grace of joy in our vocation and in our Communities and for all the priests and Religious throughout the world; also for all those who have left or are tempted against their vows.

Sr. M. Francesca has just completed 1000 copies of our Constitutions, and she has done them with great love and hard work, and I am sure you will not forget to say a little prayer of thanksgiving for her. I will be sending you copies of these Constitutions after we have put in a few changes which Rome has asked us to make. When you receive these copies don't forget to mark the changes in the copy which you received after the General Chapter.

We are hoping to carry the light of Christ to Bhubaneswar, our first house in Orissa.... It will be opened on the 21st of Nov., Feast of the Presentation of Our Lady. Two more sisters will go after Profession. They will need your prayers and sacrifices very much to help them to do God's work among the people there. Write to them....

I spent a week in Bangladesh: Sr. Priscilla in Dacca and Sr. Josephine in Khulna and Sr. Gemma in Tongi are doing great work with their Sisters for our Poor people there, who are suffering very much from the floods.

Since it is necessary that you keep close to Mother and the Mother House and I know you are all wanting it—we have therefore decided that the necessary "link" will be made through the Councillors in the Mother House....

The Regionals in India and Sister Superiors of houses outside India will renew their permissions directly with me and, in my absence, with Sr. M. Agnes, but an exchange of news and other spiritual help will be done through the link that we have created with the Councillors in Mother House; they will write to you once a month and receive news from you once a month also. The Sisters in charge of formation will renew their permissions with the Superior of the place where they are according to Constitution no. 188, which says: "those responsible for formation and their assistants depend on the local Superior for their own religious life and the discipline of the house."

God bless you,
Mother

ED 10. DECEMBER 1974

December 1974[a]

MOTHER'S MESSAGE FOR CHRISTMAS:

Happy and Holy Christmas and God's Blessing in 1975
through—
Faith in Jesus in the Eucharist and Him in each other
Hope in Jesus in each other—loving trust
Love for Jesus in the service of each other.

a. *Ek Dil* nos. 10 to 24 were sent out to the houses every month from December 1974 to December 1975. We have only re-typed versions of these *Ek Dil* issues that are bound in one document with a handwritten note on the top of the front page: "Newsletter 10–24." Mother's messages appear in only a few of them. We have inserted the corresponding *Ek Dil* number only if *Ek Dil* includes Mother's message; omitting the rest of the issues and resuming with the serial number of the next *Ek Dil* that contains Mother's message.

MGL 112. 19TH DECEMBER 1974

+ L.D.M.

Mother House
19th December 1974

My dearest children,

1st January 1975 is the beginning of the New Year—a Holy Year for each one of you and for me; also for all our Brothers and Sisters we come in contact with, our Poor. We [will] make this year a holy year by deepening our understanding of each other and so open ourselves to the Promise of Jesus:

"IF A MAN LOVES ME, HE WILL KEEP MY WORD." Jn 14:23

My new Commandment—LOVE ONE ANOTHER AS I HAVE LOVED YOU. Jn 13:34; 15:12

And—MY FATHER WILL LOVE HIM AND WE WILL COME TO HIM AND MAKE OUR HOME WITH HIM. Jn 14:23

For in loving one another through our works of love we bring an increase of grace and a growth in Divine Love. Since Jesus' love is our
mutual love,[a] we will be able to love as He loves—and He will manifest Jn 13:34; 15:12; 14:21
Himself through us to each other to help the world and by this mutual Jn 13:35
love they will know that we are His.

This year is [a] Holy Year also because it is our thanksgiving year for the 25 years of God's tender love and care for [us] and Our Lady's motherly protection.[b]

Let us try to understand each other by finding out what is good in my Sister, my Superior, the poor I serve. Try to find at least one good point and build from there. If you cannot find a good point for a particular Sister, then humbly ask that Sister, who should say it with a simple heart. Do this as a community together at a Chapter and then send me back the one paper which I am enclosing with this letter. (Only one point for each).

At your chapters you could also thank each other by mentioning the good you have seen each sister in your community do every week. I am sure this will help you.

So in January we will take: UNDERSTANDING LOVE as our target.

a. The meaning is: Since Jesus' love is the love with which we love one another.

b. The Society of the Missionaries of Charity was canonically (officially) established on 7th October 1950.

Help each other as [a] community and as individuals, to understand this "Understanding love". Let us also continue the prayer of St. Francis of Assisi ("Make me a channel of your peace") right up to the end of the year, as it is helping us all to really pray and come closer to each other.

On the 20th December, [four Sisters] are leaving for Nagpur. This will be our 51st house in India and the 12th this year. Let us thank God for all His goodness to us.

Please do not write general letters to the houses, but when you do write, send it to Mother House, as every month a letter will go from here and we will complete it and send it to all the houses. Also there is too much correspondence in India between the houses. It is unnecessary. Postage keeps increasing more and more. Please let us take care to avoid waste.

No Sister, not even the Superior, should go out alone, and all must know in the community where the Superior and the Sisters are going.

When business has to be done with men—Superior also should have a companion.

In spite of our defects, God is in love with us [and] keeps using you and me to [be His] light of love and compassion in the world. So give Jesus a big smile and a hearty thank you.

God bless You.
Mother

P.S. Those houses that have not yet sent in your statistics and feast days of the Sisters', kindly do so immediately.

ED 11. DECEMBER 1974

December 1974[a]

a. *Ek Dil* 11 of December 1974 reproduced MGL 112 of 19th December 1974 (see pp. 195–96) as Mother's message. *Ek Dil* 12 through 24 do not include Mother's messages but only the news that the Sisters sent monthly to Mother House; we have not indicated the appropriate serial numbers of these issues. In *Ek Dil* of 18th July 1975, ED 18, Mother House news reported Mother's words as a point to practice during the month. Here is the excerpt: "Mother House is infested with Novices big, short, fat, thin and small, all trying to live up to this month's MC intention, which are Mother's own words: *"I ask you, each one of you, the fruit of Holiness which comes from love, compassion and unity."* There are three *Ek Dil* issues in September 1975: *Ek Dil* 20 is the regular September issue, *Ek Dil* 21 reproduces MGL 119 of 10th September 1975 (see pp. 208–9) as Mother's message and is a special Silver Jubilee Edition, and *Ek Dil* 25 is again dated as 10th September 1975 (though it was sent to the houses after *Ek Dil* 26, December 1975 issue); this issue gives the news of the Silver Jubilee celebrations, mainly in Calcutta). This edition was given the serial number 25 (and the consecutive serial numbers of *Ek Dil* issues continue regularly after this number); however, *Ek Dil* 22, 23 and 24 were sent out to the houses in October, November and December, respectively.

1975

MGL 113. [12TH FEBRUARY] 1975

+ L.D.M.

Mother House
Lent, [12th February][a] 1975

My dearest children,

Let us thank God for all His Love for us, in so many ways and in so many places. Let us in return, as an act of gratitude and adoration, determine to be holy, because He is holy. Each time Jesus wanted to prove His love for us, He was rejected by mankind. Before His birth, His parents asked for a simple dwelling place and there was none. Because His parents were poor, there was no place. The inn-keeper looked at the poor dress of Joseph the Carpenter—thinking that he will not be able to pay, he was refused, but Mother earth opened its cave to and took in the Son of God. Lv 11:44–45; 19:2; 20:26 Jn 1:10–11 Lk 2:7

Again, before the Redemption and Resurrection, He was rejected by His own people. They did not want Him—they wanted Caesar; they did not want him—they wanted Barabbas. At the end as if His own Father did not want Him also because He was covered with our sins, for in His loneliness He cried: "My God, my God why hast thou forsaken Me?" Mt 27:21; Lk 23:18; Jn 18:40 Mt 27:46

The Yesterday is always today to God, therefore Today, in [the] world, Jesus stands covered with our sins, in the distressing disguise of my sister, my brother. Do I want Him? If we are not careful, soon the riches [will] hurt their Poverty;[b] riches with the worldly spirit will become an obstacle—we will not be able to see God, for Jesus has said: "Blessed are the Clean of heart, for they shall see God." Mt 5:8

The people at the time of Jesus rejected Him because His poverty was hurting their riches. My sisters: Do our poor reject us because our riches

a. In 1975, Ash Wednesday was on the 12th of February.

b. The meaning is: Our (the Sisters') riches will hurt their (the Poor's) Poverty.

hurt their Poverty? Are they at ease with us because we [are] so like them in Poverty? Can we look straight into the faces of our poor and say with a sincere heart—I know Poverty, She is my companion; I love Poverty, she is my Mother; I serve Poverty, she is my Mistress.

Last month, we began with Understanding love—this month we will try to pray, understand, love and live: "the Freedom of true Poverty," which was the cause of Christ's being rejected by His people. God forbid that our people reject us because of our riches.

<u>For Examen of Conscience</u>: Let us take a detailed examen of: all our personal things p. [particularly] of the things we use for the work—of the things entrusted to our care. Together with it, let us see well: Are we really, fully and sincerely giving wholehearted free service, not only to the Poor outside but also to our own Community and to each other?

- Am I faithful in renewing my general permission in time each month?—and in saying: "Please May I . . ." for the special permission I need each time?
- Is there anything with me that I know very well that I should not have (big or small), e.g., camera, wristwatch, extra ball[point] pens, etc. etc.
- Do I give things without permissions to people I know I should not give to? or to my own people?
- Did I respect personal things?[a] Did I accept personal things/gifts? Or hide things given for the work, for my personal use?
- Do I take the trouble to put down into the account book the money received or spent?
- Do I work hard like [the] poor? Do I put my hand to the common work, or do I always wait to be asked?
- When the poor are going through hard times with regard to food, light, and water—am I able to accept giving up little delicacies regarding food which are not absolutely necessary for my health, like daily chilly, pickle, etc.?[b] [Am I faithful to the rule] of not eating out of time (except in time of sickness)?
- Do I take care not to use water and light carelessly? Do I take the trouble to close the taps and put off lights that are unnecessary, or do I always leave them for someone else?

a. The meaning is: Do I take care of my personal things?

b. Mother is challenging the Sisters to notice the poverty and deprivation of the poor they serve and consequently forego at least the delicacies.

– Out of respect for our Poor, we do not eat outside—Am I faithful to this rule?

(pray often during the day the little prayer of the right wound at the bottom of the page).[a]

As you see—at the end of every month since November, I am sending you "Ekdil" with my letter or one from the Councillors.[b] I expect at least a word from you that you have received the letter. I have asked you to write every first week of the month. Up to now, very few have done so. We cannot blame the post each time. It is very necessary for us to keep up our unity and love through this regular contact. Therefore, it is a Must and not a "choosing".

At our council Meeting a unanimous opinion was given that there are grave reasons not to allow Sr.—— to make the Final Profession on 8th December—Sr.—— had therefore to leave us when her vows Expired.

On the 15th Jan. Berhampur house was opened. . . .

On the 22nd [five sisters] . . . left for our new house in Kalimpong. I will send you their address when I have it.

– O Jesus, by the wound of Your right hand (kiss it) give me a great love for my Vow of Poverty and grace to understand and observe it faithfully.

Please send the statistics at the back of A/C [account] paper each month.

A VERY SPECIAL BLESSING AND HAPPY BIRTHDAY TO:[c]

Madurai	Gaza	Berhampur
Jail Road	Jhansi	Kalimpong
Dacca	Agra	Khulna
Bhopal	Jamshedpur	Shillong

God bless you,
Mother

a. Mother is referring to the prayer: "O Jesus, by the wound of your right hand," which is found at the bottom of page 120 in the *MC Prayer Book*, and below in this same letter.

b. Mother is referring to the *Ek Dil* issues from ED 10 dated as "December 1974" to *Ek Dil* 22 dated as "December 1975." As mentioned above, after this period, *Ek Dil* was again sent out three times a year, and later twice a year, except on special occasions.

c. Mother is referring to the anniversary of the foundation day of the communities in each of the places listed. Here and hereafter, the foundation dates have been omitted from the list.

MGL 114. 10TH MARCH 1975

+ L.D.M.

10th March 1975

My dearest Children—

especially each one of you who will renew your Vows in May,

I was not going to write a letter this month, but this morning while I was making meditation the thought of you came to my mind. I prayed for you and what I write is the fruit of my prayer for you.

You are 180 MCs to renew your Consecration—your loyalty to Christ and His Church—to the Society and your community—to Mother and to
Hos 2:19 each other. In our Constitutions we read "I will betroth you to me in faithfulness." He will make you His own, only if you are faithful. You belong to Him by your Vows—

Love Christ with undivided love in Chastity,
Through freedom of Poverty
in Total Surrender to Obedience
and Wholehearted Free Service through Charity.

These are but 4 sentences—do you know them in practice? Do you live them in your daily life? Face yourselves, my Sisters—with all the sincerity of your heart and ask yourself: Am I really a true MC? One who belongs totally to God? Who gives wholehearted service to the Poor?

As our Society is still very young—in most of our houses we have mostly Junior Sisters, and in many of our Communities there is so much unhappiness and hurt created mostly by you Sisters. If you were at home or in the world you would not dare to act this way. You would have to be very careful out of fear, lest you lose your job—or if you hoped to be married, nobody would marry you.

You have just been professed and immediately you start with your health: I cannot eat—I cannot work—I cannot walk—I have backache. These are the most common diseases of my young Sisters. Some of you do so little work—that if you were to be paid, you would get nothing—and you have a Vow to give wholehearted Service.

Some of you have got into such a bad habit of answering back and creating disturbance in the Community with the hope of being changed—so you go from Community to Community, as the young Superiors cannot control you. Many of you have cut down your regular food, and are not ashamed to eat out of time, in the houses you visit or in Shishu Bhavan or Nirmal Hriday—when people are actually dying of hunger—and yet Mother can work till all hours of the night[a]—travelling by night and working by day. Is this not a humiliation for you—that I, at my age, can take a regular meal and do a full day's work—and you live with the name of being Poor but enjoy a lazy life.

Any of you who are acting like this with the hope of being sent home—need not do so, for you have only to ask and I will give you permission to go, rather than remain as a handicapped religious and disturb the Sisters who wish to live their life.

The Questionnaire I have enclosed must be answered in all its truthfulness. For your Renewal of Vows, permission will be granted only after I have received the answers from you.

A VERY SPECIAL BLESSING AND A HAPPY BIRTHDAY TO:[b]

CATIA LA MAR and KATHERINE....

All this I have written to you not to discourage you but to help you grow in love, for Mother loves you, as I love Jesus—therefore, I want you to be Christ-like.

I am grateful to each one of you for all you have tried to be and do for the Poor—but we can always love one another with greater love—AS JESUS LOVES YOU AND ME. Jn 13:34; 15:12

God bless you
Mother

MGL 115. [2ND] MAY 1975

+ L.D.M.

Mother House
[2nd] May 1975

My dearest Children,

Often you see small and big wires, new and old, cheap and expensive lined up—unless and until the current passes through them there will be no light. The wire is you and me. The current is God. We have the

a. That is, until the late hours of the night.

b. That is, the anniversary of the foundation day of the communities in Catia la Mar [Venezuela] and Katherine [Australia].

Jn 8:12; 9:5 power to let the current pass through us—use us—produce the light of the
world—Jesus—or refuse to be used and allow darkness to spread.

Our Lady was the most wonderful wire. She allowed God to fill her to
Lk 1:38 the brim, so by her surrender "Be it done to me according to thy word"
Lk 1:28 she became "full of grace"; and naturally the moment she was filled by
this current, the grace of God, she went in haste to Elizabeth's house to
connect the wire, John, to the current, Jesus. As his mother said: "this
Lk 1:39–44 child John leapt up with Joy at your voice." Let us ask Our Lady during
this month to come into our life also and make the current Jesus use us
to go round the world especially in our own communities and continue
connecting [the] wires of the hearts of men with the current, Jesus.

I am sending you this beautiful poem; learn by heart one line each day and put it into action immediately throughout the day,

A little more praising, a little less jeering
A little more trusting, a little less fearing
A little more patience, in trouble and pain
A little less willing at times to complain
A little more kindness worked into strife
Are all that is needed to glorify life.
A little more honour a little less greed
A little more service a little less speed
A little more courage when pathways are rough
A little more action, a little less bluff
A little more kindness by you and me
And oh! what a wonderful world this would be.[a]

a. This poem is found in publications as early as 1915—"Little More and Little Less," in *Confectioners Gazette* 36, no 404 (10 May 1915): 23. From then on it was also published in various other periodicals, for example, in *The Adelphian* under the title "More and Less" (*The Adelphian* 16, no. 2 [May 1921]: 150, Published by the Students of St. Bonaventure College, St. John's, Newfoundland, Canada).

"More and Less"
A little more praise and a little less blame,
A little more virtue, a little less shame,
A little more thought for the other man's rights,
A little less self in our chase for delights,
A little more loving, a little less hate,
Are all that is needed to make the world great.

A little more boosting, a little less jeering,
A little more trusting, a little less fearing;
A little more patience in troubles and pain,
A little less willing at times to complain,
A little more kindness worked into the strife
Are all that is needed to glorify life.

A little more honor, a little less greed,
A little more service, a little less speed;

A very special Blessing and a Very Happy Birthday to: DORANDA, RAIGARH, ENNORE, KANCHIPURAM, KOCHUTHURA, and GREEN PARK, GREEN VALE AND VELLORE, BANGALORE AND SANTA CRUZ, GUNTAKAL, KOTTAYAM, and MELBOURNE....

Forty-eight novices will take their first vows on the 24th at 6 A.M. in the Mother House Chapel, and sixteen Tertians, their Final Vows at the Sacred Heart Church, Dharamtala at 6:30 P.M. the same day.

I will be leaving for Melbourne on the 21st and will be away for about a month. During my absence all permissions must be got from Sr. M. Agnes.

God bless you,
Mother

MGL 116. [6TH JUNE] 1975

+ L.D.M.

Feast of the Sacred Heart
[6th June] 1975

My dearest Children,

I am just back from Australia and Papua, with deep gratitude to God and our Blessed Mother of God for all the good being done and all the love and compassion our Sisters give to each other, [and] to our Poor.—It is so very beautiful.

On the 10th May we had the 1st Profession of our four Novices.... We have closed down the home of Compassion for Alcoholics [in Melbourne] and made it into a Noviciate, and the old Noviciate will be used for our Poor children and stranded poor families....

A little more courage where pathways are rough,
A little more action, a little less bluff,
A little more kindness by you and by me,
And oh, what a wonderful world it would be.

In other contemporary publications, the author appears under the synonym "The Little Wanderer." Subsequent publications have "creed" instead of the original "speed" in the third stanza. Here the Sister typist, who might have suggested to Mother to insert the poem, has kept the first line of the first stanza, omitted the rest of the first stanza as well as the first line of the second stanza, and joined these two stanzas into one. It is also possible that the Sister typist found this version in some Catholic magazine and reproduced it as found. Eventually this shortened version was copied on a board by the Sisters and hung on the wall of one of our homes in Calcutta. The media took this shortened version, which is now circulated on the web with the "acknowledgement": "Taken from a wall hanging in the Convent of St. Teresa of Calcutta."

[Seven Sisters]...will be in Corpus Christi, Greenvale—a place like Shantinagar but for the homeless alcoholics.

On my way back we stopped at Manila, where Archbishop Sin is waiting anxiously for the Sisters.[a] What we saw is difficult to express. I have never seen people living in conditions like this. Everybody is very anxious to have the Sisters as soon as possible, and I think we will get many very good vocations—so let us hope that by August we can have the group ready to go.

The more I see the Sisters trying to grow in holiness, the more I see
the tremendous good to souls they do. Sisters that are very united to each
Jn 15:5 other in Community as the Branch to the Vine—are producing great fruits
of real holiness among the Poor. Therefore, my Sisters, my children—let
Jn 15:2 us allow the Father to prune us until we are so united as to produce the
most fruitful fruit: SAINTS—to the Mother Church. I do hope and pray
that each one of you will really try your utmost to produce this fruit of
holiness in your own life, in each other and the Poor you serve.

For the 25 years of love and service Mother has given you—I ask of you, each one of you, the fruit of holiness that comes from love, compassion and unity with each other and every house with the Society and the whole Society with the Church.

Let us ask Our Lady to help us to bring forth this fruit. Let the Rosary, which has always been the strength from the first days of the Society, be renewed with greater fervour and fidelity. The Society in a special way owes its birth to the Immaculate Heart and its growth to Her tender care. Therefore, in return let us thank Her for what she has done for us and been to us during these 25 years.

Greater love for Our Lady and
Greater Love and unity with each other in Community and
Every Community with Mother House
is the Special Gift I would be happy to get from you on the
twenty-fifth Birthday of our Society.

Each Community must do it in their own way.

a. Cardinal Jaime L. Sin (1928–2005), of Chinese-Filipino descent, the fourteenth of sixteen children, was appointed archbishop of Manila in 1974, and named cardinal in 1976. Cardinal Sin was known for advocating for the rights of the poor and uniting Filipino people in resistance to the regime of President Ferdinand Marcos. He was known as well for his great sense of humour. At his invitation, Mother established a home for the dying in the Philippines. Later, he asked her to open another house; she responded by saying she did not have enough Sisters to spare. He told her, "Mother Teresa, if I am called by St. Peter after I die and he asks me what I did for the poor, I will tell St. Peter that you denied my request." Hurriedly, Mother Teresa said, "I will send Sisters. Do not worry."

We hope soon to have a few new foundations:

Rourkela on the 6th June . . .

Meerut on the 13th June . . .

A VERY HAPPY BIRTHDAY AND GOD BLESS YOU to: DELHI, ASANSOL, ERNAKULAM AND PALERMO, AMRAVATI, JABALPUR, LUCKNOW, POONA AND BELLARY, [and] KANPUR. . . .

God bless you
Mother

MGL 117. 10TH JUNE 1975

10th June 1975

My dearest Children,

As the day of our Silver Jubilee is coming closer and closer, you must be thinking of it with great joy and love and thanksgiving in your hearts. I am sure you would like to know what you should do and what you should not do regarding the outward celebration of it.

WHAT YOU SHOULD DO: On the 7th October itself, have a High Mass of thanksgiving and invite all our Benefactors and our Poor to join with us to say Thank You to God for all He has done for us and our Society these 25 years—through the intercession of the Immaculate Heart of Mary.

WHAT YOU SHOULD NOT DO: No Money, not even one paisa, should be spent;

No celebrations like speeches, concerts, etc.

No printing of brochures, pamphlets, photos, pictures, etc.

No fundraising in the name of the Jubilee.

I am sure you will respect this wish of mine in all its details and that you will be really happy to have this chance to live according to our vocation as Missionaries of Charity and the spirit of our Society.

OUR CO-WORKERS ALSO MUST KEEP TO THIS FAITHFULLY.

Here is a Beautiful Gift for the Jubilee: reading this letter of Fr. Gorrée you will understand what I mean:

Dear Sister,

In September, 1974—Mother Teresa expressed her desire to see all the Houses of the Missionaries of Charity adopted spiritually by a convent of contemplative nuns. Mother Teresa has asked me to kindly see to this spiritual "twinning" on an international level.

Today, I wish to inform you that several monasteries of contemplative nuns have accepted to offer to God the Father their prayer and sacrifice in union with those of Jesus Christ, to obtain the graces that will render your apostolic zeal fruitful. This spiritual support is great and wonderful news, and I unite myself to you to thank Divine Providence.

In return, we would be extremely grateful if you sent your "twin" contemplative Community news of your Community and of your apostolate once a year. This correspondence could become a real stimulus for one another; this exchange of news is very precious.

We pray that this spiritual adoption will bear good spiritual fruit, and recommending myself to your prayers.

Yours devoutly in Christ,

Do not make this exchange of letters a means to ask for material things, but let it be full of the love you have for Christ and His poor through the kind of work we do. Be faithful to this writing once a year at Christmastime—to the house of Contemplative nuns who have adopted your community. The letter must be written as a community and not as an individual.

On the 11th June, I am leaving for Meerut to open our house there,[a] and then I will go on to Delhi, where I will fly to Rome, and from there to Mexico. There is a Conference of the International Women's Year which will be held in Mexico City from 19th June to 2nd July 1975, and the Church has chosen me to represent her as a member of the Delegation from the Holy See. Because the Church is everything to me and to you—I have accepted to be sent to witness Christ's Love for His Poor in the name of the Church. So I will be away for about three weeks.

I know that you will be praying for me and for one another, that we do always what God and the Church expects us to do.

HAPPY BIRTHDAY AND A BIG GOD BLESS YOU TO:

SILIGURI, VIJAYAWADA AND BRAVINGTON (LONDON), and AMMAN....

And it will be TEN YEARS since we opened our first House outside

a. A city in the state of Uttar Pradesh, India.

India in COCOROTE, VENEZUELA.... And on the Feast of the Sacred Heart Naples will be opened.

By now all must have finished the Enthronement and Consecration of the Community and the families of the poor to the Sacred Heart. The Heart of Jesus must rejoice to see the MCs all over India and all over the world—bringing so many of His Poor closer to Him. Let this thought help us to greater love and zeal so that Jesus may be better known and loved.

God bless you
Mother

MGL 118. 31ST JULY 1975

+ L.D.M.

31st July 1975

My dearest Children,

This will bring you Mother's wishes and prayers for a very Happy and Holy Feast of the Society—and also a gift from the Mother House: A novena of united efforts to grow in love through prayer and humility.

We are also preparing a special Mass for the 7th October, so that we all thank God for all the love He has given and [the] Trust He has put in each one and the Society as a whole.

I pray that your life together in Community be full of joy and so spread His fragrance of peace everywhere you go.

Please pray for our sisters and their families....

A very Happy Birthday and a Big God Bless [you] to our foundations in July and August:

SILIGUR, VIJAYAWADA & BRAVINGTON (London), PAPUA, COCOROTE, TAIZE [Taiz in Yemen], MAURITIUS, HODEIDAH, VARANASI, COIMBATORE, SHIVPUR, ROME, and BHAGALPUR....

God bless you
Mother

MGL 119. 10TH SEPTEMBER 1975

+ L.D.M.

10th September 1975

My dearest SM. Agnes, SM. Gertrude, SM. Dorothy,
SM. Clare, SM. Bernard, SM. Laetitia, SM. Francesca,
SM. Florence, SM. Margaret Mary:

After God and Our Lady, Mother wants to thank each one of you for your constant fidelity and loyalty—especially for [the] blind trust with which you followed, without knowing if the Society will live or die. There was nothing to guarantee the future. All these years of hard labour borne with so much joy; all these years of love and service to the Poorest of the
Mt 7:24–25 Poor—and it is with you all and through you that Jesus laid the foundation of the Society on solid Rock—Humility and Love.

All you others: 1100—Who have followed so generously in the footsteps of the First Group—God love you and keep you to the end of your life, deeply rooted in His Heart.

All those loved Sisters who have spent a good part of their lives in the Society and for some reason had to leave—to each one of them: God love you for the love you have given, for the work you have done with so much love, for the joy you have spread.

Also thanks for our Sisters who after finishing their work on Earth—were taken Home to Heaven to intercede for us.

The Last but not the least, I owe deep gratitude to our loyal and faithful Councillors, who, with so much fidelity and blind obedience, have served the Society—in spite of the times when it was difficult to obey.

Loving thanks to each of our Novice Mistresses, Postulant and Aspirant Mistresses and Tertian Mistresses—who spend loving hours in teaching and instilling into the hearts of our Sisters, the true spirit.

All you—Regionals, young and old Superiors—Who so bravely and so lovingly bear the burden of the Society, in spite of your age and inexperience: God Love you for the love you give to your Sisters and to me.

During these 25 years, times have been joyful and hard—we have together worked for Jesus and with Jesus, always with Mary, the Cause of our Joy, by our side. Let us thank God for all [His] Gifts and promise we will make our Society SOMETHING BEAUTIFUL FOR GOD.

I had written to all the Bishops under whom our Sisters are working—it is most beautiful what they write back. I do hope we will be able to put everything together and let you share them.

Another thing which is very wonderful is the way the different religious bodies have accepted to have the prayer for thanksgiving with their people in their own places, in Calcutta.[a] I will try to get the translation and put it all together and send it to you.

A VERY HAPPY BIRTHDAY AND A BIG GOD BLESS YOU TO:

BOMBAY, TABORA; HOWRAH; TAKDAH; GREEN PARK [and] SHISHU BHAVAN....

I am sure you will all be very happy to hear that on the 26th August Ahmedabad house was opened....

Also a house in Howrah....

On the 15th Sept. the Sisters will be going to Dumka....

God bless you
Mother

ED 25. 10TH SEPTEMBER 1975

10th September 1975

The best way to show our gratitude to God and people is to accept everything with a smile. A joyful sister is like the Sunshine of God's love, the Hope of Eternal happiness, the flame of burning love.

God bless you
Mother

a. In a very innovative manner, Mother Teresa invited the various religious groups in Calcutta, Christian denominations as well as representatives of other religions (Hindus, Buddhists, Jains, Jews, Parsis, Muslims), to hold prayer services in their own churches and temples in thanksgiving to God for the existence and work of the Missionaries of Charity. The program was published in the local newspapers. Mother, accompanied by a Sister or by a few Sisters, participated in these prayer gatherings.

MGL 120. 31ST OCTOBER 1975

+ L.D.M

Mother House
31st October 1975

My dearest Children,

I do not know how to thank God for all He has done for us during this month of thanksgiving. All the thanksgiving prayers offered throughout the world are really the best gift to God, to our Society and to each one of us. By the time this letter comes to you—Advent may begin. During this time of grace let us in a special way ask Our Lady to teach us: Her Silence, Her Kindness, Her Humility.

1. Silence of Mary speak to me—teach me how, with you and like
Lk 2:19, 51 you, I can learn to keep all things in my heart as you did; not
1 Thes 5:17 to answer back when accused or corrected as you did, to pray
always—in the silence of our hearts as you did.

Lk 1:39 2. Mary will teach us her Kindness: she went in haste to serve
Jn 2:3 Elizabeth, "They have no wine," she told Jesus. She met Jesus
carrying [the] cross.

We will learn from her this personal love—like her, let us be in haste to serve the poorest of the poor and each sister in our community.

Let us, like her, be aware of the needs of our poor and of our Sisters—be they spiritual or material, and do something, as she did. Let us, like her and with her, meet our poor—the sick, the lonely, the hungry, the naked, the homeless and each MC, and do the same thing like her.

3. She will teach us her Humility:

Lk 1:28, 38 Though full of grace—yet only the Handmaid of the Lord.
Lk 1:56 Though Mother of God—yet serving like a handmaid in the
house of Elizabeth.

Lk 1:28 Though Immaculately conceived: she meets Jesus humiliated,
Jn 19:25 carrying His Cross, and near the Cross she stands as one of us, a
sinner needing Redemption.

Like her—the greater are the graces we have received—let us, with greater and delicate love, touch the Lepers, the dying, the lonely, the unwanted.

Like her—let us not be ashamed or slow to do the humble works of the Society.

Like her—let us always accept the Cross in whatever way it may come.

Humility of the Heart of Mary fill my heart—teach me as Mt 11:29
you taught Jesus to be meek and humble of heart and so glorify Mt 5:16
our Father.

Let us during the three weeks of preparation for Christmas take each part, arrange Meditation, reading, vigils, adoration on the same point. Meditation on the Constitutions—prepared—will also help you to deepen your knowledge of these 3 gifts of God to our Society.

I will be with our Sisters in Rome for the retreat and the Profession on the 16th November. There will be 5 [Sisters taking] first vows and 2 final [vows] and 7 Postulants becoming Novices. So let us thank God. On my way back I will visit our sisters in [the] Middle East and Africa.

Pray for Mother.

God bless you,
Mother

1976

MGL 121. 22ND MARCH 1976

+ L.D.M.

Mother House
22nd March 1976

My dearest children,

As we enter Lent—the time of Christ's passion, let us enter into it with a humble open heart. It is a time of Prayer—deep personal Prayer and penance and also of sharing the Sacrifice of Jesus—by accepting deliberately and with joy the Sacrifice of:

Keeping our Virginity—Virgin
our Purity—Pure
our Chastity—Chaste.

To be holy is a simple duty for each one of us. For this we need to:

KNOW—LOVE—LIVE OUR VOW OF CHASTITY.

How to become holy through our Vows of Chastity?

1. By keeping our hearts free from all impurity and selfishness and so be able to love and live in His presence in our hearts and in
Mt 5:8 the hearts of others—for only the pure of heart can see God.
2. Mt 7:1; Jn 7:24 By keeping our Minds free from all untruthfulness, curious and
Jn 14:6 dangerous reading and rash judgments—and so allow Jesus the truth to dwell in us.
3. By keeping our touch free from all hurtful, destructive, impure touch of our own body and that of others—dangerous embraces and kisses—and so be able to touch ourselves and others with
Mt 8:3, 15; 9:29; 17:7 Christ's healing touch.

4. By keeping our Tongue free—from all idle gossip, indecent worldly talks, songs, destructive unbecoming conversations, carrying of tales and repetitions—and so be able to praise God and our neighbour.
5. By keeping our eyes free from all that is ugly and harmful—and so be able to see the Beauty of God in ourselves and others. Mt 6:22; Lk 11:34
6. By respecting our own Body—as the temple of God. 1 Cor 3:17; 6:19
7. By being Open to our Superiors and reserved with people, especially men and women who come to share the work with us.
8. By our sincerity and purity in our correspondence—never to send or receive a letter without permission.

By fervent fidelity to our life of prayer, penance and fidelity to our Constitutions, we will try to live each of these points, and make our meditation as often as possible during lent, on our Consecrated Chastity. Negligence of [our] life of prayer, penance and fidelity to the simple means to help us love Christ with undivided love in Chastity—has destroyed many a sister and will destroy you and me—if we are not [faithful], so use the means God gives us.

God bless you
Mother

MGL 122. [2ND] APRIL 1976

Mother House
[2nd] April 1976

My dearest children,

Thank God that Mother's last letter as preparation for Lent has helped each community.

This time I want to draw the attention of each one [to] Poverty, and you must help each other and Mother also.

Everywhere—money matters are becoming a concern—therefore, be very strict with spending—cut down any expense which is not so necessary. Money received as donation or rubbish[a] or otherwise must be carefully entered in the book to the last naya paisa; also receipts must be issued

a. "Rubbish money" refers to money received from the sale (and so recycling) of items such as plastic, cardboard, etc. Later, the Sisters would give these items to poor families so they could sell them.

with the date. There are very strict rules passed by the Government regarding the money received and spent.

No Sister must beg from outside India or write begging letters. Please do not accept anything from any organization without giving a receipt, nor allow anybody to ask or beg for you and use your name, nor bring up a show or any such thing without my written permission.[a] Do not sign any papers, nor documents without my written permission. [For] any dealings with the government, please contact your Regional.

In a number of houses the Sisters keep on buying all kind of things for use at Mass. For Holy Mass, you need use only two candle sticks or holders. Now we can use even the glass containers—therefore, please do not make wooden or brass candlesticks. The two of the Mass and the two more for Adoration—4 are enough. I have already written that no brass things be used in our Chapel.

There should be Holy Water in every Chapel, and the Visitor should sprinkle Holy Water in the dormitory when she says: "Praised be Jesus Christ."[b] Every Sister must be in bed—the latest [by] 10 P.M. . . .

Avoid travelling expenses and, as before[c]—Wherever you can walk, do so, or find a cheaper way [to travel]. Same for letter-writing—even for me do not send individual letters—put as many as possible in one envelope. All letters asking for Renewal of Vows should be put together in every house.

For the present, do not buy any spiritual books, but try to share with close-by communities as much as possible.

The new breviary, or the "Prayer of the Church," must not be accepted—not even as a gift—not even One Copy;[d] neither a TV set for Nirmal Hriday or Shishu Bhavan.

There is absolutely no necessity to have and to beg for a big clock for the Chapel. The Mother House also does not need it. We can always

a. To "bring up a show" means to put on some form of entertainment program for fundraising purposes.

b. The "Visitor" Sister rings the last bell at 9:40 P.M., blesses each bed in the Sisters' dormitory, and says, as the last common prayer, "Praised be Jesus Christ," to which the others respond, "Amen."

c. Mother inserted an asterisk here, linked to an added phrase: "Not even [the] Superior should travel without permission."

d. In her concern to safeguard the poverty and simplicity of the congregation, Mother wanted the Sisters to use the old Divine Office books. Eventually (in the 1980s) this decision was changed. Praying from the new Divine office book was implemented first in the houses outside of India, while the novices in Calcutta would use up the old books. After the General Chapter of 1990, the whole Society, including the houses in India, started using the new Divine Office book. Among the reasons that Mother accepted the use of the new books was the inability to find the old books that contained different texts, and ultimately the desire to be in union with the universal Church in praying the new, officially approved version of the Liturgy of the Hours.

manage with a time-piece[a]—as we have done all these years. Many houses have bought or begged for such clocks after seeing Mother House.

More and more Sisters are having the new kind of sandals with high heels and using different, even leather, handbags and suitcases—under the cover of the work. Cameras are kept and taken from house to house as a personal belonging.

Tea time—only tea except Thursday and Sunday and Feast days.

Let each one protect herself from becoming a slave to riches—and get suffocated with the food of the rich. Let us renew our fidelity to the Poverty we have chosen and for which we have become MCs. All this was our Strength before—let us help each other again.

We will write letters to our Sick & Suffering Co-workers and the Contemplative Community that has adopted the house where we are—only twice a year: at Easter and Christmas. Send your letters to Sick & Suffering Co-workers to Jacqueline de Decker,[b] . . . and for the Contemplative Nuns you may write directly but as a community only. Both these are a spiritual exchange of love, prayer, suffering and work—a most beautiful gift—which we must not spoil by asking for material things. (This letter must be read point by point and decided together as a whole Community).

N.B. Kindly send the list of the Sisters in your Community and the work they are doing.

God bless you
Mother

a. Time-piece refers to the table (alarm) clock, in distinction from a wall clock, which Mother considered unnecessary at the time.

b. Jacqueline de Decker (1913–2009) was a Belgian social worker, who, in 1948, while on a "working" visit to India, was introduced to Mother. At the time, Mother was learning the rudiments of medical care from the Medical Mission Sisters in Patna, Bihar. The two were drawn to each other by their love for Jesus and a common desire to help the poor. But a severe spinal disease forced Jacqueline de Decker to return home, making it impossible for her to join the just-formed Missionaries of Charity. Mother then asked her to become her "second self," that is, to be united with her as her spiritual sister, offering her sufferings to God for the fruitfulness of her work for the salvation and sanctification of the poorest of the poor. Jacqueline accepted Mother's invitation to the role, later called "Sick and Suffering Co-worker," and eventually took up the task of promoting for the sick this apostolate of prayer and offering of one's suffering, linking each "Sick and Suffering Co-Worker" with an individual Missionary of Charity.

MGL 123. 8th JULY 1976

+

L.D.M.

New York
8th July 1976

My Dearest Children,

I have been away in body from the Mother House and India and from each of our houses throughout the world except New York—where I am now. But I don't think distance is an obstacle for me to be with you and near each one of you, for love has no frontiers nor space, and in the Heart
Rom 8:35, 38–39 of Jesus we are One. There in the Heart of Jesus nothing will nor can separate us from the love of Christ for each other.

We have every reason to be the Happiest people in the World. To be the happiest, we have to belong to Jesus fully without any reservations [*and in total surrender*]—for He alone is worthy of our love. If we really belong fully to Him, then we must be at His disposal—that He may be free to use us and do with us whenever and whatever He [*wants*]—through our Superiors, whoever they may be. They are the instruments of His will. They may be people we like or dislike, they may be clever and highly gifted, or they may not be so, they may be of any nationality, they may be holy or not so holy—it makes no difference to us. The only thing that mat-
Lk 10:16 ters is our conviction that they are the instruments of God's Will for us
Phil 2:8; Heb 10:7, 9 and that we are infallible in obeying them.—Through our cheerful, constant and prompt obedience, we relive Christ's obedience [*to His Father*].

Lk 1:26–38 As it was in the case of Our Lady—the angel Gabriel and St. Joseph the
Mt 2:13–23 carpenter were the instruments of God's Will for her, therefore [follows] her
Lk 1:38 prompt obedience—"Be it done to me according to Thy Will." In the message of the Angel, God spoke His Will. We, too, like Her, will be pleasing to God and become carriers of His Love as she was, if we, too, like her, accept with humility and joy the message of God spoken through our Superiors.

Obedience well lived frees us from selfishness and pride, and so it helps us to find God and, in Him, the whole world. Obedience is a special grace, and it produces unfailing peace, inward joy and close union with God.

Obedience transforms small commonplace things and occupations into acts of living faith, and Faith in action is love, and love in action is Service of the Loving God. Obedience, lived with joy, creates a living awareness of the Presence of God, and so fidelity to acts of obedience—such as the bell, time table, eating of food, etc., that are the fruit of constant, prompt, cheerful, undivided obedience—become like drops of oil that keep the Light of Jesus living in our life.[a] Mt 25:1–13

If we really want to grow in holiness—Obedience is the sure way—let us turn constantly to Our Lady to teach us how to obey, to Jesus, Who was obedient unto death. "He, being God, went down and was subject to them." Phil 2:8 Lk 2:51

If we really want to obey, we must learn first to love those who have to obey us, and also whom we have to obey. For both Superiors and Subjects give and receive from each other and through each other many graces. Every Superior, if she really loves her Sisters, must herself live in the Presence of God by obeying humbly, constantly, cheerfully her higher Superiors. Only then she can, in all humility and faith, give orders and expect the same obedience from her Sisters.

Each Sister who is really concerned and convinced of her Belonging to Christ as her Vocation, will find obedience as the greatest means of growing in holiness and living in the constant Presence of God. She will love her Superior with a deep and sincere humility because she is a sure instrument of God's own Will in day-to-day life. Therefore, a Sister who lives this life of constant, cheerful, prompt, undivided obedience is like a Sunshine of God's Love in the community, the Hope of Eternal happiness to the Poor and the flame of burning love before the Eucharistic Lord, where in an act of obedience to the Father, they [*both together*] share in the Redemption [*of mankind*].

As preparation for the feast of our Society, I ask you my dear children, that each one of us really learn this Constant, Cheerful, Prompt and Undivided obedience during the coming days. Let us make our community really something beautiful for God, where the Superiors and the Sisters are one heart full of love.

I am hoping to be with you for our Feast,[b] but in case Jesus has other plans for me, my love and prayer and everything that is beautiful in me is all for you—for each one of you.

a. The handwritten draft has "Light Jesus"; however, the typed version, which is the official version sent to the houses, has "Light of Jesus," which is an obvious correction. Further, in a few instances where Mother abbreviated a word, the Sister typist chose to spell it out. We have respected this choice here. The typist also corrected some of Mother's irregular capitalization; however, we have restored it here in order to be more faithful to her style. For the reproduction of the handwritten draft of this letter as well as the typed version that was sent to the houses, please see Appendix C, pp. 544–49. The last page of the draft of this letter contains directives to Sr. Joseph Michael to prepare the letter for the houses.

b. Mother is referring to 22nd August, for the Missionaries of Charity the feast of the Immaculate Heart of Mary and the "Society Feast," that is, the patronal feast day.

I am just longing to be back, but, like you, I have also to obey, cheerfully and with undivided Love. This Sacrifice will help us all to grow in holiness.

Pray for Mother as I do for each one of you.

"SISTERS OF THE WORD"[a]

God's gift to the people of the United States of America, as a Love memorial of the 41st Eucharistic Congress,[b] and to the world. . . .

On the Feast of the Sacred Heart of Jesus, His Eminence Cardinal Cooke,[c] in the presence of Mother Teresa and others, blessed and offered to the Sacred Heart of Jesus [with Love and Reparation][d] the new born Contemplative branch of the Missionaries of Charity—to be known as "Sisters of the Word."[e]

The Sisters will live the Word of God in Eucharistic adoration and Contemplation, and will proclaim the Word to the people of God—and so,
Jn 1:14 with Mary, Mother of the Church, bring the Word made Flesh [to] dwell in the hearts of all men.

Let us praise God for His great gift of the Sisters of the Word. Sr. M. Nirmala will be in charge—there are 3 postulants with [her]. . . .

God bless you
Mother

MGL 124. 19TH JULY 1976

LDM

19th July 1976

My dearest children, Sr. M. Agnes & all in the Mother House—

I hope you got all the letters I have been writing, especially the general letter. . . .

a. After her letter was already typed and photocopied, Mother added this section with the information about the founding of our contemplative branch. The Sister typist typed this section on already photocopied pages using carbon paper.

b. The 41st International Eucharistic Congress, held in Philadelphia from 1st to 8th August 1976, had for its theme, "Jesus, the Bread of Life."

c. Cardinal Terence J. Cooke (1921–1983) was appointed archbishop of New York in 1968 and named cardinal in 1969; he served in that office until his death.

d. "with Love and Reparation" was written at the end of the sentence; however, the sentence is more understandable and better accords with Mother's mind when this phrase is placed after "offered to the Sacred Heart of Jesus."

e. Mother founded the branch of our contemplative Sisters on 25th June 1976 with Sr. M. Nirmala, MC, as co-foundress. It was initially called "Sisters of the Word," but this name was changed to "Missionaries of Charity Contemplatives" in August 1977 (see MGL 128 of 21st August 1977, p. 225).

By now you must have heard that I had a small operation on [my] leg—below the knee—for some time there has been a growth growing. Thank God it has nothing to do with cancer, so don't get excited. It is already getting better—and by the time I get home,[a] it will be healed completely.—

We have a beautiful group of Aspirants in New York. . . . In Rome they have 9 postulants and 38 Novices & 3 Tertians.

. . .

I hope all are well at the MH [Mother House] and that there is love, peace and joy among you, for without it—there is no meaning in all the Sacrifice I have to make for you.

God bless you
Mother

ED 26. 23RD SEPTEMBER 1976

LDM

23rd September 1976

My dearest Children,

Today more than ever we need to know and pray

for the Light to know the Will of God
for the Love to accept the Will of God
for the Way to do the Will of God.

This doing of the will of God is OBEDIENCE. Jesus came to do the will of His Father and did it unto death—death on the Cross. "Be it done to me according to your will," was Our Lady's answer. For you and for me who have been chosen to be His own by becoming MCs, the surest way to true holiness and [*the*] fulfilment of our Mission of Love, Peace, and Joy,—is through Obedience. Heb 10:7, 9; Phil 2:8 Lk 1:38

During the month of October, let us grow in personal love for Our Lady through the Rosary—especially—to pray the Rosary in the Streets—an act of obedience—a gift for Our Lady.

God bless you,
Mother

a. That is, to Mother House.

1977

MGL 125. 3RD JANUARY 1977

3rd January 1977

My dearest Children,

Today is already the 3rd day of the New Year. Though you may be tired, but refreshed with the graces you have each received from the Child Jesus and His Blessed Mother,—I am sure, you have all started the year with greater love and peace, unity and joy. My prayer for each and every single Sister has been a constant offering—that during this year we use all our spiritual and temporal gifts to become Holy—because Jesus our Spouse is Holy.

Mt 6:5–13; Lk 11:13 To become Holy we need Humility and Prayer. Jesus taught us how
Mt 11:29 to pray, and He also told us to learn from Him to be meek and humble of heart. Neither of this we can do unless we know what is SILENCE. Both Humility and Prayer grow from a heart, mind and tongue that has lived in
Hos 2:14 silence with God, for in the Silence of the heart God speaks.

For JANUARY we shall take THE SILENCE OF MARY: Silence of the Tongue:

TO PROCLAIM CHRIST

1. I will speak	—of the beautiful things I find in each of my Sisters.
2. I will not speak	—a) of the faults of my Sisters, nor excuse [myself] or repeat when blamed for something I have not done, but will give a big smile.
	—b) of the Community life and happenings to the people outside of our community.
	—*c) any other language but English in com. [community]*[a]
3. During this month:	—Reading, Meditation, Vigil, Instruction, Examen of Conscience, Shared Prayer, Adoration—all connected with Silence.

I shall be [going]...to Manila....From there I will go to Papua and

a. Mother added this point in her handwriting to the typed letter.

Australia, if possible. Just as we have given up Ostia,[a] we shall be giving up also: Green Vale [sic]—the Jesuits will be taking care of the Home....[b]

No Sister, not even the Superior, should write to the Co-workers or anybody outside of India for money or things before asking me or the Regional, because we have to declare everything to the Government.

Any big repairs where money has to be used, you must get a written permission from your Regional.

No Superior or any Sister should go out alone anywhere—nor without permission. Even the Superior must let the assistant know where she is going, and if the assistant is going with her, the next senior Sister.

There must be no big feeding nor entertainment and people invited and priests and nuns fed for Superior's feast, nor any other feast such as Renewal of Vows.

Renewal of general permissions with speaking of faults must be done by the 7th of each month. It is the responsibility of each Sister to do it in time.

God bless you
Mother

MGL 126. 8TH APRIL 1977

Good Friday
8th April 1977

My dearest Children,

Today Jesus on the Cross had bent His Head to Kiss you. Jn 19:30
Today Jesus had His Arms extended to Embrace you. Mt 27:35; Mk 15:5; Lk 23:33; Jn 19:18
Today Jesus' Heart was opened to Receive you.[113] Jn 19:34

Were you there?

a. The community in Ostia (Italy) was opened on 21st October 1973 and closed in January 1977. The Sisters were taking care of poor families and had a day crèche for the poor children. With time, two other congregations of nuns came (Salesian and Canossian Sisters) and began apostolates with the families and with the children. Since our poor children needed proper schooling, Mother handed over the work to these religious congregations that could provide better education for them; in this way the MCs left Ostia.

b. Mother opened a home for alcoholic men in Greenvale (Victoria, Australia) on 28th May 1974. The home was handed over to the Jesuits in January 1977, as they could help the men in a better way with organized workshops and programs, while the Sisters could continue to search for others in need and offer immediate and effective service.

And for tomorrow I, and everyone in the Mother House, wish you:

Mt 28:8; Lk 24:41, 52; The Joy of the Risen Jesus
Jn 20:20 The Joy of Jesus is the Sunshine of His Father's Love
The Joy of Jesus is the Hope of Eternal Happiness
The Joy of Jesus is the Flame of Burning Love

Easter is this Joy, and I wish you, my Children—His Joy. You cannot have Joy without Sacrifice—that is why Good Friday comes before Easter. Love for one another—is this Joy—they will know you are Mine—by the
Jn 13:35 love you have for one another.

How clear are the words of Jesus. This year, My Sisters, we will all try
Jn 15:11; 17:13 to grow in holiness through Love for one Another—by sharing the Joy of
Jer 31:3 Jesus. "I have loved you with an Everlasting Love."—"Love one another as
Jn 13:34; 15:12 I have loved you." No more—No less.

Do my Sisters in the Community—my Superior—know my love?
Do they recognise His love in me?
Can the people say—See how they love one another.

Jn 3:16 For Love, to be true, has to hurt. "God loved the world so much that He
gave his Son." His Son loved the world so much that He gave His life. And
Jn 15:9 Jesus says: "As the Father has loved me (by giving Me to the world)—I
Jn 13:34; 15:12 have loved you (by giving my life for you)." "Love as I have loved you" (by giving yourselves). This giving is Prayer, the Sacrifice of Chastity, Poverty, Obedience and Whole-hearted, Free Service.

My Sisters, the Vows bind us to our Sisters. Are the Vows alive in my life—or are they written in the book only? They are meant to be a bond of Love and Unity. To live the Constitutions together—is to live in Love with one another. Let this be not only words. Let us do—this love—

I will be a Cause of Joy in my Community:

1. I will speak well of everybody.
2. I will smile at everybody I meet.
3. I will deliberately every day make 3 real acts of love to my Sisters.
4. If I offend anyone, even if it be a little child or an Aspirant—I will ask for Pardon before I go to bed.
5. I will confess any deliberate sin, however small, against Charity and will speak my faults immediately before I go to bed.
6. I will read, meditate, speak of this love for one another.

God still keeps on loving the world by giving you to the Poor and Jesus still keeps on loving the world by giving His Body as the Bread of Life— and we too will keep [on] loving our Poor by giving ourselves to them through our wholehearted Free Service. Jn 6:35, 48, 51

Let the Superiors prepare their Instruction, their chapters on this Love for one another—and ask the Confessors to do the same. Let also the Instructions we give to the people and children be the same.

This is the Joy of the Risen Jesus I wish for each one of you,—that you love one another as Jesus and Mother love you. Mt 28:8; Lk 24:41, 52; Jn 20:20 Jn 13:34; 15:12

A Big Thank You to each one of you for your loving letters and wishes for Easter.

You will all be very happy and grateful to God to have given us Kerema. . . .[a]

In Tabora, the New Noviciate was started with 7 Novices, and Sr. M. Aloysia as their Mistress, and 19 Postulants with Sr. M. Joanna.

God bless you
Mother

ED 27. EASTER 1977

Easter 1977

A Joyful heart is the normal result of a heart burning with love, for she gives most who gives with joy.

God loves a Cheerful giver. A Sister filled with joy preaches without preaching. 2 Cor 9:7

Happy and Holy Easter to each one.

God bless you
Mother

a. Mother is referring to a new foundation in the city of Kerema, Papua New Guinea.

MGL 127. 1ST JUNE 1977

Mother House
1st June 1977

My dearest Children,

You have been all preparing for the Feast of the Sacred Heart of Jesus with so much love and care. I am sure many blessings will come to each
Jn 19:27 one of us through Mary, His Mother and Ours.

I am leaving India for Rome, England, Venezuela, Mexico, Guatemala, New York—so pray for Mother that I give only Jesus everywhere I go. During my absence SM. Agnes takes my place.

As many houses have been sending in their accounts very late, and because of this we have been in trouble, I would like you all to close up accounts by the 30th or 31st of each month. Count up how much you have in the House and in the Bank and post your account sheet to Calcutta on the 2nd of the month. Please take this as a very serious duty. All foreign cheques should be sent to the Mother House, and all foreign cash should be kept with you and sent to Calcutta through any sisters going there. We should be very careful not to make up accounts at the end of the month. It is just like stealing. If money is missing, write down how much each month. It is sinful just to add the amount somewhere and so complete your account. It should be a matter of conscience. Remember that written permission from Mother or the Councillor concerned is required each time for any project to get money or things or to have functions or taking photos to raise money. Written permission is also required for accepting any land or building for the work or the sisters.

Since the Congregation keeps on growing, we have decided to divide the regions into smaller groups under an Acting Regional, who in turn will be under a Councillor. All business matters regarding the work and the house and renewal of general permission will in future be done by the Superiors with the Acting Regional. The same trust, love and respect given to Mother and the Councillors should be given to the Acting Regional. The Acting Regional will deal directly with the appointed Councillor in all matters. Hence it will not be necessary for the acting Regional to visit the houses. In case of emergency, the acting Regional should immediately contact the Councillor concerned. . . .[a]

SM. Frederick has returned to Rome and will continue as Regional in

a. A list of the Sisters and the mission houses entrusted to their care has been omitted. By 1977, there were 69 foundations in India and 40 abroad, served by 895 active Sisters and 388 novices.

our houses in [the] Middle East, Europe, USA, Central America and South America. We are all very sorry to miss her from the Mother House, but we must do the things that are pleasing to the Father. We are all very happy to have SM. Stella back in the Mother House after so many years.

On the 31st May a new house was opened in Shawri Village near Bhagalpur....

God bless you
Mother

MGL 128. 21ST AUGUST 1977

+ L.D.M.

On the way to Addis Ababa
21st August 1977

My dearest Children, Sr. M. Agnes and All,

Happy and Holy Feast of the Society and God's Special Blessing on Nirmal Hriday on its Silver Jubilee—twenty-five years of love and compassion in service and sharing of Joy and Peace.

As the news of Addis Ababa is not good, I felt it was necessary to be with our Sisters—also to open Dire Dawa if possible.[a]

The Sisters everywhere are well and doing God's work with great love. On the 15th August we opened in Rotterdam....

On the 5th August we started Haiti....

On the 8th June we opened East End [London]....

I hope you will write to our Sisters in these our new houses and welcome them. I hope you have done so to the houses in India, Kerema and Manila.

I am sure you will be very happy and thank God for His Goodness to our Society—when you come to know that "Sisters of the Word" are no longer called by that name—just simply "MC Contemplative". This change has brought great joy into every heart.

On the 3rd June, Cardinal Polletti[b] blessed the small beginning of the Contemplative Brothers. All together we complete the Unity of Bread and Wine.

For the protection of each one of us and the Society as a whole,

a. In July 1977 war broke out between Ethiopia and Somalia and lasted until March 1978. Mother opened the house in Dire Dawa on 28th August 1977.

b. Cardinal Ugo Poletti (1914–1997), named cardinal in 1973, served as Vicar General of Rome from 1973 to 1991.

together with all the Co-workers of the whole world, we shall pray the prayer of St. Michael the Archangel (from the old prayer book). Say it after the prayer for the Holy Father at Midday. Now more than ever we need
Jn 13:34; 15:9; 1 Jn 3:23; 2 Jn 1:5 to put into life the teaching of Jesus "Love one another as the Father has loved Me." To think that we have to love as the Father loves His Son—Jesus, with all the Mercy and Compassion, Joy and Peace. Try each one for yourself to find out how the Father loves His Son and then put that into your life in loving one another. Find out in all humility how you are loved by Jesus; from the time you have realized that you are loved by Jesus—
Jn 13:34; 15:12 love as He loves you.

Mt 26:26; Mk 14:22; Lk 22:19; Jn 6:35, 48; 1 Cor 11:24 In each of our lives Jesus comes as Bread of Life—to be eaten, to be consumed by us. This is how He loves us.—And then Jesus comes in our Human Life as the Hungry One, The Other—hoping to be fed with the bread of our life, [of] our hearts, by loving, [of] our hands, by serving.—And in so
Gn 1:27 doing we prove that we have been created in the likeness of God[a]—for God
1 Jn 4:8; 16 is Love and when we love we are like God.—And this is what Jesus meant
Mt 5:48 when He said: "Be you perfect as your Father in Heaven is perfect."

Jn 15:16 Jesus has chosen us for Himself. We belong to Him. Let us so be con-
Rom 8:35; 38–39 vinced of this "Belonging" that we do not allow nor accept anything however small to separate us from this belonging—from this Love.

Let us during this month of September, when we celebrate 4 feasts of Our Lady:

8th—Birthday	15th—Sorrows
12th—Name Feastday	24th—Compassion

learn from Her: Humility, Purity, Sharing, Thoughtfulness.

Mt 17:8; Mk 9:8 We will then, like Her, become holy.—People will be able to look up and see only Jesus.—The Light of example will be only Jesus, and so we
2 Cor 2:14 will be able to spread His fragrance everywhere we go. He will be able
Mt 5:16 to flood our souls with His Spirit and so in us, through us, and with us, Glorify the Father.

I hope you are all well and that each one of you [is] sincerely trying to live the life and do the work of a true MC. Let us not forget that the Society has the power to lead us to the perfect love of God and neighbour and so make us become the presence of the Church in the world today.[b]

a. The meaning is: In feeding Him, in loving Him, in serving Him, we prove that we have been created in the likeness of God.

b. Mother is referring to the vow formula of the Missionaries of Charity.

To be able to be all for Jesus—let our Purity be pure, for only then we will be blessed and will see God. Mt 5:8

Let us pray our prayers
Live our Lives with and for Jesus
Serve our Poor with greater Love
and so become true MCs.

God bless you
Mother

. . .

MGL 129. 9TH OCTOBER 1977

Mother House
9th October 1977

My dearest Children,

During this month of Our Lady, and also during the whole of November as preparation for the great feast of 8th December, we will grow in holiness through deepening our personal love for Our Lady, especially praying the Rosary with better understanding love in the streets and when travelling. I hope you all realize that it is by our Fidelity to the simple and sincere life of prayer and action, [that] we proclaim Jesus Christ to all the Mt 28:19
nations and so make the Church fully present in the world of today.

According to our Constitution 8,[a] each one has a Constitution book for her own use and must read herself every day at spiritual reading time, and make meditation on it once a week. It is not enough that one Sister reads for the whole Community. Are you faithful to this Rule?

"The Sisters who desire to renew their Vows shall apply in writing to the Superior General at least three months before their expiration" (Chapter on Consecration: Practical Application no. 2). A number of Sisters are careless on this point. Also in future, all the Sisters wishing to renew their Vows must send in their letter in one envelope from the same house.

Many Sisters are wearing their saris in a worldly way. The sari should not touch the ground nor have so [many] gathers around the waist.[b] The forehead should be half covered with the headpiece and the hair should not be seen. . . .

a. Mother is referring to the 1973 *Constitutions*; this is no. 271 in the 1988 *Constitutions*.
b. The meaning is pleats or folds (kuchies).

All letters to and from our own family will be given and received closed, and no other letters to relatives, friends etc. should be enclosed in their letter without permission. All letters except those of our own family will be given and received opened. No letters, not even [to] your own family, must be posted by the Sister herself.

In one of my former letters I had written that no one should write directly to the Co-workers or even Sick and Suffering Co-workers and ask for help. Some Sisters have even asked for help for their relations. This becomes very difficult for Mother and the Co-workers, for each time a Sister writes to them they are surprised that the Sisters do not obey and have asked me to remind you.

Every month we have to send the Accounts to Delhi. Though I had asked you to send your Account by the 2nd of each month and to make sure it is correct, I do not understand why accounts are not coming and also some that come are not correct. This we owe to the Society. Therefore, once more, I ask you to send in your Account by the 2nd of each month and to make sure it is correct.

Any money whatsoever must be entered in the book and no money must be kept in your bag, not even [the] Superior. [The] Superior also must be very careful to enter everything she gets and spends.

Please do not give permission to people to raise money in our name. Always tell them to contact Mother House.

No Superior or any Sister must make a "project"[a] and ask money from the Bishop or priest or any organization in or outside India, for Leprosy work or any other work. Mother House for India, and Rome for outside India, holds itself responsible for the money-part of the works of the Society. So please pay great attention to this point, as this is a very grave matter. A Superior may be removed from office if she does not abide by this.

No Superior or Sister should go to any of our other houses without previous permission from Mother.

Superiors should not take on themselves to visit new places for the sake of making new foundations. All work regarding foundations must be directly dealt with [by] Mother House.

We must help our Society to grow in Holiness by our fidelity to the Spirit of Total Surrender, Loving Trust and Cheerfulness.

a. "Project" here refers to any work that is not directly an MC apostolate with the poor but involves other individuals and/or organizations and which has its own independent funding, usually solicited through some form of fundraising, publicity or advertising campaigns.

On the 1st November we are celebrating the Silver Jubilee of Nirmal Hriday. On that day we are going to feed and entertain our people in our Homes. You also do it for the children and patients, if you have a Nirmal Hriday, Shishu Bhavan or Leprosy Home.

Sr. M. Gertrude is back in the Mother House. We are all happy to have her. She is taking care of the 43 Novices preparing for their First Vows, and Sr. M. Paulette is helping her. The novices are delighted to have one of the First [Group] Sisters to prepare them.

I would like every house to send me, immediately, the name of each sister including the Superior and what work she is doing and what work needs replacement due to the Sisters coming for Tertianship or because a sister needs a change for some reason. As I need this to enable me to make the changes, please write at once. Also those who did not send the Accounts to Mother House or Rome please do it immediately.

Enclosed is the Statistic Sheet for the year October 1976—October 1977. Please fill in and return with your account sheet by the 2nd November.

God bless you
Mother

P.S.: . . .

Spiritual Reading is a community exercise and should therefore be made as a community.

Fr. W. Doyle made a Sacrifice and did not cross his legs when sitting on a chair—let us do the same.[a]

ED 28. OCTOBER 1977

October 1977

My dearest children,

Let us deepen our love for our Constitutions, for they will lead us to the perfect love of God and our neighbour, and through the fidelity to the apostolate of prayer and action we will proclaim Jesus Christ to all nations Mt 28:19
and so make the Church fully present in the world of today.

a. This sentence was added at the end of the letter and is in Mother's handwriting. Irish Jesuit Father William Doyle (1873–1917) made numerous private vows, as he found this practice a help in keeping his resolutions. One such vow was: "I deliberately vow, and bind myself, under pain of mortal sin, to refuse Jesus no sacrifice, which I clearly see He is asking from me."

Let us help each other to grow in holiness through our Love for Our Lady by praying more fervently the Rosary especially in the streets.

1st decade—For our Aspirants and Postulants
2nd decade—For our Novices
3rd decade—For our Professed, Brothers and Sisters
4th decade—For our Poor and Co-Workers
5th decade—For the Holy Father and Our Society

God bless you
Mother

MGL 130. 19TH OCTOBER 1977

+

L.D.M.

Mother House
19th October 1977

In our Constitutions, in the Chapter on Penance, "The Cross—No
Jn 15:13 Greater Love," we have in the practical application that we pray the Our Fathers in the refectory with outstretched arms on the eve of Solemn Feasts of the Church besides Fridays.

. . .

God bless you
Mother

MGL 131. 16TH NOVEMBER 1977

Mother House
16th November 1977

My dearest Children,

We have much to thank God for [for] the many beautiful vocations he has given us. In our Constitutions we have that:

> "Candidates may be rich or poor or of any nationality provided they possess the above mentioned qualities." (Please read the whole of Constitution 208.)[a]

a. Constitution 208: "Candidates desirous to join the Society must be: Free of impediments; guided

Like the Professed Sisters and Novices, our Aspirants and Postulants are also giving whole-hearted free service. I would like the following points to be observed with regard to them; because they too like any of us are the poorest of the poor, according to the Constitutions.

1. In future we will not interview girls before they join, as the aspirancy is a time to "come and see", and also to avoid double expense.[a]
2. All letters will be answered from the Mother House only.
3. Aspirants must not be accepted or sent away without written permission from the Mother House.
4. In honour of the Trinity,[b] we will not ask the girls [desiring to join us] to bring more than Rs. 300/–, and if they bring less, we will not refuse them, because it is Jesus who chooses [them] to serve Him in His Poor.
5. They must be provided [for] by the house where they are in the same way as we provide for every sister.
6. The money they bring or not, be it more than Rs. 300/ or less, must not be used to pay for their petty expenses. All money must be used from the house where they are and no separate account kept but put under Sisters' A/C [account].
7. The money must be used only for the bedding and the saris and habit, and the balance will be kept in their packet. If they have to return home or leave on their own, things must be kept and the full amount returned.

Let us pray for them and do all we can to help our Aspirants and Postulants to love Jesus and to be faithful to Him to the end.

Our Constitution no. 192 says:

> The most appealing invitation to embrace the religious life is the witness of our own lives, the spirit in which we react to our divine calling, the

by the right intention; Desirous to serve the poor according to the *Constitutions*; [Desirous] to live and work as a Missionary of Charity; healthy in body and mind, and hence able to bear the hardships of this special vocation; able to acquire knowledge; of a cheerful disposition; able to exercise sound judgment. Physically handicapped candidates may also be admitted if they fulfil the above mentioned qualities" (1973 *Constitutions*). This is no. 230 in the 1988 *Constitutions*.

a. That is, so that the candidates do not have to spend money to come for an interview and after some months spend more money to come back for "come and see."

b. Mother liked to make connections with spiritual realities, so for example here she links the number three (300) with the Trinity.

completeness of our dedication, the generosity and cheerfulness of our service to God, the love we have for one another and the apostolic zeal with which we witness to Christ's love for the poorest of the poor.

By our own fidelity to our vocation we will help the girls who come to us to be faithful to Jesus to the end.

Every house should take means to help vocations through prayer, sacrifice and contact. To obtain many holy and fervent vocations, and as a special gift to Our Lady for the Feast of the Immaculate Conception on 8th December, we will:

1. Make the Novena by using the Litany of Our Lady at the beginning of Adoration.
2. Double our penances.
3. Keep the custody of our eyes so that our eyes may see with deep
Mt 25:40 faith Christ in others, especially in the distressing disguise of our Sisters and our Poor.
4. Not touch each other, even in jest—so that when it is necessary to do so, Jesus may put into our hands and [our] touch the healing power of His love.

Sr. M. Stella has been appointed to take care of Vocations. Therefore all matters regarding vocation—candidates applying, Aspirants, Postulants—must be dealt with [by] her.[a]

God bless you
Mother

ED 29. 13TH DECEMBER 1977

LDM

13th December 1977

My Dearest Children,

Jn 3:16 God loved the world so much that He gave His Son, Jesus, to be born
Heb 4:15 like us in all things except sin. Today God still loves the world by sending
us, each one of us, to be His Love and Compassion through prayer and

a. This sentence was handwritten (but not in Mother's handwriting) in the margin of the letter. The information was probably given too late to the Sister typist, who chose to handwrite it on the margin, as there was no more space on the bottom of the page.

action, that we may proclaim that God loves the world. By doing so, we make the Church fully present in the world of today.

My prayer and wishes for Christmas and New Year for each one of you [are] that you proclaim Christ by your love for each other, so that the people will know that you are His Disciples. Jn 13:35

God bless you
Mother

1978

MGL 132. 1ST FEBRUARY 1978

L.D.M.

Mother House
1st February 1978

My dearest Children,

Let us together thank God for His tender love and care during 1977, for all the good He has done in us, through us and with us, especially for the grace of perseverance up to today.

Let us thank our Poor for accepting our love—for giving us their love and trust.

Let us thank all the people who have shared the work with their hearts, hands and in kind.

Now that we are close to Lent, where with Jesus in His Poor we can
Mt 26–27; Mk 14–15; Lk 22–23; Jn 18–19 share His Passion—we cannot do the great fasts, except on every Friday in Lent we will go without the Midday Meal. [With] the money so saved, we will white-wash and repair the houses of our Poor. Each house should keep a separate box and put in the full amount of the midday meal.

The Holy Father on the 1st January said: "NO TO VIOLENCE, YES TO PEACE". Let us take this to heart in our Society in a very real way:

NO TO VIOLENCE WITH OUR TONGUE

Violence of the tongue is very real, sharper than any knife, wounding and creating bitterness that only the grace of God can heal. And so my Children, because we all love our Society, let us, in gratitude to the Society,

- for accepting us and giving us such wonderful opportunities of serving the Poor
- for all the time the Society gives us to spend in prayer and adoration and
- for the care and concern we receive continually,

show our gratitude to the Society in 1978 by our:

No to violence with our tongue
and Yes to peace—with our tongue.

We will control our temper by saying: "Jesus I love you—come into my heart now", and if a Sister is losing her temper, say: "Jesus I love you, go into her heart now."

Whenever you meet each other always give a smile, always ready to share, always happy to meet each other.

Never repeat to a Sister what you have heard about her. Sir 19:7–8

Do not listen to uncharitable words, nor repeat them; and

When your conscience needs to represent a matter, pray and make sure that you speak the Truth.

I feel with God's grace, we will make 1978 Something Beautiful for God. My Sisters, I beg you to remember: the tongue that receives the Body Jas 3:9–10
of Christ—how can it become an instrument of violence?

Be faithful to the hour of Adoration, and make sure that at least half an hour you spend in Silence—for it is meant to bring you closer to Jesus. If you deepen your prayer life, you will be able to grow in holiness and obtain many graces for the souls entrusted to your care. Remember, a pure heart will see God. How much we need this pure heart to be able to see Mt 5:8
God in each other especially in my Community, for love begins at home.

Let us more and more deepen that love for each other, by praying for each other, by respect and thoughtfulness shown in small things, by giving a helping hand without being asked, by sharing thoughts that you have received in prayer or reading.

These will be the means to say: YES TO PEACE.

To help us understand and help each other better, we have appointed Acting Regionals all over the Society. During the retreat—which will take place from the 19th February, for the Sisters in charge of Formation and Acting Regionals, Councillors and myself—I will then explain the role of our Regionals. Let us accept them with love and respect and as a blessing. They are meant to be a bond of love, unity and peace. Pray that this retreat will also help us to make 1978 Something Beautiful for God.

As I had said before, be careful about foreign money. Some Sisters are even involving their relations to receive money from the Co-workers or from the people of [their] place. No one should make projects, close or open centres, or ask for money from outside of India without first getting a written permission from your Regional. All money and Account matters in India should be dealt with [by] SM. Camillus; outside India, [by] SM. Frederick.

I am enclosing the grouping of the houses and their acting Regionals and Councillors.[a] Contact with the Mother House is to receive the spiritual guidance and help for the Superior and Community. These Sisters being our Councillors, the Sisters from the House have full freedom to write to them and give and receive closed letters.

Last year the following [14] foundations were made . . .

I am also giving the names of the Sisters who will send you every two months the good news of the Mother House.[b] I do hope you too will send your good news. I am so anxious to make the Society Something Beautiful for God, as our Constitutions say:

TO SPREAD THE "GOOD NEWS" FROM THE MOTHER HOUSE TO OUR HOUSES IN AND OUT OF INDIA EVERY 2 MONTHS.

. . .

Our Noviciate in Manila will begin with 13 Novices on the 2nd February, with Sr. Andrea as Mistress.

God bless you
Mother—

. . .

MGL 133. 20TH FEBRUARY 1978

+

LDM

Mother House
20th February 1978

My dearest children,

On the [evening of the] 19th, on the return from Bandel, where Sr. M. Vincentia and Sr. M. Stephen took the 50 girls for picnic, their truck met with an accident.

a. The full list of the houses (here) and a list of the 14 new foundations (below), their respective foundations dates, superiors and addresses have been omitted.

b. These Sisters were assigned to write the Mother House news to the particular mission houses mentioned in the list, where the Sisters were anxious to know about Mother and Mother House.

Sr. Vincentia died on the spot. Thirty girls and Sr. Stephen were badly hurt and injured.

Sr. Vincentia was a beautiful soul. She was the sunshine of God's love, the hope of eternal happiness and the flame of burning love. Let us thank God and rejoice that she has joined our Community in heaven. Let us pray for her family. Her brother and sister came for the funeral.

Look up Constitution 10 on the practical application on community life[a]—what each of us must to do for the repose of the soul of our dearest Sr. Vincentia.

God bless you
Mother

MGL 134. 20TH MARCH 1978

LDM

Zagreb
20th March 1978

My dearest Children,

All in and out of the Mother House,

This brings you Mother's love and blessing for a very happy and holy Easter.—Easter is one of the Feasts of our Society, Feast of joy—the joy of the Lord. Let nothing so disturb, so fill us with sorrow, discouragement as to make us forget the joy of the Resurrection. Jn 15:11; 17:13; Rom 14:17; 15:13

We arrived here after a day in Germany, Frankfurt.[b]—The Archbishop & many people were waiting for us.[c]—The forgotten language is slowly returning.[d] Fr. Gabrić is like my dictionary[e]—always stands near by—to give

a. Community Life, Practical Applications: no. 10: "On the death of a sister, our superiors without delay, inform all the other houses of the death, soliciting the suffrages of the Society for the deceased sister, which consists of Holy Mass, Way of the Cross and the Rosary three times, by each sister. She also informs the deceased's relatives" (1973 *Constitutions*). This corresponds with no. 80 of the 1988 *Constitutions*.

b. Mother is referring to herself and Fr. Ante Gabrić, SJ; they visited various cities in what was then Yugoslavia, as a part of the parish missions "Zagrebačka korizma 1978" (Lent 1978 in Zagreb).

c. Cardinal Franjo Kuharić (1919–2002) was archbishop of Zagreb, named cardinal in 1983, retired in 1997. He was instrumental in the opening of our houses in Zagreb and helped the Sisters and our poor very much. His cause of canonization began in 2012.

d. Mother is referring to Serbo-Croatian, the language she spoke in Skopje before joining the Loreto Sisters.

e. Fr. Ante Gabrić (1915–1988) was a Croatian Jesuit missionary who worked in West Bengal, India, from 20th October 1938 to the day of his death, 20th October 1988. With great zeal and self-sacrifice, he served the people in the Sundarbans, being especially solicitous to the poor and the sick. Fr. Gabrić introduced professional training (carpentry, embroidery, tailoring, etc.) to promote the economic improvement of the families. He helped Mother from the early years and closely collaborated with our

me the correct word.—People are really full of Faith. Trials have purified & strengthen[ed] them in their Faith. Thank God.

They had a Mission week—a kind of living renewal. Thousands have come to confession & Holy Com. [Communion].—The whole Archdiocese—40 Parishes have had this Mission from Sunday [to] Sat. [Saturday] [inclusive].

They are anxious to have the MCs in their midst, so pray if this be the Will of God.

I do hope—the joy of the retreat that our Sisters in formation & Regionals have just finished [is being shared]. What great graces each one of us received—let us share them with our Sisters.—You, my Children—ask
Mt 7:7 from them—& you will receive—Jesus.—Seek from [them] the knowledge of Jesus, & you will find it in them. Knock at their hearts—and they will open to you the treasures of God's love within them. We have so much to thank God for [for] our Sisters who are spending themselves for our young Sisters—to give them the knowledge of our Society, love for our Society and the way of life in our Society.—The best way we can thank our Sisters spending themselves for our young Sisters is to pray for them & to trust them.

I will write again as this has to go now. I will have a little time—I will be in Rome on Wed. 29th so please send all letters there & not to N.Y. [New York].

Mt 28:8; Lk 24:41, 52; Jn 20:20 Very Happy & Holy Easter.—May the risen Jesus be always with you in His Joy & Smile.

God bless you
Mother

Sisters, especially in Maria Polli community. His efforts to improve the lives of the Bengali people earned him the title of "Apostle of the Sundarbans." His cause for canonization was opened in Zagreb in 2015.

ED 30. MAY 1978

+

L.D.M

May 1978

This EK DIL, Mother speaks to us through the Holy Father's message: "This is the best. No need for more".

<u>HOLY FATHER'S MESSAGE:</u>

Remember always, beloved daughters in Christ, the value of your religious consecration. Through consecration to the Lord Jesus you respond to His Love, and discover the needs of His brothers and sisters throughout the world. This consecration, expressed through your vows, is the source of your joy and fulfilment. It is the secret of your supernatural contribution to the Kingdom of God. It is the measure of the effectiveness of your service to the poor, the guarantee that it will last. Yes, to belong to Christ Jesus is a great gift of God's Love. And may the world always see this love in your SMILE.

Pope Paul VI[a]
Rome 6.5.1978

MGL 135. 3RD JULY 1978

+

L.D.M.

Mother House
3rd July 1978

My dearest Children,

Let us thank God for all His Goodness to us [and], in us and through us, to His people. I hope very soon to go round to the houses and see each one of you, after such a long timc. Last Junc wc got a good number of Pos tulants. I hope you are all trying your best to get vocations for our Society.

This being the month of the Precious Blood, try to increase your love
for Holy Mass and the Passion of Christ by accepting with joy all the lit- Mt 26–27; Mk 14–15;
tle sacrifices that come daily. Do not bypass the small gifts, for they are Lk 22–23; Jn 18–19

a. This is part of the message addressed by Pope Paul VI on 6th May 1978 to the Co-workers who came to Rome for their national meeting and were received in audience in the Vatican. The beginning of the message is: "As we welcome the Co-workers of Mother Teresa and those whom they serve, our thoughts turn also to the Missionaries of Charity themselves, especially to the novices and those Sisters preparing for final vows, both in Rome and in Calcutta. Remember always, beloved daughters in Christ ..." www.vatican.va/holy_father/paul_vi/speeches/1978/may/document/hf_p-vi_spe_19780506_collaboratori-missionarie-calcutta_it.html.

precious for yourself and for others. During this month, we shall often pray this prayer: "In union with all the Masses being offered throughout the
Mt 11:29 world, I offer Thee my heart. Make it meek and humble like your heart."

If we are careful of Silence it will be so easy to pray and pray fervently. There is so much talk—so much repetition, so much carrying of tales in words and in writing. Our prayer life must suffer so much because our
Hos 2:14 hearts are not silent—for as you know "only in the Silence of the Heart—
Mt 12:34; Lk 6:45 God speaks," and only after we have listened we can speak from the fullness of our hearts—our heart full of grace, full of God.

During this month we will take: SILENCE and do our reading, meditation, examination of conscience and reflection during the day on it. The fruit of that Silence will be:

—improvement of our prayer life
—love for one another especially in my community.

Let us pray [and offer] the little things I will do for Jesus:

1. I will pray the Rosary in the street
2. I will read the Constitutions everyday
3. I will cut my hair fully
4. I will use the word "Sister" before the name
5. I will speak English and not use my own language
6. I will not answer back
7. I will not carry tales
8. I will genuflect in the chapel
9. I will observe Profound Silence with great care.[a]
10. I will not speak in the washing place, staircase, dormitory
11. I will use the words "May I" with great love
12. I will not cross my feet when sitting on a chair

All these we will offer to the Father daily during Holy Mass. What powerful graces we can obtain for the world, torn with so much hatred and bitterness.

a. Profound or Grand Silence is a period of more strict silence that begins after Night Prayers and ends after Mass, or after meditation when the Mass is later, of the following day. In order to foster prayerfulness and closer union with God, the Sisters are meant to respect times and places of silence; they are to speak only in the refectory during the meals or recreation, while at other times, all unnecessary conversation is to be avoided. During the apostolate, necessary conversation is permitted. During the times of Grand Silence, the Sisters make an extra effort to move about silently, with the light of the candles or low night lights, and to speak in a low voice only if there is a real emergency. Speaking at times of silence or in places where silence is strictly observed (for example, the dormitory) is called "breaking silence."

In our Nirmal Hriday and Shishu Bhavan I want you to have morning and evening prayer. Begin the Leprosy and Medical work with a prayer and put in a little more gentleness, a little more compassion with the sick. It will help you to remember that you are touching the Body of Christ. He is Hungry for that touch. Will you not give it?

In some of our houses, our Sisters are less and less doing the humble works of the Society by employing people to do their work, under the cover of giving work to the poor. What a foolish cover—you will lose the joy of being a true MC. In some places girls are used to wash even the Sisters' clothes. I feel shy to think of what is written in our Constitutions: that every MC is the Poorest of the Poor. Are you really one? If not, try to become one.

Cream coloured sandals are the fashion. I do not know how so many got them. The Hawaii slippers have disappeared or [are] left behind in the Mother House or the house you have just left. The same applies to umbrellas. We are losing something in our Society.[a]

I hear that in some houses, priests speak of our work as a waste of time, as spoiling the poor by giving [to] them just like that. Do not take the trouble to answer, but yourself be convinced that you have chosen to make the 4th Vow, and therefore, do not allow anyone to take away from you the Gift of God—our 4th Vow.

The whole Church has come to realize the need of teaching Catechism in Schools and Sunday Schools. Though we were the first to begin regular Sunday Schools, I find that our Sisters no longer prepare their classes of Catechism—no longer have a register, and so I believe in time we'll not be needed to go to the Sunday Schools, as others who are taking the trouble to prepare and teach will take your places.

At the Mother House, on Mondays at 6:45–7:20 P.M. we are having special classes for Sisters going to Sunday Schools, in English, Bengali and Hindi. They have been grouped as follows:

Adults and Big Children
First Communion and Confirmation
Pre-First Communion

a. In India, the Sisters were wearing simple (Bata) blue and white Hawaii slippers (flip-flops). Here, Mother is correcting the Sisters about their choice of fashionable slippers, and about their lack of poverty and responsibility in discarding their old, simple slippers (and umbrellas).

You too must take the trouble and make the time to prepare your classes according to the present mind of the Church.

. . .

All reports and letters of Aspirants and Postulants should be sent to Sr. Stella at the Mother House, the latest 3 months before joining the Postulancy or Noviciate. The place where Postulants will do their noviciate will be decided by Mother and her Councillors.

All matters regarding the Noviciate and Novices reports before taking first Vows must be sent three months before—to Sr. Henrietta, who will then prepare everything for Mother and her Councillors. Reports should be short and written with great love and respect for the Sister herself and her work—her life of prayer, faith, love and service, especially the humble works of the Society.

The Novices will receive their Names and Number in the Society with the Ceremony of Cutting of the Hair, two months before Profession. Therefore, Aspirants [and] Postulants will be called by their baptismal names.

All matters regarding Renewals should be directed to Sr. Martin de Porres. The Superior of the House must enclose a short report on Sister's fidelity to prayer, to her sharing with the Community, her cheerfulness in the service of the poor. Sister's letter and Superior's report must be in one envelope and should reach Calcutta at least 3 months before renewals. All this must be done with great respect and truth and treated confidentially.

Two months before a Sister goes down for her Tertianship,[a] the Superior should write a short report regarding her good and weak points and send them to Sr. Dorothy. The new Tertians should reach Calcutta soon after they have been replaced. They should finish their retreat before they renew their Vows.

Tertians home-visit will in future be arranged during the second six months of their tertianship and no more from the houses, but from Calcutta.

Const. [Constitution] 126 par. [paragraph] 2 on the Chapter, Apostolic Life says: "For protection and to help each other to fervour and zeal in the apostolic life, we go out with permission and with a Sister as a companion." Do I know and keep this Rule?

You will be happy to know that we have opened [eight] new houses...

a. In MC parlance, this refers to coming to Calcutta.

Send in your news for Ek Dil to Sr. Henrietta twice a year so that we can really know one another and share with one another. Some houses are neglecting to do this, and so it becomes difficult for Sisters to send out the Ek Dil.

New houses should send in their address and foundation date to Mother as soon as possible.

God bless you
Mother

ED 31. 12TH AUGUST 1978

LDM

12th August 1978

My dearest Children,

I can say nothing better than what our Holy Father, R.I.P., said on the 6th May 1978.[a]

The following is His message and blessing to each one of us.—Let us pray it, love it, live it—we shall then reach perfect love of God and our Neighbour and so make the Church fully present in the world of today.

God bless you.
Mother[b]

> Remember always, beloved daughters in Christ, the value of your religious consecration. Through your consecration to the Lord Jesus Christ, you respond to His love and discover the needs of His brothers and sisters throughout the world. This consecration, expressed through your vows, is the source of your joy and fulfilment. It is the secret of your supernatural contribution to the Kingdom of God. It is the measure of its effectiveness of your service to the poor, the guarantee that it will last.
>
> Yes, to belong to Jesus Christ is a great gift of God's love. And may the world always see this love in your SMILE.
>
> To all of you goes our apostolic blessing.
>
> *Pope Paul VI*
> *Rome 6.5.1978*

a. Pope Paul VI died on 6th August 1978.

b. The same message by Pope Paul VI that was included in *Ek Dil* 30 was reprinted in this issue of *Ek Dil* as well.

MGL 136. [6TH] OCTOBER 1978

+

L.D.M.

Mother House
[6th] October 1978

My dearest Children,

Jn 15:11; 17:13; Rom 14:17; 15:13 May the joy of Jesus live in you through total surrender, loving trust and cheerfulness. I believe the last general letter was a great help to many a heart, thank God. This letter is meant to bring the Good News—that next year on the 7th Oct. we shall hold our 4th General Chapter.—As we all want to be a living expression of our Love for God and His love for the world, we shall make this Chapter Something Beautiful for God—by
Mt 5:3–11 our special preparation. I have chosen the 8 Beatitudes as our monthly preparation for the Great day—only the order will be slightly different. Therefore make your daily reading, meditation, examen, spiritual reading, Rosary, adoration on the same theme. Also your monthly recollection, and maybe once a week the priest or the Sisters could prepare the Mass. I have asked Sr. M. Bernard to prepare something—but if you have something more helpful, share it with us—but we must keep to the same theme of the month.

During these eight months I want you very specially to pray with a
Mt 5:8 pure heart—with a heart full of love for the Society and the Church, so that we really become true Carriers of God's love.

We must specially pray that the Holy Spirit will be with us when we choose the delegates for the Chapter—and also for the Chapter itself that we choose the Sisters who will govern the Society according to the Spirit of God—entrusted to the Society.—If we really pray, God is sure to guide us properly and protect the Society from anything that may destroy the gift of God, our Vocation to our Society. We shall begin our preparation with the beginning of Advent.—I would like every Community to begin the preparation on the same day.—To make sure that you get this in time in all our houses, I am writing this letter so early—for the post is very slow in some countries.

Mt 5:8 Dec.— Blessed are the clean of heart …

We shall begin our preparation by (1) a fervent confession, (2) a full day of recollection—so that really with a clean heart we Begin our Advent in our Society. During this month we will pay great attention to the

Silence—of eyes, tongue, mind and heart. For much impurity enters the soul through these Gates.

Jan.— Blessed are the Poor … Mt 5:3

To be able to love Christ with undivided love in Chastity, we must live, have and love the freedom of Poverty. We must fully examine and see—
how we have used or misused—this freedom of having nothing yet possess- 2 Cor 6:10
ing everything. Has Poverty been my strength and my joy? In a special way we shall pay attention to truthfulness—in words—in action—in thoughts, and at the end of the month make a special confession on this point.

Feb.— Blessed are the Meek … Mt 5:5

In possessing God through becoming "Clean of heart"—we possess human hearts, our own first through Meekness.—That is why Jesus insisted
that we learn from Him Meekness—kindness, thoughtfulness.—During Mt 11:29
this Month we shall very specially examine how much this Meekness of Jesus is ours—His thoughtfulness—His Sweetness—towards our own heart—towards our Sisters, our Poor. In Confession we shall specially confess all our Sins of impatience—and the hurt and bitterness we have caused to so many—through our words and actions.

March—Blessed are they that Mourn … Mt 5:4

During this month of Lent we shall in a special way and with deep
feeling meditate on the Passion of our Lord—and examine our conscience Mt 26–27; Mk 14–15; Lk 22–23; Jn 18–19
on what sin of ours caused that special pain to Jesus. On what I meditated in the morning—I will make reparation—and share that pain by doubling my penance.—I shall keep strict custody of my eyes.—I shall keep clean thoughts in my mind.—I shall touch the sick with greater gentleness & compassion.—I shall keep the silence of the heart with greater care so
that—in the silence of my heart I hear His words of comfort and from Hos 2:14
the fullness of my heart I comfort Jesus in the distressing disguise of the
Poor .—I shall confess specially my neglect of penance. Mt 12:34; Lk 6:45; Mt 25:40

April—Blessed are they that are hungry … Mt 5:6

Hungry—for God—for love.
Hungry—for the Bread of life. Jn 6:35, 48
Hungry—for Human love.
Hungry—for daily bread.

Hungry—for Holiness.
Hungry—for a life of Prayer.
Hungry—for respect and human dignity.
Hungry—for recognition as a child of God.
Hungry—for a word of sympathy, for a Smile.

Do I recognize these hungers?

In the Hunger of my loneliness, to whom do I turn?
In the hunger of my sinfulness, is Jesus the First thought?
Is prayer the food I am hungry for?
Is Jesus the Hunger of my life?
Is my love for Jesus undivided?
Is Jesus the only love in my life?

Let my examination of conscience be so delicate—so that I can see myself as Jesus sees me now and confess with great humility—anything that has
Rom 8:35, 38–39 separated me from His Love.

Mt 5:7 May—Blessed are the Merciful . . .

We all know—God's great & delicate Mercy to each one of us.—How often after a fervent confession,—we have known the joy of our sins—especially a particular sin, that has been a cause of much suffering—being just taken away, and the joy of His love [penetrating] the very heart that once was so full of sin. Each one of us must be able to tell of The Mercy of God. During this month we shall renew the fidelity to the weekly confessions and daily examination of conscience—for confession is the living action of God's Mercy. We shall examine our conscience especially on how we have forgiven those who have hurt us. Did we use moodiness opposite to Mercy—as a sign of unforgiveness? Let us confess—sins of bitterness and moodiness with great humility.

Mt 5:9 June—Blessed are the Peace-Makers . . .

I am so happy that the Peace-makers come during the month of the Sacred Heart—No other heart but the Heart of Jesus can satisfy the desire for Peace. During this month I will specially examine and see my fidelity to the Prayer life:—my love for prayer, my need for prayer—my fidelity to the spiritual duties in our society.—Have I used them to grow in holiness? Do I really want to be Holy? During this month, for confession I will especially confess all my sins that have disturbed the peace of the community.—I will confess very sincerely all the sins—of repeating, of moodiness, of carrying tales, of answering back, of finding fault, of judging—for these are the chief means of destroying peace in the community. I will take the trouble to look for what is best in my Sister.

July—Blessed are you who suffer persecution . . . Mt 5:10

We do not as such suffer bodily persecution—from outside maybe—but the persecutions caused by the devil against Chastity, Poverty, Obedience and Wholehearted Free Service is very great.—We need continual refilling—of prayer and sacrifice—of the Bread of Life, [of] the living water of my Sisters in the Community and the Poor—to be able to fight him down. We need Our Lady—Our Mother—to be with us always—to protect us and keep us for Jesus only.—Let us in our Confession be very Sincere if in any way we have persecuted others—by being a cause of bad example—of tepidity and misuse of goodness and trust.

Mt 26:26; Mk 14:22; Lk 22:19; Jn 6:35, 48; 1 Cor 11:24
Jn 4:10; 7:38

God bless you
Mother

MGL 137. [6TH] OCTOBER 1978

+

LDM

[6th] October 1978

My Dearest Children,

When we look at the Cross—we see Jesus' head bend to kiss us, His arms extended to embrace us—and He keeps looking at each of us and says—"Come to Me and I will feed you with the Bread of life—come to Me each of you, who are in pain, lonely, and let us share together My Passion for the redemption of the world. Come to Me and My Father and I will come and abide with you and fill you with our Love and compassion, so that you will bring peace in the world."

Jn 7:37
Jn 6:35, 48
Mt 11:28
Jn 14:23

So my dear Sisters, let us share His Passion to the full by accepting whatever He gives, and by giving whatever He takes, with a big smile—the sign that you belong to Jesus and that nothing will separate you from the Love of Christ.

Rom 8:38–39

God bless you.
Mother

MGL 138. 1ST DECEMBER 1978

+ L.D.M.

Mother House
1st December 1978

My dearest Children,[a]

This brings you Mother's love and blessing for a very Happy and Holy Christmas and God's blessing on 1979.

1978 has been so full of God's love and blessings. Our gratitude must
be a resolution to make 1979 a year full of love and humility—say often
during the day: "In union with all the Masses being offered throughout
Mt 11:29 the world, I offer Thee my Heart, make it meek and humble like yours."
This year being the year of our General Chapter, let us pray more fervently, deepen our humility and increase our fidelity to our Vows, by fidelity to the small observances connected with our Vows.

Let us make sure that: Our Chastity is Chaste
Our Poverty is Total
Our Obedience is Constant
Our Charity is Wholehearted.

I ask of each one of you to remember and to put into your daily life
the conviction that you are the Spouse of Jesus Crucified and that "noth-
Rom 8:35, 38–39 ing will separate you from the love of Christ." This conviction is the sure
way to great Holiness—and if you are holy, you will be able to pray the
work—*to do it with Jesus—for Jesus and to Jesus—and this praying the work*[b]
[is] the fruit of our holiness that makes us Contemplatives in the heart of
the world—to be able[c] to welcome Jesus at Christmas time not in a cold
Lk 2:7 manger of our heart—but in a heart full of love and humility,—in a heart
so pure, so immaculate, so warm with love for one another.

Mt 5:8 My children, Jesus has said: "Blessed are the clean of heart, for they
shall see God." Let us during this month make very fervent confession

a. On the handwritten draft of this letter, Mother wrote the date "30/11/78" and after "My dearest Children," she wrote, "Sr. M. Frederick and all in San Gregorio"; however, she crossed out these words. In the typed version, the date is changed to 1st December 1978, and after "My dearest Children," Mother wrote, *"Sr. M. Camillus & all in Mother House—Professed."* There are also copies of the typed version of this same letter with the addition *"Sr. M. Joseph Michael & all Jun. Tertians"* and *"Sr. M. Fredrick & all in San Gregorio,"* handwritten by Mother after the typed words "My dearest Children." Thus, even though this letter might have been initially intended as a letter to a particular house (San Gregorio), it was retyped and sent to all the houses as one of Mother's General Letters.

b. The part in italics was written in Mother's handwritten copy, but left out in the typed version, probably by mistake; thus, it has been restored here.

c. This means: "... and so we will be able to ..."

and let every weekly confession be "I will go to my Father." If we improve our daily examination of conscience, immediately we will feel the need of Jesus to forgive us: we will need confession. Lk 15:18

Let us make this resolution: Fidelity to our examination of conscience, that we may be able to make a weekly fervent confession. Confession will make us pure of heart, and we will see God in the appearance of bread and in the distressing disguise of the Poor. Mt 5:8, 25:40

God bless you
Mother

Daily to be prayed at Adoration:

O most Blessed Trinity, we lift our hearts in gratitude to You for the great gift of vocation to our Society. We thank You for all the love You have given and the trust You have put in each one of us and in the Society as a whole. As we prepare for our General Chapter we ask You, loving Father, to fill us with the Spirit of Your Son that we may understand more deeply our religious consecration and respond more truly to His love. May we understand that to belong to Christ through our vows is the joy and fulfilment of our daily life. Give us the light to know Your will, the love to accept it and the courage to do it. May our Chapter become the living expression of our Love for you and Your love for the world.

Immaculate Heart of Mary, Cause of our Joy and Queen of the World, at your pleading our Society was born,[a] through your continual intercession it grew up, with childlike confidence we now fly to you: During these months of preparation, help us to pray with a pure heart, with a heart full of love for the Society and the Church that we may truly become the carriers of God's love and spread the Kingdom of your Immaculate Heart among the poorest of the poor throughout the world.

a. From the beginning of the Society, Mother Teresa insisted that the Society was born at "Our Lady's pleading." While she did not give any details of it during her lifetime, after her death a fuller understanding of what she meant came to light: At the beginning of her new call, in a series of interior locutions and visions, first the poor, then Our Lady asks, "pleads," with her to begin the Missionaries of Charity. It was Our Lady's invitation and assurances that increased her courage to say "yes." See *Come Be My Light*, 101.

ED 32. CHRISTMAS 1978

Ek Dil, No. 32
Mother House
Christmas 1978

My dearest children,

Jn 3:16 God so loved the world that he gave us his only Son—Jesus—as a tiny
Lk 2:7 Child, born in poverty; so small, so helpless, yet true God of true God.
Jn 1:1, 14
Let us draw very close to the crib this Christmas, let us learn there
Mt 11:29 how to be meek and humble. If we really want God to fill us, we must
empty ourselves of all that is selfishness in us. Then we will be able to love
Jn 13:34–35; 15:12 each other as God has loved each one of us; then our communities will
truly become Ekdil Prempur.[a]

God bless you
Mother

a. Meaning: "One heart full of love." See ED 1, July 1966, and corresponding footnote, p. 75.

1979

MGL 139. 25TH FEBRUARY 1979

+

LDM

Mother House
25th February 1979

My dearest Children,

I am so grateful to God for all the graces we are all receiving through our beautiful preparation for our Chapter.

In a few days we begin the Passion of Christ.—As Jesus can no longer live His Passion in His Body, Mother Church gives us the opportunity to allow Jesus to live his Passion and death in our body, heart and soul. Though there is no comparison with His Passion—still we need so much grace—just to accept whatever He gives—and give whatever He takes—with joy, love and a Smile. Mt 26–27; Mk 14–15; Lk 22–23; Jn 18–19

In His Passion Jesus taught us how to forgive out of love, Lk 23:34; Jn 21:15–19
how to forget out of humility.
So let us at the beginning of the Passion of Christ examine our hearts fully and see if there is any unforgiven hurt—unforgotten bitterness.

Let us often say during the day—wash away my sins and cleanse me from all my sins. How it must hurt Jesus dwelling in our heart—to feel in our hearts this bitterness, this hurt, this revengeful feeling made of jealousy and pride. My Sisters, let us be sincere and ask to be forgiven. Ps 51:2

Is my love for my Sisters so great, so real as to forgive—not out of duty but out of love?

Is there any ill feeling in my heart against my Superiors—for the transfer they have made—for the work they have given? Has this bitterness made me speak against them or behind them?

In the Communities where I have been what have I left behind—what

do they say of me? Thank God she is gone—or we are missing her joy, her love. Do they say she was the sunshine of God's love in our community—she loved Jesus so tenderly. She was always there to give a helping hand
Mt 27:32; Mk 15:21; Lk 23:26 like Mary at the 4th Station, Simon at the 5th, like Veronica at the 6th, like
Lk 23:27 the women at the 8th, always there?

- [Was] I there to give a helping hand to my Superior[s] at the 2nd station when they took the cross—when they failed at the 3rd, 7th, 9th Station.[a]
- Were you there to give her the helping hand of your love, of your trust with respect and humility?
- Were you there when they crucified your Spouse—in your Sisters by neglect—sharp words—carrying tales—repetition?
- Were you there to give Him [the] water of Compassion, of forgiveness, in His Thirst, through your Sister?
- Jn 19:27 Were you there to receive His Mother and take her home—to your heart—in that homeless—man, woman, child?
- Mt 25:40 Were you there when they crucified your Spouse Jesus—in the distressing disguise of the Poor?

O Jesus thou hungest on the Cross
Love is draining out Thy blood
Victim to repair our love
and life by death restore.
O may my life and labour
My aim and sole desire be
To prove my ardent love for Thee
And in that love expire.

Truly He has loved me unto death.

Do I love Jesus unto death?—How can I love Jesus whom I do not see if I
1 Jn 4:20 don't love my Sister—our Poor, whom I see—St. John says: "You are a liar."

Mt 5:8 Let us enter the Passion of Christ with a pure heart—for a Pure heart can see the agony of the Heart of Jesus. During this time when we see the Poverty of Jesus to the full—let us see how did we cause it.

We get so much to give—do we really give—with a free heart for true poverty is freedom.—I hear in many houses—money is used so loosely—that the people keep questioning—they keep writing and proving that much that is given for the Poor—is given to our own people.—When

a. Mother is alluding to the hymn: "Were You There When They Crucified My Lord," and placing Superiors in the place of Jesus on the way to Calvary. In the original she wrote, "Were I there … ," but we have made a grammatical correction here for easier reading.

money is misused and missing, the amount is just added—[the] conscience does not feel disturbed—nor remember that actions like these are stealing and that it needs restitution before it is forgiven. I understand that you cannot make restitution—but you are bound in conscience to tell your Superior, and if you happen to be the Superior—tell Mother or your Regional. My Sisters, do not belittle your parents and your relations. Ask "may I have"—"may I give," and all will be well. No Superior will refuse you—if they know your family needs it.

As I have already written last [time]: All individual sponsoring must stop—in some places it is still going on. For our own children we shall pay from the General Fund.[a] Outside families—parish will do the needful; once more—all sponsoring must stop—no foreign money must be received, and if [a] cheque is sent to you, send [it] to the Mother House. Be careful not to ask money or anything from the Co-workers or any other organization. . . .

Most expensive dishes, sandals, and all kinds [of things] are being introduced. The houses do not need big clocks in the chapel. All the clocks must be removed [and given] to Shishu Bhavan or Nirmal Hriday. Half a dozen or more vases, candle-sticks, adoration oil lamps, brass stands of Indian light—all these have been introduced. In the beginning we did not have them—we were poor. Most expensive mats, electric Blessed Sacrament light [have been introduced]. In every chapel we must have a simple oil lamp burning near the tabernacle—all the rest must be removed.

Why do we have to take back what we have so joyfully given up for love of Jesus when we left home? During the Passion of Jesus—examine your conscience regarding money and things. Examine and calculate how much money you have used and given without permission. How many books bought and brought from libraries without permission. What will it profit you—if you gain and accumulate the whole world and lose your soul? The richest man of the world died alone—without his family—doctor—priest. What will happen to his millions? You and I will also die. What will happen to our poverty, chastity, obedience and charity?

Mt 16:26; Mk 8:36; Lk 9:25

I have sent a questionnaire to every Sister who wants to renew [her vows]. Keep the questionnaire for other renewals—send me only your truthful answers. I will send them back to you with my remark and permission.

a. "Sponsoring" refers to arranging for and coordinating sponsors for the scholarship of poor children. Mother asks that we pay from the general donations for all schooling needs of the children under our care instead of being intermediary between a sponsor and a child.

I am leaving for Rome on the 27th and will be back, please God, by the
Mt 26–27; Mk 14–15; Lk 22–23; Jn 18–19 10th March. In the meantime—try to enter the Passion of Christ to the full—so that in all sincerity you can say—I am the Spouse of Jesus Crucified.

Congratulations to Jesus on His Silver Jubilee:[a] The 25 tabernacles we opened in His honour are:

1. [Villa] El Salvador (Peru)
2. New Delhi
3. Tondo (Manila)
4. Jyotinagar (Lucknow, India)
5. Caracas (Venezuela)
6. T. Nagar (Madras)
7. Zarate (Argentina)
8. Shanti Bhavan (Nagpur)
9. Panama
10. Kundli (Santhal Parganas, India)
11. Dodoma (Tanzania)
12. Gauhati (Assam, India)
13. Liverpool (England)
14. Baroda (Gujarat, India)
15. Sylhet (Bangladesh)
16. Agartala (Tripura)
17. Beirut (Lebanon)
18. Secunderabad (Andra Pradesh, India)
19. Hazaribagh (Bihar, India)
20. Surat (Gujarat, India)
21. Pondicherry (Union Territory, India)
22. Amritsar (Punjab, India)
23. Hubli (Karnataka, India)
24. Sagar (Madhya Pradesh, India)
25. Bareilly (Uttar Pradesh, India)

From now on let us prepare for the Golden Jubilee of Jesus.

In Lent, we will do what we did last year: every Friday we will give up our lunch in the afternoon and give the money to the Poor.

Now the prices of blue par saris have gone up,[b] and so also other saris; let us avoid putting a join[c] except those who really need it.

In March we are hoping to open two more houses: Rajkot in Gujarat and Silchar in Meghalaya—both in India.

All Statistics inside and outside India must be sent to the Mother House and not to Sr. M. Frederick in Rome. Those of you who have not yet sent them, please send them immediately, as we need them.

God bless you
Mother

a. Since three silver jubilees had been celebrated—1975 (commemorating the foundation of the Society in 1950), 1977 (opening of Kalighat, the Home for the Dying, in 1952) and 1978 (first profession of the first group of sisters in 1953)—Mother decided to give Jesus a silver jubilee as well. In a letter to Fr. Joseph Langford, OMV (later MC), dated 11th October 1978, Mother wrote: "We are giving Jesus a Silver Jubilee also—since we all had it, the Society, Nirmal Hriday & the first group—now it is the turn of Jesus—to have His Silver Jubilee. We are giving Him 25 tabernacles, that is 25 new foundations this year."

b. "Blue par sari" is the common way that the Sisters refer to their white saris with the three blue stripes.

c. This means sewing onto one's sari an extra piece of sari to make it longer.

MGL 140. 11TH MARCH 1979

+

L.D.M.

Beirut
11th March 1979

My dearest Children,

This brings you Mother's love and blessings and also deep gratitude for the love you gave and the joy you shared. Everything went so beautifully in Beirut. I am now on my way to India. I was able to take the Sisters to their home next morning. Though the house had been well bombed; after cleaning etc., [it] became our beautiful home—big enough to have 8 Sisters, so better all get ready to make the number. They have a holy bishop.[a] I am sure [he] already [helps] them much—a picture of humility. The things the Novices had prepared—duty boards—so beautiful and with poverty. I hope you always remain faithful to the freedom and joy of poverty—which is the gift of Jesus to our Society.

There is great change in the war-torn Beirut. There is more life—more joy—many people have returned to their homes—with hope—thank God.—Do not let a single day of this Lent pass you by without really loving Jesus, in your Sisters and the Poor, with a tender delicate love as He loves you. Silence [will] help you to find ways and means to do so. Ask Our Jn 13:34; 15:12
Lady to help you—ask her often during the day to give you her heart, so pure, so beautiful, so full of love and humility.

God bless you
Mother

a. Patriarch Mar Raphael I Bidawid (1922–2003) was born in Mosul, Iraq, into an Assyrian family, was ordained a priest in 1944, and in 1957 ordained bishop of Amadiya. In 1966, he was appointed bishop of Beirut, where he served until 1989, when he was elected Patriarch of Babylon, head of the Chaldean Catholic Church.

ED 33. [MAY] 1979

[May] 1979

My dearest Children,

Let us love Jesus by joyfully accepting humiliations.
Let us love Mary by our delicate Purity.
Let us love the Poor with deep Faith through our Works of love.
Let us love each other in prayer and Self-Sacrifice.

God bless you
Mother

MGL 141. [6TH] JULY 1979

+ LDM

[6th] July 1979

My dearest Children,

This brings you Mother's love and blessing.

Thank God our first group of MC Contemplatives made their First Profession.[a] We now have a professed Community of Contemplatives. [Because of] all this, and also [because] we have opened Detroit and St. Louis, I was not able to write earlier.

As we are coming closer to our General Chapter, our prayer to the Holy Spirit must be more fervent.

I would like you to get together in your Community and go over—slowly—the first Chapters [of the Constitutions]: Name and Spirit, Vows, Community Life, Prayer and Becoming Christ, and see how you have observed them. Is there anything that entered your Community and you would like to get rid of it? Is there anything you would like to be better? add or cut off? Anything you like to write, write together and send it to me.

Also in Choosing the delegates, before choosing you may discuss—once you have written the paper, you must not tell for whom you have voted.

By the 15th September all delegates have to be in the Mother House. We will have a retreat which will be given by Fr. Neuner, SJ,[b] from the

a. On 28th June 1979, at St. Anthony of Padua Church in New York, four Sisters made vows in the Contemplative branch.

b. Austrian Jesuit Fr. Joseph Neuner (1908–2009) joined the Society of Jesus in 1926, was ordained a priest in 1936, and went to India in 1938, where he taught theology at De Nobili College in Pune. In 1950, after earning his doctorate in theology at the Gregorian University in Rome, he returned to Pune to teach theology at Jnana Deepa Vidyapeeth. He served as an expert (peritus) at Vatican II. Mother met

28th September. On the 7th October we shall—after Holy Mass—begin the Voting: first for the Superior General and after for the 6 Councillors, and then we shall speak and discuss about the Constitutions. I think we will not have so much to do as last time—since the Constitutions are very beautiful.

. . .

Each Sister will vote secretly and place her ballot in an envelope marked, "CONFIDENTIAL", which will be sealed by the Superior in front of the Community and enclosed in another envelope. Send it REGISTERED in Mother's name to Mother House.

God bless you
Mother

. . .

MGL 142. 30TH JULY 1979

+ LDM

30th July 1979

My dearest Children,

This brings you Mother's love and blessing for a very Happy and Holy Feast of the Society. How much we have to thank God for His care and love for each one of us. I have been away so long, and due to some unforeseen circumstances I have been delayed very much and so will not be able to be back before the end of August. For this reason we will have to postpone our Chapter General to the 21st November instead of 7th October.

. . .

For [the manner of voting] we have asked permission from the Holy See—so all is well.—As soon as I get the list of houses with the names of the Sisters in each Community I will send to each house a complete list of the Finally Professed Sisters to be voted for in your group together with the names of the Sisters in your Community who will vote.

The 40 delegates have to be in the Mother House by the 7th November to begin the retreat on the 12th November which ends on the 21st November, Feast of the Presentation of Our Lady, when the Chapter begins.

Fr. Neuner in the early 1960s, and he became her spiritual director. His role in helping her understand her spiritual darkness was crucial. For more details on Fr. Neuner's role, see *Come be My Light*, chapters 10 and following.

Delegates coming from outside India should bring with them all their personal belongings. On the 21st November, after the Holy Mass to the Holy Spirit, we shall begin the Chapter by voting first for the Superior General of the Society and then for the Six Councillors. After that, the work on the Constitutions will begin, so we need much prayer and penance and sacrifices to allow the Holy Spirit to use us to choose the Sisters who will be able to help the Sisters grow in holiness and give wholehearted service to the Poorest of the Poor. We must not be afraid nor be influenced by anything nor anybody but pray much that we may not spoil God's beautiful work: our Society.

The list of the Finally Professed Sisters of your group will soon be sent to you. You can then think, pray and even talk among yourselves about them before the Voting—but once you have voted you must not talk about them anymore. Also I would like you in each community to get together and discuss about the Society—the good and the bad points that have penetrated into the Society—and what you think you would like the Chapter to add or cut—[make] this as short as you can make it. Send it to me to the Mother House.

Let us all pray the Chapter prayer as often as we can especially these days when we have to prepare more intensely.[a]

My prayer is often for each one of you—especially during Holy Mass and Holy Communion. Pray much for Mother.

God bless you
Mother

P.S. Some houses may have already sent their voting papers. I will destroy all when I return—for you will have to vote again.

MGL 143. 12TH OCTOBER 1979

+ L.D.M.

12th October 1979

My dearest Children,

This brings you Mother's love, blessing and gratitude for all the fervent prayers, beautiful cards—and letters each of you have sent for my feast.

Except for the two delegates for North and Central America (we are

a. See the prayer at the end of MGL 138 of 1st December 1978, p. 249.

still waiting for the voting papers of Haiti—2 houses, Guatemala and Toluca) all the rest have been voted for—and so I am sending you the list. I hope all those voted for will be at the Mother House by the 7th November 1979.

During this month from the 21st October—right through to the end of the Chapter, we will pray this prayer to the Holy Spirit: "God our Father, through Jesus your Son, send forth your Spirit—to our Sisters in the Chapter. Give them the light to know your Will, the love to accept it and the courage to do it—so that the fruit of the Chapter becomes the living expression of our love for each other and your love for the world through us."

Through this letter I want also to thank each one of you for the love, the care and support you have given me during these 30 years in building up the Society on the Rock—Jesus, with the help of Mary our Mother. Mt 7:24–25
I pray and hope, and it is my strong conviction that it will be for the greater glory of God, the good of the Society, every individual sister and the poor—that we vote with great love for a Sister to be our Superior General among our senior Sisters. We have many wonderful Sisters who can easily take Mother's place—but on one condition only, that we all together be one heart full of love with her whom we choose. That is why we need to pray to the Holy Spirit with a pure heart, that we may see the Will of Mt 5:8
God and vote with a free heart.

Many letters have come from the houses to help with the Chapter.—In each one of them we read [about] the great need for Charity and understanding love for each other in the Community life and [of] a worldly spirit that has deprived us of the freedom and Joy of Poverty—which for us Missionaries of Charity is our strength and our protection.

Love and Poverty made Our Lady so Christ-like. Let us ask her to obtain Love and Poverty from the Heart of Her Son.

Many Bishops wrote of the work you are doing for the Poor with great love and gave great praise, but some mentioned the need for love among us in the Community. If my love for each one of you for all these years has not been what it should have been—I am sorry. The beautiful work the Church has entrusted to the Society will be completely destroyed from within, if you do not love one another as Jesus loves each one of you and Jn 13:34; 15:12
also [if you] lose the Joy of Poverty.

The Councillors and myself are fully busy with the Constitutions, and we hope to have everything ready by the 12th when we begin our retreat.

Rev. Fr. Fallon, SJ,[a] will give us the retreat. We all feel the support of your love through your continual prayer.

My gratitude to each one of you is my prayer for you that you become a true MC—a carrier of God's love, the Sunshine of God's love and compassion—the Hope of Eternal happiness, the Burning flame of God's love to all you meet, especially your Sisters and your Poor.

...

God bless you
Mother

MGL 144. 21ST NOVEMBER 1979

+

LDM

Mother House
21st November 1979[b]

My dearest Children,

Mt 26–27; Mk 14–15; Lk 22–23; Jn 18–19

Our gratitude to God our Father through the Passion of His Son Jesus and the love of the Holy Spirit, is our gift—of MOTHER to each one of us—to help us grow in holiness through the Purity and Humility of the Heart of Mary—and also the gift of the six Councillors:

Sr. M. Frederick
Sr. M. Joseph Michael
Sr. M. Shanti
Sr. M. Agnes
Sr. M. Damien
Sr. M. Andrea

With deep and loving gratitude to the [ex-]Councillors—that helped and shared with Mother the joys and sorrows of six years with so much

a. Belgian Jesuit Fr. Pierre Fallon, SJ (1912–1985), came to Calcutta in 1935 and was the first Jesuit to obtain an MA in Bengali philology from Calcutta University. He held the post of Professor of French literature at the University of Calcutta for twenty-five years and promoted intercultural and interfaith dialogue.

b. The first paragraph of this letter seems to have been written by the Sister typist (most probably one of the Councillors, who was a chapter member as well) giving information about the outcome of the Chapter elections and pledging commitment to Mother and the Society.

love and care—we all promise complete loving trust—to Mother and our [new] Councillors. May Our Lady who is specially going to be with us during the coming year—lead and guide us—to fulfil Mother's promise to give saints to Mother Church through Purity and Humility.

Sr. M. Priscilla representing North America and Sr. M. Rosemary for Central America are also in the Chapter. We are now working with the Constitutions and we are hoping to close by 30th November 1979.

On 3rd December our Sisters will make their First and Final Professions in Calcutta. On the evening of 5th December—I will leave for Rome, and on the 7th we will have the Professions there. On the 8th I will be in Oslo, God willing.[a] As the Nobel Peace Prize Committee [has] sent two more tickets besides the one for me, and above all as a mark of love and gratitude to all our Sisters of the First group for having the courage to join when there was Nothing,[b] the joy of having Nothing & yet possessing 2 Cor 6:10
Jesus to the full, & because they loved Jesus they loved the Poor, so I will be taking Sr. M. Agnes and Sr. M. Gertrude with me to Oslo.

I want you, and we all want, that we make the Society holy and [that] we give the Church holy Sisters. We make the Society—every single Sister from the biggest to the smallest. Let us make our Society a Fruitful Living Jn 15:1, 5
Branch on the Vine Jesus. So now with greater determination, greater love and humility we are going to love and serve each other, and make our Society Something Beautiful for God, through holiness of life.

God bless you
Mother

a. Mother arrived in Oslo, Norway, on 8th December 1979 and received the 1979 Nobel Peace Prize (Nobel medal and $192,000 award) on behalf of the poor from Professor John Sanness, chairman of the Norwegian Nobel Committee, on Monday, 10th December. She asked that the traditional Peace Prize dinner be cancelled and the money that the dinner would have cost be instead used for her work.

b. The Sisters of the first group are (in order of seniority): Sr. M. Agnes, Sr. M. Gertrude, Sr. M. Trinita (left as a novice), Sr. M. Dorothy, Sr. M. Clare, Sr. M. Bernard, Sr. M. Laetitia, Sr. M. Jacinta (left the Society in 1965), Sr. M. Francesca, Sr. M. Florence, Sr. Margaret Mary.

ED 34. NOVEMBER 1979–JANUARY 1980

LDM

November 1979–January 1980

My dearest Children,

This brings you Mother's love and blessing.

1979 was so full of so many graces for each one of us, and also the Cross has also been there to remind us that we are the spouses of Jesus Crucified.

1980 we begin with one strong resolution—to really make our Society something beautiful for God—Holy—through

Purity of life
Humility of heart.

Mt 5:3–11 These two points we will again use as we did the Beatitudes and so really grow in the Holiness the Church expects of us.

God bless you
Mother

Calcutta, 2/1/79

1980

MGL 145. 15TH JANUARY 1980

+ L.D.M.

Mother House
15th January 1980

My Dearest Children,

May God's Blessing of joy, love and Peace be with you all—during this year—with each one of you. I pray, hope and believe God is going to do great things in each one of us and through each one to the poor during this year. Lk 1:51; Jn 14:12

Let us begin with a strong resolution that we are going to make our Society grow in holiness—through Purity of life and humility of heart. I am enclosing for January a list of spiritual exercises prepared by Sr. M. Bernard,[a] and I hope we will be able to have it every month. Even though this comes a little late, you begin as it comes. I am sure you will be happy and grateful to have this help.

As you know, [at] our last Chapter we had decided to have Regional Superiors according to our Constitutions. After much prayer and consideration, our Councillors and myself have decided to divide the regions into five [groups]. . . .

Keep the joy of loving Jesus and the Poor in your heart, and share this joy with all you meet. Ask Our Lady again and again, often during the day: give me your heart, so beautiful, so pure—so Immaculate, your heart so full of love and humility, that I may receive Jesus in the Bread of life Jn 6:35, 48, 51
and serve Him in the distressing disguise of the poor. Mt 5:8, 25:40

God Bless you
Mother

a. These proposed "Spiritual Exercises" were sent out to the houses every month, from January 1980 to June 1981. At times these "Spiritual Exercises" had Mother's letter as a cover letter. As these were circular letters sent to the entire Society, we have included these cover letters in this volume of *Mother Teresa's General Letters to Her Sisters* in chronological order.

MGL 146. 31ST JANUARY 1980

+

LDM

Mother House
31st January 1980

My dearest Children,

This brings you Mother's love and blessing.

I am afraid many of you are hurt with my silence,[a] but it has been humanly impossible—but anyway—I am sorry for it all.

As we are preparing for Lent, I thought—the greatest penance for you and for me is interior and exterior silence. Therefore I decided to send you the Chapter on Silence, which has been added to the new Constitution.[b] I am sure you will be very happy. It will really help you to grow in love with Jesus—and this love is true holiness for Missionaries of Charity.

"God is the friend of silence."[114] His language is silence. "Be still and
Ps 46:10 know that I am God." He requires us to be silent to discover Him. In the
Hos 2:14 silence of the heart He speaks to us.

Mt 4:2; Mk 1:13; Lk 4:2 Jesus spent forty days, before beginning His public life, in silence. He
Lk 6:12; Mk 1:35 often retired alone, spent the night on the mountain in silence and prayer.
He who spoke with authority spent His early life in silence.[115]

The Word of God is speechless today—in the Eucharist His silence is the highest and the truest praise of the Father. It is the adoration of God.

We need silence to be alone with God, to speak to Him, to listen to Him, to ponder His words deep in our hearts. We need to be alone with God in silence to be renewed and to be transformed. Silence gives us a new outlook on life. In it we are filled with the energy of God Himself that makes us do all things with joy.

Silence is at the root of our union with God and with one another. Without it our whole life as Missionaries of Charity will collapse, for

The fruit of Silence is Prayer
The fruit of Prayer is Faith
The fruit of Faith is Love and
The fruit of Love is Service.

a. After the Nobel Peace Prize, Mother was heavily burdened with the "outside" world (meeting people, media, giving speeches, etc.). She had less time for the Sisters, who must have been complaining about it. Mother regretted the fact that she had less time for the Sisters and apologized.

b. The paragraphs below are from chapter 15, on Silence, in the *Constitutions* of 1980. However, at the time Mother wrote this letter the Sisters had not yet received the copy of these constitutions, so she chose to send the text beforehand in a general letter.

Therefore each one of us will take it as our serious and sacred duty to collaborate with one another in our common effort to promote and maintain an atmosphere of deep silence and recollection in our own lives, conducive to the constant awareness of the Divine Presence everywhere and in everyone, especially in our own hearts and in the hearts of our Sisters with whom we live and in the poorest of the poor.

Out of genuine love for one another, we shall provide for each other in the community an atmosphere of peace and quiet, facilitating prayer, work, study and rest.

To foster and maintain a prayerful atmosphere of exterior silence we shall:

- respect certain times and places of more strict silence,
- move about and work prayerfully, quietly and gently,
- avoid at all costs all unnecessary speaking and noise,
- speak, when we have to, softly, gently, saying just what is necessary,
- cultivate refined and quiet speech,
- look forward to profound silence as a holy and precious time, a withdrawal into the living silence of God.[a]

To help [with] real silence, we shall also discern in the light of love when to speak and when to keep silence. We shall also try to be kind and patient listeners, not monopolizing the conversation, humble hidden souls, without drawing any attention to ourselves in any way.

To make possible true interior silence we shall practice:

- Silence of the eyes, by seeking always the beauty and goodness of God everywhere, and closing [our eyes] to the faults of others and to all that is sinful and disturbing to the soul.
- Silence of the ear, by listening always to the voice of God and to the cry of the poor and the needy, and closing it to all the other voices that come from the evil one or from fallen human nature, e.g., gossip, tale-bearing, uncharitable words.
- Silence of the tongue, by praising the Lord and speaking the life-giving Word of God that is Truth that enlightens and inspires, brings peace, hope and joy, and refraining from self-defence and every word that causes darkness, turmoil, pain and death.

a. On "profound silence," see MGL 135 of 3rd July 1978 and corresponding footnote, p. 240.

Lk 2:19, 51

– Silence of the mind, by opening it to the Truth and knowledge of God in prayer and contemplation, like Mary, who pondered the marvels of the Lord in her heart, and closing it to all untruths, distractions, destructive thoughts, like rash judgments, false suspicion of others, revengeful thoughts and desires.

Mt 22:37; Mk 12:30; Lk 10:27 Jn 13:34; 15:12

– Silence of the heart, by loving God with our whole heart, soul, mind and strength, and one another as God loves, desiring God alone and avoiding all selfishness, hatred, envy, jealousy and greed.

To be alone with God in prayer and silence, we shall:

– withdraw as much as possible from our daily apostolate once a week and stay at home,
– have a day of recollection once a month, and
– make an eight days' retreat once a year.

Our silence is a joyful and God-centred silence; it demands of us constant self-denial and plunges us into the deep silence of God where aloneness with God becomes a reality.

Each time there is a death in the family of a Sister in your community please send the news to the Mother House.

Please send in your statistics for 1979 as soon as possible.

I hope you are all well and doing God's work with great love.

Keep the joy of loving Jesus in each other and the poor and share this joy with all you meet.

God bless you
Mother

MGL 147. 15TH MARCH 1980

+

LDM

Mother House
15th March 1980

My dearest Children,

Jn 13:34; 15:12 Mt 25:40

This brings you Mother's love and blessing—but especially the joy of the assurance that Jesus loves you, and I only ask you to love one another as Jesus loves each one of you—for in loving one another you only love

Jesus. This is Mother's gratitude to each one of you—my prayer—my wish for each one of you—that we all grow together and bring much fruit—the fruit of holiness. Jn 15:5, 8

May the joy of the Risen Jesus be always with you—and may you become Mt 28:8; Lk 24:41, 52; Jn 20:20

the Sunshine of His Love and Compassion to all you meet,
The hope of Eternal Happiness, and
The burning flame of God's love

through serving Christ in the distressing disguise of the poor. Mt 25:40

You will be happy to know that, with the help of God's grace, we have been able to give Jesus [four] more tabernacles in the north of India . . . and three more out of India. . . .

Pray for each of these new foundations, that our Sisters may be the good news of God's love to the poor in all these places.

The May Professions are drawing near once again, and the two months' intensive preparation will be starting in a few days in Calcutta, Rome, Manila and Tabora. I am sure you will all enter into this preparation with great love and hope that Jesus will draw you very close to Himself. They will be days of great grace for each one of you, for the Society and for the Church. Let these two months be spent in prayerful silence, for silence is at the root of our union with God and with one another.—It fills us with the energy of God Himself that makes us do all things with joy. I hope to be with you all for your profession day. I shall let you know the dates later.

God bless you
Mother

MGL 148. [2ND] MAY 1980

Mother House
[2nd] May 1980[a]

My dearest Children,

May Our Lady be a Mother to each one of us—as she was to Jesus.—May Our Lady find Jesus always in our hearts. May she help us to love Jesus as she loved Him—and may [we] love her as Jesus loved her.

During the month of May we sing the glory and praise of Mary—
Jn 19:27 as she is the Mother of the Church and our Mother, who brings about Christ's new life in us. Singing the praises of Mary fills us with God's great love—as she is the beloved daughter of the Eternal Father. We consecrate our vowed life to her and ask her to obtain for us Christ's life in greater degree. She will help us to be clothed with the humility of her Son and be radiant with joy in His Presence. On our part, we shall try to spread her devotion to all our people and teach them to pray to Mary and turn to her in [their] joys and sorrows.

God bless you
Mother

ED 35. MAY 1980

+

L.D.M.

May 1980

My Dearest Children,

This brings you Mother's love and blessing, also my prayer and sacrifice for each one of you that you must grow in the likeness of Christ through purity of life and humility of heart and become Carriers of God's Love and Compassion to each other and to the Poor you serve. Keep the Joy of loving Jesus in your heart and in each other, and share this joy with all you meet.

My gratitude to each one of you for all the love you give and [the] joy you share as MC is my prayer for each one of you—that you may become a true Spouse of Jesus Crucified.

God bless you,
Mother

a. This letter was sent to the houses as a cover letter for the prepared "Spiritual Exercises" for the month of May. The theme for this month was "My Soul proclaims the greatness of the Lord."

MGL 149. 20TH MAY 1980

+

LDM

Bombay
20th May 1980

My dearest Children,

This brings you Mother's love, blessing and prayer for each of you wherever you may be.

I do hope that the Risen Christ has filled your hearts with His Joy and (Mt 28:8; Lk 24:36, 41, 52; Jn 20:19–26 Acts 2:2–4) Peace—and while we are preparing for the coming of the Holy Spirit, I pray for you that the Holy Spirit may fill you with His Purity—so that you can see the face of God in each other and in the faces of the Poor you (Mt 5:8) serve. I ask the Holy Spirit to free you of all impurity—body, soul, mind, will, heart—that each of you become the living tabernacle of God most High, and so become a carrier of God's love and compassion. Ask the Holy Spirit to make you a sinner without sin. We are MCs, and yet we forget so often in our community life that we have been called to be His love and compassion to our own Sisters first, for no one needs that love more than our Sisters in the community, who are the very life of our life.—Often I find in so many hearts so much bitterness—on their tongues so many ugly words—in their attitudes towards each other so much pride,—and to think that, in that very heart, Jesus comes—with that very tongue we receive Jesus—that attitude, so unworthy of the Spouse of Christ. Let us keep on asking the Holy Spirit to make us true MCs in mind, heart, will and soul, and so love one another as Jesus loves each one of us. (Jn 13:34; 15:12)

I am on my way to Africa, where I hope to be present for the profession. I will be away for some time.—Sr. M. Frederick—being the Assistant General—will act in my place in all things regarding the Society, therefore all matters must be addressed to her. Give her the same love, trust and obedience you give Mother so beautifully. Do not be afraid—only trust (Mt 10:26; 28:5, 10; Lk 12:4, 32; Jn 14:27; Rev 1:17; 2:10) and obey and you will be alright.

There are a few things I want to draw your attention to. I have come to know that in some communities, the priest is brought into the refectory for breakfast, recreation and special food, and the community shares in it. If you read the Constitutions carefully, you will see that the refectory is one of the places we keep strictly for the use of the Sisters. Except the Bishop—on special occasions, if you do not have a proper parlour—no one else should enter the refectory or the dormitory. They—the priests—may tell you that other Congregations do it; you just do not enter into discussion but do not allow anyone in.

Shishu Bhavan and Nirmal Hriday left often without care of the Sisters because the Sisters go to this celebration, to this meeting—even to a cinema and parties, [and] come home late without a thought to the 4th Vow and to the decisions of the General Chapter. Thank God it is not like this in many Communities, but even if it is one—it is in our Society, our Sisters—we are all involved. There is too much time given to long conversation in the parlour—in the dispensaries with priests and others—again let us remember our 4th Vow.

In number of houses, hot pickle, chillies and limes are on the table daily, bottles of pickle are being made in many houses.—When I look at these things and look at the poor, I wonder—are we really one of them—the poorest of the poor. The way we dress—use soap, light—water—[having] the best of everything—are we one of them? Poverty and Charity are the best means to the purity of Life we are trying to grow in to become holy.

Ex 34:29, 33–35 Moses had to cover his face, take off his sandals before he could enter
Ex 3:5 the Holy Place. We too shall cover our tabernacle with a white veil—only
white, no other colour—just pure transparent cloth—to remind us how
Mt 5:8 pure our heart—the living tabernacle of God—must be, so, so transparent, so full of God; that pure veil reminds us of our purity and also of how we too must cover each other with the veil of Charity, so that we see in each other what is beautiful and not always only what is ugly.

Again and again I have reminded you of the Rosary in the streets, about calling each other Sister, cutting your hair—these are such simple things which, because many Congregations are not doing because this is not their way, some Sisters think they too can give them up—but for us this is the way. If you look up your Constitutions you will find all three mentioned there.

Due to fever and dysentery, I had to cancel my going to Africa. I hope I will soon be able to start the journey.

My Sisters, I ask you to take this letter to heart and see what is in your community that is breaking the peace and joy and unity—is it not one of those things that has crept in because we have neglected prayer—spirit of sacrifice and respect for each other? Let us carefully read Mother's letter on Silence and we will find much help from it.

As you know, we have divided our Society into regions with a Regional Superior for each Regional division....

As we see, our Society has grown, so we need to pray for our Regionals as we pray for Mother. . . .[a]

In union with all the Masses we offer You our hearts, O Jesus, make our hearts meek and humble like Yours. Mt 11:29

God has blessed the work on our Constitutions, and Rome has approved [them] for ten years. I hope we will soon be able to print them and send you each your copy.

Pray for Mother as Mother prays for each one of you.

God bless you
Mother

MGL 150. 1ST JUNE 1980

+

L.D.M.

1st June 1980[b]

My Dearest Children,

The month of the Sacred Heart is the month of God's Love. Let us make a real effort to make [it] one of true love, reparation and forgiveness. Try to make your community a place where "Our Lord can come apart and rest a while with you." Try to get as many families as possible conse- Mk 6:31
crated to the Sacred Heart of Jesus.[c]

The meditations on Jesus, the good Shepherd and Jesus our Crucified Jn 10:11, 14
Saviour, will help us to understand how God loves us and awakens in us Mt 27:26; Mk 15:15, 24–25; Lk 23:33
the desire to love one another as Jesus loves us. Use the meditations during Jn 13:34; 15:12
the novena preparatory to the feast of the Sacred Heart.

God bless you.
Mother

a. By 1980, there were 178 foundations, served by 1,355 professed Sisters, spread across 36 countries, on 6 continents.

b. This letter was sent to the houses as a cover letter for the "Spiritual Exercises" for the month of June. The theme for this month was "Jesus the Good Shepherd."

c. See MGL 92 of 1st June 1972, p. 160.

MGL 151. [4TH] JULY 1980

+

LDM

[4th] July 1980[a]

My dearest Children,

Let us thank God for all his goodness to us and through us to His People. This being the month of the Precious Blood, try to increase your
Mt 26–27; Mk 14–15; Lk 22–23; Jn 18–19 love for Holy Mass and the Passion of Christ by accepting with joy all the little sacrifices that come daily. Do not by-pass [these] small gifts, for they are very precious for yourself and for others. During this month we shall often pray this prayer:

"In union with all the Masses being offered throughout the world, I
Mt 11:29 offer Thee my heart. Make it meek and humble like Your Heart."[b]

God bless you
Mother

MGL 152. [1ST] AUGUST 1980

+

LDM

[1st] August 1980[c]

My Dearest Children,

The feast of the Immaculate Heart of Mary, Cause of Our Joy is drawing near. A very happy and holy feast of Our Lady. Let our preparation for the great day be one of deep humble gratitude to God for all we have received during this year—especially all the vocations and all the good done by the good God through each one of us. From Our Lady we will ask two special graces—

—the grace of perseverance in our beautiful vocation and
—a delicate love for God's poor.

a. This letter was sent to the houses as a cover letter for the "Spiritual Exercises" for the month of July. The theme for this month was "Bearing Wrongs Patiently."

b. See MGL 135 of 3rd July 1978, p. 240.

c. This letter was sent to the houses as a cover letter for the "Spiritual Exercises" for the month of August. The theme for this month was "Honouring the Immaculate Heart of Mary."

But let each of us try to make this love more kind, more charitable and more cheerful. Let our eyes see more clearly, in deep faith, the face of Christ in the face of the Poor. Mt 25:40

God bless you
Mother

MGL 153. 29TH AUGUST 1980

+

LDM

Mother House
29th August 1980[a]

My dearest Children,

I am just back from Europe with deep gratitude to God and our Blessed Mother for all the good being done and all the love and compassion our Sisters give to each other and to our Poor; it is so beautiful. Thank you for all your letters bringing me your love and prayers for our Society Feast Day.

This is my greeting to all of you:

> THAT YOU MAY KNOW EACH OTHER AT THE BREAKING OF Lk 24:30–31
> THE BREAD, LOVE EACH OTHER IN THE EATING OF THE Jn 6:35, 48, 51
> BREAD OF LIFE, AND SERVE EACH OTHER AND HIM IN THE Mt 25:40
> POOR BY GIVING YOUR WHOLE-HEARTED SERVICE.

When communicating with Christ in your heart—the partaking of
Living Bread—remember what Our Lady must have felt when the Spirit Jn 6:51
overpowered her, and she, who was full of grace, became full with the Lk 1:26–38
Body of Jesus. The Spirit in her was so strong that immediately she rose in Lk 1:39
haste to go and serve.

Each Holy Communion—each breaking of the Bread of Life—each Jn 6:35, 48, 51
sharing should produce in us the same, for it is the same Jesus who
came to Mary and was made flesh, Who comes to us and becomes our Jn 1:14
Jn 1:4, 9

a. This letter was sent to the houses as a cover letter for the "Spiritual Exercises" for the month of September. It was misdated as 29/9/1980 instead of 29/8/1980; that is, there was a typo for the month: instead of 8 (August), 9 (September) was typed. The theme for this month was: "The Eucharistic Presence of Jesus."

Lk 1:39–42 life. We too, like her, should be in haste to give this life of Jesus to our Sisters and the Poor.[a]

God bless you
Mother

MGL 154. 16TH SEPTEMBER 1980

+

L.D.M.

Mother House
16th September 1980[b]

My dearest Children,

Keep the joy of loving Jesus in your hearts, and share this joy with all you meet, especially your Sisters and the Poor you serve.

Mother Church has once more proved her love for our Society by giving us the Immaculate Heart of Mary, the Cause of our Joy, to be our Mother and Patroness [and] special [permission to keep the feast] on the 22nd of August. This is such a great gift for such a young Society.[c]

On the 24th Sept., I go back to Rome at the wish of the Holy Father to join the Synod on Christian Family Life.[d] I just wonder what would I be doing in the crowd of great and learned big people. My only joy is that I will have the beautiful opportunity to listen, in the silence of my heart,
Hos 2:14 for the voice of God—so pray that I let Jesus say what He wants to say through me.

Let us ask Our Lady to teach us through her Rosary to love Jesus as she

a. See MGL 94 of 15th August 1972, p. 164.

b. This letter was sent to the houses as a cover letter for the "Spiritual Exercises" for the month of October. The theme for this month was: "The Eucharistic Presence of Jesus (continued)."

c. In 1942, during World War II, and the twenty-fifth anniversary of the Fatima apparitions, Pope Pius XII placed the world under Our Lady's protection, consecrating it to her Immaculate Heart. That same year he celebrated the feast of the Immaculate Heart of Mary on 22nd August. On 4th May 1944, he officially instituted the memorial of the Immaculate Heart of Mary for the universal Church to obtain her intercession for "peace among nations, freedom for the Church, the conversion of sinners, the love of purity and the practice of virtue." When the liturgical calendar was revised in 1969, according to the norms of Vatican II, the celebration was transferred from 22nd August to the day following the Solemnity of the Sacred Heart of Jesus and made an optional memorial. Mother obtained special permission to continue to keep the celebration of the Immaculate Heart on 22nd August as a solemnity, since it is the patronal feast of the Society.

d. The Fifth Ordinary Assembly of the World Synod of Bishops was held in Vatican City from 26th September to 25th October 1980.

loved Him—to go in search of Him as she went—to stand near the Cross Lk 2:44–46; Jn 19:25
as She stood. To be able to do this, we need a pure heart—so in eating the Mt 5:8
Bread of Life in Faith and Love we shall be able to be Mary to Jesus. Jn 6:35, 48, 51

As usual, when Mother is out of India, all permissions will be asked Mt 14:27; 17:7;
from Sr. M. Frederick with love and respect. Jesus said: "Be not afraid", "I Mk 5:36, 6:50; Lk 5:10, 8:50, 12:7;
am with you", "My Father loves you because you loved me", "I have called Jn 6:20; Mt 28:20
you by name, you are precious to me, I love you". What greater proof of Jn 16:27; Is 43:1, 4
love. Do not be afraid. Mt 10:26; 28:5, 10; Lk 12:4, 32; Jn 14:27; Rev 1:17; 2:10

God bless you
Mother

MGL 155. 8TH OCTOBER 1980

LDM

Rome
8th October 1980

My dearest Children,

This brings you Mother's love, blessing and prayer—that each one of you may grow more and more in the likeness of Christ through purity
and humility of heart. We have never needed that pure heart so much as Mt 5:8
now. In our Society, which God has entrusted not only to Mother but to each one of us, Holiness is the main reason for its existence. For us holiness should not be difficult—for in giving wholehearted free service to the Poorest of the Poor, we are 24 hours with Jesus, and as every MC is the Poorest of the Poor—even when we do little things for each other in the house besides what we do outside, we live and observe that 4th Vow.

What delicate love God has had for the Poor of the World to have created the MCs; and just think for a moment, you and I have been called by Jn 15:16
our name, because He loved us. Because you and I are somebody special 1 Jn 4:19
to Him—to be His Heart to love Him in the Poor, His Hands to serve Him in the Poorest of the Poor. My children, how much love and care we must take of Him—if only we were in love with Jesus. Let us learn to pray
the work to be able to be 24 hours with Jesus, do it for Jesus and to Jesus. Mt 25:40
We need a Pure heart, a heart that has nothing [and no one] but only Jesus. Mt 5:8

There are a few things I want to draw your attention to:

Chapel—Genuflection—no bowing. Cover the tabernacle with white transparent cloth. Have the tabernacle well secured. Two candles and small cross for Holy Mass on the altar. Four [candles] for Adoration.[a] Prepare readings.—No low table for Holy Mass nor Holy Mass sitting.[b] In many houses prayers are said with such speed that it is difficult to pay attention to what is being said to God. Community Room—nowadays too many drawings and pictures. One spiritual bouquet from the house on feast days—one mala [garland]. There is a way of wearing the sari. Kindly find out and do so.

As I had written before, please do not ask the Co-workers or anybody outside India for money or anything before writing to Mother, as there are now Government regulations, and also it is causing much wrong impression when the Sisters write that Mother House did not give them the money sent. Who then sends you the money that you receive from the Mother House?

Every donation, big or small, must be written. No Sister nor Superior can use the money without writing it down. All money, even the "rubbish" money,[c] must be written before it is used. For this reason, often the A/Cs [Accounts] are completely wrong. The misuse of money is an act against the Vow of Poverty, and in time it may lead you to infidelity to the other 3 Vows, as it has done before to our Sisters who have left the Society.

I hope we will soon have the printed copy of our Constitutions. The more we know our constitutions, the more we will love them, and if we love them, we will live them, for they are the sure way to the perfect love of God—Holiness.

God bless you
Mother

a. In August 1985, Mother asked to have five candles for Adoration, representing the five branches of the Society. On 2nd August 1987, she increased the number to eight.

b. "Sitting Mass" refers to the manner of celebrating the Holy Mass on a low altar table. The priest, vested in a white alb and a saffron shawl, sits on a cushion behind the altar table, facing the congregation, that remains seated on the floor facing him. Usually the priest is welcomed with a garland. At the time of the doxology, *arati* (a dance with incense, flowers and lamps) is performed. Besides traditional *bhajans* (repetitive hymns), *arati* and *deepam* (oil lamp) and other symbols of Indian culture are used. During the entire Mass all sit on the floor (usually in a cross-legged position); thus, the name "sitting Mass." Some priests and religious congregations promoted it as a part of inculturation, and at the time it was becoming popular in India. Mother did not want such Masses in the MC chapels.

c. "Rubbish money" refers to money received from the sale (for recycling) of items such as plastic, cardboard, etc. Later, the Sisters would give these items to poor families so they could sell them.

MGL 156. 23RD NOVEMBER 1980

L.D.M.

Mother House
23rd November 1980

My dearest Children,

This brings you Mother's love, blessing and prayer for each one of you, that you may more and more grow in the likeness of Christ through Mt 11:29
meekness and humility, so that your Sisters in the Community and the Poor you serve feel His Presence and His Love—in you and through you—and learn from you how to love Jesus in each other.

I am on my way back to our Mother House after two full months. The Synod, that lasted one full month,[a] was really something beautiful for God and His Church. The concern and love shown by all present at the Synod was really very real and true—fidelity to the teaching of the Church all the time. I hope we will soon get the text. I had to speak and I asked the Holy Father to give us holy Priests, and, through their help, we, religious and families, will become holy. I prayed much to obtain the grace as to how we MCs will make our Society, and also the families we serve, holy.

The Promises of the Sacred Heart and the pleading of Our Lady came clear in my heart:[b] the Consecration of the Family to the Sacred Heart, and the First Friday devotion, and the Family Rosary.

January 5th, 1981, will be the first Friday in 1981. We will prepare in each Community with as great fervour as possible with [more] penance

a. The Fifth Ordinary Assembly of the Synod of Bishops on the theme, "The Role of the Christian Family in the Modern World," was held in Vatican City from 26th September to 25th October 1980. Mother Teresa was invited to the Synod as one of the auditors and gave a talk on 6th October 1980.

b. These are the twelve promises to those who honour His Sacred Heart, as given by Jesus to St. Margaret Mary Alacoque, a French nun, in the 1670s:

1. I will give them all the graces necessary for their state of life.
2. I will give peace in their families.
3. I will console them in all their troubles.
4. I will be their refuge in life and especially in death.
5. I will abundantly bless all their undertakings.
6. Sinners shall find in my Heart the source and an infinite ocean of mercy.
7. Tepid souls shall become fervent.
8. Fervent souls shall rise speedily to great perfection.
9. I will bless those places wherein the image of My Sacred Heart shall be exposed and venerated.
10. I will give to priests the power to touch the most hardened hearts.
11. Persons who propagate this devotion shall have their names eternally written in my Heart.
12. In the excess of the mercy of my Heart, I promise you that my all-powerful love will grant to all those who will receive Communion on the First Fridays, for nine consecutive months, the grace of final repentance: they will not die in my displeasure, nor without receiving the sacraments; and my Heart will be their secure refuge in that last hour.

during the Novena, Night Adoration from 11 P.M. to 12 A.M. on Thursday preceding the First Friday, and without lunch on Friday. In the evening, if possible, get the Parish Priest to consecrate the Community to the Sacred Heart as solemnly as possible. Give the picture of the Sacred Heart a prominent place in the Community and in the Family. Arrange things in such a way that at least 2 Sisters in your Community will, on every Friday, work at the Consecration and Devotion to the Sacred Heart, and on Saturday to the spreading of the Rosary. Try to arrange with your Parish Priest an hour of Adoration every Thursday or Friday for the families where parents and children can come together.

Do the same with the Rosary—streetwise[a]—begin every Saturday with the Sisters, and on other days the family alone. Get also non-Catholic families to pray together—a simple prayer to God. I am sure they too will be able to pray together. I know that this will need many sacrifices, but I am sure of each one of you—that you will be one heart full of love with Mother, and share this joy of loving Jesus and Mary with each other and with all we meet. I am sure Jesus will say: "Sister N. N. in my Heart, I believe in your faithful love for Me. I love you," for He has promised that our names will be written in His Heart if we spread the devotion to His Sacred Heart.

I have visited all our Middle East houses—all the Sisters are well and are doing God's work with great love.

As you know our Holy Father has given us a beautiful house in Primavalle, Rome for a Shishu Bhavan.... Marseilles, in France, was also started...

In future, kindly send the news of parents' death to SM. Frederick so that in her Mother House newsletter, which she writes every month, she may ask for prayers. Kindly send immediately the names of parents of the Sisters in your Community who have died in 1980.

Mt 2:16–18 Keep 28th December as a very special feast in all your Shishu Bhavans,
and get the children specially blessed.[b] Prepare them with a small Tri-
Mt 25:40 duum, and also give them that childlike love for Jesus.

Let us [join] together with the Holy Father, who prays the Stations of the Cross daily with great fervour....

A number of our Sisters are cutting their food—for either they do not like the food, or they are afraid they will become fat if they eat the normal

a. The meaning is: street by street; the Sisters would be praying with the people in one street on one Saturday, another street another Saturday.

b. December 28th is the Feast of the Holy Innocents.

amount. Both these reasons are very worldly motives unworthy of an MC. I am sure Our Lady never had this kind of thoughts—a thing like this can divide your love for Christ.

In some places, because the children are troublesome, many Sisters are using corporal punishment. This we never did before, believing that we do it to Jesus. Mt 25:40

According to our Constitutions we have to learn the language of the people among whom we live and work. This binds us in India also, as every State has its own language. The Superiors are bound to provide time and means to learn. In some places in and out of India Sisters cannot teach Catechism to First Communion children because they do not know the language, even after months spent in the same place. You cannot give "whole-hearted service" if you do not know the language the Poor speak, and if you do not take the trouble to learn. Where is whole-hearted?

When sick, we must remember that we are the poorest of the poor. We should not continually have the specialist and change doctors, medicine, etc., and see the Doctor for every little thing, and yet our Poor must be satisfied with what our Sisters give them with faith. Often when medicine is given, it is not taken, and yet our poor walk long distances to get the few tablets our Sisters give them. During this Advent, let us ask ourselves—sincerely and humbly: "In what can I really claim that I am the poorest of the poor? In what can I stand near them and say 'I am one of you'?" Why do we have in our Constitutions "that every MC is the poorest of the poor"—in what and how?

If Our Lady and St. Joseph were looking for a place to make a home for Jesus, would they choose our house and all it holds and is filled with? Does our Community and way of life of Poverty resemble that of the Manger Lk 2:7
of Bethlehem—which is what they are looking for? During this Advent we will in a special way try to know the Poverty we vow—love it and live accordingly. To experience the joy and freedom of Poverty as Jesus did, we need the surrender in Obedience, for if we really understand the undivided love for Jesus in Chastity, obedience is the foundation of that Love. The Poverty of Jesus will bring us very close to the Sacred Hearts of Jesus and Mary, and help us grow in their likeness through humility of heart and purity of life.

To understand what Jesus is asking from our Society and each one of us, let us ask Our Lady to give us her heart, so full of love and humility, that we may love Jesus as She loves Him.

To the Morning Offering, which you say on rising, kneeling at the foot
of your bed, add the following: "In union with all the Masses being of-
Mt 11:29 fered throughout the world, we offer you our hearts; make them meek
and humble like yours." The hymn "Sweet Lord, Thy Thirst for Souls"[a]
should be sung daily at the Adoration after the Office.

My prayer, love and blessing will be with each one of you for Christ-
Lk 2:8–20 mas, wishing you all that Jesus, Mary and Joseph, together with the Angels and Shepherds, would wish you.

God bless you
Mother

ED 36. 16TH DECEMBER 1980

LDM

16th December 1980

My dearest Children,

This brings you Mother's love, blessing and prayer for each one of you—that you may grow in holiness through

—Consecrated Chastity—

Christ's previous gift of Himself to us by which He offers us His lifelong,
Jn 15:19 faithful and personal friendship, espousing us to Himself in tenderness
Hos 2:19 and love. The Eucharist, in a special sense, is our glory and joy, and the
mystery of our Union with Him.

Jn 15:13 There is no greater love than the Love of Christ. Let us ask Our Lady
to teach us to love Jesus as She loved Him—with a pure Heart—with un-
Rom 8:35; 38–39 divided love in Chastity—that nothing and nobody will or can separate us
from the love of Christ.

Death, yes—but no Separation.

Our Christmas and New Year gift to Jesus—is our:

Chastity—Chaste
Purity—Pure
Virginity—Virgin.

God bless you,
Mother

a. See footnote to MGL 35 of 27th June 1965, pp. 60–61.

1981

MGL 157. [2nd] FEBRUARY 1981

+

LDM

[2nd] February 1981[a]

My dearest Children,

This brings you Mother's love, blessing and prayer for each one of you—that you may grow in the likeness of Christ through Purity—a humble heart is a pure heart and a pure heart can see God. Let us ask Our Mt 5:8
Lady to enclose our heart in her heart. This month specially we will try to speak the truth and to act the truth—no lies in our words—no hiding in our actions. Often during the day we will pray: HEART OF JESUS, MAKE
MY HEART PURE THROUGH TRUTHFULNESS SO THAT I CAN SEE Mt 5:8; 25:40
YOU IN MY SISTERS AND THE POOR I SERVE.

God bless you,
Mother

MGL 158. 8th FEBRUARY 1981

+

LDM

Bombay
8th February 1981

My dearest Children,

My gratitude to each one of you for the fervent and joyful way you have taken to heart to spread the love of the Sacred Heart in the families of our People. Your Adoration, MC fast and Consecration [are] the great

a. This letter was sent to the houses as a cover letter for the "Spiritual Exercises" for the month of February, with the theme "Devotion to the Sacred Heart of Jesus helped on by a Lively Faith".

gift of God to the Society, and so I pray that you may always have the love and courage to love Christ with undivided love in CHASTITY, through freedom of POVERTY, in total Surrender in OBEDIENCE and WHOLE HEARTED AND FREE SERVICE to the Poorest of the Poor, and so grow in the likeness of Christ through holiness that comes from the Heart of God Himself.

The news our Sisters have sent me is really something beautiful for God, and to think that each one's name is written in the Heart of Jesus. Our Lady must be already reading your names in His Heart, and loving you with greater love because you love Her Son Jesus. I also find that there is greater understanding love in your Communities, so one big "THANK YOU, JESUS."

The fruit of undivided love for Jesus in Chastity is our Fourth Vow—ZEAL FOR SOULS. For if we really love Jesus, that love must be put in a living action—for us it is the service of the Poorest of the Poor.—What we must do is to have and to put into the work greater love and more generous service.

- If it is the SCHOOL, then the calling of the children and the preparation of your school work and Sunday School must be done with greater care and thought for the children.
- If it is FIRST COMMUNION or MARRIAGE CLASSES, [teach] with greater Faith and conviction of what you teach—after much real preparation and knowledge of what the Church is teaching today. In preparing the families—[teach] especially the fidelity of married life and the sinfulness of abortion, the importance of Natural Family Planning as [a proof] of greater love.
- If DISPENSARY WORK, go in time and do not leave before you have attended each person. In giving medicine, give with respect; do not humiliate the poverty of the Poor by giving with harshness and being in a hurry.
- If with the LEPERS—what love, what tender courageous love you need. If you pray, you will be able to do so with faith—and if you believe, the fruit of that faith is love and compassion. They need your understanding love, full of patience and thoughtfulness.
- If at NIRMAL HRIDAY—the living Tabernacle of the suffering Christ—how clean your hands must be to touch the broken bodies, how clean your tongue must be to speak the words of comfort, faith and love; for, for many of them, it is the first contact with love, and

it may be their last. How much you must be alive to His Presence, if you really believe what Jesus had said: "YOU DID IT TO ME." Mt 25:40

- If in SHISHU BHAVAN where life begins, how much of that tender loving love and touch you must put into your work. How much we need to pray the work—not just do the work. It may become doing it for something—instead of doing it for SOMEBODY. Right there we must protect that unwanted child.
- Especially we must take special care of our BIG GIRLS—in their hunger for love and in their rejection, they are inclined to give trouble sometimes; the work with them is more difficult than with the lepers, but they are at that time Christ in the distressing disguise.— Mt 25:40
Help them to pray, pray with them—go among them as one to serve Mt 20:28, Mk 10:45, Jn 13:1–17
and not as one to be served. Never use such words as "You have been picked up",[a] or "You are a bad girl", etc. She, too, like you and me, has been created by the same loving hand of God, for greater things, to love and to be loved—therefore my Sister, my Brother.
- If VISITING THE FAMILIES, with how much delicate respect and dignity must you do this work—how much you need Our Lady's example.—When visiting her cousin Elizabeth, she went there with Lk 1:38–56
Jesus as the Handmaid of the Lord—not to gossip—not to find fault, not to hurt—but to serve. Jesus has taught us—before He could give His Body to His disciples, He washed their feet—also make sure Jn 13:4–5
your visit brings peace, joy and unity. Out of respect for the poor, do not eat nor drink outside when visiting the rich or the Poor. Come praying, pray with them, leave the place praying.

All these works of love are but the fruit of your union with Jesus—they are your love for Jesus in living action and therefore something for which we need to grow in the likeness of Christ through meekness and humility. Mt 11:29
This is the "likeness unto Christ" that Jesus has promised to give if we but ask the Father in His Name—for Jesus Himself has said that up to now we have not asked the Father in His name. So let us ask Him for the grace to Jn 14:13, 14; 15:16; 16:23, 24
be Holy as He, our Father, is Holy—to love each other as He loves each Mt 5:48; Lk 6:36
one of us. Jn 13:34; 15:12

God bless you
Mother

a. Mother is admonishing the Sisters not to humiliate the girls by reminding them that they were picked up from the street as babies.

MGL 159. 22ND MARCH 1981

+

LDM

Mother House
22nd March 1981

My Dearest Children:

Mt 26–27; Mk 14–15; Lk 22–23; Jn 18–19
Mt 28:8; Lk 24:36, 41, 52; Jn 20:19–26

During these days the Passion of Christ has been your strength. May the Risen Christ be your Joy and your Peace.

The three retreats that we had for our Superiors in India have been really a gift of God. I do hope we will be able to have it for our Superiors outside of India also. I am sure each community feels the sunshine of God's love radiating through the joy the Superior has brought to her Sisters.—If

Is 43:1, 4

you could but remember that He has called you by name—You are His, You are precious to Him, He loves you. My Sister belongs to Him, she is precious to Him. This knowledge will soon become the burning flame of love of God in our Community. My prayer for each one of you—that you grow in the likeness of Christ through love for each other and for the Poor you serve. Know each other better and you will find each other great and beautiful gifts of God, and you will love your Sister as she is and do for her and to her what you would like to do to Jesus Himself—for she [is] the Poorest of the Poor, [and] in giving her wholehearted and free service, you

Mt 25:40

are giving it to Jesus in the distressing disguise of that Sister. In the Poor, in our Sisters—it is He—and so we are 24 hours in His presence—therefore Contemplatives in the heart of the world. If we would only learn how to pray the work by doing it with Jesus—for Jesus—to Jesus, for the glory of His Name and the good of souls.

As our poor keep growing in Poverty—due to the great rise in living [costs], let us be more careful regarding the poverty of our houses. The daily needs that our Poor cannot get—let us be more careful in the use of them—so that we also feel the hardship in food, clothing, water, electricity, soap—things which our Poor often go without. Because we get these things easily, we use them in abundance, maybe more than we would use if we were at home.

Mt 10:26; 28:5, 10, 20; Lk 12:4, 32; Jn 14:27; Rev 1:17; 2:10
Jn 13:34; 15:12

Let us ask Our Lady and St. Joseph to make our Communities what they made Nazareth for Jesus. Let us not be afraid. Jesus said: "Be not afraid, I am with you" and "Love one another as I have loved you"—by this they will know that you belong to Jesus. Love does not live on words, nor can it be explained by words—above all that love which is in Him and

comes from Him and which finds Him—touches Him—serves Him—
loves Him in others.—Such love is true—burning—pure—without fear 1 Jn 4:18
and doubt.—No greater love [is there] than the love Christ Himself has
shown us—so I ask you to love one another as He has loved us. As the Jn 13:34; 15:12
Father has loved Him—He has loved us—loves us now.—He has called us Jn 15:9
by our name—we are precious to Him. Is 43:1, 4

Please, all of you pray daily for Mother's intention. The Adoration on Thursday night and the MC fast on the First Friday of each month we shall keep on—as it has brought so much consolation to the Sacred Heart and so much Joy to every Community and Peace to the Families. We shall keep the Church fast on other Fridays in Lent.

In many houses the Sisters have told me that the white [bed] sheet is cheaper, so please do not buy the grey cloth any more, but use up what we have.

I hope you are all well and doing God's work with great love. As I am most of the time out of Calcutta, please write to Sr. M. Frederick for what you need, as she, being in the house, can answer you immediately.

May the joy of our Risen Lord be your strength in your work—your Mt 28:8; Lk 24:41, 52; Jn 20:20
way to the Father, your Light to guide you and your Bread of Life. Re- Jn 6:35, 48, 51
member that the Passion of Christ ends always in the Joy of the Resurrec- Mt 26–27; Mk 14–15; Lk 22–23; Jn 18–19
tion, so when you feel in your own heart the suffering of Christ, remem-
ber the Resurrection has to come—the Joy of Easter has to dawn.

God bless you,
Mother

ED 37. 8TH MAY 1981

+
LDM

8th May 1981

My Dearest Children:

We have much to thank God for—in the 52 years of my religious life, 32 have been spent with you and the Poorest of the Poor. The best way to prove our gratitude to God is to make a strong resolution that we will grow in holiness through love for each other and the Poor we serve.

God bless you,
Mother

MGL 160. [5TH] JUNE 1981

+

LDM

[5th] June 1981[a]

My Dearest Children,

During this month of June we shall have the opportunity of thanking and praising God for His great love for each one of us through the preparation for and celebration of the two great feasts of God's love—

Acts 2:1–13; Rom 5:5 The Feast of Pentecost—when the Spirit of God's love has been poured out into the hearts of men, enabling us to become sons of God in Jesus, and

The Feast of the Sacred Heart of Jesus—which reveals to us the
Eph 3:18 "depth and the height, the length and the breath" of God's compassionate and merciful love for each one of us.

Let us spend this month in deeper awareness of God present in us, abiding
Jn 14:23 within us, living in us through the power of His Spirit of Love, dwelling in us, and helping us to discover the riches of God's love revealed to us in the
Acts 1:8 Heart of Jesus, and making us true witnesses of Jesus in the world today. May the Holy Spirit so possess us that we may never lose the Presence of God and His inestimable love.

God bless you,
Mother

MGL 161. 2ND JULY 1981

L.D.M.

2nd July 1981

My dearest Children,

My Brother has gone home to God to join our family. My Mother must be delighted to see her only Son back home.—Today at 3 P.M. they are having the burial. So let us pray for His wife & family.[b] I am leaving for

a. This letter was sent to the houses as a cover letter for the "Spiritual Exercises" for the month of June. On some of the drafts, the following was typed as a last sentence of the letter: "Theme for the Month of June: "DEVOTION TO THE SACRED HEART OF JESUS HELPED ON BY DOCILITY TO THE HOLY SPIRIT."

b. Mother wrote this from Venezuela. Her brother, Lazar Bojaxhiu, died of cancer on 3rd July 1981 in Palermo, Sicily. Mother must have written this letter as soon as she received the news (which,

England & Ireland on the 4th night and will have to be in Belfast for the Peace prayer. So pray much for Mother. I will write soon.

God bless you
Mother

MGL 162. 11TH AUGUST 1981

+ LDM

Cairo[a]
[11th] August 1981

My dearest Children,

This brings you Mother's love, blessing and prayer—that you may grow more and more in the love of God through fidelity to the humble works of the Society. Never be afraid or ashamed to be a true MC—the more you grow in the true Spirit of an MC, the more tender will be your love for Jesus in the distressing disguise of the Poor. Mt 25:40

Mary was a true MC because She was not afraid to be the handmaid of the Lord, and so She went in haste to put her beautiful humility into a living action of love, to do the handmaid's work to Elizabeth, and we know what this humility obtained for the unborn child—he "leapt with joy" in the womb of his Mother. The first human being to recognize the coming of Christ—and then his Mother sang with joy, with gratitude and praise to the Mother of the Lord. Lk 1:38–56

Humility always radiates the greatness and glory of God. How wonderful are the ways of God—He used humility, smallness, helplessness, poverty to prove to the world that He loved the world.[b]—Let the MC not be afraid to be humble, small, helpless to prove their love for God.

We have much to thank God [for] this Year—for all the Wonderful Graces our Superiors have received during their retreats....

---

because of the time difference between Italy and Venezuela, could have been the 2nd in Venezuela) or Mother could have made a mistake in writing the date and written 2nd instead of 3rd.

a. Mother wrote this letter on notepad sheets given to her on the flight to Egypt, which read: "A BORDO DI UN JET ALITALIA / ON BOARD AN ALITALIA JET." She was in Cairo from 23rd July to 1st August, so she might have begun the letter on the plane and finished it later, or just taken the notepad home with her and written later; she had used at least two different pens to write this letter. The handwritten draft is dated as "August 1981"; however, on the typed version of the letter the date is 11th August 1981, which is probably the date that the Sister typist had typed the letter.

b. Mother wrote "proof to the world" in the handwritten draft; we have corrected this obvious spelling mistake using the principle of silent correction. In the typed version of this letter the Sister typist replaced the abbreviations with full words and the ampersand sign with "and". We respected the original interpretation of the typist in this matter.

In a number of houses our Sisters are reading highly polished books—higher than the Simplicity of the Gospel. I am afraid much of it cannot be put in a living action—and also sometimes [it is] confusing by its non-understanding. In some houses Mother's letters are very little known, less loved and still less put into practice. At least once a day you should take the trouble to read the Letters or the Instructions—in common.[a] Days of Recollection should also be prepared—as far as possible—from the theme that you have chosen together. These days of recollection must, each time, bring you closer to each other—therefore always have the Chapter on the day of recollection. Try to renew your General Permissions and, if possible, write your home letter. Try to be as much as possible alone with God—so
Hos 2:14 that you can listen to Him when He speaks in the Silence of your heart.

During the retreats I have again insisted so much to make the Superiors realize that each one of them and each one in their Community [has]
Is 43:1, 4 been called by your name—you belong to Him—you are precious to Him.
Jn 15:13 He loves each one of you with a deep personal love—there is no greater
love than the love of Christ. Try to meditate on the above words. Make
them your own and remember them when you are tempted to be unkind
Is 43:1, 4 or uncharitable to each other or the Poor—[remember] they are precious
Jn 13:34; 15:12 to Him, He loves them as He loves you. Love one another with the same
love as you love Jesus and let Jesus love you as He loves His Mother. This love for your Sisters and Jesus' love for you, when united, will make you all One heart full of love.

Let us all use everything in our Power, with God's grace, to really make our Mother House, every community and all the communities, united with each other—One heart full of love with the Mother House—One with Mother—one with each other and one with Jesus: Our SOCIETY. Unity is [the] fruit of prayer—of humility—of love. Therefore if the Community prays together, [it] will stay together,[b] and if you stay
Jn 13:34; 15:12 together—you will love one another as Jesus loves each one of you, and
this is what we are going to give Our Lady on the Feast of our Society: <u>a real change of heart</u>—by making it really one heart full of love in our Community. And this one heart, make it one with Mother and offer it to Jesus, so that He will be able to give this beautiful gift to His Mother on her feast day, the 22nd August.

a. Traditionally, this is done as a reading during breakfast and during spiritual reading on day-in.

b. Mother is adapting Fr. Peyton's well-known expression: "The family that prays together stays together." Fr. Patrick Peyton, CSC (1909–1992), was an Irish priest and promoter of the rosary, also known as The Rosary Priest. His cause for canonization was opened in 2001.

I really want you Sisters to take this letter and make your own [the] parts that will help you grow in the likeness of Christ.

My brother died on the 1st Friday of July, a real going home to God. I believe He died beautifully. Pray for the repose of his Soul and also [for] his family.—

I hope to be with you before the Feast of the Society—but if [it is] not possible, I wish you all a very HAPPY AND HOLY FEAST.

God bless you
Mother

MGL 163. 29TH SEPTEMBER 1981

L.D.M.

Melbourne
29th September 1981

My Dearest Children,

This brings you Mother's love, blessing and prayer for each one of you,
that you may grow in holiness through prayer that comes from a meek
and humble heart—for a humble heart is a pure heart. A pure heart can Mt 11:29
see God, and if you see God's face in your Sister—and in your Poor—nat- Mt 5:8
urally you will love Him in her more and more. I realise why we don't
love one another as Jesus loves each one of us: because our love for Jesus is Jn 13:34; 15:12
divided—by some sin, small or big. How great and tender is the love of the
Father to have given the Sacrament of Mercy where we go as sinners with Jn 20:23
sin and we return as sinners without sin. Oh the tenderness of God's love!
If we would only allow Him to love us.

"Be not afraid—I have called you by your name, you are Mine. Water Mt 10:26; 28:5, 10;
(sin) will not drown you, fire (passions) will not burn you. You are precious Lk 12:4, 32; Jn 14:27; Rev 1:17; 2:10
to Me. I love you. I have carved you in the palm of My hand. You are Mine." Is 43:1, 2, 4; 49:16

Just think: each time God looks at His Hand He sees you. What tender
love He expresses for you, His own little one. Allow Jesus to love you—as
the Father has loved Him. No one can love nor has ever loved more than Jn 15:9
the love with which the Father has loved His Son—and to think, Jesus has
loved us as the Father has loved Him. Remember, my Sisters, that Jesus
wants us to love each other as the Father has loved Him. Jn 15:12

Do we really understand? We will understand only if we really love one
another. There is no greater love—than the love of a sister for another in Jn 15:13

the Community. There is so much hurt instead of so much love—so much bitterness instead of so much sweetness—so much repetition instead of si-
Hos 2:14 lence. We forget that in the silence of the heart, God speaks, and from the
Mt 12:34; Lk 6:45 fullness of the heart, we speak. Only when we have heard Him in the Silence of the heart—yes my Sisters, [only when] we have learned to listen to God in the silence of our heart, then only we can say: I pray.[a] There is no such a thing as prayer or love. There is no prayer without love, there is no love without prayer. If there is no love in our community, first, let us examine our prayer life:—Is it faithful, is it true, is it constant, is it full, is it really so real that in the silence of your heart you can hear Him speak? If we only knew the art, the joy, the fruitfulness of silence—our Community would become the Sunshine of God's love, the burning flame of God's love in action.

My Sisters, if you really mean to be an MC in truth—then let us really remove all uncharitableness from our hearts, our community, our society. I know you all love Mother with a tender love, but you cannot give Mother greater sign of your true love [than] by putting that love you have for her into a living action—of loving your Sisters in the Community.
1 Jn 4:20 St. John says: you are a liar if you say you love God Whom you do not see, and not your neighbour whom you see.

How can you tell me that you love me and write such beautiful letters and cards for my Feast and other times, and in your community you are the cause of destruction of love and unity and Peace? I do not know how far we can go like this—this is why I do not wish to have any feast day celebration—if you do not give me what I am asking you all the time—then I begin to doubt your love for me. In many places, people have come to know and they wonder how I speak so strongly in public on the love for one another and yet that same love is missing among you.

October is the month of the Holy Rosary—let us use the Rosary to bind us to each other. For Our Lady, I feel, is the only one who can obtain this great grace from Our Lord for us, for our Society.

I hear that in some houses my letter is just one more to be pinned on the board. Maybe once it is read by the Superior to the community—this is not enough. Each single Sister must make use of the letter

a. The original is: "Only when we have heard Him in the Silence of the heart—yes, my Sisters, unless we have learned to listen to God in the silence of our heart, then only we can say: I pray." However, the sentence seems to be incomplete. Either the typist missed something, or Mother did not complete the sentence. We have corrected the text to what Mother probably meant.

personally—take up the point that she needs most and start examining her conscience and confessing on that point.

During these last three months of this year we will use every means to grow in this love for each other at any cost and become a Cause of joy to each other. Therefore,

1. We shall first of all copy into our prayer book the Constitution on Charity.
2. We shall examine ourselves daily.
3. Take [charity] for our Particular and General Examen.
4. In Confession we shall take care to confess even the smallest sin against charity.
5. The theme of our recollection day will be on Charity.
6. At least twice a week the Superior will prepare the spiritual reading for the Community on charity.
7. . . .[a]
8. We shall mortify in a special way our eyes and our tongue.
9. Put this love for your Sisters in a living action by forgiving and by asking to be forgiven.
10. We shall often say during the day: "Heart of Jesus burning with love for me and my Sister—inflame our hearts with love for each other."

My dearest Children—I will not write to you again until Christmas, but I want from every single Community—one letter together—to write to me during Advent on the fruitfulness or failure of the 10 points in your Community.

I hope and pray that on Christmas Night I will be able to make an offering of your letters with what they contain, to the Child Jesus, and so show Him that He is precious to each one of us—and that we love Him— Jn 15:9
as the Father and His Mother have loved Him.

God bless you
Mother

a. Guidelines regarding reparation for lack of charity have been omitted.

ED 38. DECEMBER 1981

December 1981[a]

Jn 13:34, 15:12 Remember, my Sisters, that Jesus wants us to love each other as the Father has loved Him.

Mother

a. Mother's message was handwritten by a Sister.

1982

MGL 164. 23RD JANUARY 1982

+ LDM

Mother House
23rd January 1982

My dearest Children,

This brings you Mother's love, blessing and prayer for each one of you, that you may grow in holiness through love for each other in tenderness and love, as Jesus loves you. Holy Father has made a special appeal for family life and has written an exhortation on it.[a] Together with him we will help him by our first Friday Night Adoration and MC Fast, and [we will] more intensely search for families, to consecrate them to the Sacred Heart. We will bring Peace in the world through the holiness, joy, unity and love of the family. No one could help us do this better than Our Lady, the Mother of Jesus and our Mother. She will help us to grow in the likeness of Christ in such a way that when our people look up, they see only Jesus in us.

Jn 13:34; 15:12

Jn 19:27

Mt 17:8; Mk 9:8

This year we are going to work very hard through prayer and sacrifices—to grow in Purity of heart through Poverty—the Poverty of Bethlehem, of Nazareth, of Calvary. [Negligence in the practice of] poverty is something that can divide our undivided love for Christ in Chastity. To be able to be only all for Jesus—to love Him with undivided love—we need a Pure Heart—purified by the freedom of Poverty—for the less we have, the more we can give, and in possessing Jesus we possess all things. That is why we can give more, because we can give Jesus. To be like Jesus—we, too, must become poor, for He, being rich, became poor for love of us. We too, must become Poor for love of Jesus and the Poor we serve. For to be

2 Cor 6:10

2 Cor 8:9

a. *Familiaris Consortio*, On the Role of the Christian Family in the Modern World, promulgated on 22nd November 1981 by Pope John Paul II.

Lk 4:18 able to understand the Poor, to be able to proclaim the Good News to the Poor, we must know what is Poverty, therefore:

- we freely give to God our natural right and freedom to accept and to dispose freely of anything that has monetary value. Therefore, we shall never keep, give away, lend or borrow things of money value without leave of the Superior. Hence we joyfully choose to ask permissions.
- We renew our general permissions once a month.

Our Poverty should be true Gospel Poverty—gentle, tender, glad and openhearted, always ready to give an expression of love. Poverty is love before it is renunciation.

- To love it is necessary to give. To give it is necessary to be free from selfishness.

We shall begin first by taking special care of the following: (Const. 48f)

- We shall eat the <u>food</u> of the people, of the country where we live, using what is cheapest. It should be sufficient and wholesome so as to maintain good health, which is essential for the work of our vocation.
- Our <u>Houses</u> should be <u>simple</u> and modest, where the Poor feel at home.
- We shall <u>walk</u> whenever opportunity offers, and take the cheapest means of transport available to the Poor, as far as possible.
- We shall sleep in common dormitories without privacy, like the Poor.

Let every community try to free itself by using first [these] 4 points. Deliberately choosing the cheapest, the less attractive, and give to the Poor the best. A great cut must be made on the "Bill"[a] of Postage, Books, water, electricity, use of Telephone. Use of trunk Calls[b] has become so natural as if it [were] next door. [The] Telephone bill in one house alone in 1981 came up to Rs. 5470/-. Even the Postal people were surprised how Missionaries of Charity Sisters, who are supposed to be poor, can afford so many calls. We forget that we are using the money of the Poor—given to

a. Mother is instructing the Sisters that they should be careful in the use of postage, books, water, electricity and telephone, and so cut down expenses.

b. That is, long distance calls, made with the help of the operator.

us with great trust, [in the belief] that we will use it for the Poorest of the Poor. Therefore the misuse of money, etc. is an offence against the 7th and 8th Commandments, and against our Vow of Poverty. Ex 20:15, 16; Dt 5:19–20

Each time we misuse the money, or other things, or give it without permission, it is a theft and a lie. A Theft, because we use what is not ours or keep it until it goes bad. A Lie, because we pretend to be Poor and we are not.

I ask all the Superiors of every house, together with your Sisters and Houses of Formation, to take to heart Mother's appeal to help each Community and each Sister experience the joy of the Poverty of Christ.

To help our Sisters to greater love, unity and true oneness in the Missionaries of Charity Spirit, we have divided the regions [in]to smaller regions—and so many more Sisters are involved in the sharing of the responsibility of the houses with Mother. I enclose the list.[a] I hope and pray that you will accept the new Regionals with as much love and trust—and be one heart full of love with them. Superiors should ask all permissions from them.

Each Regional is under a Councillor and they will deal directly with her....

Jesus has entrusted the Missionaries of Charity not to me alone—but to you—each one—and to me. And so we must together make our Society "Something Beautiful for God"—All for JESUS.

P.S. Newsletters about our houses for Co-workers: News Letters should not be sent directly to Co-workers—but to Sr. M. Joseph Michael. Same for letters to and from our Sick and Suffering Co-workers—they should be sent to Sr. M. Paulette.

The Report of the Superior for each Sister should accompany the letter of the Sister asking for Renewal of Vows. Please write each report separately, sign and date it also, and post in the same envelope, so that letter and report reach together.

Houses outside India should write earlier, as letters are reaching very late.

God bless you
Mother

a. The list has been omitted.

Intentions—Rosary:

1st Mystery—Our Aspirants & Postulants
2nd Mystery—Our Novices
3rd Mystery—Our Professed Brothers & Sisters
4th Mystery—Our Poor & Co-workers
5th Mystery—Our Holy Father, our Society & Priest Co-workers.

ED 39. MAY 1982

May 1982

My dearest Children—

Again and again I ask Jesus:

Mt 11:29 Take our hearts and make them like yours,
Meek and humble.
Meekness for each other,
Humility with God.

How great is His love for us, to have offered His precious gift of life-
Hos 2:19 long, faithful and personal friendship, espousing us in tenderness and love.
Jn 15:13 What greater love can we have than the love of our Crucified Spouse.
Mt 25:40 What greater love can we give—than the love in action we give to Him in
His distressing disguise of the poorest of the poor.

As I am leaving for Europe and America—please write for permissions to the Councillors appointed for your area.—Address the letter directly to her. All six Councillors are at the Mother House. Sr. M. Frederick is in the Mother House also.

I pray for you that you may more and more grow in the likeness of
Christ through love for each other, and so become the true Carriers of the
Is 49:16 good news that God will not forget you.... He has carved you on the palm
Is 43:1; Is 43:4 of His hand.... He has called you by your name.... You are His.... You are
precious to Him.... He loves you.

God bless you
Mother

MGL 165. 29TH MAY 1982

LDM

29th May 1982

My dearest Children,

This brings you Mother's love, blessing and prayer for each one of you, that you may grow in the love of God through love for each other. I am very happy to know Sr. M. Frederick is back home in the Mother House. We missed her so much during the whole year.

Florence, Barcelona, and Dublin . . .are the 3 new houses we have been able to open as we did not have a group for 1st Profession.[a] Please God, in Dec. we shall do the rest.

By now all those who have been changed, I am sure they have gone to their places.—It is so wonderful to know—that where obedience sends us, that is the place where Jesus is waiting for us.

This time I do not write more, as I am sending the instruction of Rev. Fr. Brenin[b]—he is confessor of our Rome novices. It is very beautiful. I am sure you will profit much from it. I would like if a copy was sent to every house. I am hoping to [visit] this time the houses in Europe, Mid. [Middle] East & Africa, so pray that I am able to do so with great love.

Remember always—do not be afraid, you are precious to Him—He loves you—with tenderness & love He has espoused [you] to Himself. You are His, for He has offered you His lifelong, faithful and personal friendship—you have nothing to fear.

Mt 10:26; 28:5, 10; Lk 12:4, 32; Jn 14:27; Rev 1:17; 2:10
Is 43:1, 4
Hos 2:19–20

God bless you
Mother

a. Since in 1979 the Postulancy was extended from six months to one year, in May 1982 there was no regular group of novices that would make their first profession. As there were fewer Sisters who made first profession, Mother was able to open fewer new foundations than usual.

b. Fr. Brenin's talk has been omitted.

MGL 166. 19TH AUGUST 1982

+

LDM

Athens[a]
19th August 1982

My dearest Children,

This brings you Mother's love, blessing and prayer for each one of you that you may grow in the likeness of Mary through Purity and humility of heart.—This is all I ask Mother Mary to teach us—the joy of loving—
Jn 13:34; 15:12 through Purity and humility.—Do not be afraid to love each other as she loved Jesus.

We have just left Beirut.—It has been one continual action of God, loving us and His people—by continual love actions in tenderness and love.—I brought a big Easter candle with the image of Our Lady with the child on it.—On Thursday the bombing was terrible.—I lit the candle that evening about 4 P.M.—At 5 P.M. all stopped [all] of a sudden.—Since then there is perfect quiet.—We went over and brought 38 crippled and mental little children.[b]—The candle finished last night.—If you have the Easter candle please light it before Our Lady in thanksgiving—the rest I will tell you when I return.[c]

I have to leave for Mexico on the 19th.—Please pray that this my meeting with the rich of the world—[may] bring Jesus in their family life—this is the prayer of our Holy Father.[d]

God be with you all.—May His Mother and ours keep us only all for Jesus.

God bless you
Mother

a. On 19th August, Mother left Beirut, via Athens, for Mexico. She wrote this letter while in transit, at the airport in Athens.

b. "Mental children" here refers to mentally ill children, or children with mental disabilities.

c. A war between Lebanon and Israel began on 6th June 1982. On 11th August 1982, Mother travelled to visit the Sisters in East Beirut and found them safe, although the bombing was only a few miles away. The head of the Red Cross delegation in Lebanon told Mother about handicapped children in West Beirut, left in precarious conditions since the hospital they were in was badly damaged by the bombing. Mother insisted on going into war-torn West Beirut and prayed for a cease-fire. The following day, during the cease-fire, with four Red Cross vehicles, she evacuated thirty-eight children and brought them to our home in East Beirut. Two days later she brought another twenty-seven children.

d. Mother Teresa was invited to speak at the Second International Congress for Latin American Families that was held in Acapulco, Mexico, from 20th to 24th August 1982.

MGL 167. 31ST AUGUST 1982

+

LDM

Venezuela
31st August 1982

My dearest Children,

May the joy of loving Jesus through Mary—in each other and in the Poor—fill your hearts and make each one of you the sunshine of God's love and compassion wherever you are. This is my prayer for each one of you, my children—that you may, more and more, grow in the likeness of Christ through Mary, so that when you look at each other and at the Poor you see only Jesus. Mt 17:8; Mk 9:8

It has been a long time this time that I am away from the Mother House. Thank God we have Sr. M. Frederick and the other Councillors to take care of you and help you to do God's work with great love.

How much we have to thank God for giving us Jesus to espouse us in Hos 2:19–20 Tenderness and love—by giving us His life and His Heart.

Do not be afraid to love until it hurts—for only this love can help you grow like Jesus. Though I am far from you in India—but land, sea, and sky cannot separate us—nothing and nobody will divide the love of Jesus in Rom 8:35, 38–39 us—which has made us one heart full of love, all for Jesus through Mary.

God bless you
Mother

MGL 168. 12TH OCTOBER 1982

+

LDM

Rome
12th October 1982

My dearest Children,

This brings you Mother's love, blessing and prayer for all that you have been and done for me.—My gratitude to each one of you—for all the love and care you have given me, each other and Jesus in the Poorest of the Poor—is my prayer that you be Holy like Mary through Humility of heart and Purity of life so that you become a true Spouse of Jesus Crucified.

It is not possible for me to write to each one and thank you for all the beautiful letters I have received—for the joy these letters have brought to me—and, I am sure, the joy you felt in writing to Mother. I have been so long away from Mother House, but thank God Sr. M. Frederick and all the other Councillors have been there to help you and guide [you]. It is good for you and for me. I was very happy to hear how all the houses prepared for the feast of the Society and how they have grown in love for the Society by trying to live the spirit with greater fidelity. This has given me great joy, and I am grateful to each one of you.

I have visited all the houses in North, South and Central America and I
am now finishing Europe. I hope to finish [the] Middle East and then come
home. I am afraid I will have to sacrifice the joy of visiting our Sisters in
Africa, but I hope I will do so soon. In most of the places the presence
of our Sisters has created a concern and awareness of the Poor in their
country, and so [people] begin to share the joy of serving the Poor. What a
great responsibility for each one of us if we are not a true MC. More than
ever people want to see love in action through our humble works—how
Mt 25:40 necessary it is for us to be in Love with Jesus—to be able to feed Him in
Mt 5:8 the Hungry and the lonely. How pure our eyes and hearts must be to see
Him in the Poor. How clean our hands must be to touch Him in the Poor
with love and compassion. How clean our words must be to be able to pro-
Lk 4:18 claim the Good News to the Poor. That is why we need Mary, the Most
Pure Virgin, to teach us how to be Pure like Her—so that when the Poor
Mt 17:8; Mk 9:8 look up they see only Jesus in us and [so] that we remind them of Her, the
Most Pure Virgin Mother of God, our Mother.

In our old Constitutions and Explanations we had simple rules on "Modesty," how to grow in "Angelic Purity"; it was a beautiful sacrifice "not to touch each other so much as in jest," "not to call each other pet names." Since all the houses have received the Explanation of the Old Constitutions,[a] please look up these points and let us use them, and make them our own—and offer them as a gift of love to Our Lady on the 8th December, the feast of Mary's Virginity, Chastity and Purity. In my talk during the conference in Mexico—prepared by the young people—I asked them to bring the love for Purity back in the world. I believe they have started an International Movement among the youth to do so.

Much of our difficulties and loss of vocations have been caused by neglecting the simple means—that keeps our Purity—pure,
our Chastity—chaste,
our Virginity—virgin.

a. That is, the *Explanation of the Original Constitutions*.

Let us ask Our Lady to help us be only all for Jesus through being faithful to that undivided love for Jesus in Chastity through Mary.

Help each other to grow in love of God through love for each other.

God bless you
Mother

Please pray for the repose of the souls of our Sisters' dear ones.

. . .

ED 40. DECEMBER 1982

December 1982

My Dearest Children,

CHRISTMAS is not only "Doom–Dham"[a] and enjoyment but much more: It is the tenderness of God's love for us. He came to give the Good News to the Poor. If you want to get the real spirit of the Coming of Jesus try to understand Poverty. Lk 4:18

It is very strange that at His Coming He repeated TWO THINGS:

SWADDLING CLOTHES and THE DONKEY Lk 2:7
—Poverty & Humility

They were used twice: at His Birth and before He died. At His Birth, his Mother gave Him and wrapped Him up in Swaddling Clothes, and at His burial he was wrapped in them also. Mt 27:59; Lk 23:53; Mk 15:46; Jn 19:40

Mary with Child rode a little donkey to go to Bethlehem and Jesus rode the donkey when He entered Jerusalem on Palm Sunday. Only in the Holy Land you will find that the donkey—all of them, have a black cross on their back. And the donkey is always doing something humble carrying a basket of food, or a bundle of clothes. Mt 21:7; Mk 11:7; Lk 19:35

St. Bernard used to say: "Jesus, if I have to be a Donkey, let me be a Cheerful Donkey."[b]

Let us ask Our Lady to give us Her Heart so pure, so poor, so free that we may love Jesus only and do the small, humble works for Him, with Him and to Him in the distressing disguise of the Poor. Mt 25:40

God bless you
Mother

a. This is a Hindi expression meaning a grand celebration.

b. St. Bernard of Clairvaux (1090–1153) was a French abbot and a major leader in the renewal of Benedictine monasticism through the newly founded Cistercian order; he is a Doctor of the Church.

1983

MGL 169. [7th] JANUARY 1983

Mother House
First Friday
[7th] January 1983

My dearest Children,

This brings you Mother's love, blessing and prayer for each one of you in every community—that you may grow in the likeness of Mary through Purity of life and humility of heart.

To be able to grow like her in Purity and Humility we need a deep life of Prayer. We need that "Cleaving" in oneness with Jesus, as Mary was.
Lk 2:19; 51 She kept all in the Silence of her Heart. She listened and then she spoke
Jn 2:5 from the fullness of her heart: "Do what He tells you."

Today Our Lady is saying the same words to each one of us: "Do what He tells you."

Mt 11:29 What is Jesus saying to us? "Learn of Me to be meek (pure) and humble
Mt 5:8 of heart." A pure and humble heart can see God—and if we see Him, we will love Him in each other.

Jn 15:9 Jesus came to give us the good news of His Father's love for the world, for each one of us, and it is strange He used Poverty as His strength—His power.

1. A simple Virgin carried Him in Her womb—so small, so weak, so helpless, depending totally on what the simple Virgin gave Him from her own body.
2. He was born of the Virgin Mary, like any other child—only that His Mother remained Virgin even after His birth—no place, no house, no bed, just like any of our poor in Calcutta or New York.
Lk 2:7 His Mother covered Him with swaddling clothes. Thank God that she had at least that. St. Joseph, who acted as His father,

put Him in the manger filled with straw which was used as food for the donkey. When the donkeys saw the little one in the manger—they started breathing often and deeper, so that their breath could warm up the little one in the manger.

Jesus was sent by His Father to the Poor and to be able to understand the Lk 4:18
Poor, Jesus had to know and experience that Poverty in His own Body . 2 Cor 8:9

Today the Father has sent us to the Poorest of the Poor. We too, like [Jesus], must experience the joy and the freedom of Poverty, if we really want to be true MCs—carriers of God's love. That is why we need to pray,
for prayer gives us a clean heart and a clean heart can see God. A clean Mt 5:8
heart is a free heart. A free heart can love Christ with undivided love in
Chastity, with a conviction that nothing and nobody will separate us from Rom 8:35, 38–39
the love of Christ. Our negligence and carelessness in Poverty becomes "Something" that divides our love for Jesus. Once a gap has been made, it is easy for "somebody" to fill that gap. When this "somebody" comes in, it is easier for the devil to make us tell lies in action by hiding, by neglecting prayer, penance and community life. Obedience, the joy of Surrender to God, becomes a burden, and because of the time spent with "Something and somebody" we no longer can give whole hearted and free service to the Poorest of the Poor.

The Constitutions are very clear—

- regarding going alone or visiting with a woman or a child, we must be two. (C. 86c)

...

- [a number of Sisters] allow young men under the cover of volunteers—to work alone with a sister in a room. (C. 40—first paragraph)
- too many letters without permission are being written to people we should not write [to] and even posted and received hidingly. I don't think you realize the trap you are falling in by doing that. A number of Vocations have been lost in our Society and outside among priests and seminarians only through this trick of the devil. (C. 42)
- Do not humiliate your family by giving them anything without permission. Ask and it shall be given you. (C. 46)
- I have noticed in a number of our houses including the Mother House—the decorations on feast days, Profession and Superior's Feast, do not fit with our way of life and work—so much time and material wasted. (C. 64h)

Purity, Chastity, Virginity—these created a special beauty in Mary that attracted God's attention to Mary, and He showed His great love for the world by giving Jesus to her. Mary's love for Purity was so great that she was ready to forego being the Mother of Jesus. She did not want that "somebody" should divide her love for God. Only when the angel ex-
Lk 1:26–38 plained that He will be no man but God—then she said "YES".

Thank you Mary. We too have vowed to God the same purity as you. Help us protect it with our life. Let no impure and deliberate thought, word, desire or touch ever destroy the gift of God. Let no human being ever destroy this gift by any act of passionate attachment. Let my Purity be pure, my Chastity—Chaste, my Virginity—Virgin, only all for Jesus through you Mother of Jesus and my Mother.

To grow in love for Mary's Purity we will say individually before the picture or statue of Our Lady, the Three *Hail Marys* and *Our Queen and Our Mother*[a]—[as] in the Prayer we pray at Night Prayers. During the month of January and February do your community spiritual reading about Our Lady and the Vow of Chastity from Mother's instructions and letters.

God bless you
Mother[b]

MGL 170. 28TH MARCH 1983

+

LDM

Mother House
28th March 1983

My dearest Children,

This year the Holy Father has declared a Year of Redemption—a Holy Year!—to celebrate the Jubilee of Jesus' deepest expression of His love for His Father and for us—His death on the Cross—for it is one thousand,
Mt 27:50; Mk 15:37; Lk 23:46; Jn 19:30 nine hundred and fifty years since Jesus laid down His life for us.[c] Yes,

a. This refers to the prayer *Our Queen and Mother* in the *MC Prayer Book*, p. 64.

b. On the photocopied pages of this letter, after Mother's signature, the typist added the name of a Councillor and the list of the regions under that Councillor's care. This list has been omitted here in order to save space.

c. Pope John Paul II opened the Extraordinary Jubilee or Holy Year of the Redemption,

Jesus, the Son of God, came into the world to give the Good News that God is love and that He loves each one of us, and this He did by redeeming us at the price of every drop of His Precious Blood. Let us make this Year, therefore, a year of greater love. The Holy Father has empowered the Bishops of all dioceses to make the Jubilee Plenary Indulgence[a] available to all during this Holy Year.—Make sure you find out what has been decided for your diocese regarding this and instruct our poor Catholic people about it, that they do not miss the spiritual benefit of the Plenary Indulgence. 1 Jn 4:8, 16

This year, therefore, let us make it a year of greater love. Let us make a strong resolution—to live the life of greater love like Jesus—for each other and the Poor we serve by freeing—

our hearts from all uncharitable desires
our minds from all uncharitable thoughts
our tongues from all uncharitable words, of criticism, repetition, grumbling, carrying of tales, ugly, hurtful words of temper and impatience
our ears from all uncharitable listening

—in a word, living the Purity of Life to the full—with greater love.—Christ has espoused us in tenderness and love. Let us do the same to Him in each other—this is the holiness of MC—greater love for each other and the Poor we serve. Hos 2:19–20

We MCs must take this year as a special appeal of the Sacred Heart—to love one another with greater love and the Poor with greater compassion. Let there be greater understanding love between Superiors and the Sisters of the Community. Let the correction be given and accepted with greater humility; when some fault is committed, make reparation that very day—asking pardon of the Community before dinner prayer and also let the whole community [do extra penance]. I think and feel the Sacred Heart is asking something more from our Society and from each one of us: that during this year [we love with] greater love in PURITY OF LIFE AND HUMILITY OF HEART.

---

commemorating the 1950th anniversary of the Crucifixion, Death and Resurrection of Jesus, on the feast of the Annunciation, 25th March 1983. It concluded on Easter Sunday, 22nd April 1984.

a. "An indulgence is a remission before God of the temporal punishment due to sins whose guilt has already been forgiven, which the faithful Christian who is duly disposed gains under certain prescribed conditions through the action of the Church which, as the minister of redemption, dispenses and applies with authority the treasury of the satisfactions of Christ and the saints." "An indulgence is partial or plenary according as it removes either part or all of the temporal punishment due to sin." *Catechism of the Catholic Church* (*CCC*), 1471. For more information on plenary indulgences see *CCC* 1471–1479.

Lk 9:23 Do not be afraid to love like Jesus—a complete sacrifice of self.—This is what this year of Redemption will give each one—the growth in the likeness of Christ through Mary His Mother.—If you really love your vocation as an MC, if you love Mother, this is what I ask and beg of each one
Jn 13:34; 15:12 of you: Love with greater love each other and the Poor you serve.

As per our Constitution 180, I can appoint a Councillor to help me with the Formation. . . .

To help our Sisters in their work—we will offer—

1st Mystery of the Rosary for Aspirants, Postulants and their Mistresses and for Peace in India;

2nd Mystery for Novices and Tertians and their Mistresses and for peace in Middle East;

3rd Mystery for Professed Brothers and Sisters and their Superiors and for Peace in North and South America;

4th Mystery for our families, our Poor and our Co-workers and Peace in Central America;

5th Mystery for our Holy Father, Mother, Councillors and Regionals and for Priest-Co-workers and for peace in the country you are in.

Please learn by heart these intentions, as they are important for our growth in holiness.[a]

All Superiors, have regular correspondence with your Regional, and all Regionals, with your Councillors; all Mistresses of formation, with the Councillors appointed.

As the Society keeps growing, it is necessary to divide the work and help each other to do it together only all for Jesus—according to the spirit of the Society. We must also pray for our Sisters who have left the Society: Sr. M.—— and Sr. M.—— for allowing their love to be divided; Sr. M.—— and Sr. M.—— desirous to serve the Lord in a different way.

There is one very important point for which I have prayed much—"Home Going" has become a regular holiday making.—Many reasons are given and telegrams received. As we have all made the offering to Jesus of our family and all we had, let us be faithful to this beautiful sacrifice. As

a. At the 1997 General Chapter it was decided to discontinue saying these specific intentions before each decade of the Rosary and instead to say the intentions at the beginning of the Rosary, as follows: "In thanksgiving for all the graces bestowed on the Immaculate Heart of Mary and on each one of us, in reparation for all the sins committed in the world, for our Holy Father, our Mother [or, at present, Sister], and all the Branches of our Society, for peace and unity in the world and in the Church, for all our poor, our families, co-workers, volunteers, and benefactors."

according to our Constitutions we are the poorest of the poor, our people cannot do what we do. Therefore, let us accept this beautiful gift of God and, in union with our families, offer it to God and so let us help our families to share in the love of God that we profess.

I have just visited our houses in Africa. Thank God all is well with all the houses, and the Sisters are doing God's work with great love. You will be glad to know that 7[a] new foundations have been made since January: Tennant Creek (Australia), Borisal (Bangladesh), Hong Kong (Far East), Jeremy [sic[b]] (Haiti), W. Berlin (Germany), Chicago (USA), and a second house in Rwanda for work among the refugees—bringing the total number of our houses to 223. We have much to thank God for.

Let us pray for the repose of the souls of the parents or relatives of our Sisters who have died...

May the joy of the Risen Jesus so fill your hearts that each one of us may truly become the sunshine of God's love and compassion to each other and the Poor we serve. Mt 28:8; Lk 24:41, 52; Jn 20:20

God bless you
Mother

ED 41. MAY 1983

May 1983[c]

My dearest Children,

To be able to be one heart full of love in the Heart of Jesus, we need the Immaculate Heart of Mary, our Queen and our Mother. She is our way to Jesus, the Light of Jesus and the Love of Jesus and the Life of Jesus in each one of us. Let us more and more be a cause of joy to each other, the way of peace to each other and the living Love of Jesus for each other.[d] Very great holiness becomes very simple if we belong fully to Our Lady, if we only abandon ourselves to her totally and without reserve. Nothing is impossible for those whose Mother she is. Often during the day let us raise Jn 19:27

a. Originally, it was typed "6," but in some of the typed versions "Tennant Creek (Australia)" was added in handwriting (not Mother's), 6 was crossed out and 7 written over it.

b. Jeremie (Haiti)

c. On the page with Mother's typed message for this issue of *Ek Dil*, she added in her handwriting the parts that appear in italics.

d. See MGL 109 of 9th August 1974, p. 190.

our hearts to her and ask her to be a Mother to us at this moment—and above all to teach us to love Jesus as she loved Him—with a pure, meek and humble heart like hers.[a]

Is 43:1, 4 *Remember—You are precious to Jesus—He loves you.*—"Be not afraid"[b]—
Mt 28:20; Jn 14:2 *Jesus said, "I am always with you.—My Father loves you—because you have*
Jn 13:34–35; 15:12 1 *loved Me. Love one another as I love you."*

God bless you
Mother

MGL 171. 10TH JUNE 1983

+

LDM

Rome
10th June 1983[c]

My dearest children,

This brings you Mother's love, blessing and prayer that you may grow in holiness and be like Jesus and Mary through love for each other.—If
Jn 13:34; 15:12 we could love each other as Jesus loves each one of us, how like Jesus
Is 43:1, 4 we would be. We are precious to Him—He loves you and me and has
Hos 2:19–20 espoused us in tenderness & love —in spite of our weakness, sins and infidelities.

The professions in Manila, Rome and Calcutta were one of those most beautiful gifts of God: 76 Novices made their first profession, 52 Sisters made final Vows and 138 Postulants joined the first year Noviciate. See how wonderful is the Love of God in action for our young Society. At
Jn 8:44 the same time the devil—as Jesus called him—the father of lies—in his anger goes round to every house, every sister including me and you, like

a. See MGL 93 of 18th June 1972, pp. 161–62.

b. As Mother added to the message in her own handwriting, she wrote (evidently a mistake), "Be not be afraid"; we have corrected it here consistently with other instances where the same phrase appears.

c. Mother began the handwritten draft of this letter on the 9th of June 1983 and might have continued it on the next day, 10th June, the Feast of the Sacred Heart that year ("Today, the Feast of the Sacred Heart, ..."). She wrote this letter while in the hospital, due to the fall she had in Tor Fiscale and the serious heart condition that was discovered as a result. The letter was dated "16th June 1983" in the original printed version; however it seems that this date was misread from the typed version of the letter, since the Sister typist typed small letters "l" and "o" instead of numerals "1" and "0". We have changed the date to the 10th, to correspond to the original typed version.

[a] roaring lion, to see whom he can eat up—and uses all kinds of lies to divide our love for Jesus by pushing somebody or something to preoccupy our attention—affection—attachment. He never uses a strong chain, at first just a little silk thread, with a whisper not to speak about it—[*and then . . .*][a] we know the results—a number of our sisters have been caught. You and I can be caught also, if we neglect prayer—penance—humility—obedience—truthfulness. Let us learn from the others, and ask Our Lady to be a Mother to us—and let us speak in time, not tomorrow, for tomorrow may never come, but today—now. Protect each other—help each other by speaking in time, and if the Sister happens to be the Superior, help her, protect her and speak as soon as possible to the Regional or Councillor. Let us help each other to keep 1 Pt 5:8

the Purity of our heart Pure,
the Chastity of our heart Chaste,
the Virginity of our heart Virgin,

to keep it only all for Jesus through Mary. To some of us the devil may come as an angel of light, cheating us with good things as he did to Jesus. Does not matter how good it is—if it takes you away from prayer, humility, obedience and truthfulness, it's sure it is the devil who is trying to take you away from Jesus, therefore speak in time. Let each one of us examine ourselves which way the devil is trying to take us away from Jesus. Just as small things done with great love are sure means to holiness, so also small negligence of prayer, penance, obedience, purity, can lead us to hell. My children, let us beg Our Lady to protect us, let us often ask her—throw your Mantle of purity over me and keep me pure for Jesus only. 2 Cor 11:14

Today, the feast of the Sacred Heart—let us go very close to His Heart and renew with greater love our Vows, especially our Vow of Chastity, and with St. Agnes and St. Maria Goretti say—die, yes, but sin, no.[b] St. Stanislaus used to faint whenever there was an impure conversation.[c] We

a. The words in italics were in Mother's handwritten draft but were mistakenly left out in the typed copy sent to the houses.

b. St. Agnes of Rome (c. 291–c. 304) was a virgin-martyr, who suffered martyrdom at the age of twelve or thirteen during the reign of the Roman emperor Diocletian. St. Maria Goretti (1890–1902), Italian virgin-martyr, was stabbed by a young man, son of a neighbour, when she refused to submit to his sexual advances. She died forgiving him and was canonized in 1950. Mother often referred to her courage and love for purity.

c. St. Stanislaus Kostka (1550–1568), a young Polish Jesuit novice, entered the Society of Jesus in Rome at the age of seventeen. After nine months he became very sick. Early in the morning on the

will all together during the month of July—the Month of the Precious Blood

Do [more] penance (except Sundays and feast days)
and Church fast on the 3 Fridays following the 1st Friday (MC fast).[a]

Often during the day pray—"Purity of the Heart of Jesus, purify my heart." "In union with all the Precious Blood being offered throughout the world, I offer Thee my heart for all my Brothers and Sisters—especially who are tempted against Purity." "Mary, Mother of Jesus—Cover me with your Purity."

In a special way let us pray and study our Constitutions that explain Prayer, Examination of conscience, Community life, Obedience and Chastity. Let all your instructions [and] meditations fill your month of Reparation, and show still greater love for Jesus and Mary—for your Vocation and [the] Society—for each other and the Poor you serve. This is the year of Redemption, and I feel that Jesus in a special way is trying to purify and sanctify the Society and each one in it through prayer, penance, humility, obedience and Virgin heart filled with Virgin Love—only for Jesus.

While in Tor Fiscale, I had a fall from my bed. It was my Guardian Angel who pushed me, I think, to cause the pain for which I went to hospital, where they discovered I had a heart that needed medical treatment, and so I am now completely in bed. No one is allowed to visit, only our Sisters. The Priest of the hospital kindly brings the Blessed Sacrament Morning and Evening for Adoration and I have Holy Mass in my room. No greater love could Jesus show for one so small—so nothing.—All of you thank Him for loving me so much and also offer your heart again and again to love Him only, with undivided love.

Changes have all gone out. I am sure you have all received them with love and humility—even if it is the place or the people that frighten you, still go with joy and humility. It is Jesus your Spouse who is waiting for
Lk 1:39 you in that place. Go in haste with Mary and bring the Joy of the Presence of Jesus in you to the Community.

I am very grateful for all your prayers and sacrifices. Let us be ready for anything that God may decide for us all. He will take care of each one of you and the Society—for you and the Poorest of the Poor are His own chosen ones.

---

feast of the Assumption, 1568, he told a priest that he saw Mary surrounded by many angels. Shortly afterward he died.

a. "MC fast" means going without lunch, the main meal of the day.

The greatest joy you can give Mother [is] that you be holy through love for each other and the Poor you serve. Be one heart full of love in the heart of Jesus through Mary.

There will be the profession of 3 sisters for 1st Vows and two Final Vows in the Contemplatives on the 18th June.

These, our sisters, are one of the most beautiful flowers we offer to the Sacred Heart of Jesus on this His Feast.

God bless you[a]
Mother

MGL 172. 27TH JULY 1983

+

L.D.M.

Rome
27th July 1983

My dearest children,

This brings you Mother's blessing, love and prayer for each one for the feast of our Society. May Our Lady, in her great love, teach us and help us to be only all for Jesus through Her. Let us remember that we have been called to be Holy—to be so totally all for Jesus that nothing and nobody will separate us from the love of Christ. Lv 11:44–45; 19:2; 20:26 Rom 8:35; 38–39

We have been called to be Souls of prayer right in the midst of the slums—to pray the work—to do it with Jesus, for Jesus, to Jesus. I do not know who is giving you the idea, that the "vocal prayers we pray together at the call of the bell" is not prayer. This is completely wrong. I am sure Our Lady and Jesus must have prayed the psalms often together;—and in the synagogue—what did He do? An MC who is not united in heart and soul with Christ, she will not be able to live the spirit of Total Surrender, Loving Trust and Cheerfulness and so fulfil the aim—to satiate the thirst on the Cross for love of souls. [It is] this satiating of Christ's thirst that makes us contemplatives in the heart of the world—makes us like Jesus, Holy. Jn 19:28

It is true if we only "say" prayers then, naturally, you may not be

a. In the handwritten draft, Mother wrote "Go" and half of the letter "d". Probably she was interrupted and then after did not remember to continue. As there was no more place on the bottom of the page, she added the information about the vows of the MCC Sisters on the first page writing with small letters, vertically, to fit it in the small space next to the date.

praying. To pray the prayers means to completely[a] be united to Jesus in
such a way as to allow Him to pray in us, with us, for us, through us. This
cleaving to each other, Jesus and I, is prayer. We are all called to pray like
this. Much disturbance and disorder has come into the world for negligence of family prayer, religious Community prayer. Please do not allow
these wrong ideas [to] penetrate you—for it may destroy the very fruit of
Mt 18:20 Prayer—holiness. Jesus said, "where two pray together, I am there."—He
Lk 24:13–35 came to Emmaus because they were two speaking about Jesus on the way.
Acts 1:14; 2:1–4 [The] Holy Spirit came on the Apostles when they were together in prayer
with Mary. Fidelity to growing into a Soul of prayer is the beginning of
Mt 25:40 holiness. And if we remember that whatever we do, we do it to Jesus, we
are really Contemplatives in the Heart of the World. To be able to grow
Mt 5:8 in prayer we need a clean heart—for a clean heart can see God. Therefore
if you really want to pray, make sure your heart is clean—free to belong
only to Jesus—to love only Jesus—to serve only Jesus in the distressing
disguise.

When you are doing the humble works of the society, learn to pray the
Lk 2:51 work, as Jesus did in Nazareth for 30 years. The life and work, the prayer
and sacrifice at Nazareth is so much like [what] MC life in the community
should be. That peace, joy, unity that joined the Holy Family together in
prayer and work is such a wonderful living example [of] what our community should be. They grew in holiness together. We too could have deep
Jn 6:35, 48, 51 growth in Holiness, for we receive daily Jesus, the Bread of Life, and serve
Mt 25:40 and touch Him in the distressing disguise of the [*Poorest of the*][b] Poor.

In having Jesus, what else do we need? I beg you, my children, do not
Mt 6:5–13; Lk 11:1–13 have long discussions on prayer, but learn from Jesus to pray and allow
Him to pray in you and through you and put the fruit of your prayer into
Jn 13:34; 15:12 living action of love in loving one another as Jesus loves each one of you.
I am much better and hope to visit Germany, Belgium and Poland, and
maybe USA, before I return to India. In the meantime I thank you for all
your prayers and sacrifices and your beautiful letters. Through this letter I
thank you all and each one of you—for all you are to me and to Jesus, for
all the beautiful work you are doing for the Glory of God and the Good of
Jn 19:28 Souls—this is the Surest way of Satiating the Thirst of Jesus on the Cross
for love of Souls—and so fulfil Mother's promise,

a. By placing "completely" before "be" Mother seems to want to emphasize "completely".

b. The words in italics were in Mother's handwritten draft but were mistakenly left out in the typed copy sent to the houses.

"I WILL GIVE SAINTS
TO MOTHER CHURCH"

During the two novenas of Our Lady in August, pray for Mother's special intention.

God bless you
Mother

Please pray for the repose of the souls of [the Sisters' deceased family members]. . . .

MGL 173. 19TH SEPTEMBER 1983

+ LDM

19th September 1983

My dearest Children,

Thank God I am better and back home in the Mother House. It will take a little more time to be fully well but with your prayer for me, I am sure I will soon be alright.

Last year, in January 1982, we had divided the Society into smaller regions with a Councillor as a link—to be able to help and advise more of our Sisters to take responsibilities as Regionals. Now as the Society keeps growing, we need Regionals according to our Constitutions 163 and 164. (Read them carefully.) Therefore, our Councillors and I, with the advice of the Sacred Congregation for the Evangelization of Peoples (Propaganda Fide), have decided to appoint Regionals for two years until the next Chapter General—for the 16 regions. We need to pray much, that we may appoint the Sisters according to the Will of God—for His Glory and the good of the Church and of our Society. Once we have appointed them, we will accept them with deep faith and love.

Constitution 163 requires that we consult the Finally Professed Sisters of the region regarding the appointment of a Regional Superior. I am, therefore, enclosing for you a list of our Sisters in India and outside India who fulfil [the requirement of being] Finally Professed with 5 years of final profession, from among whom you may choose. After much prayer, let each Finally Professed Sister in your community including the Superior—write two names from the enclosed list.[a] The Superior will then post those

a. The list of finally professed Sisters that was attached to this letter has been omitted.

papers to me in one envelope. (Please do this immediately, as soon as you receive this letter).

According to our Constitution 165—we will also appoint two Councillors for each Regional.

During my sickness, often, very often, I prayed and offered all for each one of you, that you be one heart full of love in the Heart of Jesus—that all uncharitable words and actions leave our communities and each one's heart—for they are the greatest devilish evil—that the devil is using to destroy the work of God and each one of us.

On the 7th October will be 33 years of the Birth of our Society as a Congregation. For 33 years I have been your Mother. The greatest pain I have suffered from was and is the uncharitable words and actions towards each other in the community. In spite of all my prayers, advice and letters—the hurt and bitterness, which is the fruit of uncharitable words and actions, is deep in many hearts. Those who could not forgive have even lost their
Mt 27:50; Mk 15:37; Lk 23:46; Jn 19:30 vocation. This year is a year of Redemption: 1950 years ago, when Jesus
Jn 3:16 died—DIED BECAUSE HE LOVED, He was 33 years old and so is our So-
Mt 4:23; 9:35; Mk 1:14; Lk 4:43, 15:11–31 ciety. He had come to give us the Good News of the tenderness and love of
Gn 1:27 a Father—to whom we are precious because He has created us in His own
likeness for greater things—TO LOVE AND TO BE LOVED. I am afraid we are losing that Greatness by uncharitable words and actions.

Often I feel so helpless and sick at heart at the remarks made, words of ugly meaning repeated, tales carried from house to house, actions thrown at each other. Yes, I was sick, may be very sick—but I knew my sickness:
Mt 25:40 a wounded Mother's heart—for whatever you do to each other you do it to me also—because my love for each one of you is right in my heart—for with the love [with which] I love Jesus, I love you. So now you understand the great pain. Very often I find myself asking: Do the Sisters really love me? If they do, how can they hurt me so much by their uncharitable words and actions towards each other? I wonder what will happen to the Society in time, if you continue this way.

This is the year of Redemption—of repentance, of forgiveness. Let us all make a good general confession of all uncharitable words, thoughts and actions, and let us give our Word of Honour[a] to Jesus through Mary—that from the day we get this letter we will not say, nor think, nor do—any uncharitable word, thought or deed, and if we do, we will confess it as sin,

a. The Albanian "Word of Honor," *besa*, is much like an oath; once you give your word you must keep it with absolute fidelity.

as soon as possible without waiting for the weekly confession—and also [make reparation]. . . . The Word of Honour to God is something great and beautiful which we will offer to Jesus at the closing of the Year of Redemption at Easter 1984. It is not a Vow—but as Holy as the Vow—and for a pure heart, a Great Gift.

Say often: "Jesus in my Sister's [heart] and in my heart, I believe in Your tender love for her and me. She and I love You. Keep us in Your Heart."

If you really love me, if you really want the complete cure of my heart,—then take this letter to your heart—love it and live it and BE HOLY like Jesus through Mary.

We have over 130 applications to open new houses. I would be so happy and grateful if some of the houses could be generous to give at least one Sister from their Community. The new foundations would be such a great gift of God to the Church and the world.

"Word of honour to God"
I will not be uncharitable[a]

God bless you
Mother

MGL 174. 16TH OCTOBER 1983

LDM

Mother House
16th October 1983

My dearest Children,

This brings you Mother's love and blessings and also a loving gratitude for all the prayers [and] sacrifices you have all offered for my feast. Your letters and drawings were full of love—my prayer for each one of you is my gratitude to you. Also, I was very happy that many communities have taken my letter on Charity to heart and are determined to make their lives free of all uncharitable words and actions. Thank God and thank you, for this is the greatest proof of your love for Mother.

a. This sentence is handwritten at the end of the typed letter and before Mother's signature, but not in Mother's handwriting. It is possibly the handwriting of the Sister typist to whom Mother might have given additional instructions after she finished typing the letter and she opted to write it, instead of typing it.

After much prayer and many hours of work together we have made the full plan of regions and Regionals, which I enclose.[a] Let us read carefully Constitution 163 and 164, and we will know what to pray for, what to do, and how to accept our new Regionals.

The Councillors will no longer be the link with Mother. Regionals will take the responsibility. Superiors will deal with them, and the Regionals will deal directly with Mother in all things regarding their region. Mother will delegate the Councillors to help her with the work of the region....

I hope and pray that each community will accept with great love and trust the new Regionals as a gift of God to help them grow in holiness through love for each other and the poor they serve—for the glory of God and the good of our Society.

As Regionals can no longer be local Superiors, and as some of the newly appointed Regionals are Superiors, they will hand over the community to the newly appointed Superiors.

To make sure that we really are one heart full of love, in fidelity to the Church and to our Society [and also to grow in the love and the spirit of the Society]—we have decided to bring all the newly appointed Regionals to the Mother House for a retreat.[b] Therefore the 16 Regionals, according to the enclosed list, must be in the Mother House by the 5th of November.

As I leave for Europe on the 17th October, as usual, Sr. M. Frederick takes my place—so please deal with her in all matters. There will be the First and Final Profession of our Sisters in Rome on the 26th. Pray for them and for me.

Let us pray for the repose of the souls of the parents or relatives of our Sisters who have died....

God bless you
Mother

a. A list of the regions, the Regionals, and their respective Councillors which was sent as an attachment to this letter, has been omitted.

b. The original here read: "To make sure that we really are one heart full of love, in fidelity to the Church and to our Society—we have decided to bring all the newly appointed Regionals to the Mother

MGL 175. 16TH DECEMBER 1983

16th December 1983

My dearest Children,

This brings you Mother's love, blessing, and also prayerful wishes for a happy Christmas, filled with the Joy, Love and Peace of Jesus, newly born within us and around us.

At Christmas, Christ comes to us as a little child, small and helpless, so much in need of all that love can give.[116] Are we ready to receive Him?
Before the birth of Jesus, His parents asked for a simple dwelling place, Lk 2:7
but there was none. If Mary and Joseph were looking for a home for Jesus, would they choose your Community, your heart, and all it holds?

The world, the Church, even our Society and every Community and each one of us, have never needed holiness so much as [we do] today. To help us grow in this holiness, Holy Father has given us the Holy Year.[a] How are we benefiting by it?

This January, all our Sisters in formation will have a retreat, and then our Regionals and Councillors and myself. We need much prayer and sacrifice during the month of January, so that our Regionals will make full use of the graces they will receive and then be able to share all they receive with you.

Let us pray that we shall be able to welcome Jesus at Christmas not in the cold manger of a selfish heart, but in a heart full of love, compassion, joy and peace, a heart warm with love for one another.[b]

Pray for the repose of the souls of the parents or relatives of our Sisters who have died....

God bless you
Mother

House for a retreat, and also to grow in the love and the spirit of the Society." However, since the meaning is not obvious at first sight with this construction of the sentence, we have moved the text, enclosed in square brackets, for easier reading and understanding.

a. Pope John Paul II declared the Holy Year of the Redemption, from 25th March 1983 to Easter Sunday, 22nd April 1984.

b. See MGL 138 of 1st December 1978, p. 248.

ED 42. DECEMBER 1983

December 1983

My dearest Children,

This brings you Mother's love, blessing and prayer that you may grow in holiness through loving Jesus in each other and the Poor you serve. To be holy like Jesus you need the humility and purity of Mary.— She, being one of us, can teach us to be like Jesus—humble and Pure of heart.—The Mother and the Little One of Bethlehem will obtain this grace for us—for
Mt 5:8 the asking.— A pure and humble heart can see God and so becomes Holy like God. Be Holy—like Jesus—be only all for Jesus through Mary.

God bless you.
Mother

1984

MGL 176. 11TH FEBRUARY 1984

+

LDM

11th February 1984

My dearest Children,

We began this year with Joseph and Mary, close to Jesus. Let us continue it with greater love and humility, still closer to Jesus.

On the 29th December, our Sisters in formation had the first Retreat, given by Fr. William Smith.[a]—On the 7th January the Regionals [had theirs]—19 of them and the Councillors. We were all missing Sr. M. Frederick, whom I had to send to Yemen, because of Sr. M.—— who left the house, became a Muslim and married a Muslim. We must pray for her that she returns to the faith. Neglect of Prayer and Obedience always leads to loss of Faith and Vocation.

After the retreat of the Regionals we had two weeks full—of prayer and discussion. With this letter I am sending you the fruit of some of our discussions.

All have now gone to their places with greater love and determination to be one heart full of love in the Heart of Jesus through Mary—with each one of you, and together to grow in the holiness God expects from every MC. We must all come to a clear conviction of our duty to be Holy like Jesus—to be only all for Jesus through Mary. It is time now to fulfil Mother's promise—to give Saints to Mother Church.

Holiness is one of the most beautiful gifts a human heart can offer to God. Let us take Obedience as a sure means to great holiness. Faith

a. Msgr. William B. Smith (1939–2009), a priest of the Archdiocese of New York, served as a confessor to the Sisters and Fathers in New York and preached a number of retreats to the Sisters, including in Calcutta in 1983.

completes itself in Obedience and Obedience lives and is fruitful through Faith. Let us remember Obedience is the life of living faith—unshakable faith. So it is good that we take Obedience for our Particular Examen of Conscience. By doing this we will be able to get at the root of our Faith.
Mt 7:20; Lk 6:44 The fruit of Faith is Obedience: "by their fruit you shall know them."

As Mary was and is the most living example of this obedience, let us each one individually prepare a special gift for Our Lady: of living, fruitful Obedience, and offer it to her on the 25th March, feast of the Annuncia-
Lk 1:38 tion—the day She taught us how to obey by her example: "Be it done to me according to Thy word."

As the new Regionals have taken over their regions—you will, I am sure—take the trouble to read carefully Constitution 163 and 164, and you will know your obligations with them and towards them. I have already written to each region and each house individually. By now you must have received [the letters]. Remember they are sent to you with the Good News—how to make our Society Something beautiful for God through obedience and humility—sure means to great holiness, so that all we do be done for the Glory of God and the good of souls.

Mt 8:10, 9:22, 15:28; Mk 5:34, 10:52; Lk 7:9, 7:50, 8:48, 17:19, 18:42 Let us remember that Jesus always praised the Faith of people—therefore, often during the day we will pray:

> "Jesus in my heart Increase my Faith
> Strengthen my Faith. Let me live this Faith
> through living, humble Obedience."

Let us twice a day take the trouble to examine our Obedience—and also at night in our last prayer to Our Lady count our acts of Obedience and offer them to her with great personal love.

This year of Redemption is the greatest sign of Christ's love[a]—Jesus
Phil 2:8–11 Redeemed the world through Obedience to His Father—I have come to
Heb 10:7, 9 do the will of my Father. We too have joined the Society to do the will of
Mt 6:9 "Our Father Who is in Heaven." We all want to be holy—let us use the SUREST MEANS—OBEDIENCE.

God bless you
Mother

a. Mother is referring to the Holy Year or Jubilee of the Redemption. See MGL 170 of 28th March 1983 and its corresponding footnote, pp. 304–5.

ED 43. MAY 1984

May 1984

My dearest Children,

May the Risen Jesus fill you with Peace and make your communities—

Deeply Contemplative
Intensely Eucharistic
Vibrant with joy

And you will grow in the Holiness Mother has promised to the Church.

Be only all for Jesus through Mary.

God bless you
Mother

MGL 177. 27TH AUGUST 1984

Be humble like Mary
Be holy like Jesus
Mother

LDM[a]

27th August 1984

My dearest Children,

This brings you Mother's love, blessing and prayer that you may grow more and more in Humility. Let us learn from Mary, the Mother of Jesus, to be humble like her. Because of her humility She was, She is and She will always remain the most Beautiful of all creatures that God has ever created or will create. Mt 1:16; Acts 1:14 Lk 1:38

It is strange that Jesus has asked us that one thing only:

TO LEARN FROM HIM TO BE MEEK AND HUMBLE OF HEART. Mt 11:29

Nowhere Jesus showed so clearly that He was meek and humble as at His Birth and during His terrible Passion. At the 12th Station of the Cross we sing: Lk 2:7 Mt 26–27; Mk 14–15; Lk 22–23; Jn 18–19

No greater love, no greater love,
There is no greater love nor could there be,

a. On the top of the extant copies of this typed letter, Mother wrote, "Be humble like Mary/ Be holy like Jesus/ Mother."

Than God's great love, Infinite Love,
Love He revealed through Christ on Calvary.

I would be so happy if we could again be faithful to the daily Stations of the Cross.

We will learn Humility by looking at the humiliations Jesus went through because He loved us with that deep personal love. I can understand the Greatness of God, but I cannot understand the Humility of God that becomes so clear in His being In Love with each one of us separately and completely—as if there is no one but I in the world. HE LOVES ME SO MUCH: each one of us can say this with conviction.

We will learn humility by accepting humiliations with Joy. Therefore, say often:

Mt 11:29 "Jesus in my heart—make my heart meek and humble like Yours."

Say this prayer especially at every Station of the Cross.

Even now, my children,—when I look at you,—what you are and what you do,—and I look at myself,—I see the terrible Humility of God: He so great, so Wonderful—

Using Nothingness to show His Greatness
Using each one of us to continue to show to the world that He loves the world

as He did so clearly when He gave His Son Jesus

Jn 1:14 to become a Child,
Mt 27:50, Mk 15:37, Lk 23:46, Jn 19:30 to Die on the Cross,
Jn 6:35, 48, 51 to Become Bread of Life,
to make it easy for us to understand His love.

Humility is born as [the] fruit of Poverty and Obedience on the tree of Chastity.

Lately there has been much suffering for the Heart of Jesus by negligence of prayer. Neglect of prayer leads to an impure heart. The impure
Mt 5:8 heart stops Seeing God and instead sees "Somebody" or "something" that
Rom 8:35, 38 divides the Undivided Love for Christ—maybe just

a love letter written or received,
or hidingly meeting that "somebody",
or giving and receiving "something" without permission.

Be careful to obey Mother regarding working alone with young men. Show respect to the Priests who come in contact with you in the work but remember their total consecration to God and be reserved in your dealings with them.

Just as Fidelity to small things helps us to grow in Friendship with Jesus and in Holiness, so Infidelity to small things leads us to friendship with the devil and hell. Much of the Uncharitableness comes as [the] fruit of Pride. All harshness, all bitterness, all moodiness, all sins of the tongue come from the fullness of a heart filled with pride. Naturally we have no time to listen to God in the Silence of our heart when He speaks, neither can we see God in each other, as our heart is not clean when filled with pride.

This is why Jesus and Mary and Joseph keep on teaching us Humility,
for a humble heart is a pure heart, and a pure heart can see God, and we Mt 5:8
will for sure grow in Holiness like Jesus through Mary.

My Children, if we only had a humble heart, a pure heart—we could
see God in our Sisters and the Poor we serve. Is it not wonderful that we Mt 25:40
can be real Contemplatives 24 hours—if only our hearts were humble and pure.

My deep gratitude for the beautiful letters and cards you sent for our Society feast. Next time, I would like you to send me a holy picture that I can use.

On the 8th September I will be taking 4 Sisters to Colombo, Sri Lanka, to open—to reopen our house there.[a] Sr. Lima will be the Superior and Sr. M. Tripti has taken her place with the First Year Senior Novices.

I am sure you will all together thank God for giving us the gift of so many new tabernacles, already this year: Mysore, Calicut, Valankanni, Khandwa, Nicaragua, Pereira, Honduras, Bhiwandi (Bombay), Seemapuri (Delhi), Dehra Dun and Taiwan. The list of foundation dates and addresses of our houses each year will be sent to you at the end of each year, through your Regionals.

God has blessed us with many beautiful vocations. You must all try your best through prayer, sacrifice and contact to help young vocations.

We have had a very big number of deaths in our families. Let us always

a. Mother had opened the house in Colombo, Ceylon (now known as Sri Lanka), on 17th January 1967, but as the government of Ceylon refused to extend the Sisters' visas, she removed the Sisters and handed over the Home of Compassion to the Active Carmelite Sisters on 25th August 1971.

remember during Holy Mass—our own parents and our Sisters who have died in the Society.

I would like the Renewal letters and Superiors' reports to reach me before 15th September.

ED 44. DECEMBER 1984

December 1984

My dearest Children,

This brings you Mother's love, blessing and prayer that you may grow in Holiness through love for one another and the Poor you Serve. Be one heart full of love in the Heart of Jesus through Mary.—This is my Happy and Holy Christmas to each one of you—and God's blessing on 1985.

God bless you.
Mother

1985

MGL 178. 1ST JANUARY 1985

LDM

1st January 1985

My dearest Children,

May the little Child of Bethlehem teach us the Joy of Freedom in Poverty and the Love of the Poor in Service. He came to give us the Good News—and if we are really poor, then for sure—we have understood the Good News He brought. Lk 4:18

When we look at the Manger Lk 2:7

at the Straw
at the Animals
at the Shepherds

we understand His love—how much He loved us.

When we look at Him in the Bread of Life—we know how much He loves us now. That is why we must know what is Poverty in our own life—to be able to understand the Good News Jesus came to give us. Poverty is a Freedom—for the less we have, the more we can give. Jn 6:35, 48, 51

Poverty is also the Protector of Chastity—for being poor, our love for Jesus is Undivided: Nothing and Nobody. Lately we have had Sr. M.—— and Sr. M.—— who allowed Somebody to divide their love for Christ. Purity to be pure, Chastity to be chaste, Virginity to be virgin—needs Undivided love for Christ—Nothing and Nobody. In these last few years: Rom 8:35; 38–39

negligence of prayer,
negligence of sincerity
deliberate acts of disobedience

have been the main destroyers of the Vow of Chastity. Therefore, it is necessary for each one of us to examine our Conscience with all sincerity and humility:

> Is my heart clean? Do I see God?
> Is my Purity—pure? Is my Chastity—chaste? Is my Virginity—virgin?

If YES—THANK GOD. IF NOT, then one GOOD HUMBLE GEN-
Mt 5:8 ERAL CONFESSION will remove all and your heart will be clean and you will SEE GOD in your Sisters and the Poor you serve. Much, if not all, uncharitableness comes from our heart—because it is not clean. I would like you also to be very faithful to your regular confession every week.

As REPARATION for all the Sins Committed in our Society against Charity and Chastity: every month during the First Friday Novena we will do [more] Penance. Do it all with great love. Jesus has said that only
Mk 9:29 by Prayer and Penance, this kind of evil can be overcome.

You must have already heard that on the 30th October we have started in New York—something so Beautiful and Wonderful: MISSIONARIES OF CHARITY (FATHERS).[a] I am giving below a copy of their letter to me where you will see how each of them has made the VOW OF CHARITY for one year, and they will renew it every year. I want you to meditate on this letter and to try to make it your own:

> To our dearest Mother on this day of great joy,—from your loving sons—
>
> For the honour and glory of God, and moved by the ardent desire to satiate the thirst of Jesus within our community, fully convinced that we are called to make of this community another Nazareth from which His love may shine before men:
>
> We, as members of the Missionary Fathers of Charity, in order to complete and protect the gift of our fourth vow of Charity, which concerns our

a. In 1979, Fr. Joseph Langford, then a priest of the Oblates of the Virgin Mary (OMV), asked Mother that priests be given the opportunity to share spiritually in the charism of the Missionaries of Charity. This led to the formation of the Priest Co-Workers of Mother Teresa in 1980, known later as the Corpus Christi Movement (CCM). As the CCM grew, Fr. Joseph asked Mother to found a group of priests to oversee and direct the expansion of CCM. As a result, on 22nd August 1983, the Corpus Christi Fraternity (CCF) was approved by Cardinal Terence Cooke as a Pious Union that would aim to be a secular institute in the Archdiocese of New York. A year later, Mother and the members of the CCF agreed to seek recognition as a religious institute. She accepted the group as part of the MC family and on 13th October 1984 (now known as Name Day) gave them the name *Missionaries of Charity Fathers* with Fr. Joseph as Co-founder. The MC Fathers became a congregation of diocesan right (in Tijuana, Mexico) on 25th March 1992 (now referred to as Foundation Day). As some diocesan priests still wanted to share in the MC charism, the Corpus Christi Movement for Priests was restarted in 1997 by Mother and Fr. Pascual Cervera and received the approval of Cardinal John O'Connor of New York in May 1997 and the apostolic blessing of Pope John Paul II in July 1997, during a private audience at the Vatican.

charity of service outside the community, hereby commit ourselves to live and preserve that same charity within community: I,——, hereby vow for one year, with the help of God and trusting in our Lady's intercession, to promote and preserve the unity and Charity of this religious Family, and to refrain from ever offending against Charity in WORD, EITHER DIRECTLY OR INDIRECTLY, AGAINST THOSE INSIDE OR OUTSIDE THIS COMMUNITY.

We make this vow in response to Mother's special request of 14 October, and shall renew it every year on that date, together with all who shall ever enter our Society in the future. It is our hope that by so doing, we can be for Our Lady and for Mother "cause of their joy", as they have ever been the cause of our joy.

Missionary Fathers of Charity Noviciate,
Bronx, New York—31 October, 1984

I am sure with the help of Our Lady we will all grow in humility like Our Lady, in Holiness like JESUS.

God bless you
Mother

MGL 179. 19TH MARCH 1985

+

L.D.M.

Mother House[a]
19th March 1985

My dearest children,

This brings you Mother's love, blessing and prayer for each one of you—that you may grow and be humble like Mary—and Holy like Jesus. Thank you for all your prayers and sacrifices that you have made for my journey to China. Keep praying to Our Lady—we will especially offer the 4th Mystery of the Rosary "for peace and Unity in the Church of China." The Holy Mass is still offered in Latin, the old way—the people still pray the Rosary during Holy Mass. But I have never seen anywhere such an attitude of adoration and humility on receiving Holy Communion.—I did not see any young people—in the church, maybe because it

a. Mother probably wrote the draft of this letter while travelling ("The rest I will tell you when I return", "The sisters here and in Hong Kong . . ."). On her return she gave it to the Sister typist, who dated the letter as: "Mother House, 19th March 1985."

was a weekday, but the Church was full in the very cold morning with old and middle-aged people. The priest who offered the Holy Mass was in his eighties. He must have been ordained long before the separation. The rest I will tell you when I return. Pray much, keep on asking Our Lady to give peace and unity to the Church in China.

As I had gone so far—I decided to visit Korea, Papua and Australia before I return. So keep praying for Mother that in all my journey[s], I give only Jesus to all I meet. I visited our sisters in Tainan, the house in Taipei is already ready—we have only to send 4 sisters. So we better begin to learn Chinese, as this will be a language for the East, like English and Spanish in the West, to proclaim the Good News of Jesus. The sisters here and in Hong Kong and Macau, Korea and Papua are doing very well. The Government has given us a house in Hong Kong for Nirmal Hriday, and so all the people are very happy, as they are anxious to share in the work.

Mt 4:2; 9:35; 11:5; Mk 1:14; Lk 4:18; 7:22; 8:1; 9:6; 16:16; Acts 5:42

How privileged we are to have been chosen to be 24 hours in the presence of Jesus in the distressing disguise. Unless our hearts are clean and free from all uncharitable words, thoughts and deeds we will never be able to see Jesus in the distressing disguise of the poorest of the poor. In my last letter I sent you a copy of the Vow of Charity the MC Fathers have made. I hope and pray you have made it your own. It will help us all to greater love for each other.

Mt 5:8, 25:40

As you know, this year we will have our General Chapter. Our Constitutions have been approved for 10 years so [we] will not have to work at them. Naturally, there are points in the Constitutions we may have to consider, add or cut off. The Chapter will take place on the 7th October 1985. By the end of April you will receive information—regarding all that you have to do as a community and as a region.

The most important thing we have all to do—aspirants, postulants, novices, Junior Professed, Senior Professed, Superiors, Regionals, Councillors, and Mother:—TO PRAY. Pray the prayer that is filled with sacrifices made and offered. This Chapter is important, for at this Chapter General we have to vote [for] the MC God has chosen to take Mother's place. We must all do it, with great love for the glory of God and the good of our Society. For 35 years, each one of you [has] been the gift of God to me.—We have shared together the joy of loving Jesus in the poor. I would not have been able to do what I have done without you. My gratitude to each one of you is my prayer for you that you grow in holiness and remain faithful to the Spirit of our way of life and work. Therefore, 7th October has been chosen—the day of thanksgiving, when our Society was born as a religious Congregation. We will be one heart in prayer to choose the one God had in His mind from the beginning. Do not be afraid—do not discuss or speak of this outside your community. Only pray and do your penance with great love for this intention. In my next letter I will send you all you need to know regarding the General Chapter.

Mt 10:26; 28:5, 10; Lk 12:4, 32; Jn 14:27; Rev 1:17; 2:10

May the joy of the Risen Christ be with you. Remember that the passion of Christ ends always in the joy of the Resurrection of Christ, so when you feel, in your own heart, the suffering of Christ, remember the Resurrection has to come—the joy of Easter has to dawn. Never let anything so fill you with sorrow as to make you forget the joy of the Risen Christ.[a]

Mt 28:8; Lk 24:41, 52; Jn 20:20
Mt 26–27; Mk 14–15; Lk 22–23; Jn 18–19

God bless you
Mother

As soon as you receive this letter begin praying this prayer for the Chapter General:

> "We beseech Thee, O Lord, mercifully pour into our Society Thy Holy Spirit, by whose wisdom it was created, by whose providence it is governed and maintained and whose love may kindle in the Society that same fire which Our Lord Jesus Christ, sent down upon earth earnestly desiring that it should burn mightily."

And so:

Breathe in me, O Holy Spirit,
That my thoughts may all be holy;
Act in me, O Holy Spirit,
That my work too may be holy;
Draw my heart, O Holy Spirit,
That I love but what is holy;
Strengthen me, O Holy Spirit,
To defend all that is holy;
Guard me, then, O Holy Spirit,
That I always may be holy.[b]

a. In this letter the last phrase was typed as "Christ Risen!"; however, it seems to be an error of the typist (there is no other instance in Mother's writings of this expression being changed from her customary "Risen Christ" to "Christ Risen.") Further, it seems that the typist mistakenly typed a colon and then corrected it to an exclamation mark. Mother usually ended this saying with a period. See MGL 50 of 24th March 1967, p. 83.

b. This prayer was composed by St. Augustine.

MGL 180. 15TH APRIL 1985

+

L.D.M.

15th April 1985[a]

My dearest Children,

In my last letter I gave you the good news that we will be having our 5th General Chapter on 7th October 1985. Let us ask Our Lady to give us her heart, so pure, so beautiful, so Immaculate, a heart full of love for the Society and the Church, so that we may carry Jesus everywhere we go and give only Jesus to each other and our poor.

Pray the prayer to the Holy Spirit for our Chapter General—after Mass and Communion prayers and also at Adoration. We must especially pray that the Holy Spirit will be with us when we choose the delegates for the Chapter—and also for the Chapter itself, that we choose Sisters who will govern the Society according to the Gift of God—entrusted to the Society.

Mt 14:27; 17:7; Mk 5:36, 6:50; Lk 5:10, 8:50, 12:7; Jn 6:20

"Do not be afraid," Jesus said, again and again to the Apostles. If we really pray, Jesus will be with us and protect the Society from anything that may destroy this gift of our vocation to the Society.

Read Constitutions 135, 136 and 137.

I am sending you one Voting Paper each. All Junior Professed and Finally Professed Sisters will vote—but only Finally Professed Sisters in your region can be voted for.

See the enclosed list.

Before the Voting you can pray, think and even talk among yourselves in your community only about the Sisters on the list given you—but once you have voted you must not talk about them anymore.

Sisters, in voting, keep in mind first what is for the greater glory of God and the greater good of the Church. How much more glory will God get through my choice? I must not look at the Sister with her failures and her faults but see whether she possesses the following qualities:

1. A healthy mind in a healthy body. An open, sincere mind, a mind that can look up and see Christ and be all for God. (Mt 17:8; Mk 9:8)
2. Ability to acquire knowledge to help the Society.

a. This letter was sent out with the preparation material for the General Chapter.

3. Plenty of good common sense that does not waver—but will stand by the glory of God no matter what it costs.
4. Courage of one's convictions—courage to keep the secrecy of deliberative vote.
5. Cheerfulness and the joy of serving the Church with love and a humble heart.
6. Knowledge and love of the Society, and readiness to serve the Society to the point of giving her life for it.

Go to the chapel and talk things over with Christ. The Society is not yours or mine; it is His, and He will always protect it. God has brought us together for some good, let us, of ourselves, place no obstacles in the way of that good.

Whoever is chosen should accept it in a spirit of Faith as the will of God for the greater glory of God and the good of souls.

As soon as you receive my letter and the papers—have a Triduum of Prayers and [more] penance and at the end of the 3rd day do the Voting and immediately return the papers to me at the Mother House.

Also, I would be very happy to receive from you—as a community—or even as an individual—any suggestions or wishes you may like to present to the General Chapter. This should reach me, latest, by 15th August.

My prayer is often for each one of you—especially during Holy Mass and Holy Communion. Pray much for Mother.

God bless you,
Mother

ED 45. MAY 1985

May 1985

To be humble like Mary and Holy like Jesus we need a clean Heart—a
clean heart can see God and if we see God in each other we will love each Mt 5:8
other as He loves us—this is a true MC. Jn 13:34; 15:12

God bless you
Mother

MGL 181. 24TH JUNE 1985

+

LDM

Mother House
24th June 1985

Our Dearest Sisters,

On the 24th of June at 5:15 A.M., Sr. Clytie (Dominica Kerketta from Madhya Pradesh), age 39 years, Senior Tertian at 90 Park Street, due for Final Vows in December 1985, went home to Jesus after being hospitalized for 17 days. Her burial took place at the Convent Road Cemetery, Entally, at 5 P.M. The main celebrant was Fr. C. Van Exem, SJ.

Look up Const. no. 66 where it says the suffrages are as follows:

- Each Sister shall offer Holy Mass, Holy Communion, the Way of the Cross and the Rosary three times.
- In other houses, one Requiem Mass shall be offered for the deceased Sister.

Let us thank God and rejoice that she has joined our community in Heaven. Let us also pray for her family.

In union of prayer,
Mother and Councillors[a]

MGL 182. 4TH JULY 1985

+ LDM

Mother House
4th July 1985

Our dearest Sisters,

On the 3rd of July at about 10 A.M., Sr. M. Bijoly (Alphonsa P.V. from Kerala) a Finally Professed Sister since May 1983, aged 33 years, went home to Jesus from Bhagalpur. She was on duty till the end, taking care of the little ones in Shishu Bhavan. She received the last Sacraments and was buried in Bhagalpur on 4th of July 1985.

Look up Const. no. 66 where it says the suffrages are as follows:

a. This letter about the death of Sr. M. Clytie, MC, and the following one, about the death of Sr. M. Bijoly, MC, were sent to the houses as Mother's general letters, although they were only typed and not signed by Mother. As many houses received them, we have opted to place them here.

- Each Sister shall offer Holy Mass, Holy Communion, the Way of the Cross and the Rosary three times.
- In other houses, one Requiem Mass shall be offered for the deceased Sister.

Let us thank God and rejoice that she has joined our community in heaven. Let us also pray for her family.

In union of prayer,
Mother and Councillors

MGL 183. [2ND] AUGUST 1985

+ LDM

[2nd] August 1985

My dearest Children,

This brings you Mother's love, blessing and prayer that you may grow in holiness through love for one another especially by making your Community one heart full of love in the heart of Jesus through Mary. A very Happy and Holy Feast of our Society.

The first profession and the final Vows—both in Rome and New York:—it was really Something Beautiful for God. Everybody felt closer to Jesus. People were very touched by the prayerfulness of the whole ceremony.

On the 15th June, Fr. Brian—Sr. Sharbel's brother, was ordained Priest. Again it was really something beautiful for God. God's tender love for our Young Society is without end. How faithful we must be to this Gift of God. The Fathers are 5 Novices and 2 Postulants, but please God others are joining.[a]

Each one of us must remain

- deeply Contemplative in prayer and penance
- intensely Eucharistic in Holy Communion and Adoration
- vibrating with joy, peace and love by giving wholehearted and free service to the Poorest of the Poor.

a. In the handwritten draft, Mother wrote this sentence after the sentence below, "The Noviciate in Poland was opened..."; however, the Sister typist moved it two paragraphs later.

This faithfulness will help us

to be Humble like Mary
Holy like Jesus.

I have asked Our Lady to keep the Society hidden in the Five wounds of Jesus and in the Five Mysteries of the Rosary, when we pray the Rosary.

Lk 1:26–38	MC Sisters—Active	– The Annunciation	– in the Right Hand of Jesus
Lk 1:39–56	MC Brothers– Active	– The Visitation	– Left Hand of Jesus
Lk 2:1–20	MC Sisters—Contemplative	– The Nativity	– Right Foot of Jesus
Lk 2:22–39	MC Brothers—Contemplative	– The Presentation	– Left Foot of Jesus
Lk 2:41–51	MC Fathers	– The finding in the Temple	– Sacred Heart of Jesus

Therefore I would like[a] that in future at every Adoration, we burn five lights—to remind us to pray for our Society each Branch included.[b]

The Noviciate in Poland was opened with 10 Novices, 7 Postulants and 12 Aspirants—a real Gift of God.[c] Cardinal Polletti, in a letter to the Brothers, states that instead of Missionaries of the Word—they will be MC Brothers (Contemplative).

Let us pray always and often to the Wounds of Jesus that each one in the MC family—"BE ONLY ALL FOR JESUS THROUGH MARY". Use every humiliation to become *humble*[d] like Mary.

I am sorry to hear of so much sickness in Calcutta, but this too let us accept with a big smile—and offer all for Peace in the world, especially for Peace and Unity in the Church of China and USA.

The death of our two Sisters[e] should open our hearts and eyes to the reality—could have been any of us. Are we ready to go home to God? Is

a. In the handwritten draft of this letter, Mother wrote, "I would be grateful that..."; the Sister typist, probably in error, typed "I would like that ..."

b. Two years later, Mother asked the Sisters to burn eight lights at Adoration, adding candles to represent the LMC's, Co-workers and Our Lady (see MGL 199 of 2nd August 1987, p. 366).

c. The Noviciate was opened in July 1985 in Zaborow. The professed community, aspirants and postulants that were in Zaborow from the time of the foundation of the house (November 1983) moved to the new house in Warsaw (Grochowska) to make way for the novices and their mistresses.

d. The word "humble" is in Mother's handwritten draft, but the Sister typist must have omitted it in error.

e. Mother is referring to the two Sisters mentioned in her previous letters (MGL 181 of 24th June 1985 and MGL 182 of 4th July 1985), who died suddenly: Sr. M. Clytie, MC, died on 24th June 1985 in Calcutta, and Sr. Bijoly died on 3rd July 1985 in Bhagalpur.

our heart so clean that we can see the Face of God on our entering eternal life? Mt 5:8

Pray much for Mother, as Mother is praying for each one of you.

God bless you
Mother

Please pray for [the souls of our deceased relatives]. . . .

MGL 184. 25TH AUGUST 1985

Mother House
25th August 1985[a]

My dearest Children,

As we begin the final preparation for the Chapter, I enclose the final list of all the Society members who will share in the Chapter. Due to visa difficulties, Sr. Raphael and Sr. Joan will not be able to attend and will be replaced by the voted substitutes—Sr. Albina and Sr. Thomas. All the Sisters who have to come must be at the Mother House by the 20th of September at the latest, as we begin the retreat on the 22nd, evening, preached by Rev. Fr. Huart.[b] On the 7th Oct. we shall have only the voting at 9:00 A.M. As the 7th is our day of Adoration and Thanksgiving, we shall spend the rest of the day in Adoration and Thanksgiving after the voting is finished.—It would be good if the Sisters who are coming, both Regionals and others, bring with them all their own personal things in case they do not return to the same places after the Chapter. Arrange the work well and also the person who will replace you during your absence.

Each one of you and your Poor pray often and offer many sacrifices. Pray the prayer [for] the Chapter after Mass and at Adoration—from the 22nd Sept. to the 6th Oct. inclusive. We will all do [more] penance, and on the 6th we will have MC fast in honour of the Holy Spirit—in supplication and thanksgiving.—Kindly keep all this in your Community. No need for anybody else to get involved, only ask prayers for the Chapter.

. . .

a. This letter was sent along with the General Chapter preparations.

b. Father Albert Huart, SJ, was born in 1926, in Belgium. He joined the Society of Jesus, came to India in 1953, and was ordained a priest in 1957. He was confessor at Mother House from 1984 to 1998 and preached the retreat for the members of the General Chapter in 1985.

I am nominating [ten] Sisters, who will participate in the discussions after the elections of the Superior General and her Councillors. These sisters will not vote....

The General Chapter is a gift of God of Greater Love—so let us prepare for
Mt 5:8 *it with a clean heart—for the clean heart can see and understand the will of God*
Mt 1:16, Acts 1:14, Jn 19:27 *and do that will. Let us pray to Mary, Mother of Jesus, and our Mother.*

God bless you,
Mother

MGL 185. 31ST OCTOBER 1985

+ LDM

31st October 1985

My dearest children,

With deep gratitude and love to Our Lady for Her tender, Motherly love and help She has given us all during this General Chapter—let us all together Consecrate our lives totally to Her on the Feast of Her Immaculate Conception— 8th December—so that through Her guidance and help each of us [may] become the true Spouse of Jesus Crucified—a true MC not only in name but in life.

We owe deep gratitude and love to Sr. M. Frederick, Sr. M. Joseph Michael and Sr. M. Damien for all they have done for the Society and for each one of us—by sacrificing themselves continually for the good of the Society. Our prayer for them is our gratitude to them.

We also welcome our new Councillors: Sr. M. Agnes, Sr. M. Priscilla, Sr. M. Shanti, Sr. M. Camillus, Sr. M. Dorothy, Sr. M. Andrea. I am sure they too will help and share the work of the Society with Mother—with the same love as the others have done.

WE MUST ALL BE ONE AS THE BLESSED TRINITY: THREE PERSONS BUT ONE GOD. We too—we are many but ONE SOCIETY.

We have realized more and more during these days the greatness, the beauty and fruitfulness of our MC Constitutions and life of prayer and work.

We have also seen very clearly how this life of prayer and work has been very much destroyed through uncharitableness and pride, [*and*] so we have strongly RESOLVED to really remove all uncharitable words & actions from our Society through—

Humility and Sisterly love for each other,
Childlike love for Our Superior, and
Deep, compassionate love for our Poor.

I am sorry Sisters, if through my negligence so much uncharitableness has entered the Society.

In time I will send you all the resolutions and work of the Chapter General. From the Canon law there have been a number of changes made and additions to our Constitutions.[a]

As per Canon Law, a Second Book, called the Directory, has been made—with some practical parts from the Constitutions.[b]

As they are the Written Will of God for us, both the Constitutions and the Directory bind us equally to form one life.

One point that we have all neglected during the last six years is: a proper examination of conscience—both particular and general, and I am afraid, through this neglect, much worldliness has entered into our communities, and this has led to neglect of prayer and charity.

So let us again turn to Our Lady to help us become humble like Her, that we may become Holy like Jesus. Let us again and again remember the tenderness of God's love—that He loves each one of us with a tender, all-consuming love, and that He wants us to love each other as He loves each one of us with a tender love. Bethlehem, Nazareth, the Cross, the Eucharist speak of this love. Jn 13:34; 15:12 Lk 2:4–20 Lk 2:51 Mt 27:50; Mk 15:37; Lk 23:46; Jn 19:30 Jn 6:35–58

The other point that we all saw is: Neglect of our 4th Vow through lack of zeal and laziness:

—that "Wholehearted", that zeal binds us right in the Community Col 3:23
—and laziness in that negligence of not learning the language of the people among whom Obedience has sent us. It is nearly impossible to know and teach the Faith without proper knowledge of the language.

I enclose the list of regions and Regionals: a Sign of greater love—a Sign of growth.[c]

a. Pope John Paul II promulgated the revised Code of Canon Law on 25th January 1983. Until this time the Code promulgated in 1917 was in use. The MC *Constitutions* were therefore revised to conform to the new Code.

b. See Canon 587, 1–4.

c. The list has been omitted. At this time there were 2,071 Sisters serving in 290 foundations, which were divided into 20 regions, each region under the patronage of a different title of Our Lady. Each region could have from 12 to 16 houses; there was no fixed number.

HAPPY BIRTHDAY to our MC Fathers.

- Their Inspiration Day: 13th October 1984
- Their Foundation Day: 31st October 1984[a]

They have sent us this Beautiful FORMULA OF THE SOCIETY, which I share with you:

MISSIONARIES OF CHARITY—
FIVE WOUNDS OF JESUS IN
ONE BODY: JESUS

The two wounds in the Hands,
Sisters & Brothers—Active
Serving with active love the Poor.

The two wounds in the Feet,
Sisters and Brothers—Contemplative
Going in search of souls by their
word, prayer & penance.

The Wound in the Sacred Heart of Jesus,
The Priests—Satiating the Thirst of
Jesus by their Priesthood
by completing the work of the Sisters &
Brothers in the Poor they serve.

That is why, to show and live fully that
oneness, we light five lights at Adoration,
each separately—yet adoring one Jesus—
by the one MC Society.
Sisters, Brothers, Fathers
make one Body Jesus
one way, one life,
working at the salvation & sanctification
of the Poorest of the Poor.

To be able to do this—we need a deep
life of prayer, Community life,
together with the material & spiritual
service of the Poorest of the Poor.

a. The MC Fathers kept 13th October as their Foundation Day until 1992, when they became a congregation of diocesan right (Diocese of Tijuana, Mexico) on 25th March. Now this day is known as Name Day. See footnote to MGL 178 of 1st January 1985, p. 326.

Sr. M. Aurora (Elizabeth Macombe) a Finally Professed Sister, went Home to Jesus from Via Casilina, Rome—on 14th October, at 12:40 A.M. She was a holy Sister and right to the end she gave her All to Jesus. Her last dying words were addressed to Our Lady: "Tell Jesus I love Him."

In future, the Ek Dil will tell us a little more about our Sisters who go Home to Jesus to form our MC Community there in Heaven. A Happy Feast to all our Sisters in Heaven, for 1st November.

We will soon begin our preparation for the coming of Jesus, and in all our chapels there will be the empty crib. This year we must prepare a better crib, a crib of Humility, Poverty and Simplicity of the Gospel.[a] We need the life of Bethlehem, Nazareth—that humility and simplicity to live the life of Calvary. I beg of you Sisters let us keep things simple and not introduce things that do not fit in with our way of life. Everywhere you look it is the same thing: You look at Bethlehem, Nazareth, the Cross, the Tabernacle, it's the same thing. That is why Jesus could say: Learn of Me ... In Mt 11:29
Bethlehem, Nazareth, Calvary Jesus loved us then: In the Eucharist JESUS Lk 2:4–20, 51 Mt 27:50; Mk 15:37;
LOVES US NOW. Each one of you is Special to me because He has chosen Lk 23:46; Jn 19:30
you and with great love. Why you? Maybe some others could have done Mt 26:26; Mk 14:22; Lk 22:19; 1 Cor 11:24
better than you and me. I think God wants to prove His greatness by us- Jn 15:16
ing Nothingness. If we could really make that strong Resolution: <u>Humble like Mary, Holy like Jesus</u>. We have to satiate the thirst of Jesus on the
Cross for souls, by working for the salvation and sanctification of the poor- Jn 19:28
est of the poor—and the first poorest of the poor is myself. I must work for my salvation and sanctification first.

Let us pray

God bless you
Mother

ED 46. DECEMBER 1985

December 1985

Keep the joy of loving Jesus in your Sisters and share this joy with the
Poor you Serve. Mt 5:8

God bless you
Mother

a. See MGL 22 of 10th November 1963, p. 36.

1986

MGL 186. [12TH FEBRUARY] 1986

+

LDM

Mother House
Lent [12th February] 1986[a]

My dearest Children,

Mt 5:8; 25:40 This brings you Mother's love, blessing and prayer that you may truly obtain a clean heart, so that you can see Him in each other and in the Poor you serve. A clean heart is full of love—full of Peace, for God dwells in a clean heart. Let us ask in all the sincerity of our hearts—is my heart clean? Do I really see God in each one of the Poor I serve?

Mt 26:36–27:60; Mk 14:32–15:46; Lk 22:39–23:53; Jn 18–19 As we begin the Passion of Christ—make it a point to read the Passion from the Gospel or any other book. Archbishop Goodier has the whole Passion of Jesus in the form of meditations for every day in Lent[b]—I am sure you may find something in the library if you take the trouble—also the *Life of Christ* by Bishop Sheen.[c]

I know you all love Mother, and yet how often I have asked you to really open your eyes to all uncharitable words and deeds. We are carriers of God's love. Let us take as a real way of life—Charity that comes from a chaste life; pure undivided love for Christ.

Today God loves the world through us. Do we really give Him a free Hand to use us without consulting us? Do we make it easy for the people to see Christ in us?

Obedience is the best means to great love—because obedience is always

a. In 1986, Ash Wednesday was on 12th February and Easter Sunday was on 30th March.

b. Mother is referring to the book *The Passion and Death of Our Lord Jesus Christ* by Archbishop Alban Goodier, SJ.

c. Archbishop Fulton Sheen (1895–1979) was a very well-known American writer and preacher, especially on radio and television. His cause of canonization was started in 2002. Mother met Archbishop Sheen and read his works; he also gave her a statue of Our Lady of Fatima.

connected with sacrifice. Jesus said, "I have come to do the Will of My Father."—We know His terrible pain and surrender to His Father's will in Gethsemane.—He even perspired blood from the terrible fear of the Passion—yet He kept on saying, "My Father, Thy will be done".—His love for His Father in action was His surrender to His will—that total acceptance of all that His Father would give and take from Him. This is exactly what obedience asks of each one of us, to accept whatever He gives and give whatever He takes—with a big smile, as our Constitution says. This is the greater love—of the Spouse of Christ—of a consecrated Virgin. Let us during this Lent put our whole heart and soul in sharing in the Passion of Christ—by praying like Him—for the more the agony increased—He prayed the longer—also that total surrender in obedience as He did—"Your will be done"—Your will that comes to me—through the Church—our Constitutions—our Superiors.

Heb 10:7, 9
Lk 22:44
Mt 26:39, 42, 44; Mk 14:36, 39; Lk 22:42
Lk 22:44

So my children, let us really open our hearts to JESUS—so that like Him we too may live and glorify the Father through our love in action as the fruit of our total surrender through Obedience. During Lent we will all take for our daily examination of conscience—Charity in action through obedience.

Mt 5:16

God bless you
Mother

MGL 187. [4TH] APRIL 1986

+ LDM

Mother House
[4th] April 1986

My dearest children,

As the Church requires all Congregations to have a Juniorate programme and on-going formation, I think it would be good for us to begin with Our Lady, during this month of May. Each Sister and Superior, as well as Regionals, please see that some time be given to this at least once a week, perhaps on Thursday.[a] The work will not suffer, but will be done much better if we do this in a spirit of obedience to the Church and out of love for Jesus.

During this time also, I ask you Sisters, to please do everything possible

a. Mother is referring to the study program for the juniors.

to help each other to a greater love and acceptance of each other.—Jesus
Jn 13:34–35; 15:12 said: "Love one another as I have loved you"—"AS I HAVE LOVED YOU".
Knowing our sins and weaknesses, still He loves us. In spite of our ingrat-
itude and failures, He gave His life for us, crying out at the extreme of
Lk 23:34 pain and in His last moments: "Father, forgive them!"—it is thus Jesus asks
us to love one another. Therefore it would be most UNCHRISTLIKE for
Sisters to bring up past or present faults and mistakes. It would be most
un-Christ-like to pass remarks about each other; to ignore a Sister who
Jn 15:16 has been chosen and called by God; to make a Sister feel so lonely and
unwanted that she looks for love elsewhere; to call a Sister names and
tell her to leave the house, and so on. It would be entirely against love to
transfer a Sister, or to force our Superiors to transfer her, even to make
2 Cor 7:15, 13:11 [up] stories to get her out. As we instruct the families to live together in
harmony, drawing graces from their marriage vows, we must learn to live in peace and love, drawing graces for our own fidelity from the Sacred Heart of Jesus, to Whom we have vowed ourselves—that Heart so full of love for each one of us—for that Sister as well as for me. Therefore, we must stop spreading ugly stories and use the tongue, on which Jesus rests each morning in Holy Communion, only for the truth, for the praise and glory of God.

My Sisters, during this beautiful month of Our Lady, let us crown her with fragrant flowers—the flowers of love, gentleness, meekness and humility for one another, and ask Jesus to be truly a cause of joy to her as He was.[a]

God bless you
Mother

MGL 188. 14TH APRIL 1986

Mother House
15th April 1986[b]

My dearest Children,

As the Society keeps growing with [the] blessing of God—we have divided the Society into 27 Regions.

a. The meaning here is "... and ask Jesus that we may be truly a cause of joy to her, as He was."

b. This letter was sent both as a letter to the Superiors and as a general letter to all the houses, dated the 14th and 15th April, respectively.

The Regionals need constant contact with the Motherhouse and as I am often travelling I have divided the regions among our six Councillors. Therefore, as the Councillors are all in Calcutta, [in] all matters regarding your Region and the monthly renewal [of general permissions], when I am not in the Motherhouse, you should write to your appointed Councillor—any permissions, also deal with them.

All matters regarding formation—where there is [a] Noviciate should be dealt with Sr. M. Andrea—Tertianship, with Sr. M. Dorothy.

Give a living example to your Sisters of obedience and complete oneness with Mother.

I am grateful to each one of you for your trust and fidelity, for your Obedience and love for the Society by keeping faithful to the Spirit of our Society.—My gratitude to each one of you is my prayer for you that you and your sisters be humble like Mary and holy like Jesus.

. . .

God bless you
M. Teresa MC

ED 47. MAY 1986

May 1986

My dearest children,

Keep the joy of loving Jesus in your Sisters and in the Poor you serve and share this joy with all you meet, especially your Community—for love begins at home, and works of love are works of Peace. Make your community another Nazareth—a dwelling place of Joy, Love and Peace.— Mt 2:23; Lk 2:51–52
Be one heart full of love in the Heart of Jesus through Mary.

God bless you.
Mother

MGL 189. 14TH MAY 1986

+

LDM

Mother House
14th May 1986

My dearest children,

This brings you Mother's love, blessing and prayer for each one of you that you may during my absence all be one heart full of love in the Heart of Jesus through Mary. This is the greatest proof of your tender love for Mother—you could not give me greater love—than the conviction of your love, than by being one heart full of love in the heart of Jesus.

Do everything with the knowledge and permission of your Superior—this will help you to grow in the joy and experience the freedom of Poverty.

I only ask [you] to be one heart, full of love and humility; this will really be true joy. You know Mother's love for each one of you and how each one of you is precious to me. It is good to examine one point. Do I really love our Society? How much? How do I prove that love? [The] greatest love and gratitude you can show Mother is to show your love for the Society—the precious gift of God to each of us. In my absence show your love for the Society by your fidelity in doing small things with great love—the smaller the thing the greater the love; that is how little Therese became a great Saint.—From you I ask but one thing, to be humble like Mary, to be Holy like Jesus. This is Mother's promise to God: to give Saints to the Mother Church.

If you were to die today—what would your community say about you? What was in you that was beautiful, was so Christlike—that helped others to pray better? Face yourself with Jesus—do not be satisfied with any answer. Also—what does your vocation as MC mean to you? Do you love it? Do you appreciate it? Are you in love with it? Is your life as MC filled with joy—with expectation, with deep gratitude to God—for what He has given to you in giving you your MC Vocation? Are you really happy to be a Missionary of Charity?

Before the feast of the Sacred Heart, prepare your answers, and on the feast offer them to Jesus. You could keep a copy for me—and in my next visit to your community we will look at it together.

Often say this little prayer: "Eternal Father I offer Thee Jesus, Thy beloved Son, and with Him I offer Thee my heart in Him—with

Him—through Him to the greater glory of your Name, and so satiate the thirst of Jesus for love, for souls."

As I have started my journey of obedience,[a] pray for Mother that it really be only all for Jesus through Mary and so satiate His thirst for souls.[b]

God bless you
Mother

MGL 190. 2ND JULY 1986

+

LDM

Bronx, New York
2nd July 1986

My dearest Children,

This comes to you with much love and blessing and prayer. As we have begun the month of the Precious Blood, may the Blood of Jesus ever wash away our sins and the sins committed in our Society, and in the world, by those specially consecrated to Him. Let us often say during this month:

Blood of Christ inebriate me,
Blood of Christ sanctify me,
Blood of Christ fill me,
Blood of Christ make me holy.

Often during the day say:

"Eternal Father I offer thee the Precious Blood of Jesus
and in union with the Blood of Jesus, I offer Thee my
heart for the greater glory of Your Name, and to satiate
Your thirst for souls."

From Sister M. Frederick's letter you will get all the good news. I do not know how the days go, they go so fast—I think Our Lady still keeps being "in haste". Lk 1:39

a. From the following letter of 2nd July 1986, we learn that Mother's "journey of obedience" took her to Rome, New York, and San Francisco for Professions; to Jamaica to open a new Tabernacle; and then to Grenada, Puerto Rico, Miami, Cuba, and Germany.

b. The intended meaning is that Mother herself is satiating Jesus' thirst by her travels undertaken through obedience.

The Professions in Rome, New York and San Francisco were really something beautiful for God: all for Jesus through Mary.

I am sure all the newly Professed Sisters must have already come to their communities, and are a real gift of God and cause of joy wherever they are.

As this year is the Year of Peace,[a] in a special way let us join the Holy Father to have this peace in our own Community first, and let us remember that works of love are works of peace. Peace and love begin at home: our MC community is our home.

The surest way for us Missionaries of Charity is charity for each other — therefore if you really want to give Mother something really beautiful and real: make the vow of Charity for your Sisters in the community wherever you may be. I enclose the formula of the Vow.

> "I ______, vow and promise to Almighty God, through Mary, our Mother, and Mother of Jesus, for one year—to be God's love and compassion to my Sisters, never to speak an uncharitable word, never to make a Sister feel unloved or unwanted, but to make every effort to make my Community another Nazareth, where peace and joy, prayer and harmony can grow and unite us all with one another and together with Jesus, for the love and glory of God our Father."

Each one make it in private before the Blessed Sacrament in the presence of Mary, Mother of Jesus, as a special gift to me, your Mother, for my fifty-eight years of religious life.[b] There is no need to write or send cards: just offer this beautiful gift to Jesus for me. This is the first time I ask you "to do it for me." August 15th will be the best day to offer this gift of love.[c] Let us make our Society really only all for Jesus through Mary, by allowing Jesus to live His life of charity for each other, as he lived in Nazareth.

I beg every single Sister in the Society, including the Novices, to be really determined to clean the Society of all uncharitable thoughts, words and actions; and let us help each other to grow in holiness through this tender love for each other.

Sister M. Frederick and I have just been for two days in Jamaica, our new tabernacle. There is much apostolic work there; it is a real mission land. We are now on our way to Grenada and Puerto Rico, and then

a. The United Nations declared 1986 as the "International Year of Peace."

b. Mother is referring to her entrance to Loreto convent in October 1928.

c. Mother would begin sentences with numerals, as in this instance: "15th August ..."; we have changed it to correct grammatical norms.

Miami, and on the 8th to Cuba. Pray much for God's blessing on this visit. I will leave for Germany on the 11th, so pray much for Mother. I feel very sorry I am not able to visit our other houses in the Americas and Europe—but my prayer and blessing for each one of you is right there, from my heart to your hearts.

God bless you
Mother

MGL 191. 11TH AUGUST 1986

Mother House
11th August 1986

My dearest Children,

As we approach the feast of our Society—let us with greater zeal and love for our Society bring to the feet of Mary our acts of humility and purity, of obedience and of wholehearted service, as a gift of gratitude for being a Mother to each one of us.—The very grace of perseverance up to today is her gift, the gift of her love for each one. This year has been a year of grace, for in January and June we got 120 Aspirants.

So many Sisters took First Vows (88). So many Final Vows (87). So many new Tabernacles (19). Thank God for all the joy Jesus shared with us. There has been much pain for Jesus and for us all—as Sr. M.——, Sr. M.——, Sr. M.——, Sr. M.——[a] have left the Society. Nearly all of them said that they could no longer accept the uncharitableness they had to face. Is this true?—If it is true, what a terrible responsibility before Jesus—the loss of vocation through our lack of Charity, and we are called Missionaries of Charity. Even towards the Poor we have lost some of that zeal—that tender care and concern. How can we give it to the Poor if we do not share the joy of loving with our own Sisters. With the neglect of prayer much evil can penetrate our hearts.—First, because we cannot hear God speaking in our hearts, since we are unfaithful, and second, because our
hearts are not clean we cannot see God. Fidelity to the life of prayer is a Mt 5:8
sure way to sanctity—because a soul of prayer is a living tabernacle where Mk 6:31

a. In the handwritten draft Mother left a blank space for the number of the aspirants, probably for the Sister typist to fill in; she wrote the numbers of the Sisters that took final vows and the number of the new tabernacles with a different pen, probably later on when she verified the numbers. However, the names of the Sisters who left the Society were part of the text. It was a great pain for Mother when a Sister left, and obviously these Sisters were very much in her mind and heart.

Jesus can come and rest a while, pray in us, and with us. In us He speaks to His Father, and listens to Him when He speaks in the silence of our
Lk 1:26–2:7 Hearts. Mary was so very precious to God that He filled Her with grace, with Himself, so that Jesus could take his human body from Her, live in Her—and with Her completely as one body—for 9 months.

Let us ask ourselves: Do I pray? How do I pray? How often do I pray? Do I feel the need to pray? Do I take the trouble to pray well? When I can't pray—do I take the trouble to help myself—by finding a book that would help me? Take the trouble to pray longer and oftener? In time of trial in prayer, do I pray with greater fidelity? Do I make up the prayer I have missed? Do I [do penance] as an act of reparation and supplication?

During meditation do I follow a certain way that will help me to pray? At the end of meditation, do I make a resolution for the day?

Am I faithful to the ... daily penance? Do I ever ask permission to do [more] penance? Do I have some small aspiration that I pray often? Both these, penance and aspirations, are a very wonderful help to grow in the life of prayer.—A soul of prayer—is a living tabernacle—where Jesus speaks to His Father.

> Eternal Father, I offer Thee Jesus, Thy beloved Son, and I offer Thee myself with Him for the greater glory of Your name and the good of souls.

Once more I wish you a Happy Feast of our Society—with Mary our Immaculate Mother, Cause of our joy—may we always be a Cause of her joy through our constant fidelity to God's will, and a cause of joy to each other by our love and concern for each other.

God bless you
Mother

MGL 192. 18TH AUGUST 1986

+ LDM

Mother House
18th August 1986

My dearest Children,

I have just returned from Dehra Dun, where we laid to rest our dearest SM. Stanislaus and SM. Carrol.

On Saturday 16th Sr. Stanislaus, the Superior in Dehra Dun, and her assistant, Sr. Carrol, went out to Dispensary. It was raining heavily and the Sisters need not have gone out in such weather, but Sr. Stanislaus chose to go, because the people in that area are so desperately poor, and she did not want them to wait in vain in the rain. The road they usually went by was flooded so they took another road.—On the way home while crossing the river on an old wooden bridge, the bridge suddenly collapsed and the ambulance with the two Sisters and driver plunged into the river, swollen by heavy rains. The door opened and they fell out—Sr. Carrol fell headlong on a huge boulder striking her head on it. Her skull cracked open and she died on the spot. Sr. Stanislaus and the driver fell into the river and tried to swim against the strong current for the river bank—a policeman on duty radioed for help and rushed down to the river bank to try and help. The driver, being big and strong, was swimming towards the bank helping Sr. Stanislaus, who, though she could swim, was impeded by the sari—she caught his shirt, and both were getting to the bank when they got caught in a strong current—the driver reached the bank and reached out to the policeman who grabbed his hand to pull him in—the sudden movement broke Sr. Stanislaus' hold on the driver, and she was carried away by the current. People came from everywhere to help, and after 2 hours they found the body, sari tangled around her legs. She had swallowed much water.

As soon as we got the news from Delhi, I left to go and be with our Sisters in Dehra Dun. Sr. Margaret Mary had arranged for a car from the Home Ministry, and we left immediately, arriving at 3 A.M. in Dehra Dun. The bodies were beautifully laid out in the 2 coffins, and everything was kept ready. The Bishop came from Meerut, and the bodies were taken to the Cathedral for the funeral Mass. Eight Priests came from Delhi and nearby missions where our Sisters work—some Sisters also came from each of the nearby houses. The Cathedral was packed with Hindus, Muslims, and Christians who loved the sisters and wanted to support them by their presence. The Bishop openly wept. Sr. Stanislaus, from Calcutta, was one of the most senior Sisters, having joined the society in 1952. Her number was 27. She had a great love for the poor, and was full of life and fun. The people, priests and everyone loved her.

Sr. Carrol made her final Vows three years ago. She was from Ranchi and loved Jesus with a simple and childlike heart. Both went home to Jesus
in going beyond the mere carrying out of duty. My Children, none of us Mt 25:13
know the day nor the hour when Jesus will come for us—let us always be

ready—faithful to our duties and faithful to Jesus in all He asks of us by living the vows we have pronounced as religious, faithful to the Constitutions which bind us as Missionaries of Charity, faithful to the Spirit and Charism which God has given to our Society.

Please offer the suffrages for the deceased of our Society according to Constitution 66.

In death Sr. Stanislaus and Sr. Carrol looked so peaceful—may we all strive to attain that peace which He alone can give.

Let us rejoice—that our two Sisters have gone Home to God by giving wholehearted and free service—

God bless you
Mother

MGL 193. 15TH OCTOBER 1986

+ LDM

Dar-es-Salaam
15th October 1986

My dearest children, Sr. M. Agnes and all,

This brings you Mother's love, blessing and prayer to each one of you that you may grow in the likeness of JESUS—by imitating the humility of Mary, His and our Mother. We can never go astray if we allow Her to keep us for Jesus. Often I think what humility JESUS had to allow His Mother to teach Him the simple ways of a child. This must be the reason why JE-
Mt 18:3 SUS insisted so much on being a child if we want to enter Heaven. So let us come closer and closer to Her in humility if [we] really want to be Holy like JESUS.

These last days have been so full of pain & suffering and also deep gratitude to God—for we could have been all crushed to death, especially Sr. M. Lysa & I, and I have never felt the power of the Rosary so real and so powerful. We were praying the Rosary with greater love these days—especially as the plane started.—All was well—but all of [a] sudden the plane instead of going up—went among the Sisters & the people who had come to see us off. In less than 15 minutes—all was over—5 lay dead—2 wounded; 3 children, [the] Manager of the leprosy centre and our Sr. M. Selena covered with blood—all dead. I took the children and Sister to [the] hospital and after the doctor declared them dead, we took Sister to the convent, where we washed her and dressed her, as she was covered with blood. At 5 P.M. we had the Holy Mass, where 12 priests together with the Bishop offered the Holy Mass. He spoke of Sister as [a] Holy Sister. The Cathedral was full—then we took Sister to the cemetery. The children are missing Sister very much. Sr. M. Amrita [and] Sr. M. Grisaldia[a] were wounded. Sr. M. Amrita is still in hospital. I have sent Sr. M. Lourdes to take care of them, as the Sisters of other congregations were doing it. I can't tell you of the love and the care the Bishop and everyone gave us all.[b]

You must have come to know of the terrible suffering of the people in South Sudan. Our Sisters are in the North. Food is not allowed to come to the people, and so hundreds are dying of hunger. I am arranging to take 4 Sisters to *Wau*—South Sudan.[c] So please pray that I will be able to do so soon. Sudan and Tanzania have good relations—so they are willing to help us. I am on my way to Nairobi and from there to go to Burundi and Benin. Then go back to Dar-Es-Salaam and take the Sisters to Sudan. Will have to be in Rome on the 26th, for Assisi 27th and 28th, Professions 29th and 30th, 2nd Cuba, 8th or 9th San Francisco Professions, Blessing—[of the] Gift of Peace in Washington.[d] Hope to be in Calcutta by the 15th.

Let us pray.

God bless you
Mother

a. In the handwritten draft Mother wrote: "Grizelda (I hope this is the correct name)", but the Sister typist chose to spell correctly the Sister's name and to omit Mother's insertion about the correct name.

b. The following news report from Nairobi was sent to the houses: "Mother Teresa, the Roman Catholic missionary, aged 76, continued her tour of East Africa yesterday after escaping unhurt when a light aircraft slewed off the rough airstrip at Hombolo, near Dodoma in Central Tanzania, 200 miles west of Dar es Salaam, on Saturday, killing five people in the crowd lining the airstrip. The dead were two boys aged 8 and 12, Sister Selena, an Indian missionary nun, the director of a leprosy centre, and another Tanzanian man. The pilot, Mr. Rolf Klemenson, a Norwegian, said the plane slewed off the runway as it was gathering speed for take-off and he was unable to lift it over the crowd. Two were injured by the propellers of the plane and at least one of the dead was decapitated. Mother Teresa attended the funeral of Sister Selena at Hombolo yesterday. She was deeply affected by the tragedy, saying 'My coming is behind this accident'. She at first said she would abandon the rest of her tour, but later decided to continue and flew to Tabora, Western Tanzania, where she attended a ceremony at which seven members of her missionary Sisters of Charity took their first vows."

c Mother's handwritten draft of this letter says "Wau—S.S." [South Sudan] but this was interpreted and typed as "work in South Sudan." Wau is a city in southern Sudan, which was used as a military post by the Sudanese government during the long civil war with the Sudan People's Liberation Army (1983–2005). Severe drought had brought more than 50,000 refugees to Wau looking for food. On 16th August 1986, a plane carrying food supplies to Wau was shot down by rebels, causing all International Red Cross air shipments of food to be stopped.

d. Gift of Peace is the name of the MC home in Washington, DC.

MGL 194. 15th DECEMBER 1986

Mother House
15th December 1986

My dearest Children,

This brings you Mother's special blessing for a very happy and Holy
Christmas and God's blessing of His tender love on each one of you during
Lk 1:49 1987. Let us thank God for all He has done with you, in you, and through
you, to Jesus in the distressing disguise. During this year, three of our Sisters have gone home to God to join our Community in Heaven. Four of our Sisters have asked to go home, as they found the way of life too difficult. Let us pray for them. It is true the life of MC is difficult, but sometimes we make it much more difficult if Charity is not fully alive among
us.—Many Sisters wound and are wounded by the tongue which speaks
Mt 12:34 from the fullness of the Heart. Just think that same tongue has received
1 Jn 4:8, 16 JESUS,[a] the God of love, in the early morning—by the evening how much
Jas 3:5–6, 9–10 evil it has done by its misuse.

During this year, 304 Aspirants joined the Postulancy, 226 Postulants joined the Noviciate, 152 Novices took First Vows, 182 Sisters took Final Vows. We have much to thank God for His Great Gift.

As so many newly professed Sisters have joined your Community, try to make your Community

– deeply contemplative
– intensely Eucharistic
– vibrant with Joy—

be a cause of joy to each other—by giving good example of true MC life and spirit.[b]

We have all taken a strong resolution [*to be humble*][c] like Mary so that we can become Holy like JESUS. The surest way to great Sanctity is Prayer and Obedience. These two make you truly a holy Religious.

One of the important points that I want to draw your attention to is our 4th Vow. That Vow—Wholehearted—is as clear as Poverty, as Chastity

a. The name of Jesus was written by Mother in her handwritten draft as "Jesus," but the Sister typist chose to type it in ALL CAPS here, as well as in a few other instances in this letter. We respected her interpretation.

b. The words "life and spirit" were added by hand, presumably the typist's, on Mother's handwritten draft. Probably the Sister typist did not understand the text, asked Mother for clarification, and then wrote it as a note for herself.

c. The words in italics were in Mother's handwritten draft but were mistakenly left out in the typed copy sent to the houses.

or Obedience. We take it for granted that it is enough to have done the service, but that is not enough. We have to really give wholeheartedly.—The negligence of it is a Matter for Confession.—Work done carelessly anyhow touches the Vow, therefore, it should be confessed.—Visiting the families—only as a Visit and as a gossip touches the Vow.[a] Therefore, my children, you must be clear [about] your obligation to the Poorest of the Poor. Col 3:23

Free means completely free, not even a glass of water outside our Convent out of love and respect for the Poor.— Mt 10:8

Cuba & Nicaragua—real gifts of God to our Society.[b] This Christmas—we can offer Baby Jesus 19 new Tabernacles as our Christmas gift. You will be glad to know that now we have our Contemplatives in Calcutta also.—What a Gift of God.

Give Mary a beautiful gift for Christmas: a resolution to love Jesus as She loved Him—and our Sisters and our Poor with a more tender and compassionate love, as St. Joseph loved Jesus. Mt 2:13–21; Lk 2:4–16, 27–39, 41–51

As the Bishops keep asking for Sisters—I have decided to ask every Regional to have a group of Aspirants and junior Postulants, if possible, in her own region. This will help us to pray and work for fervent vocations.

I would be very grateful if, before writing the report of the junior Sisters who ask to renew their vows, that you both [the Superior and the junior Sister] do [more] penance for a week.

Keep the joy of loving JESUS intimately in your heart and share this joy with each other in your community.

My dearest children, God love you for all the love you have given me and each other and the joy you have shared with the Poorest of the Poor through your works of love.[c]

God bless you—and keep you,
Mother

a. The meaning is that it is against the vow to just visit the family and gossip, instead of seeing to their needs and helping them.

b. Mother had visited Cuba on 8th July 1986 and met with communist President Fidel Castro, who granted her request to bring the Sisters to Cuba. Mother opened a house in Havana on 2nd November 1986.

In November 1986, while in Nicaragua for the National Eucharistic Congress, Mother met with President Daniel Ortega, who gave her permission to establish a mission in Nicaragua, a country troubled by revolution and tensions between the Church and the Sandinista government. Mother opened a house in Managua on 7th December 1986.

c. Mother added this sentence to the typed version of the letter.

ED 48. DECEMBER 1986

+

LDM

December 1986

My dearest Children,

Holy and Happy Christmas and God's blessing on 1987.

Be one heart full of love in the Heart of Jesus through Mary. Love one
Jn 13:34; 15:12 another as Jesus and Mother loves.—Love Jesus in the Poor with a tender, Compassionate love.—To be able to do that, you need the humility of Mary—and so often say, "Mary, Mother of Jesus, obtain for me the grace to be humble like you, so that I can become holy like Jesus".

God bless you
Mother

1987

MGL 195. 2ND JANUARY 1987

+ LDM

Mother House
2nd January 1987

My dearest Children,

Happy and Holy New Year. May the New-born Child of Bethlehem Lk 2:7
be your joy, love and peace. May you grow in [the] holiness of the Little
Child through the humility of His Mother—May she be a Mother to each
one of you throughout the Year. May She teach you to pray and pray with
you. May She obtain for you the zeal of the Handmaid—so that, like Her, Lk 1:38
[you may] be always in haste to serve the Poorest of the Poor—wherever Lk 1:39
Obedience may send you.

Though she was full of Grace, full of God—the Mother of the Son of Lk 1:28
God—Jesus—yet she did not think it was below Her dignity to obey Joseph the Carpenter, in all things regarding the family life. It must have
been so difficult for Her physically and spiritually to obey St. Joseph when Mt 2:13–15
he told her to take the Child and with him hide in Egypt, just because
a proud King wanted to kill Her Child. There was no discussion on the
matter—Joseph said "take the child and come," and She took the child and Mt 2:14, 21
went. Only prayer and humility could[a] have helped her to obey without
questioning. Is our obedience like hers? Are we really so free as to be able
to accept whatever Jesus gives us, and takes from us, through our Superiors, through our obedience? In all our difficulties regarding obedience, let
us listen to Her voice—telling us "Do whatever He tells you." Jn 2:5

If the servants at the wedding did not obey the simple thing when Je- Jn 2:7
sus told them—to fill the water pots with water and serve the guests, we

a. The handwritten draft has "must" in place of "could."

would not have had the joy of knowing Jesus' LOVE for His Mother—
Jn 2:1–11 and the Mother's FAITH in the power of Her Son. She still keeps telling us
"do what He tells you" through your Superiors. Obey, and you will experience the joy of loving and being loved.

For us, who have consecrated our lives totally to God, obedience is a "must", that is why we need humility

– BECAUSE THE FRUIT OF HUMILITY IS PROMPT OBEDIENCE
– AND THE FRUIT OF OBEDIENCE IS SANCTITY.

Obedience is for each one of us the free gift we give to God, because
Gn 2:16–17; 3:6 even God Himself would not force us to obey. Adam and Eve disobeyed
God in such a small matter as eating the forbidden fruit—and we know
Rom 5:12 what that disobedience brought into the world—SIN AND DEATH—so
Ex 20:1–17 much that God had to formulate the Ten Commandments to protect us
from the evil of sin. Jesus died on the Cross

– to make reparation for sin
– to forgive sin
– to wash away sin by His precious blood.

Heb 10:7, 9 For Jesus also—who had come to do the Will of His Father—found Obe-
dience—Surrender—Acceptance of the Will of His Father so difficult, that
Lk 22:44 He perspired blood in Gethsemane. That is why He prayed the longer: to
Lk 23:33 be able to obey the will of His Father, to accept the terrible humiliation of
being crucified as a Sinner with the other two Sinners. Only His obedience
to His Father helped Him to accept all; that is why He prayed "Father, if it
Lk 22:42 is Your Will take this cup from Me; yet not My Will but Yours be done,"
Lk 22:44 and He prayed the longer. Obedience in our lives as religious consecrated to God is the most beautiful and meaningful offering to God—because our will is the only gift of God which is our own, and which God will never take by force—He will accept only when we surrender it. If we are really determined to be Holy, Obedience is a sure way and means to great sanctity—as Jesus Himself used it to prove His love for the Father and for each one of us.

On reading all this and meditating, let us face ourselves sincerely and
ask—What is Obedience in my life? How do I live it?—How much does
Heb 10:7, 9 it affect my life as a religious—as a Missionary who has been sent to do the Will of the Father—that comes to us through our Constitutions—the written Will of the Church, and the spoken Word of Jesus—through our Superiors, whoever they may be?

Yes, if we really obey—we are holy. Our Lady was so full of Grace—so Lk 1:28
Holy—because she lived her surrender: "Be it done to me according to Lk 1:38
Thy word."[a]

The coming novena for 1st Friday in February, we will offer [more] penance and deliberately make 5 sacrifices of prompt obedience in reparation for all the disobedience we ourselves and each Missionary of Charity has committed in the Society. We have much for which to thank God—for His great[b] and tender love for each one of us and our Poor. Let us show our gratitude to God the Father, God the Son and God the Holy Spirit—by
doing all things with great love—so that the Poor may see our good works Mt 5:16
and glorify the Father. Let us ask Our Lady to help us to do it.

There have been a number of changes—which have been difficult to accept with Total Surrender, Loving Trust and a Big Smile—but this is the chance for greater love, [*of total surrender*][c], of real joy and holiness.—You yourself pray, and I will also pray for you.—Don't lose the chance.

The aim of our Society is to Satiate the Thirst of Jesus for love, for Jn 19:28
Souls by working according to obedience at the Salvation and Sanctification of the Poorest of the Poor.

So let us accept whatever Obedience gives and let us give whatever Obedience takes with a big Smile. This is true Holiness. Let us pray and obey, for there is no other way to be humble like Mary and Holy like Jesus.

God bless you
Mother

a. In the handwritten draft Mother wrote "... Thy will".

b. In the handwritten draft Mother wrote: "We have much to thank God for—His great ..."

c. The words in italics were in Mother's handwritten draft but were mistakenly left out in the typed copy sent to the houses.

MGL 196. 2ND APRIL 1987

+

LDM

Mother House
2nd April 1987

My dearest children,

This brings you Mother's blessing, love and prayer that you may, each
Jn 15:16 one of you, grow in holiness—for which JESUS[a] himself has chosen you to
Mt 11:29 be His very own—like Him meek and humble.

When we read and meditate [on] the Gospel, we see clearly the prefer-
Lk 1:27ff ence of God for Poverty. The "Word of God—JESUS" was conceived in a human helpless form in the womb of a young woman, Mary—of an ordinary, simple family. Not even [*her husband*][b] St. Joseph, to whom she was engaged, knew that JESUS had come and was in her womb. God sent an Angel to explain to him—that the child conceived was by the Holy Spirit.
Mk 6:1–3 The Poverty at his birth—nothing but straw and animals. Nazareth had so little that the people were surprised at His knowledge—knowing that He was not educated as He came of a Poor family. And we all know of
Jn 18:22, 19:3 the terrible poverty of the Passion: The slap on His face; the spitting on
Mt 27:26, 29, 30, 35, 38, 60; Mk 15:15, 17, 19, 25, 27, 34, 46; Lk 23:33, 53; Jn 19:2, 18, 23, 25–27, 41–42 His face, the crowning with thorns, the scourging, the removing of His clothes, the crucifixion—putting the Cross in the centre, showing that He was worse than the other two—the burial in somebody's grave; all these and many others, especially the terrible longing to be loved—the terrible loneliness, the terrible feeling of pain for His Mother. All, all these: the love with which He loved you and me. We who have consecrated our lives to be His Consecrated Virgins—the Spouse of the Crucified Spouse—are we really true to our consecration—for which we need the freedom of
Rom 8:35, 38–39 Poverty? Or is there something or somebody that is dividing our love for JESUS?

So much of the world is trying to penetrate, is trying to destroy the simplicity and the way of life we have so beautifully taken on ourselves, to be like JESUS in Poverty. I find the simplicity of food has gone. Our Poverty was so beautiful—deliberately choosing to have the

a. The Sister typist typed the name of Jesus in ALL CAPS throughout the letter; we have respected this original interpretation.

b. The words in italics were in Mother's handwritten draft but were left out in the typed copy sent to the houses.

cheapest.—[*So much food extra and special*]—Now telephone and electric bills go higher and higher—the phone is being used without even a second thought of time—since every minute is counted. [*Five, six lights in the dormitory*]—big lights everywhere. See Constitution 64—(h) and keep to it.[a] Outsiders, Bishops and priests should not be invited, neither should we have a grand celebration with feasting in food, garlands and decorations.

Many Sisters have joined the Society because they wanted the Poverty of Jesus and Mary. It is good during this time of greater love to examine myself, my conscience, sincerely—am I really happy to be poor? not to have extras? [to have] the cheapest?—the thing that nobody wants? Am I aware of the waste? do I do something without judging?[b] Remember what our Constitution says: Our Poverty should be true Gospel Poverty—gentle, tender, glad and openhearted, a giving expression of love. To love, it is necessary to give.—To give, it is necessary to be free from selfishness. It is not that we can't have—we choose not to have. Our Poor are forced not to have. That is why Poverty is freedom for us. Are you [*and I*] really free? Am I really happy like—St. Ignatius—to have worse things? The worse place in the dormitory? less water? light? etc. St. Francis [*of Assisi*] was so much in Love with Poverty—that he used to call her—My Lady Poverty.—Is she my lady also?

Have I experienced the joy and the freedom of Poverty during these years as an MC? If yes—Thank God! If not, look at the root and work at the conversion of your heart—for only then you can love Christ with an undivided love in Chastity.

As Easter is so close—let us with Mary Magdalene look for JESUS, and Jn 20:14–16
do not rest till we find Him; and because we feel the full freedom of Pov- Song 3:1–4
erty, we can with her say: "Tell me where you have kept Him and I will go Jn 20:15
and take Him away.[c]"

I know you will pray for Sr. M.——, and Sr. M.——, who have asked for dispensation from their Vows. Let us therefore during Holy Week do

a. Constitution 64: "When two or three come together in His Name, Jesus is there—and so our means to grow in community are: (h) Celebrating the feast of the patron Saint of the Sisters including Superiors with simplicity and only within the community" (1980 *Constitutions*).

b. The original handwritten draft and the typed copy of the letter have "judging," and thus the meaning would be: "Do I judge whether it is right or wrong, before doing something?" Another possibility is that Mother could have written "judging" but intended instead to write "grumbling." By comparing this sentence to parallel passages, the meaning then would be: "Do I do without something [I need or like], without grumbling?"

c. In the handwritten draft Mother wrote: "... and I will go and bring Him." The Sister typist, however, chose to insert a different translation of the Scripture passage.

[more] penance—for our Society, that we may all understand—love and live our Vocation, to be only all for JESUS through Mary.

Happy & Holy Easter.
God bless you
Mother

MGL 197. 1ST MAY 1987

LDM

Mother House
1st May 1987

My dearest Children,

Please follow the following very faithfully.

1. Money should be handled ONLY by the sister doing the account. Not even the Superior should handle the money.
2. Whoever takes money should give a detailed account with bills. In the absence of bills, a voucher should be made listing the ITEMS and their PRICES and should be SIGNED by the Sister.
3. As far as possible avoid rough books. The cash book should be entered DAILY (not copied out at the end of the month); items you are not sure of can be entered initially in pencil.
4. Avoid buying things for other houses. Try not to LEND and BORROW, keeping the amount as Cash in Hand until the money is returned. If you need to give money for shopping to another house, try to give a round figure and write it as given to ________.The other house should enter it as G.B.F. [General Building Fund] received from ________.
5. Anything bought for or given to people outside should be entered as RELIEF in the Medical column. DO NOT add it to S.B. [Shishu Bhavan] or N.H. [Nirmal Hriday] expenses. All Relief should be entered in a book with the name of the person, amount given; purpose, signature of the Sister giving and of the person receiving.
6. Accounts of New Construction and major repairs should be kept very carefully. The details, including the wages of masons, etc., could be entered separately in the last few pages of the cash book. ALL BILLS SHOULD BE KEPT.

7. DO NOT close your accounts without getting your pass book updated.[a] It would help if you put the following details on the back of your account sheet (especially houses that have many bank transactions).

	Cash	*Bank*
Opening Balance	xx	xx
Donations	xx	xx
G.B.F.	xx	xx
Interest	xx	xx
Cash Withdrawn	xx	xx
	——	——
Total Expense	xx	xx
Cash Withdrawn	xx	xx
Closing Balance	xx	xx
	——	——

8. If there is money missing or extra DO NOT just put it in. THIS IS A MATTER OF CONSCIENCE. Look for the mistake, and if you cannot trace it, write it as missing or extra at the end of the account.
9. The SUPERIOR IS RESPONSIBLE FOR THE ACCOUNTS SUBMITTED. Before the accounts are sent, it is her responsibility to thoroughly check it and see that the daily account, vouchers, pass book, etc. are all tallied and correct. She should then sign the daily account book and the account sheet that is sent to Calcutta.
10. Cheques received from foreigners should be sent to Calcutta. Cash received (even in Indian Rupees if above Rs 500) should be kept separate. The amount, name and address of the donor should be intimated to Calcutta and then in the NEXT MONTH it should be entered as G.B.F.

I ask you to keep the accounts very carefully as a sign of your love and fidelity to Poverty.

God bless you all
Mother

a. The pass book is a small book that is used for entering cash and bank transactions.

ED 49. EASTER [19TH APRIL] 1987

Ek Dil Prem Pur[a]

My dearest children,

Be one heart full of love in the Heart of Jesus through Mary. Be holy. Only all for Jesus.

God bless you
Mother

MGL 198. 13TH MAY 1987

+ LDM

13th May 1987
Feast of Our Lady of Fatima

My dearest Children,

Let us, with deep gratitude to God, thank our Holy Father for giving us a Whole Year: TO GROW AND SHOW OUR LOVE FOR OUR
Mt 1:16; Acts 1:14; Jn 19:27 LADY—the Mother of Jesus and our Mother.[b] She who is the Cause of our joy, how deep and tender our love for Her must be.

Let us therefore, in a special way grow in love for the Mother of Jesus, our Mother. I want you to imitate and follow Her closely in:

PURITY and
HUMILITY and
SILENCE, the fruit of a Pure Heart.

Let us often meditate on the Beauty and Love of Mary from our Constitutions so that we may love Her as Jesus loved Her.

Do not let anything so disturb you, so make you restless and careless—as to make you forget that:

Jn 19:27 You are a Child of Mary
Is 43:4 Precious to Jesus
Jn 14:21, 23 Loved by the Father

a. At the top of the page Mother wrote, "Ek Dil Prem Pur," and her Easter message reflects this thought.

b. On 1st January 1987, Pope John Paul II announced that a Marian Year would begin on 7th June 1987 (the Solemnity of Pentecost) and would conclude on 15th August 1988 (the Feast of the Assumption).

because

You are the Spouse of Jesus
Temple of the Holy Spirit. 1 Cor 3:17; 6:19

Let us at the end of "MOTHER MARY YEAR" offer this Gift of gratitude to our Holy Father for giving us Our Lady, in this very special way.

I am sure by now you must have got the news about our Sr. M. Vibha, MC. She came back from Egypt a few months ago, very sick. She was in hospital and when we found that the doctors could do no more, we brought her home, where she died on 21st April, in the passage near Mother's room: a very beautiful death. Her two brothers came to see her. The burial was really Something Beautiful for God. Each one of you, offer the prayers according to our Constitution 66. We now have a beautiful community of 19 Sisters in Heaven, interceding for us.

We had also 2 beautiful days of Profession: 38 Sisters for First Vows and 72 Sisters for Final Vows. All so beautiful, which we owe to His great love for us—in giving us the Gift of so many vocations. Seventy-six Postulants became Novices. Let us pray that in June God will give us many more vocations—for the greater glory of His Name.

A Hindu family, Mr. Mukherjee and his sisters, gave us a beautiful gift of their house in Chinsura. I asked whether he wanted the Active or the Contemplative Sisters to be in his house, and he said: the Contemplatives. So right in the heart of Hindu families, the Sisters and their life of prayer and sacrifice [have] become the heart of God's Presence for the Hindus, who keep on coming to pray. In Chinsura (West Bengal, India) we have the Noviciate for our Contemplative Sisters.

This June we begin a Juniorate of 6 months for the Juniors who have finished two and an half years of their first Vows.[a] Again after two and a half years they will have six months of Tertianship before taking Final Vows. You must all pray that we really profit fully from this Gift of God.

I am hoping to visit you all this year, with Our Lady. So you must

a. The *Juniorate* is the period of temporary profession, normally five years. The explicit formation of the Junior Sisters, known as the "Junior course", began in 1987 with a six-month program in Calcutta. To avoid the difficulties of transferring so many Sisters every six months, it was subsequently decided to have the Juniorate program in every region and to distribute it to a month per year over a five-year period. This was implemented progressively. In addition, the Sisters make an annual eight-day retreat. Thus, the Sisters are absent from their communities for just over a month at a time, and the apostolate is less affected. Mother's intention was that the Sisters who would have completed the six-month Juniorate program would have had six months tertianship before final vows. However, this was not implemented; the tertianship continued to be for one year.

pray much for Mother. I am on my way to Rome and hope to visit our Sisters in as many places as possible, so pray for Mother—that my presence in our communities will bring the joy, unity, love and peace of Jesus. And together we will grow in the love of Our Society, living the Spirit of our Society, which is one of Total Surrender, Loving Trust and Cheerfulness. Through living the Spirit of our Society, we will be able to satiate the
Jn 19:28 "Thirst of Jesus" on the Cross for love of souls, by working at the salvation and sanctification of the Poorest of the Poor.

To be able to satiate the Thirst of Jesus we need:

the undivided love for Jesus in Chastity,
through Freedom of Poverty,
in Total Surrender through Obedience, and
by giving Whole Hearted and Free service to the Poorest of the Poor.

All this must be the fruit of a

Deeply Contemplative life,
Intensely Eucharistic, and
Vibrant with Joy.

Eucharist and Prayer must become the life of our life and service to the Poorest of the Poor, the fruit of that life.

This is where we need the tender love and care of Mary, to be only All for JESUS through Her.

With God's Blessing, Brother Sebastian, together with the other Contemplative Brothers, started the Lay Missionaries of Charity,[a] with Families who are consecrating their lives through the four Vows. This consecration has brought so much holiness in Family life.

God bless you
Mother

N.B. A Plenary Indulgence may be gained (under the usual conditions) when the Rosary is prayed in Church, in a family group or in a Religious community;

A Partial Indulgence may be gained for praying the Rosary in whole or in part in other circumstances.

a. The Lay Missionaries of Charity (LMC) is an international movement of the laity, approved on 25th February 1987 by the Diocese of Rome. Their special mission is to work for the salvation and sanctification of the members of their own families and of the poorest of the poor. The LMCs adhere to the spirit and charism of the Missionaries of Charity family and make private vows of (conjugal) chastity, poverty, obedience and wholehearted and free service to the poorest of the poor.

MGL 199. 2ND AUGUST 1987

+

L.D.M.

On the plane to U.S.A.
2nd August 1987

My dearest Children,

This brings you Mother's love, blessing and prayer for a very Holy and Happy Feast of our Society. This year Our Lady's Immaculate Heart is, in a special way, "the Cause of our Joy," because we have the whole year fully consecrated to her in all things. What a gift of God Her Heart is to our Society. She has done such great things for us—unworthy though we Lk 1:49
are—of such tender love. The best way to show our love for Her—is by learning from Her—humility—to be humble like Her—it is a sure way to be holy like Her and Her Son Jesus.

It was Her humility that drew Jesus to Her. She was so free—because She was so poor—so pure, so full of grace—that God could use Her very Lk 1:28
life to give life to His Son Jesus—Her Flesh and Blood, which God used to form the Body and Blood of Jesus, which He poured out from the Cross as a redeeming means of forgiveness and greater love.—And something very, very wonderful happened when the last drop of blood, mingled with water, poured out of His wounded Heart—His Mother was His last thought. His last thought was for His Mother—that she should have someone to love Jn 19:25–27
Her. And He gave Her to John, His beloved one—to take His place.—And John, in his love for Jesus, took Her—Mary—to "his own" to be His Mother. Could Jesus, during the Sacrifice of the Holy Mass, say the same to me—"Behold your Mother"? Is my love so tender—my heart so pure, as to take Her Jn 19:27
to my heart as John did? With what tenderness John took Her to his own.—At every Holy Mass, I too have a chance to take Her to my own—if only I believe. When we receive Jesus in Holy Communion let us ask Her to come with us and teach us how to take care of Him as She took care of Him in Nazareth.—We have such a beautiful opportunity to take care of Him in Lk 2:39–40, 51
the Poor and be real Contemplatives in the Heart of the World.

In my visits to our Sisters in Africa, I saw so much suffering of our Poor, and I thank God for the presence of our Sisters among them. I visited Egypt, Sudan, Ethiopia, Kenya, Zaire, Rwanda, Burundi. In Burundi, the Church is going through its Crucifixion.[a]—Thank God our Sisters are

a. President Bagaza of Burundi (in power from 1976 to 1987) imposed various restrictions on the Catholic Church, including the closing of churches, nationalizing Catholic schools, imprisoning priests, and expelling missionaries. Mother is referring to two convents of nuns who were expelled.

allowed to remain and be His love and compassion to the Poor.—I have already sent 4 Sisters to the place from where other Sisters have been sent away. I am trying to get another group—for another place from where they sent away Sisters. I know you are all praying much for Mother—for our Society.—Yes, we need to pray much so that we become true Carriers
Lk 4:18 of God's love and so proclaim the tender love God has for His people.

This year, being Our Lady's year, I want all of us to do something special for Her:

1. We will take special trouble to improve our life of prayer by our punctuality and fidelity;
2. Bring into our Community tender, thoughtful, compassionate love for each other, and if we do anything that touches charity, we will speak our fault in public before dinner;
3. Lk 1:56 We will take special care of our older Sisters—as Our Lady took care of Elizabeth,
4. We will make sure that every family, especially Catholic families, has a small altar to Our Lady and at least 1 rosary, if not more.

As the Lay Missionaries of Charity and the Co-workers are a part of our Society that belongs in a very special way to Our Lady, we will, in future, burn 8 lights before the Blessed Sacrament during Adoration—

two lights to represent the active Brothers and Sisters, who are the two hands of Jesus,

two lights to represent the contemplative Brothers and Sisters, who are the two feet of Jesus,

one light to represent the MC Fathers, who are the Heart of Jesus,

one light to represent the Lay Missionaries of Charity, who are the Holy Face of Jesus,

one light to represent the Co-Workers, who are the Head of Jesus crowned with thorns,

one light to represent Our Lady, Mother of the whole Society, interceding for us and leading us to Jesus.

It will be a wonderful gift to Jesus to have us all together in Adoration before Him.

My dearest children, be one heart full of love in the Heart of Jesus through Mary.—Protect the Spirit of our Society—and so satiate His

Thirst for souls by working at the Salvation and Sanctification of the Poorest of the Poor. Jn 19:28

Happy and Holy Feast of our Society. I hope and pray that you will prepare your Communities for the Feast of our Mother the Cause of our joy with a fervent triduum—

God bless you
Mother

P.S. We will go to Russia on the 20th Aug.—Please pray for Mother very specially on the 22nd.

MGL 200. 27TH OCTOBER 1987

+ LDM

Mother House
27th October 1987

My dearest Children,

I have a beautiful gift to give you, to each one of you—The gift of a Priest—to help him to become—only all for Jesus through Mary—a Holy Priest. A mission of love for both.

To satiate the thirst of JESUS[a] on the cross for each of His Bishops and Priests personally I offer each of you a Bishop or a Priest—individually so that each of you may offer all you are and have to JESUS through Mary, the Mother of the Church for the one who is given to you in spiritual missionary adoption, like St. Therese of Lisieux had done, so that Jesus, who is in agony in His Priests, Scourged in His Priests, Crowned with thorns in His Priests, carries the cross in His Priests, is crucified in His Priests, may find in you a Veronica to help him on His way to Calvary, so that He may be able to rise in His priests with the splendour of His Resurrection and thus bring about a New Pentecost not only in the diocese to which they belong but [in] the whole Church.

Jn 19:28
Lk 22:44
Mt 27:26, 29, 31–32, 35; Mk 15:15, 17, 20–21, 24; Lk 23:25–26, 33; Jn 19:1, 17, 18
Mt 28:6–7; Mk 16:6; Lk 24:6
Acts 2:1–4

If you wish to accept this gift of Mother to you, please send me your names immediately through your Regionals.

How holy you must be to be able to pray and offer all for the holiness of the priest given to you. Holy Father himself,[b] being the first priest, has

a. ALL CAPS in this letter are the Sister typist's choice; we have respected it, although Mother's original handwritten draft does not have ALL CAPS.

b. Pope John Paul II.

asked to be adopted also—so I have given Holy Father to Sr. M. Nirmala—who I am sure will help our Holy Father with her prayer and sacrifice.

On the 30th we begin the retreat for the Councillors, Regionals, Mistresses of formation and myself. So pray much for us all, that through this retreat we may grow in the likeness of Christ and so be His tender love to each other. Pray also for all Tertians and Novices who will take their Vows—for our Postulants who will join the noviciates, for our Aspirants who will become Postulants.

In your Rosary, at the 5th Mystery intention, add: Lay Missionaries of Charity.

I have written to every single Junior renewing her Vows. Please take the trouble to make good use of the little note.[a] I have written it with great love and with many sacrifices. Mother wants you to be a holy Sister and not just a number.

As in most of the places we are very much involved in teaching the Faith: Do we know the language of the people—do you prepare your teaching?—In time you will not be allowed to teach the faith if you don't do it properly.

If you would only obey Mother—when Mother tells you again [and again]—Love and Unity in the Community.—Superiors, in the Name of Jesus, I ask you do not use words that hurt, unworthy of the Spouse of Christ.—Some sentences told by the Superior—fill me with shivers of pain
Lk 23:31 untold.—If you speak like this now when I am with you—what will you do after. My children, we have all made the special Vow of Charity.—How it must hurt the Sacred Heart of Jesus dwelling in our hearts—those terri-
Mt 12:34 ble words that are spoken from the fullness of the heart. [*You do not know what terrible pain those words cause to my heart*][b]—Jesus & I same.[c] I have to take five different medicines for my physical heart—but I long for the best medicine—your love for one another.—Make a word of honour with Jesus and Mary that you would never offend and hurt Jesus in your Sisters with uncharitable words.

If we are going to pray for a Priest to be Holy—with what greater love we must pray for our Sisters in our Community.—The best prayer is Love for each other, with words of love that come from the fullness of the heart filled with the presence of Jesus.

a. Mother used to write a personal "little note" to each junior Sister before she renewed her vows, encouraging the Sister to work on a point or two that she needed to improve on during the year.

b. The words in italics are in Mother's handwritten draft but were left out in the typed copy sent to the houses.

c. Mother means "Jesus and I feel the same."

My children, I begin to distrust your love for me—because you are not doing what I have asked so often—to love one another. There must be ugly words and thoughts regarding me also—and this is what will destroy the Society.—It is a hidden cancer that is spreading, and one day it will just burst out—and then it will be too late to save the gift of God—Our Society.

Say often: Jesus in my heart, I believe in Your tender love for me—help me to love my Sister with the same tender love as You love me. Jn 13:34; 15:12

My Children, if you want to be holy, there is no easier, surer, quicker way than to put your hand in Mary's and allow Her to lead you to Jesus. Don't only pray to Her but really turn to Her as to your Mother, cling to Her, tell Her your needs, your fears, your desires. Whatever you do, do it with Her—asking Her help and guidance. Jesus gave Her to us as His last gift from the Cross when He said to John and to us "Behold your Mother". Jn 19:27
Make use of this precious gift—keep close to Her and you will be close to Jesus. Listen to Her.—She who told the waiters at the wedding feast "Do Jn 2:5
whatever He tells you" can and will direct you in the best way to Jesus.

Our blessed Mother calls us to fast and do penance and pray—let us be faithful to the penances practised in our Society if we are sincere in our desire to bring souls to Jesus—especially now you have the great gift to pray for a priest and sacrifice yourself in order to help him to be holy and bring souls to Jesus.

Here are the three forms of the Prayer of Offering—you are free to choose any one you wish.

PRAYER OF OFFERING

I. O my God, Most Blessed Trinity, Father, Son and the Holy Spirit, I, ________________, offer all that I am and all that I have to you through the Immaculate Heart of Mary, Mother of the Church & my Mother, for ________________, to quench Your infinite thirst for him as expressed by You through Jesus on the Cross.

Accept this, my offering, and keep us both in Your heart and fill us with Your love and treat us as You will. I ask this in the Name of Jesus. Amen.

II. O my God, Most Blessed Trinity, Father, Son and the Holy Spirit, I, ________________, offer myself to You through the Immaculate Heart of Mary, Mother of the Church and my Mother, as a Veronica to Jesus in ________________, to quench Your infinite thirst for him, as expressed by You through Jesus on the Cross.

Accept this, my offering, and keep us both in Your Heart, imprint Your image in our whole beings, and treat us as You will. I ask this in the Name of Jesus. Amen.

III. Those who wish to offer themselves as Victims:

O my God, Most Blessed Trinity, Father, Son and the Holy Spirit, I, ________________, offer myself to You through the Immaculate Heart of Mary, Mother of the Church and my Mother, as a Victim of Holocaust to Your thirsting Love for ________________, to quench your infinite thirst for him as expressed by You through Jesus on the Cross.

Accept this, my offering, and keep me in Your Heart and fill me with Your Love and treat me as You will. I ask this in the Name of Jesus. Amen.

Let us pray,
God bless you
Mother

MGL 201. 22ND DECEMBER 1987

+ LDM

22nd December 1987

My dearest Children,

Joseph and Mary and the little unborn Child Jesus in the womb of
His Mother were travelling on the back of the donkey St. Joseph owned,
through lands and hills, cold and breeze—even maybe snow—going
where? Just to obey the order of the Emperor—who out of pride—to show
Lk 2:1, 4 how many people were under him [ordered a census]. So often we find
obedience so difficult. You can imagine how difficult it must have been for
our Lady, as she knew that the time had come for her child to be born—
The Son of God. And we know what happened when they arrived—no
Lk 2:7 place in the inn. They were too poor to go to a place where they have
to pay. How easily we spend money, we do not buy the cheapest, as our
Constitution says.

So Joseph prayed and he decided to take Mary and her unborn child
to a cave; and there after a very short time, her child, Jesus the Son of
God, was born. She looked around; there was nothing but the swaddling
clothes she had brought, the manger full of straw, and the donkey. Joseph
helped her and tried to make the manger as soft as possible. The donkey
helped with his breathing to make the little one feel warm. All these sufferings [are] the result and the fruit of obedience. Is our obedience so complete, that we are ready to make any sacrifice for the sake of becoming like
Heb 10:7, 9; Phil 2:8 Jesus, who was obedient unto death even the death of the Cross? Look at
the Crib, at the straw, at Our Lady, at St. Joseph, at the donkey—what total

surrender has done to their lives—was it really necessary? Yes, because disobedience brought sin, death, and misery into this world.—So also in our lives, when did we feel most miserable?—When the sin of disobedience had entered our lives—and we could no longer love Jesus with undivided love. Gn 3:1–19; Rom 5:12

So today—while looking at the Crib with our eyes full of Faith, let us make one strong resolution: WE WILL OBEY, cost what it may. To be able to do so, we will ask Mary, the Mother of Jesus and our Mother, to pray for us, that we may, like her, say YES to God's will that comes to us through our Superiors. Mt 1:16; Jn 19:27; Acts 1:14

In our last changes we had changed quite a number of Regionals. This time also we have to do a few more.—Each time we do a few, as we cannot do it all together.

During the retreats all over there has been one strong resolution to bring back the Zeal for souls—and the love for Poverty. So in the Name of Jesus help Mother to help you bring back Zeal for souls and the love for Poverty. We have seen in Bethlehem how obedience has helped Joseph and Mary to accept poverty with joy. Obedience, I am sure, will help us to be full of zeal for souls and love poverty as our Mother—like St. Ignatius did. St. Francis of Assisi loved Poverty very tenderly and used to call it—My Lady Poverty. How joy will fill our hearts if we obey, for obedience is a sure way to great sanctity.

According to our Constitution no. 215b we will now begin to give our Senior Sisters of 10 and more years [of] final profession a period of 3 months to withdraw from their labours, for spiritual renewal and contemplation. The following sisters have been chosen for this gift of love from the Infant Jesus.

. . .[a]

I am sure all of you will be praying for each one of our Sisters to remain like Mary at the feet of Jesus during this special opportunity for spiritual growth. Lk 10:39

Let us unite in our heart—In prayer
In penance
In love

to grow in Charity especially for each other in our Society and in each community through undivided love for Christ in Chastity—Charity and

a. The list of the Sisters has been omitted.

Purity, our gift to Our Lady in a special way this year and in preparation for our two foundations in Russia and China.

Keep the joy of loving Jesus in your hearts and share this joy with all you meet, especially your Sisters in Community.

God bless you
Mother

ED 50. CHRISTMAS 1987

Christmas 1987

My dearest Children

This brings you Mother's love, blessing and prayer that you may all be one heart full of love in the Heart of Jesus through Mary. [May] this unity of love help you to become humble like Mary and holy like Jesus. Humility & Obedience are a sure way to great holiness. To Reach this holiness is Mother's prayer & desire for each one of you for Christmas & New Year.—

Happy & Holy Christmas.

God bless you
Mother[a]

a. Below Mother's handwritten message, the following lines were typed:

"What can I give Him, poor as I am?
If I were a Shepherd, I would bring a lamb,
If I were a wise man,
I would do my part.
Now that I am an M.C.
I'll give Him my heart to love
And hands to serve!"

1988

MGL 202. 17TH FEBRUARY 1988

+ L.D.M.

17th February 1988

My dearest Children,

Let us enter Lent with a pure heart—for a pure heart can see and share the terrible Suffering of Christ.—Be the one to comfort Him when He needs someone to comfort Him, especially where there is so much sin—everywhere, even in those Consecrated to Him. During this lent let us in a special way make many sacrifices through living the true Poverty we have Vowed to God.—Poverty will free us to satiate the thirst of Jesus in Gethsemane and on the Cross for love—for souls—by working with greater zeal at the Salvation and Sanctification—for each other, the Poor we serve, and our own Soul.—The world, the Church has never needed holiness so much as today.

Mt 5:8

Mt 26–27; Mk 14–15; Lk 22–23; Jn 18–19

Ps 69:20

Mt 26:36–46; Mk 14:32–42; Lk 22:39–46

What is holiness in our own life? We cannot give what we don't have, therefore what means do we use to be Holy? For us holiness is a "must", a simple duty. To be only all for Jesus through Mary.

We have been chosen to be an MC. Do I appreciate the gift of God? Do I realize the gift of God—a Contemplative right in the Heart of the world? For the Poor are Jesus in the distressing disguise—therefore whatever we do for the Poor we do it to Jesus.—"You—did—it—to—Me", He will say when we come Face to Face—after death. How precious is our Vocation to be an MC.—Do we value it? What does it mean in our life, our Vocation? What sacrifices do we make to preserve it? Infidelity to Prayer and Poverty has led many to sins against Chastity.—Once this Vow is touched—easily loss of Vocation comes.[a]

Mt 25:40

a. In the handwritten draft of this letter, Mother had continued the sentence with "—or just living a double life—what terrible suffering for the Heart of J", but she crossed it out.

The work that Obedience has given us—is our love for Jesus in action. So let us not deceive ourselves.—Do we really know the Gift of God, our Vocation to be an MC? What means do we use to preserve it, to make it grow—to grow in holiness through living the life of MC in its fullness?

I enclose with this letter points that we have to practice every day during Lent; also we will fast every Friday, the Church fast, and try to do [more] penance, if possible, during Lent.

POINTS

As a special practice during Lent and to grow in that holiness to which God calls each one of us as religious and as Missionaries of Charity, we will take and examine ourselves on the following points.

1st WEEK: POVERTY

1. Asking the necessary permissions. Renew the General permission in time. Give a correct account of the money entrusted to us. Using money with the realisation that we are
Lk 17:10; 1 Pt 4:10 stewards, not owners, and in a spirit of Poverty, and always to buy the cheapest. The money and things come for the poor, not for ourselves.
2. If your family needs, do you ask Mother or your Regional?
3. When you leave a House, do you take only the personal things given for your use?
4. For Christmas, Easter, feast days—one homemade card from the house and one garland. Are we using designed letter paper?
5. Do we carry letter paper with us when transferred?[a]
6. Am I one of those who carry boxes and boxes of things and money without permission when going home? Do I realise I am belittling my family?
7. Am I striving to grow in a spirit of total detachment from things, of emptying myself still more, to be filled with only Jesus?
8. Have I experienced the true freedom of having nothing—neither power nor earthly riches?
9. Am I totally dependent and empty of all but God?
10. Are Priests and people coming to our feast day celebrations?

a. Mother is reminding the Sisters that out of poverty, they are not supposed to use fancy letter paper, but rather plain paper; nor carry personal supplies from house to house, but use what is available wherever they go.

2nd WEEK: CHASTITY

1. Is my heart all and only for Jesus?
2. Do I really have an undivided love for Jesus?
3. Is there someone else in my mind and heart? a Sister? A Man?
4. Do I realise that person with whom I am preoccupied can make me an adulterer?
5. Do I speak in time when I sense danger for myself or my Sister?
6. Am I careless with my touch? About gossip? Reading magazines or books other than spiritual reading?
7. [Am I] bringing men into our enclosure?[a]
8. Am I friendly but reserved in my relationships with others?
9. Am I kind but prudent in my dealings with all of God's people?

3rd WEEK: OBEDIENCE

Acts of love in Reparation

1. for all the times we have failed to follow Jesus, who was obedient even to death; Phil 2:8
2. for lack of promptness and simplicity in obeying;
3. for lack of submission and answering back and making excuses;
4. for not accepting our Superior with faith and love and respect;
5. for making it difficult for our Superiors to speak to and to correct me;
6. for belittling obedience by hypocrisy and not doing it to Jesus;
7. for failing to reconcile initiative with a spirit of dependence.

4th WEEK: WHOLEHEARTED SERVICE

Acts of love in reparation for:

1. our lack of zeal in labouring for the salvation and sanctification of our poor in our visits to the families;
2. our lack of concern and love for the needs of the poor and our Sisters;
3. our failure to pick up the dying, the real street cases;
4. our seeking recompense or gratitude for our services;
5. our failure to pray for the poor entrusted to us;

a. This refers, for example, to bringing workers into the enclosure, to help in the works that the Sisters themselves could do.

6. our failure to be available to the poor and each other;
Lk 1:3 7. our failure to walk with Mary, who went in haste.

5th WEEK: HUMILITY

Jn 19:34 Jesus allowed His Heart to be opened to teach us humility:

1. in acknowledging our weakness and misery;
1 Thes 5:18 2. thanking God for everything, even for failures;
3. accepting with peace and joy to be misunderstood;
4. accepting to be looked down on;
5. accepting to be blamed;
6. accepting corrections;
7. accepting our own lack of virtue.

See Rule [no. 17]—to accept whatever He gives and give whatever He takes with a big smile.

6th WEEK: SILENCE AND PRAYER

In reparation for sins of the tongue:

1. to use my tongue to tell the truth today and avoid giving pain;
2. to praise God in everything, uniting myself to Jesus' silence in the Eucharist;
3. to allow God to renew and transform me in silence, by silence of the mind;
4. to create an atmosphere of silence and prayer in the community, avoiding all selfishness, hatred, envy, jealousy, bitterness;
5. to use the Sacrament of Reconciliation regularly;
6. to make sincere examination of conscience;
7. fidelity to meditating on the mysteries of the Rosary.

7th WEEK: THE CROSS—NO GREATER LOVE

1. To accept today to be nailed with Jesus to the Cross
   by accepting the hardships of our life;
   by joyfully accepting the Cross in our lives.
2. To rise from mediocrity to fervour by generous acts of love.
3. To rise from fervour to real sanctity by deliberate acts of love and penance.

4. To rise from sin to God by fervent acts of contrition and confession.
5. [To] fervently and generously [live] one's daily life.
   by living in the presence of God and doing everything with perfect love for God.

God bless you
Mother

MGL 203. 1ST APRIL 1988

+ L.D.M.

1st April 1988

My dearest Children,

May the Precious Blood of Jesus wash away our Sins—especially Sins of uncharitableness towards each other and the Poor we serve.

When we look at Jesus during His humiliating Passion and death we ask—why all this? For what purpose?—For whom? He loved me.—No one, not even Jesus, could have gone through all that humiliating suffering if He was not in love. He loved His Father so tenderly—He wanted to make up to Him for all the sins we have committed, and by [which] we have rejected His love—Our Father's love. Jesus loved His Father so much—that He was ready to undergo any suffering, even death—to remove sin from our lives—so that we can [*love*] the Father with a Pure heart, and that the Father in receiving our love, could say "this is My beloved Child in whom I am well pleased." Jesus wants us to love and to be loved by the Father, that is why He accepted all the most humiliating pain of the Passion—the spitting, the beating, the scourging, the crowning with thorns—to make up for each one of our sins, especially sins against Purity & Charity.—How terrible sin must be before God if Jesus went through all those terrible humiliations to forgive the fruit of pride—sin.

Mt 26–27; Mk 14–15; Lk 22–23; Jn 18–19
Gal 2:20
Mt 3:17; 17:5, Mk 9:7
Mt 27:26, 29, 30; Mk 15:15, 17, 19; Jn 19:2

We have by our Vows become consecrated Virgins.—How pure—how full of love for each other we must be to be pleasing to the Father—when we know and hear—"I have chosen you—to be Mine—I have called you by your name—you are Mine you are precious to Me, I love you." [*Jesus knew*][a] [the] Father's love for each one of us—that is why He suffered and

Is 43:1,4

a The words in italics were in Mother's handwritten draft but were mistakenly left out in the typed died for each one of us—so that we can love and be loved by the Father.

My children, let us together look at the Cross and realize how much Jesus loved us—and look at the tabernacle and see how much He loves us now—so that we can be [holy like Jesus][a]—and be filled with the Purity of His Mother and the Charity-love[b] of the Heart of Jesus, and so become His love, His purity in the world of today.

Let us make one strong resolution—not to miss our weekly confession and especially confess and make reparation for any sin [*however small it may*][c] [be] against purity and charity.

Jn 15:13 Easter is the fruit of greater love—because we could not have had Easter if we did not have Good Friday—and so I wish you and pray for each one of you to accept—all pain, humiliation, loneliness, feelings of being unwanted, unloved, for this is our Good Friday—for by accepting all
Jn 19:28 we satiate the thirst of Jesus on the Cross. Avoid touching your Vocation during the days when you are experiencing these trials—and one day—that last day [*on Earth*][d]—will be our Easter, and we shall hear Jesus say
Mt 25:34 "Come you blessed of my Father, possess the Kingdom prepared for you." This will be our Easter.

What a wonderful home-coming—the Father, the Son, the Holy Spirit, Our Lady, St. Joseph & our Guardian Angel will be all there to say "Welcome Home".

I want you all to pray in a special way that our giving Jesus a new tabernacle in Russia, South Africa and China be all for the Glory of God and the Good of Souls.

Happy and Holy Easter to each one of you MC Sisters, Brothers, Fathers.

God bless you
Mother

---

copy sent to the houses. Mother wrote "knowing", which makes the sentence incorrect; so we have corrected it to "knew", in order to fit with the grammar of the rest of the sentence.

a. It seems that Mother did not complete her thought here, however, in similar passages she said, "so that we can be only all for Jesus" or "so that we can become holy like Jesus." We have added the latter here for easier reading.

b. Mother wrote these words with a hyphen (not with her customary dash), indicating that she intends "charity-love" as one term here.

c .The words in italics were in Mother's handwritten draft but were mistakenly left out in the typed copy sent to the houses.

d. The words in italics were in Mother's handwritten draft but were mistakenly left out in the typed copy sent to the houses.

ED 51. EASTER 1988

Easter 1988

My dearest children,

Fathers, Brothers, Sisters,

This brings you Mother's blessing, love and peace.—Let us all be one heart full of love in the Heart of Jesus through Mary. Let us help each other to be humble like Mary so that we can become Holy like Jesus.

Let us ask Our Father to teach us to pray.
Let us ask the Son Jesus to teach us to be Poor.
Let us ask the Holy Spirit to fill our hearts with Zeal for Souls. Amen.

God bless you
Mother

MGL 204. 23RD JULY 1988

+ LDM

Bronx, New York
23rd July 1988

My dearest Children,

This brings you Mother's love, prayer and blessing that you all be only all for Jesus, Humble like Mary and Holy like Jesus. If you are really humble like Mary, you will possess Jesus, as She did possess Him; you will love Jesus as She loved Him and serve Him in the distressing disguise of Mt 25:40
the Poor. Oh, what [a] Gift of God are the Poor to each one of us, for in them we can serve Jesus 24 hours, and this Service of the Poor makes us Contemplatives in the heart of the world. To be able to understand and live this reality we need a clean heart—for a clean heart can see Jesus in Mt 5:8
the Poor.

Our fourth Vow reminds us of this beautiful gift. In giving whole hearted free service to the Poorest of the Poor, we touch Him 24 hours.

So, my children, pay great attention to this Vow, for it is really our love for God in action. What a gift of God. Do I really appreciate it? Do I really live this Vow? We need humility for all—especially for this Vow. We are at present the only Congregation in the Church with this Vow.

This Vow binds us first to our Sisters in Community—as every Sister, including myself, is the Poorest of the Poor. How we must love each Jn 13:34; 15:12

other—how kind and thoughtful we must be of each other. Never be uncharitable and harsh with your Sisters. Always have a pleasant smile for each other. How I pray, my [*dear*][a] children, for you—to be holy. The greatest obstacle to our becoming holy is the neglect of Charity and Humility. So I pray for you to be holy in spite [of] all obstacles. Our Love and respect for the Poor is our fourth Vow in action, so let us be grateful to the poor for giving us a beautiful chance of living the fourth Vow with Great Love.

On the 29th May we gave one more tabernacle to Jesus, in Vancouver, West Canada. I could not tell you how very happy everybody was. Very strange, we got an empty Loreto Convent. We will be able to have our Sisters and the unwed mothers in the same building. God is so wonderful in His Love for us—to give us so much to give to others. If we only remember His tender love for each one us, we would be able to do all only all for Him.

In Tijuana, the Sisters are very happy. The whole place—one big city of poverty. I am so grateful to God for giving us this beautiful gift. Our Fathers are moving out of New York to Tijuana. The Bishop[b] has given us a big plot of land for the Fathers, this will become their Mother House. Also there is a very good Seminary in Tijuana—very faithful to the Holy Father. So 15 of them will join the Seminary. I need your prayers and sacrifices for them—that we may fulfil God's will in all things. There are at present altogether 27 of them—6 priests and the rest all Seminarians. Thank God for His great love. Six Sisters and Sr. M. Fatima came also. Mr. Alberto gave us his own house—really a gift of God, just complete for a Contemplative Community. The Bishop is really full of Jesus. He radiates the joy of Christ. Thank God our MC Fathers have such [a] beautiful example in him. Our Sisters are doing very beautiful work, though they began only on the 11th Feb. So pray for all these 3 MC Communities in Tijuana. [The] people of San Diego are very kind to them.

El Salvador, we opened in July, a real Bethlehem—a small house with two rooms. Jesus got the better part—one room to Himself. The other room holds—only two beds—the other two [Sisters] with folding beds move about.[c] They too have a holy Bishop who loves the Poor and is a great help to the Sisters.

a. The word "dear" was in Mother's handwritten draft but was mistakenly left out in the typed copy sent to the houses.

b. Archbishop Emilio Carlos Berlie Belaunzarán was bishop of Tijuana (1983–1995) and later archbishop of Mérida (1995–2015).

c. This means that the Sisters move their beds to where there is place.

What we have to thank God for [is] His great personal love; His love for each one of us is so personal, so tender, so real—I am sure you will all try to make your love for Jesus more intimate, more personal, [to] feel more attached to Jesus with your whole and pure heart. All this will happen if you pray.

We have to thank God for the beautiful vocations we are getting in Central America; at present there are 18 Junior Postulants in Mexico and already four aspirants in Tijuana, and 9 in New York.

I shall be leaving New York soon after the eye surgery, which will be done on Monday, 25th, please God, and hope to be back with you in the Mother House by the end of July or beginning of August.[a]

Keep the joy of loving Jesus in each other and share this joy with the Poor you serve and the people you meet.—That is why it is necessary to be humble like Mary, and we are sure to be Holy like Jesus. Let us pray and make our Communities only all for Jesus through Mary.

God bless you,
Mother

MGL 205. [5TH] AUGUST 1988

Mother House
[5th] August 1988

My dearest Children,

I shall be very grateful if you would send me three names on a slip of paper (enclosed) of sisters whom you regard as capable of taking up the responsibility of the region, in the service of the Society.

Read Const. 163 & 164 carefully before you decide. Let your choice reflect your love for the Society—and do not name a Sister simply because you like her.

The slip of paper should be folded and put in an envelope and sealed by the Superior in the presence of the Community and then sent to me as soon as possible.

For the glory of God and the good of our Society I am trying to get the regions as far as possible in groups of ten Houses. So we have to have more Regionals, Sisters who have the real and full Spirit and the love of the Society at heart.

a. Mother had cataract surgery at St. Vincent's Hospital in New York City.

In this, as in everything else, we must be one heart full of Love in the Heart of Jesus through Mary. Remember, the Regional officially represents the Society, upholds the Superior General's authority in her region, and obeys her directions faithfully, striving by her example and her words to be the cause of unity at all levels. She promotes the spiritual and apostolic life of the Sisters in her region according to the Spirit of the Society and its Constitutions, [so] as to inspire and encourage the sisters, lovingly gives all possible help to local Superiors, guides them to fulfil their charge, and grants them the permission they need; regularly corresponds with the Superior General keeping her informed of [the] life in the different communities, and communicates to her what she foresees to be helpful solutions to concrete situations, and fosters relations between the Sisters and the Superior General and her Councillors.

My dearest children, ask Our Lady to teach you to pray as She taught Jesus.—Prayer will give you a humble heart. You & each one of us will find obedience easy—because the fruit of humility is obedience—and obedience is a sure way to great Sanctity. Let us pray.

God bless you
Mother

MGL 206. 10TH OCTOBER 1988

+ L.D.M.

Mother House
10th October 1988

My dearest Children,

Thank you—to each and every one—for your good wishes for my feast. It is so beautiful to think that each one has prayed for me. Prayer is the best gift of love you can give anyone you love. My gratitude to each one of you is my prayer for you that you grow and be humble like Mary and through humility become holy like Jesus.

I have the Good News to give you. Our Lord in His great love for our Society has blessed our Constitutions, and approved them for life through the Church. I will send a copy to each one of you as soon as possible.[a]

Our Lord, through the Church, shows His tender love for the Society

a. The Congregation for the Evangelization of Peoples (also known as "Propaganda Fide") approved the new *Constitutions of the Missionaries of Charity* on 25th March 1988.

continually. What is our love for our Society? Do we really know the Spirit of the Society—Do we live that Spirit? Do we know the reason for our existence? I feel each one should take the trouble, before Jesus in the Tabernacle, to give ourselves a written answer to these 3 questions so vital to each one of us.[a]

In some Houses Poverty has become a word—not a life. Under the cover of Shishu Bhavan and Nirmal Hriday what things have come in—opposite to our Constitutions. When we die, what will we take with us? Only our fidelity to our Poverty.

Lately, so often involvements are taking place that end with loss of vocation. I feel the best protection we could give our vow of Chastity is by really becoming deeply Contemplative—through prayer and a pure heart—by fidelity to Obedience. I find Obedience—fruit of a clean heart—the best protector to Chastity and Poverty, [*because*][b] Obedience was the way of life for Jesus and Mary, and the sure way to great holiness.

Fidelity to the Vows of Poverty, Chastity & Obedience is our 4th Vow—the ability to give Wholehearted and free Service to the Poorest of the Poor. We need that intimate personal love—a real attachment to Jesus. We cannot live a holy life unless our hearts are pure—clean, free of sin.

My Children—I beg you keep your hearts free of sin.—The sin of disobedience has brought so much evil in the world. The same sin can Gn 3:1–19; Rom 5:12
destroy the very Presence of Jesus in our hearts—Sanctifying Grace. Disobedience especially always attacks Chastity and Charity. So much impurity and uncharitableness [are] destroying the joy and the beauty of our Society.

My children, you do not know the terrible pain there is in my heart for not being able fully to answer to the terrible thirst Jesus asked me to Satiate through the Society—through each one of you. If I am feeling like this, I wonder what the Heart of Jesus must feel? Is it not at this time again—as He did on 10th Sept.—is He not looking at each one of us: "I chose you and called you to be an MC to Satiate my painful thirst, and where are you?"

a. Mother had written the sentence "Do we live that Spirit?" on a separate line between the questions: "Do we really know the Spirit of the Society—" and "Do we know the reason for our existence?" as an additional question about the Spirit of the Society. The Sister typist changed the punctuation, making two separate questions about the Spirit, and consequently changed Mother's original "three questions" to "four questions." We have restored it to Mother's original version.

b. The words in italics were in Mother's handwritten draft but were mistakenly left out in the typed copy sent to the houses.

Jn 19:28 Jesus told a priest in Rome: "Tell Mother Teresa, 'I thirst'."[a] My children, hear your own name. He is saying it to <u>you</u>.

This letter being very personal, I want you each one to make your own copy—and give yourself the answers in writing, and next time you see me we will look at it together. You know Mother's love for each one of you. I have only one desire in my heart for you—that you be humble like Mary and holy like Jesus.

Jn 15:5, 8 The Society has grown. May it grow and bring much fruit for the Glory of God and the Good of Souls. As a number of Regionals are finishing their three years, we all owe them deep gratitude for all they have given us. We welcome the new Regionals and promise to be one heart with them at any cost. Make sure you pray for the priest given to you in spiritual Adoption—by name, at Holy Mass when the priest prays for the Holy Father and the Bishop—add your priest's name.

Be very strict with the use of water, electricity, telephones and cars. Read carefully Const. 48, especially (d). I have strictly forbidden the use of television, and video is included.[b]

As per the new rules made by the Government, we must never give our children for Adoption to other Congregations or Agencies, even in India, and outside we must follow the same rule. In India foreign Adoptions will be done in Calcutta, Delhi, and Bombay only. All the other places doing local Adoption must have a written permission from [*Mother*].[c]

Today I have written much from my heart to your hearts—so let us make our Society all only for the Glory of God through Mary, and for the
Jn 19:28 Good of Souls and so Satiate the Thirst of Jesus.

We are still praying to get our visas for Russia, China and South Africa. Please pray fervently that the visas come soon.

Let us renew our fervent resolution to become humble like Mary so that we can grow in holiness like Jesus.

God bless you
Mother

a. See *Come Be My Light*, 310–11, for this account. This priest preferred not to have his name mentioned.

b. Constitution 48: "Desirous to share Christ's own poverty and that of our poor (d): We shall neither own nor keep in our convents: television set, radio, tape-recorder, projectors and cameras."

c. In the handwritten draft of this letter, Mother wrote "from Mother" (referring to herself in the third person, as was often her custom). The Sister typist changed it to read "from me"; we have restored it here to its original, as written by Mother. On Mother referring to herself in the third person, see MGL 4 of [4th] November 1960 and corresponding footnote, p. 9.

MGL 207. 9TH DECEMBER 1988

+ LDM

Mother House
9th December 1988

My dearest Children,

I know you want to do something beautiful for Jesus, and so I ask you to give Him the gift of your silence. For the fruit of silence is prayer, the fruit of prayer is Faith, the fruit of Faith is Love the fruit of Love is Service. Read and reflect carefully Const. 156 on silence.

Be faithful to your penances. Be faithful to the examination of con-
Lk 1:39 science and the daily meditation. Be full of zeal in going out in haste with
Mary to your poor. Be punctual, especially for Community exercises. Je-
Phil 2:6 sus did not feel it below His dignity [to obey], therefore:

- accept, love and respect your Superior.
- pray for them.
- show joyful trust and loyalty to them.
- make your obedience cheerful, prompt, simple, constant.

There is so much unhappiness in some Communities because we are neglecting our Constitution which is our way of life. So much time wasted in unnecessary talk with Priests, drivers and outsiders. So much money wasted. So many untruths, uncharitableness, carrying tales, criticism. So much disobedience, neglect of apostolate, getting up late, no making up the prayers.

Let us take all our miseries and give them to Jesus, let us make a firm resolution to be more faithful as we kneel before the Crib and to be really only all for Jesus through Mary.

Scc Constitution 156 on Silence:

- silence of the eyes, seeking the goodness and beauty of God everywhere,
- silence of the ears, listening to the voice of God and cry of the poor.
- silence of the tongue, speaking the truth that enlightens and inspires, bringing peace, hope and joy.
- silence of the mind, like Mary, who pondered the marvels of the Lk 2:19, 51
  Lord in her heart, and closing the mind to all untruths, destructive and revengeful thoughts,
- silence of the heart, by loving God with our whole heart, soul, mind Mt 22:37; Mk 12:30; Lk 10:27
  and strength.

Be faithful to [penance].

Jn 19:25 To [sic.] stand with Mary at the foot of the Cross in the midst of troubles great and small (Const. 160).

Jn 3:16 Make reparation for our sins and the sins of all mankind, whom Jesus
Lk 2:7; Phil 2:6–8 came into the world to save. He, being God, emptied Himself becoming small, a tiny baby, to teach us how to live, how to love, how to serve.

Do all this only for Jesus, with Jesus, to Jesus through Mary. Show great love and respect for your Superior.

You will be happy to know that we have given Jesus four new Tabernacles in Africa recently, Cape Town in South Africa, Nampula and Maputo in Mozambique and Kampala in Uganda.

Holy & Happy Christmas and New Year.—

God bless you,
Mother

ED 52. DECEMBER 1988

December 1988

My dearest Children,

Fathers, Brothers, Sisters,

This brings you Mother's blessing, love and peace.—Let us all be one heart full of love in the Heart of Jesus through Mary. Let us help each other to be humble like Mary so that we can become Holy like Jesus.

God bless you
Mother

1989

MGL 208. 27TH APRIL 1989

+ L.D.M.

Mother House
27th April 1989

My dearest Children,

God love you all for all the beautiful letters for Christmas and Easter I received nearly from every Community—for the daily prayers and sacrifices you offer for Mother. I think that is what keeps me moving—all for Jesus through Mary.

I am sure you all would like to know the exact number of Sisters, countries, places where our Sisters are—so that you can pray together. We now have 1475 Finally Professed Sisters, 1060 Junior Professed Sisters. Contemplatives: 25 Finally Professed and 22 Junior Professed. 428 Novices (active) and 18 Novices (contemplative) 275 Postulants (active) and 3 Postulants (contemplative).

We now have 389 houses altogether. In India—159, outside India—230; 8 houses Contemplative: in India—1, outside India—7. We are now in 92 Countries, and in May we will open 8 new houses.

As you know, our family keeps growing—we have now:

- Sisters—Active and Contemplative with the same Constitutions—the parts that belong only for them [the contemplatives] are in italics.
- We have 3 separate groups of Brothers
  - Active with Br. Geoff as their head
  - Contemplative with special work with Lay MC (families) with Fr. Sebastian as their head
  - Brothers of the Word (Contemplative) who work with drug addicts and alcoholics with Fr. Devanand Angelo as their head.

• Co-workers: Youth, Sick and Suffering, Contemplatives, Medical, Families,[a]
• Adoption of Priests through prayer and suffering,
• Fathers—priests with Fr. Joseph as their head.

Active Brothers and Sisters are the two hands of Jesus. Contemplative Brothers and Sisters are the two feet of Jesus. MC Fathers are the heart of Jesus. Lay Missionaries of Charity are the Holy Face of Jesus. Co–Workers are the Head of Jesus crowned with thorns.

Jn 15:5 God has blessed our Family with so many branches on the Vine—Jesus, producing His fruit of love and compassion through prayer and works of love in action.

Sr. M. Charles died a beautiful death after years of suffering. She died in Vellore a very peaceful death on the 19th April, 1989.

Sr. M. Lutgarde died in the terrible train accident on 18th April, 1989, at Lalitpur. She was brought to our convent in Jhansi. She was very badly wounded—she died on the spot. According to the Constitutions, let us fulfil our love duty to our sisters who have been such a beautiful example.

As the number of our Sisters in Heaven keeps growing—one day will be our turn too to join that Community. The hour may come at any time—are we ready?

a. Mother is referring to the various groups of Co-workers that developed over the years while sharing in the spirituality and mission of the MCs. The Co-workers of Mother Teresa, officially recognized in 1969, consist of men, women, young people, and children of all religions and denominations throughout the world, who seek to love God in their fellow men, through wholehearted service to the poorest of the poor of all creeds, and who wish to unite themselves in a spirit of prayer and sacrifice with the work of Mother and the MCs. Mother invited Co-workers to share in the work of the local MC community, encouraging them to come together as a group for prayer and sharing, and asked them especially to know and serve the poor in their own families, neighbourhoods and cities, for "love begins at home." See MGL 55 of 10th January 1968 and its corresponding footnote, p. 93.

Youth Co-workers, officially begun in 1982, was a spontaneous grouping of the young members of the Co-workers association, described as "young people of good will who are daily giving their hearts to love and their hands to serve the poor." They volunteered with the Sisters in Nirmal Hriday, Shishu Bhavan, soup kitchens, summer camps, after-school programs, etc. Mother encouraged them to "find Jesus, love and serve Him."

The Sick and Suffering Co-workers are those who, because of illness or disability, are unable to share physically in the service of the poor. They share in the MC apostolate by offering to God their prayers and sufferings for a particular Sister, Brother or Father. Initially, Mother called them "second selves." See *Come Be My Light*, 146; see also MGL 122 of [2nd] April 1976 and its corresponding footnote, p. 215.

Medical Co-workers refers to medical professionals who supported Mother and her mission, giving their services free of charge to the poorest of the poor under the Sisters' care.

Contemplative Co-workers were monasteries of contemplative nuns who adopted an MC community and prayed and offered sacrifices for the fruitfulness of those Sisters' missionary labours.

Regarding Family Co-workers, Mother is most probably referring to the Lay Missionaries of Charity. In her letter of 13th May 1987 (MGL 198), she wrote: "With God's Blessing, Brother Sebastian, together with the other Contemplative Brothers, started the Lay Missionaries of Charity with Families . . .", p. 364.

In the Heart of Jesus I am sure there is a painful thirst for love. It is painful because there are so many uncharitable words that penetrate the very Heart of Jesus. Often I wonder—what pain Jesus must have in His Heart, who loves us [*so much*][a]—with a tender love, if I feel so much the pain of uncharitable words. My dearest children, if now while I am among you, loving you—you do this to me—for in doing it to each other, you do it to me—what will happen after. This is the fear that causes me pain also, for I have promised to God "I will give Saints to Mother Church". Our Charity will improve if we only learn to be humble like Mary. A humble Sister will never allow uncharitable words to come from her heart through her tongue and wound Jesus in her Sisters. Jn 19:28

We are MC Sisters, Brothers and Fathers—how terrible it will be if we cannot see Jesus in each other. Some words uttered by Superiors, by Sisters to each other and to the Poor are like a Cancer that eats from within. Such words have been like a poison that has poisoned the heart of some Sisters in such a way that it has killed the very life of vocation. My Sisters, open your heart to the voice of Jesus saying "You did it to Me." Mt 25:40

Violence of tongue is very real—sharper than any knife, wounding and creating bitterness that only the grace of God can heal; and so my Children, because we all love our Society, let us, in gratitude to the Society for accepting us and giving us such wonderful opportunities of serving the poor, for all the times the Society gives us to spend in prayer and adoration, for all the care and concern we receive continually, show our gratitude to the Society by [our]: NO TO VIOLENCE WITH OUR TONGUE AND YES TO PEACE WITH OUR TONGUE.[b]

Our sisters need much more kindness than even the people in the street. To be an apostle of the Sacred Heart, one must be burning with love, intense love for the Sisters which does not measure—it gives. If you want peace—you cannot just say anything—the first word that comes into your head. Holiness grows where there is kindness. In religious houses, this kindness is in greater danger—for we have grown so used to each other that some think they can say anything to anybody at any time. They expect the Sisters to bear with their unkindness—why not try to control your tongue? Your holiness will help your Sister more than any great talents you may have—but talents used with such harshness.[117] Living

a. These words were in Mother's handwritten draft.

b. This paragraph about violence of the tongue is from MGL 132 of 1st February 1978, pp. 234–35.

together, working together, praying together is the greatest help we can give to our Sisters—it is a safeguard to chastity and the work for souls.

God bless you
Mother

MGL 209. 1ST AUGUST 1989

L.D.M.

1st August 1989[a]

My dearest Children,

This brings you Mother's prayer, love and blessing—that you be all
Mt 1:16; Jn 19:27; Acts 1:14 one heart full of love in the Heart of Jesus through Mary—the Mother of Jesus and our Mother—so full of tender love for each one of you. She is so beautiful, so tender in Her love for each one of us and wants us to grow in holiness—through our Love for Jesus in the Blessed Sacrament and our Love for Her through the Rosary. This is my prayer and wish for the feast of our Society. Try, during the preparation for the feast of our Society—to deepen your personal love for Mary, by learning from her to be pure and humble. These two virtues are the very foundation of holiness—so let us deepen our love for Mary by imitating her purity & humility. Much loss of Vocation [has been caused] by neglect of purity & humility. Purity and humility of Mary are the two gifts of God in Her—that have made Her so
1 Cor 3:17; 6:19 beautiful, so wonderful, so Holy—[a] living temple of the Blessed Trinity.

As by our Vows we become the Consecrated Virgin of the Blessed Trinity—let us deepen our love for Mary through imitating

Rom 8:38–39, Mt 17:8; Mk 9:8 Her Purity—No one—nothing, but only Jesus—

Her Humility, by fidelity in doing small humble works with great love.—

To remind us of our consecration—we will often say "Mary, Mother of Jesus, help me to be pure and humble like You, because I want to be Holy and pleasing to the Blessed Trinity, as you were & are."

You will, I am sure, be very happy to hear that we are giving Jesus a 4th Tabernacle in Russia.

Deepen more and more your love for Jesus in the Blessed Sacrament and also love for Mary through the Rosary. Spread this same love [to]

a. The notepad on which Mother wrote this letter has the Mother House stamp with its address, but the letter was actually written in Rome.

every house you visit, every person you meet. Show greater fidelity to praying the Rosary in the Street and fidelity to the full holy hour daily and visiting Jesus before you go out & come in and after every meal.

Senior Sisters, teach your younger Sisters by your example & fidelity.

My prayer for each one of you—that you be only all for Jesus through Mary. Pray often, pray fervently for Mother.

God bless you
Mother

MGL 210. 25TH AUGUST 1989

+ LDM

Mother House
25th August 1989

My dearest Children in Calcutta,[a]

This brings you Mother's love and prayers for each one of you.

Enclosed find the dates of the Professions in each of our houses of Formation. Please God, Mother will be soon with you once again. Keep on praying for Mother, for the Society, and let us all thank Our Lady for Her love and care for each one of us—especially for the gift of our Vocation.

Please look into the date of the Profession, and accordingly arrange with your Bishop or the Parish Priest the time for the Eucharistic Celebration for the Profession—so that when I come, everything will be in order. I shall have some time to be with you all.

All Mother House news is good. We had a very beautiful Society Feast and I am sure you too had a nice day with Our Lady.

Pray much—pray often so that you may remain very close to the Sacred Heart through the Immaculate Heart of Mary.

God bless you
Mother

a. "Calcutta" was typed in separately. Other Formation houses received the same letter with the name of their house, for example "Rome," in the greeting; thus, the names of the houses were added by a Sister typist as the letters were prepared for distribution.

MGL 211. 22ND SEPTEMBER 1989

L.D.M.

22nd September 1989[a]

My dearest Children,

Here before Jesus who has [been] and is with me through all the sharing of the Passion—I have clearly understood that the terrible pain we have caused His Sacred Heart by our many deliberate infidelities[b] to Prayer and our Vow of Chastity—due to which so many Vocations have been lost, and will be lost for want of prayer, penance and undivided love for Jesus.—

We are also too much preoccupied with big things & less & less with the humble works of our Society.—So many worldly things have penetrated hidingly or covered with the untruth.

Each one of us, especially you Regionals, take this Mother's warning to
1 Cor 5:7–8 heart—get rid of all untruthfulness to your vows.[c]—Change your heart—ask Our Lady to help you.

As Sr. M. Frederick and I are one heart in the Heart of Jesus—her coming has been the fruit of prayer.—I am not able to be with you in body, but my heart, my whole being is with you—open your heart to Sister as you would have done to me.—Let this retreat, for which Mother has paid [a] big price,[d] be really to each one of you—the joy of being only all for Jesus through Mary.

You all know Mother's love for each one of you.—Make one resolution—I will—I want to be a Saint with Mary's blessing.

I am sure you are all praying for me.—

God bless you
Mother

a. On some of the extant copies of this letter, the location of its writing, "Woodlands Nursing Home, Calcutta," was handwritten, but not by Mother.

b. In the handwritten draft, Mother wrote "infidelity," an obvious error that we have corrected.

c. This is a unique instance of Mother using this expression; its meaning is "be true to your vows," that is, "get rid of all infidelity to your vows."

d. Mother had a heart attack on 5th September 1989 and had a temporary pacemaker put in at Woodlands Nursing Home (Calcutta). She continued to have recurring fever and chest pain and was in intensive care until 7th October. She wrote this letter from the hospital—her handwriting is small and shaky, revealing her weakness. She was discharged from the hospital on 14th October 1989.

MGL 212. 13TH OCTOBER 1989

+ LDM

Woodlands Nursing Home
13th October 1989

My dearest Children,

Let us thank God and His Blessed Mother for the great tender love He has shown to me by hearing the prayers of all people and all religions and giving me back my health. This has really been the fruit of many prayers.

This will be one more reason for us all to [show] greater zeal in growing in Purity and humility and greater love for Jesus in the Blessed Sacrament and love for Mary through the Rosary.

Tomorrow morning I am leaving the hospital—after nearly 5 weeks and will be in Park Street for at least 2 weeks. So thank God for all that the doctors and the nurses have done for me and to me. It has been done purely for the love of God, not charging anything at all. See the tenderness of God's love when you have nothing, and in possessing Jesus you possess 2 Cor 6:10
all things. The love and care I received from Doctors, Nurses, even the Servants is something unbelievable. I had the Blessed Sacrament in my room and also daily Holy Mass—can you imagine the goodness of God. As I write, Jesus is right in front of me in His little Tabernacle with a beautiful red light near Him. What greater love could ever have been than this tender love of Jesus and Mary.

God bless you
Mother

Thank you also for your beautiful spiritual help for my feast. Sr. M. Agnes has kept all to show me.[a]

Let us together thank God for His great love in hearing the prayers of all the people of the world. Through the tender love and care of all the doctors, nurses and even the workers of Woodlands, God in His tender love for our Poor has restored my heart's health.

The only way I can show my gratitude is by praying for each one of you, that God's blessing be always with you all and all your families and your work.

God bless you all
M. Teresa MC[b]

a. This was written at the top of the first page of Mother's handwritten letter, as there was no more space at the bottom of the second page, with the same pen as the second half of the letter (the first pen was obviously finished); it was not included in the typed version of the letter that was sent to the houses.

b. This is a message for the public that Mother had written from the Woodlands Nursing Home. It was sent out to the Society along with this letter.

~ MGL 213. 1ST NOVEMBER 1989 ~

L.D.M.

Mother House
1st November 1989

My dearest children, in Nairobi, Rome, Poland, San Francisco, New York, Washington, Calcutta, Manila,

You have all received a beautifully prepared time table[a] regarding your Vows, but for some reason known only to the Sacred Heart of Jesus and to His Mother all has to be changed. I will not be able to come for the Vows as planned, due to sickness, though I am much better, but after much prayer I have decided to ask you all to have the first and last Vows on the 8th Dec., Our Lady's day, as usual.—

I hereby give the Power to Sr. M. Nirmala to take the Vows of our Contemplative Sisters.

God bless you
M Teresa MC

Therefore I hereby give the power to take the Vows to [one sister in each region.]

...

Therefore it is good that each one look at the Constitutions as to how the Vows are to be written, especially regarding yourself.

Try to be with the Sisters 2 or 3 days before the Vows—in that deep union with Jesus, prepare them. You know my prayer & sacrifices will be with you.

I was looking forward to be with you on your Great day—but Jesus knows what is best for us all.

As we hope to open a house in Albania—say often "Jesus, please tell Our Lady to give Mother a healthy heart so that she can take You to Albania." Heaven must be full of this prayer.

Let us pray.

God bless you
Mother

a. Mother is referring to the schedule for the profession of vows around the world attached to her letter, MGL 210 of 25th August 1989.

MGL 214. 25TH NOVEMBER 1989

L.D.M.

Mother House
25th November 1989

My dearest Children,

This brings you Mother's deep gratitude for all the prayers and sacrifices you have all offered through Our Lady to Jesus for my cure. I am much better and back home in the Mother House but still under doctor's supervision and great care of my nurse, Sr. M. Bela.

It was beautiful to see our Novices taking the first Vows in the M.H. [Mother House] and now our Tertians are preparing for their Final Vows on the 7th Dec. So pray for all of them.

In few days we begin our preparation of Christmas.

With Mary and Joseph let us prepare our hearts through purity and humility, through our tender, personal love for Jesus in the Blessed Sacrament and fervent praying of the Rosary—this will be our Birth Day Gift to Jesus.

Keep the joy of loving each other as Jesus loves each one of you. Jn 13:34; 15:12

Keep praying for Albania, that we may be able with Mary to take Jesus to Albania. Keep praying for Mother's intention.

God bless you
Mother

MGL 215. 21ST DECEMBER 1989

L.D.M.

Mother House
21st December 1989[a]

My dearest children, Sisters, Brothers, Fathers,

This brings you the Good news that we have been given with the help of the Holy Spirit and Our Lady through our MC Fathers, the light and grace of writing clearly the Charism and the essential aspects of our spirit and life in more detail, what Jesus on that 10th September 1946 entrusted to me.

a. Mother wrote this letter to all the MC branches as a cover letter to Fr. Joseph's lengthy document on the MC Charism (known to the MC Fathers as the Charism Statement).

Let this be a grace we will come to know, love and live with our whole
Rom 8:35; 38–39 heart and will, and never allow anybody or anything to ever separate us from this gift to us, to the Church and to the whole world.

May you always be only all for Jesus through Mary.

God bless you
M Teresa MC

ED 54. DECEMBER 1989

December 1989[a]

My Christmas Message for each one of you:

Love Mary—through fidelity to your life of Prayer and Obedience—for this is what made Mary so beautiful, so holy—because She was so full of humility and Purity—we too, if we want to be holy like Jesus, let us deepen our life of Prayer.

This is my prayer and blessing for each one of you Fathers, Brothers, Sisters, Lay Missionaries of Charity.

God bless you
Mother

a. We were unable to find *Ek Dil* 53.

1990

MGL 216. 25TH FEBRUARY 1990

L.D.M.

Mother House
25th February 1990

My dearest Children,

This brings you Mother's love, blessing, and prayer that you be all one heart full of love in the Heart of Jesus through Mary.

Jesus, before He was crucified, at His last Supper with His Apostles— Mt 26:26; Mk 14:22; Lk 22:19; 1 Cor 11:24
when He gave us the greatest gift of love, the Eucharist—again and again Jesus appealed to be one heart, as He and the Father are one.—That one- Jn 17:21–23
ness will help you to love each other as Jesus loves each one of you. If you Jn 13:34; 15:12
are One—there will never be any uncharitable words and actions among you.

Many times I have written and spoken that love begins at home. Our Community is our home. How do we love each other—are we a Cause of Joy to each other? A number of Sisters, not able to bear the pain of uncharitable words, have lost their vocation.—It is true—that if they had accepted the pain and offer[ed] it to Jesus—I am sure Jesus would have given them the grace of perseverance.

As per our Constitutions 86—Due to age and sickness Superior General can ask to resign.[a]

Both these—age—I will be 80 this year—and sickness—so I have asked the Holy Father to give me permission to have the General Chapter so that we can vote for a new Superior General.—Holy Father has given the permission to have the Gen. Chapter. [General Chapter]. So with God's

a. This should be not Constitution 86 but Constitution 186, which says: "Should she consider herself obliged before God to resign her charge before the end of her term of office, on account of impaired health, advanced age or any other good reason, she should make known her motives to her councillors before presenting her petition to the Holy See" (1988 *Constitutions*).

blessing and Mother Mary's help we will, God willing, have the General Chapter on 8th September 1990.

I want you to accept this decision with joy and offer all for our Society so that Mother's promise be fulfilled—to give Saints to Mother Church.

I ask one thing of you, please do not speak about this outside the Community,[a] but let us pray and do penance—that Jesus & Mary may help us to do all for the Glory of God and the Good of our Society.

Thank you for your prayers—I am much better. Be only all for Jesus through Mary.

God bless you
M. Teresa MC

MGL 217. [AFTER 25TH] FEBRUARY 1990

+

LDM

Mother House
[after 25th] February 1990[b]

My dearest Children—Regionals, Superiors, Sisters,

This brings you Mother's love and prayers for a fervent and holy Lent. In the Mother House we will have only tea in the afternoon, and standing, except on Thursday and Sunday; and on every Friday, Church fast. So you
Jn 19:25, 28 see in what way you too, can take your stand at the foot of the Cross with Mary our Mother, and satiate the Thirst of Jesus. Let us offer everything to Jesus, every sorrow, humiliation, discomfort, for the Chapter as our preparation.

For the Chapter, daily we will say the prayer for our Society "We beseech Thee O Lord ..."[c] before the Radiating Christ Communion prayer.

Please do not speak to anybody outside about the Chapter. Keep it within the family. Let us prepare sincerely and seek only God's will. For this we need to have a clean heart, a humble heart like Mary—and to be all and only for Jesus.

a. Mother's intention to resign as Superior General became public in April 1990, and newspapers throughout the world carried articles announcing that Mother Teresa was "retiring".

b. This letter was dated as February 1990 and it is a letter for the month of February (First Friday was 2nd February). However, from the context it is obvious that it was written after the letter of 25th February in which Mother announces her resignation as Superior General and convocation of an Extraordinary General Chapter, so we have chosen to date it as [after 25th] February.

c. See MGL 52 of [4th] August 1967, p. 86, for this prayer.

The Chapter will begin with a Retreat starting on 30th August evening. All the delegates should be here by 28th August. Therefore please try to finish all your Retreats, including the Superiors retreats, before the Chapter. Bring with you all the things you need and your Constitution book and Bible.

Regarding Links—as it is not in the Constitutions, we will discontinue the Links. I will ask any Sister to help me, if I need. I will be sending the voting papers and other information to you in a few days. Please address all your letters concerning the Chapter and other business of the Society to me.

Let us make some special sacrifices for the Chapter. I am sending you a simple preparation based on the Constitutions, so at the same time it will help us to know and practice them.

God bless you
Mother

P.S.: We have decided not to bring the Seniors for Renewal till after the Chapter.

MGL 218. [2ND] MARCH 1990

+ LDM

Mother House
[2nd] March 1990

My dearest Children, Regionals, Superiors and Sisters,

This brings you my love and prayers that the sacrifices you have made during Lent may deepen your love and joy in the Resurrection of Our Lord, through the most pure Heart of Mary.

I am sure you have read my last letter, in which I announced to you the Extraordinary Chapter General.

With this letter I enclose the voting papers for each Professed member of your community and a list of all the Finally Professed in your region who are eligible to be voted for as delegate to the Chapter.

Superiors, as soon as you get this letter, please read and put it up on the board with the list of names, for the Community to see, pray and reflect on.

The Voting will be done everywhere in the Society on 1st May, beginning of Our Lady's month. I will be happy if nine days before, we begin a Novena to Our Lady asking her to guide us all to vote for the Sister whom

She wants to be your delegate to the Chapter. I beg you all to remember—do not allow the spirit of the world to influence us, nor should we try to influence each other. The Society belongs to Jesus. We must seek Only His will—and through prayer, try to find the person He has chosen. Read carefully Constitution 175 and 176 during the Novena.

On May 1st, after Holy Mass, the Community should come together in the Chapel—pray to the Holy Spirit followed by five minutes silent prayer. Then write the name of the Sister whom you think should represent your region at the Chapter. Fold the paper—put it into the envelope provided. The Superior seals the envelope in front of the whole community and posts it to me the same day.

In case any name is missing from the list, kindly inform me immediately.

Let us try always to be the cause of Joy to Jesus and to be holy like Jesus and humble like Mary.

As the preparation for the chapter begins by the voting—let there be no other spirit in our Voting but the Glory of God and the Good of our Society and our Poor. That is why we must pray and offer many sacrifices, penance and Adoration, that we really pray.—My prayer and sacrifices are very close to you. Let it be all for Jesus through Mary.

God bless you
Mother

MGL 219. [JUNE 1990]

L.D.M.

[June 1990]

My dearest Children, Sisters, Brothers, Fathers,
Lay Missionaries, Co-workers,

This brings you my prayer and blessing for each one of you—my love and gratitude to each one of you for all you have been and have done all these 40 years—to share the joy of loving each other and the Poorest of the Poor.

Your presence and the work you have done throughout the world for the Glory of God and the good of the Poor has been a living miracle of [the] love of God and yours in action. God has shown His greatness by using nothingness—so let us always remain in our nothingness—so as to give God free hand to use us without consulting us.

Let [us] accept whatever He gives and give whatever He takes with a big Smile.

As the days of the General Chapter draw near, my heart is filled with joy and expectation—of the beautiful things God will do through each one of you [when you accept] with joy the One God has chosen to be our Superior General. Beautiful are the ways of God if we allow Him to use us as He wants.

I am still in Eastern Europe.[a] The living Miracles God has done during these days have been a proof of His tender love for His MC and our Poor. Let our gratitude be our strong resolution to be only all for Jesus through Mary. Let us be Pure and Humble like Mary and we are sure to be Holy like Jesus.

Humility always is the root of zeal for Souls and Charity. We see that
in Jesus—on the Cross and in the Eucharist. We see it in Mary—[who] Lk 1:38–39
went in haste to serve as handmaid—not as Mother of God.

So it is very important for us MCs to be pure and humble. No MC can
live a true MC life and the 4th vow without a pure and humble heart, because a pure heart can see God in the Poor—a humble heart can love and Mt 5:8
serve Jesus in the Poor.

Remember the five fingers—"You—did—it—to—Me". Mt 25:40

Remember—Love begins at home—our Community—our family.

Remember—Works of love are works of Peace.

Let us thank Jesus for the 40 years of tender love we have received from Him through each other—and pray that we grow in this love for each other and our Poor—by deepening our personal and intimate love for Jesus and [by] greater attachment to Jesus through Prayer and Sacrifice.

Try to be Jesus' love, Jesus' compassion—Jesus' presence to each other and the Poor you serve.

a. After World War II, the Soviet Union extended its control into various countries of Europe (Albania, Bulgaria, Czechoslovakia, Hungary, East Germany, Poland, and Romania), creating the so-called Soviet bloc, separated by an "iron curtain" from the rest of Europe to the West. The "fall of the Berlin Wall" on 9th November 1989, which was symbolic of the "iron curtain," paved the way for the fall of communist regimes in the countries of Eastern Europe. As these countries began opening their borders, Mother went there to establish new foundations.

Mother went to Bucharest, Romania, on 3rd May 1990, and opened a home for abandoned children; she opened a soup kitchen in Budapest, Hungary, on 6th May 1990; she was in Nita, Slovakia, on 13th May 1990, and in Prague on 29th May 1990, where she opened new missions. Therefore, this letter can be dated as June 1990 rather than August or April as was written on some copies of this letter found in the individual houses. It appears that the Sisters have dated the letter as August, since they probably received it in August.

Mt 1:16; Acts 1:14; Jn 19:27 All this will be possible if you keep close to Mary, the Mother of Jesus and our Mother. She will guide & protect you and keep you only all for Jesus.

Rom 8:35; 38–39 Let nothing and nobody ever separate you from the love of Jesus and Mary.—It was at Her pleading that the Society was born[118]—let it be again at Her pleading that the Society gives Saints to Mother Church.[a]

Remember, wherever you may be—Mother's prayer, love and blessing will always be with you.

God bless you
M. Teresa MC

MGL 220. 19TH JULY 1990

Mother House
19th July 1990

My dearest Children,

To fulfil our Constitution 174, with the advice of the Sacred Congregation for Religious, my Council and I have decided to add 5 more elected members to our coming General Chapter.

...

God bless you
M Teresa MC

a. In the handwritten draft of this letter that was sent to the houses, Mother wrote "beading" twice in this sentence. Mother usually wrote and said that the Society was born "at our Lady's pleading" (see the last footnote in MGL 138 of 1st December 1978, p. 249). It is possible that she intended to write "pleading" but made a mistake and wrote "beading"; in fact, it was corrected to "pleading" in some extant copies sent to the houses. However, it is more likely that in this instance she wanted to write "bidding" but misspelt it. In either case, the outcome remains the same.

MGL 221. 9TH SEPTEMBER 1990

+ L.D.M.

Mother House
9th September 1990[a]

My dearest children,

We have much to thank God for—for all His goodness and kindness to us. The retreat was really the preparation for the coming of the Holy Spirit. The priest tried his utmost to make us realize the goodness of God in giving us this wonderful vocation.[b]

The elections were made in deep recollection and full freedom and so everyone really felt the presence of the Holy Spirit.[c] On the 8th September in the presence of Msgr. Francis Gomes, delegate of our Archbishop of Calcutta, Mother was re-elected as Superior General, and was confirmed by the Holy See:

Rome, 8th September, 1990.

Dear Msgr. Gomes,

In the name of the Cardinal Prefect, this Congregation for Institutes of Consecrated Life and Societies of Apostolic Life, confirms the postulation of Mother Teresa as Superior General of the Missionary Sisters of Charity, for the term of office prescribed in the Constitutions.

Our Gratitude to God our Father through the Passion of His son Jesus and the love of the Holy Spirit:

is the gift of MOTHER to each one of us

to help us to grow in holiness through the Purity and Humility of the Heart of Mary,[d]

and also the Gift of the four Councillors:

Sr. M. Frederick, MC
Sr. M. Joseph Michael, MC
Sr. M. Priscilla, MC
Sr. M. Monica, MC

With deep love and gratitude to the Councillors—that helped and shared with Mother the joys and sorrows of six years with so much love

a. This letter, giving news of the outcome of the General Chapter, was seemingly composed by one of the councillors or Chapter members, using selections from Mother's previous general letters. Mother added "My dearest children" and the concluding greeting in her handwriting.

b. See MGL 101 of 3rd July 1973, p. 176.

c. Ibid.

d. See MGL 144 of 21st November 1979, p. 260.

and care—we will promise complete love and trust—to Mother and our new Councillors. May Our Lady, who is specially going to be with us during the coming years—lead and guide us—to fulfil Mother's promise to give Saints to Mother Church.[a]

I want you and we all want that we make the Society Holy and we give the Church holy sisters. We make the Society—every single Sister from the biggest to the smallest. Let us make our Society a faithful, Living
Jn 15:1, 5 Branch on the Vine, Jesus. So now with great determination, greater love and humility we are going to love and serve Jesus in each other and our Poor and make our Society something Beautiful for God, through holiness of life.[b]

Be one heart full of love in the Heart of Jesus through Mary. Be only all for Jesus, through Mary.

God bless you
Mother

ED 55. 30TH SEPTEMBER 1990

30th September 1990

My dearest Children,

This brings you Mother's prayer, love and blessing—that you be all one heart full of love in the Heart of Jesus through Mary.

May we receive Jesus as Mary received him, with a pure and humble heart full of love for each other.—Let us pray.

God bless you,
Mother[c]

a. See MGL 144 of 21st November 1979, pp. 260–61.

b. See MGL 144 of 21st November 1979, p. 261.

c. Mother wrote the actual date when she wrote the message, although it was her message for the Christmas 1990 issue of *Ek Dil*. On the bottom of the front page, below Mother's writing, the date "December 1990, Calcutta" is written.

MGL 222. 16TH OCTOBER 1990

+ LDM

16th October 1990

My dearest Children,

This brings you Mother's prayer and blessing to each one of you—that you may all be one heart full of love in the Heart of Jesus through Mary.

By now you must have received the fruit of our Chapter. During the whole time of Chapter you could feel Our Lady's Presence, with her humility and Purity.

At the end of all things, thanks to Fr. Joseph, MC—who helped us to understand more deeply Jesus' "I THIRST" on the Cross. As soon as we Jn 19:28
have the copies of his talks, I will send you a copy for each house.

It is good for you to know the growth of our Society: In December we will have:

FINAL VOWS:	FIRST VOWS:
Calcutta 39	Calcutta 51
Rome 16	Rome 9
Washington 17	Poland 8
	Nairobi 6
	Manila 13
	San Francisco 9

I want you all to take real trouble to work for Vocations. Though we have many, the need is great.

OUR PREPARATION THIS CHRISTMAS: "I will satiate the Thirst of Jesus on the Cross for love and for souls, by working at the salvation and sanctification of my Sisters in my Community."

This new commandment I want you to make your own: I feel this beautiful Gift of God will help us get rid of all uncharitableness in word and deed and so keep Mother's promise to give Saints to Mother Church. My Children, I have accepted to be your Mother, on condition—that all acts against Charity be removed from our Society, from every Community and each one of us. With folded hands, I beg you—don't allow uncharitableness to destroy our beautiful Society.

Let this be an act of love through Thanksgiving for all the beautiful gifts God has bestowed on our Society through this Chapter.

Be Pure and humble like Mary and you will be Holy like Jesus.

God bless you
Mother

MGL 223. 2ND NOVEMBER 1990

+ LDM

2nd November 1990[a]

My dearest Children,

The month of November begins with two beautiful days: the Feasts of All Saints and All Souls. Holy Mother Church remembers all of her children, to whom She has given the life of Jesus through Baptism—and they are now either Home with Jesus in Heaven or waiting to go there through Purgatory. We all know that during this whole month we give them extra love and care, by praying to them and for them. We too must long for that beautiful day, when our turn will come, and we do not know the day or the hour. In our MC Community in Heaven we have now our 24th member.

On the 27th October, I received the good news from Siliguri that our dearest Sr. M. Emily, MC (Aleykutty CM) born May 23, 1948, in Kerala, went Home to Jesus. As this is a difficult time in our country,[b] I was not able to send anyone from Calcutta for the burial. Sr. M. Emily made her Final Profession on 8th December, 1977. As soon as the Sisters in Siliguri send more details about her, you will receive a copy.

In our Society, the Suffrages for our dead are as follows:

a) Each Sister shall offer Holy Mass, Holy Communion, the Way of the Cross and the Rosary, three times, but in the house to which the deceased sister belonged, the sisters shall offer the Holy Sacrifice ten times.
b) In every other house, one Mass shall be offered for the deceased sister.
c) On the first death anniversary of a sister, a Mass will be offered for the repose of her soul—in the house where she died.

The Professions in Calcutta will take place on 21st November. Final—at St. Mary's, Calcutta, at 4 P.M. with our Archbishop Henry D'Souza presiding. First Profession at the Mother House at 6 A.M. with our Vicar General, Msgr. Francis Gomes, as the main celebrant.

a. This letter seems to have been written with the help of one of the Councillors or secretaries working in Mother House. The main topic of the letter is to notify the Sisters of the death of Sr. M. Emily, MC, so Mother might have asked the help of one of the Sisters to draft the letter. During her last years, in fact, it was common for Mother to ask for help from a few trusted Sisters in drafting her general letters.

b. Mother is referring to the unrest and riots, especially in Kashmir, that resulted in thousands of deaths and thousands of refugees fleeing the area.

God willing, I hope to be in Rome for their Professions on 26th November. The Professions in our other places and the Renewals will take place on 8th December.

Two Sisters from our Contemplative Branch in New York will take their First Vows on 12th December.

Let us pray for all our Sisters taking their Vows and for their families and thank God for them. Let also pray and work even harder for more Vocations and renew our own Fidelity to Jesus, as our Crucified Spouse.

By now, all of you must have received or will receive my letter of 16th October, giving you the "new Commandment" as our preparation for this Christmas. I am sure you will take the trouble to find ways to live it, and share this with each other through the Ek Dil.

I wish you a very Holy and Fruitful Advent: Ask Our Lady to help you prepare your beautiful Crib of Charity for Jesus.

Let us be one heart full of love in the heart of Jesus through Mary—the Cause of our joy—because She gave us Jesus.—May the little Child of Bethlehem make our hearts Pure and humble like His. Let us pray.

God bless you
Mother

MGL 224. 23RD NOVEMBER 1990

LDM

23rd November 1990

My dearest Children, Our Councillors & all,

As I go to Rome and other places for our Sisters—pray that it all be for the Glory of God and the Good of Souls.

In my absence Sr. M. Frederick takes full responsibility of the Society.—All permissions & letters will be seen by her—so you have no reason to do anything without permission. Help each other to be Holy—this is the best and surest way to show your love for Mother.

My prayer for each one of you is always with you.

God bless you,
Mother

MGL 225. 10TH DECEMBER 1990

L.D.M.

Rome
10th December 1990

My dearest children, Sr. M. Frederick and all in the Society,

This brings you Mother's prayer and blessing for a very happy and Holy Christmas and New Year. What wonders God has done in using nothingness to show His Greatness.

I hope and pray you are all one heart full of love in the Heart of Jesus through Mary. By now you must have all received the new commandment to work at the Salvation and Sanctification of each one in the community
Jn 19:28 and so satiate the Thirst of Jesus for love for Souls. This has been the most beautiful gift of Our Lady—the fruit of our Chapter General—let us really know it, love it, live it.

As I was not feeling too well—Dr. Bilotta[a] insisted that I come to the hospital for 2 or 3 days. I feel already much better. It is good to have something beautiful to give Jesus through Mary for the gift of Albania. The President himself has given me the date—the 4th March—when I can come, together with the Sisters.—He was kindness itself. He was so happy to ask for the Sisters. We have much to pray [for] on the 10th Feb., when they will change the laws regarding religion. Get everybody to pray. You can feel Our Lady's touch in all this.—The Albanian Gov. [government] gave me an award—a special one.[b] All for the Glory of God and praise of Mary—for She is really the One.

Something beautiful happened [a] few days [ago]—a big number of Italian families had heard that I have promised Our Lady that out of love for Her I will give 15 houses in Russia—the 15 Mysteries of the Rosary.—So the many families of a Parish—Italian—got together—and gave 15 Chalices & 15 Ciboriums—each chalice marked with the name of the Mystery of the Rosary. Fr. Forrest's[c] sister gave the money for the monstrance &

a. Dr. Vincenzo Giulio Bilotta, Italian cardiologist at Salvator Mundi International Hospital in Rome, took care of Mother when she was in Rome.

b. Mother Teresa received the Order of "Naim Frashëri te Klases I" (Order of Naim Frashëri First Class) award on 3rd December 1990 in Tirana, Albania. The award is named after Naim Frashëri, a famous Albanian poet, and is awarded for outstanding contributions to art, science, culture, or education.

c. Fr. Tom Forrest (1927–2018), a Redemptorist priest ordained in New York in 1954, worked in Central and South America and in 1978 was elected director of the International Office for the Catholic Charismatic Renewal. He organized two Worldwide Retreats for Priests in 1984 and 1990; more than 11,000 priests attended. He invited Mother to be a speaker. He was also the International Director of Evangelization 2000. In order to respond to a "divine inspiration" to start the spiritual adoption of priests ("Veronica Intercessors for Priests"), Mother turned to Fr. Forrest for guidance. He was Mother's

tabernacle for Albania; everybody is anxious to share the joy of Jesus' joy to enter these countries[a]—how grateful we should be to Jesus and His Mother for using us.

Here in Rome everybody is well—like in the M.H. [Mother House] there is always coming and going. Holy Father was so very happy to hear about Albania. He called it "First Class news—you are opening the door to Albania, converting Albania—Thank you."

Now we still have a greater resolution, we should be faithful to the spirit of our Society and deepening our love for our Society through prayer and sacrifice.

I am grateful to you all for the love and joy you have all expressed through your letters for having me as your Mother, the fruit of our Chapter.—As we begin the first year of the G. Ch. [General Chapter], let us all be one heart full of love in the Heart of Jesus through Mary. Let our hearts, our mind, our tongue, our actions, never allow uncharitableness to destroy the joy of loving in our Communities. —We must really give our "word of honour"—in Albania they say "Besa"[b]—to God that we will
really love one another as God loves each one of us. Let us pray. Jn 13:34; 15:12

God bless you
Mother

"adopted" priest, and he preached numerous retreats and conferences to the Missionaries of Charity Sisters.

a. The meaning is that everybody is anxious to share in the joy that Jesus feels upon entering these countries.

b. See footnote to MGL 173 of 19th September 1983, p. 314.

1991

ED 57. [13TH FEBRUARY] 1991

Ash Wednesday [13th February] 1991[a]

As we have entered Lent with Mary, Mother of Jesus, let us in a special
Jn 19:25 way be very close to Her so that we can share in the Passion of Jesus as She
did—right up to the Cross—with a Pure and Humble heart.

God bless you
Mother

MGL 226. 18TH FEBRUARY 1991

+

L.D.M.

18th February 1991

My dearest Children,

[*Fathers, Brothers, Sisters,*][b]

Jn 15:13 As we enter into LENT—the time of greater LOVE—let us enter it with a Pure and humble heart, CLOSE TO MARY, so that we can come as <u>close to JESUS</u> as we can.

Mary's Purity and Humility attracted the Heart of God so much that
He chose Her to be the Mother of Jesus, the first Tabernacle of God on
Lk 1:26–38 Earth. On receiving Jesus, on that day of the Annunciation—that day was
Mary's First Communion day—who can imagine the tender love shared
between Her and Her Divine Son in Her Womb; and then, 33 years after,
Jn 19:25 She stood near Her Crucified Son.

a. We were unable to find *Ek Dil* 56. At the top of the first page of *Ek Dil* 57, above the news from Motherhouse, the following was handwritten: "We praise and thank God, on the 24th May 91 we celebrate our dearest Mother's Diamond Jubilee."

b. The words in italics (here and further down in this letter) were written in Mother's handwritten draft of this letter, but left out in the typed version, probably by mistake; thus, they have been restored here.

At His coming into this world, the first act of Mary was to go in haste Lk 1:39, 56
to serve Her cousin, who was with child. [*Again, before*] [His] leaving this
world, St. John, on hearing Jesus say that Mary was "his Mother," took Jn 19:25–27
Her to His own. In spite of the terrible humiliation and bodily pain, Jesus shows His deep concern for Her and for each one of us. What a wonderful example for us to follow—when pain and humiliation come in our life.

When we feel lonely, unwanted, misunderstood or set aside—let us accept WHATEVER JESUS GIVES AND GIVE WHATEVER HE TAKES—WITH A BIG SMILE, as our Constitutions say. This is the time
of GREATER LOVE, of Greater Sharing in His Passion. This is the time Jn 15:13
when Jesus in His Suffering looks for One to comfort Him—as we read, Mt 26–27; Mk 14–15; Lk 22–23; Jn 18–19
"I looked for one to comfort Me and I found none." Be you the one to com- Ps 69:20
fort Him by accepting willingly that pain, that humiliation, that feeling of being unwanted, unloved. It is a sign that you have come so close to Him that He can share His Passion with you—that He has found you to be the one to comfort Him, by your acceptance.

During these 40 days, let us deepen our personal love for Jesus, and make it more intimate, more real and living. Be careful of temptations that touch your Vocation. Do not take decisions that will destroy your attachment to Jesus, your opportunity to Satiate His Thirst for love, for souls.

Also, let us remember that to share in the Passion of Christ is not just
a feeling but a Gift of GREATER LOVE,—of personal and intimate union Jn 15:13
with Jesus. If we but remember what Jesus said: "My Father loves you be- Jn 14:21, 23; 16:27
cause you have loved Me". During these 40 days let us love Jesus in each Mt 25:40
other and in the Poor.

With this letter I am also sending you the changes in the Constitutions that have to be made. Your Regional will help you do this.... I received [a letter about this] from the Sacred Congregation....

On the 23rd February I am leaving for Rome to open our house in Albania on 2nd March. I hope to return to Calcutta by the middle of March.

I have been able to contact our Sisters in the Middle East, and they are all safe. Continue to pray for them and our people in these countries. Let us pray even more and make many sacrifices for PEACE and that the war may come to an end.[a]

a. Mother is referring to the Persian Gulf War (17th January 1991–28th February 1991). Mother had written to President George Bush and President Saddam Hussein on 2nd January 1991, pleading with them on behalf of the poor to be reconciled and so avoid going to war (see *Come Be My Light*, 315–17, for the text of this letter.)

Happy & Holy Easter.—Let us pray to be pure and humble like Mary so that we can become holy like Jesus.

God bless you
Mother

MGL 227. 27TH FEBRUARY 1991

L.D.M.

[Rome][a]
27th February 1991

My dearest Sr. M. Frederick and all in M. H. [Mother House],

May God's blessing be with you all.

Thank God all is well. We are leaving for Albania on Saturday 2nd March at 2 P.M. by Alitalia & our things by truck. Miracle after Miracle—I do not understand this tender love of Jesus for Albania.—The Gov. [government] is changed, but the president is the same—Jane is already there.[b]— She is really a gift of God. Sandi's father is buying the house for us.[c]

It is really a first class miracle, what Our Lady is doing—where we are, this is now our house. We have to pay $20,000 for land & house, Close to the Church & to Our Poor. The Mayor has given us a beautiful house for our N.H. [Nirmal Hriday]. Can you imagine what our Lady is doing. Some received H. Com [Holy Communion] after 24 years.—It is wonderful to open a church after 25 years.—Many not baptised—many not married but faithful to the Church, though there were no priest[s].

In Shkodra I was asked to open the Cathedral; 24 priests all freed from[d]

L.D.M.

Tirana
12th March 1991

Jail after 24 years. It was so beautiful to be with them to pray with them. To protect the sacred vessels, they buried them—they gave the chalice, which was hidden for 24 years, & [it] was used at the opening of the Cathedral. I will bring it when I come. In Shkodra there are a very good number of Vocations, like in Bucharest.

a. Mother began this letter on 27th February 1991 in Rome and continued it on 12th March 1991 in Tirana.

b. Mother wrote "Jane," referring to Jan (Jeanette) Petrie, who filmed Mother Teresa for the documentaries *Mother Teresa* and *Mother Teresa: The Legacy* (Petrie Productions, New York).

c. Sandy McMurtrie, a Co-worker and benefactor from Washington, DC, generously helped the MCs in many parts of the world.

d. Mother interrupted her writing at this point and continued two weeks later in Tirana.

I am leaving for Rome on the 13th and will come back on the 16th with the eight Sisters marked for Tirana and Shkodra, and also the things they need for both these houses. Gov. [government] gave us a beautiful building.—In Tirana N.H. [Nirmal Hriday]—Gift of love—in Shkodra Sh. Bh. [Shishu Bhavan]—so pray that we do God's work with great love. On the 31st there will be the important day.[a] So pray much.

Pray that I get a priest who knows English. Only the Indian Sister is not able to confess & myself. I am sure Our Lady will do something.

Keep praying for me and all our Sisters & our people—who are hungry for God.

God bless you
Mother

MGL 228. 23RD APRIL 1991

L.D.M.

Rome, San Gregorio
23rd April 1991

My dearest Children,

This brings you Mother's love, blessing and gratitude for all the fervent prayers, beautiful cards and letters each Community has sent in for Easter.

Glory and honour to God for all He has done for us in Albania. I know you have all been praying much for Mother and sharing in the joy of having been able to give Jesus three more tabernacles where He will be loved and adored by the people of Albania. Thank you for all your letters bringing me your love and prayers and telling me how deeply you have been sharing in this time of special grace for the Church through our Society. The people of Albania are so hungry for God. People are longing for Holy Communion, but Father feels that not having been to confession for over 25 years, they have to be prepared to make a good confession. Our Sisters in the three houses—two in Tirana, the capital, and one in Shkodra—have a beautiful apostolate, opening minds and hearts to Jesus, and they are doing it so beautifully. [Two sisters] both know Albanian well and are teaching Catechism in Albanian; many people, however, also speak Italian

a. On 30th March the Sacred Heart Church was opened again for the Easter Vigil. Mother prepared the church personally for this first Easter celebration in Albania since 1967. On Easter Sunday, 31st March, the first free political elections after the communist regime were to take place.

and English, so the other Sisters are teaching in Italian and English. It is so beautiful to see the zeal of both our Sisters and the people. Except our Sisters, there is no one for the beautiful work of God's love in Albania now. In Tirana we also have a Home for destitute sick people, while in Shkodra we have a Home for abandoned crippled and mentally retarded children.

We have opened the Cathedral Church of the Sacred Heart in Tirana. All these years it was used as a cinema hall. Can you imagine the joy of the Sacred Heart as we opened the Cathedral with Holy Mass at which thousands of people participated. In Tirana we have four tabernacles now—miracle of God. Everyone has been so kind and helpful. People are really happy to have our Sisters. I will have many things to tell you when I return.

As much as I would love to be back in Mother House, as our Novices and Tertians prepare for their First and Final Professions, yet I feel Jesus and Mary want me here at this time of opening of churches in the country of Albania, where God's love has been so rejected for many years and people were starving spiritually. Let us make the sacrifice generously, it will draw down many graces upon each one and upon our Society. You all know Mother's deep love for you. My constant prayer for you all is that you may grow more and more in the likeness of Christ through purity and humility of heart. We have never needed that pure heart so much as now. In our Society, which God has entrusted not only to Mother but to each one of us, holiness is the main reason of its existence. For us holiness should not be difficult—for in giving whole-hearted and free service to the Poorest of the Poor we are 24 hours with Jesus, and as every MC is the poorest of the Poor—even when we do little things for each other in the house, besides what we do outside, we live and observe our 4th Vow.[a] It does not matter how small or how big your work is—as long as you are doing it with Him, for Him, and to Him.[b] Mother has promised to give Saints to the Church. Holiness, very great holiness, becomes very simple if we belong fully to Our Lady. Our sanctification is Her main duty. Often during the day, during the coming month of May, let us raise our hearts to Her and ask Her how She would do this or that now if She were in our place—and above all how to love God as She loved Him, that we too may love Him with Her heart.[c]

a. See MGL 155 of 8th October 1980, p. 275.
b. See MGL 97 of 13th December 1972, p. 168.
c. See MGL 93 of 18th June 1972, pp. 161–62.

The joy of loving each other in Jesus with Mary—May it become the sure way to holiness.—My love, prayer and blessing be with each one of you.

God bless you
Mother

MGL 229. 23RD JUNE 1991

L.D.M.

Baghdad
23rd June 1991

My dearest children all over the world, every one of you Fathers, Brothers, Sisters, Co-Workers and lay Missionaries of Charity,

This brings you Mother's love, blessing and prayer that you may all grow in holiness through love for each other and the Poor you serve.

It is one real living miracle of God's tender love that we were allowed by the Government of Iraq to come in and establish the MC Convent in the heart of the city of Baghdad in the house given by the Gov. [government]. Many big people[a] came to help us clean the house, which will soon be full of malnourished & crippled children.

[The] Gov. [government] has also given us a car to start the mobile clinic, as the Poor are far & unable to walk the great distances. The need is so great that I have been asked to open two more houses in two different places, so you must keep praying—whatever be the will of God for us.—The fruit of the war is so terrible; one cannot understand how any human being can do that to another—and for what?[b] Let us pray that our works of love bring Peace, unity and joy.

For the present there is a great shortage of food & medicine, and, as hundreds & hundreds of houses have been destroyed, I do not know how long it will take to rebuild—so let us include Iraq in our daily prayer.

I brought the 16 senior postulants from Bucharest to Rome. They are such a beautiful Gift of God to our Society. In Albania they have 13 Aspirants already. Our Noviciate in Rome & Poland will be full—we have much to thank God for [for] all His love for us.

a. Mother is referring to eminent or influential people, commonly referred to as VIPs (Very Important Persons).

b. This refers to the results of the Persian Gulf War; see footnote to MGL 226 of 18th February 1991, p. 411.

Looking at the people[a]—the Old Testament becomes so alive. Tomorrow we will go to see "Babilon" [sic][b]—who ever thought MC will come to these places—to proclaim the Word of God through works of love. I never thought that our presence would give so much joy to thousands of people—So much suffering—everywhere.

Among our Sisters a few know Arabic, so it will not be so difficult.

Looking at the terrible suffering & fruit of war—same thing, I was thinking, can happen through uncharitable words & actions—we do not destroy buildings—but we destroy the very heart of love, peace and unity and so break the beautiful building, Our Society—which was built with so much love by Our Lady.—

I know you all love Mother and that you would do anything to show your love & gratitude. I ask of you but one thing:

Be a true Missionary of Charity and so Satiate the thirst of Jesus for love, for souls by working at the Salvation and Sanctification of your Community and your family, the Poor you Serve.[c] Let us pray.

God bless you,
Mother

MGL 230. 28TH JUNE 1991

L.D.M.

Rome
28th June 1991

All the Sisters of the Society,

As it is difficult for me to return to India—due to unforeseen circumstances—I hereby appoint Sr. M. Frederick to deal with all matters that require my permission, and also renew all general permissions. Therefore it is important that all Regionals especially renew their General permissions

a. Mother wrote "people," but she could have appropriately meant "places," and so perhaps wrote "people" in error.

b. Mother meant the city of Babylon but misspelled it.

c. In the original handwritten letter Mother wrote: "... Sanctification of your Community and the Poor you Serve." Later she added "your family", with the "insert" symbol after the word "and" and above it the words "your family". She probably thought of the Co-workers and LMCs to whom the letter was also addressed. The more accurate meaning is rendered by reading it as "... Sanctification of your Community, your family and the Poor you Serve," as that is what Mother meant to communicate by her insertion.

in time with her. She can also hold the meeting of the Council when necessary. She will be able to contact me when necessary.

This is a beautiful opportunity for us all to practice humility and love for our Society. Do with Sister what you would do with me.

I am praying much for you all.

God bless you,
M Teresa MC

Let Sr. M. Joseph Michael go with the Sisters to the Andaman. Let her take a companion to return.[a]

MGL 231. 28TH JULY 1991

LDM

Tirana
28th July 1991

My dearest Children,

May God's blessing and His love fill your hearts as you prepare for the feast of our Society—The Immaculate Heart of Mary, the Cause of our Joy. We must all try our best to be Pure and humble like Mary, Mother of Jesus and our Mother—So that we can become holy like Jesus—for the Glory of God and the Good of our Poor we serve and our Society. Mt 1:16; Acts 1:14; Jn 19:27

It's difficult to describe the situation of Albania—a country deprived of God's presence in the hearts of the People—and so their conscience seems to be dead.—The presence of our Sisters and the opening of the Churches [have] been a real gift of God to the whole Country.—Next Month everybody is looking forward to the coming of the Nuncio, Bishops & Priests—and so re-establish the Church in Albania.—We need to pray much for the Church[b] in Albania, as it is still going through much suffering and pain.—Our 11 Aspirants are doing very well.—I think in time we will have many more—so pray for them all so that the presence of Jesus & Mary may penetrate their families.

a. The house in Diglipur, Andaman opened on 16th July 1991. Mother wanted Sr. Joseph Michael to go with the Sisters for the opening of the new foundation and to have a companion for the return trip, since the voyage by ship was about three days.

b. Mother wrote, "We need much to pray for the Church . . ." We have corrected it for the sake of the reader but note the original here.

Due to so many unforeseen difficulties it was necessary for me to be here with the Sisters. Sisters are very well, thank God, and are doing so well—twice a day they are having catechetical classes for men, women & children in Albanian & Italian, hundreds to be prepared, and we are, for the present, the only ones.—I would be very happy if I could have 2 or 3 Sisters who know Albanian to come here.—Though the Sisters are doing their best to learn the language, but it is still very difficult to speak to the people—a very beautiful Sacrifice for Albania.[a]

I hope to leave for Rome on the 1st. I believe the situation in Baghdad is not so good. Thank God our Sisters are alright.

It has been a long time since I left Mother House.—I have never had to stay in a country so long, but Albania, being legally Atheist, needs very great help to find back the way to God. We have one very great difficulty: the need of a priest. —We have one priest for all the five houses, so please keep praying.—Two others were here also—but one got very sick & had to return—the other finishing his two weeks he had to return—so please pray that we get one more priest who has the power to stay longer and knows English.

I am praying much for you all, as I have no news from Mother House or anybody that side.—So let us pray Mother[b] will soon be able to come back home.

How holy we must all try to be—[so] as to be able to be Jesus' love, compassion and presence to the people and our Sisters, so let us deepen our life of prayer, for the fruit of Prayer is always [a] deepening of faith, and where there is Faith there is holiness. For Jesus said, "Blessed are they
Jn 20:29 who have not seen and have believed." That is why our work for the Poor
Mt 5:8 is so real, so beautiful, because if our heart is Pure we can see, we can
touch Jesus, 24 hours, because He has made it so clear "Whatever you do
Mt 25:40 to the least of my Brethren You—did—it—to—Me." The Gospel in our
five Fingers[c]—that is why we need that deep life of prayer—that will help us to grow in that intimate and personal love for Jesus and complete attachment to Him—so that our Sisters & our Poor can see Jesus in us, His love—His compassion. So, my dearest children, let us ask Our Lady to teach us to pray, to help us to pray, and to pray with us and for us. Let us ask Her to be a Mother to us Now.

a. Mother is referring to the sacrifice involved in other communities providing two or three Albanian-speaking Sisters; their loss would be a gain for the communities and apostolate in Albania.

b. Mother is referring to herself in the third person. For Mother referring to herself in the third person, see MGL 4 of [4th] November 1960 and corresponding footnote, p. 9.

c. In the handwritten version, Mother underlined "You—did—it—to—Me" and "Fingers."

Happy and Holy Feast of our Society—The Immaculate Heart of Mary, Cause of our Joy.—Let us pray.

God bless you
Mother

God love you all for the beautiful letters you have written to me. I wish I could write to each one of you.

Thank you & God bless you
Mother[a]

MGL 232. [6TH] DECEMBER 1991

L.D.M.

[6th] December 1991[b]

My dearest children
Fathers, Brothers, Sisters & Our Contemplatives,

May the blessing of God be with each one of you during these days of Advent as you prepare your hearts through Prayer and penance to receive Jesus, the King of Kings, in the Bethlehem of your hearts—filled with Poverty, Chastity, Obedience and wholehearted free Service to the Poorest of the Poor, in total surrender, loving trust and cheerfulness, and so satiate the Thirst of the Little Child of Betlehem [sic] with the help of His Mother, when He is born on the 24th Midnight.

1 Tim 6:15; Rev 17:14, 19:16 Mt 2:1; Lk 2:4

Lk 2:7

This is all I wish for you—let us be faithful to the spirit of our Society.—Let us help each other to grow in holiness through love, peace and unity in our Communities and with our Poor.

The Little Child of Bethlehem will feel so warm in the Crib of our hearts if we cover him with our love and fidelity to the spirit of our Society and so satiate His burning Thirst for our tender love and affection.

This is my prayer and hope: that the Little Child of Bethlehem will feel at home in our Society and in each one of us, and that He will fill our hearts with tender love for each other and so make our Communities another Nazareth, where the Little Child of Bethlehem, together with his Mother and St. Joseph, will feel loved and feel at home.

Mt 2:23; Lk 2:51–52

a. This letter was not typed but just photocopied and sent to the houses. Mother added this part to the same handwritten letter with a different pen, probably later.

b. This letter is undated, but on the handwritten original "December 1991" was written not by Mother but by a Sister.

Let us ask His Mother to help us to be Pure and humble like Her and Charitable like St. Joseph so that we become holy like the Little Child of Bethlehem.

May God's blessing be with each one of you during the coming year.—Be only all for Jesus through Mary.

God bless you
Mother

MGL 233. 16TH DECEMBER 1991

L.D.M.

16th December 1991

My dearest Children

This brings you my prayer, love and blessing for Christmas and God's special blessing on 1992.

Jn 13:34; 15:12 Love one another as Jesus and Mary love you.

Take the trouble to deepen your life of prayer, for prayer will give you
Mt 5:8 a clean heart, and a clean heart can see God—and if you see God in each
Jn 13:34; 15:12 other, you are sure to love each other as God loves each one of you.

Take the trouble to be pure & humble like Mary, and you will be Holy like Jesus.—Let us pray.

God bless you
Mother

ED 58. DECEMBER 1991

+ L.D.M.

December 1991

My dearest Children,

May the Joy and Peace of Jesus and His Mother be with each one of you during this Christmas festival.

I want to be with each one of you on this beautiful day, but, as this is not possible, I wish you each one of you a happy and holy Christmas and God's blessing on 1992.

God bless you
Mother

1992

MGL 234. 7TH JANUARY 1992

L.D.M.

San Diego
7th January 1992

My dearest children, the whole MC family,

My dearest children, Sr. M. Frederick, Sr. M. Nirmala and both groups—Councillors,

This brings you Mother's love, blessing and prayer as a Christmas gift to each one of you, including the whole Society. The present Gift of God, my heart sickness, it is really my token of gratitude to God for the 63 years
of my being the Spouse of Jesus and entering India with the Kings[a]—and Mt 2:1–12
now that the Society is [in] 97 countries, we must also have entered one of those Kings' countries; the difference [is] that we entered with Jesus & not looking for Jesus. The kings must be happy to have the Sisters. How grateful we must be for this great Gift. That is why I am not surprised that this pain came during this time.[b]

My dear children, as a gratitude for what Jesus has done, is doing and will do with the MC family, please promise & take the real trouble to be Holy. I have promised God I will give Saints to Mother Church. This is a sure time when each one of you lives that promise & gives the Mother Church living Saints—after death, that is for others—for us is "living Saints" like Jesus & Mary were when on earth.

a. Mother is referring to her entering India on the feast of Epiphany, 6th January 1929.

b. Mother was in the MC house in Tijuana, Mexico (Juan Diego—Central), when she became very ill. She was hospitalized on 26th December 1991, with severe bacterial pneumonia and congestive heart failure, at the El Prado Hospital in Tijuana. But the doctors—and the bishop—insisted that she be transferred to Scripps Hospital in La Jolla (San Diego), which is about a 45 minutes' drive from the Mexico-USA border. On 27th December 1991, Mother suffered a heart attack and would have died had she not been in the hospital.

The care & the love I am receiving is very great. Pray for them.

With much love & my blessing.

May Mary love Jesus with your heart.

God bless you
Mother

MGL 235. 12TH JANUARY 1992

L.D.M.

San Diego
12th January 1992

My dearest children Sr. M. Frederick, Sr. M. Nirmala
and all the Sisters,

This brings you Mother's prayer, blessing and much love to each one of you.

Thank God I am much better and I hope by Wednesday I will be able to leave the hospital[a] & then for a week with our Sisters in Tijuana & then leave for Rome with the Fathers.

I cannot tell you how everyone in the hospital is just pouring love—and our Sisters who are taking care of me [too]. You must have heard that the Apostolic Carmelites gave us a house as a gift in Los Angeles for our Contemplative Sisters. Archbishop of San Diego also is giving a house for our Contemplative Sisters. They have now 15 [houses], with San Diego. I am hoping we will be able to open in Rome for them also and [for] our Fathers who need to be there for their Priestly studies.

In Baltimore they sent me word from the Bishop's house—they have 3000 AIDS children.—The Bishop is begging for at least 4 Sisters to begin something in the name of the Church. Sr. M. Dolores & Sr. M. Sylvia are willing to give 2 each. Sr. M. Sylvia thinks Sr. M. Suzane can be the Superior, so please bring this to the meeting, as I would like to do it while I am here.—

Everybody in the hospital is Kindness itself—do not accept anything for my stay, though many have offered.

a. Mother was discharged from Scripps Hospital on 16th January 1992.

You could try & see how you can make up their number from your side.[a] I hope you are all well & doing God's work with Great Love. Let us pray.

God bless you
Mother

MGL 236. 17TH JANUARY 1992

L.D.M.

Tijuana—Convent[b]
17th January 1992

My dearest Children,

Sr. M. Frederick & all,

As you see, I am back home, where I have to stay at least two weeks due to the medicines I have to take.—Also on the 27th Jan. the Juniors begin their retreat, and as I have not [had] my retreat last year I will make it with them—and so my stay will be prolonged.

In praying to Our Lady I realised that beautiful [practice] of praying the litanies of Our Lady after the Rosary—we have stopped—please let us begin again as before.[c]

In all the Churches this side [i.e., the Americas] they say Hail Mary after the intercession prayers at Mass. Find out if we can do that in India—if yes, then begin in the M.H. [Mother House]—& send word to the houses.

Let us try and make the love for Our Lady grow more & more in our Society. I am so happy to see the love for Our Lady so strong with our Fathers.—

I hope you are all well. I hope Sr. M. Dorothea is better.

All of you obey with great love Sr. M. Frederick, as she takes my place while I am sick & away from M.H. [Mother House].

Let us pray.

God bless you
Mother

a. Mother is referring to the number of Sisters that would be needed for the new community in Baltimore, which she mentioned in the paragraph above.

b. As Mother had written her previous letter from the hospital in San Diego, she is specifying that she is now at home; thus, she writes "Convent" after Tijuana.

c. At the 1997 General Chapter it was decided again not to have the litany after the Rosary so more time could be given to silent prayer.

⁓ MGL 237. 6TH MARCH 1992 ⁓

+ LDM

Mother House
6th March 1992

My dearest Children,

This brings you Mother's love, prayer and blessing, as well as my gratitude for all the prayers and sacrifices offered for me during my illness. You were all very much in my thoughts and prayers. I am now back in Mother House, thank God. You will be happy to know that soon after I arrived in Calcutta, we got the joyful news that Rome has officially erected our MC Fathers as a diocesan congregation. What great things God is doing and wants to do through our MC family! Let us thank Him, and let us allow Him to do even more by our complete openness to His loving will in all things.

Lent is once again with us, a precious time when Jesus, through His Church, asks us to keep our minds and hearts fixed on His deep longing for our loving trust in His love, expressed by our total surrender to His loving will, so as to be able to share His joy of being one with the Father. Yes, Lent, for us Missionaries of Charity, is the time when we ask ourselves how much are we truly seeking to satiate the thirst of God, our lov-
Jn 19:28 ing Father in heaven, for our holiness—the thirst which Jesus expressed on the Cross when He cried out "I Thirst" as He shed every drop of His Precious Blood with such great love and bitter pain. How much we need to keep close to Our Lady for this.

Lent is also a time when we seek to reflect more deeply on the purpose God had in creating us and recall prayerfully what our Faith teaches us, that God created us

> to know Him, to love Him, and to serve Him in this world, so as to be happy with Him forever in the world to come.[a]

God so longs to tell us about His life of Truth and Love.—How much do I long to listen to Him? What are my sincere efforts at interior and exterior silence? Examine, repent and resolve. How much do I long to learn to love God? Am I sincerely seeking to free my desires from all disorderly attachments to myself, to people and to things? Have I experienced the freedom of poverty that will protect my undivided love for Jesus lived in

a. This statement is a repetition of the well-known teaching taken from the Baltimore Catechism.

total surrender to His loving will? Do I keep united to Jesus during the
day by frequent spiritual communions? Examine, repent and resolve. Only
undivided love for Jesus will make our service whole-hearted and free. Ex- Mt 22:37; Mk 12:30; Lk 10:27
amine your love for Jesus through the way you serve Him in your Sisters Col 3:23; Mt 10:8
in community and in the poorest of the poor you minister to. Do Jesus'
words, "Whatever you do to the least of mine, you do it to Me,," find a Mt 25:40
constant echo in my mind and heart? Examine, repent and resolve.

Yes, Lent is a time of a sincere deep examination of our life as Missionaries of Charity. Often stand in spirit at the foot of the Cross with Our Jn 19:25
Blessed Mother and contemplate with her the price Jesus paid to obtain
for us the graces we need to choose to die to our sinfulness—pride, greed, 1 Jn 2:16
sensuality. Let us not take the Passion, Death and Resurrection of Jesus for
granted. They are the price of the graces Jesus obtained for us, to enable
us to choose to die to our sinfulness. Ask yourself: Am I aware of my great
need of grace to grow in holiness? Am I aware that grace is to be asked
for? That grace is obtained through prayer, the sacraments and self-denial?
What importance do I give to my prayer life? How fervently do I seek the
graces Jesus wants to give me through the Sacrifice of the Mass and the
Sacrament of Penance? Am I really faithful to weekly fervent Confession?
How do I prepare for daily Mass? Am I convinced of the importance of
voluntary self-denial in my striving for holiness? For Jesus says to us: "If
anyone would come after Me, let him deny himself, take up his cross daily Mk 8:34; Lk 9:23
and follow Me." Do I allow these words to echo in my heart frequently
and deeply during the day? Examine, repent and resolve.

Lent is a sacred time that is meant to deepen our conviction that we
are sinners, yet tenderly loved by God, who sent His only begotten Son to Jn 3:16
redeem us. To help us truly fulfil the very reason of our existence in the
Church as Missionaries of Charity, let us make this one strong resolution:

I WILL—I WANT, WITH GOD'S BLESSING—[TO] BE HOLY[a]

and so satiate the Thirst of Jesus on the Cross for love, for souls, by labouring at the salvation and sanctification of poorest of the poor.

Let us pray.

God bless you
Mother

a. Mother uses the word "will" in its sense of an active verb, the exercise of the will—"I choose to do something" (in this case, to be holy)—and not as a helping verb (either future tense or intensifier) for the verb "to be".

ED 59. APRIL 1992

April 1992

My dearest Children,

This brings you Mother's love, prayer and blessing for a Joyful Easter.
Mt 28:8; Lk 24:36, 41, 52; Jn 20:19–26 May the Risen Jesus fill each one of you with His Peace and Joy.

Jn 15:13 As Lent is a time for Greater Love, Easter is a time when we share that Love and Joy in Loving Jesus in all we meet. The best gift you can give Mother is your determination to BECOME SAINTS—that Mother promised to give Mother Church.

I WILL
I WANT
WITH GOD'S BLESSING
[TO] BE HOLY.

My prayer for you is that you may grow in the likeness of Christ through love and compassion.

Love one another
as Jesus
Jn 13:34; 15:12 *Loves each one of you.*

God bless you.
M. Teresa, MC

MGL 238. 21ST APRIL 1992

+ LDM

Mother House
21st April 1992

My dearest Children,

This brings you Mother's love, blessing and prayer that you may grow in holiness and be like Jesus and Mary through love for each other. Thank you for your letters bringing me your loving Easter wishes. I would love to be able to answer each one personally, but you know that that is impossible. You know how much each one of you is in my thoughts and prayers full of love. I do hope the Risen Christ has filled your hearts with His Joy and Peace—and while we now start preparing for the coming of the Holy
Mt 5:8 Spirit, I pray for you that the Holy Spirit may fill you with His Purity so

that you can see the face of God in each other and in the faces of the poor we serve.[a] Poverty, charity and humility are the best means to purity of life.

As the month of May draws near, let us turn our minds and hearts in a special way to Our Lady. The greatness of Our Lady was in her humility. No one has learned so well the lesson of humility as Mary did. She being the handmaid of the Lord was completely empty of self, and God filled her Lk 1:38
with grace—full of grace—full of God.[b] Love for Mary we can learn only on our knees and through our Rosary. Let us, my children, give Our Lady full liberty to use us for the glory of her Son, for if we really belong to her, our holiness is secure. Let us in this month of May improve our praying of the Rosary, especially when we are out of the house. Try to bring Our Lady fully into your life, into your communities, and into the homes of the poor.[c]

As you already know, the Holy Father is urging the whole Church to prepare a beautiful gift for Our Lord's 2000th birthday. The Holy Father knows that the gift most pleasing to Our Divine Lord is to bring as many souls as possible to know, love and serve God our Father in Him, with Him and through Him. "Go and teach all nations ... teach them to ob- Mt 28:19–20
serve all I have taught you", are the last words Jesus told his disciples before going back to the Father. So the Holy Father is urging us all to do what Jesus has told His disciples to do, to bring the Good News that God 1 Jn 4:8, 16
is love to all men. This is what Jesus came down on earth to proclaim, not only by words but by His very life of love.

Yes, Jesus not only brought the Good News, HE WAS THE GOOD NEWS. "Jesus Himself, the Good News of God, was the very FIRST AND GREATEST EVANGELIZER," the Holy Father writes in his recent encyclical Redemptoris Missio ("The Mission of the Redeemer"). I hope you have all got a copy of this encyclical; if not please try to get one. In the encyclical, the Holy Father is reminding us of our duty as followers of Christ to be evangelizers. How much more do his words apply to us as Missionaries of Charity who, according to our Constitution no. 6, are specially called "to proclaim Jesus Christ to all nations, especially to the poorest of the poor who are under our care, by:

a. See MGL 149 of 20th May 1980, p. 269.
b. See MGL 83 of 10th August 1971, pp. 145–46.
c. See MGL 93 of 18th June 1972, p. 162.

- the sincerity of our way of life;
- prayer and penance;
- our humble deeds of love;
- and also words when opportunity offers."

I am sending you a copy of a talk given us by Fr. Forrest, CSsR.[a] (a very zealous priest who is in charge of Evangelization 2000) to help you understand what the Holy Father wants us all to realize as Christians and more so as consecrated Missionaries of Charity. I want you to reflect prayerfully on what evangelization means in our lives as individuals and as communities, that in turn we may lead our poor people to do their part in bringing Christ to the world.

Pray for all our Novices and Tertians everywhere who are getting ready to take vows in May. In Calcutta, 49 Novices will take their First Vows in Mother House chapel on 20th morning, and 39 Tertians their Final Vows in St. Mary's Church on the 21st evening.

By our very name we have been Called to be His love, His compassion, His presence to each other and the Poor we serve. Therefore let us with strong determination promise Jesus, our Spouse, "I will, I want, with God's blessing, [to] be holy". Mary, Mother of Jesus, be Mother to me now, help me, guide me, protect me. I want to be only all for Jesus—Holy.

God bless you
M Teresa MC

MGL 239. 29TH MAY 1992

L.D.M.

Mother House[b]
29th May 1992

My dearest children,

This brings you Mother's love, prayer and blessing that in every Community you be one heart full of love in the Heart of Jesus through Mary.

With God's grace and blessing [we] had beautiful Profession ceremonies.

a. See footnote in MGL 225 of 10th December 1990, pp. 408–9.

b. This letter was not typed but sent out to the houses in Mother's handwriting. There are two handwritten versions of this letter, one dated 27th May 1992 and the other 29th May 1992; the only difference between them is the addition of the news about the profession of final vows by thirty-nine tertians, which was not in the letter dated 29th but has been restored here in brackets and italics.

Forty-eight Novices took their first Vows [*and 39 Tertians their Final Vows*]. Fr. Bouche[a] was the main celebrant at the first Profession. Father gave us such a beautiful talk that we made copies for the houses.[b]

As we enter into the month of June, the month of the Sacred Heart of Jesus, let us listen to Jesus as He tells us "Learn of Me for I am meek and humble of Heart". Jesus made humility His very special virtue.—Jesus, not being able to humiliate Himself for His sins—since He did not commit any sin—embraced humility out of love, by choice. As for us, we should be humble both because of our sins and for love of Jesus, who humiliated Himself for love of us. Mt 11:29 Heb 4:15

Let us ask Our Lady, the most humble Virgin, [humble] out of love, through choice, to teach us true humility. Do not be afraid, give Jesus a free hand, accept whatever He gives you, and give whatever He takes with a big Smile. Holiness is a beautiful gift of God. Mt 10:26; 28:5, 10; Lk 12:4, 32; Jn 14:27; Rev 1:17; 2:10

Let us be Holy like the Father in Heaven is Holy, Jesus said. Mt 5:48

Let us pray.

God bless you
M Teresa MC

MGL 240. [7TH] AUGUST 1992

+ LDM

Rome
[7th] August 1992

My dearest children,

This brings you Mother's love, prayer and blessing for a very Happy and Holy Society Feast. You all know Mother's love for you and how much I would love to be with you all. But as this is not possible, let us all meet each other in spirit around Our Lady and, with her, thank Jesus for the many, many graces He has showered on us through Mary's powerful intercession all these years, and let us renew our resolution—I will, I want, with God's blessing, [to] be holy.

a. Father Camille Bouché, SJ (1922–2002), left his native Luxembourg at eighteen to be a missionary in India as a member of the Society of Jesus. He was Prefect at St. Xavier's School in Calcutta from 1960 to 1988, then headmaster for five years. He was confessor of the Sisters, especially the novices at Mother House, and was known for his dedication to and affection for the novices.

b. Fr. Bouché's talk, which was sent with this letter, has been omitted.

We have just celebrated the Feast of Our Lady's Assumption into heaven, where She, the young maiden of Nazareth,

– the all PURE One chosen by God to be the Mother of Jesus because
Lk 1:28 She was full of grace,
– the HUMBLE One who uttered those beautiful words to God's
Lk 1:38 messenger, "Behold the handmaid of the Lord. Be it done to me according to Thy word,"
– the all FAITHFUL One who allowed the Holy Spirit to rule in her mind and in her heart and direct all her thoughts and all her desires—

now reigns in heaven as Mother and Queen of Virgins, our Mother and our Queen.

We now enter upon the days of preparation leading to the Feast of our Society, which is so very dear to Her Immaculate Heart. Since it was at Her pleading that the Society was born,[a] let us turn to Our Heavenly Mother and ask Her fervently to obtain for each of Her Missionaries of Charity a deeper understanding and more sincere living of the true mean-
Jn 19:28 ing of our MC vocation—which is to satiate the Thirst of Jesus on the Cross for love and for souls, especially those of the poorest of the poor.

How much we need Mary to teach us what it means to satiate God's Thirsting Love for us, which Jesus came to reveal to us—She did it so beautifully. Yes, Mary allowed God to take possession of her life by Her purity, Her humility and Her faithful love. During the coming year let us seek to grow, under the guidance of our Heavenly Mother, in these three important interior attitudes of soul that delight the Heart of God and enable Him to unite Himself to us, in and through Jesus, in the power of the Holy Spirit. It is in doing so that, like Mary our Mother, we will allow God to take full possession of our whole being—and through us God will be able to reach out His Thirsting love to all we come in contact with, especially the poor people he entrusts to us.

On the 13th [in the] evening our dearest Sr. M. Shawn, one of our Contemplative Sisters in New York, went home to Jesus. She suffered a massive brain haemorrhage two days before and expired peacefully, surrounded by Sr. M. Nirmala and all the community sisters. We will offer the suffrages prescribed by our Directory no. 47 for a deceased sister. Sr. M. Shawn was

a. For further explanation of Our Lady's pleading, see the last footnote of MGL 138 of 1st December 1978, p. 249.

one of our beautiful American Contemplative Sisters who had suffered a severe stroke two years ago, from which she never completely recovered, but was so lovingly resigned to God's will in suffering with Jesus and for Jesus.

In the beginning of August, I went to New York, where the Knights of Columbus had invited me to receive their first award.[a] They have been so very good to us and to our poor. They generously offered to print all our Constitutions and Directories for the love of God. It is truly wonderful what the love of God in human hearts can do—if only we have eyes to see.

I have just returned from Albania, where our Sisters have so much catechetical work to do, preparing hundreds of people for the Sacraments, besides seeing to the material needs of the people, which are also very great. How grateful we must be to God for giving us this wonderful opportunity to witness His Love to people who have been hungering for Him for so long.

Keep the joy of loving Jesus in each other and in your heart and share this joy with all you meet, especially your Community.

I am sending you the "litany of 'I thirst'" for your own personal devotion.

I am leaving for India tomorrow.

So keep praying for our Society, Our Poor and for me.

God bless you
M Teresa MC

ED 61. OCTOBER 1992

October 1992[b]

Keep the joy of loving Jesus in your hearts and share this joy with all you meet, especially your Community and Your Poor. The joy of loving is in the joy of Sharing.

God bless you.
M. Teresa, MC

a. Mother Teresa received the first Gaudium et Spes Award on 4th August 1992 from Supreme Knight Virgil C. Dechant at the Knights of Columbus 110th annual convention.

b. We were unable to find *Ek Dil* 60.

MGL 241. 6TH NOVEMBER 1992

LDM.

54A, Lower Circular Rd.[a]
Calcutta
6th November 1992

My dearest Children,

This brings you Mother's love, blessing and prayer. I wish I could write to each one and thank [you] for your prayers and sacrifices you have offered for my feast. I am sure Jesus is very pleased with all you have offered.

You will, I am sure, be very happy to know that 41 novices will take 1st Vows and 41, Final Vows on the 7th and 8th Dec. So please pray for them, that they be only all for Jesus through Mary.

The novena of the Immaculate Conception we shall offer in a special way in reparation for the Sisters who have left the Society. Let us renew our love for the Society and promise Jesus our Fidelity unto Death—Death
Phil 2:8 of the Cross. I wonder what Jesus must feel deep down in His Heart, the Heart that loves us so much.

As we prepare for the feast of the Im. [Immaculate] Conception, let us make one strong resolution—that we will try to be pure and humble like Mary so that we can become holy like Jesus. We have all the means that can help us to be Holy.

Pray for our Sisters who are preparing for their Vows that they may fully understand the Gift of God—their Vocation. If you want to be Holy—know, love, live the Constitutions with the help of Mary, whose Child you are.

God bless you
M. Teresa MC

MGL 242. 6TH DECEMBER 1992

L.D.M.

6th December 1992

My dearest Children of Final and First Profession,

My prayer, blessing and love are with each one of you as you go before the altar of God to consecrate your soul, body and heart to Jesus.

a. Mother wrote the Mother House address on the top of this letter, so it has been retained here.

Just think, this consecration makes you a consecrated Virgin of God. How grateful we must all be for this great gift of love.—How happy Our Lady must be to help you give yourself to Her Son Jesus.

Though I am not with you in body—You know you are very close to my heart, as I will be there in spirit with each one of you as you make your Vows.

Renew your strong resolution as you receive Jesus in your heart,

> I will, I want, with God's blessing, [to] be holy.

Let nothing and nobody ever separate you from Jesus.—Be only all for Rom 8:35; 38–39
Jesus through Mary.

God bless you
M Teresa MC

1993

MGL 243. 15TH FEBRUARY 1993

+ LDM

Mother House
15th February 1993

My dearest children,

This brings you Mother's love, prayer and blessing. I hope you are all well and doing God's work with great love and growing in holiness. By praying the work, we do the work with Jesus, for Jesus and to Jesus, and so we are in His presence 24 hours. How beautiful is our Vocation if we really
Mt 25:40 believe that He, Jesus, is in the appearance of bread, and He, Jesus, is in the hungry, the naked, the sick, the lonely, the unloved, the homeless, the helpless, the hopeless. Our lives must be more and more woven with this deep
Jn 6:35, 48, 51 faith in Jesus—the Bread of Life to be eaten with and for the poor.[a]

Mt 26–27; Mk 14–15; Lk 22–23; Jn 18–19 As we enter Lent—the time of Christ's Passion—let us enter it with a humble open heart.[b] Lent is the time when we seek, in prayer, to enter more deeply into the Passion of Christ. Let it not be just a time when our feelings are roused—but a change that comes through co-operating with
Mt 16:24; Mk 8:34; Lk 9:23 God's grace in real sacrifice of self. Sacrifice to be real—it must cost—it must hurt—it must empty us of self. Let us go through the Passion of Christ day by day. We often pray, "Let me share with you your pain; I want to be the Spouse of Jesus Crucified," and yet when a little spittle of uncharitable remark or a thorn of thoughtlessness is given to us—how we forget that this is the time to share with Him His shame and pain.[c]

Lent is also the time to remember that we share in Jesus' Passion in a special way by our living of our vows. In our Constitutions we read: "I
Hos 2:20 will betroth you to me in faithfulness." He will make you His own only

a. See MGL 105 of 25th February 1974, p. 183.
b. See MGL 121 of 22nd March 1976, p. 212.
c. See MGL 80 of 7th March 1971, pp. 140–41.

if you are faithful. You belong to Him by your vows.—Love Christ with undivided love in Chastity; through freedom of Poverty; in Total Surrender by Obedience; and Wholehearted and Free Service through Charity. These are but four sentences—do you know them in practice? Do you live them in your daily life? Face yourselves, my Sisters, with all sincerity of heart and ask yourself: Am I really a true MC? One who belongs totally to God? Who gives Wholehearted service to the poor?[a] Our vows are the precious gifts Jesus offers us in His tender love for us to enable us to know Him ever more deeply, love Him more fervently, and serve Him more generously in His humble Eucharistic Presence and in the distressing dis- Mt 25:40
guise of the poorest of the poor. Our fourth vow is the overflow of our life of oneness with Jesus—and it also protects and deepens that oneness with Jesus.

I would like you to take one of my previous Lenten letters as the subject of your weekly community gatherings and as the theme of your prayer life during these six weeks of Lent. These letters are the following:[b]

1st Week	—	Letter of 9th March 1962	—	vol. 1,	p. 13	[MGL 14, p. 25]
2nd Week	—	Letter of 19th Feb. 1970	—	″	p. 73	[MGL 70, pp. 121–22]
3rd Week	—	Letter of 7th March 1971	—	″	p. 82	[MGL 80, pp. 140–42]
4th Week	—	Letter of 19th March 1972	—	″	p. 92	[MGL 89, pp. 155–56]
5th Week	—	Letter of Lent 1975	—	″	p. 119	[MGL 113, pp. 197–99]
6th Week	—	Letter of 22nd March 1976	—	″	p. 126	[MGL 121, pp. 212–13]

I am also sending you some reflections on the meaning of Lent, which will help you to enter more deeply into this season of grace. During Lent we must change, for, as you know, holiness is not a luxury for us but a serious duty. Ask Our Lady to obtain for you the purity to see what Jesus expects of you, the humility to admit your failures, and the grace you need to work hard to become holy like Jesus during this Lent.

I would like to draw your attention to the following points:

- The monthly renewal of permissions comes under fidelity to our vow of Poverty. Be very faithful to renewing these permissions in time, by the 7th of each month. This applies also to Superiors and Regionals.

a. See MGL 114 of 10th March 1975, p. 200.

b. The page numbers and volume refer to the photocopied version of Mother's letters in circulation in the Society before this present volume. We have added MGL number and page number of the present volume in the next column for easier reference.

- More and more Sisters are asking to go home to see their relations for all kinds of reasons. We must deepen the spirit of sacrifice and joyfully choose to abide by our Constitution no. 42 and our Directory no. 17. This is also touching our Vow of Poverty. If we are really wanting to follow Jesus poor, then we must be truly poor. The poor cannot go from one town to another or from one country to another, because they do not have the money. We are using the money of the poor and we take back what we have renounced.
- We are not having retreat for the Superiors in India in Calcutta this year. . . .

During this Lent let us in a special way try to use every little sacrifice, especially the sacrifice of the tongue—to share in the Passion of Our Lord.—Let us say often during the day "Let me share with Thee your Pain, who for all my sins was slain."[a] *I love you Jesus.*

God bless you
M Teresa MC

MGL 244. 25TH MARCH 1993

+ LDM

Varanasi
25th March 1993[b]

My dearest Children—

Sisters, Brothers, and Fathers,

This letter being very personal, I wanted to write in my own hand—but there are [so] many things to say. Even if not in Mother's hand, still it comes from Mother's heart.

a. A line taken from the *Stabat Mater*, a thirteenth-century Catholic hymn to Mary, which portrays her sufferings during Jesus' crucifixion.

b. Because the origin of this letter had become a much-discussed topic, we have decided, as an exception to the rule, to insert an explanation of how this letter came about, by quoting the statement of Fr. Joseph, MC. (For the entirety of his statement, see Appendix A, pp. 523–25). Since Fr. Joseph mentions another MC Father, Fr. Gary, MC, who wrote an added explanation of the origin of the Varanasi Letter, we have decided to include that statement as well. (For this statement, see Appendix A, pp. 525–27). The working copy of the letter which Fr. Joseph mentions has not survived; however, the initial ideas that Mother wrote, and that Fr. Joseph used as a basis for his composition, did survive, and we have decided to include it. For this text, referred to by Fr. Joseph as "notes", see Appendix A, p. 528. Further, we have corrected the text of the letter to correspond to the second edition of the letter, which was printed in the form of a booklet and distributed to the Society, indicating the changes in square brackets.

Jesus wants me to tell you again, specially in this Holy Week, how much love He has for each one of you—beyond all that you can imagine. I worry some of you still have not really met Jesus—one to one—you and Jesus alone. We may spend time in chapel—but have you seen with [the] eyes of your soul how He looks at you with love? Do you really know the living Jesus—not from books but from being with Him in your heart? Have you heard the loving words He speaks to you? Ask for the grace, He is longing to give it. Until you can hear Jesus in the silence of your own heart, you will not be able to hear Him saying "I thirst" in the hearts Jn 19:28
of the poor. Never give up this every day intimate contact with Jesus as the real living person—not just [the] idea. How can we last even one day without hearing Jesus say "I love you"?—impossible. Our soul needs that as much as the body needs to breathe the air. If not, prayer is dead—meditation, only thinking. Jesus wants you each to hear Him—speaking in the silence of your heart.

Be careful of all that can block that personal [contact] with [the] living Jesus. Devil may try to use hurts of life, and sometimes [our] own mistakes—to make you feel [it is] impossible [that] Jesus really loves you, is really cleaving to you. This is danger for all of you. And so sad, because [it is] completely opposite of what Jesus is really wanting, waiting to tell you. Not only He loves you, [but] even more—He longs for you. He misses you when you don't come close. He thirsts for you. He loves you always, even when you don't feel worthy. [When] not accepted by others, even by yourself sometimes—He is the one [who] always accepts you. My children, you don't have to be different for Jesus to love you. Only believe—you are precious to Him. Bring all you are suffering to His feet—only open your heart to be loved by Him as you are. He will do the rest.

You all know in your mind that Jesus loves you—but [in] this letter Mother wants to touch your heart instead. Jesus wants to stir up our hearts, so not to lose our early love, specially in [the] future after Mother leaves you. That is why I ask you to read this letter before [the] Blessed Sacrament, [the] same place it was written, so Jesus himself can speak to you, each one.

Why is Mother saying these things? After reading Holy Father's letter on "I Thirst", I was struck so much—I cannot tell you what I felt. His let- Jn 19:28
ter made me realize more than ever how beautiful is our vocation. How great God's love for us in choosing our Society to satiate that thirst of Jesus, for love, for souls—giving us our special place in the Church. At the

same time we are reminding [the] world of His thirst, something that was being forgotten. I wrote Holy Father to thank him. Holy Father's letter is a sign for our whole Society—to go more into this great thirst of Jesus for each one. It is also a sign for Mother, that time has come for me to speak openly of [the] gift God gave Sept. 10—to explain [as] fully as I can what means for me the thirst of Jesus.

For me Jesus' thirst is something so intimate—so I have felt shy until now to speak to you of Sept. 10.—I wanted to do as Our Lady who "kept all these things in her heart". That is why Mother hasn't spoken so much
Lk 2:19, 51 of "I Thirst," especially outside. But still, Mother's letters and instructions always point to it—showing the means to satiate His thirst through prayer, intimacy with Jesus, living our vows—specially [our] 4th vow. For me it is so clear—everything in MC exists only to satiate Jesus. His words on the wall of every MC chapel, they are not from [the] past only, but alive here and now, spoken to you. Do you believe it? If so, you will hear, you will feel His presence. Let it become as intimate for each of you, just as for Mother—this is the greatest joy you could give me. Mother will try to help you understand—but Jesus himself must be the one to say to you, "I Thirst". Hear your own name. Not just once. Every day. If you listen with your heart, you will hear, you will understand.

Why does Jesus say "I Thirst"? What does it mean? Something so hard to explain in words—if you remember anything from Mother's letter, remember this—"I thirst" is something much deeper than just Jesus saying "I love you". Until you know deep inside that Jesus thirsts for you—you can't begin to know who He wants to be for you. Or who he wants you to be for Him.

The heart and soul of MC is only this—the thirst of Jesus' Heart, hidden in the poor. This is [the] source of every part of MC life. It gives our Aim, our 4th vow, the Spirit of our Society. Satiating the living Jesus in our midst is the Society's only purpose for existing. Can we each say [the] same for ourselves—that is our only reason for living? Ask yourself—would it make any difference in my vocation, in my relation to Jesus, in my work, if Jesus' thirst were no longer our Aim—no longer on the chapel wall? Would anything change in my life? Would I feel any loss? Ask yourself honestly, and let this be a test for each to see if His thirst is a reality, something alive—not just an idea.

Jn 19:28; Mt 25:40 "I Thirst" and "You did it to me"—Remember always to connect the
Mt 19:6; Mk 10:9 two, the means with the Aim. What God has joined together let no one

split apart. Do not underestimate our practical means—the work for the poor, no matter how small or humble—that make our life something beautiful for God. They are [the] most precious gifts of God to our Society—Jesus' hidden presence so near, so able to touch. Without the work for the poor the Aim dies—Jesus' thirst is only words with no meaning, no answer. Uniting the two, our MC vocation will remain alive and real, what Our Lady asked.

Be careful choosing retreat preachers. Not all understand our spirit correctly. They may be holy and learned, but that does not mean they have [the] grace of state [of our vocation]. If they tell you something different than [what] Mother is writing in this letter, I beg you not [to] listen or let it confuse you. The thirst of Jesus is the focus of all that is MC. [The] Church has confirmed [it] again and again—"Our charism is to satiate the thirst of Jesus for love and souls—by working at the salvation and sanctification of the poorest of the poor." Nothing different. Nothing else. Let us do all we can to protect this gift of God to our Society.

Believe me, my dear children—pay close attention to what Mother is saying now—only the thirst of Jesus, hearing it, feeling it, answering it with all your heart, will keep the Society alive after Mother leaves you. If this is your life, you will be alright. Even when Mother leaves you, Jesus' thirst will never leave you. Jesus thirsting in the poor you will have with you always.

That is why I want the Active Sisters and Brothers, the Contemplative Sisters and Brothers, and the Fathers to each one aid the other[a] in satiating Jesus with their own special gift—supporting, completing each other and this precious Grace as one Family, with one Aim and purpose. Do not exclude the Co-Workers and Lay MCs from this—this is their call as well; help them to know it.

Because [the] first duty of a priest is [the] ministry to preach, some years back I asked our Fathers to begin speaking about "I Thirst", to go more deeply into what God gave [the] Society [on] Sept. 10. I feel Jesus wants this of them, also in future—so pray Our Lady keeps them in this special part of their 4th vow. Our Lady will help all of us in this, since she was [the] first person to hear Jesus' cry, "I Thirst" with St. John, and I am sure Mary Magdalen. Because she was there on Calvary, she knows how real, how deep His longing [is] for you and for the poor. Do we know? Do we feel as She? Ask her to teach—you and [the] whole Society are hers. Her role is to bring you face to face, as John and Magdalen, with the love in the

a. The meaning here is "for each one (that is, each branch) to aid the other."

Heart of Jesus crucified. Before it was Our Lady pleading with Mother, now it is Mother in her name pleading with you—"listen to Jesus' thirst." Let it be for each what Holy Father said in his letter—a Word of Life.

How [do you] approach the thirst of Jesus? Only one secret—the closer
Mk 1:15 you come to Jesus, the better you will know His thirst. "Repent and be-
Mk 16:14 lieve", Jesus tells us. What are we to repent? Our indifference, our hard-
Jn 19:28; Mt 25:40 ness of heart. What are we to believe? Jesus thirsts even now, in your heart
and in the poor.—He knows your weakness, He wants only your love, wants only the chance to love you. He is not bound by time. Whenever we come close to Him—we become partners of Our Lady, St. John, Magdalen. Hear Him. Hear your own name. Make my joy and yours complete.

Let us pray.

God bless you
M. Teresa MC

ED 62. EASTER 1993

Easter 1993

My dearest Children, all in our Society,

Happy & Holy Easter. Keep the joy of loving Jesus in your hearts and share this joy with all you meet, especially your Sisters in Community and the Poor you Serve.

God bless you
M Teresa, MC

MGL 245. 14TH MAY 1993

L.D.M.

Rome
14th May 1993

My dearest children Sr. M. Frederick and all,

This brings you my love, my prayer and my blessing.—

May each one of you be only all for Jesus through Mary.—Be Holy.

All these years I never had anything direct to give to the Blessed Trinity—when Doctor told me that 3 of my ribs have been broken—immediately I offer[ed] all to the Blessed Trinity.—There is plenty [of] pain but [this] is all[a] to offer for our Sisters to be professed & Postulants to join the Noviciate. So let us thank Our Lady for helping so much with so much love.

I hope you are all well and doing God's work with great love.

Let us pray.

Special blessing to the New novices.—

God bless you all
Mother

MGL 246. 17TH NOVEMBER 1993

+ LDM

Mother House
17th November 1993

My dearest children,

This brings you Mother's love, prayer and blessing. Thank God I am back home. Thank you for praying with such faith and love for Mother's intentions. Your prayers must have helped me much, for Jesus took great care of me all along.[b] I am sure you are all anxious to know how God, in His loving Providence, directed all things, both during our visit to China and to Vietnam.

In China we first went to Shanghai, where we met with the Archbishop of Shanghai. The next day we went on to Beijing to meet with Mr. Deng Bufang, the head of the organization for the care of the handicapped. He himself is in a wheelchair as a result of an accident he had. He received us very kindly and said he looked forward to the day when China could have the Missionaries of Charity reaching out tender love and care to the poor in that vast and beautiful country. While in China we were able to visit the Cathedral of Our Lady of Sheshan, who is Patroness of China. It was beautiful to see the love and devotion that the Chinese people have to Our Lady. So continue praying that Our Lady may take this foundation under Her very special protection and make it a reality soon.

a. Mother's original handwritten letter that was sent to the houses has "but there is all to offer. . . ." For the sake of clarity when reading, we have changed "there" to "this."

b. This no doubt refers to Mother's health. On 21st August 1993, Mother was in New Delhi to accept an award from the Indian government for "promoting peace and communal harmony," but she became ill before the ceremony and was hospitalized at the All India Institute of Medical Sciences. Mother was treated for malaria and lung infection. She was discharged on 27th August and returned to Calcutta.

I was also able to go to Vietnam with Sr. M. Nirmala, where I met the Archbishop of Hanoi, who is very anxious to have a community of our sisters, as there are 20 beautiful young Vietnamese girls desirous to be Missionaries of Charity. From Hanoi we went to Saigon, where we met with the government people, who gave us great hopes that the visas for our four sisters will be granted in a short time. I left Sr. Nirmala in Cambodia with Sr. Lucina, so that as soon as the visas are issued they will take the sisters to Vietnam and help them settle down. We are hoping to have two houses and 10 candidates in each house. Both Father Petrie and his sister Jan accompanied us and were a great help all along. Let us pray and thank God for them.

You will be very happy to know that our MC Fathers have opened their first house in India in Calcutta.[a] Providence provided a temporary residence for them in the Ballygunge area. The two pioneers are Fr. Gary, MC, from Canada, and Fr. Vittorio, MC, from Malta. Two seminarians will be joining them as soon as they get the visas. Let us pray for priestly MC vocations.

Both the groups of 2nd Year Senior Novices and Senior Tertians are in intensive preparation leading up to their First and Final Professions which will take place on 3rd December, feast of the great missionary, St. Francis Xavier. Pray for them—35 First Professions will take place in Mother House chapel at 6:00 A.M., and 41 Final Professions in St. Mary's Parish at 4:00 P.M. May it all be for the greater glory of God, the good of the Church, of our Society, of every individual sister, and of the poorest of the poor entrusted to our care. I will be leaving for Rome on the 4th of December to be with our sisters for the First profession on the 7th and the Final Profession on the 8th. I hope to be able to go to Poland and, if possible, to Nairobi.

Please pray in thanksgiving for the four new houses that have opened in the last two months: Harare in Zimbabwe, Varna in Bulgaria (both are our first houses in these countries), Alwar in Rajasthan and Ranabondo, close to Krishnagar in West Bengal. How wonderful to have 4 new tabernacles where Jesus can be adored and loved.

By the time this letter comes to you, the holy season of Advent may have begun. During this time of grace let us in a special way ask Our Lady
Lk 2:19, 51 to teach us Her silence, Her humility, Her purity and Her fidelity.[b] You

a. Mother wrote: "You will be very happy to know that a community of our MC Fathers have opened their first house in India in Calcutta." But since the sentence was poorly constructed, we have changed it as little as possible to convey simply and directly what Mother intended.

b. See MGL 120 of 31st October 1975, p. 210.

will find below some points to help you stay close to Our Lady in this way as our fervent preparation for the Feast of Christ's birth. For Christmas celebrates not only Jesus' first coming in the manger in Bethlehem, but Mt 2:1; Lk 2:4
is meant to fix our attention on all His daily comings to us to live in and through us and so to satiate His Thirst to share His life with us.

We have much to thank God for—[for] His tender love for each one of us and our Poor—So let us keep the joy of loving God in our hearts and Share this joy with all we meet, especially our Sisters in our Community. Keep praying for China—where we must spread the joy of loving God.

God bless you
M Teresa MC

MGL 247. 17TH DECEMBER 1993

+ LDM

Mother House
17th December 1993

My dearest Children,

This brings you Mother's love, prayer and blessing for a very happy and holy Christmas and God's blessing on 1994. Thank you for the many letters and cards bringing me your loving prayerful wishes, together with the expression of your grateful love and earnest desire to help Mother give Saints to Mother Church.

I have just returned from Europe—Rome and Poland—where we had beautiful Profession ceremonies, thank God. All our Sisters are well and doing God's work with great love. The first news that reached me on arrival in Bombay was the "going home to Jesus" of our dearest Sr. Stephen, who was one of the pioneer sisters of our recent new foundation in Alwar, Rajasthan. She expired in the early morning of 16th December. Sr. Stephen took first vows in April 1966 and has been a faithful loving Spouse of Jesus Crucified all these 27 years. She had to be taken to hospital a week before as she had a slight heart attack, from which she seemed to be recovering nicely, when on early 16th she took a bad turn. Make sure you all offer the suffrages prescribed by our Constitutions for the repose of her soul.

My Children, Jesus has said, "Repent, for the kingdom of God is at Mt 4:17
hand," and "Blessed are the pure of heart, for they shall see God". Let Mt 5:8
us, as we prepare for Christmas, make fervent Confessions, and let every

Lk 15:18 Confession be, "I will go to my Father". If we improve our daily examination of conscience, immediately we will feel the need of Jesus to forgive us; we will need Confession. Let us make this resolution for the coming New Year:

> "Fidelity to our examination of conscience,"

that we may be able to make a good, sincere, repentant, weekly Confession. Confession will make us pure of heart, and we will see God in the appearance of Bread and in the distressing disguise of the poor.[a]

I want you to take my letter of 13/12/72 and to reflect prayerfully over the part concerning the responsibility we each must share together in
Jn 15:1, 5 building up our Society as a living and fruitful branch on the Vine, Christ in His Mystical Body the Church.[b] May the New Year, 1994, be for each one of you a year of prayer, of close union with God and deep joyful charity. Be true Missionaries of Charity in words, thoughts, and deeds. Begin with your Sisters in the Community, and it will overflow on the poor.[c] Let us thank God continually for our holy vocation[d] and strive to be humble and pure like Mary so as to be Holy like Jesus.

My dearest children—keep the joy of loving Jesus in your hearts and share this joy with all you meet, especially Sisters in your Community. This will be the best gift you can give Mother for Christmas.—My prayer for each one of you is my gratitude to each one of you.

Let us pray.

God bless you
M. Teresa MC

a. See MGL 138 of 1st December 1978, pp. 248–49.
b. See MGL 97 of 13th December 1972, p. 168.
c. See MGL 44 of 1st January 1966, p. 72.
d. See MGL 45 of 6th June 1966, p. 74.

ED 63. CHRISTMAS 1993

Christmas 1993

My dearest Children,

This brings you Mother's love, blessing and prayer that you may all be one heart full of love in the heart of Jesus through Mary. May this unity and love help you become pure and humble like Mary and holy like Jesus. Humility and Purity are a sure way to Great Holiness.—To reach this holiness is Mother's prayer for each one of you, especially during this time of
Advent—time of Greater love.—Let us pray for our Society, for our Poor, Jn 15:13
for our Holy Father and for me.

God bless you all
Mother

1994

MGL 248. 7TH JANUARY 1994

+ LDM

Mother House
7th January 1994[a]

My dearest Children

This brings you Mother's love, blessing and prayer for the New Year of 1994. Today is already the 7th day of the New Year. Though you may be tired, but refreshed with the graces you have received from the Child Jesus and His Blessed Mother, I am sure you have started the year with greater love and peace, unity and joy. My prayer for each of you is that you may become holy as Jesus is holy.[b]

This year the United Nations and our Holy Father have proclaimed as the Year of the Family. Since our Society is a family, our communities are families, let us join in this spiritual celebration of the Year of the Family with our whole heart. Throughout the world there is so much disunion and suffering in families. In this Year of the Family, let us in a special way make our communities loving and united families and so overcome this disunity and lack of love. Love begins at home. Everything depends on how we love each other. Make your communities to be families of love, and then you can spread the fragrance of this love everywhere you go,[c] to all the families you visit and with whom you come in contact. I was asked to send a message for the Year of the Family, and I am enclosing a copy of that message for you. I think it will give us all much to reflect upon and pray over. I want you to help the families you visit to pray the prayer which comes at the end, so that all families may come to live in love and

a. This is an example of an "administrative/practical matters letter" that Mother wrote, probably with the help of a Councillor or a Sister responsible for some section of administration.

b. See MGL 125 of 3rd January 1977, p. 220.

c. See MGL 87 of 3rd December 1971, p. 151.

unity as God wants. For this you will need to make copies of the prayer, and translations if necessary, to give to the families.

I want to thank you for all your Christmas letters, which brought me your love and prayerful wishes and the news of all the good that God is doing in and through each one of you. I am afraid, however, that we are losing our family spirit and the joy of poverty. I do not think it is necessary to send cards and parcels to individual sisters in the communities, not even to the Councillors. One card and one common parcel for all in the community is enough to express your sisterly love. Whatever comes to Mother House for Mother is shared among all. Though I am sure you had a good intention, I ask you to stop doing this, so that we may have that family joy of sharing all things in common. Also, when letters are sent by hand, please do not write in ink on the envelope. If you will write in pencil, the envelopes can be used again and so save the expense of buying clean ones. These are little things, but by observing them we gain a great thing—fidelity and sanctity.

You must all be anxious to get the news of the incident that took place in our house in Radha Rani, Ranchi. Just after night prayer on Monday, 3rd January, a young boy who had been hiding in our compound during the day, attacked the four Sisters—. . . who were in the house—with a knife. All were badly injured. Hearing the screams of the sisters, the people around, including our leprosy patients, came to help and caught the boy and, sad to say, killed him. This boy had been with us as a small child in Bhagalpur Shishu Bhavan and was, at the time of this incident, staying with the Jesuit Fathers in a nearby Boy's Town. It seems that he had wanted to marry a girl in the neighbourhood, but that she refused to marry him. So he, in a very disturbed state of mind, took his feelings out on the sisters. Please pray and offer Holy Mass for the repose of his soul, that Our Lady may help to obtain for him forgiveness. As soon as I got the news in Mother House, I took the first flight to Ranchi. All four Sisters had been admitted in the hospital and the doctors and all concerned were so good and kind to them, including volunteering to donate the needed blood. The Archbishop too was so very concerned and visited the sisters to encourage them. What struck me most in the sisters was their peace and acceptance of what had happened. There was no trace of disturbance or bitterness on their faces or in their eyes and no one said a word against the boy who had done it. It is a great grace that God has prevented the evil of unforgiveness from entering into the hearts of the sisters, even in the midst of so much suffering. Let us thank Him for this. As I saw that the Sisters were so well taken care of, I was able to return to Mother House the next day. The good doctors assured me that the sisters would be well cared for and would be all right soon. Please be very careful in the future to keep the doors closed when you go out of the house.

On the 14th [in the] morning, I will be leaving to go to Kerala for a few days. There will be many functions there, including a meeting for youth. Please pray that all be for the glory of God. Also I want you to ask Our Lady often to help us to bring Jesus to China, Vietnam, Laos and Burma soon. Jesus must be just longing to go to these places with the Sisters. So ask Our Lady to ask Jesus to make it possible, so that through this all may come to know Jesus better, love Jesus more and serve Him in each other.

My dearest Children, keep the joy of loving Jesus in your hearts and share this joy with all you meet, especially your Community. Come to know, love and live your Constitutions and you will be Holy.

Let us pray.

God bless you
M Teresa MC

MGL 249. 24TH JANUARY 1994

+ LDM

Mother House
24th January 1994

My dearest Children,

This brings you all Mother's love, prayer and blessing that you be only all for Jesus through Mary.

I am writing to inform you that our dearest Sr. M. Mazzarello went home to Jesus on 22nd January in Nairobi. Sr. Mazzarello took her first vows in December 1992, and left India just three months ago for Africa, where she was stationed in Burundi. There she got cerebral malaria and was brought down to Nairobi, where Jesus called her to Himself. She was 25 years old. Please offer the suffrages of the Society for the repose of her soul. Jesus seems very anxious in these days to increase the number of Sisters in our community in heaven, so let us all keep ready for our transfer from time to eternity by our faithful striving for holiness.

My journey to Kerala was a real gift of God. Everything was arranged so beautifully, and the people, especially the youth, are so hungry for real holiness. Let us pray that, by God's grace, many vocations will come from the prayers and sacrifices made during this time.

Let us be humble and pure like Mary so as to be holy like Jesus. Let us pray.

God bless you
M Teresa MC

MGL 250. 29TH MARCH 1994

L.D.M.

Vietnam[a]
29th March 1994

My dearest Sr M. Frederick and all in the Mother House and the World,

This brings you all Mother's prayer, love and blessing.

I hope and pray you are all one heart full of love in the Heart of Jesus through Mary.

As this week is a special time for Jesus and for us of greater love and
greater union, let us try in a special way to come as close as [the] human
heart can come to the Heart of Jesus,[b] and try to understand as much as
possible Jesus' terrible pain caused to Him by our Sins and His Thirst for
our love.—He has never felt this pain so much as during this week so
precious for Him and for us.—No wonder it came out so clearly in the
last moments of His human life, when He said "I Thirst". Thank God Jn 19:28
Our Lady was there to understand fully the thirst of Jesus for love.—She Jn 19:25
must have straight away said "I Satiate your thirst with my love and the
suffering of my heart. Jesus, my Jesus, I love you." How clear. Her total
surrender, her loving trust must have satiated His Thirst for love, for
souls.—That is why it is very important to keep very close to our Lady as Jn 19:25–27
St. John and St. Mary Magdalen kept. Often I wonder what they felt when
they heard Jesus say "I Thirst". That is why, my Children, this week is so
important to the life of our Society and [the] reason for our existence as
MC—to satiate the thirst of Jesus on the Cross for love, for Souls, by working at the Salvation and Sanctification of the Poorest of the Poor.—Who

a. This letter was not typed but sent out to the houses in Mother's handwriting.

b. This echoes what Mother wrote to Fr. Neuner on 24th July 1967: "Father, can you explain to me—when you have time—how to grow in the deep personal union of the human heart with the Heart of Christ" (*Come Be My Light*, 257). Twenty-seven years later, Mother has the same desire.

are the Poorest of the Poor?—My Sisters, my Brothers, my Fathers, every member of our MC family.—That's where this beautiful Gift of love—of Satiating the thirst of Jesus for love for souls—begins.

That is why, my children, let us deepen our knowledge of the thirst of Jesus on the Cross, in the Eucharist and in every soul we meet, for this knowledge will help us to be holy like Jesus & Mary.

We are here in Vietnam together with Jesus and we hope today some generous friends will give us the house—where we can begin to live our normal MC life and work for the crippled children.

For China all was ready but our going was not pleasing to the devil so he tried once more to prevent it. I am sure Our Lady will help us overcome this difficulty—as She has done in all other countries.

Sr. M. Nirmala [and] I will be soon going to the South of Vietnam to receive the 20 aspirants who have so long waited for us to come. I hope some day they will come to M.H. [Mother House] also.

I hope you are all well wherever you are doing God's work with great love.—I ask you again—please for the love of God and the love for the Society take the trouble to be Holy. All for Jesus through Mary.

Holy & happy Easter to you all.

God bless you
Mother

MGL 251. [2ND APRIL 1994]

LDM

Hanoi—Vietnam[a]
Holy Saturday
[2nd April 1994]

My dearest children—Sr. M. F. [Frederick] & all,

This brings you Mother's love, gratitude and blessing for a very holy and happy Easter.

From all your letters I understand how much you pray—and we need each of your prayers.—I am sure the evil spirit is not happy that we bring Jesus to all these places—that is why he is creating all different difficulties so that we stop trying—but with God's Grace we will not stop trying to enter China.

a. This letter was not typed but sent to the houses in Mother's handwriting.

In Vietnam things are more or less arranged.—We are hoping soon we will get our own house—at present we are in a home for crippled children [over]seen by the Government. We will share in the work until we get our own house. Sr. M. Nirmala and I will go to the South of V. [Vietnam] on Monday—so that we arrange for the house and regarding the 20 Aspirants that are waiting to join us. From what I see maybe we will need 2 more Sisters—I will try to get one from [each house] in this region—as Hanoi is where we are now and this is the capital. Ho-chi-minh is the 2nd house where the girls are—in the South. I will arrange this with Sr. M. Lucina. This country is still Communist—it is a miracle we are here. Everybody is very happy and trying to help us.

Keep the joy of loving Jesus in your hearts and share this joy with all you meet and each one in the Community.

God bless you
M Teresa MC

God love you my dearest children for all the beautiful letters I have received.[a]

ED 64. EASTER 1994

Easter 1994[b]

Ek Dil Prem Pur

My dearest children,

Be one heart full of love in the Heart of Jesus through Mary. Be Holy. Only all for Jesus.

God bless you
Mother

a. This was added at the top of the page, as there was no space at the bottom.

b. This *Ek Dil* message is identical to ED 49 of Easter 1987, p. 362. As Mother was absent from Mother House (she was in Vietnam), the Sister responsible for compiling *Ek Dil* obviously selected one of Mother's previous messages for this issue.

MGL 252. 11TH MAY 1994

LDM

Mother House
11th May 1994

My dearest children,

This brings you Mother's love, blessing and prayer that you be humble and pure like Mary so that you may be holy like Jesus.

We have much to thank God for. The Professions in Calcutta were beautiful. On the evening of 10th May, 47 Tertians took their Final Vows in St. Mary's Church, and on 11th morning, 32 Novices pronounced their First Vows in Mother House chapel. Let us keep them and all the newly professed Sisters all over the world in our special prayers that they may be faithful to their Crucified Spouse.

I was supposed to leave for Belgium on the 12th to be present for the Beatification of Fr. Damien of Molokai, who spent his life working for leprosy patients. But now that Holy Father has fallen down and is in hospital with a broken hip, the Beatification has been postponed.[a] When I spoke to the Holy Father on the phone, I told him of our two new houses in Vietnam and I asked him to offer all his sufferings for China. Please pray for Holy Father and ask Fr. Damien to intercede for him to make him all right soon.

The month of June is coming soon, the month of the Sacred Heart of Jesus. In your visits to the families, try to get as many families as possible consecrated to the Sacred Heart. See that each family has a picture of the Sacred Heart and pray with them the "Family Prayer" that Mother sent you in another letter about the Year of the Family. In this month of June also, we celebrate the Feast of Corpus Christi. Naturally, our hearts and minds turn to Jesus in the Eucharist. I have said so many times that our life must be woven with the Eucharist. From Jesus in the Eucharist we learn how much God thirsts to love us and how He thirsts for our love and for the love of souls in return. From Jesus in the Eucharist we receive the light and strength to quench His Thirst by our fidelity to our MC way of life and by our wholehearted and free service of love to the poorest of the poor. We can never thank Jesus enough for this great gift of Himself to us

Mt 26:26; Mk 14:22; Lk 22:19; 1 Cor 11:24

a. Fr. Damien of Molokai, SSCC (1840–1889), was a Belgian missionary priest of the Congregation of the Sacred Hearts of Jesus and Mary who devoted his life to the care of the physical and spiritual needs of the Hawaiian lepers. Fr. Damien was beatified by Pope John Paul II in 1995 in Belgium (Mother attended the ceremony) and canonized by Pope Benedict XVI in 2009.

in the Eucharist. Let us resolve then, during this month, to be souls of the Eucharist:

- to assist at Holy Mass and make Adoration with great faith, attention, reverence and devotion,
- to often visit Jesus in the Blessed Sacrament during the day,
- and to make many Spiritual Communions, desiring to be as closely united to Jesus as possible.

This devotion to Jesus in the Eucharist has been the strength of our Society from the first Tabernacle we opened to the two newest ones in Vietnam. If we stay close to Jesus in the Eucharist, He will use us to do great things for the glory of His Father.

My children, as you may have heard already, the Holy See has recently sent out a letter to the Bishops, giving each Bishop in his own diocese the permission to allow women and girls to serve at the altar for local reasons, following Canon Law. You may have already received a circular letter from the Bishop of the Diocese regarding this. The letter of the Holy See contains some explanations to be noted:

- It says that this is a "permissive, not preceptive" ruling, in other words, that it is allowed, but not an order, to have women or girl altar servers.
- It says that it is "very appropriate to follow the noble tradition of having boys serve at the altar", as this is a rich source of vocations to the priesthood, so that there is always an "obligation to support such groups of altar boys."
- It says that liturgical actions are carried out by lay people temporarily and according to the judgment of the Bishop, so that no lay person has the right to demand to exercise them.

I want to write to you about this so as to avoid any confusion. As Missionaries of Charity, we will abide by the following directives:

1. No Sisters or candidates will serve as altar servers in our chapels or in any other church.
2. In our chapels, no women or girls will serve at the altar.
3. We do not get involved in the training of altar girls.

Mother has many reasons for giving you these directives. I am sure, if you pray about this, you will understand them. This is like the permission of the Bishops given some years ago for receiving Holy Communion in the hand. It is allowed, but not an order, and on this point you all know that, as MCs, we have chosen to receive Holy Communion on the tongue.

In a spirit of loyalty and obedience, I ask you to be faithful to these
Ps 150:6 two points regarding altar girls and the reception of Holy Communion. If questioned about these points, do not enter into discussion—"let every spirit praise the Lord"—but let us pray that all be done for the greater glory of God and the good of the Church.

I have consulted Archbishop D'Souza about this, and he has fully approved. So I ask you to pray and be faithful in following the above points.

Keep close to Mother Mary—She will help you and guide you.

God bless you
M. Teresa MC

MGL 253. 23RD SEPTEMBER 1994

LDM

Mother House
23rd September 1994

My dearest Children,

This brings you Mother's love, blessing and prayer for a Happy and Holy Feast of the Little Flower. Like her, may we learn to do little things with great love and so become saints in Mother Church.

God our Heavenly Father, the Author of Life, has deigned to choose from our MC garden another of His chosen daughters—Sr. M. Theodore—to replant in His heavenly garden, giving her eternal life on 19th September 1994. Sister's two years of physical suffering, and especially the last few days of her life spent in silent, patient suffering, have been an inspiration to each one of us. Enclosed you will find the eulogy[a] that was read at Sister's funeral Mass, which tells of her beautiful death. Please offer the suffrages of the Society for the repose of her soul immediately on receiving this letter, as some time has gone by already. Let us thank God for the gift of Sr. Theodore, both while she was with us on earth, and now that she has gone to intercede for us close to Jesus in heaven.

a. The eulogy read at Sr. Theodore's funeral Mass has been omitted.

I will be leaving for Rome on 26th September. Holy Father himself has asked me to be present during the Synod of Bishops on Religious Life. The Synod lasts from 2nd to 29th October, so I will be in Rome the whole month of October. Let us pray much and offer many sacrifices for this Synod, which is so important for all [of us] who belong to Jesus in the Religious Life, and for the whole Church. Ask Mary, Mother of Jesus, to be a Mother to all the Bishops at the Synod and to help them to lead us all to Jesus.

She went home to God with a Smile—as She lived so she died. One of the Sisters asked her how much you are suffering—She [just] gave a Simple answer, "This is a Secret between Jesus and me".—So let us thank God for His love. Let us pray.

God bless you
M. Teresa MC

MGL 254. 1st NOVEMBER 1994

LDM

Rome
1st November 1994[a]

My dearest children
all in the Society,

I am writing you from the Synod on Religious life in Rome. My prayer is that we become true Missionaries of love—for Jesus, for the Poor, and for one another.

How precious and beautiful is our Vocation. As I wrote you already, our Charism is the only thing that keeps us going as a Society; I hope you are still praying over these letters of Mother.

I have been so pleased with all your letters in response. So many are taken up with coming closer to the thirst of Jesus—such consolation to Mother's heart.

a. Mother must have written this letter in various stages, as there are three different dates at the top of the letter. However, she crossed them out (e.g., ~~29/Oct/94~~ is readable) and wrote underneath the new date, 1st November. The letter was not typed but sent out to the houses in Mother's handwriting. Since this letter was born of controversy and added to it, something of the circumstances of its origin should be stated. Fr Joseph had received a typed letter signed by Mother expressing some points of disagreement with what the Fathers were doing (e.g., travel) and, more seriously, were supposedly teaching and encouraging the Sisters to do (e.g., extra prayer time). Mother's letter was very hurtful to Fr. Joseph and the senior Fathers, and Mother was extremely mortified by the fact the letter had been given. This letter was Mother's response written with the input of Fr. Joseph.

I want to share with you a few things, Jesus wants to tell us. Some have come to my mind during the Synod, others I have been praying over for long time, specially reading your letters to Mother.

In the Synod I see what great needs [there are] in religious life today, what difficulties. For the sake of the Church we must be ready to face and meet these needs wherever we see them, beginning in our own Society.

In your letters I see the great good that comes from learning to love and live our charism. Please do all you can to keep this desire alive. Find ways to encourage and share with one another.

Your letters tell also the pain many carry. Let us not lose hope but find help. Let us help and not hurt each other—so many carrying the crosses. Please know Mother is with you and Jesus will never leave you. Too many carry fear in their soul—this is not Mother's spirit. No one should feel forced to open their conscience outside confession. Or fear that what is told will be used against them, or shared with others. Let us respect each one as God Himself does. Only the feeling [that] we are precious and respected not only by God but by each other can bring trust—loving trust in one another. Never pass remarks about Sisters seeking help from those priests we know and trust, spending what time they need in confessional with Jesus, the doctor of Souls. All these things are against the mind of the Church, and against the Heart of Jesus.

Let us encourage and not discourage others from spending some time, even only few minutes a day, in private prayer alone with Jesus. This has renewed the spiritual life of so many. It is not harming the work. Ten minutes alone with Jesus every day will take nothing from the work—just the opposite: it will bless and add to the work. Also it will strengthen the Community in trials and temptation. Our work [is] MC only if we pray the work.
Lk 11:1 "Teach us to pray" they said to Jesus—we cannot learn to pray the work if we do not learn to pray, and we cannot learn to pray, if we do not take the time to make community prayer and [be] in touch with Jesus; we need each one to take some time alone in [the] presence of Jesus. Remember what Mother says so often, "What blood is to the body, Prayer is to the soul."

This is no danger of leading us to question our call to the MC life. On the contrary, [it] is to save our active vocation. We cannot be contemplatives in the heart of the world if we are not first contemplative in our own hearts. So many have been saved in their Vows, helped to forgive, to be healed, to grow in holiness and zeal for the work by this one thing. The time may be more or less, according to [the] need of each one and the Community—but ten minutes with Jesus will destroy nothing in the work or Community but [the] devil's traps. If ever there was a time when we need more prayer in the world and the Society it is now. Often we have chance for 10 minutes with Jesus if we only make use of them. The time has come to pray better and to pray more.

From what the Sisters have told me of the spiritual help they have received from our MC Fathers' retreats and spiritual guidance, I know it is given in our same spirit and vocation. They will help us grow in holiness as the Church has asked us to do during the Synod. Maybe [the] Fathers will not always be able to answer all our requests—but, I am sure with God's blessing and Our Lady's love for them and for us, all will be well.

Keep the joy of loving Jesus and Mary in your hearts and share this joy with your Sisters in the Community, the Poor you serve and all you meet.

Be only all for Jesus through Mary.

Be Holy.

God bless you
M Teresa MC

MGL 255. 17TH DECEMBER 1994

LDM

Mother House
17th December 1994

My dearest Children,

This brings you Mother's love, prayer and blessing for a Happy and Holy Christmas and a Bright and Blessed New Year of 1995. When we look at the crib, we see how God uses weakness and humility to do great things. So let us not be afraid to be small and humble like the Baby Jesus so that God's greatness can shine through us.

I am writing this to inform you that our dearest Sr. M. Sebastian, MC, has gone home to Jesus. Sr. Sebastian (Blandina Beng) was born on 10-3-39, and made her first profession in April of 1965. She died of a stroke in the hospital in Bhilai at 2:00 A.M. on 14th December 1994. She was a very peaceful, simple and holy Sister and it was a pleasure to live with her in community. Please offer the suffrages of the Society as given in our Spiritual Directory for the repose of her soul. May she rest in peace.

I was supposed to go to Vietnam in December, but now the government people themselves want to receive me, and so they have asked me to go in January instead. Please keep Mother's intentions in your daily prayers, especially China.

God bless you
M Teresa, MC

ED 65. CHRISTMAS 1994

Christmas 1994

My dearest Children all over the world,

Keep the joy of loving Jesus in your hearts and share this joy with all you meet, especially your Community.

Happy and Holy Christmas and New Year.

God bless you
M. Teresa, MC

1995

MGL 256. 24TH FEBRUARY 1995

LDM

Mother House
24th February 1995

My dearest Children,

This brings you Mother's love, prayer and blessing. Thank you for all your loving letters received during the Christmas Season, bringing me your love and prayers together with your sincere desire to grow in holiness—to be only all for Jesus through Mary—and so satiate the Thirst of Jesus on the Cross for love and for souls. As it is not possible for me to an- Jn 19:28
swer each one individually, this comes to tell each one of you how much you are in Mother's love and prayer.

It is my love for you in Jesus that suffers so deeply when I come to know of certain things that are going on in some communities, which hurt the Heart of Jesus so much and are also so harmful to your vocation, and which, sooner or later, could lead to the loss of the beautiful gift of your vocation to the life of a Missionary of Charity. Our beautiful Constitutions are the gift of God's Thirsting Love for us to help us free ourselves for a life of deep intimacy with Jesus. How deeply a Sister harms herself when she deliberately chooses to do things contrary to what God, in His Thirsting Love for us, has planned for our life of holiness. Superiors, as good shepherds, are gifts of God to the community. They have been entrusted with Divine Authority to help you grow in the Spirit of our Society so clearly brought out in our Constitutions. Their first responsibility is to lead you to know, love and live the Constitutions. This they do by their example first, and also by their firm loving guidance and, when necessary, gentle motherly correction. As our Constitutions say, the greatest service a Superior can render to the Community consists in living the Spirit of the Society and making it possible for the Sisters to live the life of true Missionaries of Charity. Take up again my letters of January and February 1961[a] that will help you realize better why fidelity to our Constitutions is the most precious and delicate flower of love we religious can give to Jesus.[119]

During the season of Lent, let us keep close to Our Lady and ask her to lead us to understand more deeply the true meaning of the sufferings Jesus endured for our sins. Constitution no. 164 will help us prepare ourselves to live Lent fruitfully. Each community must take those points for particular examen:

A more profound spirit of:

–silence	–recollection	–prayer
–penance	–asceticism of loving and serving one another with God's own love	

Throughout the six weeks of Lent we will also take for our daily spiritual reading and Thursday meditations the following chapters in our *Constitution* and *Directory*:

Ash Wed.	Chapter 2	Our Patroness
Week 1	Chapter 17	Silence and Aloneness with God
Week 2	Chapter 16	Prayer and Contemplation
Week 3	Chapter 18	The Cross—No Greater Love
Week 4	Chapter 9	Consecrated Obedience
Week 5	Chapter 11	Community Life
Week 6	Chapter 13	Our Missionary Apostolate

Let us resolve to live a fervent, fruitful Lent that will lead us to true repentance for our lack of loving fidelity to our Constitutions, and [lead us] to experience the merciful Thirsting Love of Jesus. Deepen your prayer life and you will find the light and love you need to satiate the Thirst of Jesus.

I want you to pray much for the Church, also in India, where today the teachings of our Faith regarding women priests are being openly and strongly opposed even by a certain group of nuns in India. I am enclosing a clear explanation of the teaching of the Church, giving the reasons why, according to God's plan, women can never become priests. Read it

a. See MGL 5 of [6th] January 1961, pp. 12–13, and MGL 6 of [3rd] February 1961, pp. 13–15.

carefully and pray over it so that you also will be convinced of the teaching of our Faith on this point, so as not to let yourself be caught by those who spread false teaching. Please be very careful also regarding the choice of priests to give retreats, seminars and spiritual help. We must pray much for priests, bishops and religious that they remain faithful to the teachings of the Church.

Our dearest Sr. Deepali, a Finally Professed Sister who had spent many years working among the poorest of the poor in Ethiopia, went home to Jesus on the 18th February. Last year she returned to Calcutta from Mekale where she was Superior, to undergo treatment for a cancerous tumour in the breast. She went to Bombay for treatment and seemed to be doing well for a few months. Then she started to complain of severe headaches. The diagnosis showed that she had developed a cancerous tumour in the brain. She was operated upon, but cancer had affected the brain. She suffered much, but prayer and the love and concern of the Sisters in Bombay helped her to accept it all in union with the sufferings of Jesus, offering all for three intentions:

- for the doors of China to open,
- in reparation for the sins of abortion,
- for the holiness of our Society.

She expired very peacefully, surrounded by the community Sisters, at 4:00 in the morning and was buried in the cemetery at the back of St. Francis Xavier's Church. Make sure to offer the suffrages prescribed by our Directory for the repose of her soul.

Ask Our Lady to help you understand, love and put into living action this letter so full of love and hope, that it will help us to be pure and humble like Mary so that we become holy like Jesus.—Let us pray.

God bless you
M. Teresa, MC

MGL 257. [16TH APRIL] 1995

+ LDM

Mother House
Easter
[16th April] 1995

My dearest Children,

This brings you Mother's love, prayer and blessing for a Happy and Holy Easter to each one of you. May the joy and the love of the Risen Jesus be always with you and in you and among you—so that we all become the
Jn 3:16 true witnesses of His Father's love for the world. "For God so loved the world that He gave His Son". Let us also love God so much that we give ourselves to Him in each other and in His poor.[a]

For a long time I have been wanting to write this letter to you. I do hope each one of you will not [just] read it and forget it, but will listen to what God is telling us, reflect over it prayerfully, so as to allow the grace of God to help each one see where and how more faithful loving care must be taken to protect the beautiful spirit of our Society. Prayer and penance will always help us to be more faithful.

As we will be having our General Chapter next year, and a General Chapter is meant to lead us to examine ourselves on how faithfully we are living up to what God expects from us, individually and as a Society, I want, in this letter, to draw your attention in a special way to our Vow of Poverty and to our 4th Vow of wholehearted and free service to the poorest of the poor, among whom, let us not forget, are our own Sisters.

Because people in the world have been so deeply touched by our humble works of love in action that bring God's tender love and concern to the unloved, the uncared for, the destitutes, this has created in the hearts of so many the deep desire to share; some do so out of their abundance, but many, and maybe the greater number, by depriving themselves of something they would have liked to give themselves, so as to be able to share with their less privileged brothers and sisters. It is so beautiful to see the spirit of sacrifice finding its way into many lives, for this not only benefits the poor who receive, but the giver is also being enriched with the love of God. This is something for which we must constantly praise and thank God, but we must also deepen our awareness of the great responsibility that is ours as guardians of what Divine Providence entrusts to us

a. See MGL 106 of Easter [14th April] 1974, p. 185.

for the poor. We are not owners, but guardians. Only deep prayer and [a] true spirit of sacrifice will protect us from [the] danger of mishandling or misusing the goods God entrusts to us for His poor. Our Vow of Poverty faithfully lived is also a great protection.

To protect ourselves from being deceived by our pride that craves for riches and power, and by the deceitful suggestions of the devil, I want you to examine yourselves on the following:

- Great care must be taken of whatever goods are brought to us. This will mean taking trouble not to let things go to waste, whether it be food, medicine, clothing, furniture, etc.
- Do not accumulate and stock goods (food, medicines, etc) unnecessarily and let things go bad or out of date and only then give them out to the poor. Remember the words of Jesus: "Whatever you do to the least of my brethren, you do to Me." Food, medicine, Mt 25:40 clothing, must be made available to the poor person in need. All these things could easily become the devil's net to catch us and lead us astray, if we are not prayerful. How easily the attitude of "mine" and "thine" can deprive the poor of what they have a right to receive from us.
- We have not made a vow of economy but a vow of poverty. Therefore, like Jesus, who chose poverty for freedom's sake, we also choose to do without things, comforts or entertainments we could have had—such as fans, radios, tape-recorders, cameras, televisions, wrist-watches, suitcases, flasks, tiffin carriers, luxury food, etc. All these things, which are not bad in themselves, we freely chose to give up on the day we pronounced our vows for greater freedom, to be able to cling with undivided heart to Jesus. Why then do we now "look for substitutes which restore to us the wealth we chose to renounce," as Pope Paul VI once said.[a] Let each one examine herself on this point.

  Be very careful about travelling. Sisters, including Superiors, must not go from one house to another distant house without the permission of the Regional Superior, and permission must be granted only when absolutely necessary. No Sister, including Superiors, must go out alone (Const. 105). Also, so many Sisters are now going on

a. See the "Address of Paul VI to the National Federation of the Italian Clergy," 30 June 1965, http://www.vatican.va/content/paul-vi/it/speeches/1965/documents/hf_p-vi_spe_19650630_clero-italiano.html.

home visit out of time and taking with them big boxes of all kinds of things intended for the poor. This must stop.

- Very strict account must be kept of monies received and spent. Do not use money at random, nor give money or things to your own people. Be happy to seize the opportunity to say "May I have."
- Be very careful not to allow partialities to spoil the beautiful work of love God has entrusted to us—giving in to likes and dislikes, treating differently people of different caste or creed. This could easily happen if we do not pray the work, doing it with Jesus, to Jesus and for Jesus. Only then the aim of our apostolate will be "to reveal and to communicate God's life to all men" (Const. 99) of whatever race, caste or creed. Also if you allow this partiality attitude to affect your dealings with the poor, it will also show itself in your dealings with your Sisters in community and be a cause of much disunity. I am sad to say that some volunteers have expressed to me their disappointment at certain un-Christlike ways shown by certain Sisters towards the poor. Learn to pray the work, and this will not happen.
- Cling to the humble works of the Society for the poorest of the poor. Our "homes" must be kept clean and tidy, but simple and humble. Our poor, sick and dying patients must be given tender care; the old, disabled or mentally sick inmates must be treated with dignity and
Mt 25:40 respect, always keeping in mind Jesus' words: "Whatever you do to the least of my brethren, you do it to Me." We must constantly beg Jesus to grant us deep Faith to be able to see the value of humble works which, when done willingly and cheerfully, reveal love and increase love. Though we need the help of outsiders, there could be a danger of our Sisters becoming just supervisors. Grab the opportunity to do the humble work that always reveals love.
- I am afraid Sisters in some communities are spending more of their interest and time on cows, goats, rabbits, pigs and ducks rather than on caring for the poor entrusted to us. I would be happy if these animals were kept only in leprosy rehabilitation centres and in isolated places difficult for co-workers to reach you or for marketing. Let us not weaken our trust in Divine Providence.
- Why are relatives and friends of Superiors and Sisters now kept in our homes for several days or even weeks? This means that time that Sisters should be giving to our poor people is spent entertaining visitors and preparing meals for them. What about our vow of whole-hearted and free service to the poorest of the poor? Please see

that this does not continue. We are normally allowed visits from our family members on the first Sunday of every month, which is also when we write our home letter.

Together with this letter I would like Superiors to read and reflect upon two of my letters to Superiors dated July 1983 and Feb. 1988, which you will find in the booklet "Feed My Lambs."[a] Do this before the Blessed Sacrament, keeping close to Our Lady, who will obtain for you the graces you need to keep faithful to the spirit of our Society and to help the Sisters entrusted to your care to do the same and so satiate the Thirst of Jesus on Jn 19:28
the Cross for love and for souls.

You will all be very happy to know that we have been able to give Jesus nine more Tabernacles where He will be loved and adored, since the last Professions in December. Outside India, the new houses are located in Hosororo in British Guyana, Puno in Peru, Esperanza in Ecuador (all of which are in South America), Tacloban in Philippines, Dwellar in Syria, Dareton in Australia, and Niamey in Niger (West Africa). In India we now have a second house in Pune, and very soon our first house in Mangalore will open. This brings the total number of our houses to:

Active Branch
In India 185 + Abroad 356 = Total 541
Contemplative Branch
In India 2 + Abroad 13 = Total 15
Grand total of houses in both branches—**556**

All these houses have been divided into 43 regions, including the newest region in South Italy with Sr. M. Prema as Regional.

By the grace of God and Our Lady's pleading, we now have 15 houses in Russia—the 15 Mysteries of the Rosary which I had promised to Our Lady in Russia, [are] now completed. How God uses our nothingness to show forth His greatness! Now please pray much for Vietnam, and specially for China so that Mother may bring Jesus to the people there.

Keep very close to Jesus and Mary and let us try to learn from Our Lady to be Pure, through Charity, and humble like Her so that we can become Holy like Jesus. Let us pray.

God bless you
M. Teresa, MC

a. The booklet *Feed My Lambs* is the collection of Mother's letters to the Superiors.

ED 66. MAY 1995

May 1995

Keep the joy of loving Jesus in your hearts and share this joy with your Community and the Poor You Serve. Be His love—His Compassion, His Presence to Your Sisters.

Be Holy.

God bless you
M. Teresa, MC

MGL 258. 15TH MAY 1995

LDM

Mother House
15th May 1995

My dearest Children,

This brings you Mother's love, prayer and blessing that the beautiful month of June, month of God's thirsting love for us, be truly a month of true love, reparation and forgiveness. Try to make your Community a
Mk 6:31 place where our Lord can "come apart and rest a while" with you. Make a real effort to get rid of all uncharitable words and thoughts. Also try to get as many families as possible consecrated to the Sacred Heart.[a]

In view of our forthcoming Seventh General Chapter in October 1996, please God, I would like you to read prayerfully the rules concerning the General Chapter in our Constitutions nos. 170–173. As we have it stated in our Directory no. 93a: "The entire Society will join in preparation for the General Chapter through fervent prayer, penance, study and reflection."

I would like this preparatory work to be carried out with one clear
Jn 19:28 purpose in view—"To satiate the Thirst of Jesus on the Cross for our love and for love of souls," which is the aim of our Society. How truly aware are we of the greatness of our vocation? How sincere are we in our earnest striving to live the aim of our Society? This aim can be realized only by our loving fidelity in seeking to know, love and live our Constitutions and Directory more sincerely, as they are the clear expression of God's loving will for us to lead us to holiness. There is no other way for us as Missionaries of Charity to fulfil the aim of our Society.

a. See MGL 92 of 1st June 1972, p. 160.

As our Constitutions have already been given final approval by the Holy See, this General Chapter will not be so much concerned with changes to be made in the Constitutions, but it is meant to be a sincere examination of conscience for each one of us that will help us see:

- whether we have been loyal to the Society and appreciative of the great gift of our Constitutions as means leading to holiness,
- or whether we have neglected these means by our infidelities, and determine to make this preparation to our Chapter a time of revival of our beautiful spirit of Loving Trust, Total Surrender, and Cheerfulness.

This preparatory work is very important to help the delegates to the Chapter see clearly the strengths and weaknesses in our living as true Missionaries of Charity, so that the delegates may know what the Holy Spirit is saying through your contribution and with prayer respond in the right way. Allow the Holy Spirit in prayer to help you see the importance of your contribution which must go beyond personal likes and dislikes, so as to focus on the good of the whole Society. We all know how much good God has been working in us and through us all these years in spite of our nothingness and weakness. So the preparation of the General Chapter must also lead us to proclaim these marvels to the praise and glory of God.

Let us all be very much aware of the responsibility we must all share together in building up our Society as a living and fruitful branch on the Jn 15:5
Body of Christ—the Church. Each one of us owes this sharing of responsibility through the Society to the Church.[a] The best one to help us with this is Our Lady. It was at her pleading that the Society was born and by her continual intercession it has grown up. Now it is up to us to plead with her to obtain for us the graces to be the Society that she had in her Immaculate Heart from the beginning and that she pleaded would be born in the Church.

I am sending you a kind of guiding questionnaire to help you with this preparatory work for our General Chapter. It would be good if each community would prayerfully study, reflect, and examine together upon how and why the various aspects of our life as Missionaries of Charity have or have not helped us to fulfil the aim of our Society.

We will spend one full year in this prayerful preparation, beginning

a. See MGL 97 of 13th December 1972, p. 168.

from June 1995. Be sure to make this preparation a prayer, for prayer gives
Mt 5:8 a clean heart, and a clean heart will clearly see the wonderful works of
God's love and our sincere response to His love. Pray and reflect individually on the Chapters of the Constitutions and Directory assigned for each period of time, and prepare any suggestions you may have. It would be good if, for each topic, you could come together as a community to share your insights. Any suggestions should reach Mother House by the month of June 1996. It will be necessary for each individual Sister to have a copy of the preparation to guide her reflections.

My dearest children—pray and allow Jesus to fill you with His love and humility so that all you do for the General Chapter be done for the Glory of God and the good of Our Society. Let us pray.

God bless you
M. Teresa, MC

MGL 259. 26TH JUNE 1995

L.D.M.

26th June 1995

My dearest Sisters,

May the Love and Peace of the Heart of Jesus fill your hearts during this time of Grace.

In your prayer try to get as close to Jesus' Heart to know Him, to love
Jn 19:28 Him better and to serve Him better by satiating His Thirst for love, for
Souls. Ask Our Lady to be a Mother to you during these days of Grace.—
Make a strong resolution to be really holy.

Let us pray.

God bless you
M. Teresa, MC

MGL 260. 9TH AUGUST 1995

+ LDM

Mother House
9th August 1995

My dearest Children,

This brings you Mother's love, prayer and special blessing for our Society Feast—the Feast of the Immaculate Heart of Mary. In these days when we celebrate the two beautiful feasts of Our Lady, of her Assumption and of her Immaculate Heart, let us pray much for our Society and for each other, that we may know better the Spirit of our Society, love it and live it more fruitfully.

We all know that Our Lady was the first Missionary of Charity. She
was so humble, so pure, so free that when the angel came to her there was Lk 1:26–38
nothing to stop her from saying "Yes" and giving herself fully to God's
plan. And immediately, as soon as she received Jesus within her, she ran in Lk 1:39–56
haste to give Him to Elizabeth and little John by works of humble service. Beautiful!

Our Lady was the first Missionary of Charity, but now she is followed by so many other Missionaries of Charity, each one of us. It is not enough for us just to admire Our Lady, not even to love her, but by God's Grace and with her help, we must become like her. Let us make the strong resolution to imitate Mary's humility and purity so that we are ever ready to
do God's will with a smile. Whenever we say "Yes" like she did, the love of Lk 1:39
Jesus, who dwells in our hearts, will move us also to run in haste to give His love to the poorest of the poor through the humble works of the Society. Mary's heart was immaculate, full of undivided love for God. When our love for Jesus is undivided, we are true Missionaries of Charity.

So many of you have written Mother beautiful letters telling how you are being helped through the preparation for the General Chapter next year. Let us thank God for this gift. It is wonderful to hear how so many of you are seeing the connection between our Constitutions and the Bible, the catechism, and the teachings of our Holy Father. I pray that this will lead each one of us to deepen our love for the Constitutions so that we can become holy by living them. I hope you have already begun to pray fervently for the General Chapter, each one by herself. In my next letter I will tell you more about what you must pray and sacrifice for as a community. Jesus is asking great things from our Society at this Chapter, and our hearts must be very pure to be able to hear Him speak and to answer with

Mt 5:8 our whole heart. So pray, pray much and fervently, for prayer gives a clean heart, and a clean heart can see God and hear Him speak.

Our Lady is giving us the great joy of giving one more Tabernacle to Jesus in Mangalore. Tomorrow I am leaving for Bombay, and then I will go on to Mangalore. We will be having the opening and blessing of the house on Our Lady's day, 15th August. With Mangalore we will have 561 Tabernacles altogether, in 121 countries, and 3,604 Professed Sisters serving Jesus in the Society. How good God has been to us! When we look at ourselves, who would think of all this? But Jesus loves to use our nothingness to show forth His greatness.

You will also be happy to know that last time I was in the United States, I was able, by God's grace, to open the new house for the adoption of unwanted babies in Washington, DC. Everyone was so happy to think that we will be able to fight abortion with adoption just in that place. So many families are ready to share the joy of loving with a child. Mrs. Clinton was also there for the opening, and she is giving us her full support. Please pray that this place becomes a real centre for radiating the love of Jesus all over America.[a]

Also pray very specially for our sick Sisters. Sr. Priscilla is having serious problems with her back, so I have sent her to New York for the necessary treatment. She should be coming back, please God, by the end of September. Sr. Magdalena, who is now in Bombay, is suffering so much with cancer. Perhaps she will soon be carrying the message to Jesus about Mother's wish to go to China. Sr. Conrad was also nearly paralyzed, but after her operation is a little better. In Shishu Bhavan we have a regular community for the sick Sisters. Just now the permanent members of the upstairs community are Sr. Sylvette and Sr. Delphinus, but there are also a lot of "changes" as Sisters come and go for operations and different treatment. Real MC!

Keep the joy of loving Jesus in your hearts and share this love and joy with each other and make your Community Something beautiful for God.

Let us pray.

God bless you
M. Teresa, MC

a. This house was opened on 19th June 1995, but was closed on 13th June 2013 because the government regulations imposed made it impossible to function.

MGL 261. 7TH SEPTEMBER 1995

LDM

Mother House
7th September 1995

My dearest Children,

This comes to inform you that our dearest Sr. M. Magdalena, MC, has gone home to Jesus at 12:15 A.M., this morning of 7th September. Sr. Magdalena took her First Vows in the Society on 24th May 1969, and served Jesus in her Sisters and the poor with faithfulness and love all these years, having also been Regional Superior of Australia and Papua New Guinea. She suffered much in these last days, but always did so courageously, keeping her eyes on Jesus. She had been in Bombay for treatment, and it was from there that Jesus took her home. As she was a deeply spiritual Sister, I know that her prayers in heaven will be of great value to the Society. Please offer the suffrages of the Society for the repose of her soul, according to Directory no. 47.

Be only all for Jesus through Mary. Let us pray.

God bless you
M. Teresa, MC

MGL 262. 27TH SEPTEMBER 1995

LDM

Mother House
27th September 1995

My dearest Children,

This comes to inform you that our dearest Sr. M. Jeevithanjali, MC, has gone home to Jesus at 7:45 A.M. this morning of Wednesday, 27th September 1995, in Budapest, Hungary. Sr. Jeevithanjali (Nirmala Kullu) was born on 19th November 1971 in Orissa. As a First Year Novice, she went to the Noviciate in Poland. She made her First Profession in Poland on 8th December 1991, and would have renewed her vows for the fourth time this coming December. Some time ago Sr. Jeevithanjali was diagnosed with T.B. [tuberculosis], and it was later discovered that it was T.B./meningitis. She suffered very bravely and cheerfully, and was an inspiration to all in her last illness. May she rest in peace. Please offer the suffrages of the Society for the repose of her soul, according to Directory no. 47.

Mt 24:36, 25:13; Mk 13:32 As we know neither the day nor the hour, let us keep our hearts clean and free and ready to meet Jesus when He comes to call. Be only all for Jesus through Mary. Let us pray.

Let us all try to love Jesus with Greater love and be more and more His Love, His Compassion, His Presence in our Communities, for we do not know when He will come.

God bless you
M. Teresa, MC

MGL 263. 7TH OCTOBER 1995

LDM

Mother House
7th October 1995

My dearest Children,

This brings you Mother's love, prayer and blessing, and also a big thank you for your letters and cards bringing me your loving, prayerful wishes for Society Feast and for Mother's feast—days of grace and unity.
Lk 1:38 Your spiritual bouquets are very precious to me, as they are the source of much grace which is so necessary to always say "Yes" to God's will as Our Lady did.

In this letter I want to ask you to pray fervently and make many little sacrifices for our Chapter General, which will be held on 7th October 1996.

This letter comes to you from Mother's heart, after much prayer and sacrifice. Today is the 7th of October, the 45th Anniversary of the Erection of our Society, and also one year before the date fixed for our General Chapter. How grateful we all must be to God and to the Church for the many, many graces that have been showered upon our Society during these 45 years, and let us entrust this coming year, preparatory to our Chapter, to the Immaculate Heart of Mary, and let us ask her to obtain for us the grace of a pure and humble heart that will enable us, when the time comes to choose the delegates, that we choose Sisters who, before God, we think will best work for the true good of our Society, according to the gift of God entrusted to the Society.

The role of the delegates at the Chapter is very important, as it includes the election of the Superior General and the Councillors General.

My dearest Children, before God I urge you to obey very strictly what is said in no. 178 of our Constitutions, where we read:

> In all elections, those voting are to avoid any abuse or preference of persons. They are to have nothing but God and the good of the Society before their eyes, and elect those whom, in the Lord, they know to be worthy and fitting. They are to avoid directly or indirectly lobbying (influencing others) for votes, either for themselves or for others (Canon 626).

I do sincerely believe, before God, that the time has come for me to hand over the governance of the Society to the one whom God has in mind, and it is right and also my heartfelt desire that this takes place during my lifetime. The Society is not mine; it is God's work entrusted in a special way to the care and protection of the Immaculate Heart of Mary. I am fully confident that what God has done in and through me, He will continue to do in and through the one who takes over, if we remain faithful to the aim and spirit of the Society. "Do not be afraid," Jesus said again and again to His Apostles. If we really pray, Jesus will be with us and protect the Society from anything that may destroy this gift of our vocation to the Society.

Mt 14:27; 17:7; Mk 5:36, 6:50; Lk 5:10, 8:50, 12:7; Jn 6:20

I ask each Regional to send in, after the December changes, the list of the Finally Professed Sisters in your region, with the date of their birth and of their First Profession. Let me also know the total number of Sisters in your region. This information should reach me by the end of January. This will enable me, with my Councillors, to prepare the papers necessary for the voting for the delegates in each region, which I will send to you in February. I would like the voting in the houses to take place on 25th March—the Feast of the Annunciation.

Meanwhile we will pray the prayer to the Holy Spirit for our General Chapter after Mass and Communion prayers and also at Adoration. We must especially pray that the Holy Spirit will be with us when we choose the delegates for the Chapter.

Please do not speak to anybody outside about the Chapter. Keep it within the family. Let us prepare sincerely, and seek only God's will.[a] Let us offer everything to Jesus, every joy, sorrow, humiliation, discomfort, for the Chapter as our preparation.

Let us pray in a special way to Our Lady to guide us and help us to know the

a. See MGL 217 of [after 25th] February 1990 , p. 398.

will of God, and put it into life—so that all be for the Glory of God and for our Society's Good.

This preparation must be strictly private & without any discussion with anyone outside the Society.

Let us pray.

God has taken such tender care of our Society, I am sure He will continue to do so.

God bless you
M. Teresa, MC

ED 67. DECEMBER 1995

December 1995

Happy and Holy Christmas and God's blessing on 1996.

Let us keep the joy of loving Jesus in our hearts and share this joy with all we meet, especially our Sisters in our Community and the Poor we serve. Be Holy.

God bless you.
M. Teresa, MC

1996

MGL 264. 26TH JANUARY 1996

LDM

Mother House
26th January 1996

My dearest Children,

This brings you Mother's love, prayer and blessing that you may be only all for Jesus through Mary.

This letter comes to inform you that our dearest Sr. Sylvette, MC, went home to Jesus on 25th January 1996 at about 8:30 P.M. from our Shishu Bhavan house here in Calcutta. Sr. Sylvette (Marcella Tirkey) was born on 11th February 1951 in Jalpaiguri. She made her First Vows in the Society on 3rd December 1979 and Final Vows on 8th December 1985. During her Juniorate, Sr. Sylvette was in Sagar and after Final Vows was assigned to Ethiopia, where she gave years of dedicated service to the poorest of the poor. She fell ill and returned to Calcutta in September 1994 for treatment, where it was discovered that she had advanced cancer.

Sr. Sylvette suffered greatly for this long period of more than a year, but did so beautifully—all for Jesus. Everyone who met her remarked on her big smile and cheerful self-giving. As she was dying, Mother and the whole community of Shishu Bhavan were around her praying with her. She went home peacefully to Jesus, who will receive her with great tenderness. Sr. Sylvette was buried today, 26th January, in the cemetery of St. John's Church, Calcutta. Please offer the suffrages of the Society for the repose of her soul.

Let us pray for the repose of the soul of our Sister. She has been a beautiful example of simple love.

God bless you
M. Teresa, MC

MGL 265. 1st FEBRUARY 1996

LDM

Mother House
1st February 1996—Decree of Praise

My dearest Children,

This letter brings you Mother's love, prayer and blessing that we may
be true spouses of Jesus Crucified. By the time this reaches you, Lent will
be beginning. Do not let this Lent go by just like that. No, this Lent
Mt 26–27; Mk 14–15; must be a special time, a time to learn to share the Passion of Jesus. We
Lk 22–23; Jn 18–19 are meant to satiate the Thirst of Jesus, and this Thirst was revealed to us
Jn 19:28 from the Cross. We cannot know or satiate the Thirst of Jesus if we do not
know, love and live the Cross of Jesus. It is not enough just to suffer. We
must be united with Jesus in our suffering, with our hearts full of love for
the Father and love for souls, as His was. Let us ask Our Lady to teach us
Jn 19:25 this. She stood by the Cross of Jesus and shared His Passion fully with her
whole heart. She did it all willingly and for souls. She will help us in our
strong resolution this Lent to be only all for Jesus, our Crucified Spouse.

With this letter I enclose the voting papers for each Professed of your community and a list of all the Finally Professed in your region who are eligible to be voted for as delegate to the Chapter.

Superiors, as soon as you get this letter, please read it carefully with the community and put it on the board with the list of names, for the community to see and pray and reflect on.

The voting will be done everywhere in the Society on 25th March, Feast of the Annunciation. I will be happy if nine days before, we begin a novena to Our Lady, asking her to guide us all to vote for the Sister whom she wants to be your delegate to the Chapter. I beg you all to remember—do not allow the spirit of the world to influence us, nor should we try to influence each other. The Society belongs to Jesus. We must seek only His Will and, through prayer, try to find the person He has chosen. Read carefully Constitutions 175 and 176 during the Novena....

I am enclosing a booklet on the patrimony of our Society that, I hope, will help us better know and love the spiritual riches found in our Constitutions so that we may live them more faithfully. This booklet can help each one of us to carry out the duty and privilege of preparing ourselves for the General Chapter. Part of this preparation must be a sincere examination of how we are living our Constitutions. If any practice or negligence is creeping in that threatens to harm the patrimony, this should be brought out, in a spirit of love for the Society, in the contributions sent to the Chapter. Likewise the many ways in which, by God's grace, the patrimony is being lived beautifully should be proclaimed for the glory of God.

No Sister who loves the Society can exempt herself from sharing in this important responsibility. Study, prayer and reflection on the patrimony as found in our Constitutions are necessary if we are to make suggestions in accord with the purposes of a Chapter in the mind of the Church. The question guiding our contributions is not to be: "What would I like?", but rather, "Does this protect and develop the patrimony?" The contributions of each one can bring great light to the Chapter. Following the guidance of Directory no. 93a, let us implore the Holy Spirit, through the powerful intercession of Our Lady, for His light and power to guide and purify us all.

Today is 1st February, the anniversary of the day on which our Society received the Decree of Praise. As we thank Jesus for this gift we have received from His Church, let us determine to be even more faithful to our MC way of life, which the Church tells us can lead us and our poor to great holiness. May Mary, Mother of the Church, be a Mother to us specially in these important days.

Think and Pray that you understand the will of God and [have] the joy to do it.
Let us pray.

God bless you
M Teresa MC

MGL 266. 29TH MARCH 1996

LDM

Mother House
29th March 1996

My dearest Children, Sisters, Brothers and Fathers,

This brings each one of you Mother's love, prayer and blessing, together with my fervent wishes for a Happy and Holy Easter.

As Holy Week draws near, let us ask Our Lady, as we contemplate the Passion of Jesus, to obtain for each one of us the graces we need to understand more clearly the words of Jesus to the disciples of Emmaus, "Was it Lk 24:26
not necessary that the Christ should suffer these things and so enter into Mt 26–27; Mk 14–15; Lk 22–23; Jn 18–19
His glory?"Remember that the Passion of Christ always ends in the joy of Mt 28:8; Lk 24:41, 52; Jn 20:20
the Resurrection of Christ, so when you feel in your own heart the sufferings of Jesus, remember that the Resurrection has to dawn.[a]

a. See MGL 50 of 24th March 1967, p. 83.

The Mysteries of Jesus that Holy Mother Church helps us to relive during Holy Week and Easter must be very specially dear to every Missionary of Charity, for it is the mystery of the distressing disguise of Jesus Crucified by sin and for sin. It is this mystery that most fully reveals the depth of God's Thirst to draw us back to His Love; the mystery that we as Missionaries of Charity—Carriers of God's Love—are called, in a special way, to contemplate, to experience, to satiate and to proclaim. How close we must keep to Our Lady, who understood what depth of Divine Love
Jn 19:25, 28 was being revealed as she stood at the foot of the Cross and heard Jesus cry out, "I Thirst."

We know that it is through Our Lady's pleading that the Society was born, has grown and will continue to grow in the Church and for the Church. It is through her special love, guidance and intercession that the Missionaries of Charity will continue her role of contemplating, experiencing and satiating Jesus' Thirst for love and for souls in His Mystical Body—the Church. This we do by our wholeheartedness in seeking oneness with Jesus in prayer and penance, by our sincerity in living our life of chastity, poverty and obedience, and by our vow of wholehearted and free service to Jesus in the distressing disguise of the poorest of the poor, by our humble works of love. Do not forget that the poorest of the poor include ourselves and our Sisters in the community. Jesus said it very clearly,
Mt 25:40 "Whatever you did to the least of mine, you did it to Me." Keep these words of Jesus deep in your minds and hearts. Please take up my letters of 27.7.83, 1.4.88, 10.10.88 and 29.3.94[a] and use them for your prayer and examination during Holy Week.

As our General Chapter draws near, let us try to understand more deeply the greatness and beauty of our call to the life of a Missionary of Charity—Carrier of God's Love—so that with the special help of Our Lady we may grow to know, love, and live our Constitutions more faithfully for the greater glory of God and the good of souls.

Let us pray.—Let us be only all for Jesus—through Mary. Be Holy.

God bless you
M Teresa MC

a. In the current volume, these letters correspond to MGL 172 of 27th July 1983, pp. 311–13; MGL 203 of 1st April 1988, pp. 377–78; MGL 206 of 10th October 1988, pp. 382–84; and MGL 250 of 29th March 1994, pp. 449–50.

ED 68. EASTER 1996

Easter 1996

Be Holy.
Let us be one heart full of love in the Heart of Jesus through Mary.
Where there is love, there is peace, joy and unity.
Let us make our Society Something beautiful for God.
Let us pray.

God bless you
M. Teresa, MC

MGL 267. 24TH APRIL 1996

L.D.M.

Mother House
24th April 1996

My dearest Children,

This brings you Mother's love, prayer and blessing as well as a big thank you for all you letters and beautiful cards bringing me your loving Easter wishes as well as your fervent prayers for a speedy recovery from the painful effects of a bad fall causing a fracture in my left shoulder bone, which happened the first day of Holy Week—something very special to offer to God in union with the sufferings of Our Lord, to make reparation for sin, and to obtain many graces for our Society as we prepare for our next General Chapter. Keep praying much for Mother.

Most of you have finished your annual retreat by now, and from the letters I received you have all made a fervent retreat. Ask Our Lady to help you to be faithful to the resolutions you have taken so as to be able to put into practice

I WILL, I WANT, WITH GOD'S BLESSING, [TO] BE HOLY.

This year we will be celebrating the 50th anniversary of what we call "Inspiration Day" . The strong grace of Divine Light and Love Mother received on the train journey to Darjeeling on 10th September 1946 is where the MC begins—in the depths of God's infinite longing to love and to be loved. How important it is for each Missionary of Charity to desire deeply to share in this same grace which Mother was entrusted with on 10th September 1946 for the Society, and through the Society, for the whole Church, but very specially for the poorest of the poor.

As a preparation for a joyful celebration of this Golden Jubilee of "Inspiration Day" on 10th September 1996, in thanksgiving to God for having
chosen us to be His Missionaries of Charity in His Church and for His
Church, I cannot think of a better way than to turn to Our Lady—for
it was at Her pleading that the Society was born—and to beg Her, one
in mind and heart, to teach us to listen deeply in fervent prayer to the
Jn 19:28 cry of Her Son, Jesus, on the Cross "I Thirst", so that with Her and like
Jn 19:25, Mt 25:40 Her we learn to stand by the distressing disguise of Jesus in the world
to-day, especially in the lives of the poorest of the poor, both materially
and spiritually, and thus satiate His thirst to love and to be loved. Our
humble works of love to the poorest of the poor are not just social works,
but they are the wonderful means the Society offers us to prove our love
Mt 25:40 for Jesus—to satiate His thirst for love and for souls. "Whatever you did to
the least of mine, you did it to me," Jesus said.

Here are a few practical points to help us prepare for the celebration of this Jubilee:

- through the fervent praying of the Rosary before Jesus, exposed in His Eucharistic presence, and in the street.
- Through frequent acts of love during the day: "Jesus in my heart, I believe in Your tender love for me; I love You".
- Through a regular, sincere examination of conscience that will lead us, with the help of Our Lady, to repent of our infidelities—our lack of love—and with the help of God's grace, to firmly resolve to uproot all pride, all selfishness preventing us from satiating the thirst of Jesus for love and for souls.

To help you with this last point, I want you to take up some of my past letters for meditation or for prayerful spiritual reading:[a]

May 1964	[MGL 27, pp. 45–47]
Oct. 1968	[MGL 61, pp. 103–5]
July 1971	[MGL 82, pp. 144–45]
Aug. 1971	[MGL 83, pp. 145–47]
June 1972	[MGL 92, pp. 160–61]
Aug. 1972	[MGL 94, pp. 163–65]
Jan. 1983	[MGL 169, pp. 302–4]
Apr. 1985 (Sup.)	[Mother's Letters to the Superiors, April 1985]
Apr. 1986	[MGL 187, pp. 341–42]

a. For easier reference we have added here the corresponding letter and page numbers.

I am also sending you a questionnaire to help you prepare your contributions to the General Chapter.[a] God has been so very good to us all these years, let us not forget to proclaim the great things He has done in us and through us for the greater glory of His Name. After much fervent prayer, try to bring before the Chapter your hopes and desires for the renewal of the life of our Society from within.[b]

I want you all to be very humble, that is very sincere and open, all for the glory of God and for the good of our Society, so that our renewal be a real work of the Spirit of God.[c] If we really take the trouble to be His Love, His Compassion, His Presence to the Poorest of the Poor, we really satiate His thirst for love by growing more and more in that intimate love for Jesus—through the works of love, both spiritual and material, to the Poorest of the Poor, for in each action we can hear Jesus' own word: "I was hungry, I was thirsty . . . I was naked . . . I was homeless . . . both spiritually Mt 25: 35–40
and physically, YOU DID IT TO ME."

Keep the joy of loving Jesus in your heart and share this joy with all you meet, especially your Family. Also always pray together.

God bless you
M Teresa MC

MGL 268. 6TH MAY 1996

LDM

Mother House
6th May 1996

My dearest Children,

This brings you Mother's love, prayer and blessing—but especially the joy of the assurance that Jesus loves you, and I only ask you to love one Jn 13:34; 15:12
another as Jesus loves each one of you—for in loving one another you only love Jesus.[d] The beautiful work the Church has entrusted to our Society will be completely destroyed from within if you do not love one another as Jesus loves each one of you and also keep the joy of poverty.[e]

As we are coming close to our General Chapter, our prayer to the Holy

a. Questionnaire has been omitted.
b. See MGL 99 of 16th March 1973, p. 174.
c. Ibid.
d. See MGL 147 of 15th March 1980, pp. 266–67.
e. See MGL 143 of 12th October 1979, p. 259.

Spirit after Holy Communion and at Adoration must be more fervent. The most important thing we all have to do, no matter where we are or how long we have been MCs, is to PRAY. Do not just say some prayers, but pray with real burning love by filling your prayer with sacrifices made and offered. We all know that this Chapter is important. There are many things we need to see together, to find out how we can renew ourselves, in fidelity to the gift God has given us and be only all for Jesus even more completely. In this Chapter also we have to vote [for] the MC whom God has chosen to take Mother's place. We must all do it with great love, for the glory of God and the good of the Society.[a] There are many wonderful Sisters in both branches—the Active and the Contemplative—who can take Mother's place, if only we all will be one heart full of love with her whom we choose.

For nearly 50 years, each one of you has been the gift of God to me. We have shared together the joy of loving Jesus, and I would not have been able to do all this without you. My gratitude to each one of you is my prayer for you that you grow in holiness and remain faithful to our MC life and work.[b] Now I am sure that you will give Mother the joy of placing the Society in the hands of the Sister whom God has chosen to take my place. How beautiful it will be to give that Sister my blessing and to pray for her while I am still with you, that she may lead you all to Jesus as Mother has done. This would be the best gift of love you could give to Mother, and I believe it is a gift that Jesus wants you to give. I ask you again not to discuss matters concerning the Chapter with anyone who is not MC.

Let every Sister in the Society realize the importance of her sharing and prepare her suggestions to the Chapter with great love according to the Questionnaire that I sent with my last letter. Please send in any contributions and suggestions before July so that there will be time to put everything together and to present all to the Chapter in good order. Pray over all you have lived in these past years, over all you have studied during this year of preparation, and over all Jesus shows you, so that your suggestions will be the fruit of prayer. Do not let the devil bring to your mind only what has hurt or disturbed you, but pray, pray much and let your suggestions come out of the truth and love and peace of the Holy Spirit.

As we begin the final preparation for the Chapter, I enclose here

a. See MGL 179 of 19th March 1985, p. 328.
b. Ibid.

the final list of the Society members who will share in the Chapter. All the Sisters who have to come must be in Calcutta by 18th September at the latest. We will have four days of seminar given by Fr. John Hardon, SJ, from the 21st to the 24th September, followed by [a] retreat preached by His Grace, Archbishop Henry D'Souza of Calcutta, from the 26th evening. On the 7th October, Archbishop will open the General Chapter by celebrating the Mass of the Holy Spirit.[a] Then we shall have the elections in the morning. The rest of the day will be spent in Adoration and Thanksgiving, for all the gifts Jesus has given us in the past, and for the gift of the Superior General and Councillors General that He had chosen on that morning. I know that it will be a day of joy and peace for all. It would be good if the Sisters who are coming, both Regionals and others, bring with them all their own personal things, in case they do not return to the same place after the Chapter. Arrange the work well and also the persons who will replace you during your absence.[b]

You will be happy to know that Professions in Calcutta will be taking place soon—14th May will be First Vows and 15th May Final Vows, both in St. Mary's. On the 17th I will be travelling to Rome, where both First and Final Professions will be on 24th May. While I am in Rome, the Mayor of Rome will be giving me Roman citizenship at a big ceremony—so I will be able to say that I am a Roman citizen like St. Paul! Let us thank God for His gifts. On 25th May, I will be flying to New York. The Professions there will be on 28th May—First Profession of the Active and Contemplative Branches—and 31st May, Final Professions in Washington. How good Jesus is to us! Since He is using every little thing to show His love for us, let us use every little thing of daily life to return that love to Him.

Acts 16:37; 22:25–29; 23:27

I am also enclosing a notice I received about the Litany of Our Lady.[c] Please read it carefully and remember from now on to add "Queen of the Family" as indicated.

Let us pray and protect Our Society from all things that may spoil the beautiful Gift of God—Our Society, its Spirit, work and the gift of the 4th Vow.

Let us pray.

God bless you
M Teresa MC

a. The Chapter was postponed to January 1997 after Mother suffered a heart attack in August 1996 and was in delicate health as a result.

b. See MGL 184 of 25th August 1985, p. 335.

c. The information on the Litany of Loreto attached to this letter has been omitted.

MGL 269. 7TH [JULY] 1996

LDM

Mother House
7th [July] 1996[a]

My dearest Children,

This brings you all Mother's love, prayer and blessing.

You will all be shocked to hear of the sudden "going home to Jesus" of our dearest Sr. M. Sylvia, MC, Regional Superior of our houses in the East of the United States, and Sr. M. Kateri, MC, Superior of our house in Bronx. Last night we received a phone call at 11:00 P.M. to let us know that there had been a serious car accident at 9:00 A.M. as the two Sisters were on their way to our house in Jenkins—and that our dearest Sr. Sylvia died on the spot, and Sr. Kateri died soon after reaching the hospital. Both were beautiful MC Sisters, deeply in love with Jesus and serving Him as Missionaries of Charity with wholehearted dedication. Jesus has now called them to Himself, and they will continue their work as Missionaries of Charity in heaven, giving praise and glory to God.

Sr. M. Sylvia, MC (Anne Mathew), from Kerala, was born in 1945. She joined the Society in May 1964 and took Final Vows in May 1973. Sr. M. Kateri, MC (Nancy Jean Turo), from the United States, was born in 1956. She joined the Society in June 1981 and took Final Vows in December 1990.

Let us remember the words of Scripture, "Precious in the eyes of the Lord is the death of His saints" (Ps 116:15). Jesus has asked for a big sacrifice from the Society, as both these Sisters were to come to the General Chapter. But they will still participate in the Chapter—and because they are now so close to Jesus, they will be able to help us even better than before.

Make sure that you offer the suffrages for the repose of their souls as soon as you get this letter. Also please pray for Sr. Sylvia's two MC sisters—Sr. Maria Lucy and Sr. Vimala—and for all the family members of our deceased Sisters, that they may be strengthened in the acceptance of this deep sorrow in knowing that God's love is at work in it all.

Let us pray.

God bless you
M Teresa MC

a. This letter was dated 7th June 1996, but this was a mistake. Sr. Sylvia and Sr. Kateri died on 6th July.

MGL 270. 31ST JULY 1996

LDM

Mother House
31st July 1996

My dearest Children,

This brings you Mother's love, prayer and blessing that you may be one heart full of love in the Heart of Jesus through Mary, real MCs.

I want you to know how much joy you have brought to Mother's heart by your sincere preparation for our General Chapter. So many letters have arrived with your comments and suggestions about how we may be better Carriers of God's love as Jesus and the Church expect us to be. Most of these letters show that you have really studied and prayed seriously during this past year over the subjects that you were given, and I am sure that this has helped each one to grow in personal love for Jesus and fidelity to our vocation. What comes out most clearly in all you wrote is your great desire to be holy—and that is the thing that gives Mother the most joy. Keep this desire burning in your hearts, my Children, and use everything that comes your way to fulfil this desire, and I am sure that Jesus will see to it that you are able to keep Mother's promise to give saints to Mother Church.

By now you must have heard about the Holy Father's new document on Consecrated Life.[a] See the tender love of God in giving this to us just as we get ready for the Chapter. It would be good if each community got a copy to read and meditate on and use the Holy Father's words to help you grow in love for our vocation.

As this letter reaches you, you will be preparing for the Feast of the Immaculate Heart of Mary—our Society Feast. The Society Feast this year must be a very special one, as it comes in the same year as we celebrate the Golden Jubilee of Inspiration Day and also our General Chapter. Even more than the exterior preparation of decorations and cooking, let your preparation for [the] Society Feast be an interior preparation of the heart. Beg Our Lady to keep us in her Most Pure Heart, so that we may love Jesus with an undivided love, an immaculate love like hers. Our Directory tells us that we have the Novena for the Feast of the Assumption and then straight we go on to the Novena for [the] Society Feast. Use the same

a. Post-Synodal Apostolic Exhortation, *Vita Consecrata,* of Pope (now Saint) John Paul II, 25th March 1996.

prayer for both—"Let us spend our lives beside you. . . ."[a] Really taste this prayer, and understand it well. We are not refusing the joys God will give us—no, we take whatever He gives. But we ask for the most important
Jn 19:25, 28 thing, to stand beside Our Lady under the Cross of Jesus, to hear Him say "I Thirst", and to learn from her to quench His Thirst. This is where we belong as Missionaries of Charity. If we stand with Our Lady, she will give us her spirit of loving trust, total surrender and cheerfulness. Offer this long Novena and all the days of the Triduum for the General Chapter, together with many sacrifices. Often say, "Mary, Mother of Jesus, be a Mother to our Chapter delegates." Let us make our community in heaven also take part, especially as now we have two Chapter delegates who have gone home to Jesus. Ask them to intercede for us all in these important days.

Soon after Society Feast comes 10th September. How grateful we must all be to God for the great, great gift He gave to Mother for the whole Church on that day—the Aim of our Society, "To satiate the Thirst of Jesus on the Cross for love and for souls." Let this Golden Jubilee really touch our hearts and take us more deeply into this gift of God—the whole reason for our existence as MCs. You must celebrate—yes. But just as the experience of 10th September is so intimate for Mother, let us make our celebration intimate also. Do not involve outsiders. Just take trouble to be
Jn 19:25, 28 close to Jesus to hear Him say, "I Thirst" to you, individually, to understand His Word, love it and live it. As Jesus did to Mother, He now does it to you. Try to hear properly. Make sure to invite Our Lady to your celebration and to be one with every member of our MC Family. To prepare for this beautiful day, make a special Novena using the following prayer:

> Mary, Mother of Jesus, you were the first one to hear Jesus cry, "I Thirst." You know how real, how deep is His longing for me and for the poor. I am yours—the whole Society is yours—Sisters, Brothers, Fathers—Active and Contemplative. Teach me, bring me face to face with the love in the Heart of Jesus Crucified. With your help, Mother Mary, I will listen to Jesus' Thirst,

a. Novena to Our Lady: "Let us spend our lives beside you, O Mother, to bear you company in your sad solitude and deepest woe; let us feel in our soul the sorrowful glance of your eyes and the abandonment of your Heart. What we ask for on the road of life is not the joy of Bethlehem, not to adore the infant God in your virginal arms; we do not ask to enjoy the sweet presence of Jesus Christ in your humble home at Nazareth, nor to join the choir of angels at your glorious assumption. Throughout our lives we beg for the mockery and jeers of Calvary. We ask for the slow agony of your Son, the scorn, the ignominy and the shame of the cross. We ask only, O most sorrowful Virgin, to be allowed to stand beside you, to strengthen our spirit by your tears, to consummate our sacrifice by your martyrdom, to sustain our hearts by your loneliness, to love our God and your God by the immolation of our whole being." (Blessed Miguel Pro)

and it will be for me a Word of Life. Standing near you, I will give Him my love, and I will give Him the chance to love me, and so be the cause of your joy. Amen.

You may also use Mother's writings to help you prepare for this beautiful day, especially Mother's Letters of 27th July 1983 and 25th March 1993,[a] and Mother's Instructions (Volume I) on pages 114 and 150.

Archbishop D'Souza has been called to Rome during the time he was supposed to preach the retreat for the Chapter, and so Fr. Gino Henriques, CSsR, will be preaching the retreat instead. There has also been a little change of dates. Delegates must still arrive in Calcutta by 18th September. Retreat will be from 20th evening through 28th September. The seminar with Father Hardon is now on the 30th September and 2nd through 4th October.

Many of our Sisters are carrying the Cross with Jesus because of serious sickness. They are a precious channel of graces for our Chapter. Let us pray much for them. Pray much also for Mother.

My dearest children—I want you in a special way—with the help of Our Lady, to come as close as you can to the Heart of Jesus, and from Your heart tell Jesus—"I want, I will with Your love and blessing [to] be Holy, so that I [may] be only all for Jesus through Mary." Let us pray.

God bless you
M Teresa MC

MGL 271. 31ST JULY 1996

LDM

Mother House
31st July 1996

My dearest Children,

This brings you Mother's love, prayer and blessing that you may be only all for Jesus through Mary.

This letter comes to inform you that our dearest Sr. M. Dominic, MC, has gone home to Jesus today at 10:00 A.M. from our Dum Dum house.[b]

Sr. Dominic (Celina Ekka) was born on 24th May 1925 in Tongo, Bihar. Upon joining our Society, she made her First Vows on 14th April 1958 and

a. In the current volume, MGL 172, pp. 311–13, and MGL 244, pp. 436–40.
b. Dum Dum is an MC Home for the mentally and physically challenged in Calcutta.

her Final Vows on 14th April 1964. Sr. Dominic was a Sister filled with undivided love for Jesus. Her one desire in life was to bring souls to Jesus, and this filled her with great apostolic zeal and caused her to spend herself tirelessly to search for souls. Sr. Dominic was a gifted catechist and teacher, and her love for Jesus filled her classes and moved the hearts of those who heard her.

In 1990, Sr. Dominic suffered a stroke, which left her mostly paralyzed. After a long struggle, she regained some movement and speech and began once again to teach catechism to the [mentally ill] girls in Dum Dum. A few days ago, Sr. Dominic had another stroke and fell into a coma. Now Jesus has called her to Himself to give her the reward of all her labours for Him.

Please offer the suffrages of the Society for the repose of her soul as soon as you receive this letter. Our community in heaven has reached 40 Sisters—maybe it is our biggest community. I am sure that Jesus has a real mission for this community in this year of our Chapter.

Keep the joy of loving Jesus in your hearts and share this joy with all you meet. Then we will all be ready for the joy of going home to Jesus when it is our turn.

Let us pray.

God bless you
M Teresa MC

MGL 272. 11TH SEPTEMBER 1996

LDM

Mother House
11th September 1996

My dearest Children,

This brings you Mother's love, prayer and blessing for each one of you—and especially Mother's great gratitude to each one for all the prayers offered during my illness,[a] all the loving preparation for Society Feast and the Golden Jubilee of Inspiration Day, all the beautiful cards and wishes that you have sent to bring Mother the joy of knowing that we are all one heart full of love in the Heart of Jesus through Mary.

a. Mother suffered a heart attack and was admitted to Woodlands Nursing Home in Calcutta on 20th August. She also had malaria and a lung infection. She was discharged from the hospital on 6th September 1996.

We had a very beautiful celebration of the Golden Jubilee of Inspiration Day here in Mother House yesterday. All five branches of the Society, plus Lay MCs, Co-Workers, friends, benefactors and volunteers really helped Mother to thank Jesus from the heart for the wonderful gift He gave through Our Lady fifty years ago, all the blessings received throughout all these years, and all the graces He is giving us just now in this moment. Through your prayers, Our Lady gave Mother the strength to be present for the Holy Mass—thank God. The celebrations began with a prayer service the night before, and the Sisters have put down what Mother said then, so I am sending it to you.

Remember that the best way to thank Jesus, Mary, and Mother is to be really holy. "I will, I want, with God's blessing, [to] be holy." Mother is not yet so strong, so keep praying much for Mother and for the Chapter.

Let us pray.

God bless you
M Teresa MC

ATTACHMENT I TO MGL 272 OF 11TH SEPTEMBER 1996

+

LDM

Mother House
9th September 1996, 8–8:15 PM

MOTHER'S MESSAGE ON THE EVE OF INSPIRATION DAY:[a]

Today our Society is 50 years old. It is so beautiful to realise that after Our Lady's birth on the 8th September Her first thought was to see that the Society would be born in the Church also. It is the claim of Our Lady—The Society belongs to Her. It is beautiful too that at the birth of Our Lady—in Her heart was also born the Missionaries of Charity. So let us thank God and Our Lady in a special way for giving birth to Our Society of the Missionaries of Charity. It was at her prayer, and [the] deep desire in Her heart to do Something Beautiful for Jesus. And today we have in

a. After a prayer service for the Golden Jubilee of Inspiration Day, Mother, though very weak after returning from the hospital, surprised everyone by giving the above message. Mother's voice was very weak, so Sr. Frederick repeated what she was saying in a loud voice. To those present, it was very moving.

heaven 28,910 poor people because of our Nirmal Hriday. Let us thank God for our Society, our Active & Contemplative Sisters, Active & Contemplative Brothers, Fathers and Lay Missionaries of Charity.

Also let us thank the first 12 Sisters who were together with Mother, who started the Society.[a] Let us thank the Poor who accept the tender love of the Sisters to help us to be really Jesus. Let us thank the Sisters who were there at the beginning when we had nothing except the poorest of the poor. Let us thank the poorest of the poor. Let us thank the first group who had the courage to join in the beginning to be one heart with Mother. Let us thank & praise God for Fr. Van Exem,[b] who is in heaven, for helping and praying for us to continue the beautiful work as Missionaries of Charity. Let us thank God for Mr. & Mrs. Michael Gomes,[c] for sheltering us, and all our Co-Workers, Benefactors and Volunteers.

I also thank all of you who have joined Mother and helped Mother to carry on the work with so much love, so much hope and so much joy, up to today. Mother thanks each one of you, and the best gratitude you can show to Mother is to be HOLY by improving [your] life of prayer, by giving wholehearted free service to the poorest of the poor, and by [your] fidelity to the Church. Brothers, Sisters & Fathers and for those who are with us—a Big Thank You. God bless you all.

Let us thank our Mother Mary for being a Mother to us, a cause of our joy, and for helping us to be true Missionaries of Charity. Let us thank Our Lady for helping us to persevere in our Society till today.

Let us pray.

God bless you
M Teresa MC

a. The "first twelve" were: (1) Mother, (2) Sr. M. Agnes, (3) Sr. M. Gertrude, (4) Sr. M. Trinita, (5) Sr. M. Dorothy, (6) Sr. M. Clare, (7) Sr. M. Bernard, (8) Sr. M. Laetitia, (9) Sr. M. Jacinta, (10) Sr. M. Francesca, (11) Sr. M. Florence, and (12) Sr. Margaret Mary.

b. See MGL 9 of [7th] July 1961 and corresponding footnote, p. 18.

c. Mother mentions Mr. Michael Gomes, since he lived at 14 Creek Lane until his death in 1999. However, it was the common agreement of the Gomes brothers (Alfred and Michael, who lived in Calcutta, and Thomas and Robert, who lived in East Pakistan, present-day Bangladesh) to make available to Mother the third floor of their home at 14 Creek Lane in 1949. This was to become "the first home for the Missionaries of Charity."

ATTACHMENT II TO MGL 272 OF 11TH SEPTEMBER 1996

+

LDM

Mother House
10th September 1996

MOTHER'S MESSAGE: "INSPIRATION DAY" (After Mass)

Let us thank God for using our nothingness, and for all the Poor, especially for the First Group who came to join when there was poverty and only the Poor.

Let us thank God for Jesus in the Blessed Sacrament—whatever you do Mt 25:40
to the least of my brethren you did it to me. We have the privilege to be 24 hours in the Heart of Jesus.

On Her Birthday She had in mind 10th September—our birthday—first work of Mary—works of love.

Not one died without love and care. It took us more than 2 hours to remove the worms and he died like an angel.[a]

To serve without any difference in religion we have [the] Fourth Vow—giving wholehearted free service. Let us thank God for our family. Family that prays together—stays together. Our gratitude to God [for all] who have shared in the work of love.

a. At this time Mother was very sick and barely able to speak. Her periodic, short instructions to the Sisters were mostly brief points that reminded them of what they had already heard many times. She was fond of repeating the story of a man picked up from the street; this event seems to have been so crucial in her life, for she overcame her repugnance in cleaning the worms (similar to St. Francis kissing the leper). She pointed out that after she spent two hours cleaning maggots from his wounds, the man died "like an angel." This phrase is actually a quote from another man who before dying in Nirmal Hriday told Mother: "I have lived like an animal in the street, but I am going to die like an angel, loved and cared for." It was very important to her that no one died without love and care.

ED 69. DECEMBER 1996

Our Golden Jubilee Year—Ek Dil, Dec. '96

December 1996[a]

My dearest children,

Open your Heart to Jesus and Mary, and this will help you to become a true Spouse of Jesus in full reality.

This is my Prayer for each one of you—Be only all for Jesus through Mary.

Let us pray.

God bless you
M. Teresa, M.C.

MGL 273. 7TH OCTOBER 1996

LDM

Mother House
7th October 1996

My dearest Children,

This brings you Mother's love, prayer and blessing that you may be one heart full of love in the Heart of Jesus through Mary.

Every day the post has been bringing Mother a flood of your wishes and cards prepared with so much love—first for Society Feast, then for Inspiration Day, then for Mother's Feast, and now for Thanksgiving Day! It is so beautiful to see how the whole Society is one family, close to each other in prayer even though far apart in miles. I would love to be able to write to each one personally to thank you, especially for all your prayers and sacrifices of fidelity to our life, but you know that it is not possible. So this letter brings to each one of you the love and thanks of Mother's heart.

You will be happy to know that Our Lady is making Mother stronger day by day. I do not know why all this had to happen just in this time, but I think it must have something to do with the Chapter. Everybody was busy preparing and sending contributions for the Chapter, so I think Jesus decided that Mother should make a contribution also![b] It is a nice chance

a. At the top of the page the following was typed: "Mother wants three copies of EK-DIL to be given to each Region, in honour of the Blessed Trinity. These should be circulated within the Region."

b. Mother was admitted to Woodlands Nursing Home from 20th August to 6th September. After her release from the hospital she continued suffering from heart pain. Then on 16th September 1996,

to give Him a beautiful gift. When we think of all that Jesus has done for us—for each one and for the Society—we should be really ready to take whatever He gives and give whatever He takes with great gratitude and love, to refuse nothing of all Jesus asks of us.

Our celebration of the Feast of the Little Flower here in Mother House was a day of rejoicing in unity and love.[a] I was able to take part in the Holy Sacrifice of the Mass, together with Novices, Tertians, Professed Sisters from the houses of Calcutta, MC Brothers and Fathers, and a large number of volunteers. In the afternoon, the Sisters had a big play with singing and dancing about Mother's life from childhood through the beginning of the Society till now. It was a good reminder of God's tender love and of how He has used nothingness to show His greatness. Our gratitude must be the firm resolution to be holy.

This month of October must be very special to each one of us, as it is the month during which Our Lady invites us all in a very special way to contemplate with her the mysteries of Jesus' life that she shared so fully, through our fervent praying of the Rosary. Yes, we must always be very faithful and never give up praying the Rosary in the street and during Adoration of the Blessed Sacrament. It is also during the month of October that, through Our Lady's intercession and protection, the Society was granted the Decree of Erection by the Church—a sure sign that God wants our Society in His Church with the special God-given mission:

To quench the Thirst of Jesus on the Cross Jn 19:28
for love and for souls,
By labouring at the salvation and sanctification Mt 25:40
of the poorest of the poor.

How grateful we must be to have been chosen to live the life of a Missionary of Charity. That is why the 7th of October is spent adoring Jesus in the Blessed Sacrament, thanking Him for our vocation and for the great things He has done in us and through us all these years, for giving us the chance to love Him

after writing letters, she fell while getting up from the chair. She was hospitalized again at Woodlands Nursing Home and discharged on 25th September.

a. The liturgical feast, on 1st October, of St Thérèse of the Child Jesus and the Holy Face, Mother's patron saint, was a big celebration in the Society.

- In His humble disguise in the Eucharist, and
- In His distressing disguise in the poorest of the poor.

Mt 25:40 Never separate Jesus in the Eucharist and Jesus in the poor.

I hope you are all well and doing God's work with great love, and so growing in holiness. Learn to pray the work—to do the work with Jesus, for Jesus and to Jesus—and you will be 24 hours in His presence. How beautiful is our vocation if we really believe that—

- He, Jesus, is in the appearance of Bread, and
- Mt 25:35–40 He, Jesus, is in the hungry, the naked, the sick, the lonely, the unloved, the homeless, the hopeless.

Yes, our lives must be more and more woven with this deep faith in Jesus,
Jn 6:35, 48 the Bread of Life, to be eaten with and for the poor.[a]

How I long and pray that you would all appreciate, love and live sincerely your beautiful vocation and your loyalty to the spirit and life of our Society,[b] for only then can Mother's promise "to give Saints to Mother Church" be fulfilled.[c] As I have often told you, holiness, very great holiness, becomes simple if we belong fully to Our Lady. The more we abandon ourselves to her totally and without reserve, the greater will be the number of Saints in our Society.[d]

How much we have to thank God for, [for] the gift of each one of you, so that together being One heart full of love we spread His love and His presence wherever we go.

I want all to grow more and more in preparing for the Chapter with great [love] and pure humble heart. Our Lady, I am sure, She will give us every possible help. So let us pray often during these days of preparation. My love and blessing to each one of you.[e]

Let us pray.

God bless you
Mother

a. See MGL 105 of 25th February 1974, p. 183.

b. See MGL 57 of 19th May 1968, p. 96.

c. See MGL 144 of 21st November 1979, p. 261, and MGL 176 of 11th February 1984, p. 319.

d. See MGL 93 of 18th June 1972, pp. 161–62.

e. Mother's handwriting is very weak and irregular, which shows the effort it must have cost her to write these few lines by hand.

MGL 274. 1ST NOVEMBER 1996

LDM

Mother House
1st November 1996

My dearest Children,

This brings you Mother's love, prayer and blessing, and also my gratitude to you for all the prayers and sacrifices offered for Mother's health. You will be happy to know that I am much better, thank God, and keeping up the hope of giving Jesus an MC "tabernacle" in China in a not-too-distant future. Keep praying to Our Lady for this to happen soon.

As the Chapter date draws closer, I want you all to feel the need of Our Lady's love and protection in a special way. Jesus gave Her to us from the Cross, and He calls us "to love Her with a most tender and filial love and devotion" (Const. 13). So devotion to Mary must be very deep in the heart of every Missionary of Charity. Was it not at Her pleading that the Society of the Missionaries of Charity was born? Our Lady, therefore, must teach us how to satiate the thirst of Jesus for love and for souls, as She did. Our humble works of love to the poorest of the poor must be, through our lives, the visible expression of God's thirsting love for souls as well as of our thirsting love for Him, for Jesus clearly said: Jn 19:26–27

"Whatever you did to the least of mine, YOU DID IT TO ME." Mt 25:40

Devotion to Mary is not built on feelings, but on Faith in God's plan of salvation. As God chose to come to us, in Jesus, through Mary, so we too must go to Jesus through Mary. Our Constitutions tell us very clearly how to go to Jesus through Mary. Yes, through praying the Rosary daily with love and devotion, and honouring Her on Her feast days, but we go to Jesus through Mary especially when we earnestly seek

to imbibe her profound reverence, adoration and deep recollection
in the contemplation of God
and
radiating her humility, kindness and thoughtfulness
towards the Sisters and the Poor we serve (Const. 15).

I want you to take up, for spiritual reading or for Meditation, some of my General letters to you, to help you know Our Lady more intimately, so as "to love and venerate Her and fly to Her with childlike confidence in all your joys and sorrows", as our Constitutions ask us to do. (4th August 1962—May 1964—31st October 1966—10th August 1971—18th June 1972—15th August 1972).[a]

The Profession dates are drawing close. In Calcutta, 43 Senior Tertians will be taking their Final Vows on the 5th December at 4:00 P.M., and 62 Novices their First Vows on the 7th December at 6:15 A.M. Keep them all in your prayers, and let us thank God for the gift of each one of them to our Society. Both Profession ceremonies will be held in St. Mary's Parish.

Many Bishops are writing to ask for Our Sisters to work for the poor in their Dioceses. The request is very great, but we need many more vocations to be able to answer the needs of the Church in different parts of the world. The best way to foster vocations is very clearly stated in our Constitutions nos. 229 & 230. Let each Community pray and meditate on this part of our Constitution and examine how we are fostering vocations to the consecrated religious life.

You will be happy to know that we have just opened our first house in the country of Mongolia, which is just north of China, where Christianity has just started to penetrate. This foundation is part of the region of Russia, where Mother promised Our Lady 15 houses in honour of the 15 Mysteries of the Rosary, so Sister M. Chantal has written to say that the house in Mongolia is the "Salve Regina." What a nice thought! In December/January new foundations will be made, please God, giving Jesus 10 more tabernacles where He will be loved and adored. That will bring the number of our foundations to 571, plus 17 contemplative houses. Let us constantly praise and thank God.

In December, 38 of our Senior Sisters—15 in different parts of India and 23 in other parts of the world—will be celebrating their Silver Jubilee: 25 years of life dedicated totally to loving and serving Jesus in His humble Eucharistic Presence and in the distressing disguise of the Poorest of the Poor. Sentiments of deep humble gratitude must fill the heart of each Jubilarian as you give thanks to God for the gift of your vocation and for the many graces received through the Society that have helped you persevere all these years. Mother will be praying for you and thanking God for the gift of each one of you to our Society. May this Jubilee celebration deepen your love for your vocation as a Missionary of Charity and help you resolve to live it ever more faithfully for the greater glory of God and

a. In the current volume, these letters correspond to MGL 16, pp. 27–28; MGL 27, pp. 45–47; MGL 48, pp. 78–80; MGL 83, pp. 145–47; MGL 93, pp. 161–63, and MGL 94, pp. 163–65.

the good of souls, and in this way you will help Mother fulfil her promise to give Saints to Mother Church. Keep in mind what our Directory no. 43 says regarding Jubilee celebrations for Missionaries of Charity:

> Jubilee celebrations are prepared and celebrated in a spiritual manner and with simplicity in the privacy of the Community. No Jubilee photos are to be taken.[a]

You will then experience true joy, the joy that Jesus wants to share with you, and that Mother wishes each one of you.

Let this letter open your heart to Jesus and Mary and help you to become a true Spouse of Jesus—in full reality. This is my prayer for each one of you. Be only all for Jesus through Mary.—Let us pray.

God bless you
M Teresa MC

MGL 275. 15TH NOVEMBER 1996

LDM

Mother House
15th November 1996

My dearest Children,

This brings you Mother's love, prayer and blessing, together with my prayerful wishes for a fervent Advent spent in the company of Our Lady, learning from her how to be pure and humble of heart. Let us all together consecrate our lives totally to her on the Feast of her Immaculate Conception—8th December—so that through her guidance and help each of us [might] become the true Spouse of Jesus Crucified, a true MC not only in name but in life.

Soon we will begin our preparation for the coming of Jesus, and in all our chapels there will be the empty crib. This year we must prepare a better crib, a crib of humility, poverty and simplicity of the Gospel. We need the life of Bethlehem, Nazareth—that humility and simplicity—to live the Lk 2:4–20, 51
life of Calvary. I beg of you Sisters, let us keep things simple and not introduce things that do not fit in with our way of life. Everywhere you look, Mt 27:50; Mk 15:37; Lk 23:46; Jn 19:30
it is the same thing: you look at Bethlehem, Nazareth, the Cross—it is the same thing. That is why Jesus could say, "Learn of Me ..."[b] Mt 11:29

a. At the General Chapter of 1997, it was decided that a few photos may be taken at Jubilee celebrations.
b. See MGL 185 of 31st October 1985, p. 339.

As the year 1996 draws to a close, we must all feel the need to thank God for all He has done with you, in you and through you to Jesus in His Eucharistic Presence and in the distressing disguise of the Poor. The following statistics will help you realize how God has used nothingness to show His greatness.

MISSIONARIES OF CHARITY—FIVE BRANCHES
AS OF OCTOBER 1996

	Act. Srs.	Cont. Srs.	Act. Brs	Cont. Brs.	Frs.
Houses Abroad	369	15	24	2	3
Houses in India	192	2	43	1	1
Total Houses	**561**	**17**	**67**	**3**	**4**
Finally Professed	2784	62	249	8	13 Priests
Junior Professed	1056	32	119	12	12
Total Professed	**3840**	**94**	**368**	**20**	**25**
Novices	438	9	57	6	5
Postulants	279	10	85	6	18
No. of Countries	121	including MCC	19	3	3
No. of Nationalities	79		23	8	11

You will also be happy to know that in December many young Sisters will have the joy of consecrating themselves to Jesus.

First Profession in Dec. 1996		Final Profession in Dec. 1996	
Calcutta	64	Calcutta	40 + 3 MCC = 43
Nairobi	16	Rome	24
Manila	7	Washington	15
Warsaw	6	Naga	11
Rome	5		
San Francisco	5		
Total	**103**		**93**

We have just received an official circular letter from His Grace, Msgr. D'Souza, Archbishop of Calcutta, communicating to us the decision of the Conference of Bishops in India regarding the English translation to be used when praying the *Our Father.* I am enclosing a copy of Archbishop's letter about this.[a] In all our communities, we shall abide by this decision, and pray the *Our Father* according to the earlier version. Following the reasoning given in Archbishop's letter, we will also return to using "thee" and "thou" in the *Hail Mary* as it is given in the Catechism of the Catholic Church.

As we begin the final preparation for our General Chapter, I enclose the final list of the formation delegates who will attend the Chapter. The voting for delegates representing Mistresses of Formation had to be done a second time in order to make it follow what is written in our Constitutions. Therefore, please replace section H on the big list of delegates with the [new information].

. . .

Each one of you and your poor pray often and offer many sacrifices. Pray the prayer of the Chapter after Mass and at Adoration very fervently from 16th January to 1st February. We will all do [more] penance and we will have MC fast on 1st February in honour of the Holy Spirit—in supplication and thanksgiving. This Chapter is important for at this General Chapter we have to vote for the MC God has chosen to take Mother's place. We must all do it with great love, for the glory of God and the good of our Society. Do not be afraid. Do not discuss or speak of this outside your community. Only pray and do your penance with great love for this intention.[b]

Let us pray to Our Lady with great love and trust that all we do in preparation for the Chapter be done with great love and humility.

God bless you
M Teresa MC

a. The text of this letter has been omitted.

b. See MGL 179 of 19th March 1985, p. 329, and MGL 268 of 6th May 1996, p. 482.

MGL 276. 20TH DECEMBER 1996

+ LDM

Mother House
20th December 1996

My dearest Children,

This brings you all Mother's love, prayer and special blessing for this Christmas, that each one of you may offer to the Father a pure and humble heart like Our Lady did, so that Jesus may be born in you and through you for the poorest of the poor.

Thank God, yesterday Jesus brought Mother out of the hospital and back to Mother House. I am so happy to be back—all the Sisters and Novices prayed and sang with Mother as I entered, and even the people were leaning out of the window across the street to share in the joy. All the doctors and nurses and everyone in the hospital took such tender care of Mother, and did everything possible to make me all right. And so many, many people were praying together with all our MC family that Our Lady made sure that Jesus answered us. I think Jesus wanted me to come back to spend Christmas in the little Bethlehem of Mother's room, where Our Lady has taught Mother how to receive Jesus in poverty and humility just like she did. Thank you, each one of you, my Children, for your many prayers and sacrifices. I saw all the letters you sent and they brought me great joy.

Soon it will be 1997. This year, especially being the year of the General
Chapter, must be a year of greater love and unity. From one of the houses
the Sisters wrote to Mother, "Up to now Jesus has used Mother's life to
create the Society, and now Jesus is using Mother's suffering to redeem the
Jn 15:13 Society." But it is not the suffering by itself, it is the love. Time of suffering
is time of greater love. Whatever means Jesus uses to make our Society
more beautiful, let us only thank Him and offer all to quench His thirst
for love and for souls.

His Grace, Archbishop Henry D'Souza, has written a circular letter for the whole Archdiocese of Calcutta about Mother's illness.[a] I thought you might like to see what he says, so I am sending it to you.

I am looking forward to seeing so many of you very soon for the Chapter, which we will have in Mother House. I don't know where we will put everybody, but God will provide, as He has always done. I wish each one

a. This letter has been omitted.

of you a Happy and Holy Christmas and a New Year full of the joy of loving Jesus. Be only all for Jesus through Mary.

Let us pray.

God bless you
M. Teresa, MC

ED 70. SEPTEMBER 1996

September 1996

Golden Jubilee of Inspiration Day
10th Sept. 1946—10th Sept. 1996

Let us give thanks to Jesus from our hearts for having chosen our Society and each one in our Society to Satiate His Thirst today and every day. Jn 19:28

God bless you all
M. Teresa, MC

1997

MGL 277. 8TH JANUARY 1997

+ LDM

Mother House
8th January 1997

My dearest Children,

This brings you Mother's love, prayer and blessing.

With the Sisters' General Chapter about to begin soon, I would like all of you to make careful note of the following:

- Please advise visitors and volunteers that beginning 13th January (Monday), Mother House will not be open to visitors for an indefinite period. You can tell them that the Sisters are having retreat and meeting.
- Since the Mother House chapel will not be open to outsiders, they will be asked to have their Mass and Adoration at our other houses.
- No Missionary of Charity is to discuss the Chapter with outsiders. Tell journalists, TV and radio people politely that we are not making any comments about the Chapter.
- During the Chapter, no press coverage, interviews or TV filming will be permitted in any of our houses.

Let us make many sacrifices of silence of tongue, mind and heart in these days, so that in the silence of the heart God may speak to the Chapter delegates and to us all. Pray much that all be for the glory of God and the good of the Society.

Let us pray.

God bless you
M Teresa MC

MGL 278. 15TH JANUARY 1997

+ LDM

Mother House
15th January 1997

My dearest Children,

This brings you Mother's love, blessing and prayer that you may take the strong resolution to be humble and pure like Mary so as to be holy like Jesus.

I know that you are always anxious to have news of Mother. As you know from my last letter, Mother came home from hospital on 19th December. Since then I have still not been so well. For some days now I have had such a terrible back pain that I have not been able to move from the bed even for Holy Mass. It is a real sacrifice for me, but I know that Jesus is asking this from Mother for the Chapter. Please continue to pray much for Mother, that Jesus may unite my sufferings to His for the greater glory of God and the good of souls, especially our Society, and that if it be His will, the pain may go away before the Chapter.

The Chapter delegates enter into retreat tomorrow. Please offer many sacrifices and prayers, and do [more] penance and fasting that I asked for in another letter, so that the Holy Spirit may be free to do great things in and through the Chapter delegates. Before, I had written to fast on 1st February, because it is the day before the elections. But afterward I remembered that 1st February is Decree of Praise, so please do the fasting on 31st January instead.

Even though the Chapter is about to begin, and the Delegates have all arrived in Calcutta, I wanted you to receive this letter quickly so that we may really be one heart with the whole Church in this year of 1997. By now you must have heard how the Holy Father wants the whole Church to celebrate the Jubilee of Jesus' birth in a very special way in the year 2000. To make us ready for this, Holy Father is giving us three full years of preparation, and this year—1997—is the first one. In 1997, Holy Father wants us to come to know and love Jesus Christ in a very intimate way. When I heard this, I was very happy, because our vocation is to belong to Jesus. So this year gives us the chance to come very close to our Crucified Spouse and, like Our Lady, to treasure and ponder in our hearts all that Lk 1:49; 2:19, 51
He has done for us and wants to give us—especially the gift of Faith and His own life in Baptism. Enclosed you will find a plan that shows you all the points that Holy Father wants us to deepen in our lives during this

Year of Jesus Christ.[a] See how you can do this during meditation and adoration, spiritual reading, your time of faith study, in the community and in the apostolate. Let us make this a year of greater love for Jesus—in the Blessed Sacrament, in the poor, in our hearts—and pray often, "Jesus in my heart, I believe in Your tender love for me. I love You."

Also enclosed is a copy of the prayer which the Holy Father wrote for the Year of Jesus Christ.[b] In union with the Holy Father and the whole Church, let us use this prayer as part of our preparation for the Jubilee. As it is quite long, it has been decided to say only a short section of the prayer every day, after the Dinner prayer. The day on which to say each part is shown on the sheet itself. It is also beautiful to make meditation on this prayer sometimes. It will help us to cleave to Jesus with an undivided heart.

The best help you can give to Mother, to the Chapter delegates and to our poor—and the greatest joy you can give to Jesus and Our Lady—is to be really holy. Put your whole heart and soul into the strong resolution—"I will, I want, with God's blessing, [to] be holy."

Let us pray. My dearest children

Give Jesus a free hand. Ask Our Lady to help you. Let us pray.

God bless you

Mother[c]

MGL 279. 16TH JANUARY 1997

+

LDM

Mother House

16th January 1997[d]

My dearest Children,

God's blessing be with each one of you. He alone matters—Mother's voice is not important but His voice—that's so important. All for His glory

a. The preparation for the Jubilee has been omitted.

b. The prayer has been omitted.

c. Mother wrote these lines in very shaky and feeble handwriting, thus revealing her very weak physical condition.

d. This letter came about from the instruction that Mother gave from her room on 16th January 1997 to the Chapter Delegates, before they began the retreat and seminar that preceded the Chapter. A few Sisters took notes of Mother's talk; subsequently it was typed and sent to the houses as a general letter.

and the good of the Society. Do not forget this retreat, it is very important for the Society. It is not an ordinary retreat. Every moment is very precious, do not miss the chance of this beautiful time. The more intimate and in love you are with Him, the more He will use you for His glory.

If we are true Missionaries of Charity, we can save souls for Jesus. Pray very specially for Mother and for the Councillors so that we can do all for Jesus and for the greater good of the Society. I want each one of you to be holy. The priests are taking great trouble;[a] take this chance to be really intimate with Jesus. Be one with Mother and the Councillors, so together we can help the Society. I want you to be holy.

This retreat is very special for our Society and to each one of us. Grow in intimate love for Jesus, this is something very special—"gift of God". Try to come closer to Him; to be able to do this, ask Mary—say "I need you, I love you, help me come closer to Jesus". Our Lady will help you to be pleasing to Him.

Be very strict with silence. Don't talk during the retreat. It is not the time for talking even if that is a good thing. Tell Our Lady to take this Chapter completely into her hands so that we can do all for the glory of God and for the good of the people.

Put your whole heart. Mother is with you all—don't feel bad. Our Lord is doing this for a purpose.

Let us pray.

God bless you
Mother

a. Mother is speaking about the priests that were preaching the retreat and giving the seminar that followed the retreat to the Chapter members.

ATTACHMENT TO MGL 279 OF 16TH JANUARY 1997

+

LDM

Mother House
18th January 1997
3:00 P.M.[a]

MOTHER'S MESSAGE:

Today we are here to honour Our Lady—love Her, cling to Her. She is the Mother, Mother of the Missionaries of Charity. Always ask Her to be a Mother to us, ask Her to protect us, teach us to love Jesus. In so many ways She has taken care of us. We show our gratitude for [her] being a Mother to us, guiding us, protecting us, for keeping us as her child—we are here now to show deep gratitude, each one of us in our own way.

Let us ask Her, Mary, Mother of Jesus, be a Mother to us now, guide, protect and keep us close to Jesus. In a special way, She is being the Mother of Jesus. Let us ask Our Lady to guide us, protect us and show us the way to Jesus. Mary, Mother of Jesus be a Mother to each one of us NOW.

The closer we come to Her, the closer we come to Jesus. Let us come closer to Her, that we will be able to grow in the tender love for Jesus. Let us thank God for His great love in giving us Our Lady to be with us. Let us remember that Our Lady is really the Mother of Jesus.

Always pray to Our Lady, turn to Her, ask Her

to be Our Mother
Our Guide
Our Protector

Let us ask Her to be a Mother to us ALWAYS.

a. Mother gave an instruction to the Sisters at Mother House, which the Sisters wrote down and sent to the Society.

MGL 280. 20TH JANUARY 1997

+ LDM

Mother House
20th January 1997

My dearest Children,

This brings you Mother's love, prayer and blessing.

This letter comes to inform all of you that our dearest Sr. M. Michelle, MC, has gone home to Jesus in the very early hours of the morning on 19th January 1997 from our house in St. Paul in Canada.

Sr. Michelle (Diane Michelle Quade) was born on 22nd May 1957 in Illinois, U.S.A. She made her First Profession in our Society on 24th October 1983 in Rome, and her Final Profession on 7th December 1989 in Washington. Sr. Michelle was a Sister who was truly meek and humble of heart, and this humility came out in her love for the humble and hidden works, in her ready acceptance of her own limitations and those of others, and in her thoughtfulness and quiet charity towards every Sister and the poor. Jesus, who made her heart like unto His, must surely have brought her very close to Himself in heaven.

Please offer the suffrages of the Society for the repose of her soul. As Jesus has called Sr. Michelle during the Chapter, I am sure that her intercession will bring many graces to the Delegates—especially humility with God and meekness with one another. Let us be humble like Mary and holy like Jesus. Please pray for Mother.

God bless you
M Teresa MC

MGL 281. 10TH MARCH 1997

L.D.M.

10th March 1997[a]

My dearest Children,

As the days for the Elections are coming closer, I hope and pray you are all praying for God's blessing, that God may give us the light and grace to vote according to His will and decision.

a. This letter, written in Mother's shaky and unstable handwriting (due to her delicate health), was not typed but sent handwritten to the houses. In this letter, as in several others from this period, the decline in Mother's health is also shown by the repetitions she makes.

As you know, we have to vote for the Superior General and the 4 Councillors. Let us decide after much prayer, that we may vote for the right people chosen by God, for the Glory of God and the good of our Society.

Keep praying, as this Voting is very important. We have to vote for a Superior General and the 4 Councillors. I am sure you are all praying that the voting be for the Glory of God and the good of our Society.

You have all been so good to me during all these years right from the beginning. I hope and pray this love and Sharing will continue with greater love and care.

With God's blessing we will vote for a New Superior General. Pray, Sisters, that you vote with great love and Faith.

I am grateful from my heart to each one of you for all the love, care and help you have all given me during these years. With your help, I have been able to do Something Beautiful for God. Let us continue the beautiful work, to serve the Poorest of the Poor with great love and care.

Let us now pray that our voting for our Superior General and the four Councillors be done with Great Faith and love. Let it be the fruit of much prayer and sacrifice.

The voting will be done on Thursday 13th March morning in the Mother House.

Let us pray and make many Sacrifices.

God bless you
M. Teresa, MC

MGL 282. 13TH MARCH 1997

+ LDM

Mother House
13th March 1997

My dearest Children,

I want to give you very special news of our dearest Sr. Agnes—who was the first to join me, on the Feast of St. Joseph, 19th March 1949, when there was absolutely nothing. Sister will be now 48 years as a Missionary of Charity on 19th March, 1997. How much we must thank God for her—so small yet with a heart full of love and trust, she let God use her nothingness to show His greatness.

Last year, after an operation, it was found out that Sister was suffering from cancer, which has now spread very fast. Like St. Agnes, she is a True Lamb with Jesus, her Crucified Spouse—and has offered her life and suffering for the Society, for this General Chapter and for China.

Our Holy Father, after being told how sick Sr. Agnes was—has sent her his words of comfort and Apostolic Blessing.

Let us thank Sr. Agnes for her beautiful example of simplicity and her tender, compassionate love for Jesus in the poor.

Sr. Agnes must always remain someone special to each one of us and let us continue to pray very, very specially for her.

Let us pray

God bless you
M. Teresa, MC

MGL 283. 14TH MARCH 1997

+ LDM

Mother House
14th March 1997

My dearest Children,

This brings you Mother's love, prayer and blessing for a Happy and Holy Easter! May the joy of the Resurrection fill each one's heart, and bring with it peace and thankfulness to Jesus for all that He has done in our Society and in each one of us.

Just now, in this Lent and Easter, it is so beautiful to see how Our Lady
was the first Missionary of Charity. At the foot of the Cross, Our Lady Jn 19:25
saw only pain and suffering—and when they closed the tomb, she could not even see the Body of Jesus. But it was then that Our Lady's faith, her Loving Trust and Total Surrender were greatest. We know that before, in
Nazareth, Jesus could not work any miracles because they had no faith. Mk 6:5–6
Now, to work His greatest miracle—the Resurrection—He asks the greatest faith from His own Mother. And because she belonged completely to God in Loving Trust and Total Surrender, He could bring to us the joy of the Resurrection, and Mary would be the Cause of our Joy.

This Chapter has been a real gift of God to each one in the Society. I am so grateful for the way that each of you did your best through prayer, sacrifice, study and suggestions to make our Society something beautiful for God. So many of the Chapter delegates have told Mother that the

Chapter was like a very long retreat, helping them to know, love and live our vocation with even greater fidelity. We all came to see more clearly how beautiful are our Constitutions and Directory, but how much we often fail to put them into practice, even sometimes to know them properly. Let us, each one, make the strong resolution to use these great gifts of God to grow holy. The decisions of the Chapter are meant to help us to live our Constitutions beautifully. They are really the fruit of the prayer and sacrifices of each one of you. Take them, together with the Constitutions and Directory, for spiritual reading and meditation so as to put them into life. Let this Chapter not remain just on the paper or in the book, but in the life of faithfulness offered to Jesus with hearts full of love.

You will be happy to know that Jesus has given our Society the great gift of a new Superior General and Councillors General. The elections were held on 13th March, with His Grace Archbishop D'Souza presiding. The following Sisters were elected:

Superior General	–	Sr. M. Nirmala, MC
First Councillor	–	Sr. M. Frederick, MC
Second Councillor	–	Sr. M. Priscilla, MC
Third Councillor	–	Sr. M. Lysa, MC
Fourth Councillor	–	Sr. M. Martin de Porres, MC

You will show your love for Mother and for your vocation by being one heart and mind with Sr. Nirmala. Give her the same love and trust, the same obedience, that you have always given Mother. Obedience is the fruit of faith. Like Our Lady, this is the time for your faith—your Loving Trust and Total Surrender—to be the greatest. If you belong completely to Jesus in
Mt 28:8; Lk 24:41, 52; Jn 20:20 Loving Trust and Total Surrender, you will see the greatest miracles of all happen in our Society now. Then you will know the joy of the Risen Lord and you will be able to share that joy with all you meet by your Cheerfulness. That will make you the cause of joy to Mother and to each other.

Only Jesus knows how grateful I am to God for the gift that each one of you has been to Mother. Every day of these 50 years, you have been Mother's strength and joy, and have given me all your love and trust. What Jesus asked of Mother could never have been done without each one of you, in-
Is 43:1, 4 dividually. Just as Jesus called Mother and then Sr. M. Agnes, He has called each one of you by name. You are precious to Him, He loves you—and you are precious to Mother and you know Mother's love for each and every one

of you. Because Mother loves you, Mother wants you to be holy—this is my love for you, my prayer for each one of you—that I may offer back to Jesus the gifts He has given to me, shining with His own holiness. That is Mother's promise: to give saints to Mother Church, and so Mother has fulfilled her fourth vow also by labouring at the salvation and sanctification of each one of you, my Children. Thank you with all my heart.

Please pray very specially for our dearest Sr. M. Agnes, MC. Her cancer is now very far advanced and she is suffering terribly, one with Jesus on the Cross. Sr. Agnes made a very big offering to Jesus yesterday when she made such great effort to be present for the elections. I know Jesus accepted her sacrifice for the good of our Society, as she was the very first one to join Mother. It seems that Jesus will soon call Sr. Agnes from this life. Pray that she may go to Him in joy.

Let us together ask Our Lady to give us her heart, so beautiful, so pure, so immaculate—her heart so full of love and humility—that we may love
Jesus in the Bread of Life and serve Him in the distressing disguise of the Jn 6:35, 48, 51
poorest of the poor. Mt 25:40

Let us pray.

Keep the joy of loving Jesus in each other and the Poor you serve.

God bless you
M. Teresa MC

MGL 284. 9TH APRIL 1997

+ LDM

Mother House
9th April 1997

My dearest Children,

This brings you all Mother's and Sr. Nirmala's love, prayer and blessing that you may be one heart full of love in the Heart of Jesus through Mary.

This letter comes to you to bring you the news that our dearest Sr. Agnes went home to Jesus this morning, 9th April 1997, at 6:10 A.M. from the Mother House. It was so striking to see the love of Jesus for His Spouse at the very last moment. Sr. Agnes had been struggling very much all through the night. At 5:45 in the morning, Father Pasquale came to celebrate Holy Mass in the room with Sr. Agnes, Mother, Sr. Nirmala and some of the Sisters, while the Novices and other Sisters were at Mass in the big chapel. Just as Sr. Agnes received a drop of the Precious Blood, she just slipped away to be with Jesus forever. So you see, Jesus did not even wait for her to reach, but He came to take her, Himself, to be His Spouse in the kingdom of heaven. We have much to thank God for.

Sr. Agnes (Subashini Das) was born on 1st January 1929. You all know that Sr. Agnes was the first one to join Mother in the very beginning, when we had nothing but the poorest of the poor. She entered the Society on 19th March 1949, made her first Vows on 12th April 1953 and Final Vows on 12th April 1959. Jesus gave Sr. Agnes the courage and love to follow Him when the Missionaries of Charity were not known, when Loving Trust and Total Surrender were daily living realities. And Sr. Agnes had the conviction to keep this way of following Jesus in humility, hiddenness and poverty all her life.

I am sure you know that Sr. Agnes had been suffering from terminal cancer very much for the last year. And yet, how beautifully she bore her sufferings—in silence and patience and real surrender to God's plan for her. That is why so many Sisters remarked on the peace and serenity that flowed from Sr. Agnes in the last weeks. In spite of pain and fatigue, she was faithful to her duties for as long as she could be—visiting houses as Regional, caring for the poor, taking part in the Chapter, right until she had to be in bed. Even in the bed, she consoled the poor and counselled the Sisters, was faithful to prayer and smiled through the pain to all who came to her. It was a real grace to have Sr. Agnes in the Mother House at the end, where so many Sisters could see Jesus in her and where she could receive the love of Jesus through the tender care and concern of Mother and the Sisters.

Please offer the suffrages of the Society for the repose of Sr. Agnes' soul. I am sure that our community in heaven will be very happy to welcome her there. Maybe Our Lady will make her Superior, since she is the most Senior, and she will lead them to give even greater glory to God in heaven, and help to us and our poor on earth.

Let us ask Our Sister Agnes to pray for the Society and each one of us. She died a beautiful death.

Let us pray.

God bless you
M. Teresa MC
M. Nirmala MC[a]

a. Sr. M. Nirmala, MC, used to sign her letters as "M. Nirmala MC" meaning "Mary Nirmala, MC" (not Mother Nirmala, MC).

MGL 285. 17TH APRIL 1997

+ LDM

Mother House
17th April 1997

My dearest Children,

This brings you Mother's love, prayer and blessing, and also the joy and hope that fills my heart on reading your beautiful letters expressing your deep grateful love for Mother and for our Society, together with your sincere desire to satiate the Thirst of Jesus for love and for souls by (Jn 19:28) a more fervent, faithful response of love to His gift of love—your vocation—which is a call to a deep intimacy in prayer and action, loving and (Jn 6:35, 48, 51) serving Him in the appearance of Bread and in the distressing disguise of (Mt 25:40) the poorest of the poor.

It is so important for us to learn to pray the work by doing it with Jesus, to Jesus and for Jesus.[a] The beautiful work of love God has entrusted to His Missionaries of Charity is God's work, not ours; that is why we need a deep life of prayer—of oneness with Jesus. It is not enough to do the work, we must learn to pray the work we do. Take great care of your prayer life—your life of union of mind and heart with Jesus.

My children, if you want to be holy, there is no easier and surer and quicker way than to put your hand in Mary's hand, and allow her to lead you to Jesus. Jesus gave her to us as His last gift from the Cross when He said to John and to us: "Behold your Mother." Make use of this precious (Jn 19:27) gift—keep very close to her, in a special way during her month of May, and you will be close to Jesus. Listen to her—she who told the servers at (Jn 2:5) the wedding feast at Cana, "Do whatever he tells you," can and will direct you in the best way to Jesus.[b]

The Chapter delegates are now all back in their regions with you they have much to share with you. Be eager to learn how lovingly God has led each one to discover more deeply the greatness, sacredness and beauty of our MC vocation and the abundance of spiritual means offered us by our Constitutions and Directory to grow holy. Desire deeply to know and understand the way of life traced out for us as MCs so as to follow Jesus closely, for only then will you grow to love it and want to live it.

The election of the MC Contemplatives' General Councillors took

a. See MGL 103 of 24th October 1973, p. 180.
b. See MGL 200 of 27th October 1987, p. 369.

place at the Mother House when all the voting papers had come in. . . . We now have the governing body of both branches as follows:

Mother M. Teresa, MC
Foundress
Sister M. Nirmala, MC
Superior General

Active Branch		*Contemplative Branch*
Sr. M. Frederick, MC Asst. General		Sr. M. Fatima, MC Asst. General & Responsible for the Contemplative Branch
Sr. M. Priscilla, MC 2nd Councillor		Sr. M. Ancy, MC 2nd Councillor
Sr. M. Lysa, MC 3rd Councillor		Sr. M. Colmcille, MC 3rd Councillor
Sr. M. Martin de Porres, MC 4th Councillor		Sr. M. Assumpta, MC 4th Councillor
Sr. Margaret Mary, MC	—	Secretary General
Sr. M. Joel, MC	—	Bursar General

In spite of all our weakness, God is in love with us and keeps using each one to light His light of love and compassion in the world. So let us give Jesus a big smile and a hearty thank you.[a] All together we must continue to make our Society "Something beautiful for God. " Our dearest Sr. M. Agnes, who has now joined the heavenly community after spending 48 years of beautiful loving fidelity in humble service to our Sisters and the poorest of the poor, so close to Mother, will obtain many graces for the Society.

. . .

I hear that the Holy Father will be going to Poland on 31st May to attend the celebrations of the Eucharistic Congress to be held in the town of Wroclaw.[b] I hope to be able to meet him to thank him and assure him of our prayer and fidelity to his teaching before I leave for USA, where 14 Senior Tertians will be taking their Final Vows on 7th June in Washington, and 5 of our Senior Novices will be taking their First Vows in New York on 11th June.

a. See MGL 112 of 19th December 1974, p. 196.

b. The 46th International Eucharistic Congress in Wrocław, Poland, held from 25th May to 1st June 1997, had for its theme: "The Eucharist and Freedom." Mother was not able to go to Poland to receive the vows of the Sisters and to meet Pope John Paul II as she had hoped; instead, the novices from Poland came to Rome for their profession.

We will keep all our Sisters preparing for their First and Final Vows very much in our prayer. Pray much for Mother and for Sister Nirmala, that all be done for the greater glory of God and the good of our Society.

Be only all for Jesus through Mary—She will help you to be all for Jesus—Holy.

Let us pray.

God bless you
M. Teresa MC

MGL 286. 12TH JULY 1997

L.D.M.

Rome
12th July 1997

Dear Sisters,

Learn of Me because I am meek and humble of Heart. Mt 11:29

If these two virtues enter our hearts, we are sure to become very dear to Jesus, and He will give us all the graces we need to be holy.—

So let us pray—

Jesus, meek and humble of heart, make my heart like Yours, so that I become a true Spouse of Jesus. Let us pray.

God bless you
M Teresa MC[a]

a. A draft letter dated 5th September 1997, that Mother Teresa was not able to sign before she died that day, was mistakenly given out as her last letter. Since it is not in fact Mother Teresa's last letter, it is not included here.

LETTER FROM SR. M. NIRMALA, MC, REGARDING MOTHER'S DEATH AND FUNERAL

+ LDM

Mother House
9th September 1997

My dearest Sisters,

In these very special days, I write to tell you how close I am to each one of you in prayer, in sorrow, and in peace. But even more I wish to share with you the joy of knowing that our dearest Mother is sending her love, prayer and most special blessing straight from the Hearts of Jesus and Mary to us, her little children.

By now all of you know that our dearest Mother went home to Jesus at 9:30 P.M. on Friday, 5th September. God in His mercy arranged everything so beautifully. In these last weeks, Mother had been quite well, and was kept very busy meeting visitors, giving instructions to the Sisters, attending to the post and the phone, and receiving the children from all our Calcutta slum schools in turn—a different school every day. No one suspected that these were Mother's last days on earth. On Thursday, 4th September, Mother had some diarrhea and vomiting, but that was soon controlled. Sometime during the day on Friday, Mother developed that same sort of back pain that she had had at the time of Chapter and later in New York. It was not so severe as to keep Mother in bed, though, and she sat at her table in the afternoon, sorting the post and telling how much work there was to do. Mother was supposed to come for Adoration, but changed her mind and rested instead. I took the Blessed Sacrament to Mother to kiss at the end of Adoration, and Mother did it with such great love and devotion. Mother ate her dinner as usual.

At about 8:15 P.M., Sr. Shanti decided to call Dr. Woodward to check on Mother, as he often did. So before phoning, Sisters began to measure heart rate, etc., in order to inform the doctor. As soon as the machines were operating, it was immediately noticed that Mother was in a heart crisis. Sisters at once began emergency medicines, and Dr. Woodward arrived soon after, but already Mother was in great distress. The Parish Priest came quickly and anointed Mother. She was having great trouble breathing and was looking around for some relief. But at a certain point her eyes focused on the crown of thorns that hangs on the wall beside her bed, and in the midst of such agony, she found the strength to lift her hand and place her kiss on Jesus' crown. Sister Gertrude was praying ejaculatory prayers, and Mother was able to repeat after her, "Jesus, I love You. Jesus, I trust You. Jesus . . ." before she lost her power of speaking. All the while the doctor, nurses and Sisters were doing their best to give medicines and do heart massage, etc. But at 9:30 P.M. the machines no longer registered any sign of life. Doctor kept working some minutes longer, but finally informed us that our dearest Mother had gone home. As soon as Mother's body could be prepared, we had Holy Mass for her in the big chapel.

Now Mother's body is lying in state in St. Thomas Church, near Loreto House, in Calcutta. Thousands and thousands of people are coming every day to pay their last respects to Mother—the very rich, the very poor and all in between. Mother will be given a state funeral—an honour that is given only to Presidents and Prime Ministers—a real sign of India's love for Mother. The funeral will be this Saturday, 13th September, at Netaji Indoor Stadium at 10:00 A.M.

You will all be happy to hear that we have received permission to bury the mortal remains of our dearest Mother here in Mother House. Preparations are already underway for making the grave in what used to be the Novices' refectories on the ground floor. So we will have Mother's spirit within our hearts and Mother's body in our house. What a great blessing from Jesus! It will in time become a shrine and a place of pilgrimage. Sisters, Brothers, Fathers, and so many other friends who loved Mother and the work for the poorest of the poor are pouring into Calcutta. Mother would have said, "See how God uses our nothingness to show forth His greatness." Many dignitaries, both ecclesial and civil, have sent messages of condolence, and many are coming for the funeral. Holy Father has also sent a beautiful message, which I am enclosing for you. Holy Father is sending Cardinal Lourdusamy as Papal Legate to the funeral.[a] Our Archbishop Henry of Calcutta had just gone to Rome when Mother slipped into heaven. He has just arrived back today. The archdiocesan Vicar General, Msgr. Francis Gomes, as well as the Loreto nuns, are giving their all in preparation for the funeral. St. Thomas Church is next to Loreto House.

Please offer the full suffrages, including ten Holy Masses, as for a Sister

a. Initially, Cardinal Lourdusamy was chosen as the pope's representative, but after the Indian government decided to give Mother the honour of a State funeral, the Holy See appropriately sent Cardinal Sodano, Secretary of State, as its official delegate to preside over Mother's funeral Mass at Netaji Indoor Stadium.

of the community, for our dearest Mother, since Mother belongs to every house in the Society.

There is so much more to say, but for now the Holy Spirit will have to speak it all to your hearts. Let us, above all, be one heart full of love in the Heart of Jesus through Mary, as Mother so desired that we be.

God bless you,

M. Nirmala, MC

Appendices

Endnotes

Concordance

Index

APPENDIX A

DECREE OF ERECTION[a]

FERDINAND PERIER, S.J.

by the Grace of God and favour of the H. See
Archbishop of Calcutta
Prelate of the Household of His Holiness
Assistant to the Pontifical Throne
To all who will see this Decree, Greetings in the Lord

For more than two years now, a little group of young women, under the guidance of Sister M. Teresa, a lawfully uncloistered religious of the Institute of the Bl. Virgin Mary, have devoted themselves with generous heart and very great profit for the souls, to helping the poor—the children, grown-ups, the aged ones and also the sick, in this Our Metropolitan City.

As they begged from Us the favour that We should now erect their Group into a religious Congregation, We have with great care scrutinised their way of living and of working, and given diligent consideration to the purpose they have in view. This earnest examination led Us to the conclusion that no other Congregation already in existence answers the purpose which this new Institute is intending; and that, consequently, its erection into a religious Congregation, for the relief of so many and such dire needs, will redound to the greater Glory of God and the advantage of the Catholic Faith in Our Archdiocese.

We have therefore, in conformity with Canon 492, Para. 1, laid our proposal before the Sacred Congregation of Propaganda, depositing at the same time before that Sacred Council the documents required according to its Instruction of 19 March, 1937.

Then, in the audience which we obtained in March 1950, the Most Eminent and Most Reverend Cardinal Petrus Fumasoni Biondi, Prefect of the Sacred Congregation of the Propaganda, graciously pronounced that nothing further precluded Us from erecting the new Congregation, a Diocesan one, to be sure, and which in virtue of Canon 492, para. 2, will have to remain diocesan, in all things subject to the jurisdiction of the Ordinary in accordance with the Sacred Canons, as long as it has not received testimonials of the H. See's approbation or praise.

In consequence, We do, by the present Decree, to the greater Glory of God and for the promotion in these parts of the Kingdom of Truth, Justice, Charity

a. Attachment to MGL 3 of [7th] October 1960.

and Peace of Christ the Saviour, institute and erect the religious Congregation that shall have for:

its name or Title: The Congregation of the Missionary Sisters of Charity

its Holy Patron: The Immaculate Heart of the Blessed Virgin Mary

its Purpose: To quench the thirst of Our Lord Jesus Christ for the salvation of souls by the observance of the three vows of Poverty, Chastity and Obedience, and of an additional fourth vow to devote themselves with abnegation to the care of the poor and needy who, crushed by want and destitution, live in conditions unworthy of the human dignity; those who join this Institute, therefore, are resolved to spend themselves unremittingly in seeking out, in towns and villages, even amid squalid surroundings, the poorer, the abandoned, the sick, the infirm, the dying; in taking care of them, rendering help to them, visiting them assiduously and instructing them in the Christian Doctrine, in endeavouring to the utmost to bring about their conversion and sanctification and performing any other similar apostolic works and services, however lowly and mean they may appear.

Thus do We INSTITUTE AND DECLARE ERECTED the above said Congregation, in accordance with Canon 492 of the Church's Law.

Given at Calcutta, under our signature and seal, on the day of the Feast of the Most Holy Rosary of the Blessed Virgin Mary, 7 October, 1950

Ferdinandus S.J.
Archbishop of Calcutta

DECREE OF PRAISE[a]

SACRED CONGREGATION FOR THE PROPAGATION OF THE FAITH

DECREE

In order that the apostolate among the poorer people might be promoted more efficaciously, the Ordinary of the Archdiocese of Calcutta, India, some years ago, instituted a Pious Union of women which he later raised into the religious Congregation of the Missionary Sisters of Charity.

As with the help of God's grace the above named Congregation has grown much and has sent its Sisters into many other dioceses of India to carry out the works of charity, the Ordinaries of the said dioceses submitted to this Sacred Council for the Propagation of the Faith a petition that the Decree of Praise might be granted to this Congregation.

Our Most Holy Father Paul VI, by Divine Providence Pope, gladly received this petition communicated to him by the undersigned Cardinal Prefect of this Sa-

a. Attachment to MGL 34 of 22nd March 1965.

cred Council at the audience of the 1st February 1965 A.D. and awarded the Decree of Praise to the Congregation of the Missionary Sisters of Charity, whose Mother House is in the Archdiocese of Calcutta.

Moreover this Sacred Council approves the Constitutions of the said Congregation for seven years according to the text which is joined to this Decree.

Given at Rome, from the Palace of the Sacred Congregation for the Propagation of the Faith, on the 1st February in the year of the Lord 1965.

G.P. Cardinal Agagianian
Prefect
Petrus Sigismondi
Tit. Archbishop of Neap. In P.
Secretary.

ATTACHMENT TO MGL 244 OF 25TH MARCH 1993

Statement of Fr. Joseph, MC, about the Varanasi Letter

A BRIEF HISTORY OF MOTHER TERESA'S 1993 "VARANASI LETTER"

In the following testimony I wish to relate what I know from personal involvement regarding the origin of Mother Teresa's General Letter of 25 March 1993, known as the "Varanasi Letter". What is stated here can be confirmed and amplified by others likewise involved at the time, especially Fr. Gary, MC, and some of the Sisters present in Mother House in November-December of 1992, and in San Gregorio, Rome, in April of 1993.

I must preface this account by relating an incident that occurred in the fall of 1984, in our (Missionaries of Charity Fathers) house in the Bronx, during one of Mother's visits to New York. At the time, I was writing the first draft of our "Founding Document" (early Constitutions), and had been reflecting long over the affirmation made to me some years prior by Fr. Sebastian, MC, that the key to understanding Mother and the Missionaries of Charity was the mystery of Jesus' Thirst.

I had been seeking a way to understand, and to explain to our candidates, the inner connection between the various elements of our MC charism. It seemed more and more to me that the source from which the Spirit of the Society, and all else, flowed logically was precisely this same mystery. At that time Mother's grace of September 10 was still seen primarily as a "command to leave Loreto and go into the slums". But if the charism, at least in seed form, was communicated to her that day, and if the elements of that charism all flowed from this one mystery, then it seemed to me that her experience of September 10 must have somehow been an encounter with the Thirst of Jesus.

I wanted to show in our Constitutions that there was a connection between the Aim and the Spirit of the Society, and that September 10 was more than a change of assignment for Mother—that it was the deposit of something precious which belonged to all of us, witnessed to next to the crucifix on all our chapel walls.

I did not want to put this in writing if it were not true, nor miss the chance to affirm it if it was. The only solution was to ask Mother herself—though her reluctance to speak of September 10 was well known. After some hesitation, and consultation with my brothers, I decided the worst that could happen was that she would not answer. After taking her aside and posing the question and the reason for asking, she paused in silence a long while, then raising her head said "Yes, it is true.... And one day you must tell the Society."

I had taken Mother's words as a kind of mandate from that day on, and done what I could, though always wishing that Mother herself be the one to "tell the Society"—whom I felt had both the need and the right to know.

It was in the light of this history that the "Varanasi letter" came to be. One day in late 1992, Fr. Gary and I had been speaking with Mother in the Mother House sacristy, and the topic came around to Mother's convictions regarding the Thirst of Jesus and MC. The conversation went on at length, and, as I had never heard Mother speak so eloquently or ardently about the subject, I begged her to "tell the Society"—to write it down and to share it in a general letter.

She agreed to do so. She asked us to pray in the chapel, and she went to her room to write while her memory of the conversation was fresh. As I recall she came back three times with bits and pieces of what she remembered. Frustrated at finding it so difficult to put in writing, she finally asked that I write it for her. I refused to do so, and for many reasons: Firstly, only Mother could know and express the depths of her own heart, and the intimate experiences with the Lord that had formed it. Secondly, what she was asking was frankly impossible—everyone would recognize the language and the letter as not being hers, and so it risked eventually doing more harm to what she wanted to communicate to the Society than good, bringing a rejection not only of the letter but, along with it, of the message it contained. But she remained adamant. After entreating her in vain to try again, I accepted to do what I could, using the scraps of phrases she had written to aid my memory (these pages have been seen by various others in MC, including the Postulator of the Cause, who can attest to their existence).

Over the next three months I attempted to do what Mother had asked. When she came to Rome in April of 1993, the Holy Father had just written for the first time on the Thirst of Jesus in his Lenten letter, and Mother took this as a kind of sign: first of all, of the timeliness of what she was about to send out, but also of the Lord's blessing on her letter. I presented what I had done, and she read it over very carefully in front of Fr. Gary and me. Since one of the topics in our conversation in Mother House had been Mother's need to communicate these things while she was still with us in this life, I referred to this in the proposed text of the letter. That was, in my recollection, the only place Mother hesitated as she read—though finally agreeing to leave it as it was. The rest she read through, and began making corrections as she went along—adding, removing, or rewriting.

After she finished her editing and revising, it was a question of writing the letter out in her own hand (which was the condition under which I accepted to contribute to the letter) and, finally, of ascribing it a date and place of origin. After repeatedly starting over, due to mistakes and pain in her hand, she gave up trying to write it longhand and asked for it to be typed instead. She wanted it known, however, that it was fully hers and claimed by her, and so she sent for the local and regional superiors (Rome) to show them what she was doing, and to ask their collaboration as well as their prudence in keeping to themselves their knowledge of the assistance she had received.

In the end, Mother wanted to date the letter on a feast of Our Lady (since it had been more than three months in the making, there was no clear date to affix). The only Marian feastday within the period of the letter's writing was the Annunciation. When Mother went ahead and dated it 25 March, I pointed out that she should also put the place where she had actually been on that day. If she were to put Rome or Calcutta, anyone would know she had not been there on that date, and would call into question Mother's authorship. If, in hindsight, the mention of "Varanasi" in the letter has actually caused confusion rather than preventing it, I take the responsibility—the idea was mine, not Mother's. In any case, it was finally signed and sent out, and Mother seemed genuinely pleased with what she had done. Personally, I was glad to see her write many of the same things in her own hand the following year from Vietnam.[a] Knowing their history, perhaps these two letters can shed light one on the other, and on what Mother so deeply wanted to "tell the Society".

I affirm before God that all the above is factual to the best of my memory.

In faith,

Fr. Joseph Langford, MC

Statement of Fr. Gary, MC, about the Varanasi Letter

After Mother Teresa's death on September 5th, 1997, I heard it said by some members of the Society that Mother Teresa (the Foundress of the Missionaries of Charity family) did not write the General Letter issued on March 25th, 1993, which has become known as the "Varanasi Letter." Because of this belief, some were not accepting the letter as representing her words and spirituality.

As the contents of this letter concern Mother's own reflections on the charism she received, this letter is very important for her Religious family of the Missionaries of Charity, especially now that Mother is no longer with us in person.

I was present on several occasions when Mother Teresa and Fr. Joseph Langford, MC, spoke about this letter.[b] I would like to recall the details from my first-hand knowledge in the hope that it will clarify any future confusion that may arise. I have already given this witness on several occasions to MC Sisters.

How did this letter come to be written?

a. He is referring to MGL 250 of 29th March 1994, pp. 449–50.

b. After reviewing this document for inclusion in this volume, Fr. Gary wanted to clarify that the "several occasions" referred to in the text actually refers to the whole process of the composition of Mother's letter. As he makes clear further in the text, the concern was to address and clarify the confusion about the essence of the Charism that was evidenced by questions among the various branches of the MC family. A few other minor edits have been made that do not affect the substance of the text.

In November or December of 1992, Fr. Joseph Langford, MC, and I met with Mother Teresa at her Mother House in Calcutta. The purpose of our meeting with her was to ask her to clarify for us (and for the Society) what she considered to be the heart of the MC charism.

Father Joseph Langford initiated the conversation, explaining to Mother his concern on our hearing from some members of our religious family that two different opinions were circulating about what was considered to be the heart of Mother's spirit and charism.

Many MCs agreed that the heart of the charism was expressed in Jesus' words on the Cross, "I thirst". But others insisted that the charism was rooted, not in the Thirst of Jesus, but rather in the Society's works—expressed in the MC 4th vow of "wholehearted and free service to the poorest of the poor."

It is true that Mother often spoke about the work and motivated us to "go in haste" to the poor, using Jesus' promise about works of charity: "Whatever you do to the least of my brothers, you do it to Me."

That day in Calcutta we met expressly to inform Mother about this confusion caused by the two separate opinions and to ask her to tell us, and the Society, exactly what was in her mind about the essence of the charism of MC.

What exactly was the essence of the Charism, for her? Did the charism center on Jesus' thirst or on the works?

When Mother heard that there was a certain division amongst us about the understanding of the charism, she was very disturbed and very animated. I remember her first expressing that yes, she had spoken mostly about the works during the years of the Society's development and growth, but these for her were the means, the way, to satiate Jesus' thirst.

She expressed amazement that everyone did not understand. "The Aim of the Society" she said in wonder, "is to satiate Jesus' thirst on the Cross for love and souls. How could anyone be confused?" "Everything exists in MC only to satiate Jesus' thirst." That was everything for Mother. "You cannot separate the means from the Aim," she said. And Mother spoke with us, in this context, for some time.

Father Joseph said that Mother had best write something, a general letter or something, to make that clear to the whole Society. Otherwise, when she died the Society would be split about the understanding of the charism.

I might add at this point that I had asked Mother on a number of occasions what she desired for all of us in the MC family (Sisters, Brothers, Fathers), and she always gave the same precise reply, "That you be one."[a] This unity and charity amongst us was always Mother's chief concern. So one can imagine the intensity of her reaction that day to learn that something as serious as the understanding of the charism itself could become the source of division amongst us after she was gone. She told us to pray in the chapel and she went directly to her room to begin writing something for a general letter.

Mother returned sometime later to meet with us, and she carried in her hand several pages of handwritten text which she showed to Father. These pages contained some of the points about which she had been speaking to us.

a. In the review, Fr. Gary added after "That you be one" "—one heart in the Heart of Jesus."

Father Joseph agreed that these points were very good, and he encouraged her to write even more and to send it out to everyone.[a] Mother hesitated and said something about it being difficult for her to write and she asked Father Joseph to draft out the points for her in letter form and she and he would review it together next time they met.

We parted that day with Mother thanking Father for bringing this to her attention.

Soon after we left Calcutta and returned to Rome. On several occasions during the following weeks, Fr. Joseph shared the draft of Mother's points and asked my opinion. He was trying to word the letter in the grammar of Mother, with her accustomed phrasing and neglect of articles. I mentioned that I did not think that was necessary, since everyone would know that this was an edited letter.

When Mother next came to Rome in the early months of the new Year (1993), the three of us met once again at San Gregorio al Celio, the Sisters' regional house in Rome.

Mother took the draft letter and read it out loud very slowly, pausing here and there in her own reflections. Only once did she raise a question. This was not about a point of hers being misrepresented, but about the introductory words that preceded her point. "For a long time Mother has been hesitant to talk to you about September 10th". "Why these words?" she asked. Fr. Joseph then said something like, "Mother, if you don't connect these thoughts back to the founding grace of September 10th, they may not be believed as yours."

Mother reflected on his words for a few seconds in silence and then continued to read the text without another word about that introduction. At the end, she was very happy with the presentation and contents of the letter.

Father next asked Mother to write out the letter in her own script, and Mother declined saying she was very tired. Father then reminded her of her custom of dating a general letter on a feast of Our Lady, and he suggested March 25th, 1993, when she had been visiting Varanasi.

Mother was hesitant to use that place, Varanasi, as the place of origin for the letter, but in the end she agreed.

Later, the letter was sent out to all the MC houses and was very well received. It came to be referred to as "the Varanasi Letter" and was accepted by most as a clear statement by our Mother on the Charism of the Missionaries of Charity.

A few may claim that Mother Teresa was manipulated into writing this letter, but I state that, to the contrary, she was very concerned to have it written.

These are my recollections. I share them only so that God's Will may be glorified in everything.

March 25th, 2002

Father Gary Duckworth, MC

a. In the review Fr. Gary added, in brackets: "(I think Mother returned twice more to her room to write more. Father Joseph then asked if she would put her points into a General Newsletter for the Society.)"

Draft of MGL 244 of 25th March 1993

LDM[a]

My dearest Sisters, Brothers and Fathers.

In reading Holy Father's letter on "Thirst" it struck me so much to realize the gift of God to our Society—from its very birth on the 10th September the Society was chosen to satiate the Thirst of Jesus for love, for souls.

How could anybody think that it is not important, since the Aim of the Society is to satiate the thirst of Jesus on the Cross for love for souls, by labouring at the Salvation and Sanctification of the Poorest of the Poor—

It is true Mother does not speak so often about "I Thirst" but she often speaks of the means how to satiate the thirst of Jesus through prayer, intimate love for Jesus, and the living of the Vows.

Sept. 10th was the birth of our Society as a whole with its aim, spirit and means. It was meant for the whole Church and it has grown like that. If it was for me alone, today [the] Society would not exist.

We have to be very careful about retreat preachers. Those who understand our spirit are very happy, as it has helped them to really come closer to God.

The MC Fathers what they have written about "I thirst" with my full permission and consent. I have all their writing with me.

The first Person to hear Jesus cry I thirst was His Mother and St. John and I am sure St. Mary Magdalen—We are only trying to imitate them.

We do not realize the greatness of God's Love and trust in choosing our Society to satiate His thirst for love for souls—The more intimate is our love for Jesus, the closer we come to Jesus, the better we understand His thirst for love for souls. So let us each one of us really try to grow in that intimate personal love for Jesus so that we can really love and live that Thirst of Jesus by satiating His Thirst with our love, our fidelity and our Holiness

God bless you

M. Teresa MC

a. This is Mother's handwritten draft of MGL 244 of 25th March 1993, mentioned in Fr. Joseph's and Fr. Gary's statements. Fr. Joseph used this draft to elaborate on the Charism, and it came to be known as the Varanasi Letter.

APPENDIX B

MC HOUSES DURING MOTHER TERESA'S LIFETIME (FROM 1950 TO 1997)

During her lifetime Mother Teresa opened 589 active and 18 contemplative houses, of which 13 were closed. At the time of her death the Sisters were serving in 594 missions established in 120 countries. The final house on this list (Manaus, Brazil) was opened three days after Mother Teresa's death; the Sisters had already been assigned and the preparations for this foundation were already made before Mother Teresa's death. Because of the actual opening date, however, this foundation is not included in the total number of houses as of 5th September 1997.

MC FOUNDATIONS DURING MOTHER'S LIFETIME—WORLD

North America (59 foundations)

- **Canada** (St. Paul, Vancouver, Winnipeg, Toronto, Montreal)
- **Mexico** (Tijuana—Postal & El Florido & Central, Tlalnepantla, Toluca, Mexico City, Cardenas, Villahermosa, Tampico, Veracruz, Merida)
- **United States of America** (Phoenix-AZ, Little Rock-AR, Lynwood-CA, San Francisco Noviciate & Queen of Peace & Gift of Love-CA, Denver-CO, Washington I & II & III-DC, Miami-FL, Atlanta-GA, Chicago-IL, Peoria-IL, Jenkins-KY, Baton Rouge-LA, Baltimore-MD, Boston-MA, New Bedford-MA, Detroit-MI, Saint Louis-MO, Newark-NJ, Chichiltah-NM, Gallup-NM, Bronx-NY, Harlem-NY, Manhattan-NY, Brooklyn-NY, Charlotte-NC, Chester-PA, Norristown-PA, Memphis-TN, Dallas-TX)

- **Mexico** (Tijuana-Libertad), contemplative foundation
- **United States of America** (Alhambra-CA, San Diego-CA, Washington-DC, Chicago-IL, Plainfield-NJ, Union Avenue Bronx-NY, Brooklyn-NY, Mahanoy-PA), contemplative foundations

Central America & Caribbean (39 foundations)

- **Costa Rica** (San Jose)
- **El Salvador** (San Marcos, Usulutan)
- **Guatemala** (Escuintla, Guatemala City)
- **Honduras** (San Pedro Sula, Santa Rosa de Copan, Tegucigalpa)
- **Nicaragua** (Granada, Managua)
- **Panama** (Colon, Panama City)
- **Cuba** (Bayamo, Cardenas, Ciego de Avila, Havana, Las Tunas, Pinar del Rio)
- **Grenada** (Carriacou, St. George's)
- **Haiti** (Gonaïves, Hinche, Jacmel, Jeremie, Les Cayes, Port au Prince—Sansfil & Delmas)
- **Jamaica** (Balaclava, Kingston)
- **Puerto Rico** (Aguadilla, Bayamon, Ponce)
- **Santa Lucia** (Castries)
- **Trinidad and Tobago** (Port of Spain)
- **Virgin Islands** (St. Croix)

- **Cuba** (El Cobre), contemplative foundation
- **Nicaragua** (Managua), contemplative foundation

South America (44 foundations)

- **Argentina** (Beccar, Zarate, Buenos Aires—Benavidez & Beccar, Frontera)
- **Bolivia** (La Paz—El Alto & San Pedro, Santa Cruz)
- **Brazil** (Brasilia, Rio—I Bonsucesso & II Realengo, Sao Paulo, Barreirinha, Manaus, Jacobina, Alagados, Malvinas, Salvador Bahia, Santos)
- **Chile** (Santiago, Batuco)
- **Colombia** (Bogota, Cali, Pereira, Cartagena, Cucuta)
- **Ecuador** (Guayaquil, Quito, Esperanza)
- **Guyana** (Georgetown, Hosororo, New Amsterdam)
- **Paraguay** (Asuncion)
- **Peru** (Juli, Chimbote, Lima, Villa El Salvador)
- **Uruguay** (Montevideo, Las Piedras)
- **Venezuela** (San Felix, Caracas–Carapita, Catia la Mar, Cocorote, Marin)

"Go into all the world and preach the gospel to the whole creation." (Mk 16:15)

"I want Indian Missionary Sisters of Charity— who would be My fire of love amongst the very poor —the sick—the dying—the little street children...."

(Jesus to Mother, quoted in Mother's letter to Archbishop Périer, 13th January 1947)

Europe (101 foundations)

- **Albania** (Dukagjin, Durres, Elbasan, Korca, Puke, Shkodra, Tirana I & II)
- **Austria** (Vienna)
- **Belarus** (Gomel)
- **Belgium** (Brussels, Ghent)
- **Bulgaria** (Varna)
- **Croatia** (Zagreb)
- **Czech Republic** (Prague)
- **Denmark** (Copenhagen)
- **Estonia** (Tallinn)
- **France** (Marseille, Paris)
- **Germany** (Berlin I & II, Chemnitz, Essen, Hamburg, Mannheim, Munich)
- **Greece** (Athens I & Athens II, Crete)
- **Holland** (Amsterdam, Rotterdam)
- **Hungary** (Budapest, Erd)
- **Iceland** (Reykjavik)
- **Ireland** (Blarney, Dublin)
- **Italy** (Bari, Bologna, Florence, Genoa, L'Aquila, Milan, Naples—Tribunali & Marianella & Ostia & Reggio Calabria, Rome—Tor Fiscale & San Gregorio & Casilina & Primavalle & Tor Bella Monaca & Nomentana, Cagliari, Catania, Palermo, Ragusa/Vittoria)
- **Kosova** (Peċ)
- **Latvia** (Riga)
- **Lithuania** (Kretinga, Vilnius)
- **Malta** (Bormla)
- **Macedonia** (Skopje)
- **Poland** (Katowice, Szczecin, Warsaw, Grochowska & St. Joseph, Zaborow)
- **Portugal** (Faro, Lisbon, Setubal)
- **Romania** (Bacau, Bucharest Milkov Mircesti & Chitila, St. Gheorghe)
- **Russia,** European part (Parkovaja, St. Petersburg, Moscow)
- **Slovakia** (Bratislava, Čadca/Žilina)
- **Slovenia** (Ljubljana)
- **Spain** (Barcelona, Madrid, Sabadell)
- **Sweden** (Stockholm)
- **Switzerland** (Lausanne, Zurich)
- **Ukraine** (Kiev)
- **United Kingdom** (Birmingham, Liverpool, London—Southall & Bravington Road & East End, Armagh, Belfast, Glasgow, Livingston/Edinburgh, Swansea)
- **Vatican** (Dono di Maria)
- **Italy** (Piombino, Acilia—Rome) contemplative foundations
- **Sweden** (Sorforsa) contemplative foundation

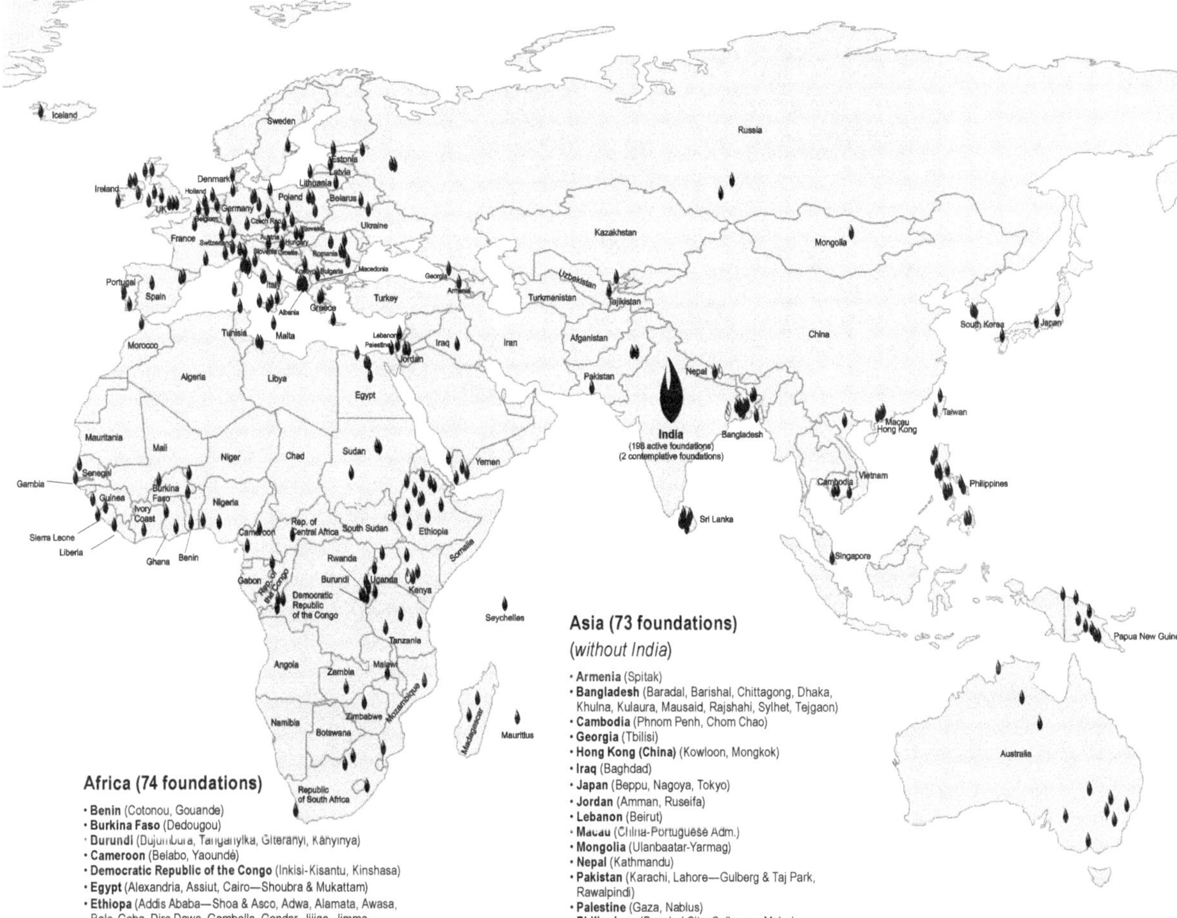

Asia (73 foundations)

(without India)

- **Armenia** (Spitak)
- **Bangladesh** (Baradal, Barishal, Chittagong, Dhaka, Khulna, Kulaura, Mausaid, Rajshahi, Sylhet, Tejgaon)
- **Cambodia** (Phnom Penh, Chom Chao)
- **Georgia** (Tbilisi)
- **Hong Kong (China)** (Kowloon, Mongkok)
- **Iraq** (Baghdad)
- **Japan** (Beppu, Nagoya, Tokyo)
- **Jordan** (Amman, Ruseifa)
- **Lebanon** (Beirut)
- **Macau** (China-Portuguese Adm.)
- **Mongolia** (Ulanbaatar-Yarmag)
- **Nepal** (Kathmandu)
- **Pakistan** (Karachi, Lahore—Gulberg & Taj Park, Rawalpindi)
- **Palestine** (Gaza, Nablus)
- **Philippines** (Bacolod City, Calbayog, Mabolo, Dagupan, Davao—Matina & Fatima, Manila—Binondo & Tondo NH & Tondo SB, Naga, Aklan, Olongapo, Taclopan, Pasil-Cebu)
- **Russia** (Asian part) (Novosibirsk, Tomsk)
- **Singapore** (Singapore)
- **South Korea** (Ansan, Inchon)
- **Sri Lanka** (Columbo I & II, Moratuwa, Galle, Kandy, Trincomalee, Madhu/Vavuniya)
- **Syria** (Aleppo, Damascus, Dwellah, Deir ez-Zor)
- **Taiwan** (Tainan, Taipei)
- **Tajikistan** (Dushanbe)
- **Uzbekistan** (Tashkent)
- **Vietnam** (Hanoi, Ho Chi Minh City)
- **Yemen** (Aden, Hodeibah, Sana'a, Taiz)
- **Nepal** (Kathmandu/Pokhara), contemplative foundation

Africa (74 foundations)

- **Benin** (Cotonou, Gouande)
- **Burkina Faso** (Dedougou)
- **Burundi** (Bujumbura, Tanganyika, Giteranyi, Kanyinya)
- **Cameroon** (Belabo, Yaoundé)
- **Democratic Republic of the Congo** (Inkisi-Kisantu, Kinshasa)
- **Egypt** (Alexandria, Assiut, Cairo—Shoubra & Mukattam)
- **Ethiopa** (Addis Ababa—Shoa & Asco, Adwa, Alamata, Awasa, Bale-Goba, Dire Dawa, Gambella, Gondar, Jijiga, Jimma, Mekale)
- **Gambia** (Banjul)
- **Ivory Coast** (Abidjan)
- **Kenya** (Maralal, Nairobi—Huruma & Otiende Kibera)
- **Liberia** (Monrovia)
- **Libya** (Tripoli, Janzour)
- **Madagascar** (Antsirabe, Tananarive)
- **Malawi** (Lilongwe)
- **Mauritius** (Port Louis)
- **Morocco** (Tangier)
- **Mozambique** (Maputo, Nampula)
- **Niger** (Niamey)
- **Nigeria** (Lagos, Onitsha)
- **Republic of Central Africa** (Bangui)
- **Republic of Guinea** (Conakry)
- **Republic of South Africa** (Cape Town, Durban, Johannesburg, Pretoria)
- **Republic of the Congo** (Brazzaville, Ouesso)
- **Rwanda** (Kigali, Ngarama-Kigungo)
- **Senegal** (Kaolack)
- **Seychelles** (Victoria-Mahe)
- **Sierra Leone** (Freetown, Makeni)
- **Sudan** (El Obeid, Khartoum, Omdurman)
- **Tanzania** (Dar-Es-Salaam, Dodoma, Rulongo, Tabora)
- **Tunisia** (Tunis)
- **Uganda** (Kampala, Moroto)
- **Zambia** (Lusaka)
- **Zimbabwe** (Harare)
- **Kenya** (Donholm Nairobi) contemplative foundation

Oceania (18 foundations)

- **Australia** (Orange, Sydney, Bourke, Dareton, Queanbeyan, Wagga Wagga, Darwin, Katherine, Tennant Creek, Melbourne)
- **Papua New Guinea** (Madang, Mendi, Tokarara, Hanuabada, Vanimo, Veifa'a Bereina, Wewak, Kerema)

MC FOUNDATIONS DURING MOTHER'S LIFETIME—INDIA

"Go into all the world and preach the gospel to the whole creation." (Mk 16:15)

"I want Indian Missionary Sisters of Charity—who would be My fire of love amongst the very poor—the sick—the dying—the little street children...." (Jesus to Mother, quoted in Mother's letter to Archbishop Périer, 13th January 1947)

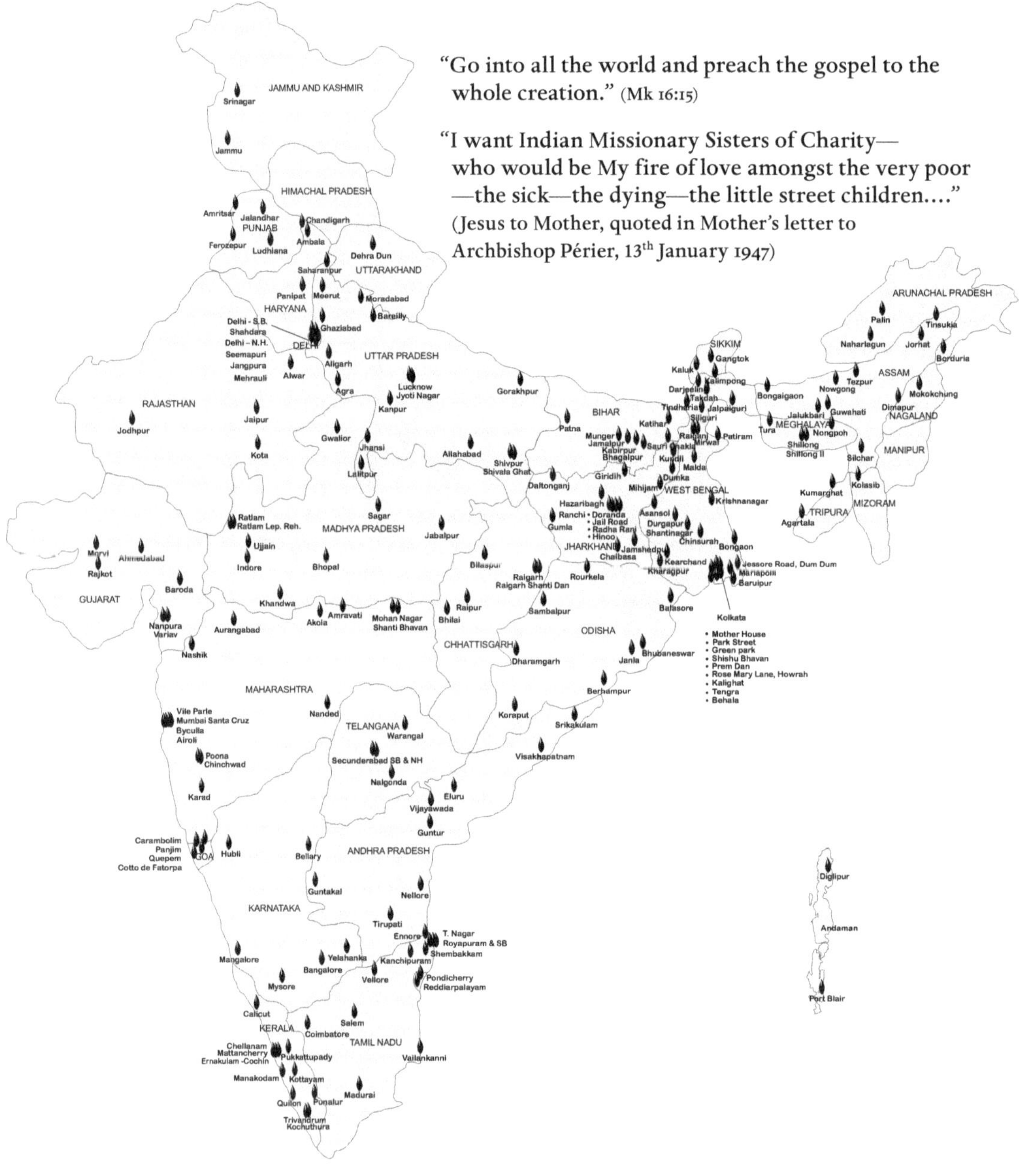

APPENDIX C

Facsimiles of some of Mother Teresa's handwritten letters

Reproduced here are facsimiles of some of Mother Teresa's original handwritten letters or drafts, and in some cases their corresponding typed versions. These examples can help us appreciate better Mother's writing style as well as the diligence and effort showed by the Sisters who helped Mother with the typing, copying, and the distribution of the general letters to the houses.

Please note that the original serial numbers of the letters that appear on the facimiles below do not correspond to the current serial numbers. The reason for this discrepancy is that the original serial numbers were added when the Sisters began the compilation for the bound version of the letters, and they did not have some of the letters that were found later. Further, some of the letters meant for particular houses were marked as general letters. We have renumbered the letters, adding those that were not included in the first bound volume; likewise, we have excluded those that were meant for particular houses. This explains the discrepancy of the numbers between the original and current version.

Please note also that Mother's General Letter is the letter that was sent to the houses (whether typed or handwritten) and not the handwritten draft that Mother wrote and handed in for typing. In this volume we have included only the General Letter into the main text, although we have noted any significant alterations that might have occurred during copying and/or typing.

LDM. Delhi 20th Sept. 1959

My own dearest Sisters, Professed, Novices, Postulants and Aspirants.

Seveth of October is a day of thanksgiving in Our Society. It is a day when the Good God erected our little society into being. As the Society is the sole Property of Our Lady, it was only right, that on Her great day - She would grant us the grace of living and growing. It is for us to grow into a straight - beautiful - fruitful tree. Let us all unite as one at the Feet of Our Mother and thank Her and also promise Her - that, as She is the cause of our joy - so we too will be the Cause of Her joy - For this we shall begin the novena of thanksgiving from the 27th Sept. in preparation for the 7th Oct. (Sing Magnificat)

My dear children - there is so much in my heart to tell You. but these two things are upper most. Charity and Obedience. Be a true Co-worker of Christ - Radiate and live His life - be an angel of comfort to the sick - a friend to the little ones, and love each other as God loves each of you with a special most intense love. Be kind to each other - I prefer you make mistakes in kindness - then that you work Miracles in unkindness. Be kind in words - See what the kindness of Our Lady brought to her. See how she spoke. - She could have easily told St. Joseph of the Angel's message - yet she never uttered a word - and then God Himself interfered. She kept all these in her heart. would that we could keep all our words in Her heart. So much suffering - so much missunderstanding for what? just for one word - one look - one quick action - and darkness fills the heart of your Sister. Ask Our Lady during this novena to fill your heart with sweetness.

SCAN OF MGL 1. 20TH SEPTEMBER 1959

Since there were no copy machines at the time of this letter, Mother was writing by hand her letters for each house. Thus, there are two extant handwritten versions of this letter. One of the copies is marked "Calcutta Pr. (Professed)"; on the other copy the name of the house has been whited out, it could have been intended for Ranchi (Doranda), Delhi, or the Noviciate (in Mother House).

On one of the copies of this letter, there is a number "2" that is probably cut out

Now that we have our 3 local Superiors - try to excel in Obedience - help them by your cheerful and prompt. blind and simple obedience - You may be more talented - more capable - better in many ways. even more holy - than your Superior. All this are not required for you to obey. There is only one thing for you "She takes the place of God for you" Some Sisters think they can do the work better than what their superiors wishes or have told them to do - Be not be blind my children, the Good God has given you His Work to do it as He wants it to be done. He wants you to do His Work in His way and that is all - Failure or sucess mean nothing to him - as long as you do His work according to His plan and His will. Since the Constitutions are the written will of God - what surer way can we follow - but the one pointed by our Superiors - You are infallible when You obey. - The devil tries his best to spoil the work of God and as He cant do it direct to Him he makes us do God's work in our way. and this is where he gains and we loose.

In all the houses and in the noviciate God is blessing the Generosity of the Sisters. Keep up this Generosity - You have every reason to be happy. Keep smiling at Jesus in Your Superiors, Sisters and Your poor.

Pray often, pray fervently for me

God bless each one of you.

Mother.

from some old calendar and pasted on the letter; it is not clear whether the number refers to the second copy of the same letter or whether it is meant as a serial number. This letter, however, is considered as Mother's first general letter.

Since this is the first general letter, we have opted to include the facsimile of both these copies, so you can appreciate Mother's effort in re-writing the same letter. There are a few minor differences between the two letters, which have been noted in the main text.

alcutta" Pr.
+LDM.

2

Delhi 20th Sept 1959.

My own dearest Sisters, Professed. Novices. Postulants and Aspiran

Seventh of October is a day of thanksgivin in our Society. It is a day when the good God erected ou little Society into being. As the Society is the Sole Proper of Our Lady, it was only right, that on her great day would grant us the grace of living and growing. It is for u to grow into a straight - beautiful - fruitful tree. Let us all u s one at the Feet of Our Lady and thank Her and also pro er. that as She is the cause of our Joy - so we too will be cause of Her joy. For this we shall begin the novena of thanksgiving from the 27th Sept in preparation for the 7th Oct (Ma

My dear children, there is so much in my heart to tell You - but these two things are upper most - Chari and Obedience. Be a true Co-worker of Christ - Radiate and live His life - be an angel of comfort to the sick - a friend to the Little Ones - and love each other as God loves each o You with a Special most intense love. Be kind to eac I prefer You make mistakes in kindness - then that You work miracles in unkindness. Be kind in wo See what the kindness of Our Lady brought to her - S how She spoke - She could have easily told St Josep of the angels message - yet she never uttered a wo nd then God Himself interfered. She kept all these in her He ould that we could keep all our words in Her Heart. So m uffering - so much missunderstanding for what? Ju

-- one word - one look - one quick action - and darkness fills the heart of your Sister. Ask Our Lady during this novena to fill your heart with sweetness.
Now that we have our 3 local Superiors - try to excel in obedience - help them by your cheerful and prompt, blind and simple obedience - You may be more talented - more capable - better in many ways, even more holy - than your superior - All these are not required for you to obey. There is only One thing for you - "She takes the place of God for you." Some Sisters think they can do the work better than what their Superiors wishes or have told them to do - Be not so blind my children - The Good God has given You His Work to do it as He wants it to be done. He wants You to do His Work in His way - and that is all. Failure or success means nothing to Him - as long as You do His Work according to His plan and His Will. Since the Constitutions are the written will of God - what surer way can we follow - but the one pointed by our Superiors. You are enfalable when You obey. The devil tries his best to spoil the work of God and as He cannot [illegible] direct to Him, he makes us do God's work in our way and this is where he gains and we loose.
In all the houses and in the noviciate God is blessing the Generosity of the Sisters. Keep up this Generosity - You have every reason to be happy. Keep smiling at Jesus in Your Superiors, sisters and Your poor.
Pray often, pray fervently for me.
God bless each one of you.
Mother

Sing for the Novena 'My soul does Magnify the Lord' and
- Prayer from the Novena in the Prayer Book

Dear. 45 San Felipe, 6th Aug 65

My dearest Children, Sisters & Brothers,
Feast of the Immaculate Heart
of Mary Cause of Our Joy is drawing
near— Let Our preparation for the great
day- be one of deep humble gra
titude to God for all we have
received during this year, especially
the 'Decree of Praise' which raised our
Society to a Pontifical right— or all the
vocations, and all the good done by
the Good God through each one of ~~you~~ us.
From our Lady we will ask 2 special
graces:- grace of perseverance in our beautiful
vocation and a delicate love for
God's Poor— I know you all love the
Poor— otherwise you would not join— but
let each one of us— try to make this
love - more kind, more charitable, more
cheerful— let our eyes see more

SCAN OF MGL 41. 6TH AUGUST 1965

Mother wrote this letter while visiting the Sisters in Venezuela.

clearly in deep Faith. The Face of Christ is the Face of the Poor –
Here we have real spiritual slum just as our people in India hunger & thirst for Food of the Body. our people here hunger & thirst for the word of God. Our Sisters will have really to preach the gospel to the Poor.

I hope to be home for the feast of the Society – but in case I cant be I send you all – my blessing and prayers – for each one of you in the Mother House, Park St. Ranchi. Jamshedpur Bhagalpur. Patna, Asansol. Darjeeling, Jhansi. Agra. Delhi. Ambala. Raigarh Amravati, Bombay. Goa. Trivandum Brothers, Venezuela and the future house of Ceylon Madras. Bhopal.

Pray much for Mother. Happy & Holy Feast.

God bless you All. Mother

Alea 57 On India - across the Ocean
17/9/67

My dearest Children

Once again I am crossing the ocean to prepare the way for you — in search of God's Poor — In search of the hungry Christ — the Homeless Christ — the Sick Christ — God's ways are very wonderful — as a very very small child — I had longed to go to Africa & work for Jesus — but for some reasons — I did not join the Convent in Africa — & now today I go as a M.C. to fulfill the desire of God in my heart. I go with different hope with different love — because of you — who will fulfill that hope & put that love into action for the Poor of Africa. It is also a beautiful preparation for our Chapter — God is so good to us

2

In reading Dom Marmion I find in him so much what our Society expects of us — Holiness. He says "Each religious order has its own beautiful spirit which delights the Sacred Heart — If we have not the peculiar spirit & training of the order to which we belong, we are out of joint in the Community, and can never be good religious, nor truly delight the Heart of Jesus — — Then to do this — through your noviciate — through your Superiors — All you have to do is to leave yourself absolutely in their hands — like wax — to cut away mercilessly all the unnecessary parts in me — that I may become a clean oblation in the altar of God's love — I would try to bear [illegible] for the love of Jesus crucified — and when temptation to leave the order came to him He prostrated himself before the tabernacle & cried out — "Let me be cut to pieces rather than leave the monastery

SCAN OF MGL 53. 17TH SEPTEMBER 1967

Mother wrote this letter on the way to Tanzania (Africa). The first house in Africa, in Tabora, Tanzania, was opened in September 1968.

3.

A religious profession faithfully observed leads infallibly to Sanctity' These are but a few sentences - from his life of faithfulness to Christ - & we my children have made the same profession to the same Christ - Are we as strong to be rooted out - then give up Christ? He achieved all these through his great love for his Rules - to which he was so faithful in very small details - He walked the way of the Rules - and the observance of the rule brought him straight to God. So many Sisters on account of a temptation or because the Superior has corrected them - or even for because of some unknown feeling so easily say - " I will go home" as in the world - so in the Convent. This is a great want of maturity - We cannot change our profession - as we

4.

we change our clothes - Vows & Rules are binding - we must use them only to fulfill God's holy will in a regard

Now a days - everything is getting looser & looser - people are trying to loosen the most sacred bindings - Are we to be guided by them - or will we cling to the rock Christ the Church by being a true MC we are faithful to his church -

Improve your life of prayer & you will find your love for the Rule increase & by this increase your stability in His service will improve also.

Be generous - love your vocation - If you really love your vocation you will appreciate & respect each other. You will love as He loves each one of you with that deep sincere love. Everything will improve if you love your vocation - God bless

Mother

94

19/3/72

My dearest Sister,

On the 22nd March I am leaving for Australia where on the 26th March we begin the Nov. & also Adoration for the old & the crippled. I am sure you will all pray much for Mother ~~and~~ Holy Week will soon begin - ~~I am sure~~ we ~~will~~ try to make it a 'real Holy Week' in sharing ~~the~~ Passion of Christ - We all have our cross. ~~to begin~~ ~~for if you are~~ if you love me - Christ said - Keep my Commandment. - Love God - Love your Neighbour. These two if we keep - we are then in love with Him - & He & His Father will come & abide with us -

To day when everything is questioned & changed let us go back to Nazareth Jesus had come to ~~redeem~~ the world to teach us the love of His Father. 2

how strange - that He should ~~be~~

spend 30 years just doing nothing wasting His time

SCAN OF MGL 89. 19TH MARCH 1972

Mother wrote this letter with a pencil on a used envelope (which she opened to gain space). Only two of the pages of the handwritten draft of this letter, reproduced here, have survived.

Not ~~showing~~ giving chance to
His personality - to His gifts - for
we know at the age of 12
He first silenced the learned
priests of the temple - who knew
so much & so well - who could
discuss the law by hours yet
this little boy Jesus - silenced
them by His answers - when His
parents found Him - He went
down to Nazareth & was subject
to them - We hear no more
of Him - only that the
people were surprised when
He came in public - to be the
carpenter's son [illegible] doing
just the humble work [illegible]
a carpenter [illegible]

PRINTED MATTER SECOND CLASS

NEW CITY
A CATHOLIC BIMONTHLY MAGAZINE
P. O. BOX 332 MANILA

GIOVANNA VERDUCCIO
119 [illegible] St.
Pasay City, R.P.

Rev. Mother TERESA
Sisters of Charity
CALCUTTA
INDIA

24

The work of the MC
is like that at Nazareth
Do I really love
my vocation -

1 — N.Y. 8/7/76

My dearest Children
I have been away in body
from the Mother House and
India, and from each of our
house throughout the world
except New York – where I am
now. but I dont think distance
is an obstacle for me to be with
you and near each one of you
for love has no frontiers nor
space – and in the Heart of Jesus
we are One – ~~and therefore~~, there
in the Heart of Jesus – nothing
will nor can separate us from
the love of Christ for each other
We have every reason to be
the Happiest people in the
world – to be the happiest – we
have to belong to Jesus fully
without any reservations and total surrender – ~~for~~ for
He alone is worthy of our love

and total Surrender – If we
really belong fully to Him
than we must be at His
disposal – that He may be
free to use us and do with
us whatever & whenever He
wants – through our Superiors
Whoever they may be – they are
the instruments of His will –
They may be people we like or
dislike – They may be clever & highly
gifted – or they may not be so –
they may be of any nationality
they may be holy or not so holy
It makes no difference to us. The
only thing that matters is our con
viction that they are the instru
ments of Gods will for us – of that we are unshakable ~~and so~~
through this our Cheerful constant and sleeping then
prompt obedience we receive Christ obedience to his Father, as it was in
Case of Our Lady. The Angel
Gabriel, St Joseph the Carpenter.

SCAN OF MGL 123. 8TH JULY 1976

Mother wrote this letter from New York. On the last page of the draft, she asked Sr. Joseph Michael to prepare it for the Sisters (please see page 8 of the draft). On that same page, Mother wrote "On the 25th June Feast of the S" and crossed it out, than wrote the instruction to Sr. Joseph Michael. The sentence "On the 25th June Feast of the S" was possibly meant as the beginning of the next part of the letter with the news about the beginning of the Contemplative branch. This part was obviously added to the letter after the copies were already made for the houses; the typing seems to be done with carbon paper and the line spacing is double (while the rest of the letter had single line spacing). We have included the facsimile of the typed letter as well.

were the instrument of God's will for Her - therefore her prompt Obedience - 'Be it done to me according to Thy Will' In the message of the Angel - God Spoke His Will " We too like Her will be pleasing to God, and become carriers of His love as she was - if we too like Her - accept with humility and joy the message of God spoken through our Superiors Obedience well lived - frees us from selfishness and pride - and it helps us to find God and in Him the whole World. Obedience - is a special grace and it produces - unfailing peace, inward joy and close union with God. Obedience - transforms - small

Common place things + occupations into acts of living faith - and Faith in action is love - and love in action in Service of the Living God. Obedience - lived with joy creates a living awareness of the presence of God - and so fidelity to acts of Obedience such as - the bell - time table eating of food, etc. that are the fruit of constant, prompt, cheerful undivided Obedience - become like drops of oil - that keep the Light Jesus - living in our life

If we really want³ to grow in holiness, ~~through~~ Obedience is a sure way, let us turn constantly to Our Lady to teach us how to obey, to Jesus who was obedient unto death — "He being God went down & was subject to them."

If we really want to obey we must learn first to love those — who have to obey us, and also whom we have to obey — For both — Superior & subject give & receive from each other & through each other many graces — Every Sup. if she really loves her Sisters — she must herself — live in that presence of God — by obeying humbly, constantly cheerfully — her higher Superiors. only then she can in all humility & faith give orders. expect the same Obedience from her Sisters —

Each Sister who is really concerned & convinced of her Belonging to Christ ~~that~~ as is her Vocation — she will find Obedience — as the greatest means of growing in holiness & living in the constant presence of God. She will love her Sup. with a deep & sincere humility because. She believes that she is ~~the spoken or written~~ Will of God ~~— & so~~ a sure instrument of God's own will — in a day to day life — Therefore a Sister who lives this life of constant, cheerful, prompt undivided Obedience — is like a sunshine of God's love in the Community the Hope of Eternal happiness to the Poor and flame of burning love before the Eucharistic Lord. where in act of Obedience to the Father — they both together share in the Redemption of mankind. As preparation for the feast of our Society — I ask you my dear ~~Sisters~~ children — that each one of us — we really learn this constant, cheerful prompt, undivided Obedience during the coming days. Let us make our Com. really something beautiful for God. where the Superiors & the Sisters are one heart full of love.

– 4 –

I am hoping to be with you for our Feast. but in case Jesus has other plans for me my love & prayer and every thing that is beautiful in me is all for you – for each one of you –

I am just longing to be back – but like you I have also to obey, cheerfully & with undivided love – this sacrifice will help us all to grow in holiness.

Pray for Mother as I do for each one of you.

God bless you

Mother

~~On the 25th June Feast of the S.~~ Sister M. Michael, please read this carefully – & correct & put things together – & also prepare as we did before the meditation & the liturgy, reading, instruction ex. of cons on obedience. I think Sr Bernard will be able ~~to do~~ it. if not you & Sr Carmel could get together & do it. The ex. of cons in the new prayer book is well done – you could use it – & put in also that during these days we take growth obedience as our particular Ex. let us more insist on that simple obedience – that helps to the awareness of God's presence let us be more busy with obedience than with disobedience.

+ 131 New York 8/7/76

L.D.M.

My Dearest Children, Sr. M. and all the 1st years

I have been away in body from the Mother House and India and from each of our houses throughout the world except New York - where I am now. But I don't think distance is an obstacle for me to be with you and near each one of you, for love has no frontiers nor space, and in the Heart of Jesus we are one. There in the Heart of Jesus nothing will nor can separate us from the love of Christ for each other.

We have every reason to be the happiest people in the world. To be the happiest, we have to belong to Jesus fully without any reservations - as He alone is worthy of our love and total surrender. If we really belong fully to Him, then we must be at His disposal - that He may be free to use us and do with us whatever and whenever He would through our Superiors whoever they may be. They are the instruments of His Will. They may be people we like or dislike, they may be clever and highly gifted, or they may not be so, they may be of any nationality, they may be holy or not so holy - it makes no difference to us. The only thing that matters is our conviction that they are the instruments of God's Will for us and that we are infallible in obeying them-through our cheerful, constant and prompt obedience, we relive Christ's obedience.

As it was in the case of Our Lady - the angel Gabriel and St. Joseph, the carpenter were the instruments of God's Will for her....therefore her prompt obedience - "Be it done to me according to Thy Will." In the message of the angel God spoke His Will. We, too, like her, will be pleasing to God and become carriers of His Love as she was, if we, too, like her, accept with humility and joy the message of God spoken through our Superiors..

Obedience well lived frees us from selfishness and pride and so it helps us to find God and in Him, the whole world. Obedience is a ~~special grace and it produces unfailing peace~~, inward joy and close union with God.

Obedience transforms small commonplace things and occupations into acts of living faith, and faith in action is love, and love in action is service of the loving God. Obedience lived with joy creates a living awareness of the Presence of God, and so fidelity to acts of obedience such as the bell, time table, eating of food, etc., that are the fruit of constant, prompt, cheerful, undivided obedience - become like drops of oil that keep the Light of Jesus living in our life.

If we really want to grow in holiness through obedience, let us turn constantly to Our Lady to teach us how to obey, to Jesus Who was obedient unto death. "He, being God, went down and was subject to them."

If we really want to obey, we must learn first to love those who have to obey us, and also whom we have to obey. For both superiors and subjects give and receive from each other, and through each other many graces. Every superior, if she really loves her sisters, must herself live in the Presence of God by obeying humbly, constantly, cheerfully her higher superiors. Only then she can in all humility and faith give orders and expect the same obedience from her sisters.

Each sister who is really concerned and convinced of her belonging to Christ as her vocation, will find obedience as the greatest means of growing in holiness and living in the constant Presence of God. She will love her superior with a deep and sincere humility because she is a sure instrument of God's Own Will in day-to-day life. Therefore, a sister who lives this life of constant, cheerful, prompt, undivided obedience is like a sunshine of God's Love in the community, the hope of eternal happiness to the poor and the flame of burning love before the Eucharistic Lord, where in an act of obedience to the Father, they share in the redemption.

As preparation for the feast of our Society, I ask you my dear children, that each one of us really learn this constant, cheerful, prompt and undivided obedience during the coming days. Let us make our community really something beautiful for God, where the superiors and the sisters are one heart full of love.

I am hoping to be with you for our feast, but in case Jesus has other plans for me, my love and prayer and everything that is beautiful in me is all for you - for each one of you.

I am just longing to be back, but, like you, I have also to obey, cheerfully and with undivided love. This sacrifice will help us all to grow in holiness.

Pray for Mother as I do for each one of you.

"SISTERS OF THE WORD"

God's gift to the people of the United States of America, as a Love memorial of the 41st Eucharistic Congress, and to the world...

On the Feast of the Sacred Heart of Jesus, His Eminence Cardinal Cooke in the presence of Mother Teresa and others, blessed and offered to the Sacred Heart of Jesus the new born Contemplative branch of the Missionaries of Charity - to be known as " Sisters of the Word", with Love and Reparation.

The sisters will live the Word of God in Eucharistic adoration and Contemplation, and will proclaim the Word to the people of God - and so, with Mary, Mother of the Church, bring the Word made Flesh... dwell in the hearts of all men.

Let us praise God for His great gift of the Sisters of the Word. Sr. M. Nirmala will be in charge - there are 3 postulants with their address:

1070 Union Avenue
Bronx, N.Y. 10459

God bless you
Mother

A BORDO DI UN JET ALITALIA
ON BOARD AN ALITALIA JET

163

Cairo August 1981

My dearest children,

This brings you Mother's love, blessing
and prayer that you may grow
more and more in the love
of God through fidelity to the
humble works of the Society. Never
be afraid nor ashamed to be
a true MC the more you grow
in the true Spirit of MC the more
tender will be your love for
Jesus in the distressing disguise
of the Poor. Mary was a true MC
because She was not afraid to
be the handmaid of the Lord
and so she went in haste to put

SCAN OF MGL 162. 11TH AUGUST 1981

Mother wrote this letter on notepad sheets, which read: "A BORDO DI UN JET ALITALIA / ON BOARD AN ALITALIA JET". They were probably given to her on her trip to Cairo (July/August 1981). This is one of the samples of the letters which was retyped while Mother was not present and then sent to the houses; since Mother was not there to sign it, the customary "God bless you" and "Mother" were retyped in all caps.

We have included the facsimile of the typed letter as well, as this is a good example of how faithfully the Sisters transcribed Mother's letters.

be beautiful humility into a living action of love to do the handmaid's work to Elizabeth and we know what this humility obtained for the unborn child — He lept with joy in the womb of His Mother the first human being to recognise the coming of Christ — and then His Mother sang with joy with gratitude and praise to the Mother of the Lord. Humility always radiates the greatness of and glory of God — How wonderful are the ways of God — He used humility, smallness, helplessness poverty to proof to the world — that He loved the world — Let the MC not be afraid to be humble, small helpless to proof their love for God

A BORDO DI UN JET ALITALIA
ON BOARD AN ALITALIA JET

We have much to thank God this Year — for all the wonderful Graces our Superiors have received during their retreats — In India we had the retreat in Bombay — for Sr M Audrey & Sr M Lourdes regions — In Delhi — for Sr M Dorothy & Sr M Albert In Calcutta for Sr M Clare & Sr M Camillus In New York for Sr M Priscilla's North Am. In Caracas for Sr M Gertrude, Sr M Dolores & Sr M Premila Central & South Am. And in Rome for Sr M Stella & Sr M Monica's Reg ~~for Europe~~ — We have now left Africa & Mid. East and far East I am hoping to be able to do it with them also.

A number of houses Sisters are reading highly polished books — higher than the simplicity of the Gospel — I am afraid much of it cannot be put in a living action. and also sometimes confusing by its non understanding

In some house Mother's letters are very little known ~~still~~ less loved and still less put into practice. At least once a day you should take the trouble to read the letters or the Instruction – in common. Days of recollection should also be prepared – as far as possible from the theme that you have chosen together. These days of recollection must each time – bring you closer to each other – therefore always have the chapter on the day of recollection – try to renew your General permissions – and if possible write your home letter. Try to be as much as possible alone with God – so that you can listen to Him when He speaks in the silence of your heart

A BORDO DI UN JET ALITALIA
ON BOARD AN ALITALIA JET

During[3] the retreats I have again insisted so much to make the Superiors realise – that each one of them and each one in their Com have been called by your name you belong to Him – you are precious to Him He loves each one of you with a deep personal love – no greater love – than the love of Christ. Try to meditate on the above words make them your own – and remember them when you are tempted to be unkind or uncharitable to ~~Some~~ each other Sister or the Poor – they are precious as we are to Him He loves them love one another with the same love as you love Jesus and let Jesus love you – as He loves His Mother. This love for your Sisters and Jesus love for you when united will make you all One heart full of love –

~~Xxxx~~ Let us all use everything in our power with God's grace — to really make our Mother House, every Community and all the Communities united with each other — one heart full of love with the Mother House. One with Mother — one with each other and one with Jesus — Our Society unity is fruit of prayer — of humility of love. Therefore if the com prays together will stay together and if you stay together — you will love one another as Jesus loves each one of you. and this what we are going to give Our Lady on the feast of our Society a real change of heart — by making it really one heart full of love in our Com. & this one heart make it one with Mother & offer it to Jesus

A BORDO DI UN JET ALITALIA
ON BOARD AN ALITALIA JET

so that He will be able to give this beautiful gift to His Mother on her feast day the 22nd Aug ~~We~~ ~~to~~ I really want you Sisters to take this letter and make your own parts that will help you grow in the likeness of Christ.

My Brother died on the 1st Friday of July. a real going home to God. I believe He died beautifully. Pray for the repose of his soul and also his family —

I hope to be with you before the feast of the Society — but if not possible I wish you all a very happy & holy feast

God bless you
M. Teresa

+ L D M Cairo, [illegible] August, 1981.

My dearest Children,

This brings you Mother's love, blessing and prayer - that you may grow more and more in the love of God, through fidelity to the humble works of the Society. Never be afraid or ashamed to be a true MC - the more you grow in the true Spirit of an MC the more tender will be your love for Jesus in the distressing disguise of the Poor.
Mary was a true MC because She was not afraid to be the handmaid of the Lord and so she went in haste to put her beautiful humility into a living action of love, to do the handmaid's work to Elizabeth and we know what this humility obtained for the unborn child: He " leapt with joy"in the womb of his Mother - the first human being to recognise the Coming of Christ - and then His Mother sang with Joy, with Gratitude and Praise to the Mother of the Lord.

Humility always radiates the greatness and glory of God. How wonderful are the ways of God. He used humility, smallness, helplessness, poverty to prove to the world - that He loved the world. Let the MC not be afraid to be humble, small helpless to prove their love for God.

We have much to thank God this year for all the wonderful graces our Superiors have received during their retreats: in India we had the retreat in Bombay for Sr.M. Audrey and Sm. Lourdes' regions. In Delhi, for Sm. Dorothy and Sm. Albert's regions. In Calcutta for Sm. Clare and Sm. Camillus' regions.
In New York for Sr.M. Priscilla's (North America). In Caracas for Central and South America : Sm. Beatrice, Sm. Dolores and Sm. Premila's and in Rome for Sm. Stella's and Sm. Monica's regions. We have now still left: Africa and Middle East and Far East including Australia and Papua-New Guinea. I am hoping to be able to do it with them also.

In a number of houses our Sisters are reading highly polished books - higher than the simplicity of the Gospel. I am afraid much of it cannot be put in a living action - and also sometimes confusing by its non-understanding. In some houses Mother's letters are very little known, less loved and still less put into practice. At least once a day you should take the trouble to read the letters or the Instructions. On common Days of Recollection - should also be prepared - as far as possible from the theme that you have chosen together. These days of recollection must each time bring you closer to each other. Therefore, always have the Chapter on the day of recollection, Try to renew your general permissions and if possible write your home letter. Try to be as much as possible alone with God so that you can listen to Him when He speaks in the Silence of your heart.

During the retreats I have again insisted so much to make the Superior's realise that each one of them and each one in their Community have been called by your name - You belong to Him - You are precious to Him - He loves each one of you with a deep personal love - there is no greater love than the Love of Christ. Try to meditate on the above words. Make them your own and remember them when you are tempted to be unkind or uncharitable to each other or the Poor. They are precious to Him, He loves them as He loves you. Love one another with the same love as you love Jesus and let Jesus love you as He loves His Mother. This love for your Sisters and Jesus' love for you when united will make you all one heart full of love. Let us all use everything in our power with God's grace to really make our Mother House, every Community and all the Communities united with each other - one heart full of love with the Mother House - One with Mother - one with each other and One with Jesus: Our SOCIETY.

Unity is fruit of Prayer - of Humility - of Love. Therefore, if the Community prays together, will stay together and if you stay together - you will love one another as Jesus loves each one of you and this is what we are going to give Our Lady on the Feast of our Society: a real change of heart, by making it really one heart full of love in our Community and this one heart make it one with Mother and offer it to Jesus so that He will be able to give this beautiful gift to His Mother on her Feastday, the 22nd August, 1981.
I really want you Sisters to take this letter and make your own parts - that will help you grow in the likeness of Christ.
My Brother died on the First Friday of July - a real going home to God. I believe He died beautifully. Pray for the repose of his soul and also his family.
I hope to be with you before the Feast of the Society - but if not possible I wish you all a very HAPPY AND HOLY FEAST.

GOD BLESS YOU
MOTHER

LDM. 10th March 1997

My dearest children,

As the days for the Elections are coming closer, I hope and pray you are all praying for God's blessing that God may give us the light and grace to Vote according to His will and decision.

As you know we have to Vote for the Superior General and the 4 Councillors. Let us decide after much prayer that we may vote for the right people chosen by God, for the Glory of God and the good of our Society.

Keep praying as this Voting is very important. We have to vote for a Superior General and the 4 councillors. I am sure you are all praying that the Voting be for the Glory of God and the good of our Society.

You have all been so good to me during all these years right from the beginning. I hope and pray this love and Sharing will Continue with greater love and care.

SCAN OF MGL 281. 10TH MARCH 1997

This is one of the last handwritten letters by Mother. The shaky handwriting and repetitions show her weak health. The letter was written during the 1997 General Chapter and voting for the new Superior General; the continuation of the beautiful work for the poorest of the poor seems to be uppermost in her mind.

ENDNOTES

MGL 2. 2ND SEPTEMBER 1960

In paragraphs 2, 3 and 4 of this letter, Mother Teresa quotes and paraphrases passages of the book *Lamps of Love* by Fr. Louis Colin, CSsR. She summarizes the author's thoughts, choosing what is essential and simplifying the language to suit the Sisters, whose first language was not English. At the same time, she adds her own ideas, in some way putting flesh over the skeleton that Colin's text presented to her. Mother rephrases the parts that Colin writes in the third person, listing herself among the "sinners" and "taking responsibility" for her own lukewarmness and lack of love.

Louis Colin, CSsR, preface to *Lamps of Love: A Recall to the Principal Sources of Love*, trans. Sister David Mary, SNJM (Westminster, MD: The Newman Press, 1959), vii–viii.

2. Colin, *Lamps of Love*, viii.

3. Colin, *Lamps of Love*, ix.

4. Colin, *Lamps of Love*, 6.

5. Colin, *Lamps of Love*, 7.

6. Colin, *Lamps of Love*, 9. In this particular instance, the author's question triggered what could be considered a classic catechism answer about the purpose of human life. Yet, Mother develops further what seems to be Colin's line of thought here, expounding on the way in which a Missionary of Charity (hereafter MC) could fulfill it, the manner to know, love and serve God in the life of an MC. In explaining how to "serve God" she shows that the Charism she received was deeply rooted in her heart. This seemingly insignificant nuance in the explanation proves her to be as mystical as she was practical; love for Jesus is expressed in the love for and the service to the Poor, "by doing to them what we would like to do to Him."

MGL 3. [7TH] OCTOBER 1960

7. Colin, *Lamps of Love*, 27. Here, and in other places, when summarizing or paraphrasing the author's thoughts, Mother changes general statements into personal ones, by using the first person.

8. Colin, *Lamps of Love*, 28. It is interesting to note that Mother uses the word "holiness" rather than Colin's original "progress in charity" and "perfection."

9. Colin, *Lamps of Love*, 29, 30. Though Colin does not mention these saints, Mother lists the saints that she considers good role models for the Sisters, indicating how much she wanted her Sisters to become saints.

10. Colin, *Lamps of Love*, 31.

11. Colin, *Lamps of Love*, 33.

12. Colin, *Lamps of Love*, 34. Mother embraces Colin's exhortation and, drawing on his words, encourages the Sisters to strive to become "Saints," an idea that Colin did not mention.

MGL 4. [4TH] NOVEMBER 1960

13. In this letter, in MGL 5, as well as in the letter MGL 14 of 9th March 1962 (in which Mother Teresa wrote, "Just as St. J. Berchmans said—a happy recreation helped him to make a fervent Holy Communion—so it should be with our letters—they should help us to love Jesus more in our Sisters"), Mother is alluding to the following excerpt from a biography of St. John Berchmans: "The very time of relaxation, the hour of recreation ordered by the Institute after dinner and after supper, was turned into a time of spiritual profit. To a heart so full of God, so opposed to the world, so empty of himself, to speak of spiritual things was no difficulty, but a simple delight; and so attractive was his conversation, that all sought and enjoyed it. His resolution, as we find it written by him under the heading, Recreation, was (i) pure intention, (2) resolve to speak on pious subjects in the presence of God. And this, faithfully carried out, made him confess that '**For my part, the after dinner recreation gives me strength for the rest of the day; and the evening recreation is a capital preparation for the meditation and communion on the morrow**.'" (here and hereafter, where the bold print appears in the endnotes, emphasis has been added). Francis Goldie, *The Life of the Blessed John Berchmans* (London: Burns and Gates, 1877), 71.

MGL 5. [6TH] JANUARY 1961

14. In this letter Mother, wanting to instruct the Sisters about the importance of observing the rule, quotes and paraphrases from Fr. Louis Colin, CSsR, who is himself quoting from Abbot Columba Marmion's, *Christ the Ideal of the Monk*. Louis Colin, CSsR, *The Practice of the Rule*, translated from the French by David Heimann (Cork, Ireland: Mercier Press, 1959), 5.

15. Colin, *The Practice of the Rule*, 11.

16. Colin, *The Practice of the Rule*, 11.

17. Tissot, *The Interior Life*, quoted in Colin, *The Practice of the Rule*, 12.

18. Colin, *The Practice of the Rule*, 4–5. Mother summarizes Colin's ideas from several paragraphs. Colin compares the peace that springs from the observance of the rule to a child's peaceful rest in its mother's arms; he urges clinging to the rule as the shipwrecked sailor clinging to a plank. In her apostolate, Mother often encountered children "desperately" clinging to their mothers, and that image was more tangible and left a deeper impression on her than that of a shipwrecked sailor. She knew that this image would have a greater impact on her Sisters as well.

19. Colin, *The Practice of the Rule*, 16–17.

MGL 6. [3RD] FEBRUARY 1961

20. Mother gives further instructions on the rule, quoting and paraphrasing from Louis Colin, CSsR, *The Practice of the Rule*, 45.

21. Colin, *The Practice of the Rule*, 46.

22. St. Alphonsus, *Oeuvres*, quoted in Colin, *The Practice of the Rule*, 47.

23. St. Vincent, *Oeuvres*, quoted in Colin, *The Practice of the Rule*, 48.

24. Colin, *The Practice of the Rule*, 48–49, quoting St. Francis de Sales, *Oeuvres*.

25. Colin, *The Practice of the Rule*, 49–50.

26. Colin, *The Practice of the Rule*, 52, quoting Jean-Marie Buathier, *Le sacrifice dans le dogme catholique et dans la vie chrétienne*.

27. Colin, *The Practice of the Rule*, 54, quoting Buathier, *Le sacrifice.*

28. Colin, *The Practice of the Rule*, 57, quoting Sister Elizabeth of the Trinity, *Reminiscences.*

MGL 8. [2ND] JUNE 1961

29. Mother encourages the Sisters with what is a rather common maxim in spiritual literature, inspired either by the phrase of Saint Ignatius Loyola "to know Christ intimately in order to love Him the more ardently and follow Him the more faithfully," (quoted by Louis Colin, CSsR, in *Jesus Our Model*, trans. Una Morrissy [Chicago, IL: Henry Regnery Company, 1959], 64), or possibly by the words of the hymn "Day by Day," attributed to Richard of Chichester (1197–1253):

> Day by day, dear Lord,
> of thee three things I pray:
> to see thee more clearly,
> love thee more dearly,
> follow thee more nearly,
> day by day.

MGL 9. [7TH] JULY 1961

30. This paragraph is a clear expression of Mother's new understanding of her interior darkness as a sharing in the redemptive mission of Jesus and a part of her mission, as she had expressed it in a letter to Fr. J. Neuner, SJ, in April 1961: "For the first time in this 11 years—I have come to love the darkness—for I believe now that it is a part, a very, very small part of Jesus' darkness & pain on earth . . . a spiritual side of 'your work.'" *Come Be My Light*, 208.

MGL 10. [4TH] AUGUST 1961

31. According to the author Robert Serrou, Mother challenged her brother Lazar in 1928, when he had protested her religious vocation, with a similar assertion: "In 1928, Lieutenant Lazar Bojaxhlu learned to his dismay that his younger sister Gonxha had decided to become a nun. Shocked, he wrote her a letter. . . . '"How could you," I wrote to her, "a girl like you, become a nun? Do you realize that you are burying yourself?" I will never forget her answer. . . . Gonxha wrote me, "You think you are so important, as an official serving the king of two million subjects. Well, I am an official too, serving the King of the whole world. Which one of us is right?"'" Robert Serrou, *Teresa of Calcutta, A Pictorial Biography* (New York, NY: McGraw-Hill Book Company, 1980), 24.

MGL 11. [27TH] AUGUST 1961

32. This novena can be found in various published sources; among the earliest is *Novena to the Holy Ghost* (Washington, DC: Holy Ghost Fathers, 1947).

MGL 15. [2ND] JUNE 1962

33. In this letter Mother quotes and paraphrases the words of Father Mateo Crawley-Boevey from the introduction of his book, *Jesus King of Love*. *"Lord, what wilt Thou have me do?" "Give Me a free hand."* (Our Lord to St. Margaret Mary). Father Mateo Crawley-Boevey, SSCC, *Jesus King of Love*, 4th ed. (Washington, DC: National Center of the Enthronement, 1945), 81.

34. Crawley-Boevey, *Jesus King of Love*, 83.

35. Crawley-Boevey, *Jesus King of Love*, 84. Mother adapts Fr. Mateo's writing to the current context of her letter "during this month of Love," that is, the month of June, traditionally dedicated to the Sacred Heart, summarizing Fr. Mateo's explanation on how to love Jesus, and adding the petition of "the courage to serve him." For Mother, service is always an expression of love or, as she would say in other places, the fruit of love; thus, she exhorts her Sisters to put their love into action by serving Jesus.

36. Crawley-Boevey, *Jesus King of Love*, 84.

37. Crawley-Boevey, *Jesus King of Love*, 84. Mother continued Fr. Mateo's thought by alluding to her decision of "letting Jesus have a free hand," a decision that was forged in the midst of her interior darkness and rooted in her desire to surrender herself fully to Him, no matter the cost. See *Come Be My Light*, 195, 242, 288.

38. Crawley-Boevey, *Jesus King of Love*, 84.

39. Crawley-Boevey, *Jesus King of Love*, 85.

40. Crawley-Boevey, *Jesus King of Love*, 86.

MGL 19. 19TH MAY 1963

41. In her advice to the Sisters, Mother might have been inspired by reading spiritual classics, like Rodriguez (see example below) or others. However, while she picks up common spiritual themes (e.g., humility), she strikes a positive note of great confidence in God. Due to our sinfulness and weakness the only constructive thing to do is to turn to God, for He is the source of all that is good. She does not leave room for dwelling on oneself and one's weakness, but rather stresses the need to be more confident and turn to action. Doing God's work is more important to her than analyzing our misery, and our weakness and sinfulness should not stand in the way. Alphonsus Rodriguez, *Christian and Religious Perfection*, vol. 2 (Dublin: James Duffy and Sons, 1882), 239–40.

MGL 23. 27TH DECEMBER 1963

42. In this letter Mother instructs the Sisters on the need of silence by quoting and paraphrasing the words of Abbe Gaston Courtois from his book *Before His Face: Meditations for Priests and Religious*, vol. 1 (New York, NY: Herder & Herder, 1962), 1–7. In quoting or paraphrasing the author's thoughts, Mother not only adapts the language to the level of comprehension of the Sisters who are just learning English, but she also tweaks his ideas to better relate to her Charism. She seems to follow a distinct pattern in her letters: she gives the teaching on a subject with the help of excerpts from books, then applies it to the MC charism, giving the Sisters practical guidance on how to live that teaching in their daily lives. At times, while possibly borrowing the general idea from an author, she seems to be translating her own personal experience into words (for example, "The energy of God will be ours to do all things well"). Courtois, *Before His Face*, 1:1.

43. Courtois, *Before His Face*, 1:2.

44. Courtois, *Before His Face*, 1:3–4.

45. Courtois, *Before His Face*, 1:5. It is interesting to note that in the passages where Courtois uses direct speech to convey Jesus' message, Mother does not quote this direct speech; instead, she changes it to the third person. This is a significant change, because in the instances when she is quoting or paraphrasing from other authors, she normally shifts from the author's third person to the first person. However, as she had heard "Jesus's voice" speak to her directly just prior to founding the MCs, she might have found it odd to appropriate Courtois' words and reproduce them as coming directly from Jesus. At this time, "the Voice" was silent (she was already experiencing deep interior darkness), so she reminded herself, along with her Sisters, that Jesus is *"always"* (emphasis added) waiting in silence, even as, for her, communication would continue in the silence of her interior darkness.

46. Courtois, *Before His Face*, 1:5.

47. Courtois, *Before His Face*, 1:7, citing Maurice Zundel.

MGL 24. [7TH] FEBRUARY 1964

48. In this letter Mother instructs the Sisters on the need for humility by quoting and paraphrasing the words of Abbe Gaston Courtois from his book, *Before His Face: Meditations for Priests and Religious*, vol. 1 (New York: Herder and Herder, 1962), 59–65. Mother introduces the letter by giving reason for such a need. She adapts to the Sisters' religious profession and their apostolate among the Poor the passages which Courtois wrote for priests and the faithful in general. Among the most significant changes in terminology is that Mother opts for simpler and more "concrete" language (e.g., "beautiful" vs. "astonishing", "empty" vs. "efface.)" One of the reasons for this could be her simplicity, but also her pragmatic disposition; she was concerned that the Sister understand and put into practice the guidance she was providing. Thus, she avoided complicated and abstract vocabulary. Courtois, *Before His Face*, 1:59.

49. (Phil. 2:6–7)." Courtois, *Before His Face*, 1:60.

50. Courtois, *Before His Face*, 1:60.

51. Courtois, *Before His Face*, 1:61.

52. Courtois, *Before His Face*, 1:61

53. Courtois, *Before His Face*, 1:62.

54. In the paragraphs that follow Mother provides an excellent summary of the author's thoughts, but also an excellent exhortation on the pedagogy of cooperation, of accepting and welcoming others with whatever they can contribute to the common good. She gives a hint, or rather a key, to understanding her profound humility: the conviction that "The Work is God's work." Courtois, *Before His Face*, 1:62.

55. Courtois, *Before His Face*, 1:63.

56. Courtois, *Before His Face*, 1:64. Mother adds the word "completely," so characteristic of her. Whatever she did, she did wholeheartedly, giving herself totally and without reserve; that was the manner she wanted her Sisters to live their life of consecration to God.

57. Courtois, *Before His Face*, 1:65. In applying Courtois's meditation on humility to MC life, which she made simple to understand, yet as demanding as the high ideal that Courtois had set for priests, she added the practice of obedience and avoidance of criticism—the points to which she had already alerted her Sisters in the previous letters (MGL 1, MGL 7, MGL 18; MGL 19, MGL 21).

MGL 25. [6TH] MARCH 1964

58. Mother instructs the Sisters about prayer by quoting and paraphrasing the words of Abbe Gaston Courtois from his book, *Before His Face: Meditations for Priests and Religious*, vol. 1 (New York: Herder and Herder, 1962). In paraphrasing Courtois, Mother gives an insight into her own prayer life: she was "straining" the eyes of her soul to "look" at Christ while an interior darkness was "hiding" Him. At the same time, she was aware that her "own voice" was united in prayer to that of Christ. In highlighting the anxiety and restlessness that result from not working with Jesus, she hints at the reason for her insistence with the Sisters in distinguishing between "social work" and "apostolate," "doing good work" versus "praying the work." Mother added childlikeness and gratitude to the requirements for prayer listed by Courtois and concluded with her own list of practical points (for Particular Examen) on how to improve one's prayer life.

59. Courtois, *Before His Face*, 1:33.

60. Courtois, *Before His Face*, 1:35.

61. Courtois, *Before His Face*, 1:37–39, citing Emile Mersh.

MGL 26. 3RD APRIL 1964

62. In this letter, Mother quotes and paraphrases the words of Abbe Gaston Courtois from his book, *Before His Face: Meditations for Priests and Religious*, vol. 2 (New York: Herder and Herder, 1962), to instruct the Sisters on joy. Mother introduces expressions that take on added meaning since she was in "darkness," experiencing desolation on the level of the senses. By positively stating "it is always hard" rather than the author's original "it is not always easy," she hints that it cost her a great deal to face the exterior difficulties of her mission and at the same time have no respite from her interior ordeal; indeed, she did succeed in being an "apostle of joy" in the midst of interior and exterior sufferings. Courtois, *Before His Face*, 2:35.

63. Courtois, *Before His Face*, 2:35.

64. The phrase, "Joy is a net of love by which you can catch many souls," that Mother coined reflects her zeal and thirst to bring many souls to God. She might have been inspired by the words of Fr. Mateo Crawley-Boevey, who said, "Grace with its manifold effects is but **the net of love** and mercy in which the God-Redeemer seeks to **ensnare our souls**" (from *Jesus King of Love*, 47). Even if that be the case, the statement shows her distinct and original thought.

65. Courtois, *Before His Face*, 2:36.

66. Courtois, *Before His Face*, 2:37.

67. Courtois, *Before His Face*, 2:39–40. The phrase, "A Sister filled with joy preaches without preaching," could have been inspired by the prayer "Radiating Christ," which Mother had composed using the meditations of St. John Henry Newman, "Make me preach Thee without preaching—not by words, but by my example and by the catching force, the sympathetic influence, of what I do," *Meditations and Devotions of the Late Cardinal Newman* (New York: Longmans, Green, and Co., 1911), 365. Mother and the Sisters prayed this prayer daily.

68. Mother may have put together the ideas presented in Courtois's text, especially in the following sentences: "Nothing brings sunshine back to a soul so quickly as a smiling act of charity. Fundamentally, joy is always the fruit of true love," Courtois, *Before His Face*, 2:44. However, the phrase, "A joyful sister is like the sunshine. . . ," is her own creation. It reflects her realization of how important this virtue is for those who are in

constant contact with suffering, but it also gives us an inkling of her own aspirations and her desire for the members of her community.

69. Courtois, *Before His Face*, 2:38–40. Mother compares sadness to gangrene, a disease that she frequently encountered in the poor she served. Again, this unique expression points to her practical way of thinking.

70. Courtois, *Before His Face*, 2:42–43. Mother's one-line summary, though quite remote from the author's words, is the fruit of her reflections and her conviction that joy (i.e., cheerfulness) should permeate every aspect of MC life, especially on account of such close contact with the sufferings of the poor.

71. Courtois, *Before His Face*, 2:41.

MGL 27. [1ST] MAY 1964

72. Mother instructs the Sisters on the importance of kindness by quoting and paraphrasing the words of Abbe Gaston Courtois in his book, *Before His Face, Meditations for Priests and Religious*, vol. 1 (New York: Herder and Herder, 1962).

Though Mother uses Courtois's ideas as a background, she paraphrases his thoughts and introduces the concept of a smile (which Courtois did not mention) as an expression of kindness and welcoming. She uses stronger language, and, as usual, applies the general points that the author makes to the apostolate with the poor. Courtois, *Before His Face*, 1:193.

73. Courtois, *Before His Face*, 1:194.

74. Courtois, *Before His Face*, 1:194.

75. Courtois, *Before His Face*, 1:195.

76. Courtois, *Before His Face*, 1:195–96.

77. Courtois, *Before His Face*, 1:196. Mother borrows the author's ideas and applies them to dealing with the poor, elaborating on the examples that she had heard of or seen and that had bothered her.

78. Courtois, *Before His Face*, 1:197. Mother captures Courtois's idea, but she takes it to a level of much deeper acceptance and love.

79. Courtois, *Before His Face*, 1:197. For Mother, everything gravitates towards the service of the poor, and while reminding her Sisters of their fourth vow, she urges them to magnanimous conduct in their service to the poor.

80. Courtois, *Before His Face*, 1:198.

81. Courtois, *Before His Face*, 1:199. At times just a word, in this case "warm," added to the author's text gives an inkling of Mother's mind. Her modifications were the result of her lived experience, conviction and practice, for she displayed great warmth in her dealings with people, especially with the poor. As always, with the poor as a backdrop on her mind, she employs two crucial terms: "the slums", and "light," which are particularly significant given her call to "be His Light" in the slums ("dark holes") of the poor.

82. Courtois, *Before His Face*, 1:199.

83. Courtois, *Before His Face*, 1:199. Mother challenges her Sisters to measure up to the paradigm of Gospel love, having none else but Jesus as their model. Characteristically, she then offers some concrete points on practicing kindness.

MGL 29. 15TH AUGUST 1964

84. Mother quotes and paraphrases the words of Fr. Louis Colin, CSsR, from his book, *Striving for Perfection*, trans. Kathryn Day Wyatt (Westminster, MD: The Newman Press, 1955), 80–85, 91, 95–96. She reiterates Colin's wording to fit the MC way life and adds many original expressions in straightforward and concrete language, relevant to the life of her community. Colin, *Striving for Perfection*, 69.

85. Colin, *Striving for Perfection*, 71–72.

86. Colin, *Striving for Perfection*, 77.

87. Colin, *Striving for Perfection*, 80–81.

88. Colin, *Striving for Perfection*, 81.

89. Colin, *Striving for Perfection*, 82, citing St. Alphonsus, *Works*, vol. 6.

90. Colin, *Striving for Perfection*, 83, quoting Teresa of Avila, *The Way of Perfection*.

91. Colin, *Striving for Perfection*, 85.

92. Colin, *Striving for Perfection*, 91, quoting P. de la Colombiere, *Notes Spirituelles*.

93. Colin, *Striving for Perfection*, 95–96, quoting St. Alphonsus, *Works*.

MGL 48. 31ST OCTOBER 1966

94. Mother instructs the Sisters on the virtue of humility by quoting and paraphrasing the words of Dom Eugene Boylan, OCSO, from his book, *This Tremendous Lover* (London: Baronius Press, 2019; New York: Paulist Press, 1947), 21, and 241–50 (citations refer to the 1947 edition). While expounding on the virtue of humility, predictably she "brings in" the poor, paralleling Mary's life to MC life, and pointing out that the poor are God's messengers to us. She puts positively the author's negative statements.

95. Boylan, *This Tremendous Lover*, 241.

96. "As Fr. Clérissac said to a friend, 'it is our emptiness and thirst that God needs, not our plentitude.'" Boylan, *This Tremendous Lover*, 243, quoting Maritain, preface to Clerissac, *The Mystery of the Church*. Note that Boylan quotes the same phrase again at 348; however, this time he uses word "trust" instead of "thirst." He writes, "In fact, to repeat Father Clérissac's words: 'It is our emptiness and trust that He needs, not our plenitude.'" The original French of Clérissac's book *Le Mystère de l'Eglise*, in Jacques Maritain's preface, has the following phrase: "C'est de notre soif et de notre vide qu'il a besoin, non de notre plénitude." Jacques Maritain, preface to *Le Mystère de l'Eglise*, by Humbert Clérissac, OP (Juvisy-Seine-et-Oise: Cerf, 1917), xxxiii. Though Mother most likely read both versions of the quotes (i.e., the correct quotation of the word "thirst" and the misquoted word "trust"), she chooses not to quote either of them, but chooses the word "lowliness" instead.

97. Boylan, *This Tremendous Lover*, 243–244.

98. Boylan, *This Tremendous Lover*, 247. "To choose always the hardest" was the point added by Mother to the list of points given by the author. This was the standard of living that she hoped for from her Sisters, but more importantly that she modeled for them by her example. The same aim is found in St. John of the Cross, *The Ascent of Mount Carmel*, in *The Collected Works of Saint John of the Cross* (ICS Publications, Institute of Carmelite Studies, Washington DC), 149.

99. Boylan, *This Tremendous Lover*, 247–49.

100. Boylan, *This Tremendous Lover*, 250.

MGL 53. 17TH SEPTEMBER 1967

101. Dom Raymund Thibaut, *Abbot Columba Marmion*, A Master of the Spiritual Life, translated from the French by Mother Mary St. Thomas, (London: Sands & Co., 1961), 50. Also found in Dom Columba Marmion, OSB, *The English Letters of Abbot Marmion*, Benedictine Studies, (Dublin: Helicon Press, 1962), 52–53.

102. Dom Raymund Thibaut, *Abbot Columba Marmion*, 50.

103. Dom Raymond Thibaut, *Union with God according to the Letters of Direction of Dom Marmion* (London: Sands & Co., 1954), 232.

MGL 54. 30TH NOVEMBER 1967

104. Mother could have been inspired by passages from Paul de Jaegher, since he has a similar approach and style. Paul de Jaegher, SJ, *The Virtue of Love* (New York: P.J. Kenedy & Sons, 1955), 99, 103.

MGL 55. 10TH JANUARY 1968

105. Note that Mother quotes here her own adaptation of Cardinal Newman's prayer. In fact, she adapted two texts of Cardinal Newman, making one prayer. The second part of Mother's version is taken from the third paragraph of his meditation, "Jesus, the Light of the Soul": "Stay with me, and then I shall begin to shine as Thou shinest: so to shine as to be a light to others. The light, O Jesus, will be all from Thee. None of it will be mine. No merit to me. It will be Thou who shinest through me upon others. O let me thus praise Thee, in the way which Thou dost love best, by shining on all those around me. Give light to them as well as to me; light them with me, through me. Teach me to show forth Thy praise, Thy truth, Thy will. Make me preach Thee without preaching—not by words, but by my example and by the catching force, the sympathetic influence, of what I do—by my visible resemblance to Thy saints, and the evident fullness of the love which my heart bears to Thee." *Meditations and Devotions of the Late Cardinal Newman* (New York: Longmans, Green, and Co., 1911), 365. Often Mother's version is incorrectly described as directly written by Cardinal Newman. However, though Mother used Cardinal Newman's meditation to compose this prayer, which became known as "Radiating Christ," the adaptations (additions and omissions) reflect her own mind and heart.

MGL 57. 19TH MAY 1968

106. Mother quotes and paraphrases the words of Louis Évely from his book *That Man Is You*: "It's impossible to know Him and not change, to recognize Him and not love Him above all else, impossible to be transformed without first losing what we think is our essential form, to be transfigured, without first being disfigured in our own sight." "God loves those to whom He can give most, those who expect most from Him, who are most open to Him, need Him most, and rely on Him most for everything." Louis Evely, *That Man Is You*, trans. Edmond Bonin (New York: Paulist Press, 1964), 34–35, 126.

MGL 58. 18TH JULY 1968

107. Mother is alluding to the line from the autobiography of St. Thérèse of Lisieux: "It should never be said that a woman in the world did more for her husband than I for my Beloved." *A Little White Flower: The Autobiography of St. Thérèse of Lisieux*, revised translation by Rev. Thomas N. Taylor (New York: P. J. Kennedy & Sons, 1925), 158.

MGL 61. 11TH OCTOBER 1968

108. A decade after she began writing her general letters, Mother had almost entirely stopped quoting other authors. It is possible that she was inspired by what she had read earlier or presently, but she seldom quotes or paraphrases. At times she might have had similar reflections as other authors or she might have been inspired by reading their works, such as this: "'Silence is a great means to help us become souls of prayer and to dispose us to treat continually with God. You will seldom find a spiritual person who talks a great deal. All souls of prayer love silence, which they rightly call the protector of innocence, the defence against temptation, and the source of prayer.'" Louis Colin, CSsR, *The Interior Life*, 28; quoting St. Alphonsus Liguori, *Oeuvre Asc.* T.X., XVI, 502, 503. However, the phrase is Mother's original expression.

MGL 66. 4TH OCTOBER 1969

109. Father Mateo speaks of making family homes "living tabernacles": "Our promoters must endeavour to secure for Our Lord many living tabernacles, so that He may not justly repeat His sad complaint: 'I looked for sympathy, but there was none; for comforters, and I found none,'" (Crawley-Boevey, *Jesus King of Love*, 1963, 239–40) and other "Nazareths": "pagan ways and pagan customs have invaded the homes that should be other Nazareths . . ." (272–73) or again: "No longer need we envy Mary and Joseph at Nazareth, for Your abiding presence in our home will make our family another Nazareth wherein we will vie with one another in giving You proofs of our love. We will do this especially by the practice of family charity, trying to love each other as You have loved us" (288–89). It is possible that Mother was inspired by reading these texts; however, she does not quote or paraphrase Fr. Mateo. Moreover, the expression was current among some religious, so Mother could have heard it from some other source unknowable to us or even coined it herself.

MGL 80. 7TH MARCH 1971

110. See Crawley-Boevey, *Jesus King of Love*, 53.

MGL 93. 18TH JUNE 1972

111. St. Louis de Montfort, *True Devotion to the Blessed Virgin* (Montfort Publications, 1980), #259.

112. St. Louis de Montfort, *True Devotion to the Blessed Virgin* #260.

MGL 126. 8TH APRIL 1977

113. St. Bonaventure, in his *Soliloquy*, said: "Christ on the cross bows his head waiting for you, that he may kiss you, his arms outstretched, that he may embrace you, his hands are open, that he may enrich you, his body spread out, that he may give himself totally, his feet are nailed, that he may stay there, his side is open for you, that he may let you enter there." Also St. Alphonsus de Liguori wrote: "Raise up thine eyes, my soul, and behold that crucified man. Behold the divine Lamb now sacrificed upon that altar of pain. Consider that he is the beloved Son of the Eternal Father; and consider that he is dead for the love that he has borne thee. *See how he holds his arms stretched out to embrace thee; this head bent down to give the kiss of peace; his side open to receive thee into his heart.* What dost thou say? Does not a God so loving deserve to be loved?" St. Alphonsus de Liguori, "Meditation XIV, For Good Friday," in *The Passion and the Death of Jesus Christ* (Brooklyn: Redemptorist Fathers, 1927), 455.

MGL 146. 31ST JANUARY 1980

114. Gaston Courtois, *Before His Face: Meditations for Priests and Religious*, vol. 1 (New York: Herder and Herder, 1962), 1. See also MGL 23 of 27th December 1963, 37–38.

115. Ibid.

MGL 175. 16TH DECEMBER 1983

116. When Mother was away from Mother House, which was frequent after her receiving the Nobel Peace Prize, and when her health began deteriorating rapidly in the 1990s, the Councillors assisted Mother with her General Letters to the Society, often using excerpts from her previous letters. This letter, using excerpts from MGL 68 of 25th November 1969, is one such example.

MGL 208. 27TH APRIL 1989

117. This paragraph is taken from the *Explanation of the Original Constitutions*, Constitution 112.

MGL 219. [JUNE 1990]

118. See *Come be My Light*, 99.

MGL 256. 24TH FEBRUARY 1995

119. Cf. Columba Marmion, OSB, *Christ, the Ideal of the Monk:* "Now the fulfilling of the rule out of love constitutes fidelity. Fidelity is the most precious and delicate flower of love here below." Quoted in Colin, *The Practice of the Rule*, 5.

CONCORDANCE

Mark

John

Acts of the Apostles

Romans

1 Corinthians

2 Corinthians

Galatians

Ephesians

Philippians

INDEX

K

L

R

T

Mother's General Letters to Her Sisters was designed in Dante with Myriad type and composed by Kachergis Book Design of Pittsboro, North Carolina. It was printed on 60-pound Tradebook Natural and bound by Sheridan Books of Chelsea, Michigan.